**UPDATED
1996 EDITION**

UNDERSTANDING MASS COMMUNICATION

A Liberal Arts Perspective

Melvin L. DeFleur

Chairman
School of Mass Communication and Public Relations
Boston University

Everette E. Dennis

Executive Director
The Freedom Forum Media Studies Center
Columbia University

Houghton Mifflin Company   **BOSTON   TORONTO**
Geneva, Illinois   Palo Alto   Princeton, New Jersey

Sponsoring Editor:	Margaret H. Seawell
Assistant Editor:	Jeanne Herring
Senior Project Editor:	Charline Lake
Production/Design Coordinator:	Sarah Ambrose
Senior Manufacturing Coordinator:	Priscilla J. Bailey
Marketing Manager:	Caroline Croley

Cover Design:	Len Massiglia, LMA Communications
Cover Image:	Michel Tcherevkoff
Interior Photographs:	Page 1: Ted Soqui/Impact Visuals; pages 36, 38, 73, 113: The Terry Wild Studio; pages 144, 146, 183, 212: Tom Benton/Impact Visuals; pages 240, 242, 281, 317, 351: Tim Barnwoll/Stock Boston; pages 380, 382, 423, 452: Bettmann Archive; pages 492, 494, 533, 570, 607: Andrew Brilliant/The Picture Cube.

Printed in the U.S.A.

Library of Congress Catalog Card Number: 95-76935

Student Text ISBN: 0-395-74681-7

Examination Copy ISBN: 0-395-76492-0

123456789–DH–99 98 97 96 95

CONTENTS

PREFACE

This updated version of the fifth edition of *Understanding Mass Communication* incorporates the latest available information about the mass media. To document recent changes in various aspects of mass communication, the most current numerical data have been added to tables, figures, and textual discussions throughout the book, and, where appropriate, other textual passages and photos also have been updated. In order to provide continuity in teaching, the chapter structure, topics, and features contained in the fifth edition have all been retained.

Focus of the Book

Understanding Mass Communication amply covers the nuts and bolts of daily media content and how it is processed and delivered to a variety of audiences who selectively attend. However, while considerable attention is given to the ways in which professional communicators function within each media setting, that is not the major focus of the book. Rather, *Understanding Mass Communication* differs from many of its competitors in that it is organized around three broad questions that go well beyond a beginner's survey of what one needs to know to get an entry-level job in the mass communication labor force. These questions place each of the media within a broad *liberal arts perspective*. That perspective draws on concepts and conclusions derived from many disciplines that have helped in understanding the process and effects of mass communications. The three broad questions to which the book is addressed are

1. *How is it that American mass media have come to be organized in the way that they are?* That is, what demographic, economic, political, and technological factors have shaped our nation's privately owned, profit-oriented mass media in such a way that they attract wide audiences mainly by presenting popular culture and entertainment?
2. *How do American mass media actually function?* That is, how do professional communicators in each of the major media decide on the content that they select, modify it, and present it in various ways using a variety of technologies so as to reach specific kinds of audiences?
3. *What effect does this flow of information from media to audiences have on us, both individually and collectively?* Does it have only minor influences on our thoughts and behavior as individuals and modify our culture and society in only limited ways? Or, is mass communication a powerful force that shapes both individual conduct and our nation's history?

New to the Fifth Edition

The fifth edition of *Understanding Mass Communication* has new chapters and distinctive features that are not found in similar books.

- A new chapter on the American audience and the effects of its demographics and diversity on mass communications
- A new chapter on popular culture that explores the characteristics of and taste publics for the entertainment content of American mass media
- A series of new boxed features that introduce and explain fourteen theories of mass communication
- A number of table-and-graph combinations that show trends in the adoption or use of the media
- A new format for the end-of-chapter summaries designed to make it easier for the student to recognize and remember the important points
- A half-dozen new boxed features that, along with another dozen that are repeated from the last edition, provide linchpins, or links, between the media and the liberal arts

The first of the new chapters—Chapter 8, "The American Population as Audience"—is organized around the demographic and cultural diversity that is such an important consideration for mass communication. An number of important trends in the population that continue to alter the nature, needs, tastes, and consumer behavior of American media audiences are discussed. Each of these trends has continuing implications for professional mass communicators. Understanding them is critical to developing insights into the process and effects of mass communication in the United States.

The second new chapter—Chapter 13, "Popular Culture: Entertainment and Sports"—discusses the origins and nature of and the taste publics served by various kinds of entertainment provided by the American media. In addition, it traces the development and functions of the spectator sports that now make up about one fifth of the content of mass communications in the United States. The chapter also discusses why the content of the American media has been so extensively criticized and why, in spite of the critics, it will probably undergo relatively little change in the years ahead.

Another completely new feature that represents an important innovation in the type of material typically presented to the beginning student is called "Explaining Media Effects." These boxed inserts are brief introductions to fourteen different theories of mass communication. The explanation and background of each theory are presented at a level that can be readily understood by students. These fourteen theories address a question that students often ask but to which they seldom receive clear answers: How do mass communications influence us, both as individuals and as a society? This feature shows students that, as a result of scholarly analyses and massive amounts of research, we can now explain many aspects of how the media function and what kinds of influences they have on us. Each theory deals with a separate kind of process or effect, is presented in simple and readable terms, and is illustrated with examples at a point where the relevant issues are discussed in the text.

Another innovation in this edition is a series of table-and-graph combinations called "Trends in Media Use." Each includes a brief explanation to aid in interpretation of the numerical information. Most of these appear in the chapters where the specific media are addressed, but others are located in later chapters where various additional trends and patterns of adoption or use are discussed. This feature of the book shows students how Americans have increasingly or decreasingly used a particular medium over the years. Tables with relevant numerical data are paired with graphs, or charts, that show the patterns in graphic form. Each combination has an extended caption that explains how the use of the medium has changed over time. The overall lesson for the student from these materials is that we live in a complex and ever-changing media environment, and that it is very unlikely that the specific media technologies that we use at present are the same as those we will use in the future.

Also new is the bulleted list format of the summary at the end of each chapter. These chapter reviews focus on the major points that have been made and are designed to help students in studying for examinations, when it is essential to be able to extract the major points that have been presented in a chapter.

The fifth edition continues to include a series of eighteen boxed essays, now entitled "Media and the Liberal Arts." Each brief essay explains a significant way in which the media are linked to issues that are central to the traditional arts, sciences, and humanities. The overall lesson for students provided by this feature is that mass communication is not just a professional field to be studied only by those who will enter its labor force to pursue careers. It is a field whose development and contemporary issues are intimately linked to major aspects of American history and closely intertwined with a host of topics that are central to the classical and liberal traditions that are at the heart of American higher education.

Issues Addressed in Specific Chapters

To begin providing answers to the three broad questions (noted above) around which the book is organized, Chapter 1 discusses the nature of, and distinctions between, basic human communication at the interpersonal level and mass communication via modern media. Then, each of the three questions is answered in greater detail. For example, influences on media organization are addressed in Chapters 2

through 7. Each of these chapters is devoted to a specific medium: books, newspapers, magazines, film, radio, or television.

These initial chapters on the several media are not designed simply to show students the kind of work environment that they will encounter if they take a job in a media field. They are intended to provide an *intellectual understanding* of how these media developed in American society and how they function today in an overall system of mass communication. This approach allows students to understand how each medium is related to the others. It also shows how it is imbedded within the ethical norms of the society, how it has been influenced by principal cultural values, and how it responds to demographic trends, economic influences, the political environment, and so on. This liberal arts perspective provides a *framework for critical thinking* about the ways in which the major media have been shaped in the past and, by the same token, how they surely will be shaped in the future.

The second major question—how the media currently function in our society to deliver their messages to their readers, listeners, and viewers—is in part answered in the first seven chapters. However, the next two chapters probe this issue more deeply. Chapter 8 on the American population as audience is new to this edition. It is a major effort to provide insights into the relevant characteristics of that audience through a detailed analysis of the population's demographic composition and a number of major trends that have occurred as ours became a media society. Each has implications for the process of mass communication. Chapter 9, on the political environment in which the media operate, has been substantially rewritten in this edition. It adds to understanding of the mass communication process by reviewing the constantly evolving laws, rules, and norms within which mass communication takes place. It includes new material on libel, obscenity, and government-press relations during the Gulf War. Chapters on economic issues and on technology have been dropped and their major points worked into the chapters dealing with specific media.

The third question—concerning the individual and social effects of the media—is addressed in Chapters 15 through 17. These chapters discuss the ways in which the influences of mass communications on audiences and society as a whole are under study by scholars using the scientific perspective. Chapter 15 reviews the research methods that are widely used in the study of media effects. Chapter 16 presents a summary of what has been found as a result of such research over a period of more than six decades. Essentially, most of that research suggests that the media have only selective and limited effects. However, Chapter 17 goes beyond the research of the past and presents important theoretical perspectives on the study of media influences that will guide scholarly inquiry in the future. These perspectives indicate that the media may have much more powerful effects on us than have been realized in the past. Indeed, they point to truly significant events in the American experience that have been shaped by the media. These influences, in particular, provide a foundation for critical thinking about the role of the media in creating change in our society.

Three chapters in this fifth edition focus directly on media content. Chapter 12 presents an overview of the news process—an analysis that is unique to this book. It shows how the understandings that each of us constructs from news reports about what is happening in the world out there do not necessarily correspond to reality. The chapter traces the decisions that are made by the news industry and the complex paths that are followed when news is presented to readers, listeners, and viewers. It shows the critical points where distortion can occur between a reporter's observations of an event and the interpretations of resulting stories by members of the news audience. Chapter 13 focuses on a different kind of content of the media. It discusses the nature of popular culture, sports, and entertainment. These, after all, make up the majority of what the media present, and it is important for students to understand the role that such content plays in the American system of mass communication. Chapter 14 continues the analysis of media content by focusing on popular music and the recording industry. New material added to this chapter discusses how technology plays a major role in the recording of hit songs and how their popularity is largely a matter of how they are marketed through air play.

Several of the chapters in the fifth edition have been carried forward from the fourth, but with careful attention to updating. For example, Chapter 10 discusses the world of advertising. It describes the critical role that the industry plays in the financial support of the American media. Chapter 11 presents an analysis of public relations as a field that is closely tied to the use of media. It discusses how mass communications and other strategies are used to achieve the goals of public relations practitioners. In particular, it reviews the credibility problems that have dogged this field as its leaders have struggled to achieve professional status for their discipline. Each of these chapters has significant new material. For example, Chapter 11 now contains a review of lobbying as public relations. This new material has been added because the role of the lobbyist has become so controversial in our society.

To close the book, Chapter 18 discusses ethical issues and the media, a topic that is assuming a new importance in understanding mass communication. The reason is that the new theoretical perspectives discussed in Chapter 17 seem to indicate that the media can have very powerful long-term influences on us as individuals as well as on our entire society and culture.

As these influences of mass communication become increasingly clear, the ethical obligations of those who control media content take on far greater significance.

Instructor's Support Materials

Understanding Mass Communication, Fifth Edition, offers the instructor a completely revised *Instructor's Resource Manual with Test Items*. It features learning objectives, chapter summaries, and a detailed teaching outline for every chapter. In addition, each chapter includes discussion questions, lecture ideas and sources, suggested writing topics, field projects, and a supplemental lecture. The Test Bank consists of approximately fifty multiple-choice items per chapter. Also available upon adoption are a computerized test generator, available for IBM and Macintosh computers, and transparencies of significant charts and graphs from the text.

Acknowledgments

The authors would like to acknowledge the contributions of Paul Anderson, not only in the instructor's manual he prepared, but for many suggestions that he has offered concerning ways to improve the book. An important contribution was also made by Tom Herling in his assistance with the section in the popular music chapter discussing the technology of modern music production and the relationship between air play and sales. Others who have made valuable suggestions are Miriam Helf, Debbie Merskin, Shearon Lowery, Jeffry Hubbard, Edward Lordan, Donna Hayes, Michael Cremedas, Mary Cronin, Lucinda Davenport, Charles Barber, Carrie Klein, Cate Dolan, Dirk Smillie, Larry Norman, and Deborah Rogers.

We appreciate the valuable comments and suggestions of the following people who kindly reviewed this manuscript: Paul Ashdown, University of Tennessee; Dean Bennett, Arizona State University; Peter Costello, Adelphi University; John Foster, Central Washington University; Earl Grow, University of Wisconsin–Milwaukee; Kenneth Hadwiger, Eastern Illinois University; Val Limburg, Washington State University; Janice Long, University of Cincinnati, Maclyn McClary, Humboldt State University; Zena Beth McGlashen, University of Texas at El Paso; John Paulmann, Westfield State University; Timothy Plax, California State University–Long Beach; Thomas Proeiti, Monroe Community College; James St. Clair, Indiana University Southeast; Paul Shaffer, Austin Peay State University; John Smead, Central Missouri State University; Douglas Starr, Texas A & M University; Dennis Stouse, Jacksonville University; Ann Wadsworth, University of North Carolina–Chapel Hill; Richard Whitaker, Buffalo State College; and B. Cleveland Wilhoit, Indiana University at Bloomington.

M.D. & E.D.

CHAPTER 1

The Nature of Mass Communication

There is no more impor-
tant issue facing us
today than the impact
of media. . . . We
receive messages—
recognized and
unrecognized—from
hundreds of sources
each day. Everything
from the television we
watch to the clothing
we wear says something
about us, or to us.

Elizabeth Thoman, Center for
Media and Values, 1992

Human beings have been communicating in one way or another for a very long time. However, their ability to use a medium to store their messages to be retrieved later or to transport them from one place to another is a relatively recent development. A *medium* is a device for moving information through time or space. It can be as simple as a carving on a piece of stone or as sophisticated as a satellite-linked television system. In either case, its function is the same. A communicator formulates a message and moves or records it by means of the medium, and a receiver in another place or at a later time constructs meanings so as to interpret the message. Thus, mediated communication is like all other human communication. It is a process linking senders and receivers who share some kind of oral or written language.[1] In this sense, media (the plural of medium) have been in use as far back as history can instruct us. However, in modern times, newly developed media have altered the overall ability of human beings to conquer time and space to such a great degree that we are into a modern "communication revolution" as profound as that which took place when human beings first learned to use language. This book sets forth the major events in that revolution—to show how these new media are organized in the United States, how they operate, and how they influence both individuals and society.

Today's mass media reach audiences that can number in the hundreds of millions, and they make use of a technology of breathtaking sophistication. Yet, our mass media still perform the same functions as their more primitive predecessors. Like the hieroglyphics, smoke signals, and jungle drums of earlier times, they move information across time or space. A major difference is that today there can be millions of receivers who simultaneously construct meanings to interpret the messages transmitted by the communicator.

The medium, however, is *not* the message. It may pose limitations on how the message is constructed; it may introduce subtle connotations that differ from one medium to another; it may enhance the communication experience with color, perspective, or imagery not present in face-to-face discussion; or it may even detract from the accuracy with which the message is received. However, the basic process that is taking place when contemporary mass media are used is *human communication based on language.*

Even in this age of technologically sophisticated media, then, people are still locked into a basic process of human communication. It is the words and sentences used by the newspaper or television reporter that determine how accurately the story is understood. Analogously, the clever and entertaining use of verbal and nonverbal language determines whether a movie or play is regarded as a success by its audience.

Language and its use, then, are the beginning point for developing an understanding of the basic process of human communication and, by extension, *mass communication.* For that reason, we must first look at how human communication takes place in the *absence* of media. That is, what are the fundamentals of face-to-face human communication? With that analysis as a basis for comparison, we next take a close look at mass communication. This, in turn, permits a comparison of the two and a fuller understanding of the advantages, limitations, and effects of communicating with contemporary media.

How Human Beings Communicate

Human beings communicate in ways that are very different from those used by any other species on our planet. Specifically, we communicate with some form of learned and shared verbal and nonverbal language that is part of a culture that has accumulated and grown increasingly complex over time. Other species communicate with signs and signals in ways that have changed little since the dawn of their existence. In spite of romantic ideas about whales, porpoises, and other animals that supposedly "talk," those creatures do not use languages based on culturally shared systems of symbols, grammar, and meanings. Animals clearly do communicate with each other, sometimes in relatively sophisticated ways. However, they do so with behavioral systems that in most cases are inherited and in some cases learned, but are never part of a culture in the true sense. In other words, no matter how one looks at it, in any realistic sense, only human beings communicate with language based on shared cultural rules.[2]

The Origins of Language

If we count a human generation as about thirty years on average, we need to go back only about two thousand grandmothers ago to come to a time when our prehistoric ancestors did not use language as we know it. Early human beings, such as *Australopithecus, Homo habilis,* and *Homo erectus,*

Although there seems little doubt that our earliest human ancestors were able to communicate, such as the *Australopithecene* family depicted here, they were undoubtedly limited to non-verbal signs and signals. The physiology of their skulls, tongues, and voice boxes resembled those of today's chimpanzees and gorillas. Limited brain size, large tongues, and heavy lip structures in earlier *hominids* prevented them from making the refined sounds required for spoken language. This did not change until the arrival of the Cro-Magnon, our more immediate ancestors. Thus, speech and language as we know them today are relatively recent human accomplishments.

clearly did not speak. In fact, they *could not* because the structure of their voice boxes was like that of modern apes and chimpanzees.[3] They could make vocal noises, as do their anthropoid counterparts today, but their anatomy did not permit them the delicate control over vocal sounds that is required for speech. That anatomical limitation continued even through the more recent era of the Neanderthal (*Homo sapiens neanderthalensis*), who inhabited wide areas of our planet starting about 150 to 125 thousand years ago. The Neanderthal apparently were able to communicate reasonably well, but they had to do so with gestures, body movements, and a limited number of sounds that they were capable of making. Then, between about 90 and 35 thousand years ago, the Neanderthal were replaced by a very different type of human being. These were the Cro-Magnon (*Homo sapiens sapiens*), our direct ancestors. If dressed in modern clothes, they would be indistinguishable from people today. Because they had the same larynx, voice box, tongue, and lip structures as modern people, the Cro-Magnon were able to generate and control voice sounds in intricate ways.[4] This made it possible for them to speak and develop language. Thus, the use of complex languages began sometime around 40 thousand years ago—a relatively recent development in the several millions of years of the evolutionary history of our species.[5] It was the first great communications revolution.

The subsequent development of increasingly efficient and flexible systems for storing, recovering, and disseminating information through the use of various media provided additional revolutions. At first, each step took thousands of years. Few people today are even aware of that long history or of the great breakthroughs that each step required—first language, then writing, the alphabet, portable media, books, print, newspapers, telegraph, film, radio, television in various forms, and the rest. But with those media in place today, human beings can use language and media together to conquer time and distance in ways that would have defied the wildest imagination of people only a few generations back.

The Use of Verbal and Nonverbal Symbols

In the current age of mass communication, we still communicate, whether face-to-face or through media, by using verbal and nonverbal symbols. A *symbol* is a word, action, or object that "stands for" and arouses a standardized internal meaning in people in a given language community. By an established *convention* (a well-established rule), each symbol—such as "dog," "child," or even the complex term "biodegradable"—is supposed to arouse parallel, that is, similar, internal-meaning experiences in everyone who uses it. In addition, actions—such as gestures and facial expressions—can be governed by meaning conventions. The same is true of certain objects, such as a cross, a star of David, or a wedding ring.

Language also includes rules for putting symbols together in patterns. The familiar rules of *grammar* establish standard ways for linking and modifying classes of symbols (such as verbs, pronouns, and adjectives) to give more precision and flexibility to their use in complex messages. Another common category of rules, called *syntax*, provides for ordering symbols so as to make the meanings clear. For example, syntax determines whether you say "The ball struck the man" or "The man struck the ball." Other familiar rules are those for *pronunciation*—socially accepted ways to make the sounds for words.

Human Communication: A Basic Linear Model

Although symbols, conventions of meaning, grammar, syntax, and pronunciation are all important, they do not provide a basic perspective on exactly how human beings communicate. To gain a more complete overview of what takes place when people engage in an act of communication, let us first analyze the process in terms of six specific stages that take place in the following order:

1. The act of human communication begins with a sender, who decides to *initiate* a message with a specific set of intended meanings.
2. That sender then *encodes* the intended meanings by selecting specific words and gestures that the receiver will presumably understand.
3. The message is then *transmitted*—spoken or written so as to cross the space between sender and receiver.
4. The receiver, the individual to whom the message is directed, attends to and *perceives* the incoming message as a specific pattern of symbols.

CONSEQUENCES OF THE FIRST GREAT COMMUNICATIONS REVOLUTION:
A Linchpin to Cultural Anthropology

When you got up this morning, dressed, ate breakfast, and traveled to school, you probably made use of a host of physical objects and technologies that were first developed by ancient people. Many were innovations that arose during what anthropologists now call the Neolithic period, or the New Stone Age. The people of that time were the beneficiaries of what we have called the first great communications revolution (to the Age of Speech and Language).

The Neolithic era began about 10,000 B.C. and was followed by the Bronze Age, beginning about 3000 B.C., and the Iron Age, which began about 700 B.C. Altogether these were times of extraordinary invention and remarkable cultural achievement, especially by comparison with the slow pace of earlier human cultural evolution.

The development of human culture quickened following the invention of language by the Cro-Magnon, who were the first human beings with anatomical features that permitted them to make the complex sounds required by speech. Using language enabled people of the Neolithic period not only to talk to each other but to think and reason in complex ways. They could classify, analyze, generalize, and reach conclusions from premises. This helped them to devise solutions to many practical problems. Furthermore, they could pass on to succeeding generations the solutions they were able to invent.

What this means for us today is that we are still using versions, albeit much improved, of many inventions from the Neolithic period. For example, if this morning you put on cotton or wool clothing and shoes made of leather, you made use of two Neolithic innovations (weaving and leather tanning). If during breakfast you drank from a cup and ate off a plate, you employed objects whose origins are truly ancient (pottery was being made in Japan by 10,000 B.C.).

If you had bacon or sausage with your breakfast, you owe a debt to these early people. They were the first to domesticate animals (by about 7000 B.C.), an event that was part of the great transition from hunting-gathering economies to farming and fixed village life. During the early part of the Neolithic period, people in various parts of the world began to plant, har-

5. The receiver then *decodes* the message by constructing his or her own interpretations of the meanings of the symbols.
6. As a result of interpreting the message, the receiver is *influenced* in some way. That is, the communication has some effect.

This is a basic *linear model* of human communication. It is obvious that such a model greatly oversimplifies the process. However, its value is that it permits us to understand each of the stages represented. Looked at in this somewhat artificial way, the communicative act begins, goes through the stages and then stops, like a tape recorder being turned on and off. In reality, the conversations that we engage in with people around us are much more complex. Most face-to-face human conversations are *transactional* in that each person encodes and decodes messages at the same time and is alert to all kinds of cues from the other person. Many factors influence the

vest, and store food from many kinds of crops. Thus, the wheat from which your toast was made, as well as the butter you spread on it, have Neolithic origins.

Another Neolithic innovation was the metal in the spoon you used to stir your cup of coffee or tea. The technology to make implements of metal (copper) was first developed about 5000 B.C. If you bought a newspaper with a coin on your way to school, you used an object that was developed about 3000 B.C.. This list could go on and on. If you traveled to school in any kind of vehicle, you were once again part of a long tradition; the wheel was in use centuries before the birth of Christ.

Perhaps more important than all of these physical artifacts and technologies was the great transformation in social life that occurred when Neolithic people began to live together in villages, towns, and cities. In time, some individuals became rich and others were forced into slavery. Occupational specialties developed, making the society far more diverse. Leaders rose to organize, coordinate, or control social life. Since productive land was valuable, military groups were organized to capture or hold it, and warfare became common. Increasingly sophisticated weapons came into use: the bronze sword, the two-wheeled chariot, the bow and arrow, body armor, and many others. Religions were devised to explain the origins of human life and the nature of the physical world. Governmental systems became increasingly complex so as to protect citizens, provide public services (such as roads), and, of course, collect taxes.

Thus, the first great communications revolution that took place after human beings learned to use language had enormous consequences with which we still live today. Still other revolutions followed with the invention of writing and of printing. We are now in the midst of an even more profound alteration of human communication based on incredibly complex technologies that include various types of mass media, electronic systems, satellites, and computers. This revolution will inevitably enrich human life, just as did the complex transitions that occurred during the Neolithic period.

Sources: Peter J. Wilson, *The Domestication of the Human Species* (New Haven, Conn.: Yale University Press, 1988); Sara Anderson, *The Neolithic and Bronze Ages* (Princeton, N.J.: American School of Classical Studies at Athens, 1971); and Robert L. Stigler, *The Old World: Early Man to the Development of Agriculture* (New York: St. Martin's Press, 1974).

process. What has already been said plays a key part in what comes next. In addition, the meanings constructed by each party are influenced by the relationship between sender and receiver (friends, boss-worker, parent-child, etc.). Moreover, the sociocultural situation and even the physical surroundings can influence the meanings constructed by both parties (for example, a conversation at a homecoming party versus one at a funeral).[6]

In spite of its simplicity and obvious limitations, the basic linear model is useful for *analyzing* the communication process, breaking it down into its distinct stages so as to understand what happens at each. Also, those stages are at the heart of the complex transactions of any conversation. That is, even if both parties are simultaneously encoding, transmitting, and decoding, they are still serving as senders and receivers, initiating and receiving messages. In other words, the six stages listed above are *embedded* within the complexities of transactional communication. Thus, the basic linear

The role-taking and feedback principles are important in human communication. If used effectively, each diminishes the incongruence in meanings that reduces accuracy. In this photo, each person is providing nonverbal feedback cues that can be used by the other in role-taking interpretations, thus helping each person to understand the meanings that are intended in the other's messages. (Nancy Bates/The Picture Cube)

model simplifies the task of looking carefully at each stage of the process separately so as to see exactly how people use symbols and conventions of meaning to accomplish the act of human communication.

We can illustrate the six stages of our linear model with a simple act of communication in which one person says "Hello" and another says "Hi" in reply. People seldom transmit messages of a single word, as in this example, but the principles do not change whether communicators use only one symbol or a complex pattern of verbal and nonverbal symbols linked by rules of syntax and grammar. Therefore, we can use a one-word exchange to keep things at the simplest possible level.

Our approach to understanding what happens at each of the six stages will be something like that of a high-speed camera tracking a speeding bullet: By slowing down a process that occurs almost instantaneously, we will look closely at each step in the process by which one human being presents a message and another constructs a subjective interpretation of its meaning.

Stage one: Deciding what to communicate   People transmit messages so as to accomplish some goal. In terms of our one-word example, the sender decides to initiate a greeting, presumably with the intention of beginning the process of getting acquainted. Usually, people decide to communicate so as to influence one or more persons in some way. People engage in face-to-face communication for thousands of different reasons, ranging from the trivial to the profound. Thus, the first stage of the communicative act is usually initiated so as to get another person to act or react in an intended way.

FIGURE 1.1   A Basic Linear Model of Human Communication

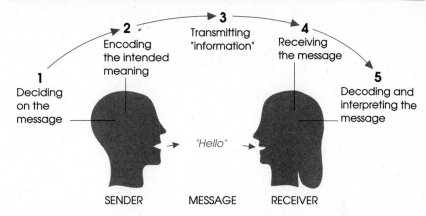

For purposes of analysis, an elementary act of human communication can be understood as a linear process of five stages in which a sender decides on a message, encodes his or her meanings using verbal and nonverbal symbols, and transmits them as physical information. The receiver then perceives the incoming information, converts it into symbols that he or she recognizes, and interprets the symbols using meanings stored in memory. Interpersonal communication also depends on complex role-taking and feedback, as well as additional transactions. These are absent in the mass communication process, in which professional communicators transmit to large numbers of receivers with whom they have no simultaneous personal contact.

Stage two: Encoding intended meanings   In the second stage of the linear model, the sender formulates, or encodes, the message. This is a complex process in which he or she selects one or more language symbols—words, actions, or objects for which people presumably share agreed-on interpretations—in order to arouse a specific set of meanings in another person. In our example, the intended meaning of "Hello" is something like "Greetings, let's get acquainted."

More generally, to achieve appropriate encoding of a message, the person must search his or her total array of remembered symbols and meanings. We can assume that this mental search involves a comparison process much like a computer's search through a vast database. When potentially suitable symbols linked to just the right meanings have been identified, they can be brought together into a message that seems to express the sender's intended meaning.

Selecting suitable symbols to express what we have in mind is a critical part of communicating, whether as an individual participating in a face-to-face conversation or as a professional communicator transmitting to a vast audience. Encoding, then, converts the intended message from internal meanings located in the memory of the communicator to symbols that can presumably be understood by the intended receiver. Selecting inappropriate symbols or meanings can lead to failure in achieving accurate communication, with potentially serious outcomes.

Stage three: Transmitting the message   How do we change language symbols in our heads to an external form that can be transmitted and received by another person? We use the parts of the anatomy involved in speaking, gesturing, writing, or typing. For present purposes, we need simply note that through such voluntary actions as speaking, the communicator converts what began as thought and imagery in memory into what we shall call *physical information*—events in the real world that conquer time or distance and can be apprehended by the receiver.[7] One example of such information is written communication, which consists of patterns of light that form visual stimuli. In our simple example, the spoken word "Hello" results in vibrations of air molecules that make up sound waves. It is these waves as physical information that span the distance between sender and receiver.

Stage four: Perceiving the incoming message   The person to whom a message is directed engages in activities that are in many ways reverse forms of the sender's activities: First, we assume that the receiver is paying attention to the communicator. This implies what psychologists call a "state of readiness" to notice the pattern of physical events—the information—that is being transmitted. Then, the receiver perceives the information. *Perception* is the mental activity by which sensory input (from our eyes and ears) is classified into recognizable categories and meanings. For example, when we perceive a spoken sound, we must first identify the incoming pattern of physical events as a known language symbol. In our example, the particular sound pattern "Hello" is perceived by the receiver as a specific English word that is distinguishable from other similar symbols.

Stage five: Decoding and interpreting the message   In this final stage, the receiver must attach *meaning* to the perceived word or words. An interpretation of the incoming message is constructed by the receiver through a process of searching through his or her memory for meanings that seem appropriate to the perceived symbol. This is a highly personal process, greatly dependent on the structure of the receiver's memory. Thus, the meanings selected by the receiver may or may not be identical to those intended by the sender. For example, the sender in our example may have intended "Hello" to mean "Greetings, let's get acquainted," but the receiver may put the meaning together as "Greetings, how are you?" Similarly, the return message of "Hi" may be constructed by the original sender (now the receiver) as having the intended meaning of "It is nice to meet you," when the original receiver (now the sender) meant "I am willing to be friendly with you."

For practical purposes in casual exchanges, such variations between intended and interpreted meanings may make little difference in how people relate to each other. Most of us get by nicely with the "deep" meanings (the basic interpretations) of the messages we send and receive. However, in critical exchanges, variations in meaning between those intended by a sender and those constructed by a receiver can have significant implications.

For example, when a woman says "No" to a man's unwanted sexual advance, and the meaning of that message constructed by the man becomes "Yes," problems for both parties are likely to follow.

Stage six: Influencing the receiver The influence of a particular sender's message on a receiver can range from trivial to profound (from "Have a nice day" to "The jury has found you guilty, and you will be hanged by the neck until dead"). Perhaps the most common effect is to prompt the receiver to become a sender and make a reply. In our example, the return message of "Hi" from the original receiver reflects such an influence. Or, the effect may be to learn new facts, to arouse emotions, or to trigger overt action. Finally, whatever the response of the receiver, it may or may not be the one that the sender had in mind.

Throughout our discussion of all of these steps taken by senders and receivers, it is important to stress that we are looking closely at activities that are virtually *instantaneous*. Indeed, human communication takes place swiftly at an "automated" level of behavior. We do not stop and reflect on each symbol we select and the meanings that it may imply. Our encoding is as fast, or perhaps faster, than the speed with which a skilled concert pianist rapidly playing a complex composition selects keys to press on the instrument.

The Contribution of Memory

Communicators cannot initiate, receive, or interpret an act of communication using words and standardized nonverbal gestures unless they have an adequately functioning memory from which to draw their associated meanings. In addition, the sender and the receiver of a message cannot experience parallel meanings unless they have learned the same cultural rules linking the symbols and what they are supposed to represent. Thus, the question arises, How do people remember meanings and rules so that they can communicate?

Memory is based in the central nervous system—in the billions of cells in the brain. It depends on biochemical and electrical processes in the molecular structures of nerve tissue. Memory is an essential part of basic human communication. Without understanding its role in the communication process, we would find it difficult to comprehend the process, effects, and limitations of mass communication.

The most important concept that has emerged from studies of the physiology of memory is that of the *trace*. The term refers to some aspect of experience stored in the brain in such a way that it can be recalled.[8] The brain is an incredible memory machine with a truly remarkable capacity to store and recall meanings. In fact, an individual's brain may be physiologically capable of remembering *everything* that ever happens to that person, no matter how trivial! Psychologically, one's memory system may block many experiences from returning to consciousness, but they remain deep in the storage system. (The fact that we all forget most of what we experience suggests that the brain might "overload" if we could remember everything at once.)

It remains a mystery why some individuals can recall experiences more readily from their traces than others. People with a so-called photographic memory appear to have almost total recall. The rest of us apparently have the same storage capacity, but only partial conscious access to our stored experiences. Psychological theories, such as those of Sigmund Freud, indicate that various kinds of emotions and inhibitions may interfere with our ability to recall some experiences.

What is the significance of these extraordinary facts about the brain and its capacity to remember? The importance is that, without our enormous ability to remember, we would be unable to learn and use verbal and non-verbal symbols and the rules of language to store, recover, and transmit messages and meanings. The number of words in the English language is mind-boggling. For example, the most recent edition of the *Oxford English Dictionary* lists meanings for approximately 500,000 words. We share with other language communities another half a million technical and scientific terms. Other languages, such as French and German, have fewer words, but their totals are still very large. It is significant for the mass communicator that the ordinary person does not carry half a million words and their associated meanings around in his or her head. Most people manage with about 5,000 words; the average college graduate uses about 15,000; and a person specialized in the use of language can use and understand about 30,000 (the number Shakespeare had at his command).[9] This extraordinary "automated" capacity to remember words, to extract them from memory storage instantly, and to arrange them without delay in patterns that make sense is what enables each of us to speak and transmit our messages to others. Their memories, in turn, permit them to attend to, perceive, and attach meanings to the incoming symbols that we have used.

The trace explanation of human memory, then, is an important aspect of communication. It enables us to understand how a communicator can formulate a meaning for a given symbol or a complex message of many words organized according to accepted rules of syntax and grammar. Similarly, it shows how a listener can instantaneously understand a particular word or untangle complex meanings for streams of words and patterns of symbols in a long message. As a result of learning the language of our culture, as well as other experiences, we have billions of traces stored in our memories. These traces can be selectively recalled or retrieved in various patterns, or configurations, and linked to words or other symbols according to the language rules we have learned. Ultimately, in a neural sense, the meaning for a given language symbol is a specific trace configuration that we have learned to recover for that symbol.

Communicating Complex Messages

Thus far we have explained the act of human communication at a very simple level. But there are three deficiencies in our explanation. First, common sense tells us that most instances of interpersonal communication are far more complex than our "Hello" and "Hi" example. Second, the meanings may not match! We have already suggested that one person may fail to understand what another person is saying, even with the simple message of "No." In other words, there are various sources of inaccuracy that are difficult to control. Finally, as we have suggested, communication is a back-and-forth, or *interactive*, process. People are not merely passive senders and receivers. They respond to the content of others' meanings, ask for clarification, and indicate agreement. Thus, we need to understand how each person shifts roles to become a sender at one moment and a receiver at another.

We know that we normally put words together into sentences, paragraphs, and various grammatical constructions using accepted rules of syntax. These patterns themselves introduce meanings that go beyond those associated with each of the words used. For example, the pattern "The boy killed the snake" implies a meaning totally different from the pattern "The snake killed the boy," even though the words used are identical.

These patterns pose no serious problem in understanding human communication. We learn the patterns and their associated meanings as part of our language, just as we learn the meanings of each word. Thus, the use of patterns by communicators and receivers follows the same general principles described for the use of one word. The patterns correspond to memory configurations that form parallel meanings for both the communicator and the receiver.

Communicating Accurately

The meanings intended by communicators and those interpreted by receivers are seldom perfectly parallel. We can use the concept of *total fidelity* to describe the situation in which the two meanings are completely congruent, that is, identical (and therefore where communication is completely accurate). However, total fidelity—that is, a perfect match between the meanings of both parties—is unlikely. In fact, 100 percent fidelity may not be possible even in the case of trivial messages. Loss of fidelity can be defined as any reduction in the congruence of, or correspondence between, the details of the sender's intended message and those of the receiver's interpreted message. In other words, when sender's and receiver's meanings do not match, fidelity is reduced.

The accuracy principle   The causes of low fidelity, or loss of accuracy between meanings, are many. Incongruence between intended and interpreted meanings can result from dim light, poor acoustics, disruptive sounds, or any other physical condition that interferes with the transfer of information. Low fidelity can also result from memory failure, faulty perception, or unfamiliarity with the language. And it can result when the sender and receiver do not share the same cultural rules for the use of language—a common problem in a multicultural society. In other words, inaccuracy can arise from any psychological, social, or cultural condition that reduces similarities between the intended meanings of the sender and the interpreted meanings of the receiver. This leads us to an important generalization concerning human communication, which we call the *accuracy principle*:

> The lower the level of fidelity (the greater the amount of incongruence) between the intended meanings of the sender and the interpreted meanings of the receiver, the less effective an act of communication will be in achieving either mutual understanding or an intended influence on a receiver.

Although the accuracy principle may seem rather ponderous, it is really a simple idea: *Inaccurate communication does not achieve intended goals.* That can be problematic in interpersonal communication and devastating in mass communication.

Clearly, it is important for both the sender and the receiver to strive for accuracy. How, then, aside from careful selection of symbols and organization of a message, can communication be made more accurate? In interpersonal communication, there are two very effective ways: by the receiver's providing feedback and by the sender's engaging in role-taking. As we will see, these two ideas have profound implications for understanding the differences between face-to-face and mass communication.

The feedback principle Usually, human communication is an ongoing process that moves back and forth between the parties. You start to explain something to a friend. At some point your friend may frown or shrug as you're talking, and you try to explain that point in a different way or provide a brief example; then you continue with your account. Your friend nods, and you understand that you have made it clear. In such a face-to-face situation, the sender is ever alert to observable verbal and nonverbal signals coming back from the receiver. These cues provide *feedback*—essentially a reverse communication by the receiver back to the communicator that indicates whether the message is getting through. In face-to-face communication, the receiver usually provides both verbal and nonverbal feedback on an ongoing basis, to influence the communicator's selection of words, gestures, and meanings. Thus, the two parties alternately become either sender or receiver as the messages of one stimulate feedback from the other.

Feedback may be deliberate or not. In any event, the communicator takes feedback into account to try to minimize incongruence of meanings and increase communication accuracy. This leads to a second important generalization, which we call the *feedback principle:*

> If adequate feedback is provided by the receiver, fidelity will be increased. That is, the intended meanings of the communicator have a better chance of being congruent with those constructed by the receiver.

Stated more simply, *feedback leads to greater accuracy in communication.* Conversely, without feedback, accuracy is likely to suffer.

The role-taking principle When a sender correctly interprets feedback cues from the intended receiver and adjusts the message to maximize fidelity and minimize incongruence, that person is figuratively placing himself or herself in the receiver's shoes. Mentally, the sender tries to *be* the receiver in order to understand how he or she is likely to respond to the message being transmitted. This process is called *role-taking*. That is, the sender evaluates how the message looks from the other person's point of view. Role-taking can be defined as the use of feedback by the sender to judge which symbols and nonverbal cues will work best to arouse the intended meanings in the receiver.

Some people are better at role-taking than others. Also, some situations are better suited for it to occur than others. Role-taking can be most effective in close, personal, and intimate situations where the communicating parties know each other well. It is most limited and ineffective in situations where strangers are trying to communicate. These considerations lead to a third generalization, which we call the *role-taking principle:*

> In communication situations in which the sender can engage in sensitive role-taking, fidelity is increased. That is, incongruence between the meanings intended by the sender and those constructed by the receiver can be minimized, with a corresponding increase in fidelity.

In less formal terms, this means that *effective role-taking increases accuracy in communication.*

In summary, these three principles tell us: (1) Face-to-face communication is accurate to the extent that adequate feedback cues are provided by the receiver. (2) Accuracy depends on the extent to which the sender uses role-taking appropriately to formulate the message in terms that are likely to be well understood by the receiver. When these conditions are met, accuracy will be at its maximum, and the prospect of influencing or changing the receiver will also be at a maximum. Thus, people are most likely to be influenced by others with whom they are in direct face-to-face contact. Not surprisingly, the potential for influence is greatest when the participants are close and intimate friends who understand each other well (effective role-taking) and who are open and disclosing in their communications with each other (rich feedback).

These principles governing the relationship between feedback, role-taking, accuracy, and influence in the case of interpersonal communication need to be kept in mind as we turn to an analysis of the nature of mass communication. As we will see, it is with respect to these issues that the two kinds of communication differ considerably.

The Contemporary Communications Revolution

Face-to-face spoken exchanges, supplemented by the use of primitive media, served as the basic human communication process for tens of thousands of years. As we shall observe in detail in later chapters, *writing* eventually evolved with increasingly portable media, such as clay tablets, papyrus, and parchment. Hand-printed scrolls and books were in use during the great classic civilizations some two to three thousand years ago.

1456

It was not until the middle of the fifteenth century, about thirty-seven years before Columbus set out on his famous voyage, that Johannes Gutenberg, an obscure goldsmith in Mainz (now in Germany), developed *printing*—a truly new communications technology that would profoundly influence human history. After experimenting with many techniques for twenty-five years, Gutenberg developed a printing press that could produce more than a hundred copies a day (of a page or document) that were meticulously alike. Printing swept so quickly through Europe that by the time Columbus returned to Spain, it was already in widespread use. Millions of books were printed during the second half of the 1400s. The printing press was one of the most important inventions of all time.

Gutenberg's invention marked the beginnings of our contemporary communications revolution. However, even though Gutenberg added a new medium of communication, for several centuries the revolution progressed slowly indeed. Furthermore, it did not displace earlier ways of communicating. The use of spoken language was then, and remains now, the primary mode of communication. Writing, and then printing, supplemented that oral tradition, but never replaced it.

Between the time of Gutenberg and today, more and more media were added to our communications tool-kit. Each was a product of some technological change. The pace of change was slow at first—almost four hundred years passed before steam-powered presses came into use (in the 1830s). But as the Industrial Revolution that began in the late eighteenth century picked up its pace, popular newspapers and magazines were developed and circulated to increasing numbers of people in all Western societies. The twentieth century witnessed still newer media. Film, radio, television, and all the sophisticated media we know today increased the methods by which human beings could conquer distance and time as they engaged in the basic process of communication through the use of shared languages.

In the less developed countries, the media arrived more slowly, and even today they may be less elaborate. But in most contemporary societies, virtually every citizen has access to news, entertainment, and other information via radio, newspapers, films, and, increasingly, television. Only in the most remote parts of the world—in a shrinking number of areas where political regimes continue to deny citizens access to information or among the poorest of the poor—are people still living in isolation from mass communications.

Whether we mark the beginnings with Gutenberg or with the turn of the twentieth century, all these developments represent a true revolution in human communication. Furthermore, the omnipresence of mass communications in the life of ordinary citizens is primarily a phenomenon of the second half of this century. That is only a brief segment in the five thousand years of recorded human history and but a wink of time in the millions of years of human evolution. Language-using human beings like us lived on this planet for tens of thousands of years before portable media (such as writing on clay tablets) came into use.

To gain perspective on the swiftness of these changes, keep in mind that some of the oldest U.S. citizens today remember living in a country where

FIGURE 1.2 Significant Transitions in Human Communication

I. The Development of Speech and Language
Between 90,000 and 35,000 B.C.

II. The Invention of Writing
Starting about 2500 B.C.

III. The Invention of the Printing Press
1456

IV. The Beginnings of Mass Newspapers
Early 1830s

V. The Electric Telegraph
1844

VI. The Introduction of Films
About 1900

VII. Beginnings of Broadcasting
Radio, 1920s; television, late 1940s

VIII. The Computer Revolution
Following World War II

there were no movies, radio, or television. Try to imagine what your life would be like without television and VCRs, CDs and stereo, or newspapers, radio, magazines, and books. Gone would be the incredible flow of information and entertainment they provide. Some people might say "good riddance" to all of it, but there is no denying that most people would miss it sorely.

For many Americans, probably the majority, the mass media are mainly a source of entertainment. People turn to television for their favorite quiz show, the newspaper for the sports pages, the radio for popular music, a paperback novel for relaxation, or the movies for an action adventure. Generally, recreational users of the media do not worry much about the effects of mass communication on society, or even on their own behavior. If they criticize the media, it is with complaints that they can't find enough of their favorite type of TV program, they didn't like the last videotape they rented, or they are bored by the news.

A more thoughtful segment of the public realizes how deeply embedded the media are in modern life and is concerned about how they influence us both individually and collectively. These people are conscious of the roles played by the media in society. They want to understand fully how the

DEPENDENCY THEORY

People in contemporary urban-industrial societies, such as ours, rely on mass communication for all kinds of information that they find difficult to obtain elsewhere. They turn to the media to be entertained, to get news, to find out where they can purchase things they need at the best prices, to locate suitable housing, to obtain many kinds of services, to seek employment, or sometimes to find someone to date or even marry.

A major reason for this dependency is that we live in a society in which networks of interpersonal ties are not as deeply established as they once were in pre-industrial societies. In contemporary "mass" societies, we do retain family ties and networks of friendships, but we receive only a limited amount of information through them. Moreover, they are not as extensive and open as was the case in older traditional societies, where people lived together in small communities for generation after generation without mass media.

In modern life, most people live in physical proximity to one another, but with extensive differences based on ethnicity, race, education, income, religion, and other characteristics. Such social and cultural differences pose many barriers to interpersonal communication. This tends to inhibit the free flow of information between people, and it leads them to turn to other sources to get the information that they need. As a consequence, in large part, it is the mass media that fill these needs today, creating a condition of dependency on mass communication. This explanation of the relationship between the content of the mass media, the nature of society, and the communications behavior of audiences is called *media*

media operate, what influences they create, and how much control we actually have over them. They are concerned about future trends and how those will affect their children. Obviously, these are very complex issues. Nevertheless, we can gain some perspective on them. Providing the necessary information to do so is a major goal of this book.

Aside from whether people like or dislike the media, our society is very *dependent* on mass communication.[10] This dependence is both social and personal. At the social level, the media play an indispensable part in economic and industrial activities. Directly, they provide jobs for millions of workers. Indirectly, they enable millions more to earn a living. For example, every business or industry selling goods or services is dependent on advertising. Large numbers of people are employed in the advertising labor force. The same is true of public relations; that professional activity would be impossibly restricted without mass media. Similarly, the music industry—both the performers and the recording business—is deeply dependent on radio, movies, and television. Since the media are large profit-making industries in their own right, they provide investment opportunities for many Americans, either through direct ownership of stock or indirect participation in retirement fund portfolios. Mass communication has also become a central part of

dependency theory, and its major propositions can be summed up in the following terms:[1]

1. People in all societies *need information* in order to make decisions about such matters as food, shelter, employment, transportation, political issues, entertainment, and other aspects of family life.

2. In traditional societies, people tend to pursue similar ways of life and are linked by *word-of-mouth* networks of extended families, deeply established friendships, long-term neighbors, and other social ties from which they obtain the information that they need.

3. In urban-industrial societies, populations are composed of unlike people brought together through internal migrations and immigrations from outside. They are *greatly differentiated* by such factors as race, ethnicity, occupational specialization, and economic class.

4. Because of their far greater social differentiation, people in urban-industrial societies have *fewer* effective word-of-mouth channels based on deeply established networks of social ties through which they can obtain the information that they need in daily life.

5. Thus, people in urban-industrial societies are *dependent* on mass communication for information needed to make many kinds of decisions. From the media, they obtain a flow of information, advice, and role models in the news, entertainment, and advertising that they use as a basis for those decisions.

1. For a more detailed discussion of dependency theory and its implications, see Melvin L. DeFleur and Sandra Ball-Rokeach, *Theories of Mass Communication,* 4th ed. (New York: Longman, 1982), pp. 240–250.

American politics. Candidates gain exposure for themselves and their ideas through the media. In fact, electing a president these days would be dreadfully cumbersome if candidates had no other means of campaigning than traveling around the country making speeches from tree stumps and railroad platforms, as they did before electronic media were available.

The list of media-dependent aspects of modern society includes not only entertainment, economics, and politics but also education, science, religion, charities, agriculture, and transportation. In one way or another, and to a greater or lesser degree, almost every major social activity in modern life depends on mass communication.

Media dependency extends to a more personal level because mass communication is woven into our day-to-day existence as individuals. We listen to the radio as a background for many kinds of work and recreation. We look to the newspaper for all kinds of consumer information, from the best buys at the supermarket and the used-car lot to stock market quotations and job openings. During the day, millions of us follow the latest adventures of a favorite soap opera. As we drive to work or do chores at home, we catch the latest tunes and news bulletins on the radio. At night, we use movies, television, and videocassettes for entertainment. Books and magazines bring us specialized information we need for school, hobbies, or in-depth understanding of public affairs. Clearly, individuals use the mass media day-in and day-out to gratify the need for entertainment or enlightenment, as well as for other practical purposes.

But there is another, darker side to this dependency. The effects of the media may be *bad*, claim some critics. They warn us that mass communication may be doing things to us that we really do not want. Some say that media content makes us more violent, weakens our moral character, controls our beliefs, attitudes, and opinions, leads us to buy things we do not need, and heavily influences many of the decisions that we think we make independently.

Other analysts claim the media are forces for *good* in society. They say that the media enrich our lives and bring us all closer together, provide us with satisfying and stress-relieving entertainment, and make us more aware of important public issues and problems. These analysts maintain that the media help us understand social problems, enlighten us politically, improve our aesthetic tastes for good music and theater, and aid in rooting out corrupt or incompetent government officials.

Most of us suspect that all these conflicting claims are true, that the media produce both positive *and* negative effects—not only on us but on our neighbors and friends and, beyond them, the nation and even the world. We understand that because the media are complex and present many kinds of content, for a variety of purposes, to people in all walks of life, there are bound to be controversies as to their influences and effects.

Defining Mass Communication and Mass Media

At first glance, a formal definition of mass communication may seem unnecessary. After all, we are already familiar with movies, newspapers, and television sets. But when film, print, or broadcasting is used to communicate with large audiences, what is actually happening? Do all the media operate according to the same underlying principles of communication, or is each medium unique in some way? And are the principles underlying mass communication different from those for a face-to-face conversation between two people? These questions are critical to understanding the nature of mass communication.

We cannot define mass communication in a quick and simple way because each medium includes its own special kinds of communicators, technologies, groups, kinds of content, types of audiences, and effects. To develop a good definition of mass communication, we must take all these aspects into account and proceed one step at a time, describing each of the major features before pulling them together. In the sections that follow, that is exactly our strategy. We shall look at each "stage" in the mass communication process before combining all the stages into an overall basic definition. The first step is to explain how and why mass communication is a *linear process*.

Mass Communication as a Linear Process

Mass communication can be conceptualized within an expanded version of the linear model that helps explain face-to-face communication. Each stage is far more complex, but, as can be seen, the basic stages are very similar:

1. Mass communication begins with senders who are *professional communicators.* They *decide on the nature and goals of a message* to be presented to an audience via their particular medium. (That message may be a news report, an advertising campaign, a movie, or some other media presentation.)
2. The *intended meanings are encoded* by production specialists (a news team, a film company, a magazine staff, etc.). The encoding process includes the selection of not only verbal and nonverbal symbols, but the special effects that are possible with a particular medium (sound, graphics, color, etc.).
3. The *message is transmitted* through the use of specialized technologies characteristic of print, film, or broadcasting to disseminate it as widely as possible.
4. *A large and diverse* (mass) *audience* of individual receivers attend to the medium and *perceive* the incoming message in very selective ways.

5. *Individual receivers* construct interpretations of the message in such a way that they *experience subjective meanings*, which are to at least some degree parallel to those intended by the professional communicators.
6. As a result of experiencing these meanings, *receivers are influenced in some way* in their feelings, thoughts, or actions; that is, the communication has some effect.

These six stages provide not only a basic identification of what takes place in the process of mass communication, but also a convenient framework for defining it carefully. After discussing each stage more fully, we can formulate a rather precise definition of mass communication, enabling us to separate it clearly from other forms.

Stage one: Deciding what to communicate to whom   The first stage in the mass communication process occurs when one or more *professional communicators* (senders) decide on the nature and goals of a message to be produced in a form suitable to be transmitted via a particular medium. Such communicators are specialists who make their living working for some part of the communication industry. There are a great many kinds— reporters, film directors, actors, authors, editorial writers, advertising executives, preachers, official spokespersons, and many more. They gather, edit, or design media content—news, entertainment, dramas, advertising messages, public relations messages, political campaigns, and so forth.

Stage two: Encoding media messages   Professional communicators depend on a host of specialists to help formulate and produce, that is, *encode,* intended meanings in their messages. Creative people—artists, authors, researchers, composers, copy writers, editors, and directors— shape and reshape messages into specific forms for eventual transmission. Technicians handle the mechanical and electronic aspects of the media. Commercial sponsors trying to sell their products supply funds to finance the production efforts. Other auxiliary groups supporting the professional communicators include agencies that prepare commercial advertising, wire services that provide news reports, polling groups that count how many people a medium is reaching, and researchers who discover better ways of getting the message across.

The motives of all these people vary. Some work solely for their salaries. Others strive to enhance their reputations. Some simply love their work.[11] Many act out of a desire for excellence or a belief in the message they communicate. The majority of professional communicators probably have a combination of these motives.

Stage three: Transmitting media messages   One of the main characteristics of mass communication is relatively *rapid dissemination*. Modern media are truly remarkable in their ability to move messages across distance and time. Even books, the slowest of the media, are disseminated rapidly by comparison with earlier times. Centuries ago, months or even years of painstaking hand lettering was required to reproduce a single *manu scriptus*; it took even longer to get it to its ultimate users. Today, high-speed presses can run off hundreds of thousands of copies of a book, which can be distributed around the country in a matter of days. The same is true of the other media: Once a film is produced, copies can be sent to theaters all over the country virtually overnight, to be seen within a few weeks by millions of viewers. Radio and television, being virtually instantaneous, conquer vast distances without delay. As many as a billion people may see a single "live" broadcast of an event (for example, the World Cup soccer match).

Besides being rapid, modern mass communication is usually *continuous* rather than sporadic; that is, the messages are sent on a scheduled basis, not on someone's whim. Newspapers appear every day, magazines weekly or monthly; publishers and movie producers provide a continual flow of books and films to the public.

The transmission of mass communication involves the use of *mass media*. We note this obvious fact because it is important to understand exactly what such a medium is, and what it is not. Recall the simple definition of a medium (of any kind):

> A medium is any object or device used for communicating a message by moving physical information over distance or preserving it through time.

Long before the age of print, film, and broadcasting, people used media that could transmit messages over distance or preserve them through time. Prehistoric people used cave drawings that have lasted for fifteen thousand years or more. Many people used flags, smoke signals, drums, or handwritten manuscripts as media to extend their ability to communicate. Some of these media are still in use. Today, the media of mass communication are usually identified as print, film, and broadcasting. They depend on sophisticated, elaborate technology, such as microwave transmission, computerized typesetting equipment, and communications satellites.

Stage four: Perceiving media messages   The "mass" in mass communication provides an important key to the way in which media messages are perceived by large and diverse audiences. It came to be part of the name of the process many years ago, and it refers to the social nature of audiences rather than to their size. The meaning of the word "mass" grew out of beliefs concerning the nature of modern society that were popular among intellectuals early in this century. Those thinkers believed that urban-industrial societies were increasingly made up of individuals whose social ties to others were eroding. Such observers saw that the extended rural family, which included grandparents, aunts, uncles, and cousins, was breaking down as people flocked to the cities. They saw that immigration resulted in a mixture of people with different national origins, ethnic and racial characteristics, and cultural backgrounds. Concentrating such diverse groups together in cities, they assumed, would result in a society where social

Many kinds of media are used in human communication. The essential feature of any medium is that it is some form of technical device that either preserves a message through time (as in print) or transmits physical information over distance in such a way that it can be perceived and interpreted by one or more receivers. The flags used for centuries by Navy signal personnel are a good example. However, although they are used by professional communicators, they lack other essential characteristics of a mass medium—wide and continuous dissemination of their messages for the purpose of influencing large, diverse audiences. (United States Naval Institute)

bonds between people would be weak, rather than strong as in earlier times. This, they thought, would lead to a society composed of people who would maintain psychological distance from one another and *would not communicate readily* on a one-to-one basis.

Theoretically, then, a "mass society" is one in which people act as socially isolated individuals rather than as members of families or other kinds of groups.[12] Thus, modern society was once thought to be a kind of "lonely crowd" made up of diverse people who did not know one another well, were not bound to one another by strong friendships, loyalties, or family ties, and did not have an open flow of interpersonal communication.[13]

This kind of society, early students of mass communication thought, would form the audiences of receivers for the media that were developing at the beginning of this century. The importance of the "mass" idea is that individuals in such large, socially diverse audiences were thought to be particularly *easy to influence*—individual by individual—with the use of propaganda and other forms of mass communication content. Because each person was supposedly isolated, the assumption was that effects of mass media messages would not be softened by social influences from other sources, such as networks of friends and family members.

Today, we no longer assume that audiences for the mass media are a lonely crowd. Research by social scientists over several decades has shown that people in an urban and industrial society still maintain strong relationships with their families, friends, and other groups. They are not psychologically isolated individual receivers at the mercy of every form of propaganda that comes along. What they interpret from the mass media is heavily influenced by the people around them. In other words, the older ideas once attached to the word "mass" just do not accurately describe these audiences.

At the same time, it is very clear that American society is culturally diverse to a great degree. Because of a long history of immigration, it is made up of literally hundreds of groups with different national, ethnic, or racial origins. Each brought, and retains to some degree, a somewhat distinct culture. The population is also highly stratified in terms of income, education, power, and prestige. Different kinds of people have more or less of each of these characteristics. If we add the influence of age, gender, region, and occupation, it is clear that receivers in American audiences for mass communication are exceedingly diverse.

This great social, economic, and cultural diversity is the basis of a huge range of tastes and interests in media content. Because of those differing tastes and interests, both attention to and perception of media messages is *highly selective*. What may appeal to and be attended to closely by an affluent resident of Italian-American origin living in a Northeastern suburb may be totally ignored by a poor Cajun farmer living in rural Louisiana. Thus, attention to and perception of media messages is closely related to the social, cultural, and psychological characteristics of each individual receiver in the potential audience.

Stage five: Decoding and interpreting media messages We have seen that the essence of human communication is the achievement of more or less parallel sets of meanings between those sending and those attending to the message—which holds true whether the communication is a face-to-face conversation or a TV show transmitted to millions of viewers. We stressed that in person-to-person communication, the receiver interprets the message by drawing on his or her stored meanings for verbal and non-verbal symbols. The result is that the meanings constructed by the receiver may or may not be identical with those intended by the sender. That is also precisely the case in mass communication.

In an audience of great diversity, it is to be expected that the multitude of receivers will have a multitude of ways in which to assign meaning to an incoming mass media message. The very social, cultural, and psychological characteristics that determine patterns of attention and perception also determine how different kinds of people interpret the meaning of such messages. For this reason, one person may be thrilled by a movie that seems boring to another. Some people will find a particular news item exciting and important; others will see it as dull and insignificant. Some will be moved to purchase a product by an advertisement that others regard as objectionable "clutter."

Stage six: Influencing media audiences The last stage in mass communication is the outcome of the preceding stages. As a result of interpreting the meaning of the message, receivers in the audience are *changed* in some way. The changes may or may not be immediately visible, and they can range from trivial to profound. Most are minor. But whatever their nature, they constitute the effects of the media, at least at an individual level. For example, a person may learn some relatively inconsequential new facts by

The term "mass communication" implies a large and diverse audience. The term derives from the concept of a *mass society*. This refers not just to the idea that large numbers of people are involved, but to the fact that they do not have as many close personal ties to one another as was the case in earlier, more traditional settings. In earlier societies, people were bound closely by ties based on family, long-lasting friendships, and traditional loyalties to rulers. In the United States, immigration brought together people from many different origins. Added to this diversity are their varied political persuasions, distinct occupations, and different income levels. Thus, the American mass audience is made up of people from many racial, religious, economic, and cultural backgrounds. (© 1993 Ted Soqui, Impact Visuals)

hearing a weather report on the radio. Thus, providing a person with information that he or she did not have is a change brought about by a medium. Or, again at a trivial level, a person may be entertained by reading the comics in the Sunday paper. In this case, causing a person to feel better is also a form of media influence.

Exposure to the content of mass media can also change individuals in far more significant ways. Under some circumstances, it can influence their beliefs, opinions, and attitudes—altering their thinking about public issues or political party preferences. Meanings aroused by media messages can also alter people's actions—influencing them to buy, donate, dress differently, give up smoking, vote, go on a diet, or engage in many other forms of behavior.

Although significant changes of this kind usually occur in minor stages over a long period, these are the kinds of influences that concern critics of the media. Some believe that rock music encourages youngsters to use drugs, engage in sex, or adopt satanism. Others charge that some TV programs stimulate children to defy authority and act aggressively. It is not easy to prove or disprove such claims. At this point, research suggests the public's fears about such influences may be exaggerated. However, as later chapters will show, such influences can occur, but as a complex and long-term process.

At a social, or *collective*, rather than a personal level, mass communication can change a culture. One example is language and its shared understandings. The media constantly introduce new words and meanings or alter the meanings of older words. For example, until about 1992, Americans did not have a shared meaning for "ethnic cleansing." But after the wars in Serbia and Bosnia (in the former Yugoslavia) received wide media coverage, millions of people learned this new term and its meaning as a form of genocide. Other examples of media-introduced words from recent times are perestroika, yuppies, crack, and sound-bite.

Mass communication can also change our feelings about social issues. The American news media's images of tanks and soldiers attacking demonstrating students in Beijing's Tiananmen Square in 1989 evoked widespread outrage toward China's leadership. Thus, the media play a part in swaying public opinion and, by doing so, help modify history. The study of the various kinds of effects of mass communication is a complex field. We will review such influences in detail in later chapters.

The last stage in the mass communication process, and for many the most important, is influencing people. Such influence can take many forms. It may be simply to make people feel better from entertainment, to provide them with facts that they need, to bring them to buy one brand over another, or to sway their vote at election time. Few communication researchers today believe that the media have no influence on their audiences. (The Terry Wild Studio; Owen Franken, Stock, Boston)

A concise definition of mass communication   Each of the six stages we have described must be part of a succinct definition of mass communication. With these stages in mind, we can define the process in the following terms:

> *Mass communication* is a process in which professional communicators design and use media to disseminate messages widely, rapidly, and continuously in order to arouse intended meanings in large, diverse, and selectively attending audiences in attempts to influence them in a variety of ways.

With this definition in mind, we must ask which media really are (or are not) mass media. This is not an idle question because it sets boundaries on what needs to be studied under the general heading "mass communication."

Which Media Are Mass Media?

Is the telephone a mass medium? How about a fax machine or personal computers linked in a network? What about a large museum? Should we include rock concerts, theatrical performances, church services, or parades in our study of mass communication? After all, each of these human activities is a form of communication. For our purposes, whether or not a medium is one of the mass media depends on whether it can carry out the process of mass communication we have just defined.

To be true to our definition, we would have to conclude that talking on the telephone is *not* really mass communication, because the audience is not large and diverse; usually, there is only one person at each end of the line. Furthermore, telephone users usually are not "professional communicators." The same is true of a fax machine or even a set of personal computers on which individuals exchange messages. A museum does not participate in mass communication because it does not provide "rapid dissemination" with "media." Neither does a rock concert qualify, because it does not disseminate messages "over distance"; it is a form of direct communication to audiences. Similarly, no situation in which live performers and an audience can see each other directly—in a theater or church, at a sports event or parade—is an example of mediated communication. Large-scale advertising by direct mail might qualify—except that it is not really "continuous." Thus, our definition turns out to be relatively rigorous. It enables us to set definite boundaries on what can be included and studied as a medium of mass communication. By definition, none of the activities listed above is such a medium, although all of them can arouse meanings and influence people.

At first glance, the record industry appears to be a mass medium; its audience is certainly large and diverse. However, the record industry is not a mass medium because artists and members of the audience interpret their meanings in a host of different ways. Some people might debate this, but we can conclude that the record industry and the popular music business in the United States depend heavily on the media and deserve extensive discus-

Although we communicate in many ways, some of which depend on the use of media, not all are forms of mass communication. Talking on the telephone certainly depends on a medium, but it is neither continuous nor does it involve a large and diverse audience. Therefore, it does not fit the definition of mass communication. (Copyright© by Walter S. Silver, The Picture Cube)

sion in this text as supportive industries. For that reason, we devote Chapter 14 to popular music and the recording industry.

Similarly, although people often speak of "the news media," this expression is misleading. As we will see in Chapter 12, news is a special form of content produced by media organizations that present their products to the public through the use of the same mass media that bring us communications about drama, music, and sports. Thus, we will treat the gathering and distribution of news not as a distinct mass medium in itself, but as an important *process* dependent on the print and broadcast media.

By exercising the criteria set forth in our definition, then, we can identify precisely what we consider to be mass media in the present text. The major mass media are print (including books, magazines, and newspapers), film (principally commercial motion pictures), and broadcasting (mainly radio and television, but also several associated forms such as cable and video cassettes). Although other kinds of media are worth study, the focus of our attention will be on those that closely fit our definition of mass communication.

Comparing Face-to-Face and Mass Communication

Having examined the nature of both face-to-face and mass communication, we can now ask how these two processes differ from each other. Our starting point is that mass communication (1) depends on mechanical or electronic media and (2) addresses a large, diverse audience. We can ask, then, do these two characteristics alter the communication process in some fundamental way? Or is mass communication just like any other form of human communication? More simply, what difference does the use of media make?

The Consequences of Using Media

Although human communication depends on verbal and nonverbal symbols and all the stages of the basic linear model, introducing a medium into communication between two people clearly alters the process. One major consequence is the loss of direct feedback. A second is severe limitation on effective role-taking because of that loss.

Loss of feedback   If we are talking on the telephone, we cannot obtain the rich return cues available when we are face-to-face with someone. In more direct interpersonal communication, we can easily detect visual, nonverbal messages such as a puzzled look, raised eyebrows, a smile, or a frown. We can also sense subtle tones of voice—small changes of pitch and emphasis that may not come through on the phone line. Exchanges of messages by fax machine or by personal computer are even more limited. The fax paper or the computer screen does not show visual, nonverbal signals, and it cannot convey nuances of pronunciation and timing. All these cues help us know how our message is being received in face-to-face interpersonal communication—or, indeed, whether it is being received at all.

Inability to engage in effective role-taking   Limitations on feedback in mediated communication reduce our ability to engage in effective role-taking. Where accuracy and congruence of meanings are critical, mediated communication is simply less effective than the direct, face-to-face, interpersonal mode—a point that most people understand very well. Each of us has at some time told a friend, "Let's not try to settle this over the telephone. Let's get together and talk it over."

Still, talking on the telephone, typing messages on a networked computer, or sending documents by fax is clearly human communication, because each depends on imprinted traces, learned patterns of meaning, labeling with language symbols, transmission of information over distance, perception by the receiver, and the construction of reasonably congruent meanings by receiver and sender. In short, interpersonal communication through virtually any medium follows the same stages as face-to-face communication. However, using a medium definitely does alter the process.

Loss of accuracy   The big difference between face-to-face and mediated communication is a loss of accuracy due to limitations on feedback and role-taking. Stated more formally:

1. The use of a medium *reduces the richness of feedback and limits the process of role-taking.*
2. Both of these limitations *increase the possibility of incongruence between meanings of senders and those of receivers.*
3. When meanings of sender and receiver are incongruent, *accuracy is reduced.*
4. Decreases in accuracy of communication *reduce the probability that the message will influence people in ways desired by the sender.*

Thus, communication via a mass medium between a professional communicator and any particular individual within an audience is very different from face-to-face communication between a sender and a receiver. In mass communication, a large, diverse audience is at the receiving end. There is no realistic way for the professional communicator to engage in any role-taking during the process of transmitting a message or for the audience to provide immediate and ongoing feedback while transmission is taking place.

These limitations are well understood by professional communicators. Dan Rather, Tom Brokaw, and Connie Chung can never place themselves mentally in our individual shoes and thus be able to understand and predict accurately how each of us will receive and interpret a news broadcast. However, broadcasters know some things about the audience in a collective sense. To provide a kind of *a priori* form of feedback, large communication corporations (for example, the major television networks) conduct extensive research on audience characteristics and behavior. The results of such research provide guidelines concerning the likely tastes and interests of the audience at a particular time. The researchers study many categories of people to get an overall picture.

The information obtained from such research is the basis for certain necessary assumptions about audiences, and it has to replace individual-by-individual role-taking. However, this approach has serious limitations, because the assumptions can be inaccurate. That hundreds of magazines, newspapers, films, and television programs have failed over the years despite extensive market research testifies to how imperfect such assumptions can be.

Feedback is similarly limited. Indeed, for all intents and purposes it does not exist. Audience members cannot interrupt what they see as a confusing or infuriating television reporter or gain immediate access to a newspaper editorial writer. Even though mass media often invite letters or phone calls, this kind of reverse flow provides only a delayed trickle of feedback from the few people who are motivated enough to go to the trouble.

Thus, by comparison with face-to-face communication, mass communication is essentially a *rigidly linear process.* Communicators try to guess how their messages will be received, with only indirect, delayed feedback in the form of advertising revenues, research findings, a few telephone calls, occasional letters, movie reviews, and box-office receipts. This delayed feedback may help them shape future communications, but it provides no basis for altering a message while it is being disseminated. As a consequence, accuracy and influencing of any particular member of the audience are significantly limited.

The Consequences of Large, Diverse Audiences

Mass communication differs from face-to-face communication and from mediated interpersonal communication not only because it involves more complex media, but also because the audience is large and diverse. Still, whether there is one receiver or a million, the basic activities of sender and receiver are the same. Even if the sender is a professional and the audience is immense, the act of communication still depends on imprinted traces in the memories of the communicator and the receivers, on patterns of verbal and nonverbal symbols linked to meanings by cultural conventions, on grammar and syntax, and all the rest. Thus, we can conclude that mass communication is not a process that depends on some exotic or unique principles of communication. It is a special form of mediated communication that is limited in accuracy and influence because simultaneous role-taking and feedback are difficult or impossible.

However, the existence of a large and diverse audience can pose still other significant limitations on the content, accuracy, and influence of the messages transmitted by a mass medium. Inevitably, much mass media content—perhaps most of it—is designed for the tastes and presumed intellectual level of "the average citizen" or, often, for the average member of a specialized category of people who are assumed to share some common taste or interest (for instance, all fishing enthusiasts, football fans, or fashion-conscious women). In forming appropriate message content, professional communicators must make assumptions about such audiences. In fact, most professional communicators tend to assume that the majority in their audiences:

1. have a *limited attention span,*
2. prefer to be *entertained rather than enlightened,* and
3. quickly *lose interest in any subject that makes intellectual demands.*

With no intention of being either critical or elitist, we can conclude that in large part these assumptions are correct. Well-educated people with sophisticated tastes and high intellectual capacity are a relatively minor part of the population, and they probably do not attend to the majority of content presented by the American mass media. However, this is not really a problem for the profit-oriented media system, because cultivated citizens are in very short supply and constitute a minute segment of purchasing consumers. Therefore, in attempting to maximize profits, professional communicators can safely ignore this small group. It is much more profitable to reach the much larger numbers of intellectually undemanding receivers, whose aggregate purchasing power is immense. In other words, as we will show in later chapters, reaching large numbers of exactly the *right kind* of people is critically important in the advertising-driven and profit-oriented American system of mass communication. Thus, all of the factors discussed above work together in a kind of system that *encourages media content that is high in entertainment value and low in intellectual demands.*

It is important to understand the conditions and principles that fit together to yield the above consequence, because they explain a great deal about why the media function as they do. Furthermore, we can then more readily understand why the media inevitably attract the attention of deeply concerned critics who have generated a long list of charges and complaints that the media are both trivial and harmful in some way.[14]

These critics urge the media to inform, enlighten, and uplift—to provide in-depth information as a basis for intelligent political decision-making, arts appreciation, and improvement in moral standards. These are commendable goals, which no thoughtful person can seriously dispute. However, the environment in which the media operate makes it very unlikely that these goals will ever be fully achieved—not because greedy people will always control the media, but because our society has defined mass communication as part of the *private enterprise system*. However, when pressed, few critics of American media would exchange our system for one such as exists in China, North Korea, or Cuba, where content remains tightly controlled by an authoritarian government.

The remaining chapters address three major questions. The first—How has American society *shaped* its media?—is answered in Chapters 2 through 7. The factors to be considered are the development of technology, the influence of a growing population with a multicultural composition, a democratic political system, and a profit-oriented economic system in which private ownership is valued. The second question is, How do the media *function?* Chapters 2 through 7 also focus on this issue, addressing the unique features of each medium. They discuss how it operates to disseminate its particular kind of information. They also describe its pattern of adoption by the American population. Finally, the third question asks, How have our media *influenced* us? The answer has two parts: One consists of influences on us as individuals, modifying our beliefs, attitudes, and behavior at a personal level; the other comprises influences on our society at a collective level. That is, how have our media brought about changes in our norms, in our political system, or in our general culture? These issues will be discussed in the final part of the book.

Finally, these broad questions are addressed within a *liberal arts perspective*. That is, the discussion of the development, functioning, and influences of the mass media draws upon a number of fields, including anthropology, the arts, economics, history, psychology, sociology, and even theater. Thus, it presents a broad rather than a narrow view of mass communication in the United States.

Chapter Review

- Human communication differs sharply from the processes used by other species. It depends on systems of learned and shared verbal and nonverbal symbols, their meanings, and conventionalized rules for their use.
- The basic act of human communication can be analyzed in terms of a linear model that includes six major stages: deciding on a message, encoding the message by linking symbols and meanings, transmitting information to span distance, perceiving the incoming symbols, constructing meanings so as to interpret the message, and experiencing some effect. In face-to-face communication, feedback and role-taking are important factors related to accuracy.

- Over several centuries, at an increasing pace in modern times, a true revolution in human communication has taken place through the use of mass media. Advanced contemporary societies are deeply dependent on mass media and probably could not exist in their present form without them.

- Mass communication is a linear process in which professional communicators encode and transmit various kinds of messages to present to different segments of the public for a variety of purposes. Through the use of mass media, those messages are disseminated to large and diverse audiences, who attend to them in selective ways.

- Members of the audience interpret the messages selectively, and the meanings they construct may or may not be parallel to those intended by the communicator. However, if members of the audience are changed in any major or minor way, the message has had an effect.

- Mass communication and face-to-face communication differ in important ways. Because of feedback and role-taking, interpersonal communication can be flexible and influential. Mass communication is largely a one-way, relatively inflexible process. Its large and diverse audiences preclude effective feedback and role-taking. In an advertising-driven and profit-oriented system, media content must be tailored to the majority, whose collective purchasing power is huge, but whose intellectual level and tastes are not very sophisticated. This tailoring of content leads to many criticisms.

- The study of mass communication must include attention to three broad sets of issues: (1) the many ways in which a society's history, values, and economic and political realities have influenced its media; (2) the unique features of each medium in the system that make it different from the others; and (3) the kinds of influences that the media have on us as individuals and on our society and culture.

Notes and References

1. In the present discussion, "language" means the entire array of verbal and nonverbal behaviors, contexts, and artifacts that can modify the meanings constructed by both senders and receivers in the transactional process of human communication. Both verbal and nonverbal dimensions are a critical part of communication using any language. See Melvin DeFleur, Patricia Kearney, and Timothy Plax, "Nonverbal Communication," Chapter 3 in *Fundamentals of Human Communication* (Mountain View, Calif.: Mayfield Publishing, 1993), pp. 67–96.

2. For an extended discussion of the basic nature of face-to-face human communication, see "Verbal Communication," Chapter 2 in DeFleur, Kearney, and Plax, op. cit., pp. 33–64.

3. Phillip Lieberman, "The Evolution of Human Speech: The Fossil Record," Chapter 12 in *The Biology and Evolution of Language*

(Cambridge, Mass.: Harvard University Press, 1984), pp. 287–329.

4. The full range of the incredibly flexible human voice comes through especially in opera. Anyone listening to the pronunciation required by Gilbert and Sullivan's *Mikado* or the range of sounds produced by Luciano Pavarotti singing the major role in *I Pagliacci* can appreciate how different our voice box, larynx, tongue, and lip structures are from those of the great apes, which can make only a limited range of sounds.

5. For a more detailed explanation of these and other changes in human communication, see Melvin L. DeFleur and Sandra Ball-Rokeach, "A Theory of Transitions," Chapter 1 in *Theories of Mass Communication,* 5th ed. (White Plains, N.Y.: Longman, 1989), pp. 7–26.

6. For a detailed analysis of linear versus transactional models of the human communica-

tion process, see "The Communication Process: An Overview," Chapter 1 in DeFleur, Kearney, and Plax, op. cit., pp. 5–31.

7. The basis for using the word "information" in this way is the classical theory of Shannon and Weaver. For their interesting treatment of the process of transmitting information, see Claude E. Shannon and Warren Weaver, *The Mathematical Theory of Communication* (Urbana, Ill.: University of Illinois Press, 1949).

8. A classic and readable work on the functioning of human memory is Alexander R. Luria, *The Neurophysiology of Memory* (Washington, D.C.: V. H. Winston, 1976), pp. 1–16. A contemporary and readable summary of scientific investigation of the ways the brain functions in human memory can be found in Mortimer Mishkin and Tim Appenzeller, "The Anatomy of Memory," *Scientific American*, June 1987, pp. 80–92.

9. Robert McCrum, William Cran, and Robert MacNeil, *The Story of English* (New York: Penguin, 1986), pp. 102–103.

10. For a discussion of the broad implications of such dependency, see Dallas W. Smyth, *Dependency Road: Communication, Capitalism, Consciousness, and Canada* (Norwood, N.J.: Ablex, 1981). For a summary of basic dependency theory, see DeFleur and Ball-Rokeach, op. cit., pp. 297–327.

11. Job satisfaction among media professionals is relatively high. A survey of over 1,500 professionals in various media industries found that people working in advertising film, journalism, photography, public relations, radio, and television were more satisfied with six dimensions of their work than similar individuals not working in media industries. See Margaret H. DeFleur, "Foundations of Job Satisfaction in the Media Industries," *Journalism Educator*, 47, 1 (Spring 1992), pp. 3–15.

12. A frequently cited analysis of the "mass" concept can be found in Herbert Blumer, "Collective Behavior," in *Principles of Sociology*, ed. Alfred M. Lee (New York: Barnes and Noble, 1953), pp. 208–210.

13. See David Reisman, *The Lonely Crowd: A Study of the Changing American Character* (New Haven, Conn.: Yale University Press, 1950).

14. Marshall McLuhan and Fred McLuhan, *Laws of the Media* (Toronto: University of Toronto Press, 1989).

PART ONE

THE
DEVELOPMENT
OF THE
PRINT MEDIA

The invention and development of printing with movable type brought about the most radical transformation in the conditions of intellectual life in the history of Western civilization . . . its effects were sooner or later felt in every department of human activity.

Myron Gilmore, The World of Humanism, 1453–1517, 1952

Books: The Oldest Mass Medium

From the time that human beings began to speak until about five thousand years ago, no system for recording and recovering ideas in written form had been devised. Human culture did develop at an ever-increasing pace, but it failed to develop *media* that could conquer either time or distance. Except for the occasional use of such artifacts as notched sticks or such devices as flags, smoke, or drums, preliterate societies were limited to the capacity of the human voice to conquer distance and to the capability of personal memories to preserve ideas through time.

In a society limited to oral communication, skilled storytellers could train new generations in myths and legends in order to preserve a group's history. However, because an accumulation of ideas could not be permanently stored, societies found it difficult to accumulate either elaborate technologies or a rich cultural heritage. Furthermore, without writing, it was very difficult for a tribe or society that had conquered another to establish efficient control over it. Conquerors could not exert close administrative supervision over large populations that were beyond their immediate visual inspection. As a result of all these limitations of the oral society, social, political, and economic progress was agonizingly slow.

Writing changed all that. It was the *second* great communications revolution, following the development of speech and language, but it took some time. The first medium people used extensively was stone. But it was very cumbersome. Stone "documents" could not be moved around easily. Within a few centuries, however, more *portable* media came into use. Ancient societies began to preserve and accumulate ideas in written form using such media as scrolls and tablets. Once it became possible to send information across great distances by using media that were easy to move, the administration of conquered lands became much easier. Larger and larger empires were established, and trade increased contacts between dissimilar peoples. These effects of writing enriched cultures and quickened the pace of social change.

The introduction of books increased portability still more. Even though early books were much more efficient than scrolls, making even a single copy was a woefully laborious process. Using a quill pen and ink, a skilled scribe might need a year or more of diligent work to copy one book. Consequently, books were in very limited supply. Few could afford them, and only a tiny segment of the population could read.

The printing press and movable type revolutionized communication, and they represent the *third* great communications revolution. Today, we have difficulty realizing what a drastic change printing brought. Compared with the dazzling color and moving images of the television tube, a printed book may seem drab and dull. However, in the broad sweep of human history, the book is undoubtedly one of the most influential inventions of all time. Next to language itself, no form of communication played a greater part in shaping human development.

Within a few years of the introduction of printing, millions of copies of books were pouring from the presses of Europe. The rich history of books—from the first primitive tablets to the contemporary book industry— is a vital part of the evolution of human culture. Books remain the most respected medium of communication. With great flexibility and simplicity, they store and make available for later recovery the most complex and significant knowledge developed by humankind. Even today's fantastic electronic marvels cannot yet do that as efficiently.

This chapter reviews milestones in the incredibly long history of efforts to develop techniques for storing and recovering information. Of great importance in the unfolding story is the evolution of *technology*. Even the earliest media represented advances in technology, for example, from stone to portable media as writing surfaces. Each major communications revolution—from the development of writing to the electronic systems of today— was based on significant solutions to technical problems.

In Europe in the fifteenth century, a few decades before Columbus sailed, a great breakthrough in technology made the printed book a reality. Today, a thriving book publishing industry continues to transmit to us everything from escapist fiction to the complex technicalities of supercomputers and high-energy physics. It seems highly unlikely that books will soon be replaced.

The Transition to Writing

The first step in understanding contemporary print media is to examine the origins of writing. The graphic representation of ideas, unlike speaking, requires a medium. Thus, the development of writing and the evolution of media are part of the same process.

A medium, as noted in Chapter 1, is simply a device for moving what we called physical information through time or space. It can be any object or arrangement of objects used to accomplish that goal so as to enable human

Among the earliest attempts to record ideas in graphic form were the cave paintings produced by Cro-Magnon people in Southern Europe and parts of Asia during the last Ice Age. Some 230 caves with wall and ceiling paintings have been found. The reindeer shown here, painted some 15,000 years ago, was found in Font-de-Gaume, Dordogne, France. It shows a high level of artistic skill. However, the meanings and purposes of such graphic representations remain unclear. (Neg. No. 15038, Courtesy Department of Library Services, American Museum of Natural History)

beings to transmit, receive, and interpret messages. Media used in writing depend on some physical representation of thoughts and ideas, either by "pictures" or by other kinds of graphic symbols that are associated with culturally agreed-on meanings. The earliest known attempts to represent ideas with pictures—the first step toward the development of writing—were cave paintings. Fifteen to twenty thousand years ago, unknown artists painted hundreds of dramatic murals on the walls of caves in what is now Europe. Well-known examples are in Lascaux in France and Altamira in Spain. The paintings show bison, reindeer, wild horses—even extinct animals—and the men who hunted them. The artists' tools were bones, sticks, and primitive brushes used to color their images. The pigments were made of animal fat mixed with charcoal and powdered earth of several bright colors.[1]

As artistic products, the prehistoric paintings are large, vivid, dramatic, and surprisingly contemporary in appearance. Certainly, they show a grasp of the complex principles of pictorial representation equaling that of modern artists. Picasso himself, after seeing the great cave at Altamira, is said to have remarked that artists today have learned nothing (about color and composition) beyond what those prehistoric painters knew. However, for all their artistic merits, as a way of communicating ideas, such paintings are extremely limited. Their meaning to the people who made them and the reasons for which they were done remain unknown.

Nevertheless, representing something *graphically* was a significant step beyond oral description of the objects and events being portrayed. Even if they were only mnemonic devices, serving loosely as memory stimulators, depictions such as cave paintings could help a storyteller provide a more detailed and accurate account, compared with unaided recall. In fact, this illustrates one major purpose of writing. In all its forms, writing is a tool for preserving ideas that were expressed earlier. In other words (to borrow today's computer jargon), writing is a system for *information storage*. Just as we seek more and more storage capacity in computers, primitive people sought systems of graphic representation of language symbols to free themselves from the limitations and inaccuracies of human memory.

Writing must also serve another purpose. Ideally, it permits people who did not record the ideas originally to recover accurately the meanings and implications of those who did. In this sense (to borrow again from contemporary computer usage), writing is a means of *information exchange*. Thus, the development of picture drawing was not enough. Only the original artist could recall accurately the intended meanings represented. The next step was to standardize both the depictions and the rules for interpreting their meaning, an advance that took more than ten thousand years.

From Glyphs to Alphabets

Even before writing was developed, people were using many complex non-verbal communication systems—hairstyles, clothing, tattoos, scars, jewelry, crowns, and other objects and ornaments—to signify rank, status, power, marital status, achievement, occupation, family membership, and dozens of additional meanings that were vital to life in their societies. However, it was not until about 4000 B.C. that people began to leave records in the form of codified writing that can be understood today. They left graphic representations on many surfaces—pottery, baskets, sticks, cloth, walls, animal skins, bark, stone, and even leaves. On these media they rendered a rich variety of signs, symbols, drawings, and decorative motifs to convey socially important ideas.

Representing ideas with written symbols At some unknown point between 5000 and 4000 B.C., people in several areas of the Near East began to use drawings to represent ideas in a somewhat more uniform way.[2] Most were agricultural people, and their early attempts at writing grew out of their need to keep accurate accounts of land ownership, boundaries, crop sales, and the like. Some were traders who needed reliable records of cargoes, profits, and commercial transactions. Generally, these people's symbols were pictures of what they knew—birds, the sun, a bundle of grain, a boat, the head of a bull, or parts of the human body. Writing in a technical sense began to emerge when such graphic signs came to represent *standardized meanings* that were agreed on by conventions among a given people. Thus, for those who understood the rules, a simplified drawing of a human form could mean "a man"; a crudely drawn rising sun might be "one day"; a stylized human foot, "walking"; and a wavy line, "water." The use of such graphic representations was a form of writing because each symbol was associated with one and only one idea or concept. When strung together

they could tell a story. For example, the drawings just mentioned might be strung together to mean "A man walked for a day along a river."

Such a system is called *ideographic writing*, or "thought writing." Because it associates specific whole thoughts or meanings with pictures, it is also sometimes called *pictographic writing*. Such a system links carefully drawn, often highly stylized representations of objects to ideas, rather than to specific sounds. Well-known ideographic systems of writing were those developed independently by the early Egyptians, the Chinese, and the Maya of the New World.

Actually, ideographic writing works quite well given enough ideograms, one of which is needed for each idea or thought that is to be recorded. However, as a culture becomes more complex, and as technology expands, more and more ideas or concepts are included in the culture, requiring an increasing number of standardized ideograms. In a complex society, such a system can become very cumbersome. And when basic symbols are combined to provide for new meanings, it adds additional complexity to the written language. For example, the Chinese combined the basic character for "female" with that for "broom" to produce the compound symbol for "housewife."

The number of characters required in a system of ideographic writing can eventually become staggering. The hieroglyphic (sacred carving) system used during the early Egyptian dynasties required only about seven hundred different ideograms. Elementary Chinese today requires knowledge of about four thousand characters, and truly literary Chinese scholars may know up to fifty thousand. Thus, ideographic systems can be very difficult to learn and use. Historically, where such systems were used, the majority of the population remained illiterate. Even powerful rulers were sometimes unable

The Egyptians produced a beautiful form of pictographic writing sometime between 5000 and 4000 B.C. Their hieroglyphs were ideograms, with each symbol standing for a separate idea. Later, they introduced phonograms into their system for consonants, but did not provide for vowel sounds. Thus, we cannot pronounce their ancient language today. (The Granger Collection, New York)

to read and write and, like others, relied on professional scribes. Because of their importance and skill, scribes often enjoyed high status and impressive financial rewards.

Graphic representation of sound　A much simpler system of writing is to link graphic symbols not to ideas or thoughts, but to sounds. Here, instead of ideograms, simpler phonograms are all that are needed. A *phonogram* is a graphic symbol linked to a specified sound by a convention or rule that prevails among those who speak a particular language. The alphabet of twenty-six letters that we use every day is the obvious example. It comes to us from ancient sources. Even its name reveals its origins—*alpha* and *beta* are the first two letters of the ancient Greek version. Alphabets, like books and printing, rank as one of the great human breakthroughs. They made reading and writing—hideously complex activities with ideographic systems—literally "child's play." All of us, when we first tackled our ABCs as children, learned the consonant and vowel sounds uniquely linked to each of the twenty-six letters. Using these along with numerals and a scattering of additional symbols representing punctuation, contractions, and so on, we can transform into written form virtually any set of ideas that need to be expressed in our language.

Origins of our alphabet　It took over two thousand years after the earliest attempts at writing to develop the alphabet that you are using to read these passages. We inherited our contemporary alphabet from the Romans. They had refined the one that they obtained from the Etruscans, who in turn copied most of theirs from the Greeks. But the Greeks did not invent the idea. They refined their alphabet from origins leading back through the

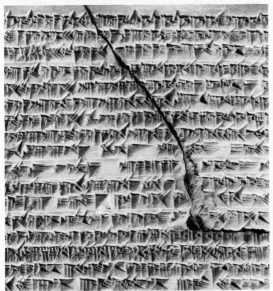

Alphabetical writing was first developed by the Sumerians between 3000 and 2500 B.C. They made impressions on clay tablets with a wedge-shaped stick to produce *cuneiform writing*. The tablets could be preserved by baking. Each of the stylized symbols stood for a particular sound, like one of our syllables, rather than for a whole idea, or concept. Combining symbols to form words meant that only a few hundred symbols were needed, rather than thousands of pictograms. By around 500 B.C., the Greeks had refined this system greatly and standardized an alphabet so effectively that only about two dozen letters were needed to represent the sounds of all the words in their language. (Giraudon/Art Resource; The Bettmann Archive)

Phoenicians, the Assyrians, and the Babylonians to the Sumerians (who probably did start the process).

Apparently, our phonetic system of writing originated when the Sumerians began to use *cuneiform writing* as a means to make records.[3] The Sumerians were an agricultural people who lived from about 3000 to around 1700 B.C. in the so-called Fertile Crescent—a region that included parts of Iraq, between the Tigris and Euphrates rivers, plus portions of present-day Israel, Jordan, Syria, Turkey, and Iran. This was the part of the ancient world where the earliest known civilizations developed.

The Sumerians found that a pad of wet clay held in a small flat box made an excellent medium, at least compared to stone. They made little drawings on the surface with a sharpened stick to represent ideas in pictographic form. They soon simplified the pictures into highly stylized forms, and the drawings eventually evolved into abstract ideograms that were unrecognizable as representations of actual objects. In part, the reason for this was that the writers sharpened their sticks to a wedgelike shape at the end, and it was hard to draw lifelike pictures with this instrument. Again, technology shaped the medium.

What the Sumerians eventually hit on was the idea of letting a particular *character* (graphic symbol) stand for a sound. In their system, sounds were usually whole syllables, rather than the much simpler sound elements of the alphabets that came later. Even though it was complex by comparison with today's alphabets, the Sumerian cuneiform system, using phonograms to represent sounds rather than ideas, was a major breakthrough. It was an innovation that other societies would soon improve on and simplify.

We can note in passing that the Egyptians, who were very powerful during the same period, worked out a similar idea. However, they did not want to

GOING TO SCHOOL AND LEARNING TO READ IN HELLENISTIC GREECE:
A Linchpin to Ancient History

When you were about six years old, you began going to school. You might not have liked it at the time, but you had no alternative because the law required it. Indeed, if your parents had not complied and made sure that you attended, they could have gone to jail! Americans realized early on that democracy requires a literate citizenry. State-by-state, beginning in the 1830s, the United States adopted a system of free (tax-supported), universal, and compulsory education.

Actually, the idea of educating every child to read, write, and calculate is an ancient one. We owe our shared belief in the importance of universal education to cultural values that were developed in Greece during the classical period (from about 490 B.C. to about 250 B.C.) and to educational policies that were implemented during the Hellenistic period (from about 250 B.C. to about 50 B.C.).

During those centuries, the Greeks were still making the transition to the Age of Writing. That is, they were making the change from being a predominantly oral society to becoming a society that routinely used writing. The standardization and adoption of the Ionian alphabet by the beginning of the classical period greatly increased the pace of that transition.

Plato (427–347 B.C.) stressed the importance of education in *The Republic*, the first well-known book of philosophy.[1] His ideas were widely recognized and respected in Greece at the dawning of the Hellenistic period. Beyond seeing learning as a noble accomplishment in its own right, the Greeks had very practical and even selfish reasons for trying to educate their children.

As Aristotle (384–322 B.C.) maintained, writing served four useful purposes in society: It was critical not only for learning things but for making money, for managing one's household, and for conducting civic affairs. Indeed, monetary transactions had become commonplace by that time and were regulated by written deeds, contracts, and receipts. Household and family documents such as wills, leases, and loans

give up the beautiful pictograms that made up their earlier hieroglyphics, so they tried to mix an ideographic system with phonograms. It was not an effective solution. Furthermore, a serious shortcoming of their system was that they had no symbols to represent vowels. For example, the Egyptians would write (the equivalent of) the word "foot" as "ft." or "beetle" as "btl." Occasionally, we do this today with abbreviations such as *blvd.* for "boulevard" and *Mr.* for "Mister." It is up to the reader, who of course knows how to pronounce the written forms, to supply the missing sounds. Unfortunately for the Egyptians, the pronunciation of missing sounds was lost over the centuries and their written language died out. Otherwise, you might well be reading the present passages in some contemporary version of ancient Egyptian hieroglyphics!

Beginning about 500 B.C., the Greeks developed a remarkably efficient alphabet (including vowels) out of many versions that had been developed earlier. Standardizing their alphabet greatly enriched Greek culture. For example, in 403 B.C., Athens passed a law making one version (the Ionian

were often recorded in writing by public officials in civil service. Furthermore, the legal codes, all lawsuits, and even testimony before the courts had to be prepared in writing.

The high importance attached to literacy during the classical period shows in the following passage from Diordus Siculus:

> For it is by means of writing alone that the dead are brought to the mind of the living, and it is through the written word that people who are spatially very far apart communicate with each other as though they were nearby. . . . Generally it is this alone which preserves the finest sayings of wise men and the oracles of the gods, as well as the philosophy and all of culture, and hands them on to succeeding generations for all time. Therefore while it is true that nature is the cause of life, the cause of the *good* life is education based on the written word.[2]

Thus, by the third century before Christ, writing was in relatively wide use throughout Greece.

One reason for the value placed on education was *ethnocentrism*. The Hellenistic Greeks thought that only they were a superior people and regarded virtually everyone else as "barbarians." They did not want to learn the languages of other people unless it was absolutely necessary. They felt that literacy in Greek was a sign of superiority and that promoting such literacy was a means of protecting their way of life. At the same time, however, literacy did not extend equally to everyone; schooling for children of the property-owning classes was deemed particularly important.

Because Greece was a society of contracts, wills, deeds, receipts, lawsuits, and many other kinds of business and legal transactions, families of even modest means had to be literate to protect their property and interests. For this reason, almost all Greek cities of any size maintained schools where both boys and girls could learn their letters and the elements of mathematics. Many schools also offered instruction in music, the arts, and oratory.

1. *The Republic of Plato*. trans. Francis MacDonald Cornford (London: Oxford University Press, 1941).

2. William V. Harris, *Ancient Literacy* (Cambridge, Mass.: Harvard University Press. 1989). p. 26.

alphabet) compulsory in official documents. The simplified alphabet promoted increased literacy, formal education, and learning. Much of Greek culture was passed on and became an important base of contemporary Western civilization because the Greeks had a written language that could easily be read.

Portable Media

Phonetic writing with a standardized alphabet was not the only innovation that enabled the Greeks to develop a rich culture. Another factor was that portable media were in wide use by their time. Although the clay tablets of the Sumerians were portable, they were heavy and bulky. As early as 3000 B.C., the Egyptians had developed *papyrus* (from which, incidentally, came our modern word "paper"). Actually, papyrus is a tall reed common to marshy areas of the Nile. Its stalks, up to two inches thick, were sliced thin and laid out in two layers at right angles to each other. When pounded together, pressed, and dried, papyrus yielded a paperlike surface suitable for writing on with brush or reed pen. The sheets were sometimes joined together at the ends and rolled up on a stick to produce a *scroll*—which was in fact an early book, although a rather cumbersome one.

It was a great technological solution, but because production was controlled by the Egyptians (and later the Romans), papyrus was often difficult to obtain and was in perpetually short supply. As the use of writing spread, alternatives had to be devised. One important writing surface that was used until relatively modern times was *parchment,* which is tanned skin of a sheep or goat. Another was *vellum,* which resembled parchment but was prepared from the skin of a young calf. They were very expensive. A single animal yielded only a few pages. However, animal skin surfaces were very durable, which helped some ancient scrolls survive into later centuries.

The Development of Books

All during the time in which writing, alphabets, and portable media were being developed, societies themselves were undergoing great changes. Sophisticated urban centers were established; techniques of agriculture were refined; technologies of war and conquest were developed; and the pace of trade and contact between unlike peoples quickened. Above all, great empires rose as a result of military conquest. An example was the huge Roman Empire, in which virtually the entire known Western world was brought together under a single government administration. Communicating to administer this vast political system was a constant challenge.

The Need for Lengthy Documents

A variety of forces led to the need for documents for recording lengthy and complex ideas. Hundreds of years before biblical times, thinkers were debating complex and perplexing questions: What is the true nature of reality, and how do people know it? What supernatural forces exist, and what part do they play in people's lives? What is a just social order? What are those bright bodies in the sky, and why do they move in such regular patterns? How do animals differ from human beings? What happens to us after death?

Human curiosity and intelligence led the search for answers, and knowledge about the physical, social, and spiritual world accumulated. This created the need to record far more than just short messages, such as edicts, land claims, and administrative commands. For example, one of the great problems for those who governed was how to stabilize the social order and make it work more justly. Ancient *codes of law* were required to provide formal guidelines for behavior and to specify punishments for deviance. A classic example is the system of 282 laws developed by the Babylonian king Hammurabi almost four thousand years ago. His laws covered everything from the regulation of commerce and military affairs to the practice of medicine and the treatment of children. In the absence of books, he had his laws carved on huge *stellae*—blocks of basalt eight feet square—that were set up in the center of each major city in his empire. But it was a terribly cumbersome system. Portable media were far more efficient, and by the time of Christ, the Romans were using books to store their famous legal codes.

The rise of great religious systems created a need to record sacred writings. The Hebrew scriptures (the Old Testament to Christians) represent an outstanding example of a long and complex set of ideas that could not have been passed on accurately in oral form over many generations. Later, Christians began to record the revelations, testimony, and injunctions of their New Testament, and Muslims followed with the sacred Koran.

What all of this meant was that for centuries there was an unfilled need for a better way to record very extensive messages. As we noted, the earliest attempts to meet this need made use of scrolls. As Rome developed, for example, libraries were established in all the empire's major cities for the storage and use of scrolls. For the most part, scrolls were used to record government transactions and various codes of law. But there were also collections representing treatises by philosophers on a great variety of topics. Unfortunately, few scrolls from Roman times survived, because invading groups who brought about Rome's decline almost always destroyed such documents in an effort to eradicate the power of those they had subjugated.

Copying Books by Hand

With alphabetical writing well developed and with the availability of efficient portable media, such as papyrus, parchment, and vellum, it was not difficult for the Romans to move beyond the cumbersome scroll to the bound book with cut pages of uniform size. It was the Romans who developed the book into the form that we know today.[4] They gave us pages with writing on both sides and bound at the edge between boards or covers.

The Romans did far more than just establish the physical nature of the medium. They also developed many innovations that shaped the formats we use in preparing books. For example, they greatly refined the alphabet and originated much of the grammatical structure we use to form sentences today. They came up with the idea of *paragraphs* and a standardized system of *punctuation*, much like we use now. Their *majuscule letters*, used extensively on their monuments, became the capital letters you see on this page. Their smaller *minuscule letters* (refined under the influence of Charlemagne in the eighth century as Carolingian scripts) became our lower-case letters. (However, the terms "upper-case" and "lower-case" came from early printers, who stored majuscule and minuscule type in separate trays—upper and lower cases—for easy access.)

Beginning in 410 A.D., illiterate tribes (the Germanic Visigoths and Vandals) began to invade Rome. Rome was quickly overrun. By 476, the last emperor was deposed, and the great empire that had dominated the world for nearly a thousand years came to an inglorious end. The Roman alphabet and the art of book production were all but lost as the Western world entered the so-called Dark Ages, which lasted for seven centuries. 700 years

It was within the Christian monasteries that the precious knowledge of alphabetical writing and books was preserved and improved. Using the Roman alphabet and letter forms (sometimes modified in various ways) and the Latin language, diligent monks hand-copied thousands upon thousands of *manu scripti*, a term we still use.[5] Most of the books produced in the monasteries were merely working documents used for practical purposes in churches and schools. However, some were exquisite works of art, illuminated (decorated) with elaborate letters and drawings. Perhaps the most beautiful book ever made is the extraordinary *Book of Kells*, created by monks around 800 A.D. in a remote monastery in the western part of Ireland. Written and illuminated using precious materials gathered from all the parts of the world known at the time, the *Book of Kells* was prepared as an act of deep religious devotion. It survives intact today as a great national treasure of Ireland, carefully preserved at Trinity College in Dublin.

As Europe slowly emerged from the Dark Ages, interest in books and writing began to grow. It was no longer only monks who were copying books by hand. In many urban centers, commercial establishments called *scriptoria* manufactured and sold books. One factor that encouraged this type of book production was the growing proportion of the population that was literate. During the thirteenth century, universities were established in the major

Producing *manu scripti* was a demanding and laborious process. Between the fifth century, when Roman civilization was destroyed, and the fifteenth century, when printing began, writing skills were preserved in monasteries and *scriptoria*, where skilled craftsmen copied books letter by letter on parchment or vellum. Many of these books were beautiful works of art executed as acts of religious devotion. Others were working copies of books needed for practical purposes in courts, schools, and churches. (The Bettmann Archive)

cities in Europe as centers of learning and the arts. Many books were produced for teaching. The wealthy student could buy books already copied from the official texts by professional scribes; the poor student had to rent textbooks, one chapter at a time, and laboriously copy each page. For the most part, Latin remained the language of the learned. But more and more, as the thirteenth century progressed, some scribes wrote in the local "vulgar" (or vernacular) languages common to the people, such as English, French, German, and Italian.

One of the technologies that would become critically important in the development of print as a medium was the manufacture of *paper.* The Chinese had developed paper and used it extensively as early as the second century.[6] During the middle of the eighth century, Persian soldiers captured a group of Chinese papermakers, who either taught the process to their captors or revealed it under torture (depending on whose version of the story one believes). In any case, the Islamic world had paper long before Europe did, and it was brought to Spain by the Moors in the twelfth century.

The use of paper caught on quickly, and within a century it was being skillfully produced in all parts of Europe. Some papermakers became truly skilled craftsmen, who made beautiful papers from linen rags. Some of the paper produced in the 1400s and 1500s rivals the best seen today. Most, however, was cruder, but it had two qualities that made it highly attractive—it was cheap (by comparison with sheep and goat skins), and it was available. It would be a long time, however, before parchment and vellum were entirely replaced for the best-quality books.

An important advance in the production of books was the introduction of paper. Papermaking technology originated in China and spread into Europe from the Arabic world after the invasion of Spain by the Moors. Until about a century ago, all paper was made from a sludge of ground-up rags. Such a sludge was boiled in the vat at the left and then filtered into the second container to remove coarse particles. In the vat at the right, a thin film of the sludge was scooped up on a screen and dumped out on a flat surface to form a sheet of paper. The sheets were squeezed in the press at the far right to remove water. Finally, after the edges were trimmed, the paper was sold in bundles such as the one against the back wall. (Culver Pictures, Inc.)

The Invention and Spread of the Printing Press

The development of printing technology did not, as we have seen, come out of nowhere. Many of the prerequisites—paper and parchment, literacy, the need for lengthy documents, and a sophisticated format for books—were already a part of Western culture. Nevertheless, the invention of a practical and efficient press marked one of those occasions when the ideas of a single person made a great difference. Furthermore, once it became available, printing with movable type was immediately recognized as a truly extraordinary technological advance.

Gutenberg's Remarkable Machine

Printing as such was not really unknown before Gutenberg's time.[7] The Chinese had begun making inked impressions from elaborately carved wooden blocks shortly after 175 A.D., when they first developed paper. Whole books were done in this manner by the Koreans and Japanese during the eighth century, and some survive today. The Koreans had even cast individual letters in metal, although very crudely, more than a century before Gutenberg perfected the process. Block printing, however, was extremely difficult and inefficient. To print from a block, an entire page of characters had to be carved (in reverse) on a single slab of hard wood. Ink was applied to the carved face, and paper or parchment was pressed onto the surface. A roller or brush was passed over the surface, and an impression resulted. The characters did not reproduce very clearly because the wood did not take razor-sharp edges. Also, the process was very laborious. Even if all went well, only a limited number of copies (perhaps a hundred or so) could be printed by this technique before the wood became too worn. In many ways it was almost as easy to copy the work by hand.

Even though all of these forerunners had been around for a long time, Johannes Gutenberg made a truly significant technological advance. He eventually managed to cast *individual letters* in molten metal in such a way that they would be as clear and sharp as those on this page. The individual letters (movable type) could be set up in lines, one letter at a time, as needed and they could be used over and over without wearing out quickly.

It took Gutenberg about twenty-five years to develop just the right process for making the letters, arranging them in a suitable press, developing the right inks, and bringing all the components together into a practical system. First, he made hard steel punches with the letters engraved in relief on the end. Then he made little molds by striking the letters individually into suitable pieces of softer brass. With the help of a special metal alloy of his own formula, he was able to cast crisp letters individually and to make many identical castings of each one. He also developed an ink made from lamp black (a soft soot) ground in a linseed oil varnish.[8] These techniques were so simple and practical that they remained in use for hundreds of years.

Gutenberg also worked out a superior system for pressing the blank pages against the inked type. It was essentially a screw-type press, much like

One of the significant transitions in the ability of humans to communicate came when Johannes Gutenberg developed movable type with individual letters cast in metal. The age of printing began in 1455 when he produced two hundred copies of his famous Bible. He worked many years to perfect his invention and feared that such mechanical reproduction would never be accepted. (Culver Pictures, Inc.)

those used for centuries for making wine. Even that invention required many years' experimentation to get just the right pressure on the parchment or paper. He experimented with many techniques, toiling to produce beautiful examples of printed copy so that when he was ready, his products would have a market among the rich. But he was filled with doubts. Would people buy what he was going to produce? He was not at all sure that mechanical printing would ever catch on. He feared that many people would still want their books copied by hand.

Unfortunately, just before he was ready to produce his first great book, he ran out of money. To continue his project, he borrowed heavily from his lawyer, Johannes Fust (whose son-in-law Peter Schöffer was the foreman in the print shop). Eventually, in 1455, Gutenberg was ready for his first great success. He designed, set the type for, and printed two hundred copies of all the pages needed for his famous 42-line Bible. It was, and still is, one of the world's most beautiful examples of the printer's art.

The work was intended for an elite and wealthy market. He even managed to produce "illuminated" letters complete with colors with his press. But before the copies were ready for binding and final sale, Fust demanded repayment of the loan. Gutenberg did not have the money, and so the lawyer took him to court. With his assistant Schöffer testifying against him at the trial, Gutenberg was stripped of his press, type, Bible, and even legal claim to his inventions. The lawyer and his son-in-law took over everything and left Gutenberg financially ruined. The poor man lost his eyesight and remained destitute until, toward the end of his life, a nobleman named

Adolph von Nassau took pity on him and made him a member of his court, providing him with a yearly allowance of cloth, grain, and wine. The brilliant inventor, whose work changed the world and enriched the lives of billions of people in later centuries, died in 1468 at the age of seventy, blind and without any recognition of his timeless contribution to humanity. Even today, little or no mention is made of his contribution in books (printed by the process he invented) used in college and university history courses.[9]

The Print Revolution

The number of books available exploded as the printing press quickly spread throughout Europe. During the *incunabula* (the period between 1455 and 1501—not even a half-century), a tidal wave of books printed in vulgar languages (not Latin) passed into the hands of increasingly eager populations. No one knows how many were published during the period, but estimates range between 8 and 20 million copies.[10] (The average press run was only about five hundred copies per book, so these figures represent a very large number of titles.)

Because more and more of these books appeared in the vernacular, printing greatly accelerated developments in science, philosophy, and religion. Knowledge of many topics became available to almost anyone who was literate in a common language and could purchase a book. Books were still expensive, but much cheaper than the older *manu scripti*. It is very likely that even before Columbus's departure for the New World (about thirty-six years after Gutenberg's first press run), more books were printed than the accumulated total of all the *manu scripti* that had been copied during the previous thousand years. As presses and printing technology were improved during the 1600s and 1700s, and as paper became increasingly available, the number of books printed each year grew sharply.

By the beginning of the 1500s, printers had established their craft in virtually every major city in Europe and were publishing books on almost every topic then known. The first press in England was that of William Caxton, who in 1476 printed the first book in English, *Recuyell of the Historyes of Troye* (a translation from the French). Caxton turned out dozens of titles, including many literary classics and translations. Other printers in England quickly followed his example.

Printing in the New World began very early. In 1539 (approximately a century before the Pilgrims arrived at Plymouth Rock), Juan Pablo set up a press in Mexico City and printed the first book in the Americas, a religious work entitled *Breve y Mass Compendiosa Doctrina Cristiana*. This book, like many others that followed, was printed under the authority of the Spanish archbishop of Mexico.

The development of education in many countries contributed greatly to the growth of book publishing. More universities were established every year until, by the sixteenth century, they were common in all parts of Western Europe. Religious changes (primarily the rise of Protestantism) brought a considerable demand for Bibles and other religious works. In addition, the Renaissance, with its expansion of art, science, philosophy, and literature, contributed to the demand for more and more books. Gutenberg had unleashed a powerful medium indeed.

At first, books were not recognized as a political force. But as soon as those in authority realized that printing could be used to circulate ideas contrary to those of the ruling powers, presses came under strong regulation. In 1529, for example, Henry VIII of England established a list of prohibited books and a system of licensing. In spite of these measures, many documents expressing political opinions were circulated. Still, the Tudors, who ruled in the mid-1500s, were effective censors of England's presses. This suppression was to last more than a century.[11]

Book Publishing in North America

The first printing press in the English colonies was set up at Harvard College in Cambridge, Massachusetts, where the first book was published in 1640—the *Whole Booke of Psalmes* (most often called the *Bay Psalm Book*). The college controlled the press until 1662, when the Massachusetts legislature took it over.

Book publishing was slow to develop in the colonies, partly because of restrictions imposed by the Crown. But political dissent around the time of the American Revolution stimulated all forms of publishing. In the decades following the Revolution, New York, Boston, and Philadelphia became established as centers of a budding publishing industry. Books published early in American history included religious works, almanacs, and political and social treatises.

Before the 1800s, only a small proportion of the American population was able to read. Most people lived on farms, where literacy was of little significance. This held back the development of a large book-publishing industry. After the turn of the century, however, the new political system spurred an increasing interest in reading and writing. Democracy required an informed citizenry if it was to survive as its architects hoped. Voters needed to be able to read about candidates and issues. Also, as the century moved on and industrialization progressed, it became apparent that a more literate work force would be required to manage factories, work in banks, and serve in various parts of a more specialized and expanding economy.

For these reasons, advocates of public education such as Horace Mann fought for statewide school systems that would provide free, universal, and compulsory education. The concept of tax-supported public schools was thought by many wealthy property owners to be both radical and dangerous. They saw it as a sure way for them to lose the political power they had traditionally exercised. However, at Mann's urging, the Commonwealth of Massachusetts established just such a system in 1834. Other states soon followed, and most Americans began educating their children in the new public schools.

A press was established at Harvard College in Cambridge, Massachusetts, in 1640. *The Whole Booke of Psalmes* ("Bay Psalm Book"), produced that year by Stephan Day, is American's most precious piece of printing. (By permission of Houghton Library, Harvard University)

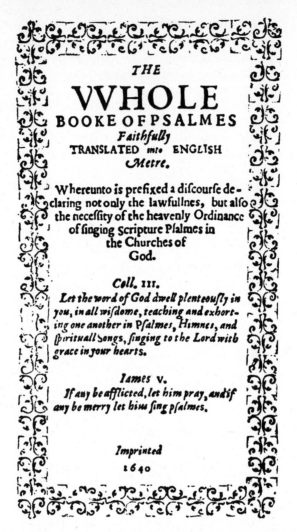

THE
VVHOLE
BOOKE OF PSALMES
Faithfully
TRANSLATED *into* ENGLISH
Metre.

Whereunto is prefixed a difcourfe de-
claring not only the lawfullnes, but alfo
the neceffity of the heavenly Ordinance
of finging Scripture Pfalmes in
the Churches of
God.

Coll. III.
*Let the word of God dwell plenteoufly in
you, in all wifdome, teaching and exhort-
ing one another in Pfalmes, Himnes, and
fpirituall Songs, finging to the Lord with
grace in your hearts.*

Iames v.
*If any be afflicted, let him pray, and if
any be merry let him fing pfalmes.*

Imprinted
1640

By the 1840s, a growing reading audience existed in the United States. In addition to scholarly and religious works, cheap paperback reprints of popular books appeared, and then sensational fiction. By 1855, the United States far surpassed England in the number of books sold. That year saw the first publication of Whitman's *Leaves of Grass*, Longfellow's *Hiawatha*, and Bartlett's *Familiar Quotations* (which is now in its fifteenth edition). Probably no other American book had as much impact on its time as one published during this period—Harriet Beecher Stowe's antislavery novel, *Uncle Tom's Cabin*. Thus, as the nineteenth century progressed, book publishing in the United States became well established as a business, as a shaper of American culture, and as a form of mass communication.[12]

Although numerous advances in technology have continued to alter the mechanics of producing books, the industry has changed surprisingly little since the nineteenth century. It is more commercialized and larger today, and more than fifty thousand titles are published each year. Of these, fiction makes up only about 10 percent. College textbooks account for a large portion of the books published; nearly 80 million copies are sold each year. In recent years, many publishing companies have merged, and others have been acquired by large corporations.

Today, books are still our most respected medium. They allow the slow, thorough development of ideas that serious and complex subjects demand. At the same time, they are also a diverse medium. Everything from Einstein's theory of relativity to hard-core pornography is available in book form. At this point, the future of books seems secure. But so did the future of radio and general circulation magazines in the 1940s. New media continue to appear, and it is not impossible that books may some day be replaced by competing technologies. A long-term decline in reading ability poses another challenge. Today's college textbooks, for instance, must be easier to read than were those twenty years ago. Both factors could cause the publishing industry problems in years to come.

Books as a Contemporary Medium

The truly remarkable nature of books—and the irreplaceable services they provide to individuals and society—can be seen in the fact that they have not only survived but prospered in the face of increasingly sophisticated competing media. Movies, television, and VCRs combine both audio and visual presentations as well as color. They would seem to pose vigorous competition with the comparatively unexciting format of a book. Yet people still buy and read millions of books every year. They remain a medium of entertainment, the principal repository of our culture, our guides to technical knowledge, the source of teachings on many subjects, and our basic reference for religious doctrines.

The Unique Character of Books

Books obviously have distinctive characteristics that set them apart from other media. Certainly, they differ from other print media, such as newspapers and magazines, in that they are bound, covered, and consecutive from beginning to end. Because books (such as the present text) often take years to write and a year or more to produce, even after the author gives the finished manuscript to the publisher, they are less timely than newspapers and magazines. Nevertheless, like other mass media, they are encoded by professional communicators and generally transmitted to relatively large and diverse audiences. One obvious difference from several other media is that, like movies, books are not basically supported by advertising (although some publishers are experimenting with this idea). Thus, books have to earn profits for their producers on the basis of their content. Moreover, books are made to last longer than any other medium, and this durability lends itself to in-depth exploration and development of a topic or idea.

Adam Smith, *The Wealth of Nations* (1776) This work set forth the basic theory of capitalism that served as a guide for the early Industrial Revolution. Even today, many of his ideas are fundamental to the values guiding business and industry throughout the world.

Karl Marx, *Das Kapital* (1867) This analysis of history and the relationship between owners and workers provided the philosophical foundations on which were developed huge communist empires in the twentieth century. They had profound influences on millions of people who lived within them and on millions who resisted them.

Gunnar Myrdal, *An American Dilemma: The Negro Problem and American Democracy* (1944) This respected Swedish scholar's analysis of race relations in the United States accurately identified as the nation's greatest problem its structure of laws and deeply institutionalized beliefs and practices justifying prejudice and discrimination against African-Americans. Myrdal's ideas made important intellectual contributions to the civil rights movement of the 1960s and consequent changes in federal and local laws.

Rachel Carson, *Silent Spring* (1962) This book provided a wake-up call regarding the impact of pesticides on the environment. It was a powerful message that is widely credited with stimulating the environmental movement that has been so important in recent decades.

Betty Friedan, *The Feminine Mystique*, (1963) This book revived the women's movement that flowered during the nineteenth century and then faltered after women won the right to vote in 1918 (with the 19th Amendment to the U.S. Constitution). Friedan decried the stereotyping of women as little but homemakers and sex objects. Her ideas led to the current trend of reshaping women's roles in society.

These characteristics suit the book to a special role among the mass media. Most books sell only a few thousand copies. Even a national runaway best-seller will probably sell no more than 10 million copies over its effective life—less than the audience for soap operas during a single day of television. Yet the social importance of books can hardly be overestimated. Like opinion magazines, books often persuade the influential, and they can have an impact far beyond their actual sales and readership. In addition to serving as a major channel for transmitting our cultural heritage, they have promoted powerful ideas and inspired changes, even revolutions.

Books are often seen as entertaining, but some people also see them as dangerous. For that reason, even today, some books are removed from approved school district lists, banned from libraries, and burned by dictators. In 1989, author Salman Rushdie was condemned to death (in absentia) by the Ayatollah Khomeini of Iran for his book *Satanic Verses*. He has remained in hiding for several years. In 1992, he made two rare appearances—in New York City and Washington, D.C.—and returned to his hermitic life in a heavily guarded compound in Britain. No other medium has attracted persecution to the extent that books have.

The Publishing Industry: An Overview

Between the authors who prepare the manuscript and the public that receives its messages lies the publishing company. The publisher's role is threefold: (1) to *select* and help shape what books will be published, (2) to *produce* the book as a physical artifact, and (3) to *distribute* the book to booksellers for a profit. Authors prepare the content, but publishers take the risks involved in investing the money to convert a manuscript into a book and to promote and distribute it to its ultimate consumers. Because most publishers are private businesses, they must earn a profit. In recent years, the industry's changing economics have influenced the way publishers carry out their other roles.

Table 2.1 shows the changes in the output of book publishers in the United States during this century. Clearly, publishing is a growing industry, with more copies of books in publication in recent years than at any time in the nation's history. There are several reasons for this. During the first half of the century, book publishing took an important turn toward *commercialism*. What it offered the public was determined more and more by a sharp focus on profits. Many kinds of books were found to be unprofitable, and the number of titles published declined steadily. In the 1920s, the Book-of-the-Month Club and the Literary Guild were founded, expanding the market for novels and other works by reaching those who lived far from bookstores. Following World War II, more and more Americans pursued higher education. Demand for textbooks soared as returning veterans, helped by the G.I. Bill, filled colleges and universities. And the postwar baby boom meant that more children entered school than ever before.

One of the significant innovations in book publishing in the United States was the introduction of the now-familiar small *paperback*. Even during the nineteenth century, following the development of cheap paper and high-speed presses, paperback "dime" novels were widely available and an important part of American publishing. However, until well into this century, more "serious" books were always published in hardcover form. In Europe, less expensive paperbound books came into wide use well before World War II, but they did not catch on in the United States. But as books in their traditional form became increasingly expensive, book sales were not keeping pace with population growth. (Note the period 1910–1945 in Figure 2.1.) Then, cheaper printing and binding processes were introduced during the 1950s. The small paperback format made it possible for all kinds of books to reach much larger audiences than ever before. The dollars Americans spent for books increased by a whopping thirty-seven times from mid-century to the present: Total sales went from just over $435 million in 1947 to more

TABLE 2.1
Books Published in the United States during the Twentieth Century

Year	Number of Titles Published	Titles per 1,000 Households
1900	6,356	0.40
1905	8,112	0.45
1910	13,470	0.67
1915	9,734	0.43
1920	8,422	0.34
1925	9,574	0.35
1930	10,027	0.33
1935	8,766	0.27
1940	11,328	0.32
1945	6,548	0.18
1950	11,022	0.25
1955	11,901	0.25
1960	15,012	0.29
1965	28,595	0.50
1970	36,071	0.58
1975	39,372	0.55
1980	42,377	0.48
1985	50,070	0.58
1992	44,528	0.47

Sources: U.S. Bureau of the Census, Statistical Abstracts of the United States *(Washington, D.C.: U.S. Government Printing Office, 1986 and 1992. Also,* The Bowker Annual, *1993.*

Early in this century, when radio and television were not available, Americans bought and read more books per capita than at any period since that time. Then, as alternative media became available (and as societal conditions changed, with the Great Depression and World War II), book publishing declined sharply. Since 1960, with the coming of the inexpensive paperback, book publishing and consumption have shown a strong upward trend. These data seem to contradict the generalization that Americans no longer read.

FIGURE 2.1
Trends in Book Publishing in the United States, 1900–1992

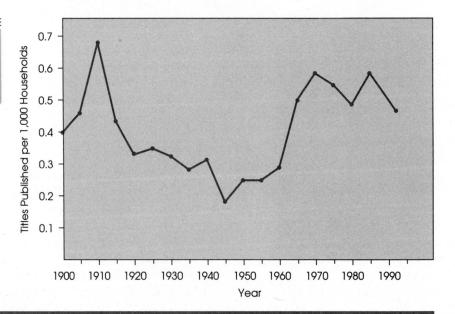

than $22.6 billion in 1993! The number of places where one could buy books also increased: Books were sold in 8,360 stores in 1957 compared to 26,787 in 1992.[13]

These trends reflect significant changes within the industry. Book publishing had long been something of a dignified "gentlemen's" profession. It had not been the place to find either "big money" or shrewd business practices. Much of the industry had consisted of family-owned enterprises passed on from one generation to the next. To take advantage of the new opportunities for growth, however, publishers needed new resources, so they "went public." This means that they sold stock in their companies. That was an important turning point. Banks and other profit-oriented investors began to buy the stock. In addition, since the 1960s, many publishers have merged or been acquired by communications corporations and conglomerates. As a result of such buyouts, publishing firms gained financial resources along with more sophisticated business and marketing skills. However, there was a cost. Many publishers lost autonomy in decision-making. They had to show constant profits for their stockholders and new owners. Publishing was no longer a dignified club, but an objective business. Today, mergers and sales of companies take place at a dizzying pace. Publishing companies are now no different from other businesses, being subject to buyouts, takeovers, and, above all, concern about annual profits. Also, the publishing industry was the first media industry in the United States to be subject to heavy foreign investment (from British and German publishers mainly)—a trend that continues today.

These economic changes forced publishers to alter the ways in which they acquired, produced, and sold books. Until recent decades, publishers ran their own printing plants, binderies, and bookstores. Now, they contract with independent printers and binders to work on specific books. They may also hire people outside the company to design the book, draw illustrations, edit and proofread copy, and do many of the other tasks that are part of the process of producing books.

Critics of publishing's new economic realities most fear the increasing role of market research in determining what will be published. Traditionally, publishers produced many meritorious works simply because they valued their high literary or scientific quality. They knew that such books would never yield large profits, but they published them anyway because they felt obligated to maintain high standards and to contribute to the accumulation of knowledge. But, as publishing houses passed into the hands of owners interested mainly in profits, they had to adopt a completely businesslike approach, together with modern management techniques.

Today, few book publishers are likely to express interest in noteworthy but unprofitable manuscripts. Instead, they are more likely to consider themselves simply as profit-makers, little different in principle from producers of beer, soap, or soup. Their aim is to manufacture a product that they can persuade consumers to buy, regardless of its other qualities. Thus, publishing today looks less like a craft or an intellectual enterprise and more like any other modern industry. Critics fear that neither the meticulous craftsmanship nor the intellectual standards of traditional publishing will survive, and that in their place we will soon find only "conformity to the median of popular tastes."[14]

The Publishing Process

In addition to publishers, the key people in the production and distribution of books are authors, editors, book manufacturers, bookstores, and sales personnel. Naturally, many kinds of specialists and technicians have supporting roles. Since nonemployees do so much of the work of developing a book, contemporary publishers have to a great extent become orchestrators, hiring and coordinating the work of many outside suppliers.

Types of Publishers and Types of Books

Like theatrical producers, publishers (to some extent, at least) have styles and reputations. In part, these come from how they organize the publishing process, how they deal with authors, and the physical appearance of their books. Some publishers produce books as quickly and cheaply as possible, publishing "instant" books shortly after news events. During recent years, books came onto the market almost overnight on such topics as the Challenger disaster, the Alaska oil spill, the Chernobyl meltdown, and the San Francisco earthquake. Such books take advantage of headlines while they are still freshly in mind. In contrast, other publishers are known for their craftsmanship. Often they are small and concentrate on producing books of high quality. Perhaps even more companies are known for the topic of the books they choose to publish—for example, science, fiction,

TABLE 2.2
Types of Books

Type	Description
Trade	Includes literature, biography, and all fiction and nonfiction books for general reading. These books are usually handled by retail bookstores.
Textbooks	Includes books for elementary and high schools, colleges, and universities. These books are usually sold through educational institutions or college bookstores, but publishers make their sales pitches to state or local school boards or faculty members.
Children's	Sold through bookstores or to schools and libraries.
Reference	Includes dictionaries, encyclopedias, atlases, and similar books. These require long and expensive preparation.
Technical and Scientific	Includes manuals, original research, and technical reports.
Law	Involve the codification of legal materials and constant updating.
Medical	Also require frequent updating.

Source: Smith, Guide to Book Publishing, pp. 128–129. Used by permission of University of Washington Press.

**FIGURE 2.2
Estimated Book Sales
by Category, 1993**

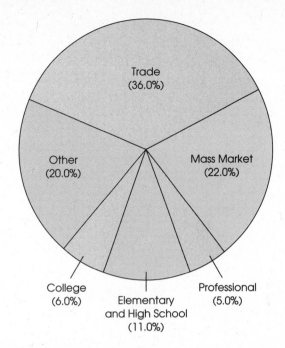

Trade
(36.0%)

Mass Market
(22.0%)

Other
(20.0%)

College
(6.0%)

Elementary
and High School
(11.0%)

Professional
(5.0%)

Note: "Other" includes religious books, book clubs, and mail order business.
Source: Veronis, Suhler and Associates, 1993.

fine arts, medicine, law, or religion. There are other bases of specialization among publishers. Table 2.2 presents a classification of books according to audience and function.

As the pie chart in Figure 2.2 indicates, trade books account for the largest share of books sold by publishers. Trade book sales, totaling about $4.4 billion, make up more than one-third of publishers' total book sales—and that share is rising.[15] Included are books published by university presses, but their output is a very small part of the overall business. However, university presses, associated with and often subsidized by a particular educational institution, are often far more important than their dollar sales suggest. Their books are aimed primarily at scholars and scientists. However, in recent years, many university presses have become more profit-oriented and have been expanding their lists to include topics of popular interest.

Like the movies, books mix business and art. The trade magazines, especially *Publishers Weekly*, monitor industry trends. At a recent symposium on book editing, it was concluded that "the emphasis in book publishing has shifted from the book's artistic value to its news content, a trend partly the result of television promotion." Some other trends also seem likely:

1. Because of escalating production costs, hardcover books may be on the way out, as publishers find it increasingly difficult to compete in today's mass market in both trade and textbook publishing.

2. Highly diversified small publishing houses and university presses with far lower marketing and distribution costs will flourish, while big labor-intensive commercial houses may decline.
3. Because of rising costs, direct-mail sales to customers may begin to replace retail marketing in both textbook and trade publishing.[16]

From Manuscript to Finished Book

Since the time of Plato, whose *Republic* is the earliest surviving book-length work, books have had their first stirrings of life as ideas in the heads of their authors. However, authors are in a very real sense "outsiders" in the publishing world. That is, they are rarely employees of the publisher. But since publishing is a competitive business, the author represents an important resource. Publishers must have a continuing flow of new manuscripts to process and sell, and therefore authors are key players in the process. Without manuscripts, publishers would have no reason for existence. Although publishers have little trouble finding fiction manuscripts—indeed, the publisher of fiction is often inundated—that is not the case for technical works and textbooks.

Beginning novelists may have a difficult time getting their works read by a publisher. Once a work is accepted, however, and especially if an author has previously produced successful works, things get better. The fiction author often receives a substantial advance (against royalties) from the publisher, ranging from a few thousand dollars (for a beginner) up to several million dollars or more (for a well-known writer). *Royalties* are some agreed-on small percentage of the publisher's earnings from selling books to retailers. If the book is successful, a novelist may receive huge additional income from paperback contracts and even movie or television rights.

In trade-book publishing, authors normally use literary agents to represent them. The literary agent ferrets out book ideas, negotiates with the publisher for the author, and contacts publishing houses and particular editors who may be interested in what an author is working on. The agent receives a percentage (usually 15 percent) of the author's share from a book's earnings. Agents also secure advances.

Either an author, an agent, or an editor may initiate the idea for a trade book. As publishers have increased their use of market research, the editor's role in initiating or reshaping the idea for a book has grown. For example, Time, Inc. sometimes sends prospective readers elaborate brochures describing a proposed book or series of books and eliciting responses. The replies received may lead editors to cancel the project or to change its proposed content, format, and promotion.

On the textbook side of publishing, the relationship between publishers and authors differs somewhat. Textbook authors are often sought out and asked to undertake a work that the publisher thinks will sell. They are offered contracts before writing the book on the basis of a detailed outline and perhaps a draft of a chapter or two. However, textbook authors must be specialists in the field in which they are writing, and publishers carefully screen prospects. The financial incentives are also different. Textbook authors usually command lower advances than novelists or writers of other trade books, but a good textbook can often go through several editions, providing a continuous source of income for both the writer and the publisher.

Clearly, publishers are risk-takers. Publishing executive Dan Lacy, commenting on the "essence of publishing as entrepreneurship," notes, "The publisher pays the costs and assumes the risks of issuing each book, and hence he occupies a highly speculative position."[17] Of course, authors also take a risk. Writing a successful novel or textbook can take years. The author may receive advances from the publisher before book publication, but almost all the money comes much later from royalties. If the book does well, the author gets paid; if it does not, he or she has toiled a very long time for very little.

Once the publisher receives the author's original manuscript, several kinds of editors work on it. Publishing companies have many specialized editors, often with impressive-sounding titles, who are responsible for such activities as bringing in manuscripts, analyzing and editing them, and preparing the final copy for the typesetter. One kind is an acquisitions editor, whose work may be devoted mainly to generating ideas for books and finding able and willing authors. Other editors may evaluate the quality of manuscripts and their sales potential. Some work directly with the author as developmental editors to organize the book and help make it the most effective statement of its topic. There are also copy editors, whose main task is to check the spelling, syntax, grammar, and punctuation of a manuscript. Other specialists develop illustrations and design the print style, cover, and format of the book.

To set the manuscript into type, publishers hire outside companies called *compositors*. They also buy paper and contract with printers and binders. Sales representatives from a publishing company persuade independent booksellers to carry the company's books, school boards to adopt them, or college and university faculty members to assign them. A few publishers also run chains of bookstores of their own.

Thus, the publisher brings together and coordinates a complex team including authors, editors, designers, compositors, printers, and booksellers. Through the various stages of bookmaking, publishers try to control the cost, schedule, and quality of the work. Their role, in Dan Lacy's words, is "somewhat analogous to that of a theater producer, or an independent film producer."[18]

The Publisher as Entrepreneur

Like the other media industries in the United States, the book-publishing industry largely pays its own way. One of the few exceptions is the U.S. Government Printing Office, the nation's largest publisher. It turns out thousands of documents, pamphlets, and books each year, but it does not do so for profit. As Table 2.1 shows, in 1992, American book publishers produced over 44,000 titles. The great majority of these were new titles; the rest were reissues of old titles. Some publishers are subsidized by religious, political, or educational organizations, but for the most part books in the United States are published by private companies trying to make a profit.

The mainstream of American publishing is found in the large publishing houses, many of which are located in New York City. In fact, just 2 percent of the nation's publishers account for about 75 percent of book sales. However, small publishing houses flourish across the country. A publishing company can begin with only one or two people and little equipment, hiring outside suppliers on a book-by-book basis. Unlike the small radio or TV station, the small book publisher needs no federal license, and unlike a small newspaper, the enterprise is not limited to a local audience. Through selective promotion and direct-mail advertising, a new firm can command national attention and sales. Book publishers can thus begin with limited capital, publishing only a few titles until they begin to show a profit.

In view of what we have said, it may seem surprising that many books—perhaps most—*never turn a profit*! However, publishers survive because the earnings for a good seller can be high enough to pay for other books that lose money or barely break even. It is very difficult to forecast whether a book will succeed, so publishers are forced to gamble. Some economists have observed that book publishers would be better off publishing fewer books and concentrating on obtaining higher sales for those they do publish. Some critics attribute the tendency to produce a wide range of titles to optimism. Others say it results from vigorous competition. After all, the author rejected by one publisher can go in search of another. In any case, if the advice of economists recommending concentration were followed, many truly important but highly specialized books would never be available.

The contemporary book industry uses a variety of marketing techniques. Included are direct-mail advertising, telephone marketing, book clubs, and magazine ads. Publishers sometimes offer a reduced rate to purchasers who buy a book in advance of the publication date. Virtually every promotional device used to market other products has been tried. However, traditionally, publishers have tiny advertising budgets compared with manufacturers of other consumer products. Perhaps more than other forms of print, books depend on other media. For example, they depend on magazines and newspapers for promotion in the form of reviews and paid advertising. Authors frequently appear as guests on TV and radio talk shows, where they promote their books.

Book publishers operate under a number of limitations. It has been said that there are too few retail bookstores, but chains have become a major force in bookselling. "The large chains are the power behind book publishing today," says Joan M. Ripley, a former president of the American Booksellers Association.

The problems of profit-making are quite different on the trade and textbook sides of publishing. Publishing college textbooks is not a large industry. Total dollar sales were only $2.5 billion in 1993, about one-third as large as total sales of trade books. Moreover, it is an industry with an uncertain future. For example, Table 2.3 shows that the number of trade books sold each year between 1982 and 1994 has increased each year, for a total increase of about 70 percent. The sale of new college textbooks, however, exhibits a different pattern. Table 2.3 shows that the number of textbooks sold each year has fluctuated during the same period, for a much lower overall increase of 17%.

A slight drop in college enrollments over the last decade may account somewhat for the smaller increase in numbers of new college textbooks sold. However, another trend that has affected new college textbook sales has been a great rise in the price that publishers charge retail bookstores for each book. As Table 2.4 shows, that price averaged $8.99 in 1982. By 1994, it had risen to an average of $17.40—an increase of 94 percent. How can this increase—which exceeds the rate of inflation during the period—be explained? The trend in textbook costs reflects not publishers' greed but

TABLE 2.3
Trade Books versus Textbooks: Millions of New Books Sold by Publishers, 1982-1994

Year	Trade Books	Textbooks
1982	459.2	115.2
1984	519.7	112.2
1986	562.6	111.1
1988	609.7	130.2
1990	704.5	136.9
1992	760.4	136.6
1994*	779.0	135.2
Increase *Estimated	70%	17%

Source: Veronis, Suhler and Associates, Communications Industry Forecast, 1994.

TABLE 2.4
Retail Prices Charged by Publishers for College Texts

Year	Price
1982	$ 8.99
1984	10.42
1986	11.88
1988	13.75
1990	15.13
1992	16.16
1994*	17.40
Increase *Estimated	94%

Source: Veronis, Suhler and Associates, Communications Industry Forecast, 1994.

the growth of a highly sophisticated *used-book trade*. This phenomenon poses a serious problem, because it is students as captive consumers who suffer the most. The problem begins when publishers produce new or newly revised textbooks, which instructors adopt for their classes. Textbooks are expensive to produce, and since knowledge in most fields advances regularly, new books and updated versions of ones previously published are constantly required. However, at the end of the semester, bookstores buy used copies very cheaply from students who bought them new. Students watching their budgets have little choice but to sell at the price offered by the bookstore (there are no alternative buyers). Once the used books are obtained, the bookstore sells them back to the next wave of students after holding them for a few weeks at most. Those that are not sold locally are wholesaled at a profit to companies specializing in swift nation-wide redistribution of used books. This process is repeated after each semester.

At first glance, the used-book trade looks like it ought to be a boon to students—after all, they do not have to buy new books. They can get a used copy for slightly less. But, in fact, the system is the engine that is relentlessly driving up both new *and* used textbook prices. What happens is that the bookstores price the used copies just below the cost of a new book. This is logical enough; they buy low and sell high—the classic formula for success in a capitalist system. And, since they have no production costs (which are all borne by the publisher), their profits are very high.

An unfortunate consequence of the system is that the costs of both new and used books for the student rise sharply for two reasons: First, publishers have to compensate for their loss of markets by revising books more often so as to create more new products. A few years ago, textbook revisions were on a four- or even five-year cycle. Today, the cycle is three years at most, and it will soon go to two. It may grow even shorter. Each revision adds to the publisher's costs. Second, publishers have to price all new books high enough to cover their costs, knowing that sales of used books will eat up their market within a year or two at most.

This situation has produced a kind of spiraling escalation that has already made textbooks very expensive, whether new or used. This spiral poses serious problems for *publishers* whose profits shrink, for *authors* who lose their financial incentive for writing them, and above all for *students* who have to pay increasingly high prices for both new and used books.

Tremendous controversy surrounds this situation. No one blames the students for trying to stretch their dollars. No one blames bookstores for being efficient capitalists. No one blames publishers for wanting to stay in business. But the present system artificially forces both new and used textbook costs sky-high and they are likely to go higher. Some analysts maintain that prices would come down if publishers were allowed to share at least some of the profit on used as well as new texts. This would extend time between revisions and allow price relief on both new and used books. However, such a system would require legal changes to define books more narrowly as intellectual property (of the producers), as is the case with sheet music, records, tapes, and video cassettes. This controversy is now receiving congressional attention. If this problem is solved, the runaway cost of textbooks may slow down.

Another factor pushing textbook costs upward is the unauthorized reproduction of copyright-protected work of authors and publishers using photocopying machines. Although individuals are allowed to copy material for personal use under the "fair use" provisions of copyright law, reproducing copies to sell for profit is illegal. One well-known firm (Kinko's) has been successfully sued by a coalition of publishers for extensive reproduction of copyrighted material that was sold to students.[19] The number of such suits is increasing. Several professors have also been sued for similar practices.

Outlook for the Future

What is the future of books? All in all, they are reasonably profitable today, and they play a substantial role in American intellectual life and entertainment. Clearly, the book industry remains robust, especially publishers of trade books, even though critics once claimed that the public would tire of all forms of print. In fact, a new wave of "superstores"—book stores stocking up to 100,000 titles and owned by large conglomerates—is coming.[20] These are likely to replace small chain-owned stores in malls as well as privately owned neighborhood operations. The superstores may do to bookselling what Home Depot, Kmart, MacDonald's, and supermarket chains did to the hardware, general merchandise, fast food, and grocery industries.

The retail book industry is undergoing a pattern of change that took place for many other kinds of products in earlier years. Today, the sale of groceries, office supplies, hardware and home improvement products, and even clothing is dominated by supermarkets, superstores, and discounters. Mom-and-pop bookstores and the relatively small establishments in shopping malls are being replaced by elaborate and economically efficient retail outlets owned by large chains and conglomerates. These new superstores stock four to five times as many titles as the typical mall bookstore. (© Andrew Brilliant, The Picture Cube)

In short, with expanding markets, new retailing and vigorous publishers, books will remain a powerful force, even in the face of the electronic media. For the foreseeable future, books will continue to be printed on paper. At some point, an increasing number of books may be available on CD-ROM. However, the survival and continued popularity of the traditional paper-based medium seem likely because of three features: *portability*, *permanence*, and *cost-effectiveness*.

First, portability is an attractive attribute—one can carry a book anywhere without need for electronic circuitry or a cord to plug into the wall. Electronic miniaturization may reduce this advantage of books but probably won't eliminate it any time soon. Books also have permanence; we can save them on our shelves for decades and refer to them conveniently whenever we want. Books are "user-friendly"—they require little effort to open and read, and the user does not have to have complex technical skills. That is not true of alternative media. As yet, it remains difficult to thumb leisurely through an electronic system, which requires complex and expensive machines. Although we have deplored the surge in costs of textbooks, even an expensive book is cheap on a cost-per-word basis compared with the computer and associated software needed to read print on a screen. These features, along with the fact that education is becoming more and more important in our society, indicate that books appear to be here to stay.

Chapter Review

- Cave paintings were human beings' first attempts to represent ideas graphically. Such efforts represent a transition from purely oral description to the graphic depiction of ideas.

- Ideographic systems based on pictographs began about 4000 B.C. Improvements came slowly over about two thousand years until phonograms came into use. Eventually writing was greatly simplified when alphabets were invented. Our alphabet is based on early forms standardized by the Greeks and passed on to the Romans.

- Solutions to technological problems have always been the basis of more effective media. When portable media replaced stone, longer documents and even libraries of scrolls became possible. The Romans made the first books with letters on both sides of cut and bound pages and end boards or covers. They also developed many of the formats for written language that we still use in books and other printed material.

- The skills of writing and manuscript preparation were kept alive during the Dark Ages by the Christian monasteries, but after the twelfth and thirteenth centuries they passed into lay hands as well. Meanwhile, paper had come into use, and the stage was set for print.

- A great technological advance came when Johannes Gutenberg developed both a workable press and cast-metal type. His invention was enormously important and quickly spread throughout the Western world.

- Book publishing came late to North America, but once it caught on, books had a powerful influence on the spread of literacy and on popular opinions and ideas.

- As a medium, books are slow to produce, but they provide permanent storage of ideas that can be repeatedly referred to at a pace convenient for the user. They remain society's most influential medium—and the major repository of civilization's most significant ideas.

- A publishing house processes the content of a book from author's manuscript to finished product. A publisher, which risks capital in the hope of making a return on its investment, fills the role of bringing together individuals with diverse talents to create an end product, somewhat in the manner of a movie or theater producer.

- There are many kinds of books and publishing houses. A major division is between textbook and trade publishers.

- Publishers are entrepreneurs who use different strategies to make a profit on what they produce. Many books published do not make a profit, and the ones that do have to support those that do not.

- Textbook publishers' profits are hurt and the cost of books is forced up by the resale of used books, from which only the bookstores benefit, and by illegal reproduction of copyright-protected material.

- Books in their traditional form are likely to survive because of their portability, permanence, and cost-effectiveness. The changes that lie ahead are more likely to be in their production and retailing than in their basic form.

Notes and References

1. Miguel Angel Garcia Guinea, *Altamira and Other Cantabrian Caves* (Madrid: Silex, 1979), p. 4.
2. The sections on writing, the alphabet, early books, and the invention of printing are based on the following sources: Albertine Gaur, *A History of Writing* (London: Scribner's, 1984); Joseph Naveh, *Early History of the Alphabet* (Jerusalem: Magnes, 1982); Donald Jackson, *The Story of Writing* (New York: Taplinger, 1981); and Douglas McMurtrie, *The Book: A History of Printing and Book-Making* (New York: Oxford University Press, 1943).
3. Hendrik D. L. Vervliet (ed.), *Through Five Thousand Years* (London: Phaidon, 1972), p. 18.
4. McMurtrie, op. cit., pp. 76–77.
5. Francis Falconer Madan, *Books in Manuscript: A Short Introduction to Their Study and Use,* 2nd ed. (Oxford: Oxford University Press, 1920).
6. Robert Hamilton Clapper, *Paper, An Historical Account of Its Making by Hand from the Earliest Times Down to the Present Day* (Oxford: Oxford University Press, 1934).
7. James Moran, *Printing Presses: History and Development from the Fifteenth Century to Modern Times* (Berkeley and Los Angeles: University of California Press, 1973), p. 17.
8. Ibid., p. 18.
9. David Stebenne, Seth Rachlin, and Martha FitzSimon, *Coverage of the Media in College Textbooks* (New York: Freedom Forum Media Studies Center, 1992).
10. The actual number will forever remain elusive. But it was clearly a great communications revolution, rivaling that which has occurred in this century. For a detailed analysis of the implications of that revolution, see Elizabeth Eisenstein, *The Printing Press as an Agent of Change*, vols. 1 and 2 (Cambridge: Cambridge University Press, 1979).
11. Frederick Seibert, *Freedom of the Press in England, 1476–1622* (Urbana: University of Illinois Press, 1952), Chapters 1–3.
12. John Tebbel, *The Media in America* (New York: Crowell, 1974).
13. Veronis, Suhler and Associates, *Communications Industry Forecasts* 1994. See also "Books by the Number" (compiled by Charles Barber), *Media Studies Journal* (New York: Freedom Forum Media Studies Center, Summer 1992), p. 15.
14. Charles A. Madison, *Book Publishing in America* (New York: McGraw-Hill, 1966), p.

402. See also Benjamin A. Campaigne, *The Book Industry in Transition* (White Plains, N.Y.: Knowledge Industry, 1978).

15. There is considerable lag time in the process of gathering and reporting such figures because publishers are often reluctant to disclose current sales trends. Therefore, completely up-to-date unit and dollar sales are not always available. The figures for trade and college textbook publishing in this chapter were obtained in part from the 1989 *Communications Industry Forecast,* an annual industry information publication, by Veronis, Suhler and Associates.

16. Dan Lacy, "The Economics of Publishing, or Adam Smith and Literature," in *The American Reading Public* (New York: Bowker, 1965), based on an issue of *Daedalus.* For a more recent view of the publishing industry, see "Publishing Books," *Media Studies Journal,* Summer 1992, in which agents, authors, industry executives, critics and scholars offer an upbeat prognosis on the future of books.

17. Lacy, op. cit.

18. Lacy, op. cit.

19. See "8 Publishers Charge Copyright Violation, Sue Copying Chain," *Chronicle of Higher Education,* May 3, 1989, p. A1.

20. David Berreby, "The Growing Battle of the Big Bookstores," *The New York Times,* Business Section, November 8, 1992, p. F5.

CHAPTER

3

Newspapers: The First Medium for the Mass Society

Newspapers are the spring of knowledge, The general source throughout the nation, of every modern conversation. What would this mighty people do, If there, alas! were nothing new?

The New York Journal, 1770

ince the earliest use of language, people have been interested in gossip and tidings about others in their midst, people outside their group, and events in other places. For millennia, the only way they received such news was by word of mouth from travelers or roving troubadors and at social gatherings, taverns, and fairs.

The first *published* news (in the sense of being formally "made public") came shortly after the birth of Christ. Every day, the Roman Senate posted handwritten information sheets, called *acta diurna populi Romani* (daily transactions of the Roman people), in public places.[1] These announcements provided reports about the Senate's current actions and decisions, along with more general information on political and social life in the capital. Scribes made their living by copying these bulletins and delivering them to interested citizens in the city or abroad. For many centuries, however, the delivery of news in written form was confined to private correspondence and newsletters circulated among diplomatic envoys, the aristocracy, and merchants who required detailed reports relevant to their activities.

Ultimately, it was *technology* that spurred the development of newspapers, as has been the case with each of the mass media. Gutenberg's inventions provided a critical foundation. Later, the ability to print improved swiftly as steam was linked to a roller-type press. Then came cheaper paper, zinc engraving, the telegraph for news-gathering, the typewriter, photography, the electric press, typesetting machines, and finally computers to assist both in gathering news and in controlling many of the mechanical functions required to produce and distribute a newspaper. This chapter traces the influence of these events on our newspapers.

But technology is only part of the story. Various social systems had to be designed in order to use new technologies to deliver news and other content that people wanted. Like everything else, gathering news, preparing it for the press, and printing and delivering a newspaper cost money. Ways of paying the related costs had to be invented. Finally, newspapers, like books, have the potential of shaping people's ideas. That seemed to pose a threat to those in power. Thus, the relationship between rulers and the ruled seemed at risk, unless newspapers were controlled. The control of newspapers by government was a significant issue in the American colonies during the eighteenth century as part of the events that led to the American Revolution. Freedom from such control was established as a central principle in the new Constitution. Control of the press still poses a problem in many parts of the world.

The Development of Newspapers

Essentially, the story of newspapers begins with Gutenberg's press. Soon after its invention and initial diffusion, printed descriptions of important events began to appear. These brief documents, the forerunners of newspapers, were sent relatively quickly to distant places. For example, the story of the voyage and discoveries of Columbus spread throughout Spain in the form of printed copies of the explorer's accounts within a few months of his return. From there, by word of mouth and private correspondence, descriptions of what had been found (often grossly exaggerated) traveled relatively swiftly to all the major cities in Europe.

The First Newspapers

The printing press was used in a variety of ways to provide news, even during its earliest years. In the mid-1500s, the leaders of Venice regularly made available to the public printed news sheets about the war in Dalmatia. To receive a copy, Venetians had to pay a *gazetta*, a small coin. (The word "gazette," so frequently used in newspaper titles, comes from that source.) An obscure forerunner of what we call a newspaper was apparently printed in Germany in 1609. Not much is known about it. Better known is the *coranto* of the same period. The coranto was a brief printed news sheet whose form originated in Holland. During the early 1600s, corantos were being published periodically for the commercial community in several countries. The oldest surviving example, printed in 1620, is shown on page 76. It could be regarded as the first newspaper in English, although it lacks certain features of a true newspaper as we define it today.

Newspapers of more modern times have several characteristics not found in these earlier publications. Edwin Emery, a distinguished historian of journalism, has defined a newspaper in the following terms. A true newspaper:

1. is published at least weekly,
2. is produced by a mechanical printing process,
3. is available (for a price) to people of all walks of life,

The oldest known newspaper in English of which a copy survives was printed on November 21, 1620. It lacked a title, suggesting that it was not published regularly in the manner of a true newspaper. However, as you can see, this page provided relatively current reports about events in several European countries. The difficulty of obtaining news is reflected in the note at the top of the page: "The new tydings out of Italie are not yet com." (The British Library)

The new tydings out of Italie are not yet com.

Out of Weenen, the 6 November.

THe French Ambaſſadour hath cauſed the Earle of Dampier to be buried ſtately at Preſburg In the meane vvhile hath Bethlem Gabor cited all the Hungeriſh States , to com together at Preſburg the 5. of this preſent , to diſcourſe aboute the Crovvning & other cauſes concerning the ſame Kingdom.

The Hungatians continue vvith roveing againſt theſe Lands. In like manner thoſe of Moravia , vvhich are fallen upon the Coſackes yeſter night by Hotleyn, ſet them on fire , and ſlaine many dead , the reſt vvill revenge the ſame.

Heere is certaine nevves com , that the Crabats , as alſo the Lord Budean, are fallen unto Betlem Gabor.

The Emperour ſends the Earle of Altheim as Ambaſſadour to Crackovv in Polea, to appeare upon the ſame meeting-day.

Novv comes tidings, that Betlem Gabor is at Thurna, there doe gather to gether great ſtore of States.

The Emper. Maj. hath appoynted heere a meeting-day upon the 1. of Decemb. thereupon ſhould appeare the 4. Proclaimed States. The appoynted taxing ſhall bring up a great ſom of money.

Out of Prage, the 5 of November.

Three dayes agone are paſſed by, a mile from this Cittie 6000 Hungarians (choſen out Soldiers) under the General Rediſerens, vvhich are gon to our Head-camp, & the Enimie lieth yet neare unto ours by Rackonits , though the crie goeth, that the enimie cauſed all his might to com togither, to com this vvayes againſt Prage, if that comes to paſſe, it ſhall not run off vvithout blovves, the vvhich might be revealed vvith in ſevv dayes.

It continues , that in the Satſer Crais are gathered togither 10000 Contrie-men, moſt highdutch-men, againſt Meiſſen , & no Bohemians , they vvill help the King, to drive the enimie out of the Land. In like manner ſom certaine 1000 Contrie-men rebel in the LentmaritſcherCrais, but it is feared that thoſe Contrie-men are ſtarred up , through practiſe of the Adverſarie , that the enimie in the meane vvhile might com to Prage. We underſtand, that Bucquoy hath not been in the Camp, but by the Duke of Saxen ſom certaine dayes , therefore vve are to looke to our ſelves, for feare of Trecherie. And it is thought that the Emperour vvill leave Auſtria to the Hungorians, & ſee to effect his intention only uppon Praghe.

Out of Ceulen, the 21. Novemb.

Writing from Marpurg in Heſſen , that the Earle of the ſame Land, doth cauſe the foreſaid Cittie to be ſtrongly fortified , there on doe vvorke many 100 men dayly , and there is muſtered in the Earleſhip Zigenheym not long ſince 1. Governement of foote-men , & 6. Cornets of horſe-men , the foote-men are ſent to Marpurg & Rijnſels. But the horſe-men are lodged in the Villages about the Cittie , & thereafter are alſo muſtered the Duke of Saxen Lauvvenburgs Governement in Tries-Zigenheym, novv further vvhere they ſhallbe laid & uſed, is yet unknovvn. The ſames Brothers Governement, there quarter is laid by Caſſel , the Souldiers vvhich are taken on about Hamburg. Lubeck, in the Dukeſhip of Holſteen , & Meckelenburg, ſhould alſo be muſtered about Caſſel , & be uſed vvhere neede ſhall require.

Since the laſt vve cannot enquire, that there is any thing of any importance paſſed betvvixt the Marquis Spinola & the Vnited Princes. We underſtand that the foreſaid Spinola vvil lay his Souldiers in Garniſon vvith the firſt , & deale them unto divers places, on part to Oppenheym, Altzey, Ingelheym & Cruiſinach, the other part at Summeren & Bacharacht , the ſpeech goeth that there ſhalbe layed vvith in Ments a good Company in Garniſſon.

The Biſhop at Halberſtadt, Duke Chriſtiaen at Bruynſvvyck, doth cauſe to be taken on 2000 Muſquetters, to ſend to the Vnited Princes.

Heere is tydings , that betvveen the King of Bohemia & the Emperours folke hath beene a great Battel about Prage , but becauſe there is different vvriting & ſpeaking thereuppon , ſo cannot for this time any certainety thereof be vvritten, but muſt vvayte for the next Poſt. As alſo of the Cittie Pilſen , vvhich the Earle of Manſvelt (ſo the ſpeech goeth) ſhonld have delivered into the Emperours hands.

From Cadan in Bohemia , 4. mile from Raconits, the 12. November.

From Solts is certaine adviſe that the Emperours folk have made them ſelves vvith all theire might out of theire Camp, & taken their vvay to vvards Praghe, like as they vveare then com to the long mile , but as the King underſtand ſuch , he is broken up vvith his armey, and com to the log mile beforen the enimie, vvhere they have had a very ſtrong Battelle & on both ſides more then 6000 men ſlaine, though moſt on the Kings ſide, alſo hath the enimie gotten of the King ſom peeces of Ordentaunce and vvaggens vvith amunitie, ſo that the King muſt retire back to Praghe , and the enimie to the Weiſſenberg , there he lies yet and roves from thence to the Leut Maritſcher Crais unto Brix,

---

4. prints news of general interest rather than items on specialized topics such as religion or business,
5. is readable by people of ordinary literacy,
6. is timely,
7. is stable over time.[2]

By this definition, the first true newspaper was the *Oxford Gazette* (later called the *London Gazette*). First published in 1665 under authority of King Charles II, the *Gazette* appeared twice a week and continued publication well into the twentieth century. This was an *authorized newspaper*, which means that its content was controlled and screened by the Crown.

The first daily newspaper in English, the *Daily Courant* (from *coranto*), began publication in London on March 11, 1702. A newspaper of high quality and considerable integrity, the *Courant* was not really a mass medium, because it maintained a sophisticated literary level and appealed primarily to an affluent and educated elite. However, like the more popular newspapers that would come in the nineteenth century, it recovered its costs mainly from advertising.[3]

After the late 1600s, censorship was rarely enforced in England. But it was a different story in the American colonies. The colonial press was tightly controlled. The reason was that insurrection was always regarded as a possibility in such remote colonies. Thus, relatively strict control of printing presses was exerted by the Crown-appointed governor of each of the colonies. But in spite of those efforts, colonial governments soon confronted lively and independent newspapers.

The Press in the American Colonies

The growth of newspapers in the American colonies was tied closely to cultural, economic, and political circumstances that existed at the time. Both the population and commerce grew steadily, creating a market for news of shipping and trading as well as a need for a limited amount of advertising. As political tensions over such issues as taxes and control of trade grew, the colonists often published criticisms of the Crown's government. One of the more significant of such criticisms appeared in Boston on September 25, 1690—the first (and last) issue of a paper titled *Publik Occurrences Both Forreign and Domestick*. This four-page paper was the work of Benjamin Harris, a printer who had fled to Boston from London, where the authorities had first jailed him and later seized one of his publications. In it, Harris managed to insult both the Indians, who were allies of the British, and the French king. The governor of Massachusetts banned Harris's paper on the grounds that it had been published "without authority" (without prior review by the Crown's representatives) and that it contained material not approved by the government.

Even though it survived for only a single issue, *Publick Occurrences* was important, not only because it was first chronologically but also because it spoke against the government. However, because it was not published continuously, it does not really fit our definition of a newspaper. The honor of being the first American paper in that sense goes instead to a dull publication called the *Boston News-Letter*, which first appeared—"published by authority"—in April 1704. John Campbell, the publisher, was also the postmaster of Boston; as postmaster, he was able to mail the paper without postal charges. For early colonial papers, a connection with a post office was almost indispensable, because there was no other practical way to distribute copies.

The *Boston News-Letter's* content consisted mainly of dull treatises on European politics, shipping reports, and some advertising. The result, according to Edwin Emery, was a paper that was "libel-proof, censor-proof, and well-nigh reader-proof."[4] Because of a lack of public interest, the paper never really became a financial success, but it did survive for seventy-two years. Somewhat better was the *Boston Gazette*, which William Brooker began in 1719. It was much like the *Boston News-Letter,* but both its printing and its news information were crisper.

Establishing Traditions in American Journalism

The manner in which the press in the United States operates today—protected by the First Amendment's provision for freedom of the press and by a body of law developed over two centuries—is the end product of a long chain of events started during the colonial period. As the eighteenth century progressed, colonial governors continued to suppress articles that spoke against the government. However, their control was gradually subverted by rather bold printers and publishers in a long struggle marked by numerous conflicts and harsh repressions.

The press as watchdog of the public interest In 1721, James Franklin—an older brother of Benjamin Franklin—started his own paper, the *New England Courant.* It was something of a departure from the restrictive colonial tradition because it was not published by authority and had no connection with a post office. Aimed at a well-educated and prosperous elite, it appealed mainly to those who liked literary essays and controversial political opinions. It also contained shipping reports and information from nearby towns.

The *Courant* was the first newspaper in the colonies to "crusade" on a public issue. During an outbreak of smallpox in Boston, it argued strongly against the newly invented medical procedure of inoculation. Although its position turned out to be wrong from a medical standpoint, using the newspaper to "speak out" against a situation seen as harmful to the public began an important tradition that would come to characterize American newspapers. Increasingly newspapers would become "watchdogs of the public interest," a role they continue to play vigorously.

The *Courant*, successful and bumptious, criticized this person, poked fun at that one, and finally attacked the governor himself. As a result, the governor cracked down, and Franklin was thrown in jail for a month. He was ultimately forbidden to publish the *Courant* or any paper "of like nature." Franklin was clever, though, and he got around the restriction by making his brother Benjamin the publisher (a move that later had significant consequences for the emerging nation).

Young Ben Franklin was apprenticed to his brother at thirteen and began to gain firsthand experience with printing. He worked as a "printer's devil," setting type for the paper, and did all the other chores of an apprentice. At a tender age, he even tried his hand at writing essays, signing his first works "Silence Dogood" and craftily slipping them under the door of the print shop at night. They were cleverly written and when published provoked many replies by other essayists. When his brother was in jail, young Ben operated the print shop and paper. By 1729, he had moved on to take over the *Pennsylvania Gazette* in Philadelphia. Franklin not only made that paper a success but anticipated another tradition that would come to characterize journalism—he established a small chain of newspapers.

Establishing the principle of freedom of the press   Of great importance in the unfolding struggle to establish a free press was the conflict that developed early in the 1700s between John Peter Zenger, a printer, and William Cosby, governor of New York. Zenger was persuaded by a group of businessmen in New York to establish a newspaper, the *New York Weekly Journal.* They wanted to have a paper in opposition to the officially authorized *New York Gazette*. Zenger began publication in 1733, and his paper ran articles openly critical of the governor and his policies.

That was too much for Governor Cosby, and he had Zenger clapped in jail on a charge of "seditious libel." *Sedition* means promoting disaffection with government—inciting people to revolt against constituted authority. *Libel* means publicizing untruths. However, under British law of the time, it really did not matter whether what the defendant published was true; it was the seditious intent that was the major offense and that was the central legal issue of the case.

Zenger was brought to trial before a jury in 1734. The governor's case seemed airtight. Zenger had, in fact, broken the existing law. However, Andrew Hamilton, a distinguished lawyer, undertook his defense. Hamilton freely admitted that Zenger had published articles criticizing the government. But he argued with great conviction that the articles were *true* and that in spite of what the law said, no one should be punished for printing the truth. In a stunning upset, Hamilton's argument convinced the jury that they should ignore the judge's instructions and declare Zenger not guilty. They did so, and the governor was furious. The significance of Zenger's trial was not that it set an important legal precedent, but that it was a symbolic victory of press over government and was frequently mentioned by those arguing for freedom of the press. Law books ignored the Zenger case for years, and when asked about it, legal scholars maintained that the jury had exceeded its authority. Juries are supposed to decide matters of *fact* (whether or not something happened), not matters of law (which are left to judges). The idea that the press should be allowed to criticize government would eventually find its way into the First Amendment to the Constitution, which would be formulated a half-century later.

Characteristics of the Colonial Press

The colonial papers were small, usually about four pages measuring a mere ten by fifteen inches each. By 1750, most Americans who could read had access to some kind of newspaper. However, even though many newspapers were started during the period, few were successful. The problem was that they were difficult to support financially, and distribution remained a problem. The majority failed after only a few issues.

The colonial papers were very limited in many ways: Their news was seldom up to date; they were published infrequently; and they were slow to reach their subscribers. The papers were usually delivered by mail, traveling to subscribers by horse and carriage, pack trains, or sailing vessels. Rapid delivery of newspapers would have to wait until the next century. In addition, until 1783, when the *Pennsylvania Evening Post and Advertiser* was started, the colonies had no daily newspaper.

The colonial papers were also limited by existing technology. The hand press used by Benjamin Franklin and others in the late 1700s was little different from that used by Gutenberg in the mid-1400s. Paper was still made from rags, not wood, and it was expensive and always in short supply. Compounding the problem, literacy rates were very low by comparison with later centuries; no systems of free public education had been established. Schools were available mainly for the children of affluent people of larger towns and cities. Little schooling was available for the vast majority who lived on farms.

We noted earlier that advertising is an important source of financial support for newspapers. However, there was a limited need for advertising in colonial times. The great consumerism that we know today had not yet arrived. It was a product of the Industrial Revolution, the advent of easy distribution by improved transportation, and the development of well-coordinated retail systems. Thus, there were not many products to be advertised, and few markets could provide a solid financial base for the support of newspapers.

Another factor limiting colonial newspapers was that they restricted their own audiences. Many were *partisan papers*; that is, they consistently argued for only one point of view. When political parties developed at the end of the eighteenth century, each had certain newspapers under its control. Some even subsidized papers. After the Revolution, the number of *commercial newspapers* increased, but they were also intended for a restricted audience. They recorded commercial transactions and business matters, such as shipping and foreign economic news, which mainly interested merchants.

All the papers, commercial and partisan, were aimed at comparatively well-educated and relatively affluent subscribers, who made up only a small part of the society. Newspapers were also very expensive, which made them unavailable to the common people. Around the time of the Revolution, a newspaper might cost six to ten dollars a year, about as much as a worker's salary for one or two weeks. In today's terms, that would be like paying several hundred dollars for a year's subscription. Few people would be able or willing to pay that much.

In spite of these limitations, the colonial press established valuable traditions that were to become an important part of American journalism. Many papers defied local authorities and spoke out on behalf of the public. They showed that the press could be a political force. Writers such as Thomas Paine and Samuel Adams helped build public support for independence. After the Revolution, the most famous treatises debating various features of the Constitution (the *Federalist Papers*) were first presented in newspapers. From its colonial beginnings, then, the American press established itself as an important political force—a monitor and critic of government. In many respects, it retains that position today.

Newspapers for the Common People

By the early nineteenth century, the Industrial Revolution had started. Innovators were beginning to solve the technological and other problems that had prohibited wide circulation of newspapers among the public. It was a time when all kinds of new machines were being driven by steam power to accomplish many tasks with astonishing rapidity and uniformity. The printing press was no exception. With the old screw-type press, a well-trained team of two printers working full speed could put out only two hundred sheets per hour at best. By 1830, steam-powered rotary presses were introduced. They were a truly significant improvement in technology. Even the earliest could produce four thousand sheets per hour printed on both sides.[5]

At first, the new presses benefited only book publishing. But their existence meant that newspapers would be able to greatly increase their circulation if the right combination of content, subscribers, and financial support could be found. Both the population and the percentage of people who could read had increased, but existing newspapers were still expensive at six

A technological limitation holding back the development of the mass newspaper was the hand-powered printing press. This engraving shows how newspapers were produced shortly before the introduction of steam-powered presses in 1830. Note the typesetter at the left rear using the upper and lower cases for majuscule and miniscule letters. The compositor in the foreground is arranging the lines of type in a frame.

The man near the press is applying ink to a frame of type, and the one in the center is checking a printed page prior to hanging it up to dry.

By the mid-1800s, with the Industrial Revolution well underway, printing technology had advanced greatly. Not only was cheap paper available, but new high-volume presses incorporating roller technology were being constructed. This Hoe cylinder printing press, driven by steam power, used ten rollers with entire pages cast in metal stereotype. It could turn out an astounding 18,000 copies of a newspaper per hour. (Brown Brothers)

cents a copy. For a working person who made only four or five dollars a week, they remained a luxury. If a daily newspaper wanted to multiply its circulation, it had to overcome this price barrier—recovering its costs in some other way.

The Emergence of the Penny Press

On September 3, 1833, a strange little newspaper appeared on the streets of New York. It was published by Benjamin Day and was called the *New York Sun*. Its masthead carried the slogan "It Shines for All." That slogan was somewhat misleading; the *Sun* was not designed to appeal to everyone, but specifically to the less sophisticated. Day offered his readers news that was nearest at hand—the incidental happenings of New York life. The *Sun* was filled with human interest items about common people. In its first issue, on page one, Day declared: "The object of this paper is to lay before the public, at a price within the means of everyone, all the news of the day, and at the same time afford an advantageous medium for advertising."

Day began an important newspaper tradition when he hired a salaried "reporter," who wrote lively stories about local happenings, with an emphasis on crime, human interest, accidents, and humorous anecdotes. Another feature of the new paper was that it was sold on the streets by *newsboys* for only a penny. (Historians have discovered, however, that some of these newsboys were actually girls dressed in boys' clothes.) This system of distribution worked well. The newsboys bought the papers in lots of a hundred for sixty-seven cents. If they sold the whole hundred, they earned thirty-three cents, which was quite a profit for a youngster at the time.

One of the most important features of the *Sun* was that advertising played the central financial role in Day's system. The penny that buyers paid for their copy did not recover the costs of production. The *Sun* made its profit by selling advertising space for a great variety of products and services. This was possible at the time because the new factories were producing a greater variety of goods, and new retail establishments were selling to larger and larger markets.

The paper was an instant success, selling more than eight thousand copies per day. Its sales soon doubled, and within three years, it was selling thirty thousand copies daily. Other journalists were astounded.

The *Sun* spurred a revolution in newspaper publishing. Within a few months, it had competitors, and the mass press was a reality. Together, all the competing newspapers who adopted Day's basic formula were known as the *penny press*. Particularly noteworthy was the *New York Herald*, founded in 1835 by the colorful James Gordon Bennett. Bennett imitated Day, but he also added many features that became part of modern newspapers—for example, a financial page, editorial comment, and more serious local, foreign, and national news. Horace Greeley's *Tribune* and Henry Jarvis Raymond's now famous *New York Times* were also started during this period.

The penny papers had distinctive characteristics that made them completely different from the colonial press. They were vulgar, sensational, and trivial in many respects. But publishers after Bennett began to carry increasing amounts of basic economic and political news, as well as editorial viewpoints regarding public matters. As they developed, then, the penny newspapers brought at least some significant firsthand information and ideas to large numbers of people who had not been readers of newspapers up to that time.

Using enterprising newsboys to distribute papers began in the 1830s. It was part of the innovative systems used by the penny press to reach new and much larger audiences. This form of distribution was relatively rapid compared to delivery by mail, which was the only means available during earlier periods.

These turn-of-the-century newsboys not only had regular routes for both morning and evening papers, but hawked special "extra" editions in the streets, providing quick dissemination of breaking news. (Library of Congress)

HOW THE TELEGRAPH GAVE US STANDARDIZED TIME:
A Linchpin to History and Technology Studies

With the coming of new technologies, there is often much speculation about what their ultimate impact will be. In recent years, for example, the computer's capacity to store and process information has had a revolutionary impact on modern life. Such earlier technologies as the telephone and telegraph, although profoundly important, have been with us long enough to be taken for granted.

"The most important fact about the telegraph," writes communications scholar James W. Carey, "is also the most obvious and innocent: it permitted for the first time the effective separation of communication from transportation."[1] Before the telegraph, letters and other messages were carried by horse, by boat, or even by pigeons. Transportation was the primary means by which communication traveled.

The development of the telegraph had a great impact almost immediately. Messages could now be sent over wires to distant points in the country and eventually around the globe. There was an economic impact, since futures markets depended on the transmission of timely information. There was also an impact on language: Spare messages written in short takes to save money replaced the longer and more flowing prose of letters.

Perhaps the most significant impact of the telegraph, however, was in the establishment of standard time. As Carey has pointed out, until late 1883 there were almost an infinite number of time zones in America. Every community could have its own sundial set by the local jeweler or courthouse, church, or other town official. In some cities, a ball dropped from

The Impact of Society on the Growth of Newspapers

During the nineteenth century, three great changes took place in American society that had significant influence on the growth of the nation's newspaper industry. One was the rapid expansion of the *population*. The second was the remarkable evolution of *technology* that increased enormously the ability of journalists to gather, transmit, print, and distribute news. The third was the influence of the *Civil War*, which stimulated a great demand for news and the development of increasingly efficient systems for getting it to newspapers and from there to subscribers.

Rapid population growth   The rate of population growth in the United States during the nineteenth century was unprecedented in history. During the two decades preceding the Civil War (1840–1860), millions of people arrived, especially from Northern Europe. Most settled in the eastern states. At the same time, steady streams of internal migrants moved westward, settling along a continuously expanding frontier, establishing new towns and cities where newspapers were needed. Even higher levels of immigration, especially from Southern and Eastern Europe, came during the last half of the century as people were needed to occupy the vast lands that had been

the highest building each day at noon signaled the hour for miles around. The variations in times from city to city raised havoc with railroad schedules. The state of Michigan alone had twenty-seven time zones!

From the 1870s on, scientists and government officials conferred about how to simplify this bedeviling array of time zones. Delegates to the Philadelphia General Time convention asked a young civil engineer named William Frederick Allen to develop a plan. He divided the United States into four time zones centering on the 75th, 90th, 105th, and 120th meridians. It was agreed that November 18, 1883 would be the date when the United States would move from local to standard time. When people realized that railroad time had, in fact, become standard time, many mass meetings were held: Some of the protests were from religious groups who felt that imposing this kind of human standard on time was tampering with the forces of nature and with God's will.[2]

Later, after educational campaigns and many newspaper editorials, the public generally accepted standard time, which was made possible by the latest technological invention: The telegraph transmitted the accurate and correct time across the nation. Although this function was later taken over by radio waves now transmitted from the naval observatory in Maryland, the telegraph was vital to the initial establishment of standard time. The telegraph also brought us wire services, telegrams, and other forms of communication.[3]

1. James W. Carey. *Culture as Communication* (Boston: Unwin Hyman, 1989). See especially Chapter 8, "Technology and Ideology, the Case of the Telegraph," pp. 201–230.
2. Ibid., pp. 201–230.
3. Ibid. Also see Daniel Czitrom, *Media and the American Mind: From Morse to McLuhan* (Chapel Hill, N.C.: University of North Carolina Press, 1982).

taken over. As they learned English, they subscribed in ever-increasing numbers to daily newspapers.

The revolution in technology   As the nineteenth century progressed, the industrial and mechanical arts flourished to a remarkable degree. After about 1830, ever larger and more elaborate steam-powered rotary presses could print, cut, and fold increasing thousands of finished newspapers per hour. Cheap paper to feed these presses was being made from wood as early as 1867.

In another great advance in technology, the telegraph wires along the rail lines linked major cities and made possible the rapid transmission of news stories to editors' desks. The same day Samuel F. B. Morse sent the historic message "What hath God wrought?" from Washington to Baltimore (May 25, 1844), he also sent over the wire the news of a vote in Congress. Soon, *wire services* would be established, and newspapers in all parts of the country began to receive a flow of stories from the "lightning lines."

The telegraph truly opened a new era. It was the beginning of a *fourth* great revolution in human communication (following speech, writing, and printing). It ushered in an era of *instantaneous communication* across great distances. From the dawn of human awareness until the invention of the steam-powered train, communication between two people over a distance had been limited to the speed of a swift runner (about fifteen miles an hour), or a galloping horse (about twenty-five miles an hour) or at most a flying pigeon (perhaps thirty-five miles an hour over distance). But by the early l840s, trains had achieved the awesome speed of forty-five miles per hour. Many people regarded this as a final limit, and that any further increase would be a violation of God's plan for humankind. They warned that people might fly apart if such dangerous speeds were exceeded.

It is difficult today to imagine what people thought when it was announced that a means had been devised to send a message at the mind-boggling speed of a lightning bolt, *186 thousand miles per second*, a mere wink of the eye. It was, in the words of moon astronaut Neil Armstrong, more than a century later, a "giant leap for mankind." As we will see later in the chapter, the telegraph opened a new era in the history of newspapers as associations were formed to transmit news along the new network of wires.

The rapid expansion of the railroads and steamboat lines also promoted the growth of newspapers. Now daily papers printed in a city could be delivered across substantial distances so that people in surrounding communities could receive the news in a timely manner. The ancient dream of conquering both time and distance with an effective medium of communication was becoming a reality.

The Civil War The great conflict between the North and the South enormously stimulated the development of newspapers. Its battles resulted in terrible slaughter—the worst loss of life this country has ever known. People on both sides of the conflict were desperate for reports of the battles and news about the fate of their loved ones. The hundreds of reporters in the field often devised ingenious methods to get their reports out ahead of their competitors. Faster and faster steam presses across the nation churned out millions of copies daily.

By 1839, photography had been invented. It would be more than three decades before photographs could be printed in newspapers, but the existence of the technology stimulated the beginnings of pictorial journalism as photographers captured the nation's history on their plates. During the Civil War, one of the country's leading photographers, Mathew Brady, persuaded President Lincoln to let him make a photographic record of the battlefields. Brady was given unrestricted access to military operations, as well as protection by the Secret Service. He and his team made some 3,500 photographs, one of the most remarkable photographic achievements of all time.[6]

By the end of the century, the newspaper was a technologically sophisticated and complex mass medium. Newspaper publishers had at their disposal a rapid telegraphic news-gathering system, cheap paper, linotype, color printing, cartoons, electric presses, and, most important, a corps of skilled journalists. The newspaper had settled into a more or less standard format, much like what we know today. Its features included not only

During the Civil War, newspapers sent hundreds of reporters to the fields of action. The reporters lived and traveled with the military forces. The officers in charge wanted favorable publicity. The top photo shows the portable field headquarters of the *New York Herald*, with its staff being briefed on the next engagement. The grim side of the war is shown in Mathew Brady's photo of soldiers killed in battle. Although the printing of photos in newspapers was still a decade away, Brady's 3,500 photos of the conflict became American classics of great significance. (Smithsonian Institution Photo No. 73-5137; Library of Congress)

domestic and foreign news, but also a financial page, letters to the editor, sports news, society reports, women's pages, classified sections, and advice to the lovelorn. Newspapers were complex, extremely competitive, and very popular. Furthermore, they had no competition from other media.

The Era of Yellow Journalism

Because newspapers in the United States were profit-oriented, privately owned businesses, they were very competitive. It was this competitiveness that led to a brief era of so-called yellow journalism, which was one of the most colorful periods in the history of American newspapers. It came about because the key to financial success of a newspaper, then as now, was to attract as many readers as possible. By showing advertisers that more people would see their messages than in a competing paper, a publisher could sell more ad space at higher prices and enjoy greater revenues. During the last decade of the nineteenth century, the competition for readers led to a rise in sensationalism in the press.

The penny papers had taken the first steps, with their emphasis on crime, human interest, and humor. Then, by the early 1890s, Joseph Pulitzer succeeded in building the circulation of the Sunday edition of the *New York World* to over 300,000. To do this, he combined good reporting with "crusades," plus an emphasis on disasters and melodramatics, sensational photographs, and comic strips—all to intensify reader interest. Pulitzer crusaded against corrupt officials, for civil service reform, and for populist causes, such as taxes on luxuries, large incomes, and inheritances. He pioneered the use of color printing of comics in newspapers, which did much to spur the circulation of his Sunday editions.

One popular cartoon in the *World* made history. It featured a bald-headed, toothless, grinning kid, clad in a yellow sacklike garment. The "Yellow Kid," as the character came to be called, appeared in settings that depicted life in the slums of New York and was soon at the center of a controversy. William Randolph Hearst, who founded the *San Francisco Examiner,* set out to master the art of attracting readers. Hearst expanded to the east and purchased the *New York Journal* in 1895, determined to build its flagging circulation to surpass that of Pulitzer's *World*. Hearst lured the Yellow Kid's cartoonist from his rival with a large salary and added other writing and editorial talent. Then he published *more* comics, *more* sensational reports, and *more* human interest material—all of which led to greater circulation.

As the circulation of Hearst's *Journal* began to rival that of Pulitzer's *World*, the two newspaper barons led their papers further into practices that would significantly influence the style of American journalism of the period. For more than a decade, many newspapers came to be preoccupied with crime, sex, sob stories, exposés of "sin," disclosures of corruption in high places (many of which were gross exaggerations), sports, dramatic photographs, misrepresentations of science—indeed, anything that would attract additional readers.

It was said that each issue of Hearst's paper was designed to provoke one reaction from its readers: When they saw the headlines, Hearst wanted them to say, "Gee whiz!" Responsibility to the public seemed to have been abandoned. The new style came to be called *yellow journalism*. Many historians believe the label derived from the Yellow Kid cartoon character because it symbolized the newspapers' mindless intellectual level.

As the nineteenth century came to a close, yellow journalism in the Pulitzer and Hearst tradition died with it. Essentially, newspapers had saturated the market, and it was no longer possible to gain large increases in circulation through such tactics. In addition, people tired of that type of newspaper and wanted a more responsible press. However, as we will see, sensational journalism is alive and well in some of the metropolitan newspapers and (especially) in the curious tabloids commonly sold in supermarkets.

Trends That Have Shaped Today's Newspapers

As daily newspapers became available to the public, they were not immediately subscribed to by every family in the nation. Like other innovations, the number of people who adopted them was limited at first. Soon, however, the number grew rapidly. Then, after reaching a high point, it leveled off. One important trend we might follow, then, is the ever-changing relationship over time between the number of subscriptions to daily newspapers and the number of households in the country.

A second trend that began in the last century is the development of two major *auxiliary services* that supply newspapers with content that they do not generate themselves. One such auxiliary consists of the wire services, mentioned earlier, that bring to local newspapers a daily flow of stories from beyond their communities. Another is made up of a number of *feature syndicates*—commercial groups that contract with publishers to provide a great many of the features that make up the content of today's newspapers.

A third major trend has been the changing pattern of ownership that has characterized American newspapers in this century. Only a small proportion of the nation's papers remain in the hands of the families of those who started them. Increasingly, newspapers are owned by newspaper industry corporations or media firms, which typically organize their holdings into groups, or *chains*, for economic efficiency and management convenience.

Newspapers as Cultural Innovation

Scholars who study patterns of social and cultural change have noted that inventions introduced into a society or items borrowed from other societies follow a typical pattern as they are taken up—that is, adopted and used.[7] Specifically, when the proportion of a society that begins to use such an innovation is plotted against time, a *curve of adoption* is described. Figure 3.1 shows the curve of adoption for newspapers in terms of the proportion of U.S. households who subscribed to a daily paper over succeeding decades.

Subscriptions to a daily newspaper followed the classic curve of adoption well into this century, but did not do so in later years. The classic curve is an S-shaped pattern that starts slowly, rises swiftly, and then levels off. As Figure 3.1 shows, after a slow start during the nineteenth century, subscriptions to daily newspapers per household did increase sharply during the last decades of that century, reaching a peak early in this century. However, after about 1930, a significant reversal of the trend began, and newspaper use declined.

These major features of the pattern can best be understood in terms of the relationship between newspapers and other mass media in the United States. By the time of World War I, circulations had grown to a point where many households in the country were subscribing to both a morning and an afternoon paper. Thus, during the early decades of the new century, newspapers enjoyed a kind of golden age. However, as the curve of adoption indicates, it did not last. As newer media arrived, newspapers showed a pat-

**TABLE 3.1
Newspaper
Subscriptions per
Household, 1850–1992**

Subscriptions to daily newspapers rose at an increasing pace during the last half of the nineteenth century, especially during the era of yellow journalism. Newspaper usage peaked around the time of World War I, when many households subscribed to both a morning and an afternoon paper. It was the medium's golden age. People urgently wanted news, and there were no competing sources. Later, as radio, magazines, and then television began delivering news, subscriptions declined steadily. At present, about two households in three maintain a subscription to a daily newspaper.

Year	Subscriptions to Daily Newspapers (in thousands)	Total Number of Households (in thousands)	Subscriptions per Household
1850	758	3,598	0.21
1860	1,478	5,211	0.28
1870	2,602	7,579	0.34
1880	3,566	9,946	0.36
1890	8,387	12,690	0.66
1900	15,102	15,992	0.94
1910	24,212	17,806	1.36
1920	27,791	20,697	1.34
1930	39,589	29,905	1.32
1940	41,132	34,855	1.18
1950	58,829	43,468	1.24
1960	58,882	52,610	1.12
1970	62,108	62,875	0.99
1980	62,201	80,776	0.77
1990	62,324	93,347	0.68
1992	60,164	95,669	0.62

Note: These figures do not include Sunday editions.

Sources: U. S. Bureau of the Census, Historical Statistics of the United States (Washington, D.C.: 1960), Series 255; U.S. Bureau of the Census, Statistical Abstracts of the United States (Washington, D.C.: 1973, 1983, 1992); U.S. Bureau of the Census, Current Population Reports: Population Characteristics (Washington, D.C.: 1967, 1989); U.S. Bureau of the Census, Facts about Newspapers (Washington, D.C.: 1986); Newspaper Association of America.

FIGURE 3.1 The Curve of Adoption of Daily Newspapers in the United States, 1850–1992

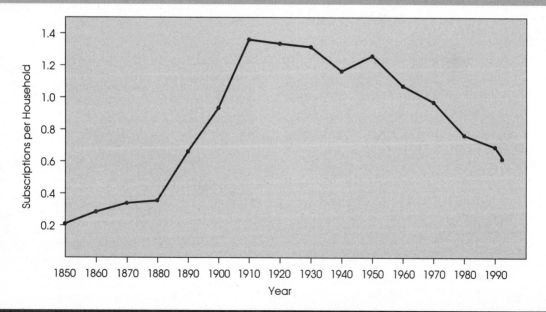

TABLE 3.2
Daily Newspapers Published in the United States, 1909–1993

Year	Number of Daily Newspapers Published
1909	2,600
1920	2,042
1925	2,008
1930	1,942
1935	1,950
1940	1,878
1945	1,749
1950	1,772
1955	1,760
1960	1,763
1965	1,751
1970	1,748
1975	1,756
1980	1,745
1985	1,676
1991	1,616
1993	1,556

Sources: U.S. Bureau of the Census, Historical Statistics of the United States (Washington, D.C.: 1975), Series R224-231; U. S. Bureau of the Census, Statistical Abstract of the United States (Washington, D.C.: 1978, 1991); Editor and Publisher International Yearbook, 1994.

The number of daily newspapers published in the United States has declined sharply since the early part of this century. During the first decade, the daily paper had no competition as a source for news. As other media began competing, not only for the news audience but for advertising revenues, a long-term trend of consolidation and concentration of ownership began. Today, many cities have only one newspaper, and most papers are owned by chains. The trend toward concentration of ownership continues as papers merge or are purchased by chain owners.

FIGURE 3.2
The Decline in Number of Daily Newspapers Published in the United States, 1909–1993

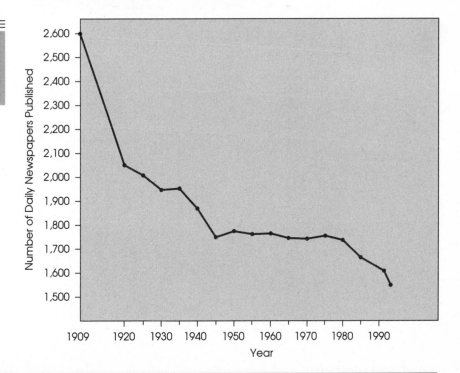

ADOPTION OF INNOVATION THEORY

In a changing society, there is a constant flow of new technical products, solutions to problems, interpretations, and other kinds of innovations. They can range from the trivial, such as a new dance step, to the profound, such as a new political philosophy (for example, communism or democracy). Sometimes the origin of an innovation is well-known. A specific person may invent something at a particular point in time, as when Thomas Edison invented the phonograph on July 18, 1877. At other times the origins of an innovation are lost. For example, it is unclear exactly who invented the hamburger, although that delicacy has been almost universally accepted by the American population. Many innovations are adopted by a population after having been invented elsewhere. For example, many in the world eagerly adopted the powered aircraft after Orville and Wilbur Wright first flew one in 1903. Other borrowed innovations are adopted by people in a society by a far less obvious process. For example, the now-popular pizza was virtually unknown in most of the United States before about 1945.

But whether invented or borrowed, every innovation is taken up by people in a particular society in a rather regular process that is well-described by the theory of the *adoption of innovation*. That theory is important for the study of mass communication for two reasons: First, each of the major mass media was originally an innovation that had yet to be adopted and widely used. That is true of the mass newspaper (which began in New York in the early 1830s), the motion picture (beginning at the turn of the century), home radio (early 1920s), television as a mass medium (after World War II), and so on. The spread of each through the society followed a curve of adoption. A second reason why innovation theory is impor-

tern of decline in subscriptions per household. That trend continues today.

As a consequence of these changes in usage, there has been a corresponding pattern of change in the *number* of daily newspapers published in the United States. Between 1880 and 1900, that number more than doubled, from 850 to 2,226. But after 1910, when the country had over 2,200 English-language and nearly 400 foreign-language dailies, the number of papers began to decline. (See Table 3.2 and Figure 3.2.) Some papers merged; some dailies became weeklies; others suspended publication completely. As a result, the number of daily newspapers declined from 2,042 in 1920 to just under 1,600 in 1993.[8]

As Figure 3.1 showed, the golden age of the newspaper was between about 1910 and 1930. Subscriptions per household were about twice what they are today. The great decline was a consequence of several factors. Obviously, as the 1930s began, television was not yet a reality, and radio was neither a serious contender as a news medium nor a strong competitor for the advertising dollars of business and industry. Furthermore, as we pointed out earlier, the mass newspapers had both impressive technologies and elaborate news-gathering systems. After 1930, however, the costs of news-gathering and all other aspects of publishing increased. Furthermore, com-

tant to the study of mass communication is that the media are often largely responsible for bringing new items to the attention of people who eventually adopt them.

The theory of the adoption of innovation was originally formulated by sociologists, but it has been widely applied to many fields.[1] It can be summarized briefly in the following set of propositions:

1. The adoption process begins with an *awareness stage* in which those who will ultimately adopt an innovation learn of its existence (often from the mass media), but lack detailed information about it.

2. Awareness is followed by an *interest stage*, during which those who contemplate adoption will devote increasing attention to the innovation and seek additional information about it. The media are often providers of some of this information.

3. In an *assessment stage*, interested individuals use the information obtained to evaluate the applica-

bility of the innovation to their present and expected future situations.

4. In a *trial stage*, a small number of these individuals acquire and apply the innovation on a small scale to determine its utility for their purposes.

5. Finally, in an *adoption stage*, a few innovators actually acquire and use the innovation on a full scale. After that, increasing numbers adopt it and the accumulation of users follows a characteristic S-shaped curve that has started slowly, but rises quickly and then levels off.

Not all adopters go through all of these stages in acquiring every innovation. In addition, some innovations spread swiftly and are taken up by virtually everyone, while others are adopted more slowly, to be used by a smaller final proportion of the population.

1. For an explanation of the origins of the theory of the adoption of innovation and its current status, see Everett Rogers, *Diffusion of Innovations*, 3rd ed. (New York: Free Press, 1983).

petition for advertising dollars from radio, and eventually television, rose relentlessly. Consequently, papers began to fail financially or were purchased by their rivals to consolidate production and other facilities. These trends have continued up to the present.

The Growth of Wire Services

The second trend influencing newspapers is the growth of two kinds of national organizations that supply them with much of their daily content. These are the wire services and various feature syndicates. If you doubt the extent to which modern papers depend on these sources, take your local newspaper, clip all the stories that come from wire services and the material provided by syndicates, and put the clippings aside. You will probably be left with some stories from your community, a lot of advertisements, and little more.

Thus, even though most newspapers are still geographically local, they depend on the wire services and syndicates to bring them national and international news, cartoons, comic strips, columns, crossword puzzles, and other familiar features found in the daily paper. The advantages of these services are many. One is lower costs. For example, hiring a full-time comic artist is well beyond the means of most small newspapers, and even some large ones. But a syndicate can hire such an artist and sell the strip to papers across the country, greatly reducing the amount charged to each.

Today's wire services grew out of an agreement in the early 1840s among several newspapers in New York, Baltimore, and Philadelphia, which pooled their resources to provide faster, cheaper, and more comprehensive news of the Mexican War.[9] This temporary but innovative agreement set a precedent in that the papers were cooperating rather than competing in covering the news. Then, in 1848, several small papers in upstate New York agreed to share the cost of having a reporter telegraph news stories from Albany, the state capital, to each paper along the wire.

The idea of a wire service worked well, and others decided to try it on a larger scale. A few months later, six New York newspapers signed an agreement to share the costs of telegraphing foreign news from Boston, where ships first arrived with the latest dispatches from Europe. This agreement was the forerunner of the modern Associated Press (AP). During its earliest years, AP was mainly an organization linking eastern newspapers. But as Americans moved westward and railroads grew, the new wire service began to cover the nation rather than just the East. During the Civil War, AP covered the great battles and troop movements, providing subscribing papers with detailed accounts.[10]

By the early twentieth century, various AP groups had consolidated in a reorganization of the Associated Press, and competing wire services had begun to appear. Edward Wyllis Scripps, the owner of the Scripps chain of newspapers, founded the United Press Association (UP), which began operation in 1907. William Randolph Hearst formed his own press association, the International News Service (INS), in 1909. In 1958, UP and INS merged into United Press International (UPI), which was able to provide more vigorous competition for AP.[11] In addition, since the early 1960s, a number of *supplemental wire services* have been organized to provide a variety of news and feature material.[12] Examples are the New York Times Service and the Washington Post/Los Angeles Times Service. In recent years, Reuters, the venerable British service, has begun to compete vigorously in the United States.

From their beginnings, the "wires" changed American newspapers. In the early days, sending stories by telegraph was very expensive, and clarity and precision were essential. The correspondent in the field had less time for the flowery language and elongated sentences common to early nineteenth-century newspapers. Before long, reporters and editors began to distinguish between "telegraph" and "newspaper" stories. The concise writing needed for wire stories eventually produced AP's famous prescription for a lead: "who, what, where, when, and why." Stories transmitted by wire were organized in the *inverted pyramid style*, in which the most important elements were first, the next important second, and so on. Thus, if a local newspaper needed to save space, a story could easily be shortened by dropping less important details from the tail of the pyramid.

Another consequence of the system resulted from the fact that wire stories had to appeal to newspapers in different regions with various political persuasions. This meant limitations on opinionated and controversial interpretations of the news. To achieve this goal, AP pioneered what would later be called the *objective report*.

Thus, almost from the beginning, the wire services broadened the content of news—allowing more newspapers to have a wide range of coverage from distant points—tightened journalistic style, and increased the level of objectivity in news coverage. Today, stories are not sent by telegraphic wire but transmitted via computer networks linked in various ways by telephone lines, optical cables, and even satellites.

The Development and Role of Syndicates

The feature syndicates, like the wire services, trace their origins to the mid-nineteenth century. Early on, journalists recognized the importance of *entertaining* readers as well as informing them. Entrepreneurs among them surmised rightly that they could make a profit by offering newspapers a package of ready-to-print features, including opinion columns, poetry, cartoons, short stories, and many other kinds of non-news content. They formed companies to provide such material.

The first syndicate was organized by two Wisconsin newspapermen just after the Civil War. By the late nineteenth century, several more were offering services to newspapers. By the early 1900s, syndicates were offering opinion pieces, political cartoons, comic strips, and columns on fashion, personal problems, politics, and other topics. Almost from the beginning, the syndicates played an important role in making the work of particular writers and artists popular among millions of readers. Today, there are more than three hundred syndicates, ranging from those with billings of more than $100 million a year to small firms that represent one or two writers.

The syndicates are not without their critics. Some are concerned that they exert too great an influence on newspapers.[13] Certainly, the syndicates provide a remarkable variety of entertainment and opinion material for newspapers, including editorial cartoons, serializations of popular books, columns by noted political commentators, comic strips, puzzles and games, movie reviews, and columns on astrology, automobiles, books, bridge, politics, gossip, consumer advice, human relations, music, religion, and television. In addition, some syndicates sell design services, graphics, and even newsstand racks. They promise that their material will bring circulation gains, and readership studies indicate that they are sometimes right. For example, "Dear Abby" and "Ann Landers" often head the list of the most-read items in a newspaper, and the comics have always had strong appeal. Newspapers have occasionally fought vicious court battles to retain a particular columnist or cartoonist.[14]

Because relatively little is written about syndicates and all are privately held companies, even their size and scope are something of a mystery. One way to measure the *reach* of a syndicate (number of people who read it) is by the number of newspapers or magazines it serves. The top five by this criterion are King Features Syndicate (started in 1914 by William Randolph Hearst), United Media (owned by Scripps-Howard), North American Syndicate (owned by Rupert Murdoch), Tribune Media Services (owned by The Tribune Company), and Universal Press Syndicate.

Changing Patterns of Ownership

A third major trend that has shaped today's newspapers is the consolidation of their ownership. This has taken place because, in spite of the facts that newspapers have lost the enviable position they held early in the century as the *only* source of news and that they now must compete for advertising dollars with other media, they continue to earn a great deal of money. Although information on newspaper profits can be hard to obtain, the data that are available indicate that these profits are almost twice what is being earned per dollar of investment by the nation's five hundred leading corporations![15]

The growth of chains   The profitability of American papers is due largely to the buying up of individual papers by chains. Like the mom-and-pop hamburger stand, the independently owned newspaper is very close to extinction. Economic forces—soaring costs of labor, materials, and services—have led to a great expansion of chain ownership of newspapers. For example, by 1994, the Gannett Corporation owned 133 newspapers as well as 9 television stations and 11 radio stations, in more than thirty states. Such chains also own other kinds of businesses.

Determining the relative size and scope of a newspaper chain or group is more difficult than it may seem. Some critics are fond of counting the number of newspapers owned, whereas others look more to circulation figures. What is easier to assess is the pattern of change over time. In 1920, during the period when newspapers were enjoying a virtual monopoly on the news industry, there were only 31 chains in the United States, and each owned on the average fewer than 5 newspapers.[16] By 1960, 109 chains controlled an average of 5 newspapers each. By 1986, there were 127 chains with an average of 9 dailies per chain. Looked at another way, the number of daily papers owned by chains rose from 153 in 1920 to 1,235 in 1994—about 78 percent of all of the daily newspapers published in the United States.[17]

The trend will slow in the years ahead because in 1994 only 346 independently owned newspapers were left to be absorbed. Chains are not likely to establish additional papers because they would then be competing either with themselves or with well-established papers that already dominate local markets. However, in the decades ahead, big chains will be likely to continue gobbling up smaller ones. A pattern will probably emerge that looks very much like what happened to American automobile manufacturers. In 1920, there were more than a hundred brands of cars being manufactured in the United States. By 1993, only Ford, Chrysler, and General Motors remained.

A modern counterpart of the nineteenth-century newspaper baron is Rupert Murdoch. He is a controversial figure who has developed an international communications empire that includes newspapers—such as the *New York Post* and the London *Times*—and television stations, as well as holdings in film, book publishing, and magazines. Originally from Australia, he lived in England and later became an American citizen in order to meet U.S. requirements for media ownership. He has many critics in the world of mass communications. (Peter Marlow/Magnum Photos Inc.)

During the next century, we may see a "Big Three" (or some other small number of chains) controlling our nation's newspapers.

The implications of chain ownership This change in newspaper ownership has certain ominous implications. It implies an ability on the part of the chains to control the news and thereby (potentially) to shape how we think about events. Most communications enterprises are owned by companies that specialize in communications, but lately other corporations have moved into the field. Media critics warn that in a few years a handful of corporate conglomerates might have a "stranglehold" on the nation's newspapers. There are three reasons why control by such "absentee" owners is even more alarming than dominance by large communications industries. One is that these owners, with far-flung and diverse economic interests, have little commitment to local communities. Second, it is argued that they are not likely to be committed to journalistic (watchdog) traditions. And third, a conglomerate is designed primarily to make profits on products, and news should not be defined as only one of many products in a conglomerate's portfolio.

Those who plead the cause of media diversity argue that chain ownership greatly limits the number of independent local voices. They also note that family-owned, locally controlled papers are often better papers. This view is disputed by William H. Henry III, of *Time*, who has written that family-owned newspapers are often marked by nepotism and parochialism.[18] Moreover, both minorities and women benefit from strong equal opportunity programs at papers owned by conglomerates. Defenders of chain ownership say that more news-gathering resources—such as chain-run news services—are available and that economies of scale are achieved, which lead to better newspapers. Ironically, some of the country's best and most honored papers are part of chains—as well as some of the worst.

When all is said and done, however, the big question is whether the trend toward consolidation of newspaper ownership will actually restrict debate and robust discussion of issues in such a way that it will change the mission and quality of the American press. In the days of William Randolph Hearst, the corporate offices in New York dominated his chain's newspapers. As our account of yellow journalism showed, that *did* change their mission and quality. Today, however, only a few newspaper conglomerates issue direct orders to local editors about editorial policies, although they do firmly control finances and have generally high expectations about local newspapers' profits.

Overall, the implications of chain ownership remain an open question. At some point in the future, Americans may find that the papers they read have about as much local autonomy in what they print as a Kentucky Fried Chicken franchise does in what it cooks. On the other hand, as we have seen, the search in the past few decades has not been for ways in which to dominate readers' opinions regarding political or moral positions, but for ways to maximize profits by giving readers more of what *they* want and think they need. In other words, newspaper content in a profit-oriented economic system is audience-driven rather than owner-driven. Although that fact may limit corporate control of news, it may mean that, in the search for greater returns on investment, the focus on entertainment will increase at the expense of providing information to the public.

The Newspaper as a Contemporary Medium

The difference is great between the simple colonial newspaper run by a single printer in a tiny shop and the complicated computerized operations of today's major dailies. As we have noted, about 1,600 newspapers sell some 62.6 million copies every day. To examine this huge medium from a contemporary perspective, this section begins by examining various *types* of newspapers currently published. We then identify the *functions* that these newspapers serve for their readers. Our focus then turns to the *dual identity* that is shaped by the political and economic environments of newspapers. And finally, we summarize briefly the way newspaper work is *organized*.

Critics claim that one of the potential consequences of chain ownership is an emphasis on the entertainment function in order to increase profits, at the expense of the information function. If true, this would reduce the credibility of the press. During the 1980s, many of these critics maintained that people no longer trusted newspapers and other media to present full and unbiased accounts of the facts. Various newspaper professional organizations and chains conducted large-scale research studies to see if this was true. The results were mixed. One chain, Times Mirror, reported that the press did not have a major credibility problem. (Courtesy of The Times Mirror Center for The People & The Press)

Types of Newspapers

Contemporary American newspapers come in all types and sizes, but most, past and present, have shared at least one characteristic: They are very local in their orientation and coverage. Although most American dailies cover national and international news, community and regional events receive far more space. In contrast, newspapers in many other nations emphasize national news and concerns. The United States does have a few national newspapers—for example, *USA Today*, the *Christian Science Monitor*, and the *Wall Street Journal*. In addition, the *New York Times* and, to some extent, the *Washington Post* are read nationwide, although both depend on their respective cities for most of their readers and each gives special attention to its metropolitan area. Both carry at least some news of their city on the front page and devote a section to their region. Other large American papers, such as the *Boston Globe* and the *Seattle Times*, are regional papers with a distinctive local stamp.

We can divide almost all of this country's thousands of newspapers into two very broad categories: *general newspapers* intended for readers within their area, and *specialized newspapers* aimed at a particular kind of reader, such as people in a specific minority group, of a particular religious faith, or with a well-focused interest. Both can be further classified in terms of how often they publish (daily, weekly, etc.) and their circulation (number of copies sold). Using these criteria, most U.S. newspapers fall into one of the following categories.

Metropolitan dailies   Newspapers in the nation's largest cities have circulations that usually exceed 250,000, and the probable readership is several times larger. Most metropolitan newspapers are printed full size—usually fourteen by twenty-two inches, with six or seven columns—and published seven days a week. Their Sunday editions typically devote considerable space to books, travel, the arts, personalities, and similar topics. Examples are the *Chicago Tribune* and the *Los Angeles Times*. Such papers reach readers not only in their metropolitan areas but also in a large, multistate area. Others, such as the *Kansas City Star*, serve a more limited region round their cities. Still others, such as the *Riverside Press-Enterprise* (in Southern California), have a primarily local readership. All, however, are distributed house to house by carriers, on the street in coin boxes or from newsstands, and occasionally by mail.

The major metropolitan dailies include news, features, entertainment, sports, and opinion. Much of their content comes from syndicates. They rely on the wire services for much of their national and international news, although a few have national staffs (usually based in Washington) and foreign correspondents in important cities around the world. Several have set up special investigative teams that put together detailed stories on local or even national issues, problems, or scandals.

Some metropolitan dailies are *tabloids*. Today, the term refers mainly to a special size—approximately twelve by sixteen inches, with five columns. At one time, a tabloid newspaper was one of low quality and sensational content. The big-city tabloids were usually splashy, designed to capture attention and produce high street sales with large bold headlines. Today, the distinctions are less clear because tabloids (in the sense of size and format) include papers that mix sensationalism and professionalism (the *New York Daily News* and the *Boston Herald*), as well as the more sedate *Christian Science Monitor* and *Chicago Sun-Times*.

Quite another category of tabloids are those that are displayed and sold at the checkout counters in supermarkets and that feature unusual or bizarre stories that often defy the imagination. Examples are the *National Enquirer*, the *Globe,* the *Star*, and the even more extreme *Weekly World News.* Perhaps because of their remarkable content, which many readers find interesting, these tabloids earn a great deal of money. The *Enquirer* earns a profit of over $17 million a year, with sales of well over $4 million a week.[19]

Medium-sized and small dailies   Medium-sized dailies have more modest circulations (from 50,000 to 100,000), but they are often physically hefty. They may have fewer of their own editorial resources than the major dailies, and they use wire service news and subscribe to syndicates that provide much of their feature material.

Small dailies have a circulation under 50,000. They are even more locally focused than medium-sized dailies and sometimes are meant to be read along with a larger nearby regional paper. Usually small relative to other dailies, they use less material from external sources.

Weekly newspapers   Sometimes called the *community*, or *grassroots, press*, the weeklies were once exclusively rural or suburban publications. They ranged from suburban papers that featured life-style stories (for example, on apartment living or how to fund day-care centers) to small country papers dominated by local events and subscribers' correspondence. During the 1980s, an increasing number of new urban weeklies were founded. Some concentrate on their own neighborhoods; others are sophisticated, cosmopolitan publications that review such topics as politics and the arts. Alternative news weeklies such as New York's *Village Voice*, the *Boston Phoenix,* Chicago's *Reader*, San Francisco's *Bay Guardian,* and Portland's *Willamette Weekly* are mainly supplemental reading for people who are already informed about news and public affairs from other media.

Free-distribution newspapers   Papers that were originally called *shoppers* by the commercial press have been published for decades. Beginning in the 1980s, many of these papers took a more aggressive stance in competing with traditional daily and weekly newspapers by adding more news and entertainment material, as well as calendars of local events and various features. Many have been willing to print publicity items for local organizations and groups without much editing. These papers, once dismissed by the mainstream press, have become formidable competitors for advertising. Indeed, a number of conventional papers have begun their own free-distribution versions.

The ethnic press   During those periods of American history when massive numbers of immigrants were pouring into the country, the foreign-language press was substantial. In colonial times, French-language papers were common. During the late nineteenth century, German and Scandinavian papers prospered. But as immigrant groups assimilated into the general population, their foreign-language papers tended to die out.

Today, both foreign-language papers and papers written in English but aimed at a particular ethnic group make up the *ethnic press*. African-American papers form a large part of the ethnic press. However, because of continuing immigration from Mexico and other Latin American countries, the number of Spanish-language papers is increasing. The same is true of papers aimed at Asian immigrants. In fact, virtually every ethnic group that has emigrated to the United States—including Vietnamese, Haitians, Lebanese, and others—has at least one newspaper of its own. However, many of the papers serving racial and cultural minorities are now published in English rather than in foreign languages.

The African-American press began in the nineteenth century. From 1827 to 1829, John B. Russwurm and Reverend Samuel Cornish issued the periodical *Freedom's Journal* to counter attacks on African-Americans by New York papers. In 1847, Frederick Douglass began publication of his *North Star*, later called *Frederick Douglass' Paper*. Today, the United States has several black-oriented newspapers, including the *Baltimore Afro-American*, New York City's *Amsterdam News*, and the *Chicago Defender*.

Most of these newspapers emerged because of segregationist policies of the white press, which virtually ignored African-American people and their concerns. For many years, it was difficult for blacks to get jobs within the mainstream media. This began to change as a result of the civil rights movement of the 1960s, and the trend has continued in part because of federal legislation promoting minority hiring. By and large, the press itself has also supported this goal. Many industry and professional newspaper organizations have developed special programs for recruiting and training minorities, although many fall short of their goals. There has also been greater emphasis on reporting about minority communities, although many media critics consider this coverage inconsistent.

Papers for Hispanics have a long history. In 1855, Francisco P. Ramirez founded *El Clamor Publico* to give Mexican-Americans a voice. Prominent Hispanic newspapers today include *La Opinion* (Los Angeles), *La Informacion* (Houston), *El Nuevo Herald* (Miami), and *El Diario* (New York). The Hispanic (or Latino) press is diverse—with Mexican, Cuban, Puerto Rican, and other perspectives represented.

Native American papers include the *Navaho Times* (Arizona), the *Cherokee Advocate* (Oklahoma), and the *Indian Country News* (South Dakota). These papers include dailies as well as community weeklies, but they all take on the broad issues affecting their readers.

Other specialized newspapers The list of specialized papers can go on and on. There are industrial and commercial newspapers, labor newspapers, religious newspapers, and those serving environmentalists, feminists, gays, special hobbyists, members of voluntary associations, and of course college students. There are even prison newspapers. Some of these papers are supported not by advertising but by membership fees or an organization's profits.

Changing Functions and Content

Whatever the size of a newspaper, running it as a business means knowing how to make a profit, which means knowing how to sell the paper to the largest possible audience. Nearly three-quarters of a century ago, sociologist Robert E. Park pointed out that the "natural history" of the press is the story of how the strong survive in the struggle for existence:

> It is an account of the conditions under which the existing newspaper has grown up and taken form. A newspaper is not merely printed. It is circulated and read. Otherwise it is not a newspaper. Furthermore, it has to derive income to survive. The struggle for existence, in the case of the newspaper, has been a struggle for *circulation.*[20]

To win this struggle—to maintain a flow of income from advertisers—newspaper publishers have had to adjust to the changing demands of their audience; they have had to do this by fulfilling a variety of needs among their readers and offering them many kinds of content that provide gratification. The ways in which they do this can be called the functions of the newspaper. Although they change from time to time, at least six major functions can be identified.

Persuading, informing, and entertaining Around the time of the American Revolution, the number of functions served by newspapers was limited. As we have indicated, one major category of papers at the time comprised politically partisan ones, whose main function was persuading readers (or at least reinforcing the views of those already committed to the paper's point of view). To some extent, today's newspapers continue to serve this *persuasion, or opinion, function* by supporting particular political candidates, promoting public policies, endorsing programs, and taking positions in their editorial pages. Some provide favorable or unfavorable news coverage of institutions, candidates, and issues. However, contemporary papers are far more restrained and balanced in performing this function than were their counterparts a century ago.

The second category of early newspapers was made up of the commercial papers, whose main function was providing information about the arrivals and departures of ships, the availability of cargoes and goods, insurance matters, and so forth. In modern times, the *information function* of the newspaper is especially alive and well. It is served in part by that portion of the paper that is devoted to actual news. This can be surprisingly small. After all the other material, such as feature stories, comics, syndicated columns, and advertising, is given space, some room remains for important and unimportant news stories. This space—referred to as the "news hole"—makes up only about one-fifth of the paper. Other parts of the paper, such as weather forecasts and stock market reports, also serve the information function.

To stay alive financially, contemporary newspapers must also perform an *entertainment function*. For this reason, a large amount of their content has little to do with news. It is designed to amuse and gratify readers. Thus, newspapers offer human interest stories, crossword puzzles, recipes, gardening hints, sports scores, and advice on everything from medical problems and fashions to how to rear your child.

One might be tempted to criticize newspapers for providing entertainment so as to boost circulations. This is obviously a strategy intended to generate the advertising revenue from which the newspaper makes much of its profit. However, a good case can be made that advertising messages are a necessary part of the newspaper's information function. People need a source to find out where in the local community they can apply for a job, lease an automobile, go to a movie, rent an apartment, buy a bed, and get clothing and food at reasonable prices—and all these kinds of information are provided by various categories of advertising. Thus, advertisements by retail establishments and the classified sections are more than just promotional propaganda. They are basic to many of the consumer choices of daily life and to the economic viability of the local community.

Providing detailed coverage and analysis   The *detailed coverage and analytic function* is closely related to the information function. However, in performing this function, a newspaper goes beyond transmitting information by providing background details relevant to the news, explanations of related events, and analyses of their importance and implications. Newspapers are able to do this better than most other media. They placed increasing emphasis on this function when radio began to broadcast news reports. This posed a real threat, because newspapers lost their edge in

Modern survivors of sensational journalism are splashy daily newspapers that capture reader attention and promote sales with bold headlines. They use the tabloid format and devote a large amount of space to human interest stories of a melodramatic nature, but they also contain serious news. This sets them apart from the tabloids sold at supermarket counters, which feature bizarre stories and creative photos that many enjoy as entertainment. (Copyright © *New York Post.* Reprinted with permission from the *New York Post.*)

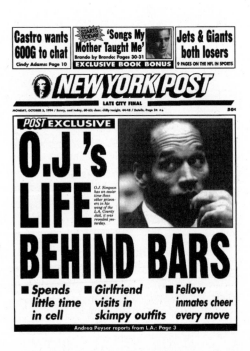

timeliness. Radio (and later television) could always get the news out faster, but its restricted time formats allowed for little more than a summary of the day's events. Consequently, newspapers began to place less emphasis on the news "scoop" and more on details and discussions of the meaning and significance of events.

As part of their function in providing detailed coverage and analysis, many journalists are now using computers as part of their basic tool-kit. Huge amounts of data on virtually every conceivable subject are available through vendors that assemble and manage on-line databases, such as Lexis/Nexis and similar computerized systems. Most newspapers in the country (except the smallest) subscribe to such services. Today, reporters routinely access on-line databases to search for background information that can be helpful in developing stories. New occupational roles for computer specialists skilled in managing such information systems are becoming increasingly common at newspapers, and reporters themselves must command searching skills.

Another important application of computers to journalism is in what is now has called *CAIR analyses* (CAIR is short for Computer-Assisted Investigative Reporting).[21] This is essentially the use of systematic strategies for computer analysis of the electronic records of government agencies at all levels to develop news stories on their activities. CAIR was developed because few such agencies continue to keep massive paper files and have switched to keeping their records in electronic form, making it difficult for investigative reporters without computer skills to monitor their activities—thus hampering the press's watchdog role. (This issue will be discussed in more detail in Chapter 12.)

Serving as the official communicator   Increasingly over the years newspapers have worked out a special function as their local government's *medium of public record*. According to *Black's Law Dictionary*, an "official" newspaper is one "designated by a state or municipal legislative body, or agents empowered by them, in which the public acts, resolves, advertisements, and notices are required to be published." For example, the laws of a city or state may require that the government publish (in the sense of making public) notices of candidates filing for elections, auctions of property seized for failure to pay taxes, or building contracts open for bids. When a local government designates an official newspaper, it pays that paper to print these notices as a means of placing them in the public record. Local governments often subsidize a selected newspaper to serve as their official communicator in this manner. Sometimes the subsidy has made the difference between survival and bankruptcy. In many cities and towns, the official newspaper is simply the community's main daily or weekly, but in large cities, it is often a specialized legal or commercial publication.

Appealing to specialized interests   Another change came during the second half of this century, when newspapers took on the function of *appealing to specific reader interests* with whole sections devoted to particular kinds of content. For example, even the *New York Times*, known for its coverage of hard news in a staid, serious, and reliable fashion, now includes special sections each week called "Home," "Living," and "Weekend." Other papers appeal to readers' specialized interests with sections on food, automobiles, and travel. Today, a typical newspaper might allot 20 percent of its space—about the same as for news—to various kinds of interest-related sections, plus sports, comics, and so on. (The rest, about 60 percent, goes to advertising.)

A number of such interest-related topics have been aimed at one group in particular—the youth market, or those in their late teens to late twenties. Newspaper executives have been increasingly alarmed by studies showing that fewer and fewer young people are newspaper readers, much less newspaper buyers. The trend suggested a bleak future for newspapers, and it did not please advertisers. People in this age group, after all, are among those whom many advertisers most want to reach. As a result, the Newspaper Advertising Council urged newspapers to provide more material of interest that would provide gratifications to young people. The result has been special sections and more coverage of youth-oriented entertainment, such as rock groups, and clothing trends.

In an effort to make it easier to serve all six of these functions, newspapers have made many changes in format. Older papers had rather dreary formats with as many as nine columns of rather small type. By the 1990s, however, most papers had reduced the number of columns, added white space between them, and cut the size of the page. The result is a newspaper that looks livelier, has more color, and is easier to read.

A Dual Identity with a Built-in Conflict of Interest

Earlier in this chapter, we defined newspapers with a simple list of characteristics. However, not everyone sees newspapers in those terms. In fact, they can seem like different things to different people: Some simply see profit-oriented businesses whose main goal is to make money for their owners. Others see an important source of information serving the public as a guardian of democracy. Still others see newspapers as some combination of the two. For example, the U.S. Department of Commerce defined newspapers in both business and public service terms:

> Newspaper publishing is the nation's tenth largest industry and its fifth largest industrial employer. The United States Constitution and its interpreters see newspapers as conveyors of information and opinion vital to the operation of government and the maintenance of freedom. . . . The millions who read newspapers see them in myriad roles. . . . The newspaper is at once a private enterprise struggling in a highly competitive economy and a quasi-public institution serving the needs of all citizens.[22]

There is considerable merit to this complex view of the nature of newspapers. As we have indicated, whatever else they may be, newspapers are private, profit-making businesses. At the same time, however, they have a special obligation—delivering information to citizens to allow robust discussion of public affairs. As a result, newspapers not only have to earn their keep financially, they also bear a special responsibility to serve the public. Indeed, to enable them to do this well, they are granted special freedoms protected by the Constitution and other laws.

Thus, the contemporary newspaper has a *dual identity*: On the one hand, the newspaper is a quasi-public institution charged with being the watchdog of the public interest and often an antagonist of government and other forces in power. This identity is a product of the responsible traditions of journalism established over the last two hundred years. On the other hand, as a business, the newspaper seeks to make a profit and function as a member of the business community, a major employer, and a member of the chamber of commerce.

This dual identity automatically brings with it an inherent conflict as business values and those of serious journalism clash. For example, the advertising department and news editors may compete for space, or they may argue over how some stories should be covered. Or, a publisher who sees the paper as only, or primarily, a business may not want to investigate a local scandal that is likely to antagonize advertisers. Why pay the kind of salaries that will keep good reporters if the gossip columns, the comics, and the sports section can maintain circulation and advertising? Yet if the publisher does not see the paper as a business, it can easily go under financially. Thus, the dual identity of the newspaper can pose a serious dilemma.

How Newspaper Work Is Organized

In the early 1920s, Walter Lippmann, a renowned journalist and scholar, marveled at the rich offerings of American newspapers: "The range of subjects these comparatively few men [editors] manage to cover would be a miracle, indeed, if it were not for a standardized routine."[23] Although much has changed since Lippmann made that observation, the organization of newspaper work still follows the basic routine that he understood. This section looks at the newspaper's basic organizational structure and division of labor.

Although newspapers range in size from the *New York Times*, with a staff of about six thousand employees, to the country weekly with a staff of three or four, one aspect of their organizational structure is the same: All papers have two basic divisions, the *business* and *editorial operations*. Generally, the business side manages the paper's financial affairs and its advertising—which generates income and keeps the paper alive. The editorial side includes reporters, editors, and all the others who acquire and process the information that goes into the paper's news stories and other editorial (non-advertising) content.

Overview of departments   The larger the paper, the more complex the organization. On the business side, several essential activities are often organized as separate departments. The *advertising department* handles both display advertising from merchants and businesses and the classified section (containing such announcements as apartments for rent, used autos for sale, and help wanted). The *production department* is responsible for type-setting (which today is done largely by complex computerized systems) and printing. The *circulation department* is responsible for arranging for home or mail delivery or sale by street vendors. A general *business department* handles such things as accounting, personnel, and building maintenance.

The editorial staff The people who produce the news content of the paper are those who gather, write, and edit stories, handle photographs, select what to publish from the wire services and syndicates, and prepare final selections for printing. They are organized into a ranked system of power and prestige. A number of supervisory people have titles that include the word "editor," and this can be confusing. However, each editor has a different level of authority, is responsible for different parts of the paper, and supervises workers who prepare distinct forms of content.

Heading the entire editorial department is the *editor-in-chief*—sometimes called simply the *editor* or, with the advent of chain ownership, the *executive editor*. The editor works directly for the *publisher* (either the owner or the principal owners' representative) and is responsible for all the paper's content, with the exception of advertising. Reporting to the editor-in-chief is the *editorial page editor* (sometimes called the *associate editor*), who is responsible for the editorial page and the "op ed" (opposite the editorial) page. The editorial page editor reports directly to the editor because newspapers try to separate "opinion" from "news" to the greatest extent possible. Also reporting to the editor is the *managing editor*, who is responsible for the day-to-day operation of the newsroom. The managing editor is a relatively powerful figure who hires and fires staff members and supervises various specialized editors. For example, the *city editor* (or *metropolitan editor* in large papers) works under the direction of the managing editor and is responsible for local news coverage, including assignments for local reporters.

Depending on the size of the paper, other news-gathering sections such as sports, business, entertainment, and features also have editors supervising them. The number of separate sections working within a newsroom is determined by the size of the paper more than any other factor. Also working for the managing editor is the *news editor*, who is responsible for preparing copy for insertion into the pages. The news editor supervises *copy editors* (who really edit stories and write headlines). The news editor also oversees the design of the pages and decides where stories will be placed. On major stories, the news editor will often consult with the managing editor and other lower-level editors before a decision is made. Finally, the *wire service editor* (or *news service editor*) selects, edits, and coordinates the national and international news from the wire services, such as the Associated Press (AP). Although smaller papers may not have personnel with all of these specific titles, someone on the newspaper staff must perform each of the activities in order for the paper to get produced.

A familiar part of the editorial staff are the *reporters*—journalists who seek out news information and initially write stories. There are basically three kinds of reporters. *General assignment reporters* cover a wide range of news as it happens, regardless of the topic. They also rewrite stories. *Beat reporters* are assigned to particular areas of government, such as the courts, police, and state government. *Specialist reporters* cover fields such as business, science, and urban problems. A special category, which is discussed in detail in Chapter 12, consists of *investigative reporters*, whose probes help the press fulfill its vital watchdog role.

Larger and more complex newspapers obviously have greater specialization in the reporting and editing functions. For example, large newspapers have specialized business reporters, columnists, and editors, who monitor commercial and industrial events. Some papers have local columnists who write about colorful people or events and reflect on the general character of the city. Other columnists specialize in politics or race relations.

Other specialists Photojournalists have played a major role in the American press since before the turn of the century. Today, their work is indispensable, since stylized, illustrative photography has become more vital to overall design. Photography came into its own when newspapers began to use more and more color. Earlier, up until about the end of the 1970s, most newspapers (except Sunday editions) were produced in black and white. Spurred by *USA Today's* eye-catching color photography and elaborate graphics, many other papers followed suit during the 1980s and "repackaged" themselves. They made greater use of drawings, photos, and color in an effort to become more attractive to readers. As a result, many papers now employ art and design directors who work with editors to design regular pages and special sections.

People who work for newspapers as editors, reporters, or photojournalists, or in other professional capacities, appear to enjoy it. Studies show that people who have graduated with degrees in journalism or mass communication and who have gone into the mass media labor force are relatively satisfied with their work on a number of dimensions. There are differences in the satisfaction levels of people who work in the various media (television, magazines, advertising, public relations, film, etc.), but *all* are more satisfied on average than similar graduates who work in industries not related to mass communications.[24]

The Future of the Newspaper

As we noted, newspapers are slowly declining in terms of the percentage of the population that subscribes to them. Nevertheless, they remain quite profitable for their owners. This is because newspapers command the largest share of American advertising dollars—spent by local businesses who must advertise their goods and services to local customers. Moreover, newspapers remain a personal and local medium, where readers find information about events, people, and institutions in their own community. Thus, newspapers continue to serve needs that are difficult for other media to fulfill.[25]

Those who own and control newspapers constantly seek new services to provide for their subscribers so as to fill the needs of people dependent on media as sources for information to use in their daily lives. Thus, many newspapers now have sections in which people can place ads about themselves and seek compatible people for social relationships. More than a hundred newspapers are now offering free-to-call voice services. Callers can dial a central number and get many kinds of information on stocks, weather, sports, soap opera summaries, election results, and even horoscopes. Newspapers continue to experiment with fax-on-demand for the latest news, and some are even offering on-line computer versions.[26]

However, three factors will probably continue to reduce both the proportion of Americans who read newspapers and newspaper revenues in the future. First, many newspapers are owned by corporations that also own radio and television stations. That could reduce competitive efforts. Second, there is a finite number of advertising dollars available in the U.S. economy, and these revenues are being chased by an increasing number of competitors (newspapers, radio, television, cable, magazines, direct mail, and perhaps phone companies and computer systems in the future). Third, media consultants maintain that consumers will spend only a certain, constant percentage of their income on information and entertainment, no matter how many outlets and services are available. Thus, that revenue pie is also only so large, and as the number of media competitors increases, they will have to cut it into smaller and smaller pieces. Inevitably, these factors will decrease the profitability of newspapers. However, in spite of these problems, it seems clear that newspapers will survive for the foreseeable future.

Chapter Review

- The origins of newspapers lie far back in history. The first newspaper in English that meets contemporary criteria was the *London Gazette*, the official newspaper of the British Crown, which began publication in 1665.

- Newspapers were slow in coming to the American colonies. The first to publish more than a single issue was the *Boston News-Letter* of 1704. A succession of small colonial newspapers followed, and a tradition of free expression was slowly established. The dramatic trial of Peter Zenger in 1734 was an important landmark in establishing the concept of a free press.

- The colonial papers were small, slow in reaching subscribers, aimed at affluent and educated readers, and limited in coverage. Some were partisan papers published to express and support a particular political position; others were commercial papers of interest mainly to merchants and traders. Nevertheless, these papers established the important journalistic tradition of guarding the public interest and played a key role in spreading ideas that became important to establishing the new nation.

- Newspapers for the common people became increasingly possible as the Industrial Revolution brought new technologies and as immigration, the growth of cities, and increased literacy led to larger potential audiences. In the *New York Sun,* Benjamin Day put together the necessary components of printing technology, advertising support, news content with wide popular appeal, and an effective distribution system. Quickly, the penny papers spread to other American cities.

- A number of changes in American society spurred the growth of newspapers. These were rapid population growth through immigration, increasing literacy, and technological changes including the steam-powered press, telegraph, trains, and steamboats. Intense competition for readers among competing urban newspapers fostered an era of yellow journalism.

- Early in the new century, the newspaper was the nation's only mass medium, and it had been adopted by most American households. However, as other media arrived, the number of newspaper subscriptions per household declined. That trend continues today.

- Both wire services and feature syndicates developed to supply newspapers with news stories from many sources and with non-news features that had great appeal to their readers. This made newspapers increasingly popular, but more and more oriented toward entertainment.

- Even before World War II, chains began buying up independently owned papers. That pattern of ownership now predominates, and less than one-third of all newspapers are still in the hands of families and other independent owners.

- There are many types of newspapers, classifiable according to size, the area they cover, the nature of their readership, and the kinds of content they emphasize. These types include metropolitan dailies, medium-sized and small dailies, weekly papers, free-distribution papers, and ethnic newspapers.

- The functions of newspapers began to change with increased emphasis on corporate profits. The older function of informing readers is still there, but entertaining them has assumed new importance. Newspapers increasingly emphasize their function of in-depth coverage and analysis because of competition from radio and television, which get the news out much faster.

- Newspaper work is organized around two broad divisions—editorial and business. Within these are a number of departments, including advertising, production, and circulation. The editorial division has a hierarchy of editors who have specialized assignments and responsibilities for various categories of content. Several kinds of reporters cover different beats and develop stories to be processed and published.

- Finally, although readership and profits may continue their slow decline, there is little doubt that newspapers will be with us in the foreseeable future because they meet needs and serve interests that currently cannot be met in other ways.

Notes and References

1. C. A. Giffard, "Ancient Rome's Daily Gazette," *Journalism History*, 2 (Winter 1975–76), pp. 107–108.
2. Edwin Emery, *The Press in America*, 5th ed. (Englewood Cliffs, N.J.: Prentice-Hall, 1972), p. 3.
3. Marvin Rosenberg, "The Rise of England's First Daily Newspaper," *Journalism Quarterly*, 30 (Winter 1953), pp. 3–14.
4. Emery, op. cit., p. 31.
5. For an excellent discussion of the development of early press technology, see John W. Moore, *Historical Notes on Printers and Printing, 1420–1886* (1886; reprint, New York: Burt Franklin, 1968).
6. An excellent selection of Brady's photographs is reproduced in Phillip B. Kunhart, Jr., *Mathew Brady and His World* (New York: Time-Life, 1977).
7. For a thorough analysis of patterns in the adoption of innovation, see Everett M. Rogers and F. Floyd Shoemaker, *Communication of Innovations, A Cross-Cultural Approach* (New York: The Free Press, 1971).
8. U.S. Bureau of the Census, *Statistical Abstract of the United States* (Washington, D.C.: U.S. Government Printing Office, 1991); *Editor and Publisher International Yearbook* (New York: Editor and Publisher, 1994).

9. (For an account of the history of wire services, see Victor Rosewater, *History of Co-Operative News-Gathering in the United States* (New York: Appleton-Century-Crofts, 1930).

10. A thorough history of the development of auxiliaries can be found in Richard A. Schwartzlose, *The Nation's Newsbrokers*, 2 vols. (Chicago: Northwestern University Press, 1989).

11. At present writing the future status of UPI is uncertain at best.

12. Michael W. Singletary, "Newspaper Use of Supplemental Services," *Journalism Quarterly,* 52 (Winter 1975), pp. 750–751.

13. Milt Rockmore, "Do Syndicates Exert Undue Influence?" *Editor and Publisher,* February 3, 1990, p. 18.

14. David Astor, "A Features Controversy Erupts in Dallas," *Editor and Publisher,* August 12, 1989, pp. 42–43. See also "A High-Priced Feature Switch in Dallas," *Editor and Publisher*, September 23, 1898, p. 43.

15. This situation has prevailed for decades. For example, see Arnold H. Ismach, "The Economic Connection: Mass Media Profits, Ownership and Performance," in E. E. Dennis, D. M. Gilmore, and A. Ismach, eds., *Enduring Issues in Mass Communication* (St. Paul: West, 1978), pp. 143–259. For a more recent discussion that comes to the same basic conclusions, see Robert Picard, *Media Economics* (Newbury Park, Calif.: Sage Publications, 1990).

16. John C. Busterna, "Trends in Daily Newspaper Ownership," *Journalism Quarterly,* 65 (Winter, 1988), pp. 831–838.

17. The sources for figures on trends in ownership are Lynch, Jones and Ryan, Inc., John Morton Research, Inc., and the Newspaper Association of America.

18. William H. Henry III, "Learning to Love the Chains," *Washington Journalism Review,* September 1986, pp. 15–17.

19. Antonio N. Fins, "Alien Beancounters Invade the *Enquirer,*" *Business Week,* September 11, 1989, p. 35.

20. Robert E. Park, "The Natural History of the Newspaper," *American Sociological Review,* 29 (1923), pp. 273–289.

21. See Margaret H. DeFleur, "Supporting the Watchdog: Aiding the Press through Computer-Assisted Investigative Reporting," in Keith R. Billingsley, Hilton U. Brown III, and Ed Derohanes, eds., *Computer-Assisted Modeling on the IBM 3090: The 1989 Contest Prize Papers*, vol. 2 (Athens, Ga.: The Baldwin Press, University of Georgia, 1992).

22. Ernest H. Hynds, *American Newspapers in the 1980's* (New York: Hastings House, 1980), p. 11.

23. Walter Lippmann, *Public Opinion* (1922; reprint, New York: Free Press, 1965), p. 214.

24. For comparisons of dimensions and levels of job satisfaction of communications alumni who work in advertising, film, newspaper journalism, broadcast journalism, photography, public relations, radio and television, see Margaret H. DeFleur, "Foundations of Job Satisfaction in the Media Industries," *Journalism Educator*, 47 (Spring 1992), pp. 3–15.

25. Guido H. Stempel III, "Where People *Really* Get Most of Their News," *Newspaper Research Journal*, 12 (Fall 1991), pp. 2–9.

26. Randy Bennett, "Newspapers Go Interactive Again," *Online Access*, 7, 4 (Winter 1992), pp. 46–49.

CHAPTER

Magazines: Voices for Many Interests

This is the age of Magazines
Even Skeptics must confess it:
Where is the town of much reknown
That has not one to bless it?

The Cincinnati Literary Gazette, 1824

The word "magazine" entered the English language in the late 1500s, but it did not refer to a printed medium. The term comes originally from the Arabic *makhasin*, which means "storehouse." Thus, a magazine in ancient times was a place containing a collection of different items, usually military stores. We still use the word to describe many kinds of military enclosures where explosives are kept. In the 1700s, when the early printed periodicals began to appear, they eventually came to be called magazines because they were in a sense storehouses of writings about various topics.

Obviously, magazines depended on the same technological developments in movable type, presses, printing, and paper as did books and newspapers. However, magazines are not like other print media. Although they have some of the features of books and are published on some regular schedule like newspapers, they comprise a unique medium in their own right.

Magazines were originally established in London, where they prospered in a great city with many urbane and educated residents. The very different societal conditions prevailing in the American colonies during the eighteenth century held back their development. However, as the new nation expanded, became more urban, and developed improved transportation, American magazines began to prosper. By the end of the nineteenth century, they were a serious and respected medium serving millions of readers.

During the early twentieth century, magazines played an important role in exposing unacceptable social conditions and stimulating social reform. Between the two world wars, before television became a household medium, they were one of the major mass media advertising nationally distributed products. After World War II, the growth of television had a significant impact on the magazine industry. Large-circulation general magazines were severely hurt financially, but new kinds of magazines were founded and the industry thrives today.

Magazines have always served specific functions in society that differ from those of either newspapers or books. Furthermore, those who subscribe to and read magazines constitute a distinct segment of the U.S. population. Magazines' functions and audiences have a long and colorful history, and although they have changed greatly over time, at least some remain remarkably similar to what they were from their beginnings.

The First Magazines

The history of the magazine started in London in 1704 with the first issue of a small periodical called *The Review*.[1] In some ways, this little publication resembled a newspaper of the time; it was printed on about four small pages and (at first) was published weekly. Yet it was different from the early newspapers because it was much less concerned with news; it focused mainly on articles about domestic affairs and national policy. In England at the time, people could still be jailed for writing and publishing material contrary to the policies of the Crown. As it happened, the founder of *The Review* had been doing precisely that just before starting his magazine. The founder was the outspoken Daniel Defoe (who later wrote *Robinson Crusoe*), and he wrote the first issue while he was in Newgate Prison. He had been arrested because of his critical writings denouncing certain policies of the Church of England.

Thus, the magazine was born as an instrument of politics. *The Review*, like many of the magazines that would follow it, was a vehicle for political commentary and intended to influence its readers' beliefs and opinions. At the same time, it was an instrument of entertainment—at least for sophisticated readers—in that it also contained essays on literature, manners, and morals. Both of these functions were central to this medium from the beginning, and for many magazines, they remain so today.

After his release, Defoe continued to produce *The Review* on a more frequent schedule, about three times a week, until 1712. The significance of Defoe's little publication was that it was almost immediately imitated, and the idea of magazines as a separate kind of print medium began to catch on. By 1709, Richard Steele had begun publication of *The Tatler*, offering a mixture of news, poetry, political analyses, philosophical essays, and even coffee house gossip. Within a short time, Joseph Addison joined Steele and together they produced *The Spectator*, which quickly became a favorite of London's urbane elite, enjoying a circulation of several thousand.

Although these early publications are now seen as the first magazines, they were not called that at the time. The term was not applied to a periodical until 1731, when Edward Cave, a London printer, first published his monthly *Gentlemen's Magazine*. Cave's use of the term was appropriate because his publication was a kind of printed "storehouse" of reports, articles, and treatises that had already appeared in other journals. In some ways, it was an early form of today's *Reader's Digest*, which serves similar functions. The *Gentlemen's Magazine* was quite successful and eventually reached some fifteen thousand subscribers, truly a remarkable circulation for the time.

What made these early magazines so different from newspapers of the period was both their content and their authors. The magazines presented material by some of the most able writers of the time. The pages contained essays, stories, and entertaining commentaries by such figures as Samuel Johnson, Alexander Pope, and, as noted, Daniel Defoe, Joseph Addison, and Richard Steele—among the most respected English writers of the eighteenth century.

As the form and substance of the new medium came together by the middle of the 1700s, the functions it was serving in the society were unique. The magazine was clearly designed to make a profit. It depended on subscription payments by its readers and, to a limited extent, on advertising revenues. It sought to attract readers with a mixture that was heavy with political commentary, but it also included discussions of controversial topics and issues and opinion-shaping essays. Its literary quality was high, and its typical reader was a member of the affluent, well-educated elite. It was not a medium for the masses. By the middle of the century, a number of rival magazines were being published successfully in England, and the concept was spreading to other parts of the world. Thus, by the time of the American Revolution, hundreds of publications that we would recognize today as magazines were being produced in the major cities of Europe.

The Development of American Magazines

Magazines were slow to develop in the United States. Although attempts to produce them started even before the American Revolution, they almost always ended in failure. The central reason for this was that the conditions of society required to support this kind of medium did not exist in the United States until after the beginning of the nineteenth century. Then, as education, transportation, printing technology, and other conditions improved, many magazines were started, and some of them became extraordinarily successful.

Barriers to Development in the Eighteenth Century

The magazines that had been established in England were impressive models. To some intellectuals, it seemed like a great idea to begin the publication of such a periodical in the colonies. In fact, Benjamin Franklin, ever the innovator, tried to get one started in 1741. It had the awesome title of *The General Magazine, and Historical Chronicle, for All the British Plantations in America*. And it even had a competitor with an equally awesome title, Andrew Bradford's *The American Magazine, or A Monthly View of the Political State of the British Colonies*. Franklin's effort lasted for six issues; Bradford's failed after only three.[2]

Generally regarded as the first American periodical of its kind, *The General Magazine, and Historical Chronicle* was published by Benjamin Franklin in Philadelphia in 1741. An inexpensive postal system for delivering magazines to subscribers did not exist then, and there were too few educated and affluent colonials to support such a medium. The magazine was an idea whose time had not yet come, and this one lasted for only six issues. (Boston Public Library, Department of Rare Books and Manuscripts)

After that, attempts to produce a magazine were sporadic.[3] Several, including *The American Magazine and Historical Chronicle* and the *Christian History*, also appeared during the 1740s. None lasted more than two or three years. Then, a whole decade went by with no attempt to publish a magazine. Somehow the idea was not working as it had in England.

If Franklin, Bradford, and the others had been able to hire a modern market researcher, he or she would have looked carefully at colonial "demographics," as we say today, to try to determine if there was a sufficient market for a magazine. It would not have taken much research to reveal that such projects were doomed before they even got started. There were four major conditions that created barriers to the successful establishment of magazines in the United States and caused their development to lag considerably behind that of their European counterparts: (1) the nature and dispersion of the population, (2) the economics of publishing at the time, (3) the state of transportation and the postal system, and (4) the characteristics of the readers themselves.

The population factor   When Franklin and Bradford brought out their rival magazines, the population of the entire thirteen colonies was only about 1 million, and few inhabitants were village or city dwellers. During the colonial period, people were spread over a huge land area, extending about 1,200 miles along the coast and a few hundred miles inland. The majority of the colonists lived on farms, often in isolated locations. Although there was some commerce, the principal industry was agriculture. There was no manufacturing of the kind that would later draw laborers to factory locations to form industrialized cities, and there were only a handful of communities of any appreciable size. Even a half-century later, in 1790, when the first official U.S. Census was taken, only 3.9 million people (not counting Native Americans) lived in the entire original thirteen states. There were only twenty-four "urban places" (larger than 2,500 inhabitants), and only Philadelphia and Boston had populations in excess of 25,000. Altogether, city dwellers made up only 3.5 percent of the entire U.S. population.[4]

As a consequence of these population conditions, no accessible market existed for a magazine in the American colonies in the eighteenth century. If Franklin and Bradford and those who later tried to start magazines had understood how these factors were related to the success of their medium, they probably would not have even taken the trouble.

Obstacles to magazine delivery   Besides a sparse and dispersed population, colonial transportation was another factor that retarded the development of American magazines. The colonies' primitive roads prevented overland movement of almost anything. It is difficult for us to imagine what it was like to take a trip then. Traveling from New York to Boston today requires a few minutes by air and just over four hours on expressways by car. By contrast, in the middle of the eighteenth century, it was a rough eight- to ten-day trip by stagecoach, and just getting there was an accomplishment. Hauling goods (such as bundles of magazines) by wagon or pack animal was much slower. In many parts of the country, mud or snow made the rude tracks that did exist impassable during long periods of the year. Even near population centers, such as Boston and Philadelphia, travel was difficult. In the less settled areas, there were few roads of any kind, and most travelers went by horseback, sailing vessels, or even canoes. In 1790, the steamboat was decades away, and railroads would not link the nation's cities until after the 1840s.

Today, we receive magazines in the mail routinely and reliably. Subscribers seldom think about postage because it is paid by the publisher (and is really quite inexpensive). Getting magazines to subscribers in the

Early in this nation's history, the development of magazines was impeded for a variety of reasons. One was the problem of how to get magazines from where they were published to subscribers who lived elsewhere. It was not until just before the Civil War that the United States provided for reliable and inexpensive delivery of magazines by mail, with postage paid by the publisher. Today, inexpensive postal rates allow magazines to be sent even to remote areas. (T. Tracy/FPG International)

eighteenth century was a different matter. As early as 1710, a mail system had been established by the Crown. It was mainly for letters that were carried by postal riders, and service was not available for bulky magazines. By the 1790s, however, the new Congress did allow magazines to be sent by post, but this was not practical because the cost was based on weight. Postage at letter rates was required, and this made mailing heavy magazines prohibitively expensive. A few years later, the Congress changed to a system based on the number of pages plus the distance required for delivery. This did not work well either, because magazines became very expensive for people who lived far away. Postage, which had to be paid in advance by the subscriber, added from 20 to 40 percent to the cost of the periodical.

It was not until 1852 that postal rates for magazines could be paid at the point of mailing by the publisher. By that time, roads had been greatly improved, and both steamship lines and railroads were operating on regular schedules to carry mail quickly, cheaply, and efficiently. The lower costs led most publishers to absorb the postage as part of the subscription price.

The cost of subscribing   A magazine in the early days of this nation was a real luxury. It is difficult to try to convert the various colonial currencies into today's dollars. However, the first magazines produced by Franklin and Bradford, for instance, sold for a shilling per issue in the currency of the time, and this was the going rate up until the time of the American Revolution. At that time in New England, that was about half a day's wages for a farm laborer. A year's subscription equaled what a laborer could earn in about four to five days. Added was the cost of delivery, about another day's wages. Today, a laborer working for five to six days at five dollars an hour makes at least two hundred dollars. Few among us would be willing to pay that much for a magazine subscription. For the same reason, few in the eighteenth century were willing to pay the going price.

Magazines were then, and would remain for a substantial period, a medium for the well-to-do. They were just what was needed in European cities such as London and Paris where, even though the majority of residents were poor, those who did have wealth were concentrated. Affluent enclaves made these cities centers not only of commerce and political power, but of fashion, the arts, and literature—exactly the topics discussed in the magazines. In other words, the elite of the population centers made up a pool of potential subscribers. In contrast, the farmers and laborers of the American colonies, thinly scattered over a vast area, did not constitute a potential market.

Catalysts for Development in the Nineteenth Century

Virtually every imaginable factor conspired against the development of magazines in America during the 1700s, but the situation started to change significantly after the 1800s began. As noted, transportation improved greatly, and the postal system changed. In addition, printing technologies developed quickly, the population increased rapidly, people were better educated, cities expanded, and there were great issues about which the population urgently needed detailed information. These were just the conditions needed for a great flowering of magazines.

Rapid population growth   A significant factor in the development of American magazines during the nineteenth century was the rapid growth in the population. The first U.S. Census (1790) counted only 3.9 million people. Ten years later, the figure had increased to 5.3 million. Then, during only five decades, the population soared to 23.2 million, which represents an increase of over 337 percent. By the end of the nineteenth century, owing in large part to massive immigration, the population had skyrocketed to 75.9 million. Few nations in history have ever recorded such an astonishing rate of population growth.

Population expansion remained a factor helping to decide the fate of magazines well into the present century. Massive immigration continued into the 1920s before it was slowed by legislation. All during the nineteenth century, and into the twentieth, the birth rate was also high, adding to population growth. The rate finally dropped during the Great Depression of the 1930s but climbed sharply again after World War II, when the so-called baby boom generation was born. (The U.S. population is now more or less stable with just over 250 million.) The golden age of magazine growth during the nineteenth century would never have occurred without these long-term population trends. As we will see, that population growth also provided the market base for the large-circulation general magazines that were prevalent in the first half of this century.

Urbanization   Not only did the population grow geometrically, but it became more urban; that is, increasing numbers of citizens lived in villages, towns, and cities rather than on farms. In part, this trend toward urban living arose from the spread of transportation networks that made it possible to move farm goods to domestic and foreign market centers. Starting in 1815, the great Erie Canal was dug (without power machinery) across an incredible three hundred miles, connecting Albany on the Hudson River with Buffalo on Lake Erie. By this route, combining horse-drawn barges and Great Lakes steamboats, travelers and goods could journey cheaply along a network from New York City to the new city of Chicago.

As farm products and consumer goods moved over this great transportation system, hundreds of communities sprang up in the Midwest and in northern parts of Pennsylvania, New York, Indiana, and Ohio. Southward links allowed barge traffic to move from Lake Erie down the Miami River into the Ohio and on into the Mississippi. Thus, before the middle of the nineteenth century, people could travel by canal barge and paddle-wheel steamboat from New York City to New Orleans by way of the Great Lakes. New York City itself, at the eastern end of the system, grew into a great port for exports and imports. It became the largest and most important city in the United States—and because of that, eventually the center of the nation's mass communication industries.

Between about 1840 and 1870, the railroads, too, had spread to most parts of the country, fostering their own share of towns and cities. The United States was developing into one of the most productive agricultural and industrial powers the world had ever known. Steel mills, factories, and hundreds of other kinds of production facilities were established by the end of the century, drawing more people into concentrated communities. Thus, although all segments of the population were growing, the mix was changing. Increasing proportions of the population lived in towns and cities and earned salaries and wages. During the same period, smaller and smaller proportions were living on farms.

The growth of towns and cities meant more concentrated populations with larger cash incomes and higher levels of education. These were precisely the conditions required for an expanding market for magazines. To give some idea of the shift, in 1790, more than 95 percent of American families lived on farms. By 1820, this figure had dropped to 80 percent. At the time of the Civil War, it was about 70 percent. The flow of people from farm to city continued and even accelerated in this century. By 1920, only half of the nation's families lived on farms. Today, it is 2 percent. The United States is truly an urban nation. Over half of Americans live on only 1 percent of the land mass.

Increasing education   Sheer numbers and their concentrations are important, but the quality of the population is also a factor shaping the market for a product like a magazine. In its early years, the United States was a nation whose citizens for the most part had received little or no formal instruction in reading. Even at the beginning of the nineteenth century, education beyond the rudiments was largely available only to the elite. Few ordinary people went to secondary school, and only the wealthy attended college.

Nevertheless, a remarkable and uniquely American idea at the beginning of the nineteenth century was that of education for all citizens (at the time, that meant all white citizens). Here, after all, was a new kind of society, based on assumptions of personal freedom, equality, and participation in the political process. A literate citizenry was essential to the system. Furthermore, as industrialization began, it became increasingly clear that reading, writing, and arithmetic were skills needed to improve a person's chances in life. Free public education was vigorously promoted by reformers and enthusiasts early in the century. The most prominent among them was Horace Mann of Massachusetts who, as noted in Chapter 2, had by 1834 persuaded his state's legislature that a system of universal and mandatory education was a good idea. Essentially, Mann's concept consisted of three basic principles: (1) Tuition-free (that is, tax-supported) elementary and secondary schools should be available to all children; (2) teachers should receive professional training in special schools devoted to their education; (3) all children should be required to attend school (either public or private) until a minimum age.

In those conservative times, Mann's system was widely regarded as a wild and radical scheme. It was vigorously opposed by large numbers of the wealthy and the propertied, who feared that universal education would foster too many critics of the prevailing system (which they for the most part controlled). Many religious leaders also fought it, holding that too much book learning would clearly lead to godlessness.

In spite of the controversies, the Massachusetts system for educating all citizens quickly spread to the other states. The Civil War disrupted society greatly, including educational development. Following the conflict, however, increasing proportions of the nation's children were enrolled in free elementary and high schools. Table 4.1 shows the spread of education over

TABLE 4.1
The Growth of Education in the United States, 1869–1988

Period	School Enrollment*
1869–1870	57.0
1889–1890	68.6
1909–1910	74.2
1929–1930	81.7
1949–1950	83.2
1969–1970	86.9
1977–1978	88.7
1987–1988	96.5

*Percentage of population aged 5–17 enrolled in elementary and high school.

Sources: *U.S. Bureau of the Census, U.S. Department of Health, Education and Welfare, Statistics of the School Systems, 1986–87.*

more than a century. This great social change had profound implications for the development of magazine markets.

The great issues   As population changes occurred during the 1800s, demands for specialized information played a part in the spread of the modern magazine. Providing that information became its special task. It was a medium that could present positions, details, opinions, and analyses in ways quite different from those of the newspaper, and in much greater depth. It was from magazines that Americans learned about important trends, controversies, and significant issues that were affecting their society.

The entire century was marked by extraordinary events, sweeping changes, and truly significant movements in thought, politics, and religion. For example, there was no more important nineteenth-century event for Americans than the Civil War, with its accompanying debates over slavery. Works such as Harriet Beecher Stowe's *Uncle Tom's Cabin* were serialized

During the nineteenth century, magazines were a major medium for informing people about great issues that confronted the population. It was a time of great social change, political controversy, and intellectual ferment. One issue that divided people sharply was Darwin's theory. On one side were those who accepted the evolutionary explanation of the origins of species, including human beings. On the other were those who held that human beings, along with the entire natural world, were created by God as described in scripture. Magazines were the medium of choice for airing all sides of such issues. Cartoons such as this one were often used as a means of expressing a point of view. (The Granger Collection)

in magazines and reached a reading public that far exceeded the number who had access to the book.

Intellectual debates of monumental significance provided unique content for magazines. An example was the explosive conflict over Darwin's explanation of the origin of our species. Magazines were an important forum for both sides in the debate over evolution versus creation. Magazines also delved into topics such as financial panics and depressions, controversial discoveries in medicine, great religious revivals, and the continuously expanding frontier.

During the middle part of the nineteenth century, no issue stirred the population more than the question of the proper place of women in the society. Many magazines were aimed directly at women, and women's suffrage and women's rights in general were hotly debated topics. Even the subject of women's dress could generate a heated argument almost anywhere. The issue of women's clothing had become controversial before the Civil War, when Amelia Bloomer proposed that women abandon the clumsy hoop skirts of the time and wear instead "Turkish pantalettes" (baggy trousers gathered tight at the ankle) with a knee-length overskirt or jacket. (Decades later, a particular women's undergarment, worn well hidden under skirts, came to be called "bloomers.") All in all, abundant issues great and small generated lively topics for magazine debate.

Characteristics of Magazines in the Nineteenth Century

Because of the catalysts noted above, the magazine industry flowered during the nineteenth century. It was a dynamic industry, constantly seeking new formats, new audiences, new appeals, and new ways to increase profits. Although thousands of magazines were started only to die within a short time, some lasted for generations.

Numbers and circulations The number of magazines published in the United States showed a remarkable pattern of growth over a period of seventy-five years. In 1825, there were fewer than 100 magazines in circulation.[5] By 1850, there were 685 periodicals, other than newspapers, being regularly published. The Civil War held down magazine growth, but by 1870 the number had risen to 1,200. It then doubled in a single decade to 2,400. By the end of the century, 5,500 magazines were circulating.

Paralleling this rapid expansion in the number of magazines published was growth in circulation rates. Actual circulations were not systematically recorded during the century, but various figures are available that show a sharply increasing trend. For example, during the late 1700s, a magazine would have been lucky to have 1,500 subscribers. Most had fewer. In contrast, the *Country Gentleman* in 1858 had 250,000—apparently the largest audience of the time. By the eve of the Civil War, *Harper's Weekly* had 120,000 subscribers. Other magazines of the time were within the same range. *Godey's Lady's Book*, a very popular magazine among women, had a circulation of 150,000. Within fifteen years, circulations had risen sharply. For instance, in 1885, the *Youth's Companion* was the leader with 300,000 subscribers. The more literate *Scribner's Monthly* had a respectable 200,000.

A magazine for every taste and interest   During the last years of the nineteenth century, magazine publishers came to understand their markets very well. "Every interest had its own journal or journals—all the ideologies and movements, all the arts, all the schools of philosophy and education, all the sciences, all the trades and industries, all the professions and callings, all organizations of importance, all hobbies and recreations."[6] In other words, while newspapers were providing their readers with a daily cafeteria of many different types of content, magazines zeroed in on specific social categories—on people who shared an interest in a particular subject.

As the century came to a close, the world of magazines was varied indeed. There were a number of religious periodicals. In fact, by 1885, there were some 650 aimed at different groups, from the main denominations to those interested in every obscure religious practice and philosophy. Scores of magazines were devoted to the arts, including music, theater, and literature. Short stories, travel accounts, and virtually every other conceivable subject of interest were served by a periodical. Many of what are now the nation's most prestigious professional and technical journals were started during the last years of the nineteenth century.

Generally, then, by the end of the nineteenth century, the magazine had become a mature and important medium. For many citizens, magazines were the major source of opinions and analyses concerning complex issues and topics that were not covered in depth by the newspapers. For other people, they offered amusement and trivial entertainment. Some read them to reinforce their religious views or to gain insight into complex political questions. Others subscribed simply as a means of gaining information about a particular hobby. Magazines were as varied as were readers' interests and concerns.

Magazines in the First Half of the Twentieth Century

Magazines gained additional respect early in the twentieth century when a number of them became vehicles for exposing political corruption, social problems, and economic exploitation. During the first decade of the new century, prestigious magazines took the lead in pricking the nation's social, moral, and political conscience as their writers, editors, and publishers probed into economic and political life. As we shall see, the conditions revealed during this muckraking period resulted in many needed reforms and corrective legislation.

Yet ultimately, magazines, like all the other American mass media, were produced and distributed for the most part because they made a profit for their owners. It was true that some were started because of some special communication mission—for example, to provide religious information to the faithful. Even so, revenues to support the magazines had to be found.

EARLY MAGAZINES AS MEDIA OF LITERARY EXPRESSION:
A Linchpin to Literature

Long before cheap books became widely available to the public, magazines served as the main medium of literary expression. Some of the first literary magazines, such as *The Spectator* and *The Tatler*, were created in eighteenth-century England as journals of satire and criticism. By virtue of the genius of their founders, these journals raised the discursive essay to an art form, one that still enjoys a popular following in many modern magazines.

By the mid-nineteenth century a relatively new literary form, the novel, had become the most popular form of literature in Europe and the United States. By the 1870s, fiction dominated the content of most American magazines. Indeed, magazines were often the first to publish, in serialized form, many important works that achieved lasting critical importance. For much of the nineteenth century and well into the twentieth, magazines played a major role in raising the cultural awareness of subscribers scattered across a vast country, many of whom lacked access to schools, colleges, books, and libraries.

Even the great muckraking magazines of the period, such as *McClure's* and *Collier's*, would routinely include short fiction by writers such as Arthur Conan Doyle, Jack London, Booth Tarkington, O. Henry, Frank Norris, Edith Wharton, Owen Wister, and Zane Grey. Many other magazines of the period were created precisely as vehicles for short stories. Magazines such as the *Golden Argosy, Story Teller, Pocket Monthly*, and *Short Stories* were given entirely to short fiction, most of it sentimental tales of romance and adventure now thankfully lost and forgotten. Other magazines of the period—*Black Cat, Gray Goose*, and the *Owl*—sponsored short-story contests, published the winning entries (some of them quite good), and were very successful. Another type of periodical immensely popular during the 1890s was the "dime novel"; it featured a short novel, usually of the action and romance variety.[1] Many of these publications were considered somewhat racy by contemporary standards, and their cheap price and special appeal to the young often caused them to become the target of censors and urban anti-vice societies.[2]

Nonetheless some of the nation's best narrative talents also published their short stories in magazines. Mark Twain published his comic tale "The Jumping

If none were available, they died. Subscriptions were very important, paying a considerable portion of the costs of producing and distributing the magazines. However, as with newspapers, the real profit was in attracting advertisers.

As an advertising medium, the magazines of the nineteenth and early twentieth century were formidable. There were no other widely distributed media for touting wares to the national market. Radio would not become a household medium until the 1920s; television would not be a reality until decades later. Newspapers were local, and neither books nor movies used advertising in the same way. In a very real sense, magazines were the national advertiser's only hope. For the cost of the space, a magazine circulated nationwide could guarantee that potential customers all over the country would be exposed to the message. This advertising function led to the large-circulation general magazines of the first half of the twentieth century.

Frog," later rewritten as "The Celebrated Jumping Frog of Calaveras County," in the *Saturday Press* in 1865. Bret Harte published his great stories "The Luck of Roaring Camp" and "Outcasts of Poker Flat" in an 1868 issue of *Overland Monthly*; and the classic American parable "The Lady or the Tiger?" by Frank Stockton, first appeared in the November 1882 issue of *Century*. *Scribner's* magazine, one of the great magazines of this period, published by the New York book publisher of the same name, enjoyed a near monopoly of the short fiction and poetry of Robert Louis Stevenson and published other American poets and fiction writers as well, among them Thomas Wolfe, Ernest Hemingway, and Stephen Crane—whose 1897 *Scribner's* story "The Open Boat" is now regarded as an American masterpiece.

Other magazines, such as *Harper's* and *The Atlantic*, published in serial form novels by such popular European writers as Charles Dickens, George Eliot, Victor Hugo, William Thackeray, and Thomas Hardy. These magazines also published the work of then lesser-known American novelists such as William Dean Howells, Henry James, and Bret Harte. Of these, Howells was considered the preeminent writer of the day, though there were other, more popular American novelists at the time. Mark Twain, for exam-ple, did not publish his longer work in magazines, though in the mid-1880s *Century* reprinted in serial form both *Tom Sawyer* and *The Adventures of Huckleberry Finn*, both of which in book form were widely banned from library shelves.

The literary tradition in magazine publishing found new voices in the early twentieth century with such publications as *The Saturday Evening Post*, which pub-lished some of the early work of William Faulkner and Ben Hecht, among others. In 1936, the *Post* published Stephen Vincent Benet's classic short story "The Devil and Daniel Webster."[3]

The role of the literary magazine declined greatly after newer media came into being and as Americans gained greater access to books and other sources of information during the twentieth century. However, there are still a number of influential maga-zines devoted to literature, among them *The New Yorker*, *Harper's*, and *The Atlantic Monthly*, as well as several literary journals.

1. Frank Luther Mott, *A History of American Magazines*, vols. 3 and 4 (Cambridge, Mass.: The Belknap Press of Harvard University Press, 1957).
2. Paul S. Boyer, *Purity in Print: The Vice Society Movement and Book Censorship in America* (New York: Scribner's, 1968).
3. Theodore Peterson, *Magazines in the Twentieth Century* (Urbana, Ill.: University of Illinois Press, 1964).

Aimed at a nationwide readership drawn from all walks of life, they truly were magazines in the original meaning of the term. They had something for everyone in every issue—fiction, biography, travel, humor, advice for the homemaker, a sprinkling of political commentary (but not much), and sports. Magazines such as *Collier's*, *Cosmopolitan*, *Liberty*, and *The Saturday Evening Post* would come to dominate the industry during the mid–twentieth century.

The Muckrakers: Magazines as a Force for Social Reform

One of the most important periods in the history of magazines began just before the turn of the century and lasted until the end of World War I. It was a time when a limited number of magazines took the lead in what we now

By the end of the nineteenth century, a rich variety of magazines was being published and read by Americans. Magazines contributed greatly to the development of the nation's culture, with some published for almost every category of people. Magazines were an important source of information about literature, science, geography, religion, politics, and virtually every other topic. (The Bettmann Archives)

call investigative reporting. At the time, it was called *muckraking*, a term coined by President Theodore Roosevelt to characterize journalists who, instead of extolling the virtues of the United States, were determined to expose its dark and seamy side. Roosevelt compared such journalists to the "Man with the Muckrake" in John Bunyan's classic *Pilgrim's Progress*, who would not look up from the filth on the floor even when he was offered a glittering crown.

Particularly forceful in the muckraking movement were *McClure's, The North American Review, Forum, The Atlantic Monthly*, and even *The Saturday Evening Post*. These were national publications with a huge combined circulation. A number of their writer-investigators probed political, social, and economic conditions as a part of the popular reform movement that was sweeping the country. Those investigative writers were vigorous, relentless, and thorough. As early as the 1870s, *Harper's Weekly* had campaigned to oust New York City's political dictator "Boss" Tweed. Another nineteenth-century magazine, *Arena*, had attacked slums, sweatshops, and prostitution, demanding sanitation laws, birth control, and socialized medicine. By the turn of the century, thorough exposés of corruption in the cities and abuses by industry had been published and widely read.

With the new century, the movement to expose unsatisfactory social conditions moved into even higher gear. Perhaps the best-known example of muckraking was a series in *McClure's* by Ida M. Tarbell on the giant Standard Oil Company. Tarbell was a remarkable woman, whose accomplishments illustrate the best traditions of journalism as the watchdog of society. Samuel S. McClure (who published the magazine of the same name)

McCLURE'S MAGAZINE

APRIL, 1904

Enemies of the Republic
By LINCOLN STEFFENS

The Breaking Up of the
Standard Oil Trust
By IDA M. TARBELL

The Negro—Part Two
By THOMAS NELSON PAGE

SEVEN SHORT STORIES

Illustrations in Color

S. S. McCLURE CO. NEW YORK AND LONDON

One of the most important magazines of the muckraking era was *McClure's Magazine*. On its staff were both Lincoln Steffens and Ida Tarbell, both of whom left indelible marks on the history of investigative journalism. Steffens's investigations of political corruption in American cities resulted in many reforms, and Tarbell's reporting about the Standard Oil Trust brought her world fame. (Clockwise: State Historical Society of Wisconsin; Culver Pictures, Inc.; The Bettmann Archive)

had confidence in Tarbell because she had already written very good biographies of Napoleon and Lincoln for him. She was an outstanding writer and a thorough researcher. McClure hired her as a staff writer and assigned her to produce a series about Standard Oil, expecting a portrayal of the high achievements and efficiency of American industry in producing and distributing an important product.

As it turned out, he got something very different. Tarbell spent five years preparing and writing seventeen articles about the giant trust. She dug into every public record that she could find, interviewed people, and examined letters, court transcripts, and thousands of other documents. She did report that Standard Oil was superbly organized and that it achieved its objectives with great efficiency. However, she also showed in merciless detail how John D. Rockefeller and his corporation had used "bribery, fraud, violence, corruption of public officials and the railroads, and the wrecking of competitors by fair means and foul."[7] The public was outraged, and *McClure's* circulation soared. Tarbell's series gained worldwide recognition as an example of thorough investigative reporting.

The names of other reform-minded writers such as Lincoln Steffens and Ray Stannard Baker also became household words. Steffens produced the widely praised "Shame of the Cities" series, showing how corrupt governments worked in a number of American communities; Baker's "The Right to Work" was a series on the problems of workers and corruption in labor unions. These writers and dozens of others of the muckraking period made a tremendous impression on the public and became the conscience of the nation. Powerful political figures took up their cry for reform, and both federal and state governments acted to correct the political and economic abuses that had been exposed. Muckraking, the forerunner of investigative journalism, was definitely out of fashion by the 1930s when Steffens published his autobiography, now regarded as a journalistic classic.

Eventually, a great many magazines turned to this kind of material. Some did it well, but many churned out poorly researched criticisms of virtually everything about which stories could be written. Eventually the public tired of this tidal wave of criticism, and magazines had to change. The muckraking period ended with World War I, but it may have been the high point in the social and political importance of magazines.

The Challenge of Television

After interest in muckraking declined, new classes of magazines began to appear. One was the *newsmagazine*, a term coined by Henry Luce and Briton Hadden when they founded *Time* in 1923. New concepts arose, too (or more accurately, old concepts were revived), such as the digest—a collection of excerpts from other publications. Even today, *Reader's Digest* remains one of the most successful magazines of all time. *The New Yorker* was also founded in the 1920s. In 1936, the picture magazine *Life* was first published and met instant success. In 1945, the picture magazine *Ebony,* aimed at African-Americans, was founded. For almost thirty years, from the 1920s into the 1950s, large-circulation general magazines such as *Life*, *Look*, *Collier's*, and *The Saturday Evening Post* dominated the market. National circulations reached into the tens of millions. Magazines were far ahead of newspapers and books in the effective, sophisticated use of photographs, color, and graphic design. They were beautifully printed, efficiently distributed, rewarding to read, great as an advertising medium, and enormously profitable for their owners. People loved them, and they seemed to be a part of the society that would last forever.

Then came television! As this new medium's popularity grew, the large-circulation general magazine found its subscriber pool shrinking and its advertising revenues dwindling. Television was its own kind of "magazine," and it was much easier to use. Furthermore, after the initial investment in a set, it was free to the user. Those who were marketing products nationally began turning in droves to the networks and TV commercials. Within a few years, the magazine industry had to make major adjustments. As it turned out, most of the big general magazines with the "something for everybody" approach died. For example, *Collier's* and *American* were early casualties, succumbing to economic pressures in the 1950s. In the 1960s, many others failed, including the large picture magazines *Life* and *Look*. Some, such as *Life*, returned in the 1970s and 1980s, but in a new form with smaller, more carefully targeted circulations.

There are still a few immensely popular magazines appealing to the general population, including *Reader's Digest* (circulation over 15 million), *TV Guide* (over 14 million), and *National Geographic* (over 9 million). But most magazines today are not directed to a broad heterogeneous audience preferring a "storehouse" of mixed content, but rather aimed at a more defined group with distinct interests. In place of large-circulation general magazines, there are now thousands of more narrowly focused, special-interest magazines. Some enjoy huge circulations, such as *Modern Maturity*, the publication of the American Association of Retired Persons (with a circulation of over 22 million). Others that are also very popular are *Parents*, *Playboy*, *Skiing*, *PC* (for personal computer enthusiasts), and *Gardening*.

Meanwhile, the venerable newsmagazines such as *Time*, *Newsweek*, and *U.S. News and World Report* are experiencing difficulties. Although their circulations have been increasing slightly (18 percent during the past twenty years), the demographic category at which they aim—college-educated readers between twenty-five and forty-four—has nearly trebled during the same period. Thus, they have lost a large share of their target group during a time when their circulations should have boomed. Whether this type of magazine can survive in today's competitive news and advertising environment remains to be seen.[8]

The Growth of Specialty Magazines

In 1993, there were 10,857 periodicals of all kinds in circulation in the United States, and as noted above, most of them focus on special interests. There is a specialty magazine (in fact, there are often several) for every conceivable interest, hobby, and taste—from tennis, fly fishing, and model trains to wine collecting and wooden boats. There is even one called *Prison Life* for convicts.[9]

Advertisers love specialty magazines because they are so effective in reaching precisely the categories of consumers who buy their kind of product. For example, no maker of expensive hand-crafted bamboo fly rods will advertise those wares on national television, in a newspaper, or on local radio, because most people using those media will not be interested. The product should be brought to the attention of relatively affluent potential buyers of such equipment scattered all over the nation, and perhaps even in foreign countries. Such contacts can be reached by placing an ad in one or more of the magazines devoted to fly-fishing enthusiasts. Not only will subscribers see the ad, but the magazine will likely be passed on to other fly-fishing enthusiasts. Thus, a single advertisement can reach precisely the targeted potential customers for the product. Furthermore, such advertising is

Regularly published in the United States are thousands of individual magazines that appeal to various categories of readers with specialized interests and tastes. However, as is the case with other media, ownership is becoming increasingly concentrated. Large corporations, such as Times Mirror Magazines, regularly acquire successful magazines started up by others and thus publish a great variety of periodicals. In this way, a single corporation can potentially connect with a huge audience. Many critics fear that this phenomenon may place too much media power in the hands of too few. (The Terry Wild Studio)

cheap by comparison with other media. It is because of these factors that so many narrowly focused magazines can make a profit today; by following this pattern, the magazine industry has adapted to and survived the challenge posed by television.

The Magazine as a Contemporary Medium

After reviewing the history of magazines over more than two centuries, it may seem an idle question to ask just what a magazine is and how it differs from a newspaper. Actually, this is a necessary question, because in contemporary publishing it is sometimes difficult to distinguish between the two. Generally, a magazine is published less frequently than a newspaper. It is also manufactured in a different format—usually on better-quality paper, bound rather than merely folded, and with some kind of cover. There are exceptions to all these characteristics, but for the most part they satisfactorily distinguish the form of magazines from that of newspapers. To these differences in form, we can add differences in the audiences, content, functions, and influences of contemporary magazines.

We have already seen how magazines usually probe issues and situations more carefully than newspapers; however, with an increasing interest in investigative reporting on the part of today's larger newspapers, that is not always the case. What we do find in magazine content is less concern for the details of daily events and more for interpreting topics in a broad context. Historically, magazines have appealed to a regional or national audience and have been free of the fierce localism of newspapers. Theodore Peterson offered this thoughtful description of the modern magazine:

Although the magazine lacked the immediacy of the broadcast media and the newspaper, it nevertheless was timely enough to deal with the flow of events. Its timeliness and continuity set it apart from the book. As a continuing publication, it could provide a form of discussion by carrying responses from its audience, could sustain campaigns for indefinite periods, and could work for cumulative rather than single impact. Yet its available space and the reading habits of its audience enabled it to give fairly lengthy treatment to the subjects it covered. Like the other print media it appealed more to the intellect than to the senses and emotions of its audience. It was not as transient as the broadcast media, nor did it require attention at a given time; it was not as soon discarded as the newspaper; its issues remained in readers' homes for weeks, for months, sometimes even for years. In short, the magazine by its nature met well the requirements for a medium of instruction and interpretation for the leisurely, critical reader.[10]

Magazines today, then, retain their traditional functions. They are a major medium of *surveillance*—keeping track of events in the society—often delivering information ahead of the rest of the media. Some magazines, such as *Time*, are intended mainly to inform; others, such as *Spy*, to entertain. But among the various functions served by magazines in contemporary society, the most notable is still *correlation*—interpreting society and its parts, projecting trends, and explaining the meaning of the news by bringing together fragmented facts. Other print media also inform and entertain, but it is in performance of the correlation function that magazines stand out. Magazines, in other words, are the great *interpreters*.

The long-held distinction among newspapers, published magazines, and electronic magazines is becoming increasingly blurred. Indeed, when newspapers have made major changes in packaging and presentation, it is often said that they are adopting a "magazine format." Thus, newspapers have become more like magazines, both in marketing methods and in writing style. Even television has been influenced: CBS's *60 Minutes* and its current imitators call themselves "television newsmagazines"; and various TV stations produce local "evening magazine" shows.

The distinction in format between printed magazines and other media may become even less clear in the future. With the spreading use of online information services such as Lexis/Nexis and CompuServe, people may eventually be able to create their own specialized magazines without benefit of paper or magazine editors. However, for the foreseeable future, most analysts think, the magazine will continue to exist in its present printed form, because of its portability and its permanence.

The Magazine Industry

To reach specialized audiences, magazine publishers sort potential readers into neat demographic categories with the help of computers; then they refine their products to match those readers' interests. In other words, they target their content and tone to attract specific audiences, thereby appealing, as we have noted, to many advertisers, who like to direct their advertising to likely consumers.

For magazines, as for other media, audience ratings and audience surveys are important in determining advertising rates. But as Philip Dougherty has pointed out, there is an interesting twist for magazines:

> If an editor creates a magazine that is so on target that subscribers refuse to part with it, that's bad. If, however, the editor puts out a magazine that means so little to each individual that it gets passed from hand to hand to hand, that's good. Reason: the more the magazine is passed along, the higher the total audience figure will be. In that way, the ad agency rates will look more efficient to agency people, who would be more likely to put the magazine on their . . . schedule [for advertising].[11]

Thus, like all other media that are supported by advertising, a magazine must pay keen attention to its audience in order to survive. In fact, American magazines seem to be in a continual process of birth, adaptation, and death. Because magazine publishers rarely own their own printing presses, the initial investment needed to found a magazine is rather modest, and so starting a magazine is comparatively easy. Maintaining it is much more difficult. Most leading observers agree that many magazines die because the publisher failed to strike a balance between revenue from circulation and revenue from advertising. Some magazines die because the publisher failed to fine-tune the product to meet changing fashions and interest. The most successful magazine publishers produce more than one magazine. If one magazine fails, they still have others to keep their company alive.

Types of magazines   As noted, the American magazine industry today provides a periodical for just about every interest. Magazines also target categories defined by income, age, education, and occupation. There are various ways to categorize magazines, but the industry typically speaks of two broad categories: consumer magazines and business magazines. *Consumer magazines* are those readily available to the public by subscription—to be received through the mail—or by direct purchase at newsstands. *Business magazines*, on the other hand, cover particular industries, trades, and professions and go mainly to persons in those fields. Table 4.2 describes the main types of consumer magazines and the leading business magazines.

Writer's Digest, a publication with a considerable focus on magazines, classifies them into four major types: trade journal (such as *Billboard* and *Modern Machine Shop*), sponsored publications (such as *American Legion*), farm publications (such as *Southern Hog Farmer*), and consumer magazines (such as *Consumer Reports* and *Food & Wine*).

Many consumer magazines are mass-circulation magazines, but a subcategory, the secondary consumer magazine, includes broadly circulated magazines that concentrate on a specialized topic or a specific interest; examples are *Private Pilot*, *Yachting*, and *Gourmet*.

During the 1980s, about seven hundred new consumer magazines were established; reportedly, the number of titles grew by 68 percent. Typically,

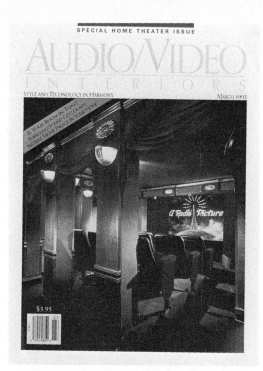

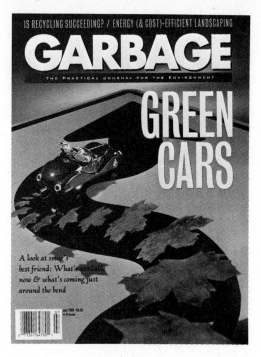

entrepreneurs who want to start a new magazine develop a business plan charting a course for the magazine and "proving" with statistics (on potential readership and related market research) that there is a niche (market) for the new publication. Then a staff is hired and offices established. Typically, printing is contracted out, as are arrangements for distribution and circulation. Advertising space can be sold either by the magazine staff or by national advertising media representatives. Many new magazines start with high hopes, only to find that no significant niche exists to make the new publication profitable. Often, new magazines that do succeed are quickly sold to large magazine or media companies, whose economies of scale make it profitable to publish many different magazines under the same corporate roof.

The number of new magazines that appear each year has grown sharply in recent times and is now nothing short of phenomenal. However, the failure rate is equally phenomenal. Industry sources indicate that 789 new consumer magazines were introduced in 1993 alone. Of that number, only two in ten were expected to survive for more than ten years. The 1994 edition of *Consumer's Guide to New Magazines* reported the numbers of start-ups in the following nine categories:

Sex, 95 (the largest category); sports, 84; lifestyle and service, 34; media personalities, 22; crafts, games and hobbies, 33; metropolitan, regional, and state, 18; gay and lesbian, 16; fishing and hunting, 13; home service, 45.[12]

TABLE 4.2 Types of Magazines

Consumer magazines: Periodicals purchased on newsstands or subscribed to by the general public for home delivery. Examples are *Reader's Digest, Life, Ebony, TV Guide,* and *Sports Illustrated.*

Trade journals: Magazines aimed at a particular trade or industry (also called the businesspaper press). Examples are *Electronic Business, Modern Machine Shop,* and *Publishers Weekly.*

Sponsored publications: Internal publications of particular organizations, unions, and other groups, including college and university magazines, customers' publications, and employee magazines. Examples are *Elks, American Legion,* and *Ambassador.*

Farm publications: These magazines are given a category of their own because of their large number and the degree of specialization within the farm press. Examples are *Farm Journal* and *Agribusiness.*

Newsmagazines: Serving as national newspapers in America, newsmagazines include *Time,* which was once known for its strong Republican bias but is now more moderate politically; *Newsweek,* a less doctrinaire publication, with a generally liberal bias; and *U.S. News & World Report,* with a strong business orientation.

City magazines: Publications such as *New York, Philadelphia Magazine, The Washingtonian,* and *Boston* exemplify city magazines, which tend to concentrate on the activities of a particular city or region. Most major cities (such as Columbus) and many smaller ones (for example, Albuquerque) now have city magazines that investigate public affairs and try to critique the local scene (especially entertainment and restaurants).

Sex magazines: These publications have substantial circulations and generate considerable revenues. They take pride in their fiction and nonfiction articles and interviews as well as their suggestive photographs. This group includes such general-interest sex magazines as *Playboy, Playgirl,* and *Penthouse.* Publications such as *Hustler* and *Screw* cater to people with unusual sexual appetites, There are also sex magazines for homosexuals and bisexuals as well as heterosexuals.

Sports magazines: Americans are preoccupied with sports of all kinds, and there are scores of magazines to satisfy their interests, ranging from *Sports Illustrated* and *Sport,* which cover a variety of sports, to specialized magazines covering just one sport, such as *Runner's World, Racquetball,* and *Skiing.* A new sports fashion will quickly generate magazines. When racquetball gained enthusiasts in the 1980s. several racquetball magazines appeared. Sports magazines, like sex magazines, once seemed to be intended for men only; but women now make up more and more of the audience for general sports magazines, and some sports magazines are designed especially for women.

Opinion magazines: These include some of the oldest and most respected journals in the United States. They range from the venerable *Nation,* which has been publishing since the Civil War, to the *National Review,* a conservative magazine founded in the 1950s by columnist William F. Buckley. Some others are the liberal *New Leader, New Republic,* and *The Progressive,*

Intellectual magazines: These small-circulation publications are very similar to opinion magazines, but they usually have denser copy and are aimed at a more intellectual audience. Examples include *Commentary, American Scholar,* and

TABLE 4.2   Types of Magazines (continued)

The New Leader. Both opinion magazines and intellectual magazines pride themselves on "influencing the influential."

Quality magazines: Although these magazines are similar to opinion and intellectual magazines, they usually have slightly larger circulations (perhaps as much as 500,000) and reach a more general audience. Some examples are *Atlantic Monthly, Harper's, Esquire, The Smithsonian,* and *National Geographic.*

Men's interest magazines: These publications, such as *True: The Man's Magazine* and *Argosy,* sometimes overlap with sex magazines and sports magazines. *Gentleman's Quarterly* and other similar magazines represent men's new preoccupation with fashion.

Women's interest magazines: Some of the most successful magazines in the country, with the highest circulations, are aimed at women. The first American magazine in the nineteenth century to have a circulation of more than 1 million was *Ladies' Home Journal,* which continues today. Other magazines in this class are *Savvy, Better Homes and Gardens, Good Housekeeping,* and *McCall's.* A women's interest magazine that departs from the traditional mold of women's periodicals is *Ms.,* which reflects a moderate feminist viewpoint (*Ms.* led the way for feminist magazines, and today there are several available with varying editorial formulas and viewpoints).

Humor magazines: Taking hold in the 1870s with *Puck, The Comic Weekly,* humor magazines have been with us ever since and include *National Lampoon, Mad,* and *Harpoon.* A highly successful humor magazine of the 1980s and 1990s is *Spy.* Related to humor magazines are comic magazines and comic books, forming an industry in themselves. Many of these publications are not humorous at all, but use cartoon-style artwork to present complex plots and characters and diverse views and social commentary.

Business magazines: Few subjects are more compelling to the American audience than business. Among leading business magazines are *Business Week,* published by McGraw-Hill; *Fortune,* a Time-Warner publication; and *Forbes,* which uses the whimsical slogan "A Capitalist Tool." *Barron's* is published by Dow-Jones, which also produces the *Wall Street Journal.* Some business magazines offer broad-based news coverage; others are designed to advise their readers on the machinations of the stock market. There are also many specialized business magazines, especially those covering high technology and electronics, such as *Byte* and *Computer World* (in fact, the publishing industry has benefited a great deal from changes in technology; there are many new publications just on computers).

The greatest increase was in the categories of sex, home service, and sports. Some of the newcomers on the list were established by large publishing companies; others were low-budget projects begun by private individuals.

Making a profit   Consumer magazines are the industry's major money makers. According to Veronis, Suhler and Associates (a firm monitoring the industry), revenues from magazine advertising and circulation totaled $20.8

billion in 1994, and of that amount consumer magazines generated $14.1 billion, or 68 percent.

The vast majority of magazine sales occur through mailed subscriptions. In fact, this number dropped slightly from 66 percent in 1977 to 65 percent in 1992. This is important, because about half of the total earnings of consumer magazines comes from subscriptions (and newsstand sales); the other half comes from advertising. For business magazines, the revenue picture is radically different. In 1991, business magazine revenues were $5.5 billion, of which approximately 90 percent came from advertising. Thus, subscriptions are not a significant part of the profit picture in the business magazine. In fact, many business magazines are actually given away free! That is, they have controlled, nonpaying distributions. Those magazines using this pattern of distribution can afford to do so because they blanket the relevant field or industry, making them especially attractive to advertisers. Magazines aimed directly at a given industry tend to be read by a large percentage of people in that field—exactly the people that the advertisers want to reach.

In recent years, magazine starts and failures have paralleled changes in the general economy. As the United States has moved from an economy based on heavy manufacturing and extractive industries (such as coal, iron, and oil) to one based on information, communication, and services, a corresponding decline has occurred in business publications serving the older industries, along with an increase in magazines aimed at covering computer, electronic, and financial services.

Like other media, magazines are creatures of the marketplace. They can be a powerful medium for precise, demographically defined advertising, but they are also susceptible to fickle consumer demands. As Chapter 10 explains, media advertising is a complex and dynamic process that links together specific forms of advertising content, specific media, and consumer demands for particular products. Thus, when consumer demands change, advertising content in magazines moves up and down in volume, causing the magazine industry to prosper or decline accordingly.

For example, although both the numbers and readership of magazines rose sharply during the 1980s, the profitability of magazines in the United States grew only slowly from about 1985 until 1990. In fact, in this sense, the industry lagged behind the nation's general economic growth. The question is, Why? One answer is that in 1984 several major industries (computers, cigarette/tobacco, gasoline/fuel, and liquor) reduced their expenditures for advertising. Before the cutback, these industries accounted for 20 percent of total consumer magazine advertising.

Why did those industries reduce their expenditures for advertising? Analysts believe that several factors converged at the same time. One was the decline of the home video game fad. The corresponding decline of public interest in home entertainment computers in effect killed some new computer magazines. A second factor was what happened in the tobacco industry. When the ban against cigarette advertising on television went into effect, the magazine industry hoped to gain advertising revenues displaced from television. However, public consumption of tobacco products declined—and so did the industry's overall advertising expenditures. A third factor was an increase in gasoline prices and a reduction in miles driven by Americans. With respect to the liquor industry, increasingly health-conscious Americans reduced their consumption of alcohol—and down went magazine advertising revenues from that source (hard spirits cannot be advertised on television). Even though there were some countertrends in such products as soaps, cleansers, and pet foods, as well as real estate and entertainment, these did not balance out the income losses in the other areas.

Ownership trends Much of what was said in Chapters 2 and 3 about trends in media ownership also applies to magazines. Today, many are owned by chains. Large corporations and conglomerates, whether multinational firms from abroad or large media corporations in the United States, regularly buy them up and incorporate them into their financial empires. The resulting concentration of magazine ownership appears to be unabated. Especially noteworthy was the 1989 merger of Time, Inc. with Warner Communications, which overnight created the world's largest media company. Although Henry Luce originally established Time, Inc. in the 1920s exclusively as a magazine publishing company, by the end of the 1980s it was far more. In fact, one high-level Time-Warner executive recently remarked, "If you thought that Time-Warner was mainly about magazines, you were wrong—I'd say it is more accurately called a cable company with some publishing interests."[13] That may be a slight exaggeration, but certainly the combination of Time and Warner interests means that magazines have become only a part of a far-flung empire of movie studios, cable companies, programming services, business information, book publishing, broadcasting, and other interests. Writing in the magazine *Manhattan, Inc.*, in a tongue-in-cheek piece mocking *Time* magazine's style, Robert Sam Anson offered this obituary:

> Died. In the eighty-ninth year of the American Century, after a long muddled management illness of chronic miscalculation complicated by acute greed, outsize ego, and corporate hubris; proprietor of the nation's leading newsmagazine and assorted lesser publishing and electronic properties; in a Wall Street boardroom, by its own hand, with Wall Street sharks attending. *Time*, Inc.[14]

Ironically, *Manhattan, Inc.* itself died in 1990 as a result of lack of advertising.

The Influence and Importance of Magazines

As we have shown, magazines differ greatly in their circulations. However, size and importance are not the same; nor can total revenues be equated with power and influence. Under such an evaluation, *TV Guide*, perhaps the

Opinion magazines have limited circulation compared to more popular periodicals, but their influence often goes far beyond mere numbers. Such magazines are often read by people who fill important decision-making roles in society and who seek a more in-depth understanding of important issues, events, and trends. *The New Yorker* is one such magazine. (Cover drawing by de Michiell; © 1993 The New Yorker Magazine, Inc.)

nation's most financially successful publication, boasting the largest circulation, would seem more important than a magazine such as *Foreign Affairs*, a quarterly with a very modest circulation. But although millions read the former and only a few thousand the latter, the smaller magazine may influence a much more powerful audience.

Editor Hendrik Hertzberg addresses the issue of the relative importance and impact of magazines in this earthy comment:

> Browse through any newsstand and you will be obliged to conclude that journals of opinion occupy a laughingly piddling place even in that relative backwater of "the media" known as magazine publishing. General magazines of any kind—that is magazines read for their own sake rather than as adjuncts to cooking, masturbating, riding dirt bikes, wearing clothes, or collecting guns—take up less and less shelf space; and journals of opinion (never big sellers at the drug store to begin with) are a next-to-invisible subset. Yet, no student of American society and its power relationships would dispute that *The Nation* (circ. 80,000) is somehow more important than *Self* (circ. 1.2 million), *National Review* (circ. 120,000) and *The New Republic* (circ. 96,000) more important than *Weight Watchers* (circ. 950,000). [15]

Hertzberg's analysis may seem elitist, but he does have a point. The journals of opinion exert influence far beyond their numbers. They are read by government officials, business leaders, educators, intellectuals, and others who affect public affairs much more than does the average person. The opinion magazines set agendas, shape ideas, start trends, and offer labels for everything from types of people (for example, "yuppies") to time spans (such as "the Me decade" for the 1970s). Perhaps more important, they speak to what it is that magazines do better than almost any other medium. Clearly, magazines inform, but compared with the reach of television news or the immediacy and impact of daily newspapers, this function is of modest importance in any overall assessment. The same is true for entertainment, where television and the movies are the champions. Even fiction, a genre in which magazines were once very important, accounts for little of their content today. In none of these is the magazine a strong contender.

It is in the realm of *opinion* that magazines triumph. They have the luxury of expressing their biases, being openly liberal or conservative, as grumpy or savage as they choose. Other media, trying to court larger audiences, could never accomplish this. Magazines also can make long investigations and present their findings in equally lengthy form. For example, *The New Yorker*, a widely respected analytical magazine, can present lengthy articles that take up such topics as law and justice in a cerebral and philosophical sense and articles about the United Nations that severely challenge the moral authority of that institution. *The New Yorker* does this kind of thing in the context of an eighty-year history during which it has earned a high reputation for such analyses. As with other respected opinion magazines, when *The New Yorker* speaks on an issue, people listen. And the ideas it presents are picked up and diffused by more popular magazines, newspapers, and even television to audiences far beyond its readership. Thus, a respected opinion magazine can have an influence far beyond what the number of its subscribers suggests.

Generally, then, the magazine is not only likely to survive as a medium, but may thrive in the decades ahead. It has faced many challenges over its long history and has survived by adapting to an ever-changing system of mass communication. The great diversity to be found in the industry provides something for everyone, and in a form that is current, portable, permanent, and presented at a level within the readers' capability. That is a formidable formula. So even though the medium may have to meet new challenges over time, it seems at this point that Americans will continue to support these voices for many interests.

Chapter Review

■ Magazines as we know them today started in London, where there was a concentration of urbane, affluent, and literate people. The earliest magazines were mainly instruments of politics, both in England and in the United States.

■ It was difficult to establish magazines in the American colonies because people were spread out, literacy was not widespread, and the population was not affluent. In addition,

such factors as transportation and mail service were uncertain at best.

■ During the 1800s, societal changes encouraged the growth of magazines in the United States. The population grew; cities became larger; more citizens were educated; the mails became more reliable and less costly; and all forms of transportation improved. In addition, it was a century of great issues.

- The magazine flourished early in the twentieth century during the era of the muckrakers. Prestigious magazines took the lead in exposing corruption in business and government as well as unacceptable social conditions.

- New kinds of magazines appeared in the 1920s. One category was the newsmagazine. Another was the large-circulation general magazine containing something for everyone. Such magazines had huge circulations, making them important vehicles for national advertising. They were very successful, and it seemed that they would be a permanent feature of society.

- When television arrived, it absorbed much of the advertising revenue that had previously gone to the large general magazines, many of which failed in consequence. However, the industry adapted remarkably well by developing a host of specialty magazines aimed at markets with well-defined interests and characteristics.

- The magazine as a contemporary medium continues to serve the surveillance, information, and entertainment functions. Its most notable function, however, is correlation—that is, interpreting the society by bringing together diverse facts, trends, and sequences of events.

- The magazine business today is fiercely competitive and very dynamic. An impressive variety of magazines are published. Every year, many are started; however, the majority fail. The two basic types are consumer and business magazines; of the two, the consumer magazine predominates.

- Trends in magazine ownership parallel those for other media; that is, most are owned by chains. Large conglomerates, with many kinds of businesses, buy magazines and add them to their diverse holdings. The consequence of such consolidation of ownership is difficult to predict.

- The sheer number of people who subscribe to or even read a magazine is no indicator of either its ability to make a profit or its influence. The most influential periodicals are the opinion magazines. Their circulations are small compared with more popular magazines, but the people who read opinion magazines tend more than others to occupy positions of power and leadership, where their decisions can markedly influence public affairs.

- Generally, the magazine is likely to survive in its present form. It is a medium that presents material tailored to the interests of specific kinds of people in a manner that they prefer. It is likely that Americans will be reading magazines for a long time to come.

Notes and References

1. Many of the details in this section concerning the first magazines were drawn from James P. Wood, *Magazines in the United States* (New York: Ronald, 1949), pp. 3–9.
2. Ibid., p. 10.
3. The details about early American attempts to produce magazines are drawn from Frank Luther Mott, *A History of American Magazines, 1741–1850*, vol. 1 (Cambridge, Mass.: Harvard University Press, 1930), pp. 13–72.
4. Melvin L. DeFleur, William V. D'Antonio, and Lois DeFleur, *Sociology* (Glenview, Ill.: Scott, Foresman, 1972), p. 279.
5. The various figures in this section were painstakingly assembled from historical accounts and various early government documents by Mott in his five-volume *A History of American Magazines*. As he notes, many are approximations.
6. Ibid., vol. 4, p. 10.
7. Wood, op. cit., p. 131.
8. Fleming Meeks, "God Is Not Providing," *Forbes*, October 30, 1989, pp. 151–158.
9. *Prison Life* is aimed at the million people in the United States who call state and federal prisons home. Regular columns include "In-

Cell Cooking," and "Ask the Law Professor." Advertising focuses on such products as body-building supplements. Jolie Solomon, "Putting the 'Con' in Consumer," *Newsweek*, October 26, 1992, p. 49.

10. Theodore Peterson, *Magazines in the Twentieth Century*, 2nd ed. (Urbana, Ill.: University of Illinois Press, 1964), p. 442.

11. Philip Dougherty, "Saturday Review's New Drive," *New York Times*, April 2, 1979.

12. Samir Husni, *Consumer's Guide to New Magazines 1994* (published by *Folio* magazine, Hanson Publishing Group).

13. Personal communication.

14. Robert Sam Anson, "Greed and Ego in Gotham City," *Manhattan, Inc.*, August 1989, p. 45.

15. Hendrik Hertzberg, "Journals of Opinion, An Historical Sketch," *Gannett Center Journal*, Spring 1989, p. 61.

PART TWO

THE DEVELOPMENT OF FILM AND BROADCASTING

The Movies: Popular Culture for Mass Consumption

In superficial ways, movies and television are alike. They both have moving images in color and sound. But the similarities end there. We have long had—and still have—a dynamic, separate industry that makes films. It existed before television was even a dream in the heads of electronic engineers. By the time of World War I, the motion picture was a fully developed form of popular entertainment. Although the movie industry has had to change in many ways to adjust to the impact of television, it remains thriving and vital today. Above all, the movies have left an indelible stamp on this nation and its culture.

The history of the motion picture as a mass medium is short, spanning less than a century. But the events that led to motion pictures go back many centuries. The first steps in this story involved solving a series of complex technical problems. A motion picture, after all, is a series of still pictures rapidly projected on a screen in such a way that the viewer perceives smooth motion. To achieve this illusion of motion, problems in optics, chemistry, and even human physiology had to be overcome. Lenses, projectors, cameras, and roll film had to be invented. Only then were "the movies" born.

Magic Shadows on the Wall

The first problem to be solved was how to focus and project an image. Convex quartz lenses for magnifying and concentrating the sun's rays were used as early as 600 B.C. Centuries later, Archimedes earned fame by frightening the Romans with a lens during the defense of Syracuse. He is said to have mounted on the wall of the city a large "burning glass" that could set fire to the Roman ships. The story may or may not be true, but it indicates that the ancients had begun to grapple with one of the main problems that would later be associated with cameras and projectors—how to use lenses to focus light.

The idea that light rays could be focused with lenses and mirrors has ancient roots. This fifteenth-century drawing explains how Archimedes could have focused the rays of the sun on Roman ships off Syracuse so as to set them on fire. Whether or not the story is true, this principle played an important part in the eventual development of photography. (The Granger Collection, New York)

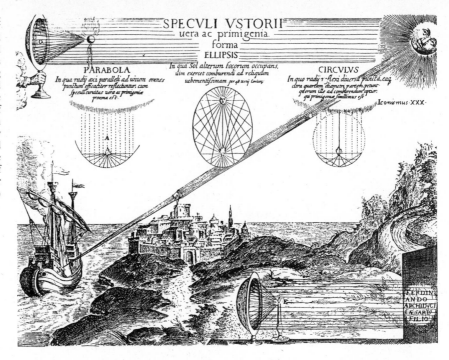

A major advance came in the mid–seventeenth century. A German priest, Athanasius Kirscher, conducted experiments in projecting a visual image by passing light through a transparency. In 1645, he put on a "magic lantern" show for his fellow scholars at the Collegio Romano, using slides he had painted himself. His projected images of religious figures could barely be seen, but his show was a sensation. No one had ever seen anything like it. In fact, there were dark rumors that he was in league with the devil and was conjuring up spirits through the practice of "black arts."[1]

In the eighteenth century, the public became increasingly aware of the idea of the projected image. Showmen entertained audiences with shadow plays and projected images of ghostlike figures. By the mid-1800s, improved lanterns with reflecting mirrors and condensing lenses were fairly reliable sources of light. The simple oil-burning lantern was eventually replaced by a powerful light produced by burning hydrogen gas and oxygen through a cylinder of hard lime (hence the word "limelight"). Ultimately, of course, electric lights provided the necessary illumination.

Developing the Technology

Because movies are associated so strongly with popular entertainment, it is easy to think of them in less than serious terms and to overlook the fact that they depend on a highly sophisticated base of scientific knowledge. The technological components of the motion picture are far more complex than those of print, and they were a very long time in coming.

Photography   The science of lenses and projection advanced more rapidly than that of photography. Until the nineteenth century, people could project images, but no one had been able to capture images to form a still picture. However, advances in chemistry in the late 1700s and early 1800s set the stage for the development of photography. Several experimenters worked to perfect a photographic process, but a French artist and inventor, Louis Daguerre, and a chemist, Joseph Niepce, arrived at the best method after years of work. Niepce died shortly before success was achieved, but his partner, Daguerre, carried on.

In 1839, Daguerre announced the success of his work and showed examples of his sharp, clear photographs to the public. He called his process the *daguerreotype.* Each picture was made on a polished copper plate coated with gleaming silver. In total darkness, the plate was exposed to iodine fumes to form a thin coating of light-sensitive silver iodide. When the plate was then exposed briefly to a scene, the image registered in the silver iodide. Chemical baths then "fixed" the image on the plate. Because Daguerre's pictures were much clearer and sharper than those of others (who tried to use paper), his process was adopted all over the world.[2]

Photography was received enthusiastically in the United States. Soon there were daguerreotype studios in every city, and itinerant photographers traveled the back country in wagons making portraits. By the 1880s, as chemistry and technology improved, such pioneers as George Eastman transformed photography from an art practiced by trained technicians to a popular hobby. More than anything else, it was Eastman's development and marketing of flexible celluloid roll film that made photography a popular success.[3] The availability of flexible film also made motion pictures technically feasible. But before they could become a reality, the development of photography had to be matched by progress in understanding visual processes and the perception of motion.

The illusion of motion   Motion pictures, of course, do not "move." They consist of a series of still pictures that capture the moving object in progressively different positions. When the stills are run through a projector at the correct speed, the viewer perceives an illusion of smooth motion. At the heart of this illusion is a process called visual lag, or *visual persistence*: "The brain will persist in seeing an object when it is no longer before the eye itself."[4] We "see" an image for a fraction of a second after the thing itself has changed or disappeared. If we are presented with one image after the other, the visual persistence of the first image fills in the time lag between the two images, so they seem to be continuous.

After the discovery of visual persistence by Dr. Peter Mark Roget in 1824, its study by eminent scientists of the time led to widespread interest in the phenomenon. Toys and gadgets were produced that were based on visual lag. For example, a simple card with a string attached to each end can be twirled with the fingers. If, for example, a bird is drawn on one side of the card and a cage on the other, the bird will seem to be inside the cage when

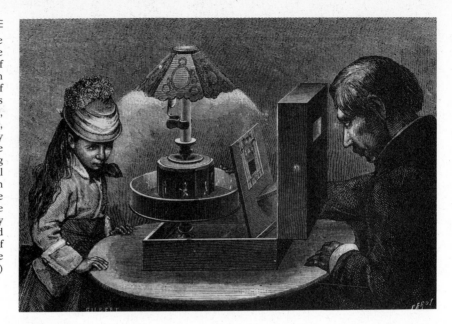

During the latter half of the 1800s, a variety of devices were developed to take advantage of the principle of visual lag in order to create the illusion of motion. Each inventor gave his apparatus a complex name, such as phenakistascope, mutoscope, or zoetrope. They all worked on the same principle, however—showing the viewer a succession of still drawings that when seen in rapid sequence produced the illusion of motion. Shown is the praxinoscope developed by Émile Reynaud, who astonished Paris with his displays of moving images. (The Bettmann Archive)

the device is spun. The reason for this is that both the bird and the cage are retained by the human retina for a brief period during the rotation.

The illusion of motion came under intense study by such scientists as Joseph Plateau, who studied timing, color intensity, and other matters related to the perception of movement. By the middle of the century, the wheel of life (or *phenakistoscope*, as it came to be called) was highly developed. It consisted of a large disk, about three feet in diameter. A series of still pictures showing an object in different positions as it moved were mounted around the rim. The individual viewed these through an aperture as the wheel turned and perceived smooth motion. When the principles of this device were elaborated and combined with the photography of things in motion, they provided the basis for movies.

Capturing and projecting motion with film   During the closing decades of the nineteenth century, a number of people tried to photograph motion. One major advance was the result of a bet. Governor Leland Stanford of California and some of his friends made a large wager over whether a running horse ever had all its feet off the ground at once. To settle the bet, they hired an obscure photographer named Eadweard Muybridge. Muybridge photographed moving horses by setting up a bank of twenty-four still cameras, each of which was tripped by a thread as the horse galloped by. His photographs showed that a horse did indeed have all four feet off the ground at once.

The photographs created such interest that Muybridge took many more, refining his techniques for photographing moving things. He eventually traveled to Europe to display his work and found that others had been making similar studies. Interest in the photography of motion became intense, but in 1890 no one had yet created actual motion pictures. Further advances in both cameras and projectors were needed.

During the late 1880s and early 1890s, various crude motion picture cameras were under development, and a number of showmen were entertaining people with moving pictures based on serially projected drawings. Then, during the 1890s, advances in filming and viewing procedures virtually exploded. By 1895, greatly impressed French audiences were seeing brief motion pictures projected on a screen by August and Luis Lumière. Other applications of the new technology soon followed, and several individuals claimed the title of inventor of the motion picture. But it was William Dickson, assistant to Thomas Alva Edison, who perfected the motion picture camera.

Meanwhile, Edison and Thomas Armat developed a practical and reliable projection system. Edison and his partner obtained U.S. patents and began to manufacture their projector, which they called the *Vitascope*. Edison also set up a studio to produce short films—mostly of vaudeville acts. Although it had many shortcomings, the *Vitascope* worked reliably. Its major flaw was that it projected at a wasteful forty-eight frames per second, whereas sixteen frames are sufficient to provide the illusion of smooth motion.

Because Edison, ever the penny-pincher, declined to spend $150 to obtain foreign patents, his machines were quickly duplicated and patented in Europe. In fact, numerous improvements soon made Edison's original machines obsolete. Furious fights in the patent courts later threatened to kill the new medium.

Edison decided to exhibit his moving pictures in a peep-show device that he called the *Kinetoscope*. For a nickel, a single viewer could turn a crank, look inside the machine, and see a brief film on a small screen. This one-viewer-at-a-time approach, Edison thought, would bring a larger return on investment than projecting to many people at once. Edison's approach did not catch on; in the end, instead, the industry developed along the lines of the theater model. Such pioneers as the Lumière brothers and others in Europe had seen this clearly. By 1896, however, Edison was projecting motion pictures to the public in New York City for the first time in the United States.

In general, by 1900, all the scientific and technological underpinnings of the motion picture were in place, and the new medium was ready for mass use. Millions of people were eager to pay to be entertained.

The Movies Become a Mass Medium

The first few years of the fledgling medium in the new century were marked by experimentation. Many of the early films ran for only a minute or two. Yet just the sight of something moving on the screen could thrill an audience. Then the motion picture makers began to try longer films offering more interesting content.

By 1903, both American and European producers were making *one-reelers* that lasted ten to twelve minutes and told a story. One-reel films were produced on every conceivable topic—from prize fights to religious plays—for exhibition at vaudeville halls, saloons, amusement parks, and even opera houses. Some have become classics, such as *Life of an American Fireman* (1903), *The Great Train Robbery* (1903), and *A Trip to the Moon* (1902). Many others have been lost or simply were not worth preserving. Several years later, two-reelers became increasingly common, lasting up to twenty-five minutes. These were even more interesting for audiences, and as the popularity of the new films increased, their production and distribution expanded at an extraordinary pace.

The nickelodeons   The idea of renting films may seem to be of little significance, but it made the local motion picture theater possible as a small business venture. The required investment was modest, and the profits could be high. One could rent a film and a vacant store, add some cheap decorations, install folding chairs, buy a projector, piano, and screen, and open the doors for business. In 1905, two entrepreneurs from Pittsburgh, Harry P. Davis and John P. Harris, did just that. They charged five cents for admission and called their theater "The Nickelodeon." In a week they made $1,000, playing to near-capacity houses. At the time, this was the next best thing to owning an Alaska gold mine.

The success of the first nickelodeon greatly impressed the entertainment world, and there was a stampede to set up others in cities across the nation. Within a year, a thousand were in operation, and by 1910, ten thousand were showing films. National gross receipts for 1910 have been estimated at $91 million.[5]

By 1910, there were some ten thousand motion picture houses exhibiting silent films in the United States. Most were modest establishments whose audiences were poor people in urban centers. The operators of these *nickelodeons* rented the hall, the film, and even the chairs and the piano. These establishments were generally very profitable. The motion picture was developing rapidly as mass entertainment. (Brown Brothers)

Most of the early theaters were located in the industrial cities of the Northeast. Movies were made to order for that time and place. The United States was a nation of immigrants, most of whom were newly arrived and many of whom lived in the Northeastern cities. A large proportion spoke either no English or very little. Since the early movies were silent, language posed no barrier for an immigrant audience. Going to the movies was cheap, so they provided entertainment for people in the bottom strata of society. Even the illiterate could understand their stereotyped plots, overdramatized acting, and slapstick humor. Because of their near-universal appeal and modest price, the nickelodeons have been called "democracy's theaters."

The early movies proved to be popular beyond the wildest dreams of their pioneers. In New York City alone, more than a million patrons attended the nickelodeons each week in the early part of this century. Although the nickelodeons were associated with slums and ghettos, movies had become big business, and corporations were quickly formed to produce, distribute, and exhibit films.

Movies for the middle class The nickelodeons brought the motion picture to the urban poor, but the industry was anxious to lure other kinds of customers into the theaters—especially the huge mass of middle-class families. But at first such people viewed movies as vulgar and trivial. The young medium not only bore the stigma of low taste but was associated with the least prestigious elements of society. Efforts to shake this image and bring middle-class patrons to the box office included building attractive theaters in better neighborhoods and opening movie "palaces" in the business districts. Movie makers produced longer, more sophisticated films to exhibit in such improved surroundings. While striving for a better product, producers discovered that they could increase attendance by creating *stars*. They gave prominent roles to particular actors and actresses and publicized them as artists and important personalities. To less sophisticated fans, these movie stars became idols and love goddesses. Thus, the *star system* was born—and it gave a tremendous boost to the popularity of motion pictures.

By 1914, an estimated 40 million patrons attended movies every week, including an increasing number of women and children. The movies had been accepted by the middle class, movie theaters were respectable, and the era of the tacky nickelodeon was over. Meanwhile, as Europe entered World War I, Hollywood had been established as the center of American movie making. The film industries in Europe had to stop production because of the war, leaving the world market to U.S. film makers. They took advantage of the opportunity, and a huge growth in film attendance occurred all over the globe. American films have been popular in the world market ever since.

The talkies Since the 1890s, inventors had tried to combine the phonograph and the motion picture to produce movies with synchronized sound. Few of their contraptions worked well. The sound was either weak and scratchy or poorly coordinated with the action in the film. The public soon tired of experiments, and movie makers thought that talking pictures posed insurmountable technical problems.

But the difficulties were overcome by the mid-1920s. American Telephone & Telegraph (AT&T) used its enormous capital resources to produce a reliable sound system. Recently, controversies have arisen over who really invented the key devices, such as the vacuum light tube and the photoelectric cell, that made it possible to develop practical sound movies.[6] In any case, by 1926, Warner Brothers had signed an agreement with AT&T, and the transition to sound was underway. Warner produced a new feature including sound for the 1927–28 season. Starring Al Jolson, *The Jazz Singer* actually did not have a full sound track. It included only a few songs and a few minutes of dialogue; the rest of the film was silent. But it was an enormous success, and other *talkies* followed quickly.

Almost overnight, the silent movie was obsolete; the motion picture with a full sound track became the norm. As technical quality, theaters, acting, and other aspects of the medium improved, motion pictures entered their maturity.

Portrayals of the fast life   The 1920s were a time of great transition. The old Victorian codes of morality simply crumbled following World War I. As the twenties progressed, there was a great emancipation from—some said deterioration of—the old rules. Women, who had been confined to full-length dresses and prim codes of behavior for generations, could now smoke, wear short dresses and cosmetics, cut their hair short, and even drink alcohol without being branded as harlots for life. It was a time of fast music, fast cars, fast bucks, and, many thought, fast women.

It is hard to say whether the movies of the time contributed to these changes in social norms or merely portrayed them as they developed. In any case, in its struggle for increased profits, the movie industry began to introduce subject matter that was sexually frank and that portrayed modes of behavior unacceptable by the standards of the older generation. Within a short time, major religious groups actively opposed portrayals in the movies of easy money, gangsterism, alcohol use, and sexual themes. These were powerful critics, and the industry was forced to take steps to police itself. As we shall see in more detail later, in 1930, the industry adopted its first voluntary code for censoring films before exhibition.

The golden age   During the 1930s, the movies increasingly tried to appeal to entire families and become their major form of entertainment. In the process, the standards in the motion picture code made movies about as sinful as a Norman Rockwell painting. By the mid-1930s, for example, the code banned words such as "broad" (for woman), "hot," fairy," "pansy," "tart," and "whore." Bedroom scenes always showed twin beds and fully clad actors. The code was rigidly enforced, and by the 1940s the movies had become a wholesome, if bland, form of family entertainment.

It was during this same period—from 1930 to the late 1940s—that American movies in many ways reached their peak. During those two

As the movies matured during the 1920s and after, elaborate and ornate theaters with large seating capacities were built. The era of the nickelodeon and the peep show thus ended abruptly. In the movie palaces, families and dating couples could enjoy an evening in glamourous surroundings viewing a black-and-white film featuring their favorite movie stars. The program usually included a newsreel and a cartoon. The movies had entered their golden age. (Culver Pictures, Inc.)

decades, movies were the most popular form of mass entertainment in the United States. During the Depression decade of the thirties, there was not much else one could do for so little money. The price of admission for adults was usually about 25 cents. Children could get in for half price or less. A whole family could go to the movies together, have a snack afterward, and generally have what was regarded as a "swell time" while barely denting the hard-earned family resources. The golden age of movies had arrived, and people loved them.

Before World War II, a few major studios dominated movie making—the "big five" being MGM, Twentieth Century–Fox, Paramount, RKO, and Warner Brothers. However, several other companies also produced films, including Columbia, Universal, and Republic. Although Universal Studios distributed films made by independent producers, one of the major features of the time was that the studios generally controlled the process from the

TABLE 5.1 Motion Picture Attendance in the United States, 1922-1992

Year	Average Weekly Movie Attendance (thousands)	Weekly Attendance per Household	Year	Average Weekly Movie Attendance (thousands)	Weekly Attendance per Household
1922	40,000	1.56	1948	90,000	2.22
1924	46,000	1.71	1950	60,000	1.38
1926	50,000	1.78	1954	49,000	1.04
1928	65,000	2.23	1958	40,000	0.79
1930	90,000	3.00	1960	28,000	0.53
1932	60,000	1.97	1965	21,000	0.37
1934	70,000	2.24	1974	17,904	0.26
1936	88,000	2.71	1976	19,992	0.27
1938	85,000	2.52	1983	22,558	0.26
1940	80,000	2.29	1985	22,084	0.25
1942	85,000	2.33	1988	20,933	0.23
1944	85,000	2.29	1990	18,883	0.20
1946	90,000	2.37	1992	18,538	0.19

Note: Figures do not include Alaska or Hawaii.

Sources: U.S. Bureau of Census, Historical Statistics of the United States, Colonial Times to 1957 (Washington, D.C., 1960), Series H 522, p. 225; Series A 242–244, p. 15. U.S. Bureau of Census, Historical Statistics of the United States, Continuation to 1962 and Revisions (Washington, D.C., 1965), Series H 522, p. 35. U.S. Bureau of Census, Statistical Abstract of the United States (Washington, D.C., 1968), tables 11, 302, pp. 12, 208 (1973); tables 53, 347, 349, pp. 41, 211, 212. U.S. Bureau of Census, Current Population Reports: Population Characteristics, Series P-20, No. 166 (August 24, 1967), pp. 1, 4. Variety, Jan. 11, 1984, p. 7. Motion Picture Association of America, Jan. 19, 1990. International Motion Picture Almanac (New York, NY: Quigley Publishing, 1994).

**FIGURE 5.1
The Curve of Adoption
of the Motion Picture**

People began to purchase tickets to the early motion picture theaters, such as the nickelodeons, a number of years before systematic data were collected by the U.S. Bureau of the Census and by the motion picture industry. However, beginning in 1922, more systematic estimates became available. As can be seen, the peak period for paid movie attendance was the golden age, between about 1930 and the end of World War II. After that, television cut into ticket purchases, and the movie industry had to adapt to the new medium.

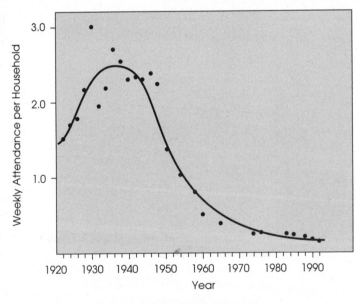

conception of an idea to showing the final product in chains of local movie theaters.

The decline Box office receipts held steady until the late 1940s. Movies were especially popular during the war years (1941–1945). By 1946, some 90 million tickets were being sold weekly (see Table 5.1 and Figure 5.1). Then, with extraordinary rapidity, a new medium came on the scene that was to have a devastating impact on motion pictures as a family entertainment industry. With the rise of television, the movies in their traditional form underwent a precipitous decline. By the early 1970s, only about 17 million tickets were being sold during an average week. To try to draw patrons back to the theaters, movie makers turned to a variety of gimmicks and innovations. They tried increasing the use of color, escalating levels of violence, making sexual portrayals increasingly explicit, and employing horror themes, spectacular special effects, space fantasies, and even an occasional three-dimensional (3D) production.

To a very limited extent, those efforts helped. In 1983, the most recent peak year, average weekly ticket sales rose to more than 22.5 million, but there has been a small decline since then. In 1992, weekly attendance was 18.5 million. It is clear, then, that on a per capita basis, movie attendance is still declining. And as we will see later, movie exhibitors (those who own theaters and show films) are plagued by a number of negative trends. In addition, audiences today do not consist of entire families, as in earlier decades, but mainly of young people. The older neighborhood theaters and drive-ins closed long ago, when television became popular. Today, multitheater cinemas, often located in or near malls, offer young viewers a range of films from which to choose. Nevertheless, for a variety of reasons, the movie business is here to stay. It has survived by adapting to smaller, younger audiences and by producing movies for broadcast and cable television. Even more important, the rapid growth in movie rentals for home VCR showings has greatly improved the profit picture.

Film as a Contemporary Medium

Perhaps more than any other medium, the motion picture has attracted the popular imagination. Screaming supermarket tabloids, gushing movie magazines, and caustic television commentators pass on the latest Hollywood gossip and speculation to a fascinated public. The pictures themselves—from *The Birth of a Nation* to *Jurassic Park*—are seen by tens of millions during their peak years. The stars have always been in the public eye. Enthusiastic followers have been fascinated with the smallest details of their lives. This nation's standards of female beauty and sexual attractiveness have been derived in some part from movies. It started early in the century when Lilian Gish began to set the norms. It continued with the "vamps" of the 1920s and great beauties such as Greta Garbo and Ingrid Bergman in the 1930s. By mid-century, "sex goddesses" such as Marilyn Monroe and Elizabeth Taylor served as models. Similarly, American conceptions of handsome manliness have been influenced by such figures as John Wayne, Clark Gable, and, more recently, Tom Cruise and Mel Gibson. These standards can have a profound influence on the behavior of millions, in everything from using cosmetics to selecting a mate. All the publicity and popularity may do more to hinder than help our understanding of movies. Behind the gossip and the glamour lie complex realities. In addition to being a medium of mass communication and a social force, motion pictures are both a huge and diversified industry and an intricate art form.

As art, film takes in the whole spectrum of forms that the term implies: It is a performing art, like the theater and dance; it is representational, like painting; and it is a recording art, like music. Evaluating the artistic merit of films, however, is beyond the scope of this book. As a social force, the motion picture gives rise to issues concerning the industry's presumed influences, which we consider in later chapters. In this section, we are most concerned with film as a contemporary medium of mass communication with different kinds of content that serve distinctive functions. Both the content and the functions are determined by professional communicators—the industry that produces the pictures—and their large and diverse audience.

The Functions of Films

For the people who make films, the medium provides an avenue for expression and an opportunity to practice a complex craft. It is also a means to wealth for some and simply a livelihood for others. The end product may be frivolous and diverting; it may provide information or training; it may make a social or political statement; it may have important aesthetic qualities. That is, a film may seek to amuse or *entertain* by providing diversion and enjoyment; to *educate*, as many documentaries do; to *persuade* or influence, as in the case of wartime propaganda films; or to *enrich* our cultural experiences. Most often, a film will have combined functions, seeking to entertain while it also enriches, informs, or persuades. For the audience, a film may be an escape and an engaging lesson in history, morality, or human relationships. For their producers, films are a source of profit. For directors and actors, films can be a means of supporting artistic values, whereas for writers, films may be a way of raising consciousness about social causes.

Film's function is, of course, partly in the eye of the beholder. Most people consider vintage Walt Disney films to be wholesome family entertainment; but others interpret them as rigid ideological statements that praise an unrealistic image of the United States, showing artificial, antiseptic WASP communities devoid of social problems. It is safe to say, however, that the main function of American films has been, throughout their history, to entertain. In one very important respect, movies differ from the print and broadcast media. We refer not to their obvious mechanical aspects, but to the traditional functions inherent in their origins. The origins of magazines and newspapers were related to the functions of providing information and influencing opinion. But films grew from the traditions of both theater and popular amusements. These traditions had far less to do with transmitting information and opinion; their central focus was always on entertainment. Films, then, continue those traditions, and their principal function has always been to take their viewers away from the pressing issues and mundane details of everyday life, rather than to focus attention on them.

The Development of Themes and Styles

The early movies looked to the established forms of drama (comedy, tragedy, and musical) for their themes. They often turned to books for ideas and screenplays. Early silent film comedies relied on the art of mime. But soon American films developed their own forms and traditions. In the silent period, Mack Sennett, Charlie Chaplin, Buster Keaton, Harold Lloyd, and others created their own forms of acting and story-telling; later, directors such as Eric von Stroheim and Cecil B. De Mille added their mark. These and later film makers who have created films with a distinctive style are known as *auteurs*.

Eventually, films' content and style were influenced less by material from plays or books and more by the medium's own emerging traditions. The 1930s research of Edgar Dale provides a glimpse at those traditions. Dale analyzed the content of five hundred films that had been released by 1920,

Directors who put their personal stamp on a category of movies are called *auteurs*. Starting in the 1930s, film directors such as Eric von Stroheim and Cecil B. De Mille played major roles in creating personal styles. Alfred Hitchcock continued the tradition after World War II. Today, auteur Steven Spielberg produces films such as *Close Encounters of the Third Kind*, *E.T.*, *Star Wars*, and *Jurassic Park*, with complex special effects. (Copyright © by Universal City Studios, Inc. Courtesy of MCA Publishing Rights, a Division of MCA Inc.)

another five hundred released between 1921 and 1925, and yet another five hundred released between 1926 and 1930. He found that three major themes—crime, sex, and love—accounted for approximately three-fourths of the movies produced during the period.[7]

In general, directors were the dominating force shaping films until the 1930s. Then, in the 1930s and 1940s, the studios became dominant. Several studios came to have recognizable styles. MGM was well-known for its richly produced, glossy epics aimed at middle-brow tastes. Paramount was said to give its films a European sensibility. Warner Brothers often shot on location because creating the sets was too expensive; so Warner developed a reputation for realism.[8]

Today, these differences in production styles have disappeared as the influence of the major studios has declined. But even in the heyday of the studios, some individuals—directors, actors, or cinematographers—marked their films with their own distinctive stamp. Different members of the film-making team may dominate at any time and in any film. During the 1970s and 1980s, the director once again held sway as the king of film. Today, on the whole, there is a greater awareness of varying directorial styles.

The Content of American Films

A film's content is almost always shaped by conflicting forces. The audience, technology, economics, and the film makers themselves play a part. Producers look carefully at the balance sheet, continually worrying about audience interests. They ask, What is technically and economically possible, and what does the audience want? Perhaps no single concept can capture all that, but one film historian has suggested the phrase "efficient dream-building" to describe the process:

> *Efficient* means meeting production demands of cost and time while developing an intelligible visual narrative within the prescribed single-double or multi-length reel length. *Dream-building* means satisfying audiences' appetites for formula structure in comedy and melodrama with accepted standards of moral and philosophical thought.[9]

Which films constitute efficient dream-building varies with the times. The search for efficiency led, for example, to standardized lengths for films, though these lengths have changed through the decades. Efficient dream-building also calls for coherent plot structures. Old westerns, for example, were usually melodramas with a hero, a villain, a beautiful girl, a sidekick, a handsome horse, and perhaps inaccurately portrayed Indians. The audience had particular expectations of what they would see, and plots usually conformed to those expectations.

But old formulas can become trite. Over time audiences change, in terms of both their characteristics and what they want to see. Anxious to keep track of audience composition and tastes, studios hire the services of organizations such as the Opinion Research Institute of Princeton, which puts together a profile of moviegoers. Since 1989, for example, at least 55 percent of those attending movies have been under thirty and less than 10 percent over sixty.[10] Making movies for the young, therefore, has become a more certain way to make money than making them for mature audiences.

The theme of a film to be made is determined by many factors. For example, producers often assume that if particular subject matter has been popular in a book or on the stage, then a movie on the topic will be a winner. Another example of Hollywood thinking is that a successful formula should be repeated. If no fresh ideas are available, make a sequel, or even better, make a series. Thus, in recent decades, the public has been blessed with a long list of notable repetitions: *The Godfather* (1972), *The Godfather II* (1974), and *Godfather III* (1990); *Jaws* (1975), *Jaws II* (1978), and *Jaws III* (1983). A record of some kind was set with *Rocky I, II, III, IV and V*. We could add the various installments of *Star Trek*, *Rambo*, *Aliens*, the Indiana Jones adventures, and *Batman I* (1989) and *II* (1992). The runner-up for all-time leader in sequels was *Friday the Thirteenth*, versions *I* through *VIII*. However, the all-time winner is the James Bond series. Beginning with *Dr. No* in 1962, the Bond films progressed (dropping and replacing lead actors as they aged) up to *License to Kill* in 1989—the sixteenth in the series!

Still, the balance sheet is not the only factor that determines the shape of films. Directors, actors, and even producers may also want to put the mark of their own imagination on a film. According to one film historian, the workings of these opposing forces—bottom line versus personal expression—"drove the Hollywood cinema: the clash between the artist's sensibility and the classic mythic structure of the story types that were identified and popular."[11] Out of this clash came a broad range of films and film genres.

Genres   Balanced against the film maker's desire for individuality, then, is the need to give the audience a message it will understand and accept—the need for successful dream-building. As a result of this need, plots become more or less standardized. Story types, or genres, develop. A *genre* is a category of films with the same basic kind of characters, settings, and plots. The gangster film is an example. Another is the war film. Still another is the slapstick comedy. Literature developed genres, and so did American films.

Probably the most popular film genre of all time is the western. It was a completely American invention, with brave men and women living the rugged life of the range or moving across the frontier, where they met hardship in battle with the elements, Indians, and outlaws. (The Republic studio in particular made large numbers of early westerns.)

Musicals were once immensely popular, and some studios, such as Warner Brothers, virtually specialized in this genre. It was Warner Brothers that produced Busby Berkeley's elaborate, geometrically choreographed dance films of the 1930s, featuring dozens of dancers forming intricate patterns when photographed from overhead. Many of Berkeley's "dancers" knew nothing (and did not need to know anything) about genuine dance. All they had to do was to move precisely together for a few steps. He used unusual camera angles and fast-paced editing to create spectacular effects.

LITERARY CLASSICS AND THE MOVIES:
A Linchpin to World Literature

The modern Hollywood blockbuster movie, critics say, is often lacking in any real story-telling vigor. In the blockbuster, narrative is less important than concept, which is usually developed through flashes, crashes, and an ever-louder soundtrack—all of which lead, randomly and unconvincingly, to something resembling an ending.

It wasn't always so. Many of the earliest American movies made for commercial showing were based on classic and popular novels and plays and brought these works to life for moviegoing audiences who otherwise might not have had the opportunity to enjoy them.[1] In 1912, the Famous Players Film Company, the forerunner of what would become Paramount, produced its first feature-length film, *The Count of Monte Cristo*, then one of the most popular and longest-running plays in American theater history. The film starred James O'Neill, who had made fame and fortune in the stage production of the play and whose son, Eugene, would later see his own great works for stage made into classic films.

Movie studios routinely turned to popular books and plays for their stories in the early years of movie making, resulting in such early box office triumphs as D. W. Griffith's *Birth of a Nation* and *The Four Horsemen of the Apocalypse*, starring a then unknown Rudolph Valentino.

But in 1923 box office success and critical acclaim alike came for Universal Studios' production of Victor Hugo's novel *The Hunchback of Notre Dame*, starring Lon Chaney in a poignant portrayal of the suffering Quasimodo. In 1924, the newly formed Metro-Goldwyn company made the first film adaptation of Lew Wallace's famed novel *Ben-Hur* for the unheard-of cost of nearly $4 million. That same year the Warner brothers—Samuel, Harry Albert, and Jack—produced *The Sea Beast*, based on Herman Melville's classic *Moby Dick* and starring the eminent stage actor John Barrymore. By the end of the decade a new age in film making would bring Quasimodo, Judah Ben-Hur, and Captain Ahab to the big screen again—the age of sound.[2]

Throughout the 1930s, Hollywood studios turned regularly to classic and popular literature and drama for material. The romantic adventure novels *The Three Musketeers* and *Captains Courageous* were made into popular films in the 1930s. Metro-Goldwyn-Mayer made highly successful films from Charles Dickens's

Comedies have always attracted wide audiences. They have ranged from dry-witted, British-inspired parlor comedies to screwball films by the Marx Brothers, the Three Stooges, and Laurel and Hardy. Other genres are horror films, historical romances, and detective thrillers. Occasionally, public taste dictates development of a new genre, such as the science fiction thrillers of the 1950s and the teen-horror movies of the 1980s.

Public attitudes and social conditions have often influenced (some would say dictated) the treatment of racial and ethnic minorities in film. For many years, it was difficult for African- and Hispanic-American actors to get good film roles. They were often depicted in subservient positions that reinforced racial stereotypes. In more recent years, there have been new images for minorities in screen roles. Beginning in the early 1970s, several

David Copperfield and A Tale of Two Cities, and in 1938 MGM released Gone with the Wind; based on the Civil War epic by Margaret Mitchell, it was the biggest box office success thus far in film history. In 1930, Universal Studios produced one of the great anti-war films of all time, All Quiet on the Western Front. Based on the controversial novel by Erich Remarque, the film received that year's Academy Award for best picture.

With some exceptions, Hollywood turned to war as its creative source during the 1940s. Most notable among the exceptions were John Ford's 1940 film adaptation of John Steinbeck's The Grapes of Wrath, with a young Henry Fonda as Tom Joad, and John Huston's 1948 production of Hamlet, starring Laurence Olivier. Hamlet went on to take best picture at the annual Academy Awards, with Olivier winning as best actor.

Hollywood returned to literature and the stage for its inspiration in the 1950s and early 1960s. In 1951, Vivien Leigh and Marlon Brando brought Tennessee Williams's A Streetcar Named Desire alive on the big screen, and two years later Brando gave a memorable performance as Marc Antony in the film adaptation of Shakespeare's Julius Caesar. MGM in 1959 released its highly profitable remake of Ben-Hur, starring Charlton Heston, then followed with a hugely suc-

cessful film adaptation of Boris Pasternak's Doctor Zhivago in 1965. Gregory Peck re-created Captain Ahab in a 1956 remake of Moby Dick, and in 1962 won an Academy Award for best actor for his stirring portrayal of Atticus Finch in the film adaptation of Harper Lee's great novel To Kill a Mockingbird.

In every decade, screen and video adaptations of literary classics continue to delight audiences. Although it was not regarded as the best of its genre, actor Mel Gibson's version of Shakespeare's Hamlet revived that often produced play for the movie screen. James Fenimore Cooper's Last of the Mohicans and E. M. Forster's Howard's End also played to appreciative crowds in 1992. Virtually every generation enjoys a new version of Sir Arthur Conan Doyle's Sherlock Holmes, and the popular play Front Page, depicting Chicago newspaper reporters in the 1920s, has had four revivals.

1. Richard Schickel, "The Crisis in Movie Narrative," in the Gannett Center Journal (New York: Gannett Center for Media Studies, Summer 1989), pp. 17–28.
2. Robert Stanley, The Celluloid Empire: A History of the American Motion Picture Industry (New York: Hastings House, 1978).
3. Ephraim Katz, The Film Encyclopedia (New York: Putnam Publishing Co., 1979).

major studios distributed films that portrayed African-American heroes, unity among blacks, and victory over the white establishment. Some, such as Sounder (1972), were sympathetic portrayals; others, such as Shaft (1971) and Superfly (1972), had less sensitive macho themes. However, despite their portrayal of blacks and their themes, and even though blacks often wrote, directed, and acted in these films, they were actually owned and distributed by white-run studios. During the 1980s, another black genre appeared, featuring comedians such as Eddie Murphy and Richard Pryor.

Although such efforts have provided opportunities, black performers and artists still complain, justifiably, that there are not enough roles for them and for members of other racial minorities. The situation may be improving.

Films such as *A Soldier's Story* (1985), *The Color Purple* (1985), *Glory* (1989), and *Driving Miss Daisy* (1990) have provided unusual and important roles for African-American actors. New ground has been broken by black directors in such films as Spike Lee's *Do the Right Thing* (1991) and *Malcolm X* (1992) and John Singleton's *Boyz N the Hood* (1991).

Films depicting women and women's issues have also gone through a number of phases. In the early films, women were usually melodramatic heroines—pretty girls threatened by evil villains and saved by virile heroes. In the 1930s and 1940s, actresses such as Bette Davis, Joan Crawford, and Barbara Stanwyck portrayed very strong women. In the 1950s, the role of sexy blonde, most prominently associated with Marilyn Monroe, brought a different and much weaker image of women. During the 1970s and 1980s, women returned in less demeaning film roles. Indeed, a number of popular films took on clear feminist themes, with actresses playing important roles dealing with issues and problems of special interest to women; examples include *Nine to Five* (1982), *Terms of Endearment* (1983), *Out of Africa* (1987), *Working Girl* (1988), *Beaches* (1989), *Thelma and Louise* (1991), *Fried Green Tomatoes* (1991), and the 1994 remake of *Little Women*.

Documentaries The public overwhelmingly identifies the movies (both as an industry and as products for consumption) with the entertainment function. Indeed, the vast majority of films that have ever been produced do have that as their primary goal. For this reason, most of the films we have discussed in this chapter have fictional, entertainment themes. But an important category of nonfiction films, called *documentaries*, are also significant in that they fulfill an education function. From an intellectual perspective, documentaries may have a lasting importance, far exceeding entertainment films, as records of human culture in particular periods. Imagine what you might see if someone at the time could have made documentaries of the ancient Egyptians building the pyramids, of Gutenberg developing printing, or of the first encounters of Columbus with the people of the New World. At some point in the future, some of the documentaries produced in this century, such as World War II films that recorded that conflict for future generations or the film and video records of the first human beings on the moon, will have that kind of value.

Although this type of film had been produced earlier, the term "documentary" was first introduced by British film maker John Grierson, whose nonfiction film *The Drifters* (1929) depicted the lives of herring fishermen in the North Sea. In the documentary's purest form, the film maker intrudes as little as possible; the director, for example, does not direct actors or set up scenes. The controversial technique of *cinema vérité* takes this idea further; it is spontaneous, direct filming. To make *Titicut Follies* (1967), for example, Frederick Wiseman wandered through a state mental hospital capturing representative snatches of life in the institution; then he edited these snatches into a coherent portrait of what he saw. Some directors feel that it is impossible not to intrude on the subject in some way, not to include one's own interpretation, consciously or unconsciously. Others feel that intrusion and interpretation are necessary to give a documentary coherence. The courts took a draconian view of *Titicut Follies,* ruling that it could only be shown to professional audiences. Not until 1993 was the film available to the general public.

Through the years, documentaries have dealt with people at work, the efforts of nations at war, social problems, and other issues. Some are timeless and artful classics that are now intellectual treasures, such as Robert Flaherty's *Nanook of the North* (1922), which depicted Eskimo life just before the native culture was transformed into a more contemporary form. Some documentaries take bits and pieces of a process and weld them into a film. For example, Emile de Antonio and Daniel Talbot's award-winning *Point of Order!* (1963) used sequences from the McCarthy hearings that others had filmed. The directors creatively put together the work of other film makers and of camera operators not under their direction to produce an outstanding film. Documentaries often carry a powerful message; an example is Peter Davis's *Hearts and Minds* (1975), which traced the painful relationship between the United States and Vietnam. Future generations of Americans will find these films of great value in understanding the nation's history.

By the late 1980s and early 1990s, documentaries began once again to reach audiences. Some were shown in movie theaters, including *Mother Teresa* (1986), *Roger and Me* (1989), Madonna's *Truth or Dare* (1991), and *Hoop Dreams* (1994). Others came via television. In 1990, a four-part documentary about the Civil War, based mainly on still pictures from the period, electrified Americans when it was presented on public television. An outstanding TV "docudrama" was *Stalin* (1993). Nevertheless, there are ample reasons to question whether the documentary is becoming an endangered species. If it is on the wane, that is a loss to us all.

Public preferences No other kind of motion picture has been able to challenge the dominance of the fictional film whose purpose is entertainment. It is by far the category of choice for the majority of the public. Many entertainment genres have been popular, including science fiction, adventure-thriller, gangster, supernatural, musical, and historical epic. During the early 1950s, just before the beginning of the attendance downslide, the studios seemed to prefer to make westerns.[12] Recently, public response to comedies and films with spectacular special effects (like *Jurassic Park*) has been high.

Many factors influence preferences: trends in morality, current fads and recent events, as well as various styles and standards. The 1930s fostered stark realism and grim themes of the Great Depression, as well as cheerful musicals that helped the public escape from its troubles. Historical and patriotic themes as well as war films were popular during World War II and after, but so were light comedies. In the 1950s, films seemed to reflect the light-hearted mood of the country. Comedies and westerns were increasingly popular, and sexual themes were becoming more explicit. In the late 1960s, during a period of dissatisfaction with prevailing standards and styles, some films successfully celebrated the antihero and began to take on controversial social topics. Films from the late 1960s through the 1990s explored such themes as racism, drug use, war, and homosexuality. But there was still time for the screwball comedy and the light-hearted musical. Recent films have also explored international espionage and organized crime, as well as labor strikes, sports, and the supernatural.

The Movie Industry

Above all, makers of motion pictures want profits. Art has never really been a prime mover of the industry. Charlie Chaplin, whose "Little Tramp" films are now regarded as art, put it bluntly in 1972: "I went into the business for money and the art grew out of it. If people are disillusioned by that remark, I can't help it. It's the truth."[13] There can be no doubt that movie making is an industry in which money talks. To sketch a profile of this industry, we will look briefly at its organization—owners, studios, and employees—the source and size of its financial rewards, the number of its theater screens and films, and how many people watch films.

The Film Makers

By the late 1920s, the movies were a billion-dollar-a-year industry employing thousands and claiming a lion's share of Americans' entertainment dollar. Because of its benign weather and abundant sunshine for filming, the early studios of the 1920s chose Hollywood as the home for their huge dream factories. They filmed on extensive "back lots" that could be made into a Western town or a jungle paradise. However, as the industry matured, films were made in many locations. Hollywood became in some ways more of an administrative than a production capital. Nevertheless, it remained a symbol of glamour. As editor Peter Buckley wrote, "Hollywood was synonymous with everything that came out of the U.S. film industry, yet few films were actually made there. . . . Hollywood was a wonderful, fanciful state of mind: the film capital that never really was."[14]

Owners and studios The glamour myth of Hollywood overstated the geographic concentration of the film industry. From its beginnings, the industry forged financial links with Wall Street as well as artistic and production ties with European countries, and movies were often filmed on location. Nevertheless, concentration of control and ownership was always part of the equation in American film making. Major studios, such as the big five, have been the dominant force in Hollywood since its early days. The studios organized early and gained tight control over the whole production process, as well as over distribution and exhibition.

Founded by legendary motion picture moguls (such as Samuel Goldwyn and Louis B. Mayer), the studios ran their huge production plants in high gear. If you wanted to work in the movies in the heyday of the 1930s and 1940s, you worked for a studio, which had its own writers, directors, actors, and actresses under contract, as well as its own technicians, equipment, and lots. Through a practice known as *block booking,* each studio forced theater owners to show its bad films if they wanted a chance to show the good ones. The studios even owned their own chains of theaters. Thus, they had an assured outlet for their films—good or bad—while other smaller producers found it difficult to have their movies exhibited. In short, the studios had control from idea to camera to box office. It was little wonder that smaller companies had difficulty breaking into the business.

Then the federal government stepped in. The courts ruled that major studios must stop block booking and give up their theaters. Because of this decision, film making was to be a riskier business, and the major studios became less powerful.

In the 1960s, various large corporations bought up studios and theaters, integrating these holdings with other kinds of investments. For example, Gulf & Western bought Paramount. In the early 1990s, Columbia Pictures was purchased by Sony, the Japanese conglomerate. Warner Brothers was bought by Kinney National, which also owned funeral parlors, parking lots, and magazines, among other things. In 1990, that conglomerate became part of Time Warner. In the 1970s, the trend toward conglomerate ownership of studios abated in favor of emphasis on independent production companies, which continued during the 1980s.

The mix keeps changing. Today, the top motion picture studios, such as Sony (Columbia–Tri Star), Buena Vista (owned by Disney), MGM, Universal, and Twentieth Century–Fox, dominate theatrical film distribution. But although the names have survived for many decades, these studios are no longer what they once were—the private empires of single movie moguls. They are now publicly held by numerous stockholders.[15] Thus, the movie industry is more diverse and scattered today than it was in the first half of the century. Although independent producers are making many films, the major studios continue to lead the industry, financing and distributing most films produced by independents as well as producing their own. They collect more than 90 percent of the total income of movie distributors, although they share this income with the independent producers and directors whom they hire for particular services or assignments.

Making a movie Making movies is a communal process. They are the product not of one person but of many. As a result, according to Professor John L. Fell:

> The substance of any particular production is likely to change appreciably between its early idea stages and the final release print. These changes may be dominated by some individual's vision, ordered by his own evolving understanding of what the movie is, but such a happy circumstance is never altogether the case, . . . even if most of the time someone pretends to be in charge.[16]

Moreover, every film requires the solution of both mechanical and aesthetic problems. The many people who are part of the team making the film must have different skills. Just consider the various unions involved in film making: the Writers Guild of America, the American Cinema Editors, the

Directors Guild of America, the Screen Actors Guild, and the International Association of Theatrical and Stage Employees. In other words, films are put together under chaotic conditions by a variety of artistic, technical, and organizational personnel.

Fell has identified seven stages or elements in the process of film making:

1. *Conceptualization.* The idea for a film may come from any one of various people. Early directors often wrote their own scripts.
2. *Production.* To produce a film means to get the money together, organize all the people involved in the schedule, and continue supervising the process until the film is ready for distribution.
3. *Direction.* Once financial backing is secured and the script is acquired, then the director is chosen.
4. *Performance.* Actors must be chosen and their performances calibrated to the script and to other personnel involved in the film.
5. *Visualization.* The planning and execution of the actual filming involves cinematographers, lighting technicians, and others.
6. *Special effects.* Everything from camera trickery to monsters to stunts comes under this heading.
7. *Editing.* This process involves choosing takes from all the film that has been shot and processing a finished film.

The producer is a key figure in putting all these elements together. In most cases, he or she is part of a film studio that has the space, facilities, and personnel to complete the film. It is the producer who carries the responsibility for most of the central decisions, other than technical ones about acting, editing, and so on. The producer initiates the development of a film by acquiring a story or a script or by merely taking an *option* on a story (that is, an agreement giving the producer the right to purchase at a later date) until he or she sees whether the talent and the money are available to produce the film. If financial backing is available and suitable acting talent can be placed under contract, then the producer finds a director and assembles the rest of the film-making team. Directors are in charge of the shooting.

Employees   Working for the studios is a host of specialists: electricians, make-up artists, property workers, grips, projectionists, studio teamsters, costumers, craft workers, ornamental plasterers, script supervisors, actors, extras, film editors, writers, composers, musicians, camera operators, sound technicians, directors, art directors, and set directors, not to mention the stars. Almost all the technical workers are unionized. The Bureau of Labor Statistics estimated that in 1991 about 386,200 people were employed in the movie industry. The total payroll in 1992 was approximately $6.6 billion. Some superstar actors make many millions of dollars per film. (Sylvester Stallone reportedly received $27.5 million plus 35 percent of profits—totaling $63 million—for each for his Rocky and Rambo films.)

Recently, the number of those employed in the motion picture industry has steadily increased. As Table 5.2 shows, most of these people are engaged in making films or advertising and distributing them to exhibitors.

TABLE 5.2
Number of Persons
Employed in the
Motion Picture
Industry, 1980–1993

Year	Production/ Services	Distribution*	Theaters	Total
1980	80,811	11,000	128,511	220,322
1981	71,911	10,778	131,478	214,167
1982	76,756	10,544	125,156	211,456
1983	84,200	10,367	116,166	210,733
1984	96,633	10,389	109,100	218,122
1985	101,400	11,411	108,156	220,976
1986	103,044	11,300	105,010	219,356
1987	115,167	12,500	103,489	231,156
1988	114,800	131,478*	107,922	354,200
1989	132,592	137,750	106,658	377,000
1990	154,800	131,800	107,900	394,500
1993	171,900	141,200	104,600	417,700

*In 1988, the U.S. Department of Commerce added the video distribution sector to this category (which had covered motion picture theaters only). This accounts for the sudden increase.

Source: Motion Picture Association of America, Inc., 1994.

Note that although the total labor force increased from 1980 to 1993, the number of movie theater employees declined. This is because movie attendance decreased, theaters became smaller and were consolidated into multi-screen establishments, and equipment was automated.

Wages, of course, are only part of the cost of movies. By one estimate, the stars and other cast members account for only 20 percent of the costs, whereas sets and physical properties account for 35 percent.[17] The average cost of making a film in 1991 was $26.1 million. Many cost far more. Advertising and other costs were an additional $12.1 million per film on average. The money that the studios take in to balance such costs obviously depends on the number of films they distribute, the size of the audiences, and the cost of admission. The industry took in $4.8 billion dollars at the box office in 1991, a new all-time high.[18] However, what accounts for the increase is not more people going to the movies but continuing inflation in the price of admission.

Showing the Product to Its Audience

After a film is made, the next step is to distribute it in such a way that a maximum number of people will pay to see it. This boils down largely to renting it to exhibitors who operate theaters. Some are independent, but like newspapers, more and more are owned by chains. Furthermore, during the Reagan administration, some of the older antitrust restrictions that kept movie studios from owning their theaters were dropped. As a result, at least four of the major studios now own theaters or shares in companies that do.[19] To understand the current situation of distribution, we need to look at the number of films that are being released, and the number of theaters that show them to the public, and the cost of admission.

Number of films released   The number of films released per year has been declining rather drastically since Hollywood's peak years ended. This decline is especially noticeable with respect to the major studios. According to the *Film Yearbook Daily*, the studios released over 300 films per year during the peak period of 1931–1942. From 1943 to the late 1950s, the number stayed around 250; then it dipped under 200. Since 1980, the major studios have released fewer than 150 films per year. However, many films are produced and released by other studios as well. For example, in 1993, a total of 450 new films were released.

Theaters and the cost of admission   In the late 1940s, there were 20,000 theaters in the United States. By 1993, there were 25,737 (indoor and outdoor) screens. Although that looks like an increase, keep in mind that the U.S. population expanded from about 150 million to approximately 253 million during the period. Thus, the per capita decline in movie going has been truly significant. Even the number of seats per theater has declined. Whereas in 1950 the average indoor movie theater had about 750 seats, by the 1990s the average theater had approximately 500.

The average weekly attendance at movies reached a peak of more than 90 million in the late 1940s; it was down to just over 18 million by 1990. Clearly, television has been the major factor in this precipitous decline, but the

Great changes have occurred in the movie industry during recent decades. The older pattern centered on an independently owned movie theater in which rented films were shown on a single screen. The movie changed every week or so to provide variety and attract customers. Today, movies are shown in theaters that have a number of screens. Many are located in or near shopping malls, and few of these multiscreen establishments are independently owned. They are usually part of a large corporation or conglomerate, illustrating the pattern of concentration of ownership of the media. (The Terry Wild Studio)

increasing price of admission may also have discouraged moviegoing. The price of attendance (a single adult ticket) rose from an average of only 23 cents in 1933 to $5.05 in 1994. Admissions to first-run motion pictures are more expensive. At a typical mall theater in most mid-sized U.S. cities, a ticket now costs between $5.00 and $7.00. In large cities, it is even more. For example, to attend a first-run picture in a major movie theater in New York City, the typical price of admission in January 1995 was $8.00.

Overall, Americans are now spending more money on movies than ever before. However, in real terms, the industry is attracting a much smaller part of the family entertainment dollar than before. For example, in 1943, Americans spent more than 25 percent of their recreational expenditures on movies. By the beginning of 1990, this figure had dropped to less than 5 percent.

The film industry, however, is not about to go broke. To adapt to declines in traditional moviegoing, the industry is marketing in new ways that have helped it financially. The growing use of movies by network, independent, and cable television systems, plus the expanding market for movies on video cassettes, have improved the picture significantly. Because of this, the movie industry is more likely to prosper in the future than to disappear.

The Movie Audience

Like the other mass media, the movies have a large and diverse audience. As indicated above, the size and composition of that audience determine the economic health of the industry as well as film content. Here we look more closely at the kinds of people who go to a theater and pay to see a movie and at the other main pattern of viewing that is emerging, namely home viewing using television and VCRs.

Who pays at the box office?   As indicated earlier, movie theaters draw a youthful audience and appeal less to those who are older (see Table 5.3). The youthful vitality of the theater audience and its relative stability in make-up constitute an important force in keeping the industry alive and well. Most mass communication industries see young audiences as very desirable, because it is that portion of the population that in the future will buy goods and services and participate in the political process. Unfortunately, as we have suggested earlier, the young movie audience has been shrinking for a long time, and that decline continues at a slow pace.

How often do people pay to see a movie in a theater? Among most people, not very frequently, according to national studies, but those who do go attend and pay quite often. So-called frequent moviegoers make up only about 21 percent of the public over age twelve, but they account for 83 percent of all movie admissions.

Detailed data on the social characteristics of moviegoers are not easily obtained, but a 1992 Gallup poll showed that single people are more frequent moviegoers than those who are married: Only 19 percent of married

		Percentage of
	Percentage	Total Yearly
Age Group	of Population	Admissions
12–20	16	27
21–29	17	22
30–39	21	19
40–49	15	15
50–59	11	7
60 and over	21	8

**TABLE 5.3
Movie Admissions by
Age Group**

Source: Motion Picture Association of America, Inc.,
1994.

people said they went frequently to the movies, compared with 32 percent of single people. And at the other end of the scale, 35 percent of married people sampled said they never went to the movies, whereas 26 percent of single people said they never went. More males than females describe themselves as frequent moviegoers (21 percent versus 16 percent of those over eighteen). Finally, movie attendance tends to increase with higher educational levels among adults, suggesting that the moviegoing audience tends to be better educated than those who do not go.[20]

The age structure of the movie audience may change in the future. Some observers of the industry have noted a trend toward more adult film fare, such as *Awakenings* (1990), *The Silence of the Lambs* (1991), *Glengarry Glen Ross* (1992), *The Piano* (1993), *Forrest Gump* (1994), and *Quiz Show* (1994). These are films that appeal to baby-boomers—people born in the decade following World War II, who are now entering midlife.

The audience at home Some critics argue that a movie seen in a theater and a movie seen on television are not really the same thing. That may be true, but millions of people watch movies at home on TV sets. As we show in a later chapter, TV networks and cable programming services have become heavy exhibitors of movies. Ownership of VCRs has climbed enormously in the past decade, and their primary pattern of use has been for home viewing of rental movies. A large grassroots industry came into existence during this period to provide rental services. Stores from corner shops to mall outlets rent and sell video cassettes, and chains, such as Blockbuster Video, have started to expand across the country.

Many of the economic problems that have been squeezing the movie industry since the 1940s are eliminated through video rentals and cable. Unlike the theater trade, they involve no expensive physical plants to maintain, no elaborate system of distribution, and relatively few union problems. Of course, as movies become more a part of TV fare, they cease to be a medium of their own and are a subset of a larger programming context in which they compete with news, sports, and half-hour and hour TV programs.

The Financial Picture

The shifts and adjustments made by the movie industry in order to go beyond deriving income only from box office receipts are reflected in its current financial picture. In general, the major studios' profits declined in the 1950s, when they lost their theater chains and then faced competition from television. But profits began to regain ground in subsequent years. The British journal the *Economist* traced a detailed picture of the studios' profits through the difficult period. From 1932 to 1976, there was a cyclical pattern of boom and slump. Although television was a major cause, the pattern resulted in part from overstocking films as the studios rushed to imitate earlier successes. For example, efforts to imitate the success of *The Sound of Music* (1965) in the late 1960s led to losses in the early 1970s. As commentator Cobbett Feinberg wrote:

> Although the industry throughout its history has attempted to find ways to reduce the horrible risks of spending millions of dollars up front without knowing whether a film will succeed or not, none of those ways have been foolproof. The star system has worked often, but not in a consistent and predictable fashion. Studio ownership of theaters was another way to reduce risk, but that policy was declared illegal almost thirty years ago. Stepping up investment to make films noticeably better than television fare has also failed to work regularly. Movie making remains a risky enterprise.[21]

In spite of the industry's problems, the possibility of making great profits on films still exists, a fact that has not been lost on the corporations that have bought studios and theaters. Some films can earn hundreds of millions of dollars in gross revenues for their producers over a span of years. Not all that is profit, of course. After great glory followed by hard times, the motion picture industry is now generally on the mend, at least in terms of its financial condition. Still, making a movie remains a high-risk business. Of all the movies exhibited in theaters in 1991 (424 new films, 31 reissues, and an additional number of older movies), only 94 grossed more than $10 million, and a mere 64 exceeded $20 million.

Even with the new sources of income, movie revenues still depend heavily on domestic box-office receipts. For the producer, that means rentals to exhibitors. Rental fees are usually the main way of making back the investment associated with completing a film to its final negative, including overhead and interest costs. Added to the costs of production are those of marketing and advertising the film, which can be very high.

Although it is true that there are very high costs associated with producing and distributing a film, some films make remarkable profits. It is for this reason that producers continue to be willing to gamble startling sums of money. Consider, for example, a recent film that ran up $28 million in direct production and marketing costs.[22] As it turned out, it was quite successful at the box office and substantial revenues were derived from film rentals to domestic exhibitors. It also earned revenues from foreign releases, home video, pay television, network television, and syndication. Taken together, these added up to a total of approximately $40 million, yielding a net profit of $12 million before taxes, which is a startling 42.9 percent of investment! About the only other investments yielding such a return would be illegal narcotics deals or junk bond scams that swindle widows and orphans! Unfortunately, though, for every box office smash such as *Jurassic Park*, the industry produces a large number of uninspired films. Many make nothing, and some are total turkeys on which their producers lose their proverbial shirts.

There are other gambles for film producers. We saw in our review of the book industry that unethical and often illegal practices cut into the earnings of those who create the product and take the risks. The same is true in the movie industry, where one serious problem is *pirating*. Movies are copied illegally and shipped abroad for film and video cassette distribution. This results in millions of dollars of lost potential revenues for motion picture producers. The elaborate network of pirates who steal and redistribute films is said to involve organized crime, both in the United States and abroad. Christine Ogan, a journalism professor at Indiana University and an authority on such piracy, says that the illegal system is so efficient that newly released motion pictures are being seen in obscure Third World locations only days after they open in American theaters. Not surprisingly, the Motion Picture Association of America is actively trying to counter this trend by urging enforcement of copyright laws here and abroad and by calling for stiff trade agreements.

Cleaning Up the Movies

As the movie industry grew rapidly earlier in this century, much of the public feared that films were having both powerful and harmful effects. A number of people believed the new medium was negatively influencing children and teaching them unwholesome ideas. Many civic and religious leaders concluded that the movies would bring a general deterioration of moral norms and harmful political changes to American life. The industry was pressured to "clean up" its product, and efforts to suppress certain kinds of content in the movies have continued. Most of the criticism now centers on films with excessive violence and "mature" themes—by which people usually mean those that deal with sex.

Sex and the Movies

During the 1920s, when the first strong pressures arose to censor films, the industry responded by cleaning up its own house. The Motion Picture Producers and Distributors Association appointed a former postmaster general, Will H. Hays, to head their organization. Part of Hays's charge was to develop a system of self-regulation and to create a better public image for the movies. Hays and his group cooperated with religious, civic, and women's groups that had set up motion picture councils. During this early period, Hays's office was a buffer between the film industry and the public. Hays finally developed a tough self-censorship code, which all producers in the association had to follow. Without code approval, a film could not be shown in American theaters. Film producers who tried to defy this dictum were subjected to costly legal battles. The code restricted depictions of sex in particular. From the mid-1930s until the rise of television threatened the industry, movies avoided direct treatment of sexual themes and sexual behavior.

Meanwhile, a number of local governments screened and censored films. Even into the 1960s, Chicago gave this assignment to its police department, which called on a group of citizens to screen controversial films. Among the private groups most active in efforts to censor films was the Catholic Legion of Decency, which was established in 1934. It developed a list of recommended and nonrecommended films, and it promoted the list to both Catholics and the general public. The ratings carried a special moral force and occasionally were reinforced by bishops who warned Catholics to stay away from certain films. Eventually, the Legion of Decency was replaced by the Catholic Church's Office for Film and Broadcasting, which published regular newsletters and film guides. A group within the U.S. Catholic Conference continues to promote this system, publishing ratings in Catholic diocesan newspapers as advisories for Catholic parents. The ratings and their assessments are as follows:

A–1: Morally un-objectionable for general patronage
A–2: Morally un-objectionable for adults and adolescents
A–3: Morally un-objectionable for adults
A–4: For adults with reservations
A–5: Morally objectionable in part for all
  C: Condemned

Efforts like those of the Legion of Decency and other critical groups stimulated creation of a set of guidelines that Hays developed for the industry, the Motion Picture Production Code. Although the code was not tough enough for groups such as the Legion of Decency, others regarded it as harsh, repressive, and too legalistic. Some film historians think the code hindered the development of American motion pictures.

By the late 1960s, the Production Code had been modified greatly. Numerous legal actions had broken efforts to apply rigid censorship. The industry entered a new era of self-regulation by establishing a movie-classification system. Instead of barring certain films from theaters, the new system required that the public be warned of what to expect in a film. The result, which has been modified four times since it was adopted in 1968, is the following:

  G: All ages admitted, general audiences
  PG: Parental guidance suggested, for mature audiences
PG–13: Parents are strongly cautioned to give special guidance to children under thirteen
  R: Restricted, children under seventeen must be accompanied by a parent or other adult
NC–17: No one under seventeen admitted (until 1990 this category was rated X)

The classification does not indicate quality; it is only a guide for parents in deciding what motion pictures their children should see. The industry, through the Motion Picture Association of America, in effect puts its seal of approval on the first four categories of films and denies it to the fifth. This system won public support and stilled some criticism, but some film producers feel that the system is too restrictive. There has been no active move to overturn it, however. Interestingly, there are far fewer G- and PG-rated films produced than films with PG–13, R, and NC–17 ratings.

Efforts to suppress a particular motion picture can backfire. Perhaps no film in recent times has aroused such an outcry as *The Last Temptation of Christ* (1988), a low-budget movie that became something of a financial success at the box office largely as a result of the furor. Various church groups and other disapproving people threatened and carried out boycotts and protest demonstrations. These efforts were thoroughly covered by both national and local TV news, and of course by newspapers. The publicity brought crowds of curious viewers to the theaters to see what all the fuss was about. Some observers have speculated that if the film had been ignored, it would quickly have died as a dud.

Censorship and Politics

Although their treatment of sex has been at the center of most of the outcry against movies over the years, politics too has been the basis for censorship

In our mass society, many categories of people with differing values, interests, and preferences exist. Almost any film not suitable for general family entertainment will be seen as objectionable by one group or another. However, some movies provoke especially vigorous outcries because of their themes or content. A recent example that deeply offended many Christian groups was *The Last Temptation of Christ*. Many theaters showing the film were picketed by demonstrators who deemed it blasphemous. Media attention given to such demonstrations may have resulted in larger box office receipts than if the film had been ignored. (AP/Wide World Photos)

efforts. Many films with political themes were widely criticized during the 1930s. Battles to organize unions, fights between unions and producers, charges that some unions were tools of Communists, and accusations that some films were Communist propaganda split Hollywood in the years before World War II. During the war, political differences were submerged as the industry united behind the war effort. But when fear of communism ignited again in the late 1940s and 1950s, political censorship came to Hollywood as never before. The House Un-American Activities Committee, an official arm of the U.S. Congress that had been active since the 1930s, held hearings and charged scores of people, including many in the film industry, with being Communists. The hearings were followed by some prison sentences and *blacklisting* of people in the film, broadcast, and print industries.

Blacklisting was the work not of government but of private groups. It was decidedly not a democratic activity. Various lobbying groups put together lists of people they suspected of being Communists, circulated the lists privately, and threatened to boycott advertisers who sponsored shows, newspapers, or magazines that hired anyone on the list, as well as producers who gave listed people work. Most of those blacklisted were not publicly accused, so they had no chance to defend themselves. Some actors, producers, writers, and others did not even know they were on such a list until no one wanted to hire them and their careers crashed. For a time, performers had to be cleared by one of the anti-Communist groups before they would be hired. This period, when unsupported charges were frequent, is one of the darkest in media history. Postwar fear of communism was the culprit, and the film industry was hard hit by the informal censorship that resulted.

The blacklisting of the 1940s and 1950s may have seemed like an unlikely worry in the 1980s, but Warren Beatty was quite cautious when he directed, produced, and acted in *Reds* (1981), a film about the life of American Communist writer John Reed. When asked why he granted no press interviews during the making of the film, Beatty said, "It was like making a giant soufflé and not wanting anyone to stomp on the floor." Some critics suggested that Beatty was being very careful in presenting a film that treated a Communist as a hero. In the end it all worked out very well. The film won both commercial success and critical acclaim, in spite of the fact that it was produced during the conservative Reagan era.

Many groups outside the movie industry have exerted influence on the content of films. Congress has summoned actors and directors to public hearings; the Supreme Court has tried to define what is and is not obscene; church groups and local officials have tried various strategies to shape, suppress, or ban American movies. The result is a constraint on the artistic freedom of film makers, but little if any useful feedback for them. The groups pressuring the film makers are too small and their interests too narrow for their efforts to constitute effective feedback for a medium intended for a mass audience. Nevertheless, their efforts can seriously distort communication between film maker and audience. On the other hand, consumers of films have the same First Amendment rights as film makers do, including the right to protest against content they do not like.

Evaluating Films: Criticism and Awards

Film ratings are only one of the many assessments that film makers receive. The writings of critics, the selections made for film festivals and awards, and surveys of public opinions of films provide other evaluations and also give the public help in judging films. These assessments might suggest that there are uniform standards of excellence in films, but that is not the case. Although occasionally there may be widespread agreement on which film was the best of a year or decade, there are about as many standards for criticism as there are critics and awards.

The Critics

Some people distinguish between *reviewers*, who make assessments for a general audience, and *critics*, who judge a film by more artistic and theoretical criteria and try to ascertain its social importance. The terms are used interchangeably by most people, as they are in this book.

All critics have standards against which they judge a film, although the standards vary from one individual to another. Table 5.4 shows the results of asking twenty-three critics to rate the best films of the 1980s. Each critic, using his or her own criteria, assigned points ranging from 0 to 10 to the films. The resulting list is quite different from one based on public popularity.

Because film has gained status as an art form, a good deal of the criticism of a particular example is based on aesthetic criteria. Some critics judge a film on the basis of artistic potential and compare it with other films and theatrical productions. They consider factors such as the film's originality and its ability to project universal themes. A critic might be interested in any number of things about a film: the technical aspects, such as photography, sound, use of close-ups, and color; the quality of the screenplay as a piece of writing; the performance of the actors; and the unity and cohesiveness of

TABLE 5.4
The Ten Best Movies of the 1980s*

Title of Film	Total Points Earned
Raging Bull	105
Wings of Desire	59
E.T.: The Extra-Terrestrial	46
Blue Velvet	40
Hannah and Her Sisters	29
Platoon	29
Fanny and Alexander	28
Shoah	26
Who Framed Roger Rabbit?	26
Do the Right Thing	25

*As nominated by the twenty-three best-known film critics.

Source: Kitty Bow Hearty, "The Decade's Best: Film-World Notables Pick Their Perfect 'Ten'," Premiere: The Movie Magazine, November, 1989, pp. 106–107.

the production. Some critics discuss the film in terms of the way it fits into a particular actor's or director's career. For example, a critic might discuss whether the direction and acting in the latest Woody Allen film are as good as in his previous films.

Film criticism appears in many places. Specialized industry magazines speak mainly to the movie community and to film scholars. Many magazines and newspapers have movie reviews and criticisms. Local TV and radio stations review films on the air. Sometimes it seems like more energy is devoted to reviewing and criticizing films than to making them. There are even annual awards for the best film criticism.

The Awards

Most organized human endeavors offer various kinds of symbolic rewards to individuals or groups that perform well. It may be a medal for wartime bravery, a diploma for completing a degree program, a plaque for selling the most insurance, or a cup for catching the biggest fish. Individuals who organize and control such awards understand their importance. As long as people take them seriously, awards satisfy needs for status recognition and give both prestige and publicity to whatever happens to be the arena of competition.

Movie making is no exception. It has its own system for recognizing high performance and for publicizing those accomplishments. The granddaddy of all the movie awards is the Oscar—the gold-plated statue about a foot high awarded each year in a nationally televised spectacle by the Academy of Motion Picture Arts and Sciences. The Oscars are prizes from the industry itself to its honored few, and even though the little statues themselves are rather tacky, they are the most coveted of all the movie awards. Receiving the awards has real economic value, since films that win them are usually re-released, with attendant publicity, and draw thousands more viewers and box-office receipts.

The Academy makes awards in an almost mind-boggling list of categories: It includes best picture, best director, best actor, best actress, best supporting actor, best supporting actress, best screenplay adaptation, best original screenplay, best cinematography, and best foreign-language film. There are also awards for art direction, sound, short subjects, music, film editing, and costume design, as well as honorary awards, scientific and technical awards, and various awards for service to the industry.

The Academy Awards have not been without their critics. Some charge that those giving the awards concentrate on the most popular films rather than on the best or most socially significant. There is some truth to this argument. For example, one of the best films of all time—Orson Welles's brilliant *Citizen Kane* (1941)—got only one award, for best screenplay. Still, the list of Oscar winners is a kind of "Who's Who" of well-known films and film makers.

Other honors and prizes are less well-known. Both the Writers Guild and the Directors Guild give awards, and there are a number of awards by

Systems of competition in which winners receive symbolic awards can be found in almost every arena of human endeavor. These contests range from catching the biggest fish to winning the most ball games. The awards prompt attention to the events and confer status on the winners. The movie business is no exception. Foot-high gold-plated Oscars are awarded once each year by the Academy of Motion Picture Producers to actors, directors, technicians, and others involved with films. Here Jessica Lange and Tom Hanks have received Oscars as Best Actress and Best Actor of 1994. (Bettmann)

groups independent of the industry. The National Board of Review Awards are given for films that are recommended for children. Both the National Society of Film Critics and the New York Film Critics Society give annual awards for exemplary films, and the foreign press corps covering Hollywood gives annual Golden Globe Awards. The awards at these festivals usually honor artistic quality. With the rise of globalism, international recognition has also become very important, as evidenced by the Cannes Film Festival and others.

Finally, there have been a number of efforts to identify the greatest films of all time by surveying directors and critics. One of the most ambitious efforts to identify such a film was carried out by the American Film Institute in 1977. The 35,000 members of the Institute across the nation—including film scholars, critics, and industry people—were asked to select five choices, in order of preference, for the best American film. Some 1,100 titles were mentioned in the balloting, and the institute compiled a list of the top fifty films. The list was heavily weighted with films produced since 1970, and the silent era, in particular, was underrepresented. Andrew Sarris, critic for the *Village Voice*, commented, "I suspect that many AFI voters were simply not familiar with many great films."[23]

Nevertheless, the Institute unveiled the list of the top fifty films at a dazzling ceremony attended by the president of the United States. The top ten films on the list (keep in mind that no film listed was made after 1977, when the survey was conducted) were

1. *Gone With the Wind* (1939)
2. *Citizen Kane* (1941)
3. *Casablanca* (1942)
4. *The African Queen* (1952)
5. *The Grapes of Wrath* (1940)
6. *One Flew Over the Cuckoo's Nest* (1975)
7. *Singing in the Rain* (1952)
8. *Star Wars* (1977)
9. *2001: A Space Odyssey* (1968)
10. *The Wizard of Oz* (1939)

To balance all the self-congratulation of the movie industry and its friends, the *Harvard Lampoon*, with tongue in cheek, presents annual worst movie awards. There has been no great study to identify a list of all-time turkeys. However, films have been produced and released that are so bad that it is difficult to imagine what possessed people to produce them. Perhaps the worst film of all time was an unbelievably tacky western with the title of *Terror of Tiny Town*. It had an all-midget cast, including very small ponies for the hero and villain!

Chapter Review

■ Motion pictures have a technological history that includes inventions in optics, photography, and electronics and discoveries in the psychology and physiology of the perception of motion. By 1886, short primitive pictures showing motion were being exhibited in the United States.

■ The movie theater as we know it began after the turn of the century with the nickelodeons. Within a few years, movies were being made for the middle class, and the industry expanded to become a popular mode of family entertainment.

■ As the society changed rapidly after World War I, the movies mirrored the new ways of life. Conservative people were alarmed at portrayals of alcohol use, easy money, fast cars, and sexual themes. Extensive efforts to control the movies arose, and research on their effects began.

■ Between 1930 and 1960, the golden age of movies dawned and then declined. The U.S. movie industry has gone through many changes in its short history. For the most part,

film has been a medium for entertainment. Despite technological and artistic changes and competition from television, that is still its primary function today.

■ Every film is a product of technology, artistry, managerial skill, and showmanship. Making a film involves a wide range of professionals and craft workers. At various times, different members of the film-making team have tended to dominate in shaping films.

■ The content of a film is influenced by conflicting forces: the desire for efficiency, a view of what the audience wants, and an individual's desire to shape the film. The result of this conflict has been a wide range of genres and styles in American films.

■ Traditional film (shown in theaters) was once a more important medium of entertainment than it is today, but the industry has responded to the demands of new competition, changing technology, and changing audiences. Because it has adapted so well, the moving picture show, in one form or another, will remain a large, lively, and significant medium.

Notes and References

1. Martin Quigley, Jr., *Magic Shadows: The Story of the Origin of Motion Pictures* (Washington, D.C.: Georgetown University Press, 1948), pp. 9–10.

2. Josef M. Eder, *History of Photography* (New York: Columbia University Press, 1948), pp. 209–245, 263–264, 316–321.

3. There were several claimants of the invention of celluloid roll film in the late 1880s. Eventually the courts decided a case on the matter in favor of the Reverend Hannibal Goodwin. However, George Eastman produced the film in his factory and marketed it to the public. See Frederick A. Talbot, *Moving Pictures: How They Are Made and Work* (London: Heinemann, 1923).

4. Talbot, op. cit., p. 2.

5. Tino Balio, ed., *The American Film Industry* (Madison: University of Wisconsin Press, 1976), p. 63.

6. In 1988, the work of Theodore Case, of Auburn, New York, came to light. Very early sound films (1923) were discovered in a coal bin in his home, along with documents and equipment. It now appears that Case, rather than Lee De Forest, may have first developed the critical elements in the sound movie. At this point, however, it remains an open question.

7. Edgar Dale, *The Content of Motion Pictures* (New York: Macmillan, 1935).

8. Ibid., p. 208. See also an excellent summary of the history of the major studios, in Cobbett Feinberg, *Reel Facts: The Movie Book of Records* (New York: Vintage, 1978), pp. 376–389.

9. Thomas W. Bohn and Richard L. Stromgren, *Light and Shadows: A History of Motion Pictures* (Port Washington, N.Y.: Alfred, 1975), p. 170.

10. *International Motion Picture Almanac*, 64th ed. (New York: Quigley Publishing, 1993), p. 18A.

11. James Monaco, *How to Read a Film*, rev. ed. (New York: Oxford University Press, 1977), p. 246.

12. John Cogley, *Report on Blacklisting*, vol. 1 (New York: Fund for the Republic, 1956), p. 282.

13. Feinberg, op. cit., p. xiii.

14. For an excellent abbreviated analysis of the movies, see Garth Jowett and James M. Linton, *Movies as Mass Communication* (Beverly Hills, Calif.: Sage, 1990).

15. See Thomas Guback, "Theatrical Film," in Benjamin M. Compaign, ed., *Who Owns the Media?* (White Plains, N.Y.: Knowledge Industry, 1982), pp. 199–286. See also *Variety*, January 1 and January 8, 1986.

16. John L. Fell, *An Introduction to Film* (New York: Praeger, 1975), p. 127.

17. These estimates were obtained by one of the authors in an interview with the National Association of Theater Owners in 1992. We wish to thank the organization for its assistance.

18. These data were obtained from the National Association of Theater Owners in 1991.

19. All data in this section come from the Motion Picture Association of America, Inc., "Incidence of Motion Picture Attendance, July 1986," a study conducted by Opinion Research Corporation, Princeton, N.J.

20. See Christopher Sterling, ed., *The Mass Media: Aspen Guide to Industry Trends* (New York: Praeger, 1978), pp. 184–185.

21. Feinberg, op. cit., p. 392.

22. These data were provided to the authors on the condition that the name of the film and its producer would remain anonymous.

23. Andrew Sarris, "The Night They Left Garbo Alone," *Village Voice*, December 12, 1977, p. 51.

The development of the electromagnet early in the (nineteenth) century made the telegraph possible. The growth of mass production and distribution made it necessary. . . . Wherever industrialization was going on, (people) were becoming dependent on events in distant places. . . . Rapid intelligence became a life and death matter.

Eric Barnouw, 1956

U ntil a little over a century ago, lack of communications technology was a severe handicap in coordinating complex human activities. It had been since the dawn of history. In fact, inability to communicate quickly over distance had more than once altered the fate of the entire world. For example, in 1588, Philip II of Spain sent the Armada, a great fleet of 130 warships under the command of the Duke of Medina Sidonia, to crush the English, who were helping Spain's enemies. The plan was for the Spanish ships to pick up the army of Alessandro Farnese, the Duke of Palma, on the shores of Flanders and take them across the English Channel to invade and conquer England.

It was the greatest naval and military venture in the history of the world up to that time. With effective communication, it undoubtedly would have succeeded. However, the rendezvous failed miserably. English ships harried the Armada in the channel, doing little actual damage, but forcing them northward. Problems of coordination mounted. Unable to contact the leader of the nearby army he was supposed to meet and, indeed, uncertain that it was even there, Sidonia abandoned the invasion plan. Bad storms arose as the ships tried to return to Spain by way of the Atlantic west of Ireland. Dozens of vessels foundered with great loss of life, and the whole effort ended in disaster. If the commanders of the Armada and the shore-bound army had possessed just one little CB radio each, they could have coordinated their efforts effectively. The entire history of the world would have changed, and you would probably be speaking, reading, and writing Spanish today!

Communication devices that could conquer distance at high speed were a dream extending back to ancient times. Giovanni della Porta, a sixteenth-century scientist, described the "sympathetic telegraph" for which learned men had long been searching.[1] It was a device that would be able to "write at a distance" (in Greek, *tele* means "far off," and *graphos*, "to write"). In the imagination of those searching for a way to do this, the instrument would consist of a lodestone (a magnet) that would sensitize two needles so they would act "in sympathy"—that is, in unison—but at different locations. The needles were to be mounted on separate dials, something like compasses, in such a way that if one needle were to be moved to a given position on its dial, such as to point to the letter A, the other would move to a similar position immediately, even though the devices were far from each other. With the alphabet arranged around each dial, messages would be sent and received over distances.

It was a great idea. Unfortunately, the special lodestone was never found. However, the slow accumulation of science during the next three centuries, followed by the more rapid acceleration in technology during the nineteenth and twentieth centuries, eventually yielded communication devices that would have astounded Giovanni della Porta.

Starting in the 1840s, the new technologies came quickly, one after the other, within a span of about fifty years. The first was the electric dot-and-dash telegraph (1844). It was followed by the telephone (1876), the wireless telegraph (1896), and finally the radiotelephone (1906). Then, with adaptations of radiotelephone technology in the early 1920s, radio became a mass medium for household use. We saw earlier that the movies also came into existence during the last decade of the nineteenth century. By the mid-1920s, even the principles needed for television had been developed.

To appreciate how rapidly all of this took place, think about a person born in 1843. That year, a message could move only as fast as a galloping horse, or at best a flying pigeon. Few increases had been made since prehistoric times. Then, suddenly, remarkable changes came. Earlier, crossing the Atlantic could take a month or more by sail, but that was reduced to around two weeks by the new paddle-wheel steamships. When a person born in 1843 was only 10 years old, the telegraph was regularly sending messages at a mind-boggling 186,000 miles per second between distant points in a large network. By the time our individual was about 40, he or she could telephone friends at distant locations. By 85, he or she could listen on a home receiver to regularly scheduled radio programs transmitted over a nationwide network. If that same individual had survived to an unusual 105 years, he or she could have watched news, sports, and entertainment on a TV set at home.

These swift changes can be seen from another perspective by contrasting them with the time needed for previous transitions in human communication. As we noted in Chapter 1, early prehistoric human beings were restricted to the use of signs and signals. The biological requirements for speech took about 3 million years of evolution before language could come into use. Once people could talk, writing required perhaps another thirty to forty thousand years to develop. Printing did not arrive for another four thousand years. From printing to the telegraph took only four hundred years. Then, going from the telegraph to network television took just over a century— the potential span of a human lifetime, a mere moment in history. The new media of communication that emerged from this incredibly swift transition changed the workings of societies and had a significant impact on the personal lives of millions of people all over the world. Because it all happened so quickly, and on such a large scale, this hundred-year transition is often identified as a "revolution" in instantaneous communication.

This chapter focuses on only part of that revolution—the development of radio. As will be clear, radio and television share a common background of technological development. They also share a common economic base and a system of societal control. For that reason, the events of history common to both media are reviewed in this chapter, and what is unique to television will be presented in the next.

The Growth of Broadcasting Technology

To show the ways in which the development of communication by broadcasting was a part of more general trends taking place, we need to review very briefly what we have said in earlier chapters about society itself at different times during the nineteenth century. Few citizens at the beginning of the period could have imagined the changes in life-style that would soon take place in the industrializing countries. During the early nineteenth century, people still traveled between towns on foot or by animal power. Trips to distant places often took months. Goods to be purchased were hand-crafted rather than factory-made; food was either grown at home or produced on nearby farms; only a limited selection of items came to a community from distant places. Long-distance communication was by slow postal or courier services. The pace of society was slow, and most people lived a simple rural or small-town existence.

The century was not even half over before travel time had been drastically reduced. Awesome machines, belching smoke and steam and pulling long strings of wagons, were rolling across the countryside on iron rails at what were then considered incredible speeds. Powerful ships, thrust forward by steam-driven paddle-wheels, were plying the nation's waterways. Power-driven factories spewed forth standardized goods. The scope and pace of commercial activities had increased greatly. Thus, even before the Civil War, the Industrial Revolution had transformed the nation.

After the war ended, railroads connected most major American cities with scheduled service, and steam-driven ships regularly crossed the great oceans. In addition, hundreds of factories were producing shoes, farm implements, clocks, guns, cooking pots, woven cloth, tools, and a great variety of other manufactured goods. Small towns had become cities, and large metropolitan centers existed. Food came not just from local farms but by rail from more distant sources. The Industrial Revolution had generated a parallel revolution in the production, distribution, and consumption of goods and services of many kinds.

The development of radio was a part of these great changes. As we have already suggested, it was by applying principles discovered in the basic sciences that practical devices were developed to communicate rapidly over long distances. For example, unraveling the mysteries of electricity was a first step toward broadcasting. The Greeks marveled at static electricity but did not understand its nature. By the 1700s, Europeans were generating

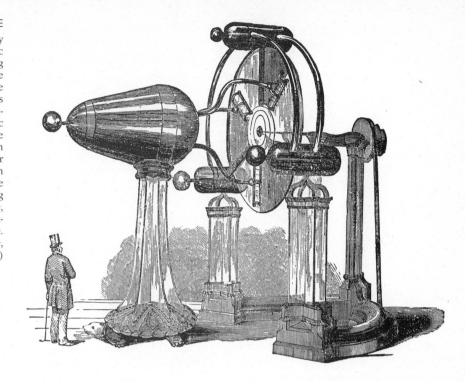

During the late 1700s and early 1800s, massive blasts of static electricity were generated using machines such as the one shown here. The lightning-like jolts delivered by such devices impressed experimenters greatly and stimulated scientific investigation. This is the same kind of electrical phenomenon that we experience on a smaller scale in our clothing or when walking on a wool rug. At the time, however, virtually nothing was known about the nature, principles, or possible applications of the mysterious force. (Historical Pictures Service, Chicago)

gigantic static charges, but they still did not understand the nature of electricity. Then, researchers succeeded in revealing how electricity works, how it could be stored in batteries, and how it could be used in practical applications. Discoveries of scientists such as Volta, Ampere, Faraday, and Maxwell laid the foundations for the telegraph and, later, radio and television. The scientific principles they discovered were applied to produce practical devices for instantaneous long-distance communication.

Communicating over a Wire

The American Samuel F. B. Morse is usually credited with inventing the long-distance telegraph. What he actually did was develop a better system than those of earlier innovators. The first important discovery came in 1819 when Hans Oerstead found that a wire carrying a pulse of electrical current over a considerable distance could deflect a magnetic needle. He also noted that reversing the direction of the current would reverse the deflection of the needle. Once ways of patterning and interpreting the deflections of the needle had been developed, the device served as a crude telegraph. This led a number of scientists, including Andre Ampere and Karl Gauss, to study and improve the process. By 1837, Wilhelm Cooke and Charles Wheatstone had developed a working telegraph system based on this needle-deflection principle. It was actually used by railroads in England.

A much more efficient system, based on the electromagnet, was developed by Morse in 1844. The electromagnet itself was discovered by William

Sturgeon in 1825 and then refined by Michael Faraday and Joseph Henry. It was a rather simple device: If a bar of soft iron, about the size of a thin wiener, is wrapped in copper wire, and a steady flow of electricity from a battery is passed through the wire, the bar becomes a fairly strong magnet. Stop the electricity, and the bar loses most of its magnetic property. By starting and stopping the flow of electricity, an operator can make the electromagnet attract and release another piece of iron. Using this principle, Morse constructed a telegraph machine and devised a code for each letter based on long and short pulses of electricity. He was also able to attach a pencil to the piece of metal that his electromagnet attracted so as to leave a record of the transmission on a moving strip of paper.

By today's standards, Morse's was a crude system. But by comparison with what was available at the time, it was a fantastic practical advance in communications technology. After the device proved workable, Morse was able to obtain a grant from the U.S. government to field-test the system. He had a copper wire strung on poles between Baltimore, Maryland, and Washington, D.C., a distance of about forty miles. From Baltimore, on the morning of May 25, 1844, he sent the dramatic message "What hath God wrought?" It was received in Washington with wild cheering and awe. No longer was the movement of a message limited to the speed of a train or a carrier pigeon. Information could be flashed to a distant location at the speed of lightning. It did indeed seem to many observers like something that God had personally wrought.

Within a few years, with wires on poles along the railroad lines, most of the major cities of the United States were connected by telegraph. Business, the military, and, as we saw in Chapter 3, newspapers began to depend on the system for rapid communication. Undersea cables were laid, even before the Civil War. Regular service between the United States and Europe was available by 1866. Yet the telegraph obviously was not a medium for the general public. It would be more than half a century before ordinary people would have a device in their homes for instantaneous mass communication without wires.

The telegraph not only initiated the era of instantaneous communication; it also set the model for the structure of ownership that would eventually characterize the electronic media in the United States. Even though the federal government had paid for Morse's experimental line between Baltimore and Washington, it declined to exercise control over the telegraph. The medium became the property of a private corporation to be operated for profit. This was a critical decision because it set the pattern followed by telephone, radio, and television as they developed.

Communicating with Radio Waves

Meanwhile, a German scientist, Heinrich Hertz, had been experimenting with some curious electromagnetic phenomena that he had produced in the laboratory. By 1887, he had demonstrated the existence of what we know today as radio waves. The accomplishment electrified the scientific world, and experimentation with these new waves that traveled at the speed of light began in laboratories in many countries. This discovery in basic science was to become the foundation of radio broadcasting.

Marconi's wireless telegraph A few years later, Guglielmo Marconi, a twenty-year-old Italian youth from a wealthy family, had read everything he could find about the Hertzian waves. He bought the necessary parts and, on his father's estate, built his own devices to produce and detect them. He experimented with different wavelengths, types of antennae, and other features of the system. His idea was that by systematically interrupting the wave as it was being generated, he could send and receive messages in Morse code—without wires.

Finally, in 1895, Marconi succeeded in sending coded messages over a considerable distance across his father's estate. Thinking that his invention could have great social consequences, he offered it to the Italian government and tried to persuade them to help finance his work. But that government, deciding the device had no importance, was not interested. Undaunted, and at the urging of his English mother, Marconi took his ideas to London, where in 1897 he was able to obtain a patent as well as financial backing to develop his wireless telegraph further. Soon after, by 1901, he had built a much more powerful transmitter and succeeded in sending a message across the Atlantic.

Radio, in this dot-and-dash form, had enormous practical advantages over the land-based telegraph that required wires. Ships at sea could communicate with each other and with stations on land. A number of remote stations could receive the broadcast of a central station simultaneously. For England,

By 1895, Guglielmo Marconi had found a way to transmit a message via radio over an impressive distance on his father's Italian estate. He synthesized Heinrich Hertz's discoveries of electromagnetic waves that traveled instantaneously without wires and the concept of transmitting messages encoded into dots and dashes via the electric telegraph. The result was a telegraph that worked without wires. It was one of the great inventions of all time—the starting point for the modern era of electronic media. (Culver Pictures, Inc.)

as for other nations with numerous colonies, a large navy, a huge merchant marine, and far-flung commercial enterprises, the wireless telegraph was a godsend.

The principal drawback of the earliest sets was that they required large, heavy equipment to achieve long-range transmission. An early set could barely fit into a room. Not being a scientist, Marconi had chosen the wrong end of the frequency band. He reasoned that long radio waves would go farther than short ones. But it took great electrical energy to transmit them over long distances. Thus, his system required powerful electric currents, heavy wiring and switches, and massive antennae. If he had used the very short waves, he could have developed a much smaller, more portable machine. However, within a few years, that became evident.

Marconi was not only an inventor, but also a shrewd businessman. He successfully fought patent challenges to protect his ownership and established profit-oriented corporations to exploit wireless communication. He founded the American Marconi Company in 1899, and by 1913, it had a virtual monopoly on the use of the wireless telegraph in the United States. By that time radio had come into worldwide use, and Marconi became a very rich man. As with telegraph by wire earlier, the principle of private ownership and profit in broadcasting was established from the outset.

Marconi also invented a device for generating and detecting a particular wavelength for the more precise transmission of signals. He patented it in 1904. This was important because it allowed the transmitter to broadcast on a specific wavelength or *frequency*. With the receiving instrument "tuned" to the same wavelength, signals of other frequencies could not interfere. We still tune radios to specific frequencies in this manner for transmission and reception.

The radiotelephone During the first decade of the new century, radio quickly became more than a wireless telegraph. On Christmas Eve in 1906, radio operators along the lonely Atlantic sea lanes could not believe their ears when suddenly they heard a human voice over their sets. A man read from the Bible, then played a phonograph record and a violin. Up to that time, only dots and dashes had ever come out of their earphones. It was Reginald A. Fessenden broadcasting from an experimental station near Boston. He used a telephone mouthpiece as a "microphone" and a special alternator to generate his radio waves. The dot-dash receivers were able to detect his complex signals.

It was Lee De Forest who brought the radio into its own in 1906 by inventing the *audion*, a three-element vacuum tube, which allowed much more sophisticated circuits and applications. De Forest's tube made amplification of radio signals possible. This, in turn, permitted the development of small reliable receivers. As a result, portable radio transmitters and receivers about the size of a bread box played important roles in World War I. By 1918, radio communication had advanced sufficiently for a pilot to receive and transmit from an airplane to people on the ground. Basically, however, radio at this time was either the older dot-dash wireless system introduced by Marconi or a laboratory device used for experimental purposes. It was by no means something that people used at home to listen to scheduled broadcasts. In other words, it was a private rather than a public medium.

Nevertheless, radio captured the imagination of the public in the early days. It seemed like a scientific marvel at the cutting edge of new technology. People had the same fascination with it that later generations would have with early space vehicles. For example, when ships got into trouble, it was possible to summon aid by radio. One of the first such cases occurred in 1898, when radio signals were used to bring aid to a vessel in difficulty. But a really dramatic rescue at sea took place in 1909. When the _SS Republic_ began to sink off New York, the wireless operator sent out a distress signal. Other ships detected it and came as quickly as possible to the position indicated. All the passengers were rescued. It made newspaper headlines, and the public was enthralled.

A historic rescue effort in 1912 was less successful. When the "unsinkable" _Titanic_ struck an iceberg in the North Atlantic, the wireless operator tried to alert nearby ships, but their radio crews had gone to bed for the night. However, he was able to make contact with a shore station (in Wanamaker's department store in New York City), whose stronger signal could reach more distant points. The young operator, David Sarnoff, stayed at his post for many hours, making contact with other vessels. Unfortunately, by the time those ships arrived the next morning, the great passenger liner had gone to the bottom. Some 1,500 people drowned, including the _Titanic's_ heroic wireless operator, who tried all night to summon aid until he went down with the ship.

The Development of Radio as a Mass Medium

In increasing numbers, amateur radio fans were attracted to the medium after World War I. Although assembled sets could be purchased, they were expensive; so thousands bought parts and put together their own receivers. Plans for radio receivers called crystal sets appeared in popular magazines aimed at the home mechanic and tinkerer. Companies marketed kits through the mails for crystal sets that even a bright child could put together. With a length of copper wire wrapped around a Quaker Oats box, a device to slide along the resulting coil to "tune" the device, and the right kinds of crystal, battery, earphones, and aerial, the home listener could pick up audible signals. Radio was the scientific wonder of the age, and the public expressed a broad interest in the medium even before regular broadcasting began.

The Period of Transition

Before radio could be a mass medium, it had to make the transition from a long-range, rather cumbersome system for maritime, commercial, and governmental communication to an easy-to-use device that would bring program content to people in their homes.[2]

First, radio sets had to be small enough for use in the home. In part, the home-built set helped fulfill that need, but many people wanted to purchase their sets ready-made. Second, therefore, the price had to be brought within the means of large numbers of families. Third, there had to be regularly scheduled programs to which people would want to listen. This was a real barrier, because there simply were no stations providing content that would interest most potential listeners. Fourth, reception had to be reasonably clear—that is, without annoying static and overlap between stations. This meant that there had to be a means of regulating the use of the airwaves, either by voluntary agreements or through some government licensing scheme. Not everyone who wanted to broadcast would be able to do so without interfering with others on the same wavelength. Fifth, and perhaps most important of all, there had to be a means of paying for the broadcasts. Although, by today's standards, the transmission equipment itself was not all that expensive, space had to be provided to house the station, which brought attendant costs of heat, light, rent, and so forth. Also, salaries had to be paid to engineers, to people who said things over the air, and even to janitors who cleaned up.

Within a few years, all of these barriers were overcome, and the transition to a true mass medium took place very quickly. In 1916, David Sarnoff (who played a part in trying to summon aid for the *Titanic*) went to work for the American Marconi Company. He wrote a now famous memorandum to his boss that outlined the way in which radio could become a medium for home use:

> I have in mind a plan of development which would make radio a "household utility" in the same sense as a piano or phonograph. The idea is to bring music into the house by wireless. . . . The receiver can be designed in the form of a simple "Radio Music Box" and arranged for several different wave lengths, which should be changeable with the throwing of a single switch or pressing of a single button.
>
> The "Radio Music Box" can be supplied with amplifying tubes and a loud-speaking telephone, all of which can be neatly mounted in one box. The box can be placed on a table in the parlor or living room, the switch set accordingly and the transmitted music received.[3]

Sarnoff went on in his memo to suggest that people listening at home could receive news, sports scores, lectures, weather reports, and concerts. He also suggested that such machines could be manufactured and sold by the thousands. All his scheme needed was the addition of advertising as a source of financial support for regularly scheduled broadcasts and government control over frequency allocation. Those would have made it a very accurate description of the future of radio as a mass medium. Sarnoff's proposal was rejected by his superiors as impractical and too visionary. However, by 1919, he had become the commercial manager of a new company called the Radio Corporation of America (RCA), and he played a major role in bringing radio to the public.

Scheduled programs begin   The broadcasting of regularly scheduled programs over the airwaves did not begin in all parts of the country at the same time. A sort of amateur version of such broadcasts started in Pittsburgh in April 1920. An engineer, Dr. Frank Conrad, was developing transmitting systems for the Westinghouse Corporation. He needed to test equipment after hours, so he built a transmitter over his garage at home. It was licensed as station 8XK, and with the help of his family, Conrad began making regular broadcasts two evenings a week. People sent him postcards and called on the telephone requesting particular musical selections. This feedback from the audience enabled Conrad to discover the reach of the signal.

Westinghouse, seeing the growing public interest in home radio in 1920 and intrigued by Conrad's example, decided to establish a radio station to produce regularly scheduled broadcasts in the Pittsburgh area. The idea was to provide programming for people who bought the home receivers that Westinghouse was manufacturing and selling. The firm built a transmitter in a tin shack on top of its building in Pittsburgh and licensed it as radio station KDKA. To dramatize the establishment of the station, Westinghouse announced that for the first broadcast it would transmit the returns of the 1920 presidential election (Harding versus Cox). Actually, the station received its election information from a local newspaper by phone. Nevertheless, several hundred people with sets in the Pittsburgh area learned from signals sent over the evening sky that Harding had won, and the event was a dramatic success, greatly stimulating the sale of receivers. The station continued to broadcast during the year, presenting music, religious services, sports information, political talks, and even market reports. Its signal carried over a long distance, and people in many parts of the country tuned in. Station KDKA is still on the air and is recognized as the oldest commercial radio station in continuous operation in the nation.

On November 2, 1920, KDKA became the nation's first commercial radio station to begin continuous scheduled operation. Its first broadcast consisted of news about the Harding-Cox presidential election. A running account of the returns was phoned in from a newspaper office and read over the air. Between announcements, banjo music was played. (Courtesy KDKA Radio 1020, Westinghouse Broadcasting, Inc.)

Within months, dozens of other stations went on the air in various cities. Soon there were hundreds, and the infant mass medium became a chaotic mess. Transmitters were paid for and operated by just about anyone who wanted to transmit messages, including department stores, wealthy individuals, automobile dealers, corporations, churches, schools, and, of course, manufacturers of radio equipment. By the end of 1922, some 254 federal licenses had been issued for transmitters that complied with the provisions of the Radio Act of 1912. By 1923, dozens were going on the air every month. About six hundred were broadcasting by the end of the year. There simply were not enough locations on the frequency spectrum to accommodate everyone. Each position had at least one and sometimes several stations. Furthermore, the system for broadcasting that was in use could carry over very long distances, especially at night. People trying to listen to a local station would at the same time hear a jumble of broadcasts from other parts of the country.

Regulating the airwaves Since radio transmissions respect no national boundaries, it was clear from the beginning that international agreements of some sort were needed to maintain order on the airwaves. An international structure designed to regulate telecommunications already existed, long before radio was developed. It was the International Telegraphic Convention, organized in 1865 by twenty-five European countries to work out agreements on telegraphic and cable operations. It was quite successful and provided a model that by extension could be used to forge agreements on radio broadcasting.

The first conference devoted specifically to radio was held in Berlin in 1903, and important rules were agreed upon. For one thing, it was decided that humanitarian and emergency uses of the medium would get the highest priority. Thus, when ships needed aid or during other emergencies, commercial interests were to be set aside. In 1906, a second Berlin Convention set forth further restrictions and rules on international and maritime broadcasting.[4] However, all of this had nothing to do with home radio.

The U.S. Congress confirmed these international rules in the Radio Act of 1912, which replaced a number of earlier attempts to develop regulations suitable for radio. One feature of the 1912 Act was that it provided for licensing of transmitters. However, as it turned out, that feature failed to solve enormous and unanticipated problems in the development of a home radio industry. Although it required citizens to obtain a license to operate a transmitter, it provided no way for the government (actually the Secretary of Commerce, who was head of the licensing agency) to turn anyone down. Furthermore, it established no criteria for the operation of a new transmitter, such as a broadcasting frequency, power, and time on the air.

Since the 1912 legislation did not prescribe a frequency for a new station, its owner could choose the one that he or she preferred. If several operators decided to use the same frequency, as often happened, interference and overlap increased. Some stations solved the problem by agreeing informally to broadcast only on certain days or hours. Others, less cooperative, simply increased their power sharply to blast competing stations off the air. There was some experimentation with networks, with several stations sending signals on the same frequency. However, none of these solutions were effective.

As more and more stations began transmitting, the overlapping of frequencies and broadcast hours finally made it virtually impossible to tune in any clear signal. Many signals were lost in a chaos of noise. The chaos first brought the establishment of new stations to a halt, then sharply reversed the growth trend. Hundreds of stations simply went off the air and never returned .[5] They had no way of recovering their costs.

Obviously, some sort of tight government control was needed to make the system work. However, the federal government was very reluctant to try to control the new medium. It was still a time when Americans looked on government regulation of anything as unwanted interference. Decades earlier, Congress had shied away from taking over the telegraph, and it was not about to step in and be charged with trying to limit free speech through control of the airwaves.

The Secretary of Commerce at the time was Herbert Hoover. He tried to assign frequencies to new stations on an informal basis as licenses were granted, and it did seem to help for a while. However, the courts decided in 1926 that his agency lacked the legal power to do even that. The chaos that had prevailed earlier started to return and again threatened to ruin the fledgling industry.

Finally, Congress stepped in, held lengthy conferences and hearings, and provided new legislation—the Radio Act of 1927. This act established a very important principle: *The airwaves belonged to the people.* Thus, the government had the right to regulate their use in the public interest. The Radio Act of 1927 temporarily gave the government new authority to regulate virtually all technical aspects of broadcasting. The act provided for a Federal Radio Commission (FRC) with broad new powers. In particular, the rules for licensing became very stringent, and those who wanted to transmit had to agree to do so on assigned frequencies, at specified power levels, and at scheduled times. Even though the 1927 act brought strong and effective controls to the medium, it was applauded by the industry, which had been totally unable to regulate itself.

The Radio Act of 1927 prevailed during the new mass medium's early years of growth and development. Within a few years, it was replaced by the Federal Communications Act of 1934, complex legislation administered by a permanent Federal Communications Commission (FCC) that could oversee licensing and issue rules as needed. The 1934 act remains the legislative foundation governing the broadcast industries, as well as all other forms of radio transmission in the United States.

Establishing the Economic Base of the New Medium

Radio was so new that no one was sure how to pay for the costs of transmitting or how to make a profit from the broadcasts. Each of the other media available at the time—newspapers, magazines, the movies, and even the telegraph system—paid their way and made money. And there seemed to be a number of alternatives.

Paying for the broadcasts   At first, the costs of acquiring and operating a transmitter were not great. For about $3,000 one could set up a station and start broadcasting. Operating expenses ran about $2,000 a year. Almost immediately, however, expensive, technically trained personnel and greater transmitter power were needed. Costs began to escalate. How to recoup those costs was an important question.

Clearly, operation by the government was one possible answer. That was the solution settled on by many societies in different parts of the world. In such a system, radio and television are operated by government bureaucrats and the content of the media is rigidly controlled. In the United States, however, few citizens wanted that kind of arrangement. The basic values of democracy conflict with government intervention in the flow of information. Therefore, such a system was never seriously considered.

Some visionaries thought it would be best to use a subscription system, which meant that each owner of a radio receiver would have to get an annual license to operate it and pay a fee that would support the programming. Although that system was adopted in Great Britain, it was never seriously attempted in the United States.

One system that was tried (by AT&T) was the common carrier approach. The principle here was similar to providing a truck or train line to carry whatever goods people might want transported and delivered. Applied to broadcasting, the transmitter was to be leased to whoever wanted to go on the air to broadcast whatever content they prepared. There were not enough takers, and the idea was abandoned.

Another possibility was the endowment idea. Rich philanthropists would be invited to endow stations with large money gifts, and then the stations could use the earnings on investments to pay the costs of broadcasting. That system had worked well in funding universities, museums, and libraries. However, no rich philanthropists stepped forward.

Advertising as the source of profit   The challenge, then, was how to make a profit by broadcasting programs to a general public who could tune in and listen for free. About the only obvious possibility was to transmit advertising messages over the air and charge the advertiser for the time, just as newspapers made a profit by presenting such messages in print. However, there was great resistance to the use of the airwaves for advertising, at least at first. Radio seemed to most people to be a wonderful new medium at the forefront of human accomplishment and destined for nobler purposes. To use it for advertising seemed a crass idea. Herbert Hoover strongly opposed it, saying, "It is inconceivable that we should allow so great a possibility for service, for news, for entertainment, and for vital commercial purposes to be drowned in advertising chatter."[6]

**TABLE 6.1
Radio Set Ownership in
the United States,
1920–1994**

Year	Total Number of Households (in thousands)	Households with Sets (in thousands)	Percentage of Households with Sets
1920	24,352	—	—
1922	25,227	60	00.2
1925	26,528	2,750	10.4
1930	29,905	12,049	40.3
1935	31,982	21,456	67.1
1940	34,949	28,048	80.3
1945	37,503	33,100	88.3
1950	43,468	40,411	94.6
1955	47,874	45,302	95.8
1960	52,610	50,193	95.4
1965	57,521	55,200	96.0
1970	62,875	62,000	98.6
1975	71,120	70,124	98.6
1980	80,776	78,600	99.0
1985	86,789	85,921	99.0
1990	93,347	92,800	99.4
1994	(saturation reached)		99.9

Sources: U.S. Bureau of the Census, Historical Statistics of the United States: Colonial Times to 1970 *(Washington, D.C.:1989); U.S. Bureau of the Census,* Statistical Abstract of the United States *(Washington, D.C.: 1994).*

**FIGURE 6.1
The Curve of Adoption
of Household Radio,
1920–1994**

The acquisition of radio sets by American families followed a classic adoption curve after the beginning of regular broadcasts in the l920s. Virtual saturation of households was reached after about mid-century. By the time of World War II, almost every household had at least one radio. Many acquired portable sets, and there were many in automobiles. Miniaturization greatly increased the number of sets owned after about 1960, and the average now exceeds 5.5 sets per household.

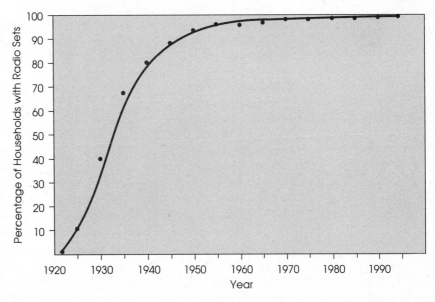

In spite of such early airwave "environmentalists," advertising won over good taste. There simply did not seem to be any alternative solution that could make the medium financially viable. Although scattered uses of advertising over the airwaves had been tried earlier, the system as we know it was initiated by station WEAF in New York, which made the decision to lease time to present advertising promotions. There was no particular limit on the amount of time (the idea of brief commercials sandwiched in between segments of a program would come later). In the summer of 1922, a real estate firm leased a ten-minute segment to extol the virtues of some apartments in New York. It cost the firm $50.

After the idea caught on, advertisers warmed to the idea of becoming regular sponsors of weekly programs. These included dance music, readings of the news and ball scores, and so on. With the number of home-owned receivers growing astronomically (see Table 6.1 and Figure 6.1), it soon became clear that radio was a very important medium by which advertising messages could reach consumers. However, early advertising was very polite and restrained. The initial model was institutional advertising; that is, the corporation sponsoring a particular presentation or program was identified by name, but no information was provided about a specific product that it produced. For example, an advertisement in the early days of radio might have consisted of a dignified voice saying, "This program is sponsored by the XYZ Pharmaceutical Corporation, and we are pleased to present the following program." That was it! Today, advertising messages openly identify a specific product, such as a brand of laxative, and go into grim details about such matters as "constipation," the "softening effects" of the product, the time it takes to "gain relief," and feelings of comfort and joy that result. The public in radio's early days would have been truly horrified by the mention of such matters over the air, and the resulting outcry would have caused the station's license to be withdrawn. Obviously, times and standards of taste have changed.

Acquiring receivers for home use   All during the early 1920s, manufacturers marketed various kinds of sets, and the public eagerly bought as many as could be produced. For several years, demand often outstripped supply. By 1922, an estimated half-million sets were in use. In 1925, that number escalated to about 5 million. By the end of the decade, some 14 million radio receivers were in U.S. homes. (They no longer required batteries and were operated on house current.) In 1926, the National Broadcasting Corporation (NBC, led by David Sarnoff) initiated network broadcasting. The Columbia Broadcasting System (CBS) and others soon followed, and near the end of the decade, people all over the country could simultaneously hear a broadcast of the same radio program.

Thus, in the brief span of a single decade, radio was transformed from a long-distance signaling device serving limited interests into a medium that served an entire nation with broadcasts to home receivers. A great industry had come into existence. It was privately owned, dedicated to making a profit, and linked firmly to the world of commercial advertising. Unlike

By 1925, radios were being manufactured and sold to the public for use at home. The sets were powered by batteries and made use of primitive exponential-horn speakers. They caught on like wildfire, and by the end of the decade radio had become a national medium. (Brown Brothers)

other media, it was regulated to a considerable degree by government, especially in terms of the mechanics of broadcasting. Listening to the radio was rapidly becoming one of everyone's most important leisure-time activities. Marconi's device had truly become a mass medium.

The Golden Age of Radio

During the years between 1930 and the entry of the United States into World War II in December 1941, radio continued to develop into a medium of increasing national and worldwide importance. Following the great conflict, radio enjoyed only five additional years, from 1945 to about 1950, of unchallenged dominance as the nation's major broadcast medium. It then had to meet the challenge of television. Thus, we can identify the fifteen-year period between the mid-1930s and about 1950 as the golden age of radio.

The programs and diversity that we see on television today are contemporary versions of much of what was on radio during its golden age. The medium offered an enormous variety of content. Its comedians became household names and made the nation laugh; it promoted popular dance bands and singers who gained national followings; it presented sports events to which millions of fans listened; it was used by politicians to get elected and to persuade the public to support new programs; it was an important and immediate source of news for huge audiences; it brought a constant flow of fads; it promoted ever-changing dance styles and new forms of popular music; it amused millions of housewives with soap operas during the day. Above all, it sold the nation's goods. Radio's advertising revenues soared to stupendous levels. It was, in short, a great medium that became a significant part of almost everyone's life.

During this period, American society underwent two experiences that had an impact on radio. One was the Great Depression, and the second was World War II. Radio played a special role in each.

Radio during the Great Depression

If ever there was a population in need of free entertainment, it was the people of the United States during the Great Depression of the 1930s. At the depths of the economic collapse, 15 million people, about 20 percent of the labor force, were unemployed in a population numbering about half of what the U.S. population is today. There was no national system of public welfare, no unemployment compensation, and no government programs of public works (all would come later in the 1930s). Farmers could not sell their crops; factories could not sell their goods; many businesses simply shut down and locked out their employees. Mortgages went unpaid; families were evicted from homes and farms. People went without meals, without medical treatment, and even without shoes. Hundreds of thousands of children wandered without adult supervision; hungry people foraged in the streets. Anyone who had a steady job was among society's fortunate, no matter how mean the work.

But people did have radio. It was free in the sense that all one needed to do was plug a box into a socket. It brought comedy broadcasts by such former vaudeville stars as Fred Allen, Jack Benny, Eddie Cantor, and Ed Wynn. Listeners laughed at the antics of "Amos and Andy" (a show with two white actors working in blackface in the old minstrel tradition). They thrilled to the heroism of the Lone Ranger, who brought simple justice to the Old West; they were kept in suspense by The Shadow, a mysterious figure who repelled the forces of evil; they were excited by the airborne adventures of Sky King and the incredible space exploits of Buck Rogers. For those with more rural tastes, there were regular programs of country music. Urbanites probably preferred the dance music of the "big bands," which transmitted live swing music from various hotels and ballrooms. News programs reported the latest policies of the Roosevelt administration and called attention to events overseas, such as the military buildups of Hitler in Germany and Mussolini in Italy. All that did not seem very important to most listeners; few Americans were interested in the political problems of places such as Europe and Japan.

Although one might think that the Depression should have held back the development of the medium, that was not the case. An increasing number of stations came on the air and an ever-growing number of homes purchased radio sets. Advertising revenues grew sharply, from about $40 million per year in 1930, just as the Depression began, to over $112 million in

1935, as it reached bottom. Programming became more and more diversified and sophisticated, attracting a swelling number of listeners. The networks continued to expand and dominate broadcasting.

In the mid-1930s, two things happened that were very important to the future of broadcasting. One was the enactment of the federal legislation we noted earlier (the Federal Communications Act of 1934), with a new government agency (the FCC) to supervise broadcasting in the United States. The other was the development of an entirely different technology for broadcasting called frequency modulation (FM).

Frequency modulation (FM) broadcasting In 1933, a relatively obscure inventor, Edwin Armstrong, developed and patented a new kind of radio signal based on frequency modulation (FM) rather than amplitude modulation (AM). The world took little note because Armstrong did nothing to publicize his innovation. The advantages of the new signal were that it was static-free and it could carry much higher and lower audio frequencies, making it an ideal carrier for music. At first, it seemed that its disadvantage was that at most parts of the frequency spectrum, FM signals are not capable of bending over the horizon. In contrast, AM signals travel upward from the transmitter to the ionosphere where they are reflected back to earth, and they can bounce back and forth between the two far beyond the horizon. Thus, AM can carry signals over very long distances (such as across the Atlantic). The FM signal is different. At very high and ultrahigh frequencies (VHF and

UHF), it simply goes in a straight line in all directions and does not bounce up and down. Since the earth is not flat, such broadcasts cannot be effectively detected beyond the horizon. Furthermore, a big building or mountain that gets in the way of FM signals can garble or even stop them.

These might sound like serious limitations, and for some purposes they were. However, FM turned out to be exactly what was needed as a basic carrier of the audio signals for the new medium of television, with which RCA and other corporations were experimenting. The FM audio carrier was ideal for TV broadcasts because it could confine a signal to a local area and not interfere with other transmitters some distance away, meaning that TV channels could be kept from interfering with each other. The same was true for radio stations that wanted to confine their broadcasts to a local area.

Unfortunately, Armstrong had to fight RCA in the courts when they started using his system for TV broadcasts. His case was ultimately won, but his bitterness and frustration led him to commit suicide some years before the settlement.

Radio and the news   Another great battle fought during the 1930s was over who had proprietary rights to the news. In 1930, Lowell Thomas, who was to become a well-known radio personality, began a trend by reading the news over the air. Frightened by the competition radio was giving them, newspapers tried to stop local stations from using the early editions of papers as the source for their news, claiming that the radio stations were violating copyright laws. But the courts ruled that although the particular expression of a writer can be copyrighted, the factual content of news is in the public domain—thus, no one "owns" the news. The radio stations could broadcast news shows even if they could not afford to hire their own reporters.

As it turned out, radio coverage actually stimulated rather than deterred interest in newspaper reading. The brief news broadcasts and bulletins provided by radio caused people to want to follow up with more detailed accounts in print. Before long, the major networks had developed their own news-gathering operations—a system that still brings us the broadcast news today.

Radio during World War II

Radio became a global news medium as the world was plunging into war. Even before U.S. entry into World War II, reporters around the world were able to transmit live, eye-witness reports on major events by short wave to New York. From there they were picked up by the major networks and relayed over standard frequencies to listeners at home. Americans heard dramatic first-hand accounts from Edward R. Murrow, reporting from London in 1940 during the bombardment by the German air force. Later, such news personalities as Robert Trout, H. V. Kaltenborn, and Elmer Davis used the medium to bring reports and interpretations of the war in Europe.

On Sunday, December 7, 1941, Americans could scarcely believe their ears when they learned by home radio that the Japanese had attacked Pearl Harbor. Japanese bombers devastated the U.S. Pacific Fleet and killed more than two thousand American servicemen and a number of civilians. Radio played a key part in mobilizing the nation. As the war progressed, first-hand news reports came from battlefields in strange places people had never heard of—Guadalcanal, Attu, Anzio, Iwo Jima. Throughout, President Roosevelt calmed the American public with frequent radio talks, reassuring the nation of ultimate victory and setting the goal of "unconditional surrender." Finally, the Allies defeated Germany, and then U.S. atomic bombs forced the Japanese to surrender and the dreadful conflict came to an end. By this time, radio was the unchallenged news medium of America.

The importance of the expansion of radio news to worldwide coverage is that it built the foundation of audience expectations of news on a global basis, which contemporary broadcasters provide. For example, when CNN Headline News presents summaries of what is happening "Around the World in Thirty Minutes" on a 24-hour basis, it is following a tradition that was pioneered by radio broadcasters during the late 1930s and the dark days of World War II.

Radio and the Challenge of Television

After World War II, radio lived on in its glory for roughly five years. But, starting in 1948, TV stations went on the air with regular broadcasts. Early in that first year, only seventeen stations were in operation. Before the end of the year, however, the number more than doubled (to forty-eight). Sales of TV sets increased 500 percent, and the audience for TV broadcasts grew at an astounding 4,000 percent in only two years! Coaxial cables began to connect communities, and the same networks that had fostered radio enthusiastically developed the new medium. No one in radio knew quite what to do. Many radio executives announced that television was only a fad and that audiences would remain loyal to the original broadcast medium that had served them so well.

Then, as we will see in Chapter 7, beginning in 1948, the FCC imposed a freeze on granting new licenses for TV broadcasting stations. The freeze was to last until 1952, and by its end, some 17 million TV sets were in use. After it was lifted, the number grew astronomically.

Radio was in deep trouble. In fact, it was in danger of disappearing as a mass medium. Profits dropped, and radio audiences melted away as talent and interest switched to television. Radio might have died completely had it not been for its resourceful response to the challenge of television. At first, the medium tightened its belt and took on advertising accounts that could not afford costly TV commercials. Then it made changes across the board that permitted it to survive on a more permanent basis.

The major form of adaptation was that the content of radio broadcasts changed sharply. Out went the well-developed radio drama, the soap opera,

RADIO AND THE MOBILIZATION OF AMERICA IN WORLD WAR II:
A Linchpin to the Sociology of Public Opinion

In 1941, the United States was a relatively isolated society separated by vast oceans from troubled Europe and Asia, where wars were already in progress. The nation was also isolated in terms of public opinion about foreign affairs. Americans were preoccupied with their own internal problems that had been created by the Great Depression of the 1930s. The United States had not yet played a major role as a world power in the sense that it does today.

As the year went on, Americans remained sharply divided in their thinking about the nation's foreign policy. Some people thought that we should help the British and others in their fight against Nazi Germany. Many others were convinced that we should follow George Washington's advice and stay out of foreign entanglements. Still others, by far in the majority, knew little and cared less about foreign affairs of any kind. These were the working people who had less contact with news from abroad and whose deepest concerns were with making a living in difficult times. Most were still suffering lingering effects of the Depression.

On Sunday, December 7, 1941, everything suddenly changed. That morning over 250 carrier-based airplanes of the Empire of Japan swooped down on Pearl Harbor, near Honolulu, and repeatedly bombed the U.S. Pacific Fleet. The surprise attack, which lasted for over two hours, had a deadly effect. Most of the U.S. warships in the harbor were either sunk or so badly damaged that they would be useless for months. More than 2,200 American servicemen were killed, plus many civilians.

The news came swiftly, simultaneously, and directly to American homes in every farm, town, and city. It came via radio, a medium that had been in widespread use for only about fifteen years, and whose worldwide news-gathering and distributing systems had barely reached maturity. It was the existence

the quiz program, and other amusement fare that had been the mainstay of radio entertainment. All of that type of programming could now be heard and seen on television. In came the disc jockey, continuous music, frequent spot news, weather reports, and call-in talk shows. For the most part, radio ceased to be a national medium. Network-type programming decreased, and radio became a medium providing services to local rather than national audiences. In effect, then, radio drastically changed its functions. It gave more emphasis to news summaries, music, and talk, and less attention to its earlier forms of entertainment. In this way, radio survived as an intimate and community-oriented medium.

One additional set of changes that influenced radio (as well as television) was the development of public broadcasting. As early as 1941, the FCC had reserved a number of FM channels for "noncommercial" use. In effect, this meant "educational" broadcasting. However, Congress provided no funding for such programming. A number of small radio stations eked out an existence with support from churches, colleges, and universities. Some lived on public funds, some on donations or foundation support. In 1967, however,

and functioning of that radio news system that played a key part in shaping the response that Americans made to the Japanese attack. It provided for a massive restructuring of U.S. public opinion about involvement in war.

For the first few hours, the nation was in shock. By the next day, outrage became evident. Almost every citizen who had access to a radio heard President Franklin D. Roosevelt declare to a joint meeting of Congress that "December seventh, 1941, is a date that will live in infamy." Not a single citizen disputed that claim, and the entire nation cheered when Roosevelt formally declared that "a state of war exists" between the United States and both Japan and Germany.

During the days that followed, a new and unifying public opinion swept through the nation. Recruiting offices were overwhelmed. In many cities, fistfights broke out in lines where young men were trying to enlist ahead of others. During the war years, more than 15 million U.S. citizens donned the uniforms of their country. Millions more worked in war industries,

and still other millions made sacrifices at home to hasten victory.

The most remarkable feature of the early days of the war was the rapidity with which members of the public received the news, came to define the war as a noble purpose, and willingly altered their lives in major ways to contribute to the joint effort. The unprovoked nature of the Pearl Harbor attack was, of course, a major factor in determining attitudes toward the war. However, the existence of the radio network as an almost instantaneous news medium unified a divided nation into one that saw the war as a great moral cause. At no other time in history has any medium of communication played such a significant part in transforming the public opinion and behavior of an entire nation.

Sources: Mitchell Stephens, *A History of the News: From the Drum to the Satellite* (New York: Viking Penguin, 1988), p. 278; Tom Lewis, *Empire of the Air: The Men Who Made Radio* (New York: Harper Collins, 1991); and Christopher H. Sterling and John Kittross, *Stay Tuned: A Concise History of American Broadcasting*, 2nd ed. (Belmont, Calif.: Wadsworth, 1990).

Congress passed the Public Broadcasting Act, creating the Corporation for Public Broadcasting (CPB), serving both radio and television. It was not really a corporation in the sense of a profit-oriented business, and it was not exactly an arm of the government. It was set up as an independent, nonprofit organization that receives federal funds and allocates them to local stations within networks. The radio part of the CPB package is National Public Radio (NPR), which not only links radio stations into a network, but also produces various kinds of noncommercial programming for broadcasts. Today, there are about two hundred FM radio stations in the NPR system. They all produce some programs and make at least some use of the nationally produced material. Such stations also solicit local donations and sponsors. For the many people who tire of regular AM or FM stations—with their continuous broadcasts of rock 'n' roll, country-western, or classical music and frequent commercial advertising—NPR is a pleasant relief. The nationally produced content is heavy on news, public affairs analyses, and information about music, theater, and the arts. There is even some attention to sports.

Radio adapted to the development of television during the 1950s by changing the kind of programming it delivered. It is a medium that does not demand the level of concentrated attention required by print or television, thus allowing people to drive, jog, sunbathe, or do any of a number of other things while listening. Popular music plays a dominant role, appealing largely to younger listeners. However, AM and FM programming includes fare for other segments of the American audience, including news, talk shows, and classical music. Because of these features, radio will probably survive as a medium. (Spencer Grant/Photo Researchers, Inc.)

In its various formats, radio is surviving the challenge of television. FM broadcasting has been growing and now accounts for more than half of the radio stations operating in the United States. FM stations tend to present less news, more oldies, low-key background-type music, and classical music. NPR is thriving, with a small but dedicated following. In contrast, AM radio tends to be more oriented toward faster-paced popular music and talk shows, with some news summaries.

Radio as a Contemporary Medium

Radio continues in the 1990s to be the most widely attended to medium of communication in the United States. A total of 11,334 radio stations stretch across the country, with numerous signals reaching every community and neighborhood.[7] Studies show that 96 percent of the population over age twelve listens to the radio during an average week. This compares favorably to television viewing (90 percent) and newspaper reading (76 percent). Among the reasons why so many people listen is that radio is the most portable of the broadcast media, being accessible at home, in the office, in the car, on the street or beach, virtually everywhere at any time. Because listening is so widespread, radio has prospered as an advertising medium. Radio stations reach local rather than national audiences and are thus attractive to merchants who want to advertise their wares and services to people in their community. Furthermore, radio serves small, highly targeted audiences, which makes it an excellent advertising medium for many kinds of specialized products and services. As we explained for magazines (Chapter 4), this feature appeals to advertisers, who realize it would be inefficient and prohibitively expensive to tout a special-interest product to the heterogeneous audiences drawn to nationally popular entertainment programs.

Radio's Survival as an Industry

Between 10 and 11 percent of all money spent on media advertising in the United States goes to radio. This percentage has remained quite stable for more than a decade, which has meant substantial growth in actual dollars brought in by radio. In 1977, for example, total radio advertising amounted to about $2.6 billion per year. By 1993, it was $9.6 billion—representing more than a threefold increase.[8] Industry analysts predict that it will exceed $11 billion by 1996. According to Veronis, Suhler & Associates' 1994 *Communications Industry Forecast,* this growth has exceeded that of the overall economy, reflecting the radio industry's robust progress.[9] Surveys show that radio gets about 75 percent of its revenues from local advertising, about 24 percent from national advertising, and a tiny sliver (around 1 percent) from network compensation.

What accounts for radio's renewed economic success? Experts say it is the high cost of commercial television time, which is still prohibitive for many local advertisers who can afford radio's more reasonable ad rates. Another key factor may be the emergence of remote control devices and VCRs, which allow viewers to avoid watching TV commercials and are cutting the effectiveness of television advertising. The radio audience, on the other hand, is more captive, not able to tune out commercials easily. In addition, the advertising sales forces for radio stations offer a good deal of assistance to local advertisers in preparing their spots for broadcasting. It is thought that radio's ability to attract local advertisers hurts mainly newspapers, since television is less attractive to the small, local advertiser.

Radio's changing formats Today's radio stations offer their listeners a complex mix of formats. Some stations specialize in a particular form of music—classical, country, Dixieland, classic jazz, rock, new age, or folk. These musical offerings have loyal followings. Similarly, there is a good deal of talk radio, with many kinds of interviewers having different styles. Talk shows offer programming for personal problems, auto repairs, financial matters, handling pets, and even plant care. NBC radio's "Talknet," for example, offers its listeners advice and instruction on these topics and more, throughout the day and night. Conservative commentary is offered nationally by Rush Limbaugh on ABC radio from WABC in New York.

Local radio stations determine just what their formats will be, usually based on how they have fared in comparative industry audience ratings. However, they get their programming from a variety of national and regional radio networks, some of which own their own stations. The programming services these networks supply are paid for indirectly by national advertisers.

Of course, a good many radio stations have a mixed format, with music, news, sports, and advertising as well as some commentaries. Such stations mix and match network sources and features with their own locally originated programming, which often involves a disk jockey playing popular music. Furthermore, radio stations are forever changing their formats, tinkering with the mix of programming they offer and sometimes making sudden radical changes from classical to rock or easy-listening tunes, much to the consternation of their loyal listeners.

Radio also serves many ethnic communities. There are Spanish-language, Native American, and African-American radio stations (and even a national African-American network), as well as stations that feature programming in Greek, Irish, Scandinavian, Chinese, Japanese, and other languages. (Cable television, too, serves widely as a medium for ethnic programming, but radio is cheaper to produce than cable.)

Public radio, especially NPR, mentioned earlier, and other forms of noncommercial broadcasting provide important services and typically reach a large, upscale market, especially in university communities. Many noncommercial stations are owned by educational institutions, religious organizations, cities and towns, and other groups. However, most U.S. radio, like

Radio talk shows have become enormously popular, delivering information about everything from politics to health care. Talk show personalities, or hosts, constantly seek new audiences by focusing on such matters as car repair, investment tips, and child care. Some such as Rush Limbaugh, shown here, have attracted large and loyal followings. (AP/Wide World Photos)

U.S. television, consists of commercial stations that rely on advertising sales to stay on the air.

The shift to FM listening As the history of radio recounted earlier in this chapter indicates, radio technology has not stood still. In recent years, however, the changes have been rather subtle. The quality of radio sound has probably been the greatest single influence in the changing fortunes of AM and FM radio stations in the United States. Because of AM signals' great power and range, the nation's seven most dominant individual stations are AM broadcasters. However, even though AM signals have always had the advantage of reaching across vast distances, FM signals are free of static and thus provide better listening quality to a limited geographic area. With the growth of FM stereo broadcasting, audiences over the years have steadily switched to FM stations. In 1973, about 70 percent of the radio audience in the United States tuned in to AM, with about 30 percent listening to FM. By 1993, the situation had totally reversed, with only 22 percent of listeners in the AM column, while FM claimed 78 percent. These figures have considerable meaning because they are the basis for advertising revenues, profits, and even the value of individual radio stations.

According to *Broadcasting* magazine the survival of AM radio will require an all-out effort by station owners and their personnel. For AM stations, the problem seems to be that today's adults who grew up listening to teen-oriented music on FM stations have not changed to AM, as has been the trend in the past. Listening to AM radio does still have an advantage in the car, however, especially if one is driving more than twenty-five miles and traveling outside of a central city.

The Future of Radio

Today, radio is prospering. As we have noted, it still commands the largest cumulative audiences in the United States, and it is gaining strength. As cable television and VCR usage intrude on the efficiency of television, local advertisers are turning to radio. If revenues from local advertising continue to increase, the worth of radio stations will increase, and this will help their prospects for future profitability. It is hard to say how far this trend will extend into the future. However, radio has proved itself a versatile medium, one that supplies a good deal of information and entertainment, some opinion, and effective local advertising. It will probably continue to readjust and recalibrate itself as audience tastes and interests change. Like all media today, radio is sometimes owned by medium-specific companies (that have mostly radio properties). Increasingly, however, stations are being purchased by large media companies that are likely to own newspapers, magazines, TV stations, databases, and other communication enterprises. Radio continues to have a market niche due to both its command of audiences and its ability to sell advertising and generate other revenues.[10]

Chapter Review

- Radio developed as a logical extension of the electric telegraph, which became a reality in the 1840s. Reliable electric telegraphy was not possible until after the invention of the electromagnet, which was at the heart of the system developed by Samuel F. B. Morse.

- When Morse sent his famous message, "What hath God wrought?" between Baltimore and Washington, D.C., the speed with which information could move increased from that of a train or a carrier pigeon to that of lightning. It was a truly startling advance.

- Radio shares its early history with the telegraph. The wireless represented the achievement of an ancient dream of conquering both time and distance to communicate quickly without wires. The first wireless patent went to Guglielmo Marconi, who spanned the Atlantic Ocean with a wireless telegraph message in 1901.

- The new form of telegraphy was an enormously useful device for communicating with ships at sea and with far-flung business, military, and diplomatic enterprises around the globe. Radio took on an aura of glamour very early when it played a critical role in rescue efforts at sea. Although it would be many years before it would even start to become a household communications medium, it quickly gained a large and enthusiastic following in the population.

- Under existing legislation during the early 1920s, virtually anyone could obtain a license, build a relatively inexpensive transmitter, and go on the air. Hundreds did just that. Soon, the airways were cluttered with conflicting signals. With considerable reluctance, Congress passed the Radio Act of 1927 and then the Federal Communications Act of 1934, which brought radio broadcasting under the technical control of the federal government.

- An important problem that had to be solved before radio could become a household medium was how to pay for the broadcasts. After several alternatives were considered, the answer came in the form of selling air time to advertisers—a close parallel to selling space to advertisers in the print media. This permitted the development of sponsored shows, regularly scheduled broadcasts, and a star system.

- The golden age of radio lasted from the 1930s, after the medium had matured, until it was almost displaced by television during the early 1950s. Many important features developed during the period, including worldwide radio news, FM broadcasting, and the ultimate adjustment of radio to its current format and style.

- As a contemporary medium, radio is surviving, largely as a local medium. Listening is widespread, and radio captures about 10 percent of the nation's expenditures for media advertising. Its content ranges from various kinds of music through talk shows, news, and sports. The majority of listeners today tune in to FM stations.

- Radio's future seems secure. It has worked out its own niche in the system of mass communication. It is a flexible medium capable of responding to changes that may come in the future. At present, in financial terms, radio is enjoying a period of relative prosperity.

Notes and References

1. John Baptista Porta (or Giovanni Battista della Porta), *Natural Magik* (New York: Smithsonian Institute for Basic Books, 1957). This is a modern reprint of a book first printed in the late sixteenth century, just after the invention of the press.
2. The details of the history of radio presented in these sections are a summary of several

chapters devoted to a more extended treatment of the subject in Melvin L. DeFleur, *Theories of Mass Communication*, 1st ed. (New York: McKay, 1966), pp. 44–69.

3. Gleason L. Archer, *History of Radio to 1926* (New York: American Historical Society, 1938), pp. 112–113.

4. For an excellent discussion of these early developments (from which the authors have drawn many insights), see Sydney W. Head and Christopher H. Sterling, *Broadcasting in America*, 5th ed. (Boston: Houghton Mifflin, 1987), pp. 62–65, 435–499.

5. For the most thorough and contemporary discussion currently available of the entire broadcasting industry and the details of its development, see Head and Sterling. The present chapter incorporates many insights from this classic work.

6. Alfred G. Goldsmith and Austin C. Lescarboura, *This Thing Called Broadcasting* (New York: Holt, 1930), p. 279.

7. *Broadcasting Magazine*, February 22, 1993.

8. Radio Advertising Bureau, 1994.

9. *Communications Industry Forecast* (New York: Veronis, Suhler & Associates, 1994).

10. For an extensive contemporary review of the medium, see "Radio: The Forgotten Medium," *Media Studies Journal*, Summer 1993.

Television: The Most Popular Medium

A welter of media
developments
surrounded and
confronted the
television world: cable
systems, satellites,
cassettes, videodiscs,
lasers, optical-fiber
technology—all with
the potential for
hugely expanded
communication systems,
new transmitters of
the culture. Their
implications were a
vast uncertainty.

Eric Barnouw, *Tube of Plenty*,
1975

elevision was born in controversy, and it remains controversial today. The controversy began with claims to its invention. Following World War I, scientists in various parts of the world—England, Japan, Russia, and the United States—began experimenting with the idea of sending visual signals over the air using radio waves. (Thus, several nations now maintain that television was invented by citizens of their country.) Although the early technology may not have been exclusively American, there is little doubt that in the United States, within a very brief period, television was transformed from a scientific phenomenon into an enormously popular mass medium. It began as an experimental electronic technology in the late 1920s and became a fledgling broadcast medium during the late 1930s. Its development was temporarily halted during World War II, but by the end of the 1940s, it was poised to sweep through society as a mass medium for home use. During the 1950s, it did just that.[1]

During its brief history, television has been a remarkably volatile medium. Its technology has steadily changed; its content has constantly evolved; its audiences have grown; and its critics have continued a flow of condemnation denouncing its presumed effects. In spite of all of that, it quickly became and remains Americans' favorite medium.

At first, the typical home receiver offered a small black-and-white picture hardly larger than a wallet. It was of poor quality by today's standards, but people were fascinated with the idea that moving pictures could be broadcast over the air and into the home. Even the commercials seemed interesting, because they *moved*. Before long, however, the novelty wore off—audiences became more selective and demanding. They wanted clearer pictures, and then color, and then larger screens, and then greater control over what they viewed.

As new technologies arrived to satisfy these wishes, Americans quickly adopted them. Screens grew much larger than the early versions. Better transmitters and receivers made the picture more stable. Color made television more pleasurable to watch. Cable hookups brought greater choices of programs. VCRs transformed the TV set into a little movie screen in the living room. Hand-held remote controls, routinely supplied with new sets, enabled audiences to excise ruthlessly the bothersome commercials sandwiched between segments of programs. As we will see, that upset advertisers, who started to turn to alternative media. That move reduced the earnings of the networks, eroded the income of advertising agencies, and generally threw the whole television industry into turmoil. It remains in a condition of "vast uncertainty" today.[2]

The Birth of Television

The history of television goes a lot further back than many people suppose. In fact, in 1884, a German experimenter, Paul Nipkow, developed a rotating disk with small holes arranged in a spiral pattern that, when used with a light source, had unusual properties. Aiming a strong light at the disk so that light passed through the holes produced a very rapid "scanning" effect. That is, pinpoints of light came through the holes in the whirling disk and across from left to right or right to left, depending on whether the disk was whirling clockwise or counterclockwise, in a pattern that was somewhat like the movements a human eye makes while scanning across a page. It was realized quite early that the perforated whirling disk could produce electrical impulses that could be sent along a wire so as to transmit pictures. The *Nipkow disk* became the central technology for further experimentation on the transmission of images, both by wire and later by radio waves. Its scanning concept is at the heart of television, even today, although it is accomplished by electronic means rather than by a mechanical disk.[3]

Although the scanning disk was unique to early experiments with television, the entire histories of radio and television are closely intertwined. All the inventions and technologies that made radio broadcasting possible are also part of the history of television. In addition, the social and economic organization of the industry was already set before television became a reality. The medium is supported by advertising. That was never an issue. It is governed by the Federal Communications Commission (FCC). That, too, was never an issue. Its content is an extension of that developed in radio. The three major television networks were radio networks first, and the same companies that pioneered commercial radio broadcasting also developed television.

Early in the 1920s, such corporations as General Electric and RCA allocated budgets for experiments with television, and other corporations soon followed. The idea seemed far-fetched and futuristic to many, but the research was authorized in the hope that it would eventually pay off. General Electric employed an inventor, Ernst Alexanderson, to work exclusively on the problem, and within a short time he had developed a workable system based on

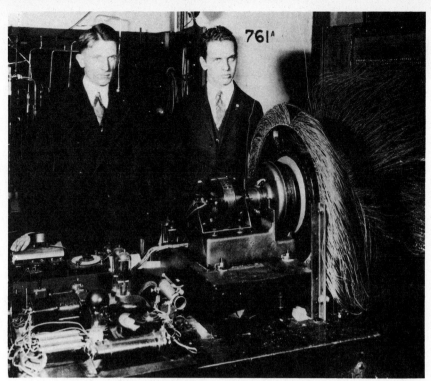

Often the early forms of a new technology are cumbersome, and their output less than impressive. Here, for example, is an experimental television system developed in the mid-1920s. It made use of hundreds of wires connected to different segments of neon-filled tubes. Current flowing from the transmitter through the wires created a pattern of light and dark areas on the tubes, forming a picture such as that of Felix the Cat shown here. A system in this stage of development is obviously not ready for use as a mass medium. (RCA Corporation; Courtesy of AT&T Archives)

the Nipkow disk. However, it was not to be the system that the industry finally adopted. What was needed was a completely electronic system.

Developing an Electronic System

Perhaps the most remarkable of the inventors who played a key role in developing the needed electronic technology was a skinny high school boy in an isolated part of the United States. Philo T. Farnsworth was a poor youngster from a large family in Rigby, Idaho, a small farm community. As a child, he had started reading about electricity, and in 1922, he astounded his high school science teacher by showing him diagrams for electronic circuits that would make it possible to transmit and receive moving pictures over the air.

Farnsworth had studied reports of television experiments that were based on the Nipkow disk. He correctly reasoned that such a system was primitive and clumsy. He had reached the conclusion that electronic devices were needed to sweep across a scene rapidly in a series of horizontal lines, detect points of light and dark along these lines, and transform those variations into signals that could be broadcast over the air. Parallel electronic devices for reception and viewing were also needed. He had come up with designs of circuits for each apparatus and calculations as to how they could function. Farnsworth's teacher enthusiastically encouraged him to try to perfect and patent the system.

During this same period, just after World War I, a talented Russian, Vladimir K. Zworykin, had come to the United States to work on radio research at Westinghouse. He had been a communications specialist in the army of Tsar Nicholas, where he had worked on early television experiments, before the Russian Revolution. He asked for permission to continue development of television at Westinghouse. Directors of the huge corporation thought it was a long shot but decided to finance the work. Like Farnsworth, Zworykin was unimpressed with the mechanical-disk approach and believed that electronic systems were needed for practical television transmission and reception. He set out to work on them with the full facilities of the Westinghouse laboratories.

Meanwhile, as Zworykin was closing in on the solution, a friend of Farnsworth took him to California and provided him with funding for his experiments. There, on a shoestring budget, Farnsworth transformed his circuits and drawings into a working apparatus, which he built in an apartment where he kept the blinds drawn. (The neighbors thought he was a bootlegger running a still, and he was raided by the police.) In 1927, the young man was able to make actual transmissions. He showed his friend how his apparatus could broadcast and receive both fixed images and small scenes from motion pictures.

Having created a working system, Farnsworth took his drawings to federal authorities and applied for the first electronic television patent. His application created an uproar. The great radio corporations, taken completely by surprise, were shocked and outraged that an obscure teenager had invented, built, and asked to patent a system that Westinghouse, RCA, and others had spent fortunes trying to develop and were themselves about to patent. They immediately contested the application.

After a great deal of controversy and legal maneuvering, Farnsworth won. To regain control, RCA haggled with Farnsworth, who held out for a very profitable royalty settlement. Although Farnsworth reached his solution just before Zworykin did, the latter invented some of the most critical components of television technology—the iconoscope (electronic picture tube) and the image orthicon camera, without which television would not have been workable as a mass medium.

The Early Broadcasts

The earliest experimental TV receivers used tiny screens, based on cathode ray tubes about four inches in diameter. Cameras were crude and required intense lighting. People who appeared on the screen had to wear bizarre purple and green make-up to provide contrast for the picture. Nevertheless, in 1927, a picture of Herbert Hoover, then Secretary of Commerce, appeared on an experimental closed circuit demonstration.

By 1932, RCA had built a TV station, complete with studio and transmitting facilities, in New York City's Empire State Building. RCA set aside a million dollars to develop and demonstrate the new broadcast medium. In

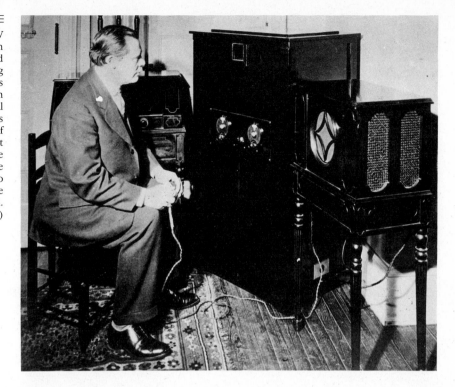

By the end of the 1920s, TV broadcasts were being made on an experimental basis, and receivers somewhat resembling their modern counterparts were being developed with an eye toward an eventual consumer market. In this 1928 version, the screen of the cathode ray tube is about the size of a business card. The speaker is at the right, and the man is using the controls to adjust the picture's quality. The set received only one channel. (The Bettmann Archive)

1936, it began testing the system, broadcasting two programs a week. By that time a few hundred enthusiasts in the New York area had constructed or obtained TV receivers and were able to pick up the transmissions in their homes. Meanwhile, the federal government had developed procedures for awarding licenses to transmitters and had granted a limited number. Thus, by 1940, the medium was set to take off.

Suddenly, the whole world changed. After the Japanese attack on Pearl Harbor in December 1941, the war effort completely monopolized the country's attention. Along with almost every other aspect of American life, the manufacturing of the new TV receivers was temporarily delayed. All the electronics manufacturers turned to producing equipment for the armed forces and did not return to making products for the civilian market until 1945. In the years immediately following the war, however, TV stations were quickly established in a number of major cities, and the public was ready to buy sets. Television was finally ready for home use.

The Period of Rapid Adoption

By 1946, the FCC had issued twenty-four new licenses for TV transmitters. The networks and advertising agencies were eagerly waiting for the new medium to enter American homes. It seemed clear to all concerned that television might become a truly important broadcast medium. There was a great scramble to take part.

The manufacture and sale of home receivers began that same year. As sets became available, Americans rushed to buy them. However, they were quite expensive. In 1947, a set with a picture about six by seven inches cost around $400. That was more than a month's wages for many blue-collar working families, and it did not include the special antenna that had to be installed on the roof. A truly deluxe set, with a fancy wood cabinet and a mirror system for making the picture seem larger, sold for about half as much as a modest car. Obviously, only more affluent families could afford such a luxury, and so a TV set became a new kind of status symbol. Families who had one often invited their envious neighbors in to watch the transmissions (and to see visible evidence of their affluence). Stories circulated of people who put up an antenna to make their neighbors think that they had television, when all they really had was the antenna. In fact, television was regarded as such a luxury that if a family that was receiving welfare was found to have a television set, it was regarded as a moral outrage.

One establishment that could afford a set was the local tavern. By 1948, a TV set was a central feature in almost every tavern in the country. Sports programs were the favorite, and big crowds would gather to watch the games. It is probably no exaggeration to say that the local tavern played a significant role in demonstrating and popularizing the new medium.

Television began to become available as a home medium just after World War II. Sets were expensive and had high value as status symbols. This deluxe "big screen" model cost about half as much as the average new car in 1949. Screens were still small, but with mirrors they could be made to seem larger. In spite of the high price, the public bought TV receivers as fast as they could be produced. (The Bettmann Archive)

The Big Freeze

By the beginning of 1948, the FCC had issued approximately one hundred licenses. Some cities had two or even three stations, although many still had none. Soon, however, problems developed of the kind that had troubled radio in the early years. The signals of one station sometimes interfered with those of another. This led the FCC to conclude that drastic action was needed to avoid upcoming difficulties. Beginning in 1948 and extending through 1952, the commission ordered a freeze on the issuing of new licenses and construction permits (previously licensed stations were allowed to start up). As a result, TV transmitters could not be built in many American communities until after the freeze was lifted. The FCC wanted to study thoroughly the technical aspects of television and related broadcasting so that it could appropriately allocate frequencies to television, FM radio, and other kinds of transmissions.

During the freeze, the FCC developed a master plan that still governs TV broadcasting today. The system prevents one television station from interfering with the broadcasts of another, thus avoiding the chaos that characterized early radio broadcasting. When the freeze was lifted in 1952, television spread quickly throughout the United States. Within a remarkably short time, it became so ubiquitous that most American families had a set. Social commentators began to speak of the "television generation" of Americans born after World War II who never knew a world without television. The medium is presumed to have shaped their lives in significant ways.

Becoming a Nation of Television Viewers

Table 7.1 and Figure 7.1 show how rapidly the American public adopted television. In 1950, less than 10 percent of American homes had a set. In 1960, only ten years later, nearly 90 percent had a receiver. By 1970, that had risen to more than 95 percent, and by 1980, ownership of sets had virtually reached saturation level in American households. Today, it is very unusual to find a family without a TV set, and most have more than one.

Another index of the popularity of television can be seen in terms of viewing time. Table 7.2 and Figure 7.2 show that the TV set has been in use during an ever-growing number of hours per day for almost four decades. In 1950, those who owned sets had them on four and a half hours daily on average. That number rose sharply year after year to more than seven hours per day in recent years. Today, it is becoming increasingly difficult to determine patterns of television viewing because a TV set can be used in so many ways. One can watch regular broadcasting, cable, and of course, video cassettes. And with multiple sets in about two-thirds of American homes, one person may be watching a broadcast of a ball game, another a soap opera on cable, and still another a movie on a VCR.[4] No matter what the specific time allocations among these various forms are, it is clear that Americans are spending a huge amount of time with their TV sets turned on.

Year	Number of Households with TV (in thousands)	Percentage of Households with TV
1950	3,880	9.0
1952	15,300	34.2
1954	26,000	55.7
1956	34,900	71.8
1958	41,920	83.2
1960	45,750	87.1
1962	48,855	90.0
1964	51,600	92.3
1966	53,850	93.0
1968	56,670	94.6
1970	58,500	95.3
1972	62,100	95.8
1974	55,200	96.9
1976	69,600	97.4
1978	72,900	97.6
1980	76,300	97.9
1982	81,500	98.1
1984	83,800	98.1
1986	85,900	98.1
1988	89,300	98.1
1990	90,680	98.2
1993	93,100	98.3

Sources: Nielsen Media Research; U. S. Bureau of the Census, Statistical Abstract of the United States, 1991, 111th ed. (Washington, D.C., 1991); Television Advertising Bureau, 1992.

FIGURE 7.1
The Curve of Adoption
of Television,
1950–1993

The adoption of television by U.S. households followed a classic adoption curve, although it took place very rapidly by comparison with other media. Television was introduced about 1947, when a limited number of stations went on the air. The big freeze of 1948 to 1952 slowed early adoption slightly. However, as soon as it was lifted, adoption soared as new transmitters went on the air. By 1970, television had reached virtual saturation, with only a few late adopters still holding out.

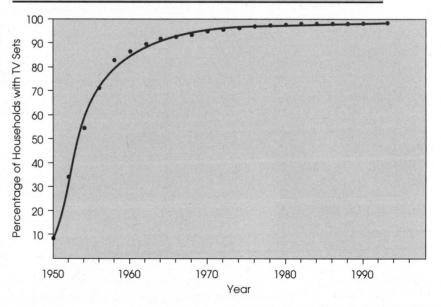

TRENDS IN MEDIA USE

	Average Daily
Year	Time with Set On
1950	4 hrs. 30 min.
1955	4 hrs. 51 min.
1960	5 hrs. 6 min.
1965	5 hrs. 31 min.
1970	5 hrs. 59 min.
1975	6 hrs. 12 min.
1980	6 hrs. 34 min.
1985	7 hrs. 7 min.
1990	7 hrs. 10 min.
1993	7 hrs. 12 min.

**TABLE 7.2
Use of TV Sets in U.S. Households, 1950–1993**

Source: The above figures represent estimates obtained from combining figures from the following: Television Bureau of Advertising, Inc; A. C. Nielsen; Corbet S. Steinberg, TV Facts, 1980; Motion Picture Association of America, 1992–1993.

**FIGURE 7.2
Trends in the Use of TV Sets in U.S. Households, 1950–1993**

For decades, American families increased their daily use of their TV sets. In the early days of television, with a limited number of channels to view, the set was on only about four and a half hours per day on average. As the number of over-the-air and cable channels increased, that average time increased to over seven hours a day, where it has apparently leveled off. However, this does not mean that people always pay close attention to programs. We now know that people do many things—visiting, eating, cooking, tending to children, etc.—with the television on in the

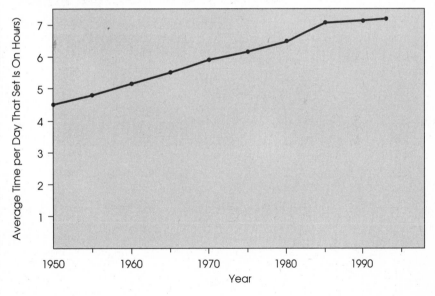

The Coming of Color

Color television got off to a slow start. Experiments had been performed with color test pictures as early as 1929, and there was much talk about commercial broadcasts in color, even as early as 1940. But there were problems in settling on the best technology. By 1946, two separate color systems had been perfected. CBS had developed a system based on a rotating disk that actually gave very good results. However, it had one major problem: The FCC insisted that the system for color transmission be such that existing black-and-white sets could still receive a picture (though not in color), and with the CBS system, they would not be able to do so. In 1953, the FCC approved a different system, developed by RCA. Although it produced less refined colors, it did allow existing black-and-white sets to receive programs.

For a variety of reasons, the networks exercised a great deal of caution in delivering color broadcasts. At first they transmitted only a few programs in color. By 1967, though, most network programs were in color, and even local stations began to produce programs in this mode. As a result, all the black-and-white cameras had to be phased out and new technicians trained. But the industry made the transition to the new technology smoothly. By 1992, some 98.6 percent of U.S. households with a receiver had color television.[5]

Television's Golden Ages

Two different periods can be called the golden age of television. The first is the time when the medium was experiencing its most rapid period of growth—roughly from 1952 to around 1960. The second is a longer period—from about 1960 to around 1980—when network television had few competitors.

Those who identify the earlier period do so not only because of the rapid growth of the medium, but also on the basis of some of the programming. Some point to it as a golden era because of its high-quality dramatic programs, such as "Playhouse 90." These appealed to more sophisticated viewers. Others note that it was a time when family situation comedies, sports, and variety-vaudeville shows were new features of home viewing that had very wide appeal. Among the latter, Milton Berle's "Texaco Star Theater" and Ed Sullivan's "Toast of the Town" are often cited as examples of how great television programs were in those "good old days." Among the performers often identified as among the "greats" of the period are Sid Caesar and the late Jackie Gleason. Today, the long-running series "I Love Lucy" (starring the late Lucille Ball) is routinely mentioned as a classic. Many younger people who view these programs today are at a loss to understand the glowing classifications. To them the early shows can seem naive and even dull. Whether the programming of the period should be regarded as simple slapstick, as art, or as just mindless and trivial pop culture of a particular era could be debated endlessly.

On other grounds, the two decades between 1960 and about 1980 can be regarded as a different kind of golden age of television. It may not have been so in some ideal sense of audience satisfaction or in terms of classic programming. On the contrary, the public at the time showed many signs of frustration and dissatisfaction with the medium. The period was one of turmoil in American society, beset by such issues as civil rights, the Vietnam

War, and increasing crime and violence. Many blamed television for social ills, believing it to be a powerful medium that was eroding the moral standards and stability of the nation. As we will see later, such charges generated a great deal of interest in the effects of television.

The same two decades constituted a time when the medium was dominated by three major networks that had virtually no other competition, whose profit margins were very high from advertising revenue, and who had the attention of virtually the entire viewing audience during prime time. Cable had yet to spread to more than a small proportion of American households, and there were no VCRs for home use. The networks were competitive, but the three of them almost totally dominated the medium. If one wanted to watch television during this period, there were very few alternatives to viewing network programming. A small proportion of Americans did view programs on educational stations and the Public Broadcasting Service (PBS, the television arm of the Corporation for Public Broadcasting, which was set up in 1970), but they had to do so in inconvenient ways on UHF channels. Thus, it was a golden age for the networks, in the sense that their profits were at a maximum.

Network television was widely criticized for broadcasting too much violence and for keeping the intellectual level of its programs low. Programs presented during the period were often designed with the tastes of the lower middle class in mind. Violence and fantasy were persistent themes. The lower-middle-class viewers in the United States were the ones who purchased the most beer, soap, detergent, toothpaste, soft drinks, and other nationally distributed products that could be advertised so effectively on television. The cumulative purchasing power of this vast majority was mind-boggling, and it was toward that aggregate monetary bonanza that programming was directed. That translates into simple tastes and material that was not at a demanding intellectual level. Americans loved that kind of

Television is a global medium that reaches even into remote regions. Through the use of satellites and VCRs, images of American culture have been brought to people in virtually every society on earth. What is transmitted is not always flattering and in many cases is criticized or denounced. Nevertheless, there is almost universal interest in the music, technology, clothing, political ideas, and general way of life of the people of the United States. (Owen Franken, Stock, Boston)

TELEVISION BRINGS LIVE DRAMA TO NEW AUDIENCES— THE CASE OF "PLAYHOUSE 90":
A Linchpin to Dramatic Theater

During the 1950s, the period many critics remember somewhat romantically as the golden age of television, dramatic series flourished on commercial television as they never have since. Shows such as "Studio One," "Philco Playhouse," "Kraft Television," "Armstrong Circle Theater," "The Alcoa Hour," and "The U.S. Steel Hour" all produced distinguished original material and gave voice to a new generation of artists, At a time when television was the ascendent medium, its great dramatic shows served as the fountainhead of creative talent and story-telling for both Broadway and Hollywood.[1]

Of all these dramatic series, however, one weekly show stood out for its original work, its quality, and, for a time, its willingness to take on controversial and technically difficult material: CBS's "Playhouse 90." First aired in October 1956, "Playhouse 90" was perhaps the most ambitious and best of the dramatic TV series of its time and remains the standard by which other such shows have been judged. The show featured original plays written, produced, and directed by some of the finest dramatic talent in the United States, including John Houseman, Rod Serling, John Frankenheimer, Sydney Lumet, J. P. Miller, and Paddy Chayefsky. Some of the plays they wrote for "Playhouse 90" are today regarded as American masterpieces.[2]

Many of this country's best-known actors also got their start in "Playhouse 90" presentations, among them Robert Redford, whose memorable depiction of a sensitive young Nazi soldier in In the Presence of Mine Enemies helped launch his career. Actor Art Carney, who had costarred in CBS's "The Honeymooners" with Jackie Gleason, moved to more serious drama in several "Playhouse 90" productions, performances that eventually brought him to Broadway and later to Hollywood. Other actors who appeared in "Playhouse 90" dramas include Rod Steiger, Jason Robards, Paul Newman, and Geraldine Page.

In its first season, each of the show's ninety-minute dramas was taped live, and the year included some of the show's most memorable performances. In only its second show, in October 1957, "Playhouse 90" presented Requiem for a Heavyweight, an original work by Rod Serling that starred Jack Palance as a wrecked and washed up, dumb but endearing boxer. Through masterful camera work the producers managed to defy many of the spacio-temporal problems that limited live television in those days. "It was so good," said one critic, "it was hard to believe it was live." Four months later "Playhouse 90" presented another original, Charles Gibson's The Miracle Worker, with Patty McCormack playing the blind and deaf Helen Keller. In one of the show's most celebrated productions, Paddy Chayefsky's Marty, young Rod Steiger played a lonely Bronx butcher who falls in love

TV content; at the same time, however, many understood that, in the words of Newton Minow, then chairman of the FCC, network television was a "vast wasteland" of mindless comedy, unrealistic soap operas, staged wrestling, violent cartoons, spectator sports, quiz games, and shallow portrayals of family situations.

Somehow, though, for both of the golden ages of television, time has transformed what many critics regarded at the time as "trash" into the

with a homely girl at a dance. Later productions included stage adaptations from George Bernard Shaw and Joseph Conrad, as well as original works by Serling, William Saroyan, and others. To avoid interrupting the dramatic flow of the plays, CBS founder and chairman William Paley directed that commercials be bunched at the beginning and end of the show rather than interspersed throughout.[3]

By its second season in 1957, the series' principal director, John Frankenheimer, was filming some "Playhouse 90" presentations in advance, but most were still done live. This required the utmost precision and planning by the production crew, which almost always performed impeccably. In 1959, the show was cut back to an alternate-week status and produced such original plays as *Point of No Return; Bitter Heritage; The Plot to Kill Stalin*, which got CBS expelled from the Soviet Union; J. P. Miller's play about alcoholism, *Days of Wine and Roses; Judgment at Nuremberg;* critically acclaimed adaptations of William Faulkner's story *Old Man* and Ernest Hemingway's novel *For Whom the Bell Tolls;* and a George Balanchine production of Tchaikovsky's ballet *Nutcracker Suite* as a Christmas special.

"Playhouse 90" pioneered in other ways as well. Critics who today note the blurring of network news and entertainment functions often forget the realism CBS newsman Eric Sevareid added by narrating John Houseman's *Seven Against the Wall*, a story of the Chicago St. Valentine's Day massacre. "Playhouse 90" devoted another show to a celebration of the film *Around the World in 80 Days*, narrated by newsmen Walter Cronkite and Jim McKay. Unfortunately, this show was garish and self-conscious; the *New York Times* called it "a dreadful bore."

Despite its triumphs, "Playhouse 90" and the other live network drama series slowly lost ground to filmed Hollywood adventures—particularly a new and conspicuously successful television genre, the western—and to game shows. Television drama also fell prey to the demands of network advertisers, who complained about the sometimes depressing themes of the dramatic shows and who increasingly favored the lighter and shorter half-hour dramas that were gaining in popularity. Shortly after its success with Serling's *Requiem for a Heavyweight*, CBS infuriated the playwright by tampering with two of his plays after sponsors complained. *Aftermath*, Serling's story of a black lynching in the contemporary South, was changed to a lynching of a Mexican in the 1880s, and *Panic Button*, the story of an airline crash, was changed so many times to appease the airlines that the play never aired. Not long afterward Serling left the show to begin work on a new half-hour series for CBS titled *The Twilight Zone*. In January 1960, CBS stopped production of "Playhouse 90," and the show aired for the last time in September 1961.

1. Harry Castleman and Walter J. Podrazik, *Watching TV: Four Decades of American Television* (New York: McGraw Hill, 1981).
2. Tom Brooks and Earle Marsh, *The Complete Directory to Prime Time Network TV Shows, 1946–Present* (New York: Ballantine Books, 1988), pp. 628–629.
3. Lewis J. Paper, *Empire: William S. Paley and the Making of CBS* (New York: St. Martin's Press, 1987), p. 198.

"good old days." That revised assessment may arise in large part from the fact that the content of the period was carefully designed to fit the limited tastes and intellectual preferences of the majority. Those same people are now older, but their tastes have not become noticeably elevated. It is little wonder, then, that as they look back, they see the programs of the earlier periods as classics and the people who starred in them as significant performers.

Alternatives to Broadcast Television

Two technological advances are playing a critical role in the reshaping of the American television industry. One is the growth of cable television, and the other is the widespread adoption of the video cassette recorder. Both are relatively recent developments.

The Spread of Cable Systems

Cable television began innocently enough. It was needed in certain locations because of the line-of-sight nature of the TV signal. For example, a community that is blocked by a large hill between it and the nearest TV transmitter cannot receive the signal. The same is true for people who live in a valley or among a lot of tall buildings that block transmissions.

In the 1950s, a number of local and very small systems were set up to overcome such obstacles. The solution was to put a large community antenna in a favorable location and wire people's homes via coaxial cable to this central facility. Usually, the signal was amplified to make reception very clear. It worked just fine, and it was especially attractive to people in rural areas and other hard-to-reach locations.

At first, the number of households that were wired in this way was very small (less than 2 percent of households with TV sets in 1960). It was actually a kind of "mom and pop" industry, with some 640 small systems each serving only several hundred or a few thousand clients. Then, the whole thing began to expand, largely because cable brought better pictures and more selection. This angered the broadcasters, who saw the cable operator as a "parasite" who was pirating their programs off the air and selling them for a profit. Then, as the cable companies developed better technology, they began to offer their clients TV signals that had originated in cities a long way off—effectively diminishing attention to local broadcasters. Even worse, some of the cable companies started originating their own programming!

Lawsuits were filed by everyone against everyone else. Finally, it was resolved that the FCC had the right to regulate the cable companies, just as though they were broadcasting over the air. The broadcasters persuaded the FCC to impose stiff, complex regulations that effectively stopped the growth of more cable systems. By 1979, however, many of those restrictions had been relaxed, and local governments were given the right to grant franchises to private cable companies to provide service in the local community. Out of that came a great surge of development. In 1980, less than 20 percent of American homes with television were wired. By 1993, the proportion had soared to 62 percent as the adoption curve continued to rise. (See Table 7.3 and Figure 7.3)

The increasing adoption of cable by American households has significantly altered the whole TV industry. First, it has reduced the share of the total audience that views regular network television. Second, it has begun to segment the viewing public along the lines of tastes and interests. With dozens of channels to choose from in a typical system, a viewer no longer needs to watch whatever the networks happen to be broadcasting at the moment. At any given time, it is possible to find on most cable systems some form of

Year	Percentage of TV Households with Cable	Percentage of TV Households with VCR
1960	1.5	—
1965	2.3	—
1966	3.3	—
1968	4.7	—
1970	6.7	—
1972	9.2	—
1974	11.6	—
1976	14.5	—
1978	17.1	0.3
1980	19.9	1.1
1982	29.8	3.1
1984	39.3	10.6
1986	45.6	36.0
1988	49.4	58.0
1990	56.4	68.6
1993	62.0	77.0

Sources: Nielsen Media Research; U. S. Bureau of the Census, Statistical Abstract of the United States, 1991, 111th ed. (Washington, D.C., 1991); Television Advertising Bureau, 1992.

**FIGURE 7.3
The Curve of Adoption
for Cable Television,
1960–1993**

Cable television started on a small scale with community antenna systems wired to households in local areas where there was difficulty in receiving an over-the-air signal. The expansion of cable was held back during the 1970s by legal fights over federal regulation and lawsuits concerning the right of cable companies to transmit network programming and other content. As the 1980s began, those difficulties were resolved and a great expansion in cable systems took place. The majority of Americans are now connected to a cable system. In spite of these conflicts and limitations, the adoption of cable television has followed a rather typical s-shaped curve.

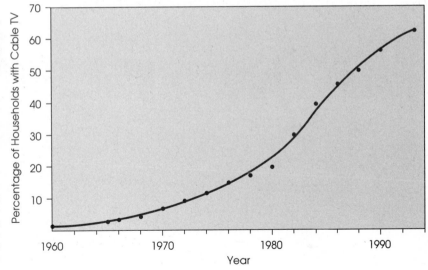

Alternatives to Broadcast Television ■ **227**

program content that will fit almost anyone's interests. Thus, a pattern is developing much like that for magazines when the large-circulation general periodicals gave way to the more focused specialty magazines. Advertisers are following these developments with keen interest. If one has a special product to advertise, it is more than likely that a program interesting potential customers can be found in the cable TV line-up.

Currently, there is considerable criticism of cable channels such as HBO, USA, and MTV. The programming is often repetitive. Monthly fees are said to be too expensive, and such channels incorporate almost as much advertising as traditional over-the-air broadcasts. Furthermore, critics complain, there has been no noticeable elevation of aesthetic tastes or intellectual standards. One used to find such content as wrestling, bowling matches, and soap operas on broadcast channels. Now one finds them on cable channels, along with new contenders, such as direct marketing, real estate ads, and rock music videos.

These appear to be valid criticisms. However, cable is still serving the same tastes that broadcast television always has. There is little reason to assume that the majority audience professional communicators seek to reach want programming to be more sophisticated just because it is being delivered by cable. We can safely conclude, therefore, that the intellectual level and aesthetic tastes of most programming on cable will remain similar to what has always been found on broadcast television.

The Video Cassette Recorder

Like so many electronic devices, the video cassette recorder (VCR) is an American invention and a Japanese success story. The original machine was developed by the Ampex Corporation in New York. In 1952, Charles Ginsberg, along with several other Ampex engineers, set out to develop a device that could be used to record television programs on magnetic tape.[6] Four years later, they had succeeded. The first video tape recorder was about the size of an upright piano and used large reels of two-inch-wide tape. It was quickly adopted by the TV industry as a means to record material for later broadcasting. Used in this way, it was very practical. No longer did all shows have to be broadcast live. Programming errors could be edited or changes spliced in, allowing mistake-free programs at air time.

At the beginning of the 1970s, a number of U.S. companies saw the consumer potential of the device and set out to manufacture and market a small home version. However, they could not agree on the size and standards of the tape and other aspects of the system. By the middle of the decade, some five different standards were used in the machines on the market. All were very expensive, and the prerecorded material available might or might not fit the machine purchased.

The Japanese stepped in. They standardized the systems and technology, brought prices down, and sold millions of the machines in just over a decade. Today more than three-fourths of U.S. households with television have a VCR. Table 7.3 and Figure 7.4 show the pattern of adoption of

The compact VCR (Video Cassette Recorder) that is so common in American homes today started out as a VTR (Video Tape Recorder). Its principles and technology were developed in the early 1950s by this team of six American engineers of the Ampex Systems Corporation. This original model was ready for use in 1956. Its major application at the time was in professional television studios and stations, where programs could be recorded on tape for rebroadcasting at a later time. The Japanese refined and standardized smaller machines for home use. Almost all VCRs today are made in Japan. (Courtesy of Ampex Systems Corporation)

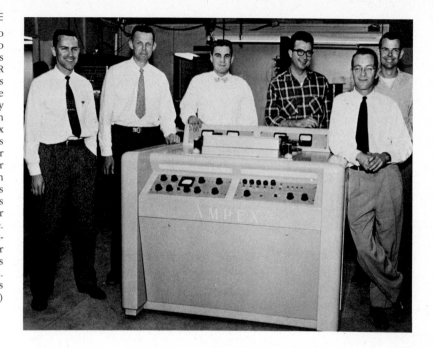

the VCR for home use. The device gave birth to a whole new industry. Today, one can rent a movie for a very modest fee at a rental agency specializing in video cassette tapes or in a supermarket, convenience store, or even a gas station. To feed this market, the movie industry has begun to distribute films in this form. A movie on video cassette can generate enormous profits long after the film has exhausted its market at regular theaters. A host of other kinds of cassettes—with content ranging from exer-

**FIGURE 7.4
The Curve of Adoption
for VCRs, 1978–1993**

The home use of the VCR as a device for recording television programs or viewing other content was delayed for many years after its invention in 1952. In its earliest form, it was used mainly by the TV industry to record programs for replay. After unsuccessful attempts by U.S. manufacturers to standardize the device for home use, the Japanese took over its development and manufacture. During the last half of the l980s, its use soared. The majority of American homes now have a VCR, and there is a classic curve of adoption.

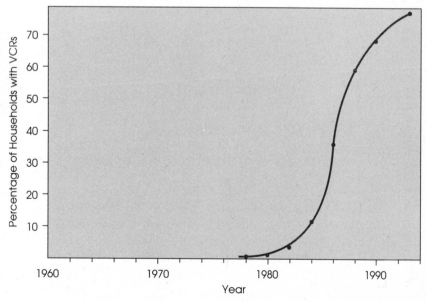

cise programs to bass fishing and home repair instructions—have made the VCR even more popular.

Earlier, the proliferation of home VCRs was seen as a threat by movie makers and broadcasters, who feared that people would record movies and programs off broadcast or cable television, reducing video rentals and the effectiveness of TV advertising. That fear turned out to be unfounded. For the most part, VCRs are used to play rented or purchased cassettes. Studies show that the majority of VCR users do not even know how to program their machines to record material off the air.

Developments in viewing technology have brought great change, and there is more to come. The VCR and cable television, along with the hand-held remote control that can mute sound or change channels, have made serious inroads into traditional broadcast television. We have seen the impact of new technology on existing media in previous chapters. Earlier, alternative sources for news brought a significant decline in newspaper subscriptions. The large-circulation general magazine was a victim of the shift to TV advertising. Television viewing almost destroyed radio, and it seriously displaced moviegoing. Today, it is network television that is in trouble—or more precisely, broadcast television of all kinds—undercut by the VCR, cable, and the hand-held remote control. Numbers of viewers are down, and consequently advertising revenues are declining. Many who advertised their products almost exclusively on broadcast television are turning to direct mail, to cable, to specialty magazines, and to any other medium where they can still reach their potential customers.

Television as a Contemporary Medium

Like radio, from which it was derived, television is both a technology and a complex medium of mass communication. As its history amply demonstrates, it is also an economic system made up of communicators, advertisers, programs or content, and a large and diverse audience. And it has become an omnipresent medium—the form of mass communication most preferred by the American public. As indicated earlier, on average, the TV set is on more than seven hours a day in American households. At the same time, television is a medium that is little understood by its public. The majority of viewers know little about the behind-the-scenes dramas involving the individuals and groups that make up the TV industry.

The Economics of Competing Systems

Television signals are received from local stations over the air (or via cable). These local stations are still the backbone of the system. In 1994, the country had 1,512 operating TV stations. Of these, 561 were commercial VHF stations (which appear as channels 2 to 13 on the television band). An additional 584 are commercial UHF stations (in the higher numbered channels). There were 126 noncommercial (that is, public) VHF stations and 241 noncommercial UHF stations. Some of these were operated by schools or other institutions.[7]

In this system, the networks play a key role. Two-thirds of the commercial TV stations get the major part of their programming from one of the networks, with which they are affiliated. Thus, the networks are major *suppliers* of content to chains of local affiliates. At the same time, the networks are also broadcasters. A number of stations are owned and operated directly by networks (these are called "O & O's" in the industry).

The three major networks are, of course, ABC (American Broadcasting Corporation), CBS (Columbia Broadcasting System), and NBC (National Broadcasting Corporation). All three have been in business for decades. Much newer are the Fox network and CNN (Cable News Network). The Fox system is owned by Rupert Murdoch, whose holdings also include a newspaper empire (as noted in Chapter 3). CNN is a specialized operation that delivers programming to cable systems. In addition, there are regional systems formed of local stations that band together and share programming and promote advertising. The noncommercial Public Broadcasting Service (PBS) is also a network, of course. Finally, the U.S. government operates a large television network overseas. Ostensibly for members of the armed forces, AFRTS (Armed Forces Radio and Television Service), as it is called, reaches into seventy countries and is seen not only by people in the armed forces, but also by millions of U.S and foreign civilians.

Over the years, the number of independent (not network-affiliated) stations has increased. This has given rise to *barter syndication*. (The idea of syndicates for newspapers was discussed in Chapter 3. The same structure exists for broadcasters.) Thus, a local station can get taped content from program syndicators who lease their wares to independent, non-network stations, creating what amounts to a series of small networks. Such syndicated programming competes directly with network offerings.

From the standpoint of a family viewing their TV set at home, the sources that deliver programs can be a confusing jumble. What they see on their screen at any given time may originate from one of several networks, from an independent local station, from PBS, from their basic cable service (perhaps with add-on subscription fees), or from a cassette in their VCR. This variety in sources makes little real difference to viewers. A given movie provides the same viewing experience regardless of who delivers it. The same is true of a ball game, cartoon, or nature documentary. What do viewers care how it comes to them? Since it looks the same on the screen, regardless of what delivery system is being used, most families do not attach a great deal of importance to the various vendors and systems from which they get their entertainment, sports programs, or even news. The main thing for them is that the programming they want to view is *there*.

However, for the players involved, what source viewers use is of paramount importance. It is the basis for consuming battles for profit and economic survival within the system. Thus, *competition* among the sources that deliver programming to audiences is the central factor in understanding the economics of contemporary television.

Competition has always existed among the various networks. Every year, they vied for dominance in terms of commanding the largest audiences. And in recent years, competition started between network television and its alternatives (cable television and the VCR) as these systems came on line. That competition resulted in significant changes.

From the early days of television up until the mid-1980s, regular broadcast television was very popular because of the relationship among networks, advertisers, those who produced the content, and the audience. That is, advertising revenues brought high earnings to the major networks, permitting them to produce expensive programs that were well received by audiences. Thus, a kind of reciprocal system was in place. Television advertising was very costly. But since the commercial messages shown on the popular programs reached huge audiences, advertisers were willing to pay enormous fees for tiny segments of air time (such as 30 seconds, or even 15). And because of this great income, the networks were able to produce still more expensive programs with even greater appeal to the public. Thus, advertising revenues spiraled up and up, along with the size of the audience.

The significance of audience attention   At the heart of this mutually profitable system is *audience attention*. The worst nightmare of both the advertiser and the television network executive is that people will not view the programs on which their wares are advertised. Media audiences are measured in terms of ratings, and various kinds of survey and polling techniques have been used to determine what kinds of people view what kinds of television programs during what periods of time. For many years, the techniques used were rather simple. Some were based on diaries that carefully selected panels of people kept at home or on verbal reports of people contacted by phone or mail about what they had been watching. Whatever their limitations, those ratings became *institutionalized*, that is, deeply established, as the ultimate measure of whether a given program would be kept on the air. They remain so today. Thus, what can be called the *law of large numbers* was the prevailing principle determining the TV agenda presented by the major networks. That is, the more eyes and ears a program attracted, the more valuable it was to an advertiser whose message was displayed during the transmission and to the broadcaster who profited from the sale of the time. If a program's ratings fell, even by a few points, it was in jeopardy. Many programs were simply dropped from the air if their ratings did not seem to justify what it cost to produce and broadcast them, and especially if they did not draw enough advertisers to generate sufficient profits.

The use of such ratings as the ultimate criterion by which the networks assessed the worth of a particular program was just fine with the advertisers who supported the system. It ensured that the programs on the air, and therefore the advertisers' commercials, were commanding the attention of the largest possible numbers of potential consumers. For several decades, this was how the system worked. Thus, in spite of competition among networks, the system as a whole remained rather stable for many years, and the networks continued to dominate television. The law of large numbers continues to prevail today.

The "blab-off" and the "zapper" In recent years, a new factor has entered the competitive arena. Another nightmare of the advertiser and the television network executive became a reality. It came in the form of the "zapper"—the hand-held remote control, with its buttons for muting the sound or changing the channel without leaving the chair or couch. It has brought a significant reduction in the amount of attention that viewers give to TV commercials. Actually, the zapper idea had been around for a long time before the more contemporary versions came into wide use. The earliest version (as far back as the early 1950s) was called the "blab-off." It had a long wire between the viewer and the speaker circuit in the set, and by pressing a single button, the viewer could turn the sound on and off. A limitation of the device was that it had to be purchased separately and installed by a technician. That was a lot of trouble, and not many people used the blab-off. In later years, however, manufacturers began building remote controls directly into the set, with infrared light beams providing the link between set and hand unit. Today, remote controls are extremely common.

The zapper deeply troubles advertisers, who worry that the expensive commercials they are paying for are not getting through to TV audiences. That is an especially serious issue for network television, which is still where the bulk of the most expensive advertising messages appear. The networks have had a hard time countering the charge that the zapper is eroding attention to TV commercials.

The hand-held remote control, now in almost universal use, poses a problem for network television. In the late 1980s and early 1990s, many considerations have reduced the percentage of total viewers who tune in to network broadcasts. Although their audiences are still large, the networks have been hurt by the growth of cable systems, the rapid adoption of the VCR, and the "zapper," which mutes the sound. Advertisers, worried that TV audiences are not attending to their messages, have increasingly turned to other media to promote products. (Dick Luria/FPG International)

In recent years, a new device has created headaches for network television. It is a relatively simple recording device called a "people meter"—a gadget operated by the home viewer, who is part of a panel of hundreds of people carefully selected and managed by one of the audience-measuring services. The system provides a more reliable way of obtaining relatively accurate records of who watches what.

When the people meter was introduced, it created a great stir because it revealed patterns of viewing that were quite different from those that had been indicated with the older ways of calculating ratings. This was very disturbing, particularly when the new device seemed to show that the actual audiences for certain programs were really much *smaller* than had been suggested. In particular, the people meter made it possible to determine rather accurately when people were viewing cable or using their VCR, rather than being tuned to network television. It was very clear that overall attention to network television was on the decline. This caused many advertisers to reconsider how much of their advertising budgets they wanted to devote to network television, as opposed to other media.

The significance of the zapper and the people meter in the economics of television is easy to document: For the first time in history, advertising rates went *down*. (Later they did recover, though.) Pundits began to debate whether the networks that had dominated the medium for so long were dinosaurs ready for extinction. Such conclusions appear to have been premature. Today, network television is in a slow decline in terms of its share of the total viewing audience. But at the same time, as Table 7.2 and Figure 7.2 indicate, the total amount of time that American families spend with their sets has been rising ever since the medium was first introduced. Thus, network television still commands a huge audience, and it will very likely be an important player in the system for some time to come. Still, the viewing mix continues to change, and the ultimate impact of cable TV, the VCR, or any other system cannot be predicted at this time.

The Television Industry in Transition

It is difficult to separate television as technology from the medium as an economic institution. Increasingly, television is a global industry with programming cutting across national borders. As we have pointed out, many TV stations in the United States are owned by large corporations, although the number that a single owner can have is limited by law to twelve stations not covering more than 30 percent of the population of the country. Media ownership, like that of many other business enterprises, is global. Although FCC regulations place limits on foreign ownership of broadcast properties, complex patterns of conglomerate ownership are common. For example, some of the large organizations and multinational corporations that are involved in ownership of TV stations in the United States are Time-Warner (United States), Bertelsmann (Germany), Gulf and Western News

Corporation (Australia, United Kingdom, and United States), Capital Cities/ABC (United States), Hachette (France), and Gannett (United States).

Television profits are a function of the total annual revenues of the whole industry—advertising sales, annual volume of advertising, network and station television billing, market ratings, and other indicators. The major players are networks, local stations, and barter syndicators, which provide independent sources of programming. As mentioned earlier, the competition from cable, VCR, and syndication services has brought a downturn in the economic fortunes of TV networks. But the networks nevertheless can still deliver impressive audiences, even though their share of total audience viewing time is down.

In spite of the fact that a great deal is known about the social, cultural, and economic structure of the U.S. population (as we will see in Chapter 8), one of the poorly charted aspects of TV audiences is their actual composition. For example, TV industry market researchers give only superficial attention to the demographic characteristics of network viewers. Cable services and public television sometimes claim to deliver "quality," or upscale, audiences of viewers who are relatively well-educated and affluent in comparison with the general population. However, those claims are not backed with data from well-designed studies, and television as a whole does not conduct precise and careful research on audiences in the same detailed ways as marketers of many other products and services do.

An important concept for TV stations is the market as an area. A *market* in this sense consists of a community and a contiguous area in which a substantial number of people live who can be reached by a station's signal. In practical terms, this translates into a metropolitan area that includes a city. Some markets are relatively small, such as that in which Little Rock, Arkansas, is located. Others are huge, such as that of Los Angeles or Philadelphia.

Finally, the economic fortunes of television in all its forms, as we have stressed, revolve around *advertising*. Today, the revenues from that source are by no means evenly distributed among the competitors. For example, cable—which receives its basic support from subscriptions and fees—receives only about 7 percent of all advertising spent on television. Television stations broadcasting to markets receive a whopping 54 percent. That is understandable because they account for virtually all of the local or community-level advertising. Still, the networks, whose advertising is mainly for nationally distributed products and services, retain 32 percent of the total. Barter syndicators are a minor player, with only 7 percent.

As we suggested earlier, patterns of television advertising are changing. As noted, the ratio between advertising revenues of local stations and those of the networks is 56 to 36. Ten years ago, the percentage was about the same, 55, for the stations, but it was 45 for the networks. This brings into sharp focus the problems now faced by the networks that have resulted from such factors as the zapper and the people meter and such alternatives as cable. A decade ago, none of these advertising revenues went to cable or to syndicators. The drop from 45 percent of the total to only 36 percent works out to a 22 percent reduction in revenues—a truly substantial loss for any business—and it means very difficult times for the networks.

The Future of Television

The future of television will be one of constant and somewhat unpredictable change. The zapper will continue to trouble advertisers, and they will actively explore alternative media, such as newspapers, magazines, radio, and even direct mail. However, offsetting these negatives for TV advertising is another trend we showed in Table 7.2 and Figure 7.2. That is, the total time people spend using their television sets has increased over the years. However, it now appears to have stabilized, presumably because there is only so much time that people can devote to television. Overall, then, television today faces a complex situation, and there is little doubt that further changes are in store. The fortunes of the industry will continue to shift as new players arrive on the scene.

Another aspect of television's future that is difficult to predict is its technology. Looming on the horizon are a number of technological systems that will vastly extend the number of choices viewers will be able to make in their homes. These include a number of new ways of delivering the signal via optic cables and telephone lines. Other innovations will enlarge and clarify the picture that viewers see. Many new devices for improving the viewing experience are under development, such as wall panel screens and more elaborate sound systems.

One technology that is about to arrive is *HDTV*, or high-definition television. The Japanese began the development of this new kind of broadcasting and receiving system a number of years ago. It is based on the transmission technology in use today, but it provides for a much clearer picture. The screen is somewhat wider than the ones we use today, and since it has from 50 to 100 percent more lines (depending on which system is considered), it gives a much sharper image—a picture equal to a fine photograph.

There is little doubt that HDTV is coming. It is just a matter of when and whose standards will be used. The European Community has decided to use a different number of lines on the screen than in the Japanese system (probably for political reasons related to manufacturing and marketing opportunities). The FCC has vacillated but has now settled on the basic features of the U.S. system. At present, it appears that the United States will use a different number of lines than in either the Japanese or the European system. The reason is that the FCC wants to make HDTV broadcasts compatible with present receivers so that all of us do not have to throw away our present sets. This was the FCC policy when the shift was made from black-and-white to color, and it makes a great deal of sense. We will continue to see the same picture quality on our present sets, and when we buy a new one, it will be able to receive HDTV.

Television continues to undergo technological development. It was strictly a black-and-white medium for some time after its introduction in the late 1940s, but color broadcasts became standard during the 1960s. Cable and the VCR were widely adopted during the 1980s. The next major innovation will be HDTV, shown here. The new screens are wider, and the picture is clearer. Much larger screens and interactive systems will become common soon, and cable systems capable of delivering five hundred channels are already being developed. All of these technological developments will have an impact on the TV industry and on competing media. (© Gerry Davis/Phototake NYC)

Moreover, U.S. companies have been developing a *digital* system for HDTV that is technologically somewhat different from the *analog* approach used in Japan. This system, based on computer technology, is an excellent choice because it will be more compatible with other computer-based technologies that will develop in the future. Thus, by lagging behind the Japanese in this case, the United States may in the long run actually come out ahead.

Another unknown that may have profound implications is *direct broadcast satellite* for home reception. A small disk (about the size of a large dinner plate) in the attic allows homes to receive transmissions that networks send up to suitably located satellites directly, without ever going through a local station. This technology, which is now available, can provide up to five hundred channels in subscribing homes and may set the TV industry in the United States on its ear. There may be less and less need for network affiliates, and local TV stations as we know them would, like radio, have to redefine their roles and functions.

One thing about the future of television is entirely clear. The tastes and preferences of the TV audience in the United States will undoubtedly remain *precisely what they are*. Therefore, we will not undergo a revolution in program content that will parallel the new technological developments. Thus, whatever spectacular home TV sets are in store for us, perhaps with wall-sized pictures as clear as the real world and with hundreds of choices of channels, we will be seeing the usual array of soap operas, sitcoms, human interest news, quiz games, sports, home-shopping opportunities, religious evangelists, negative political campaigns, and so on. Mixed in will be a scattering of offerings for the more serious viewer, but the great number who support the industry through their consumer purchases of breakfast foods, laxatives, and other commonly advertised products will want more of the same. Thus, the law of large numbers will prevail in the future as it has in the past.

Chapter Review

- Pioneering experiments on sending pictures by radio were begun in several countries just after World War I. The earliest attempts made use of a revolving Nipkow disk, a mechanical system that created a picture by recording an image through small holes punched in a whirling circular device. It was not until electronic scanning was developed that television became practical.

- The first patent for an electronic television system was awarded to Philo T. Farnsworth, an obscure inventor, who had worked out the basic design while still a high school student. With minimal funding, he built a working model in a small apartment in Los Angeles. Vladimir Zworykin, of Westinghouse laboratories, also invented an electronic system. Court battles resulted, but Farnsworth won.

- By 1932, a transmitter was installed in the Empire State Building in New York City. Regular transmissions began on a limited basis in 1936, with two broadcasts per week. A few hundred amateur enthusiasts who had built or purchased sets could receive the signals in the New York area.

- By 1940, television was capable of becoming a mass medium for home use. However, when World War II began in 1941, the need for war production temporarily halted development of the new medium.

- The period of rapid adoption of home receivers began just after the war. Between 1950 and 1960, nearly 90 percent of U.S. households acquired a television set. This happened in spite of a freeze on the licensing and construction of new TV stations imposed by the FCC between 1948 and 1952.

- Television quickly became a part of family behavior patterns across the nation. The number of hours during which the average household set was in use climbed from about four and a half per day in 1950 to over seven in recent years. During the 1970s, color sets all but completely replaced black-and-white.

- Two periods can be identified that might for different reasons be called television's golden age. One, based on the popularity of certain programming and TV personalities, was roughly from the early 1950s to about 1960. The second, defined more in terms of the predominance and profitability of the networks, was from about 1960 to 1980.

- Alternative ways to use the TV set at home have now become a significant part of the total picture. Cable systems were not a major factor in the industry until the 1980s. During that decade, the proportion of U.S. homes receiving cable transmissions increased sharply. The VCR was developed in the 1950s by a U.S. company. Since the mid-1980s, the Japanese have sold millions of the sets in the United States. HDTV and direct satellite broadcasts may change the picture still further.

- As an industry, television is undergoing a number of changes. New patterns of ownership are emerging. Large corporations and conglomerates are increasingly making TV stations and even networks part of their holdings. The result is a changing pattern of competition within the industry. Also, the original networks have lost a large share of the market in terms of advertising dollars. Both cable and VCRs are more widely used than ever before. Further changes lie ahead as this dynamic industry continues to evolve.

Notes and References

1. See "The Development of the Television Industry," Melvin L. DeFleur and Sandra Ball-Rokeach, *Theories of Mass Communication*, 5th ed. (White Plains, N.Y.: Longman, 1989), pp. 110–122.
2. Randall Rothenberg, "Change in Consumer Markets Hurting Advertising Industry," *New York Times*, October 3, 1989, pp. A-1, D-23.
3. For a thorough history of television up to the mid-1970s, see Eric Barnouw, *Tube of Plenty: The Evolution of American Television* (New York: Oxford University Press, 1975).
4. "Trends in Television," A Research Trend Report of the Television Advertising Bureau, 477 Madison Avenue, New York, NY 10022, April 1989.
5. Nielsen Media Research, Inc., 1992.
6. *Newsweek*, July 10, 1970, p. 42.
7. These figures on the numbers of stations are from *Television Fact Books* (Washington, D.C.: Warren Publishing, 1994).

PART THREE

FORCES THAT SHAPE CONTEMPORARY MEDIA

The American Population as Audience

Like Thoreau's marcher in the quotation on the previous page, we all step to a different drummer when it comes to attending to mass communications. We do so because each of us is a unique individual, with distinct preferences in what we want to read, hear, and view. That uniqueness is derived from our past learning experiences in our family, among friends, at school, and in the community at large. These experiences, in turn, are strongly influenced by our positioning in particular kinds of *social categories* and various *groups* in our community and society. It is the resulting *individual differences*—in our personal psychological organizations of beliefs, attitudes, values, tastes, and interests—that determine what we will select and attend to from the vast flow of mass communications that is available to us every day. Those personal characteristics, shaped and influenced by our social locations and memberships, will determine what meanings we will assign to the media messages we receive, how much we will like and use them, and what actions we will take as a result.

This chapter focuses on those sources of individuality—the distinctions that can be found among Americans in terms of such characteristics as age, gender, income, education, race, and ethnicity. It also discusses ongoing changes in significant social processes such as urbanization, migration, and family composition. All of these *demographic characteristics and trends* make the audience for mass media psychologically as well as socially heterogeneous. They need to be understood because they lead different kinds of people to select, interpret, and act upon different kinds of content from different media. The sections that follow, then, discuss the general demographic features of the American population that define the nature of the audience for the complex system of mass media. Also discussed are various ways in which professional communicators obtain delayed feedback from their audiences through the use of assessments of their size, composition, and patterns of attention.

In Chapter 1, we discussed a linear model of human communication that could be applied to the process of mass communication (pp. 21-28). In describing the six stages of that model, we noted that the process began with professional communicators who decided on the nature and goals of the message; additional steps were encoding the intended meanings and transmitting the message via the specialized technologies of print, film, and broadcasting. In Chapters 2 through 7, we have discussed those technologies and indicated how they transmit messages. We will return to the encoding issue in later chapters and discuss more fully how this takes place in such areas as advertising, news, popular culture, and music. Meanwhile, this chapter looks at the *receiving end* of the model, that stage in which members of the large and diverse audience selectively attend to, perceive and assign meanings to what they read, view, or hear. In other words, as we indicated in our discussion of the linear model, the "multitude of receivers will have a multitude of ways in which to assign meaning to incoming mass communicated messages."

As we have made clear, the American system of mass communication rests solidly on individual ownership, free enterprise, and competition in the marketplace. Although there are exceptions, the bottom line in this system is that it is designed to earn money from its audiences, either directly or indirectly, in the form of profit. That is, content is prepared for the media that audiences will buy directly or that will attract their attention to advertising designed to motivate them to purchase goods and services. Thus, an understanding of the tastes and interests of the audiences that bring them to make selections from the media are the *sine qua non*—the absolute necessity—for anyone who attempts to be successful in the mass communication business. And, since audience tastes and interests are linked to the personal and social characteristics of individuals, we need to look closely at the population itself. This means examining its demographic structure, including its trends and changes.

The sections that follow do not try to sort out details about which specific media reach how many people. We have tried to do that in previous chapters. Instead, the discussions focus on the nature of audiences and the techniques used by the major media to assess them. These sections also do not try to identify the kinds of influences mass communications have on audiences. That will come later (in Chapters 16 and 17). Instead, this chapter focuses on the great *diversity* that exists in the American population, its sources, and how the population is undergoing changes that will have implications for mass communications.

Essentially, the first section of our discussion of the American population as audience reviews three major factors: One is the *size* of the population and how that continues to change. A second is its complex *composition*. By composition, we refer to such factors as age, gender, education, income, race, and ethnicity. A third factor is *migration* or population movement from one area to another. All of these factors lead to multicultural and personal diversity in American media audiences, providing the basis for modern counterparts of what Thoreau had in mind when he posed his metaphor. Because each of us is different in our personal combination of social identities, we do indeed hear different drummers as we select our content from the media. This leads each of us, as we think about or act on these selections, to step to music that may not be perceived in the same way, or even heard at all, by others.

The Changing American Population

The sheer number of people in a population can be critical to the success or failure of particular kinds of media at particular times. We saw earlier that one of the reasons that magazines failed during the colonial period was that when they were introduced, the population was too small and too scattered to provide a viable market. In addition, we saw that it was the growth of population in such urban centers as New York City, and generally along the more populated Eastern seaboard, that provided the initial audiences for the penny press—the forerunners of modern newspapers.

Today, with a population exceeding 250 million, there is little danger that there will be too few people in the nation as a whole to support any major medium. On the other hand, that population is not evenly distributed among the states and local areas. Furthermore, the size of any population—local or national—*changes* over time, and that can have significant influences on the viability of particular media. That is especially true at the local level. If a town or city is gaining or losing population, its newspapers, radio stations, and even its movie theaters will be affected.

A History of Rapid Growth

The shift in population size in any particular area during any particular period of time is a product of three specific factors: These are the number of *births* that add population during the period, the number of *deaths* that occur during the period and remove people from the population, and the pattern of *migration* into or out of the area that results in a gain or loss of residents. If the past trends of these three factors are known and their nature in the years ahead can be anticipated, predictions of population size are not difficult, at least on a short-term basis.

The problem is that all three of the above factors can change rapidly and rather sharply. The birth rate in a particular area can rise or fall as people make decisions about starting, expanding, delaying, or stabilizing the size of their families. The death rate generally rises or falls with the availability of medical treatment and as public health measures (clean water, effective waste disposal, and food inspections) deteriorate or improve. Migration can be a wild card as people move into or out of an area because of the availability of work, welfare benefits, housing, protection from crime, religious or racial intolerance, and so forth. In fact, the American population as a whole has changed during the century as a product of just such factors.

To demonstrate how population size, and numbers of people available for media audiences, can change as a result of the above three factors, we can review the pattern of population change at the national level during the twentieth century. As Table 8.1 shows, there has been a long-term expansion of the American population since the beginning of this century.

TABLE 8.1
Size of the U.S.
Population, 1900–1990

Year	Population (thousands)
1900	76,094
1905	83,822
1910	92,407
1915	100,546
1920	106,461
1925	115,829
1930	123,077
1935	127,250
1940	132,122
1945	139,928
1950	151,684
1955	165,275
1960*	180,671
1965	194,303
1970	204,879
1975	215,973
1980	227,757
1985	239,279
1990	248,710

*Alaska and Hawaii added after this date.

Sources: U.S. Bureau of the Census, Historical Statistics of the United States, Colonial Times to 1970, Series A, Nos. 23–28; Statistical Abstract of the United States, 1990.

The American population has been characterized by one of the fastest rates of growth in history. Even during the twentieth century, population continued to rise sharply as wave after wave of immigrants arrived from Europe and other parts of the world. Immigration has continued during the 1990s, with most immigrants arriving, either legally or illegally, from Mexico, Asia, and South America. These patterns of population movement have been the source of the great diversity of the American population, as the offspring of immigrants maintained many of their ethnic, racial, and national cultures.

FIGURE 8.1
Growth of the U.S.
Population, 1900-1990

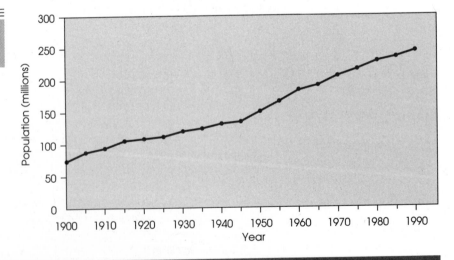

Actually, that expansion started earlier, as soon as the 1800s began. By 1840, large numbers of immigrants were already pouring into the United States. By the end of the century, the population had reached over 76 million from a mere 5.3 million in 1800. That is an impressive 1,334 percent increase in essentially three generations (of about thirty years each).

All during the nineteenth century, attracting immigrants was a deliberate national policy. The United States acquired vast territories, and undeveloped land is an open invitation to external aggressors. Settlers were needed to secure millions of square miles when the nation's geographic boundaries expanded as a result of two huge land acquisitions: The first was the Louisiana Purchase of 1803, which for a mere $15 million added what are now the states of Arkansas, Iowa, Kansas, Missouri, Nebraska, North and South Dakota, and most of Minnesota, Montana, Oklahoma, Louisiana, and Wyoming. The second, following a successful war with Mexico, was the result of the 1848 treaty of Guadalupe Hidalgo. It permitted the United States to acquire, for another $15 million, what became California, New Mexico, and Utah, plus major parts of what are now Arizona, Texas, and Colorado, and smaller sections of other states. These monumental real estate bargains opened enormous territories to settlement.

In 1862, during the Civil War, the federal government established the Homestead Act, which allowed any citizen, or even an alien who had filed a declaration to become a citizen, to acquire ownership of up to 180 acres of public land free of cost by residing on the site and farming for five years. Entire regions were populated by immigrants taking advantage of this extraordinary offer.[1] To develop the nation's agriculture more rapidly, the Congress, through the Morrill Act of 1862, granted tracts of land to the states to establish colleges where offspring of the settlers could study the "agricultural and mechanical arts." (These have become our great land-grant colleges and universities.) Thus, during the nineteenth century, the majority of the population lived on farms. The nation did not reach the 50 percent urban and 50 percent rural point until the 1920s. Today, only about 2 percent of Americans live on farms.

Immigration and Cultural Diversity

In 1993, the American population was an estimated 253 million, up by 177 million from the beginning of this century. Though the population has expanded far more slowly in this century than in the previous one, the rate of growth is still enormous. It was during this period that the mass media saw their major patterns of growth. Although the print media were already well established as the century began, radio, the movies and television in all its forms developed after 1900.

One of the important features of the current rate of population growth is that it is largely a result of immigration, through which the United States continues to add population. In fact, according to Bureau of the Census estimates, another 25.4 million people will be added during the 1990s alone.[2]

Although births are declining, large numbers of immigrants (legal and illegal) will come from Mexico. Others will arrive from Asian countries, South America, and the Caribbean.

People who came as part of the earliest large-scale immigrations in the 1800s settled in the Northeastern and Midwestern states. Vast parts of these regions were virtually empty of farms and settlements at the time, and those in charge wanted immigrants from Europe very badly. The fact that Native Americans were already there did not trouble the young nation. They were either pushed aside, forced onto reservations, or killed. The immigrants who replaced them during the early and mid-1800s were mainly from England, Ireland, Scotland, France, Scandinavia, and Germany, plus large numbers of Africans brought as slaves.

Toward the end of the nineteenth century, the origins of the immigrants shifted to Southern and Eastern Europe as millions of Italians, Poles, Russians, Czechs, and Hungarians arrived through Ellis Island in New York harbor. Many remained in cities on the Eastern seaboard, but others went on to the Upper Midwest and found work in mines, mills, and factories. These immigrant groups, along with the offspring from previous waves of immigration, have produced a nation of great ethnic, racial, and cultural diversity.

As Table 8.2 shows, the population of the United States is now one made up largely of the offspring of immigrants. The parents or grandparents of most contemporary Americans arrived in this country during the twentieth century. Many of the cultural values and life-styles they brought with them are still to some degree alive and well in the United States. We can see that in our ethnic neighborhoods, foods, folk festivals, and diverse religious groups.

Just before and after the turn of the century, unprecedented numbers of immigrants poured into the United States from all parts of the globe, but mainly Europe. Shown here, eating lunch in the main dining room, is a group of immigrants passing through Ellis Island. Some called it the "Golden Door" to their life in the New World. The result of this massive immigration was a society of great ethnic, racial, cultural, and religious diversity. Such diversity remains an important feature of the audiences for mass communications in the United States. (AP/Wide World Photos)

TABLE 8.2
U.S. Population by
Ethnic Group

Ethnic Group	Population (thousands)	Ethnic Group	Population (thousands)
European		**Hispanic**	
English	49,596	Mexican	7,693
German	49,224	Puerto Rican	1,444
Irish	40,166	Cuban	598
French	12,892	Dominican	171
Italian	12,184	Spanish/Hispanic	2,687
Scottish	10,049	Colombian	156
Polish	8,228	Spanish	95
Dutch	6,304	Ecuadoran	88
Swedish	4,345	Salvadoran	85
Norwegian	3,454	Total	13,017
Russian	2,781		
Czech	1,892	**Asian**	
Hungarian	1,777	Chinese	894
Welsh	1,665	Filipino	795
Danish	1,518	Japanese	791
Portuguese	1,024	Korean	377
Total	207,099	Asian Indian	312
		Vietnamese	125
Middle-Eastern		Total	3,384
Lebanese	295		
Armenian	213	**Other**	
Iranian	123	Jamaican	253
Syrian	107	Haitian	90
Total	738	Hawaiian	202
		Native American	6,716
African		French-Canadian	780
Afro-American	20,965	Canadian	456
African	204	Total	8,497
Total	21,169	Grand Total	253,904

Source: U.S. Bureau of the Census, Statistical Abstract of the United States, 111th ed. (Washington, D.C.: 1991).

During the period of the great immigrations, the national policy was based on the "melting pot theory," in which all immigrants would drop their foreign ways and merge into a single American culture. It was a policy intended to unify the nation politically and reduce the risk that age-old blood hatreds and ethnic animosities would create destructive political conflict in the United States. (Such ethnic strife has recently reared its head in the former Soviet Union and Yugoslavia.) In that sense, the melting pot policy worked very well. Americans share a common language, even though others are also spoken. Moreover, although there are people in this country with almost every conceivable ethnic and religious background, we are able to function very well within our secular democratic institutions, which separate church and state. In other respects, the melting pot was a dreadful idea that brought disrespect to other people's cultures and led to prejudice, discrimination based on ethnicity, and conflict between parents and children. Our contemporary policy of cultural pluralism is aimed at avoiding these consequences. However, it may also produce problems.

Internal Population Movements

A factor that works in the other direction, to reduce certain kinds of differences between people in audiences, is internal migration. Major shifts in population within U.S. borders have taken place during the present century. They resulted in redistributions of the population into various regions of the country. The most visible of these internal migrations have been the following:

1. The great westward movement—which has been extended into modern times. This has caused high rates of growth in most of the Western and Southwestern states during recent decades.
2. The farm-to-city movement that occurred as millions of rural people were attracted to cities and factory towns as opportunities arose through the growth of industry. This greatly accelerated the growth of the urban centers of the Northeast.
3. A large south-to-north movement of population that took place as African-Americans left the harsh conditions of the South to seek work in the industrial North. The majority of the urban black communities that exist in Northern cities today grew sharply as a result of this trend. It was accelerated greatly during the two world wars, when factory hands were badly needed in war industries.
4. A continuous exodus to the suburbs as the white middle class escaped from crime, racial tensions, and other stressful conditions of the city. This led to vast expansion of suburban communities in all parts of the nation.

During the past two decades, some of these trends have been partially reversed. Increasing numbers of people have moved to the Sun Belt states. They sought economic opportunities as Southern states changed from agriculture to other types of industries. Many older Americans sought more favorable weather conditions and lower living costs for their retirement. There has also been an expansion of small towns that are within commuting distance of large cities. Finally, with the gentrification of formerly run-down areas in some cities, many younger middle-class families have moved back to more urban areas.

Implications of Population Changes for Mass Communication

Both the massive immigration and internal migrations of population that have characterized the American population have had implications for mass communication. Adding millions of people from a long list of foreign coun-

Four great streams of internal migration have characterized the American population over the last century. One was the westward movement, which brought people to newly acquired territories, displacing Native Americans. A second was the South to North movement of African-Americans, from subsistence farming or sharecropping to urban ways of life. A third was the farm to city movement, bringing rural people into urban environments. Finally, an exodus from the cities to surrounding areas concentrated middle-class whites in the suburbs. All of these movements played a part in structuring the American audience for mass communications. (Joe Munroe, Photo Researchers, Inc.)

tries to the population of the United States left a legacy of cultural diversity, resulting in racial and ethnic co-cultures that continue to exist. This is a factor that can create conflict and animosity, both of which create barriers to communication. For example, racial and ethnic groups are sensitive to their treatment in the media. This has become abundantly clear over the years. To be politically correct, communicators must encode media messages with a clear understanding of the beliefs, attitudes, and values of people from diverse backgrounds. Professional communicators ignore this principle at their risk.

Although, as we have shown, immigration from abroad has been a significant factor in creating diversity, the American population is also one that has constantly been on the move, migrating and relocating within the nation's expanding borders. Over the generations, this has mixed diverse people in ways that have reduced their differences, producing a strong and unifying *general American culture*. Thus, internal population shifts have to some extent resulted in a kind of "homogenization effect" on national tastes for certain kinds of media content. Because of the relatively predictable nature of the general American culture, the media have been able to present entertainment—soap operas, evening crime drama, game shows, films, and other kinds of content—that is not bound to particular ethnic co-cultures. Each major socioeconomic level has media products that appeal to its tastes and interests in all parts of the country, creating a true national audience for the print, film, and broadcast media.

Contemporary Sources of Diversity

We have reviewed the great diversity among Americans that has resulted from two centuries of large-scale immigration. However, additional contemporary sources of social differentiation and individual differences in the population, and consequently in media audiences, are very obvious demographic factors. Important among them are age, gender and education. There are others as well, but these three have a particularly strong influence on what people select from the mass media.

Age

No factor is more important in the process of mass communication than age. Significant trends have taken place in the American population with respect to this demographic factor. The most pronounced among them is that Americans are now living much longer on average than was true at the beginning of the century. And there is every likelihood that the aging trend will continue. As Table 8.3 shows, in 1900, the average life expectancy at birth was 47.3 years.[3] By 1991, it had risen steadily to 75.7. Figure 8.3 illustrates how this has meant an increasingly aging population, which, of course, has significant implications for interests, tastes, and preferences of media audiences.

The causes behind this extension of average human life expectancy are not difficult to understand. For the most part, they are a result of public health measures and preventative measures that have reduced the influence of infectious diseases as the leading causes of death. At the turn of the century, such diseases regularly struck large numbers of people. For example, in 1900, 200 people for every 100,000 in the population died of influenza and pneumonia. During the influenza epidemic of 1918–19 alone, more than 500,000 Americans died of the dread disease.[4] By 1960, the rate of deaths due to this cause was down to a mere 0.2 fatalities per 100,000. The number of deaths from small pox, tuberculosis, diphtheria, typhoid fever, dysentery, whooping cough, scarlet fever, and malaria showed similar declines.

Older people were particularly vulnerable, and mortality from these diseases kept the average age of the population low, as it had been for centuries. Preventative measures that now seem simple and obvious to us were not understood. However, medical experts increasingly discovered the microorganisms that caused these diseases and took steps to control them. These steps included sanitary sewage disposal, purification of water, quarantining those who were already infected, and the use of effective vaccines.

These public health measures, coupled with more attention to industrial accidents (a major cause of deaths among males in particular), began to extend the average life expectancy of the American population. Today, this trend continues. The effects of smoking have been uncovered, and we are moving rapidly toward a smokeless society. The relationship between diet, exercise, and health is now clearer to many Americans, and they are taking steps that will extend their lives. Thus, the composition of the population in

**TABLE 8.3
Changing Life
Expectancy of
Individuals, 1900–1991**

Year	Average Age at Death*
1900	47.3
1910	50.0
1920	54.1
1930	59.7
1940	62.9
1950	68.2
1960	69.7
1970	70.9
1980	73.7
1991	75.7

*This is the number of years that a person born in a particular year can expect to survive on average if death rates remain the same as during that year.

Source: U.S. Bureau of the Census, Statistical Abstract of the United States, 1992; U.S. Bureau of the Census, Historical Statistics of the United States, Colonial Times to 1970, Series B, Nos. 107–115 (Washington, D.C.: U.S. Government Printing Office, 1975).

Americans are now living much longer than they were at the beginning of the twentieth century. Life expectancy (the average age at death of people born during a given year) has risen by nearly thirty years. For the most part, this rise has been due to relatively simple measures, such as improving water quality, more effective disposal of human wastes, inoculation and vaccination to prevent the spread of diseases, and related public health measures. Life expectancy will continue to rise, however, as scientists continue to discover ways to keep older people in better health. This has significant implications for mass communication as audiences will be made up of older individuals.

**FIGURE 8.2
Rising Life Expectancy
of Individuals,
1900–1991**

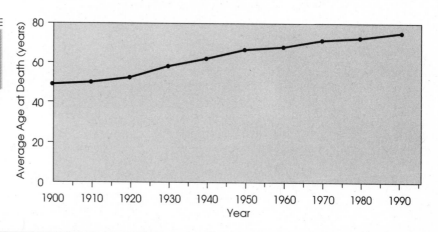

terms of age will continue to change, with more and more older people among the media audiences.

Table 8.4 and Figure 8.3 show the trends for four age groups in the United States between 1900 and 1990. The number of seniors in the society has increased steadily, but the numbers of middle-aged people, young adults, and youths has fluctuated from one decade to the next. These fluctuations are due to increases and decreases in the birth rate from time to time. For example, during the Great Depression of the 1930s, the number of births per family declined sharply, and many postponed having children. World War II came right after that, continuing a low birth rate. This is reflected in the decline of the number of young adults in the population between 1945 and 1970. Similar considerations account for the drop in the number of youths, shown in Figure 8.3. Then, the postwar years were characterized by an accelerated birth rate. This shows up in Figure 8.3 as a rise in the number of young adults (the baby boomers) in the population between 1960 and 1980. More recently, a dropping birth rate caused a decline in the number of youths.

Gender

Males and females do not select identical kinds of content from the mass media. This means that gender is an important demographic factor in trying to determine what kinds of material will work well to achieve the goals of professional communicators. A review of past trends and the current composition of the American population in terms of gender can help in understanding media audiences.

For reasons that are not entirely clear, there are more males than females born in all human populations. About 106 baby boys arrive for every 100 girls. Perhaps this is nature's way, based on long evolution. In earlier times, many males were killed in the hunt and in battle. Consequently, the death rate for men was higher than that for women. In fact, it still is! Today, females outnumber males in our population. As Table 8.5 shows, for every 100 females there are only 95.2 males. The number of males per 100 females in the population is called the *sex ratio*. As can be seen in Figure 8.4, it has dropped steadily during the twentieth century.

One reason for the changing sex ratio is that the number of males in the society at the beginning of the century was greater because of the typical pattern of immigration. That is, males came in larger numbers than females. Some—but not all—later sent for their families. Then, as the factor of immigration declined in importance, the higher risks for males in the labor force and in wars altered the ratio. Today, many women survive their husbands and live on as older widows. Thus, the imbalance between the two gender categories is less at younger ages than for seniors. Among the elderly, women greatly outnumber men.

Education

Educational attainment in the American population has been rising sharply for many decades. The overall trend is illustrated in Figure 8.5, showing the median years of formal schooling for all categories of Americans. Table 8.6 shows the various levels of education attained by Americans since 1940. As can be seen, the percentage of the population with only elementary education has declined significantly. At the other end of the scale, the proportion who have gone to or completed college has risen sharply. Therefore, we

TABLE 8.4   Changes in the U.S. Population by Age Categories, 1900–1990*

Year	Youths (15–24)		Young Adults (25–44)		Middle-Aged (45–64)		Seniors (65+)	
	Number	% of Total	Number	% of Total	Number	% of Total	Number	% of Total
1900	14,951	19.2	21,434	28.2	10,463	13.8	3,099	4.1
1905	16,526	19.7	24,092	28.7	11,867	14.2	3,505	4.2
1910	18,212	19.7	27,033	29.3	13,555	14.7	3,986	4.3
1915	18,844	18.7	29,710	29.5	15,484	15.4	4,501	4.5
1920	18,821	17.7	31,798	29.9	17,124	16.1	4,929	4.6
1925	20,691	17.9	34,296	29.6	19,126	16.5	5,786	5.0
1930	22,487	18.3	36,309	29.5	21,573	17.5	6,705	5.4
1935	23,130	18.2	37,987	29.9	23,947	18.8	7,804	6.1
1940	24,033	18.2	39,868	30.2	26,249	19.9	9,031	6.8
1945	23,709	16.9	45,521	32.5	28,630	20.5	10,494	7.5
1950	22,260	14.7	45,489	30.0	30,764	20.1	12,362	8.1
1955	21,667	13.1	46,993	28.4	33,410	20.2	14,489	8.8
1960†	24,546	13.6	47,140	26.1	36,203	20.0	16,675	9.2
1965	30,773	15.8	46,912	24.1	38,916	20.0	18,451	9.5
1970	36,496	17.8	48,435	23.6	41,974	20.5	20,085	9.8
1975	40,812	18.9	54,302	25.1	43,781	20.3	22,696	10.5
1980	42,743	18.8	63,294	27.8	44,515	19.5	25,704	11.3
1985	39,801	16.6	74,077	31.0	44,934	18.8	28,540	12.0
1990	37,074	14.9	80,596	32.5	46,169	18.5	31,078	12.5

*Population figures are in thousands.   †Alaska and Hawaii added after this date.

Sources: U.S. Bureau of the Census, Historical Statistics of the United States, Colonial Times to 1970, Series A, Nos. 23–28; Statistical Abstract of the United States, 1991.

**FIGURE 8.3
Trends in U.S.
Population by Age
Categories, 1900–1990**

The age composition of a population is of vital concern to professional communicators. The various age categories in media audiences constitute distinctive markets for different kinds of consumer products. In addition, various kinds of media content appeal to different age segments. The percentage of older people in the American population continues its rise; the percentage of youths is now in decline. The proportion who are young adults continues to rise, and this group now makes up a significant proportion of the population.

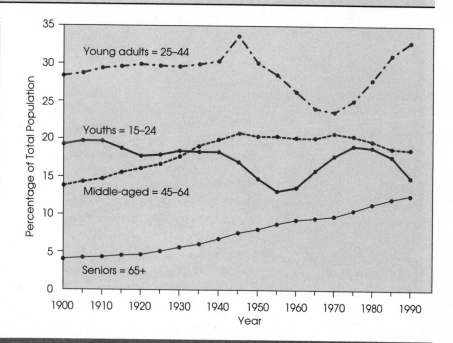

TRENDS IN THE AMERICAN POPULATION

**TABLE 8.5
Numbers of Males and
Females in the U.S.
Population,
1900–1991***

The gender composition of a population is of great importance to mass communicators. More males are born in any given year than females. However, by the time they reach retirement years, females outnumber males. This influences the gender composition of older audiences. Moreover, during this century, the proportion of the population that is male in any given year has declined steadily. The earlier surplus of males was a product of immigration. More males than females left their native lands to immigrate to the United States.

Year	Number of Males	Number of Females	Males per 100 Females
1900	38,867	37,227	104.4
1905	42,965	40,857	105.2
1910	47,554	44,853	106.0
1915	51,573	48,973	105.3
1920	54,291	52,170	104.1
1925	58,813	57,016	103.2
1930	62,297	60,780	102.5
1935	64,110	63,140	101.5
1940	66,352	65,770	100.9
1945	70,035	69,893	100.2
1950	75,539	76,146	99.2
1955	82,030	83,246	98.5
1960	89,320	91,352	97.8
1965	95,609	98,694	96.8
1970	100,266	104,613	95.8
1975	105,366	110,607	95.3
1980	110,888	116,869	94.9
1985	116,648	122,631	95.1
1991	122,979	129,198	95.2

*Population figures are in thousands.

Source: U.S. Department of Commerce, Bureau of the Census, Current Population Reports, Series P-25, Nos. 519, 917, 1045, 1057, and 1095.

**FIGURE 8.4
Number of Males per
100 Females in the U.S.
Population, 1900–1991**

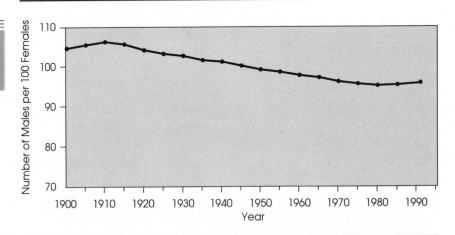

have, as a nation, become far more educated than was the case before World War II.

This great advance in education is a product of several factors. One is the history-making concept of free (tax-supported) and mandatory education for all children, which was introduced by Horace Mann in Massachusetts in 1834. Before that, it was mainly the children of the affluent who became educated. At the time, it seemed to conservative elements a wild and radical idea, and they opposed it bitterly. However, it spread to all the states, and as a result, we have a population deeply devoted to education today. Our system of state-supported education extends beyond secondary school to community colleges, four-year institutions, and great research universities that are all funded in part by tax revenues. We also enjoy the largest number of private schools, colleges, and universities in the world. These, along with government supported programs, such as the G.I. Bill, Pell grants, and student loans, have opened educational doors to almost all individuals who have the motivation and intellectual capacity to earn degrees. In that sense, the United States is unique.

Implications of Diversity for Mass Communication

Age, gender, and education are basic demographic factors that have a truly significant influence on the media habits of American audiences. It has been very well-established that older people have very different preferences and media habits than younger people. They follow the news avidly (both in print and broadcasting); they attend fewer movies and select ones different from those that appeal to youths and young adults. Seniors also watch more television, perhaps because they have more time. They have very different preferences in music, and therefore, their radio listening tends to be very different from that of younger people. They also have more money.

Gender is not as powerful a factor in determining selections from media as age and education. However, women do have different preferences in content from men in many ways. As a category, they have less interest in sports, and they tend to dislike violent films. They are more likely to read romance novels than adventure or war stories, and they watch the daily soap operas much more than men. For understandable reasons, they attend more closely to presentations about child-rearing, fashions, and beauty products. At the same time, women are similar to men within specific age and educational categories. They have about the same interest in public affairs and political news.

No factor plays a greater role than education in determining what selections people make from available media content. Those who are well-educated, as compared to people with limited schooling, select different books, read different parts of newspapers, attend different films, prefer different types of TV programming, and listen to different radio programs.

In summary, as the above sections have shown, age, gender, and education, as well as race and ethnic background, are factors that have a significant influence on what people select from the daily flow of media content as well as how they interpret and respond to those messages. Professional communicators must take these factors into account as they design and encode messages.

TABLE 8.6 Percentage of Population Completing Various Years of School, 1940–1990*

| Year | Population (thousands)† | Elementary | | | High School | | College | | Median Number of Years Completed |
		0-4 Years	5-7 Years	8 Years	1-3 Years	4 Years	1-3 Years	4 or More	
1940	74,775	13.5	11.4	34.6	15.0	14.1	5.4	4.6	8.4
1950	87,885	10.8	15.9	20.2	17.0	20.2	7.1	6.0	9.3
1960	99,438	8.3	13.8	17.5	19.2	24.6	8.8	7.7	10.6
1970	109,899	5.5	10.0	12.8	19.4	31.1	10.6	10.7	12.1
1980	132,836	3.6	6.7	8.0	15.3	34.6	15.7	16.2	12.5
1990	156,538	2.3	4.0	4.9	11.2	38.4	17.9	21.2	12.9

*Not all respondents reported their educational attainment, so percentages total less than 100%.
†Population is defined as those aged 25 years and older.

Source: Statistical Abstract of the United States 1948, 1950, 1960, 1970, 1991, and 1992.

**FIGURE 8.5
Growth in the
Educational
Attainment of the U.S.
Population, 1940–1990**

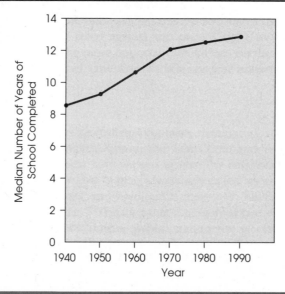

The level of educational attainment of the audience is of critical concern to professional communicators. Educational level is a rough index of income. Those with a college degree, for example, make about $1,000 a month more than those who only completed high school. Those who did not complete high school have far lower incomes. Educated audiences prefer and can deal with more sophisticated mass communication content. During the last half-century, the proportions of the population completing high school and college have risen sharply. At the opposite end, the proportion dropping out before high school has declined significantly.

The Changing American Family

Media messages are received and interpreted mainly within the context of our families. They influence not only what we attend to but also how we understand and act upon what we receive. American families have changed significantly during the twentieth century—and especially since World War II—in terms of size, decision-making, women working outside the home, and aggregate purchasing power. All of these trends have had important consequences for mass communications.

Trends in Family Size

At the beginning of the twentieth century, when Americans were mainly a rural people, the extended family was common and households included a larger number of individuals. That is, grandparents, parents, and their children—three generations—often lived in the same house. Other relatives, such as a widowed aunt or aging father-in-law, might have also lived with the family. In addition, families included on average a larger number of children than they do today. For example, in 1940, the average size of a family in the United States was 3.76 persons. By 1990, this had fallen to 2.63, a decline of over 30 percent. Today, there are far more single-parent families, persons living alone, and couples with no children. Obviously, such smaller families attend to and use almost all forms of mass communication differently than do those with larger numbers of members.

Relationships between Husbands and Wives

During this century, the American family changed from one that was male-dominated to a more egalitarian pattern. As the century began, few husbands wanted their wives to work outside the home. Men were supposed to be the breadwinners, supporting the family by their earnings alone, and they accepted that obligation. In their capacities as providers, they felt entitled to make the major decisions in the family, and for the most part, their views and preferences prevailed over those of their wives and children. Women were supposed to be submissive and to serve as child-bearers and home-makers. They had little power and no right to vote. Until relatively recently, they were not even allowed to own property. Women could not initiate a divorce, take out a mortgage in their own name, or obtain credit at a store.

One of the most significant changes in the American family since the turn of the century has been a reduction in the number of people in an average household. In earlier times, the norm was the extended family, consisting of several generations and often including aunts, uncles, or other relatives who had to be provided for in a society without a national welfare system. Today such large family units are the exception, and many families consist of a single parent and one or more children. This change has greatly altered the family as a consuming unit and modified the mass communication audience. (Stock Montage, Inc.)

In general, then, the traditional family was almost completely male-centered. It had a clear-cut division of labor—one in which neither wives nor children had much of a voice in their own destiny.

Because of these characteristics, the American family at the beginning of the century was a very different economic and consuming unit than it is today. Because few women had control of the family purse-strings, they played only a minor role in purchasing decisions. Typically, their husbands doled out an allowance for them to purchase their clothing and the family food. As Table 8.7 shows, only 18.8 percent of women were in the labor force. Most of these worked as teachers, secretaries, domestic servants, or factory hands. There were almost no professionals, such as doctors, lawyers, or professors.

Today, drastic changes have taken place. The movement for equal rights for women began to coalesce in 1848 when the first women's rights convention was held at Seneca Falls, a community in upstate New York. In the present century the movement's greatest achievement was women's suffrage. Women gained the vote when the Nineteenth Amendment to the Constitution was ratified in 1920. The movement waned for several decades, but women began to change their job status during World War II, when many entered the labor force temporarily, replacing men who had joined the armed forces. They earned high wages and learned to enjoy financial independence. During the years that followed, a new feminism evolved that has drastically altered the status and freedoms of women in contemporary American society.

Although patterns of sexual harassment and limitations on women's economic opportunities remain, the American family is now very different from what it was just a few decades ago. Power tends to be shared, and husbands increasingly take responsibility for household chores, including shopping for domestic products. Women have a much greater voice in decisions about major purchases. For example, auto makers have found out that women constitute a large market and have changed their designs and products accordingly. Even children have money to spend and freedom to make choices—a fact not lost on those who advertise such items as food, clothing, athletic shoes, popular music, and films.

Female Participation in the Labor Force

No feature of family life has undergone more drastic change than the movement of women into the world of work. As Table 8.7 shows, there were relatively few women in the labor force at the beginning of the century. But as the century moved on, the proportion of females of working age who held jobs outside the home steadily increased. Figure 8.6 shows the upward trend.

This trend toward two-income families had a heavy impact on the mass media industries. For one thing, it considerably increased the aggregate purchasing power of American families. Perhaps it is more accurate to say that it kept disposable income from eroding as inflation in the society increased. And, in spite of the financial difficulties of the early 1990s, families with both

**TABLE 8.7
Women in the U.S.
Labor Force,
1900–1992**

The role that women play in American society is of great concern to professional mass communicators. One of the most significant trends in this century has been the movement of women into the labor force. This has altered their disposable income, their media habits, and their patterns of consumption. Today, more women work outside the home than at any period in U.S. history. This leads them to select different media content, attend to different advertisements, and purchase different kinds of products than during earlier periods.

Year	Number of Females of Working Age*	Number of Females in Labor Force†	Percentage of Women Who Work
1900	28,246,000	5,319,000	18.8
1910	34,553,000	8,076,000	23.4
1920	40,449,000	8,550,000	21.0
1930	48,773,000	10,752,000	22.0
1940	50,688,000	12,887,000	25.4
1950	54,293,000	18,412,000	30.9
1960††	61,582,000	23,240,000	37.7
1970	72,782,000	31,543,000	43.3
1980	88,348,000	45,487,000	51.5
1985	93,736,000	51,050,000	54.5
1986	94,789,000	52,413,000	55.3
1987	95,853,000	53,658,000	56.0
1988	96,756,000	54,742,000	56.6
1990	98,399,000	56,554,000	57.5
1992	100,035,000	57,798,000	57.8

*From 1900 to 1930, the U.S. Department of Labor defined those of working age as "noninstitutionalized civilians aged 16 years and older." From 1940 to 1960, 14-year-olds and older were included in the working age population. After 1960, the definition became "noninstitutionalized civilians aged 16 years and older" again. From 1940 to 1970, those of working age included people in the armed forces, as well as civilians.
†Includes both unemployed and employed.
††First year for which figures include Alaska and Hawaii.

Sources: U.S. Bureau of the Census, Historical Statistics of the United States, Colonial Times to 1970, Series D, Nos. 11–25; Statistical Abstract of the United States, 1992.

FIGURE 8.6   The Rising Proportion of Women in the U.S. Labor Force, 1900–1992

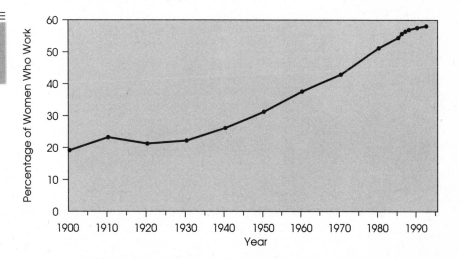

As more and more women have entered the labor force, relationships between husbands and wives have changed. Power tends to be shared, and husbands have taken greater responsibility for domestic chores. Women who earn a share of the household income are much more involved in purchasing decisions. These changes have altered advertising directed at women as consumers of various products and generally changed the nature of the audience for mass communications. (© James H. Karales/Peter Arnold, Inc.)

the husband and wife employed will continue to have more discretionary income than if we returned to the male breadwinner pattern.

Many women who work today are single, largely as a result of divorce. The proportion of Americans who are divorced has risen sharply in recent years. For example, in 1970, only 3.2 percent of the population were divorced. By 1989, that had risen to 8.1 percent, a 153 percent increase in just twenty years! There are more divorced women in the society than men—largely because divorced men tend to remarry rather quickly. If children are involved, the courts tend to follow legal tradition and award custody to the woman. This has created a significant number of American families in which a working mother provides the sole or major support for her children. These are largely low-income families, because women lose the purchasing power of the husband as the marriage is dissolved, even if child support is paid. There are other single-parent families, with some made up of never-married women and others of divorced men. In all of these families, patterns of media usage tend to differ from those in intact families.

Implications of Family Trends for Mass Communication

Of all of the above factors that influence the functioning of the media in American society, it is the purchasing power of consumers in the audience that is of greatest interest to professional communicators. Because of their heavy dependence on advertising, newspaper publishers want their papers to get into the hands of and be read by those who are likely to buy what is advertised. The same is true in the worlds of magazines, television, and radio. It is those categories of consumers that (1) exist in large numbers and

TABLE 8.8   Percentages of U.S. Households at Various Income Levels, 1992

| Group | Number of Households (thousands) | Income Level | | | | | Median Household Income (dollars) |
		Under $9,999	$10,000–$24,999	$25,000–$49,999	$50,000–$74,999	Above $75,000	
Total	95,669	14.9	26.8	32.5	15.4	10.4	30,126
White	81,675	12.8	26.4	33.3	16.3	11.2	31,569
Black	11,083	30.8	29.8	27.2	8.4	3.7	18,807
Hispanic	6,379	20.7	33.7	30.6	10.0	5.0	22,691

Source: Statistical Abstract of the United States, 1993.

The income of different categories of people in the society is of great interest to professional communicators. Those who make up the white majority earn the most money and consequently make up the largest block of purchasing consumers. However, Hispanics and African-Americans taken as a whole make up a significant block of people with enough purchasing power to form a very large market for many kinds of goods. These groups may prefer different media content, attend to different advertisements, and purchase different kinds of products than the majority do.

FIGURE 8.7   Median Household Income of Groups within the U.S. Population, 1992

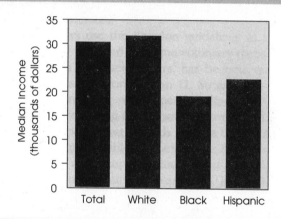

(2) have available income to spend that are of greatest interest to those who produce and present media content.

In exercising purchasing power, it is the family that is the most significant *unit of consumption*. Individuals make purchases independently, to be sure, but it is families that buy most of the food and purchase homes, automobiles, furniture, appliances, and even recreation.

Family incomes differ greatly on average, depending on what demographic categories are considered. One of the most obvious differences is that prevailing between white, Latino, and African-American households. As Figure 8.7 shows graphically, whites dominate. It is also clear from Table 8.8 that African-Americans are twice as likely to be at the lowest income level. At the other end of the income scale, whites are twice as likely to be at the highest level. Hispanics fall in between. Thus, economic resources, and therefore family buying power, are concentrated among whites. There are not only ten times as many of them in the audience, they are far more likely than either blacks or Hispanics to be above the national median in income.

The changing American family is the foundation for understanding many of the purchasing decisions and media habits of contemporary Americans. For that reason, understanding the size, structure, and processes of decision-making within families is critical for media professionals who want to influence purchasing decisions using advertising and other persuasive appeals. Today, the family is smaller, less likely to include members other than the parents and children, and far more democratic in its decision-making. The majority of women of appropriate age are employed outside the home, and they are now much more important as consumers of a variety of products than they were just a few decades ago. Even children have a considerable amount of spending money if considered in aggregate.

Generally, the trend toward two-income families has increased family purchasing power, or at least kept it from serious erosion during a lengthy inflationary period. At the same time, other family-related trends have had a negative impact on women's aggregate purchasing power. In particular, the increase in the number of single or divorced mothers raising their children alone has created a growing number of consumer households with very limited income.

Overall, these changes in the American family, along with all of the demographic factors of population growth, race, ethnicity, age, gender, and education, have created a complex and constantly changing audience for mass communicators to sort out as they try to discover and chart who attends to their messages. Since all of the trends we have described will continue in various ways, the audiences of the future will be *unlike* those of yesterday or today. But whatever the size and composition of a given audience at any given time, the many social categories involved will continue to play a significant part in shaping the beliefs, attitudes, and behavior of every individual who turns to the mass media for news or entertainment and who receives information about products to buy. The bottom line is that at any particular time there are many audiences of varying size and diversity in the heterogeneous and multicultural population, each composed of its unique pattern of demographic factors and individual differences.

Assessing Audience Composition and Attention

Each of the media faces the task of discovering and continuously *assessing* the size and composition of its audience. If professional communicators did not know the nature of their receivers and how they were responding, they would soon be out of business. But as this section will show, the assessment of audience size and composition is carried on in a variety of ways.

In principle, there could be three kinds of information flowing back to professional communicators from their receivers. Having effective feedback would make it easier for professional communicators to reach the largest number of people, tailor the nature of their messages to the capacities and interests of their audience, and prompt members of the audience to take some form of desired action (buy, vote, donate, etc.). One very limited kind of such information is *simultaneous feedback*, such as takes place in face-to-face, or interpersonal, communication. A second, more common, one is *delayed feedback*, such as occurs in letters to the editor or phone calls to the studio after a broadcast. Finally, the most widely used is *audience-assessment information*, obtained from various agencies and services that make a business of measuring audiences for the various media. These kinds of data are systematically gathered in the form of circulation audits, ratings, and polls.

Only in a very limited sense is simultaneous feedback a part of the mass communication process. As we pointed out in our discussion of the linear model of mass communication, there are very few occasions when receivers are actually visible to a professional communicator while he or she is delivering a message. It can happen, as in the case of a live audience in a studio, a news report where a reporter is among a crowd of people, or a call-in program on radio or television, where at least some members of the home audience can be in direct touch with the communicator. For the most part, however, simultaneous feedback from the audience is not available as the media message is being formulated or transmitted.

Delayed feedback is another matter. Indicators of approval or disapproval come from many sources. For example, a considerable amount of commentary and criticism often flows from individual members of the audience back to the communicator. Newspapers regularly print at least some letters to the editor, in which individuals denounce or applaud news stories or other material that has been printed. Large metropolitan newspapers get several thousand of these letters a year (but print only about 10 percent). Most other papers receive from a hundred to about five hundred a year, depending on their size. Similarly, people write to or call radio and television stations to air their views about particular broadcasts. Even film makers receive mail with comments on their products. The limitation of such material is that it is scarcely representative of the views of the majority of the audience. Such delayed feedback tends to come mainly from disgruntled people with an axe to grind who are sufficiently motivated to write or call to take issue with the communicator.

Sometimes such delayed feedback takes a more organized form. From time to time, various groups take strongly critical positions on the content of mass communications. A religious group may object to the way in which sacred ideas or events are depicted in a film and organize demonstrations at theaters where it is being exhibited. An organization representing a minority group concerned about the way its people are portrayed may put pressure on local or national media through threats of boycotts. An organization of educators, mothers, or physicians may deplore the content of television and seek the assistance of Congress to bring about change. Many professional groups, such as police organizations, seek change in the content of television, the movies, and even recordings. Some mount nationwide petition

HOW THE AUDIENCE RULES IN "ADOPTING" NEW TECHNOLOGIES:
A Linchpin to the Spread of Material Culture

John Carey, a genial communications technology expert, has a favorite question. He seriously asks his audiences, "Would you buy a dog that could fly?"

He then explains, "It's an odd question, but no more odd than questions people are asked everyday in telephone surveys that try to determine the likelihood of consumers buying futuristic communications services." Says Carey, "In responding to a question about a hypothetical, genetically engineered flying dog, you might respond positively on the grounds that you would be the envy of all your neighbors, or negatively if you considered the problems associated with walking such a dog." In either instance, Carey wonders aloud with his audiences, "How much confidence should the person asking the question put in your answer?"[1]

Carey and other advisers to high-technology companies producing new media try to get the best possible intelligence for their clients. After all, no one wants to manufacture a new device, appliance, or service that people say they want but will not pay for. In a sense, new technological devices ranging from VCRs to picture phones and electronic notebooks are like

orphans when first introduced by manufacturers. They are produced because they are technologically possible and because the manufacturer wants to make money. The big question is, Will the public buy the new product? In some instances, new technologies start out as institutional services. For example, when the telephone was first introduced, it was not practical for individual households but used in offices. Eventually, it was "adopted" by people in their homes and then even in their cars. By contrast, early facsimile machines in the 1930s and 1940s were test-marketed in people's homes. Consumers reacted by saying "This is interesting, but why should I pay for it?" and for decades the fax was dead. It came back in the 1980s, first in offices and institutions and later in private homes. Today, people can get faxes through their laptop computers and electronic notebooks on airplanes.

Carey, a guru of consumer adoption of new technologies, says there are four factors worth watching when considering the possible success or failure of a new technology.

First, the price has to come down dramatically from where it started. Phone calls were exorbitantly

drives to put pressure on professional communicators for change. For example, the illustration on p. 268 is an advertisement that was published in a number of newspapers in December 1992 by a group called the American Family Association, headed by the Reverend Donald Wildmon, with headquarters in Tupelo, Mississippi.

Are the media sensitive to such pressures from their audiences to a point where they actually alter the nature of their messages? The answer is "sometimes." We saw in Chapter 5 that, in its early years, the film industry became very concerned about public criticism and adopted a strong production code that completely cleaned up the movies—for a while. However, during the 1950s, the code became ineffective when television reduced movie attendance sharply. Films then turned to violence, sex, special-effects, gore, or whatever would result in paid admissions without creating too much of

expensive when first introduced (as much as a full day's pay for a three-minute call between New York and Chicago), as were radios, color TV sets, and pocket calculators. Affordability is key.

Second, technology needs to reach a point of explosive growth so that it can penetrate a significant number of households to be a serious contender for audience affections. For some devices, such as radio and television, the explosion came immediately, but for others, such as the VCR, growth came more slowly. VCRs were once seen as a luxury for the rich who could afford to *buy* a whole library of videotapes. The *rental* store was the trigger that made the technology affordable and useful for ordinary people. Today, 75 percent of Americans own a VCR.

Third, some technologies get off to a fast start only to fail later because they are fads and the public is fickle about them. Citizen-band (CB) radios in the 1970s and 3-D movies of the 1950s are examples of fast-moving, exciting new technologies that had short life spans. This does not mean that a new technology, like the fax, won't come back when there is public demand.

Fourth, sometimes small competitive disadvantages perceived early at the start may escalate and eventually spell doom for a new technology—for example, the battle between VHS and Beta formats in the video cassette market ended with the dominance of VHS. The public, says W. Brian Arthur, senses even a tiny competitive edge in a product and favors winners over losers. People watch publications such as *Consumer Reports* or TV consumer shows that indicate what will be the best product in the long run. Here, the role of information is crucial and critical.

Brilliant inventors, enthusiastic manufacturers, and skilled marketers all work in concert to curry public support, but it is the consumer in the end who votes at the cash register and determines which of the thousands of "orphans" in the marketplace will be "adopted." As David Poltrack, head of research for CBS, says, "for the commercial television industry, (the product) is its audience."[2]

1. John Carey, "Looking Back to the Future: How Communication Technologies Enter American Households," in John V. Pavlik and Everette E. Dennis, *Demystifying Media Technology* (Mountain View, Calif.: Mayfield, 1993), pp. 32–39.

2. David Poltrack, "The Big Three Networks," *Gannett Center Journal* (now the *Media Studies Journal*), Summer 1988, p. 53. See also W. Brian Arthur, "Positive Feedbacks in the Economy," *Scientific American*, February 1990, pp. 92–99; "Measuring the Audience," an entire issue of the *Gannett Center Journal* (now the *Media Studies Journal*), Summer 1988, which includes articles about the people meter and audience preferences and how they are determined.

an uproar. At one time or another, codes and conventions pertaining to virtually all of the media have been formulated by various groups. The problem with almost all such agreements is that they are voluntary and lack effective enforcement provisions. The result is that when financial pressures arise, the agreements become ineffective or are forgotten.

Awards and prizes are still another form of delayed feedback, although it comes from judges and other media professionals. Each industry has its contests in which its products are judged for various (largely symbolic) recognitions. The movies have their Academy Awards; the newspapers have Pulitzer Prizes; the advertising industry awards Clios for ads judged by various professional criteria; and so on.

The ultimate form of delayed feedback to the media is *profit*. If a particular kind of film brings in the dollars at the box office (or video rental store),

Delayed feedback often takes the form of simple letters or phone calls to the media, expressing the views of the person who writes or calls. Sometimes, however, such attempts at influence are far more elaborate. From time to time, nationwide efforts are mounted, such as boycotts of advertisers that sponsor programs that offend particular groups or letter writing campaigns to influence Congress. As this ad shows, Reverend Donald Wildmon and his group hope to change the media through a nationwide petition and letter drive. (Reprinted with permission of American Family Association)

it is likely that others will be produced within the genre. If a television series fails to attract the advertisers that the network needs, it will not be on the air very long. If a magazine's circulation falls below a certain level, it will be out of business. Thus, in the final analysis, audience approval in the form of paid admissions, rentals, subscriptions, purchase of products, and so forth is the only truly effective form of delayed feedback.

The media themselves understand very well the need to assess their audiences in terms of size, composition, interests, tastes, and purchasing power. In order to do that, a number of organizations providing such services have been developed over the years to measure the numbers of people who attend to media and to determine their demographic characteristics. This is critical information to all of the media, and they use this form of delayed feedback continuously to design and redesign their presentations in order to gain the attention of their audiences, to satisfy the audiences' interests and needs, and to elicit from the audiences behavior they deem desirable. In the sections that follow, we outline briefly the major forms that such audience assessment takes for print and broadcast media.

Measuring Circulations of Print Media

The basic assessment of audience size for a newspaper or a magazine is its *circulation*—paid subscriptions plus other sales by mail or single copies. Obviously, large numbers of readers attract advertisers who want their message seen by as large a number of people as possible. Early newspapers and magazines were often guilty of exaggerating the numbers of their readers and subscribers. To end this practice and promote reliable, impartial reports, a group of advertisers, advertising agencies, and publishers formed the Audit Bureau of Circulations (ABC) in 1914. It is essentially a combination research organization and auditing firm that makes periodic checks on circulations reported by the newspapers and magazines that make use of its services. Today most newspapers and magazines in the United States are ABC members, though several competing firms offer similar services. The data provided by ABC yield an important form of delayed feedback to the medium, and critical data to advertisers and advertising agencies who want precise numbers before deciding whether to place their ads. Market penetration, as represented by circulation, is an important indicator of audience composition and the apparent value of the medium to the advertiser.

ABC sets standards for circulation (such as solicitation methods and subscriptions) and requires a publisher's statement of circulation and other data every six months. The statements are checked, processed, printed, and distributed by ABC. Once a year, an ABC auditor goes to the offices of the newspaper or magazine and examines all records and materials necessary to verify the claims of the publisher's statement of circulation. Information provided by ABC in its semiannual reports includes audited, paid-circulation figures for the six-month period, with breakdowns for such things as subscriptions versus newsstand sales and data on regional, metropolitan, and special edition circulation. The report also includes an analysis of a single issue of the publication in terms of the market area it reaches and much more.

Assessing Movie Audiences

As we suggested earlier, the most significant means of gauging the response of any audience to any message transmitted by any medium is by determining the amount of profit that it eventually derives for its owners. For films, measuring profit—and thereby the response of the audience—is relatively straightforward. The total number of dollars derived from paid admissions to movie theaters—the box office receipts—is the major form of delayed feedback.

A daily trade newspaper, *Variety*, keeps track of the earnings of each film released and shown in the United States. Every week, a report is prepared showing the earnings of and several other kinds of information about the fifty films that lead the list. Each is followed week-by-week until its earnings are low enough that it falls out of the top fifty. The necessary data for *Variety's* "Weekly Box Office Report" are derived from a systematic survey, by an independent research firm, of some 1,600 theaters that are located in approximately twenty cities. It is a simple and reliable system and the results are closely followed by the entire industry. They provide a clear-cut means of assessing whether Americans like what has been produced well enough to pay for a ticket. However, it is not the only form of delayed feedback indicating a measure of a film's success. Once a movie has been shown in most theaters around the country, it is released in video cassette form for purchase and rental. In addition, many American films are shown in large foreign markets. A movie may not be a top box office success at home but do well in the home video market or in other countries.

A number of other approaches to analyzing audience response to films are used—both before release and after. Some studios make use of *focus groups.* These are composed of from a dozen to about twenty carefully selected people who see the movie before it is finally edited. If they dislike certain parts of it, it may be edited. Some consultants analyze film scripts even before they are produced in an attempt to forecast whether it will have audience appeal and why. Still other analysts interview people or persuade "sneak preview" audiences to fill out a questionnaire right after they have seen a film. All of these techniques can provide useful information.

Ratings and the Broadcast Audience

The paid circulation of a magazine or newspaper, or the amount of money people pay to see a movie, can be audited rather easily. But getting reliable information about the audience for a broadcasting station or a network is more difficult. Here, no physical object, such as a ticket, newspaper, or magazine, passes from one hand to another. Moreover, broadcast messages can occupy long periods of time and reach their audiences in different ways and at varying levels of intensity. Consequently, wrote broadcast historian Sydney Head, "no single universally accepted way of measuring broadcast consumption has evolved. Instead, several research companies using rival methods compete in the audience measurement field."[5] They use different procedures to chart audience size, characteristics, and behavior. Over the last twenty or thirty years, they have frequently changed these methods to keep pace with new techniques for using surveys and statistics.

Broadcast audience assessment, in one form or another, has been around a long time because radio, from its early days, and later television have had to justify their worth to advertisers who agreed to sponsor certain programs.[6] In addition, *ratings*, which involve audience as well as program and advertising analyses, have played a central role in determining the shape of broadcast content in America since the 1930s. The first ratings were done by advertising agencies, but before long the networks organized their own research departments. Later, independent research rating services joined in. Today, each of the major TV networks has a large research department that investigates such topics as the influence of television on children as well as trying to determine which programs will succeed with the audience.

In the world of television, the influence of ratings has gotten more intense in recent years, as cable and other new technologies have attempted to capture the traditional broadcast audience. For decades, the various techniques of assessment were quite crude. They were based on telephone interviews and a number of other procedures, such as diaries. Essentially, such efforts measured simple factors, such as when TV sets were turned on, not who actually watched and with what degree of attention. (As we will note, that limitation has now been reduced somewhat through the use of new devices and techniques.) An amused Albert Gollin, of the Newspaper Advertising Bureau, called the broadcast rating efforts a "drive to count every last pair of eyes watching TV in what purport to be representative samples of American homes." This, he said, might be an extreme example of "the American passion for numbers."[7]

At one level, broadcast ratings have generated increasingly complex quantitative assessments of who is watching, when, for how long, and with what intensity. At another, these "number crunching" ratings have inspired the ire of critics, who have called for new assessments. Their objections may be justified as dense numerical ratings are quite limited in what they tell us about the *quality* of television and its overall effect. The issue of critical examination of the social and cultural consequences of television raised in industry circles is echoed in universities, where scholars argue that quantification can lead to self-fulfilling results and does not necessarily yield much new knowledge about either the medium or its audience. For example, a Columbia University conference in 1985 explored this topic and urged the networks to develop *qualitative* means to make sense out of public reaction to television.

Types of ratings   One way to measure the audience in an area is to relate the number of receivers in working order to the total number of households; the result is the relative saturation, or *penetration,* of the broadcast medium in a particular area.[8] Obviously, this figure is not a precise measure of the audience, because it says nothing about the viewing habits of people, who may or may not be using their TV sets regularly. Penetration (or saturation) measures reveal the *potential* audience.

The search for more precision in calculating the broadcast audience led to systems in which the *relative audience size* for a particular time slot or program is calculated. Various measures are used in this approach. One kind is *instantaneous rating reports* that indicate the audience size at a particular moment; another is *cumulative reports* that give figures for a period of time, thirty minutes, for example.

More specifically, three measures frequently provided by audience measuring services are the rating of a particular program, the share of the total audience that is tuned to a station at a given time, and an index of households using television (again at a given time). These provide a set of comparative indices that tell within a specified market area how well a particular station is attracting viewers, as well as how well the programs that it offers are competing for the audience that is viewing at a particular time.

The differences among these forms are important. They can be expressed as follows.

A program's *rating* is defined as the number of households receiving the program, divided by total TV households in the market area (times 100). Or, in terms of a calculating formula:

$$\text{Rating} = \frac{\text{Households watching a particular program}}{\text{Total households with TV sets}} \times 100$$

Thus, in general terms, the rating is the *percentage* of the potential audience, made up of TV-set–owning households in an area, that could be watching or listening to a particular program aired in a particular time slot. It is a critical measure of program popularity.

Another important index is *HUT*, which stands for "households using television." This percentage does not tell much in itself, but it is needed in order to calculate the share of the active or viewing audience at any time that a particular station or program is attracting. HUT is defined as the number of households in the area with their TV sets turned on, divided by the total number of households that own sets (again, times 100). In terms of calculation, the formula is

$$\text{HUT} = \frac{\text{Households in the area with the TV set on}}{\text{Total households with TV sets}} \times 100$$

Still a third index is a program's, or a station's, *share*. This can be defined as the percentage of the audience presumed to be viewing the programming offered by a particular station at a particular time. This is often used as a measure of the success of the station (rather than the program) in competing for its slice of the available audience pie. This index can be calculated with the following formula:

$$\text{Share} = \frac{\text{Households tuned to a particular station}}{\text{Households in area with TV sets on}} \times 100$$

These measures may seem complex, or at least a bit confusing, but each provides somewhat different information that is helpful to both broadcasters and advertisers in sorting out how many people are attending to a station or a program at any given time. Rating services also provide estimates of the composition of the audience, with some demographic data about age, sex, education, and so on.

Research on the broadcast audience has undergone many changes over the years; today, the audience is examined in terms of its overall size potential, its actual size, its stability over time, how much time it actually spends with particular programs, and the degree of viewer loyalty, which is called *tuning inertia*. In addition to national television and radio ratings, there are also local station and market ratings for broadcasting, as well as relatively new services that measure the cable audience.

Cable ratings have proved difficult. They involve measures of cable penetration (the percentage of overall viewers on the cable) and audience viewing patterns across many more channels than is the case with conventional broadcasting. Radio research typically measures a much smaller audience than TV research does, because there are so many radio stations, and they aim at limited segments of the audience with their specific formats (rock, country-western, news, etc.).

Obtaining ratings   Radio and TV ratings are obtained in rather similar ways. In all audience research, after the area or market has been designated, some more or less representative set of people—a sample—must be selected. The people are contacted; data obtained from them are recorded in some way so that it can be analyzed; and reports are prepared for users. More than fifty companies conduct research on a national level, and scores of others do local and regional research that leads to ratings of some kind. Their first step is to define the local population or area of interest. Two major broadcast rating services, *Arbitron* and *Nielsen*, provide national and local ratings. Arbitron developed one method for defining the areas of interest in the television industry. It divides the United States into more than 260 market areas called *areas of dominant influence,* or ADIs. Nielsen uses another term, *designated market areas.* Each of the nation's 3,141 counties is assigned to one of the areas, and the markets are ranked according to the number of TV households. The ADIs range from New York, with more than 7 million TV households, to Pembina, North Dakota, with just over 6,500. The information is used by media advertising buyers to try to capture specified audiences.[9]

Researchers use various techniques: telephone interviews, in-person interviews, listener/viewer diaries, and receiver meters. Arbitron, which conducts research for both radio and television, asks a sample of about four thousand listeners or viewers to keep a weekly diary of their daily listening or viewing behavior. Radio listeners, for example, are asked to indicate the amount of time spent listening and the stations they listen to, including the specific program and the place where they are listening (for example, at home or away from home, including in a car). Samples are drawn from each market area and are weighted to provide a picture of the listening or viewing habits of the people who are asked to keep diaries. Needless to say, the system has many limitations. People forget to fill out the diaries. Some put in data to make it seem as though they listened, even if they really did not. Less than half of the diaries distributed to the sample come back to Arbitron with usable data.

For years, the Nielsen ratings, from which the network TV programs were ranked, were based on data accumulated from a device called an *audiometer*. It was attached to TV sets in a sample of about 1,700 American homes. All it recorded was how long the set was on and to what channel it was tuned. It provided no information as to whether someone was actually viewing. However, the device delivered the information to a central computer through a telephone-wire network. This allowed rapid daily processing of data, which were analyzed for the national prime-time ratings. For ratings of local programs, Nielsen also used diaries. In addition to diaries and audiometers, a considerable amount of telephone sampling was used to provide the electronic media with information about their audiences.

The people meter controversy In the late 1980s, as computer-driven audience research became more precise, a new technique for audience assessment was introduced by Nielsen, Arbitron, and other firms. The *people meter* consists of a small box that sits on top of the TV set and a hand-held gadget (like a remote channel-changer) with which people can record what they say they are viewing. Nielsen uses about four thousand such systems in a supposedly random sample of households. Each provides information on various demographic factors for the rating company. While viewing, members of the family press buttons that record times and stations. As viewers turn on their people meters and record their viewing, the information goes instantly over phone lines to a central computer, which yields almost instantaneous rating analyses. Originally tested on an experimental basis, people meters were so popular by 1987 that they had replaced the diary system. They seem to work well, with about 90 percent of the households providing usable data.

Although people meters attracted little sustained attention outside of the trade press, experts regarded this new tool as the most dramatic development in audience measurement in decades. However, it was not immediately accepted by all parties because it gave different results from earlier techniques. CBS especially objected to some of the earliest findings derived from

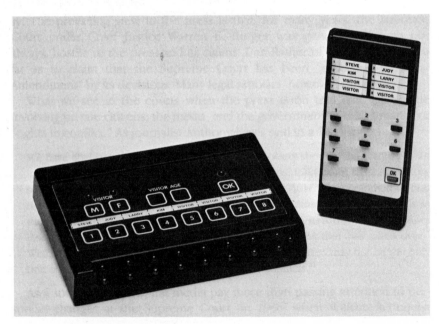

The introduction of the people meter by companies that provide rating services created a controversy about actual audience size. Some critics maintain that these devices underestimate the TV audience. As shown here, people record what they are viewing by signaling a box on top of the set using a hand-held device. The information goes instantly over telephone lines to the rating service, providing rapid indirect feedback and demographic information about the audience for a particular program. (Courtesy Neilsen Media Research)

the people meter, feeling that the new system undervalued part of the TV audience that had typically been loyal to CBS, namely people in the Midwest, especially in small towns. Corrections were made, and eventually all the networks, advertising agencies, advertisers, and other parties accepted the new system. People meters, with their presumably more precise records, also helped the cable industry, since for the first time cable and VCR use received serious ratings attention.

A new data-gatherer called the *pocket people meter* is now on the horizon. Arbitron is testing this small device, which is *worn* by members of the sample, who merely need to press a button to turn it on or off. The device does the rest. Based on sophisticated technology developed by the military, it monitors what the individual is listening to on radio or viewing on television, whether at home or elsewhere, keeps track of the information and sends it to Arbitron for analysis. Whether or how soon this will replace other systems in not known at present.[10]

Problems remain with the use of people meters to obtain ratings. Some critics are concerned because any system of sampling has its flaws. For example, they maintain that young, urban viewers with a "high-tech" orientation would be more likely to let Nielsen come into their homes and wire them for people meters. It was also thought that people who would cooperate with the people meter measurers would be more likely to be cable viewers. Finding a reasonably accurate assessment of the viewing audience from which generalizations can be drawn is always a problem. As Peter Boyer of the *New York Times* wrote of the people meter:

> And, for all the technological advances and apparent improvement in accuracy, there remains a certain murky aspect to the process of audience measurement. Viewers still fall asleep while watching Johnny Carson, two-year-olds punch buttons incorrectly, and the tastes of a few thousand people will determine the viewing options of a nation. There remains something quite unnerving about that.[11]

Over $15 billion a year is spent on advertising on national television. Thus, in the people meter debate, huge sums of money are at stake to be won or lost on the basis of the ratings revealed. Before it came on the scene, and as long as cable viewing and VCR usage were not easily determined, the three major networks could claim great dominance and dismiss cable as a limited service with no "hard numbers." To advertisers, these arguments were powerful and important. With the adoption of the people meters, however, the growing importance of cable and other services was documented and thus gained credibility. These developments caused the networks significant financial difficulties as their share of the advertising revenue pie began to shrink.

Audiences for the news News programs have not been immune to the probes of researchers and rating services, and their audiences are regularly measured in the same way as other programming. But in addition to the rating information, news broadcasters frequently make use of *consultants*. These are individuals and firms who, for substantial fees, analyze a station's news operation and advise as to how its ratings and share can be improved. Thus, such companies as Frank N. Magid Associates and McHugh and Hoffman are really marketing experts concerned mainly with "packaging" the news to achieve the greatest possible audience. Their recommendations often have much less to do with journalism as such than they do with theater and nonverbal communication. As two educators have written:

> Few [of the consultants' suggestions] deal with the complexities of news writing, best uses of resources, lines of communication, controversial reporting, or other journalistic topics. They have traditionally convinced station managers that the anchorwoman needs to convey more warmth on the air, the sportscaster needs to have silver teeth fillings replaced with more telegenic porcelain fillings, the weathercaster needs to practice getting rid of his lisp.[12]

Outrageous and superficial as these examples seem, they do reflect the kinds of recommendations that the consultants make. They may urge the station to build new and better sets, suggest more elaborate weather-forecasting equipment, and tell the anchorman to get a new hairpiece or wear a sweater vest. In recent years, the most visible sign of the news consultants' work for local stations has been "happy talk" news, in which anchorpeople deliver the news in chatty fashion with frequent friendly comments to sidekicks who are on camera. Other evidence of the consultants' advice is the "action news" format, which includes more stories of shorter length. This format is the result of the consultants' conviction that viewers are not too bright and have short attention spans.

Station managers take these recommendations seriously, although many news directors have resisted them. In some places, the consultant's recommendations have virtually dictated major changes; in others, the information is used advisedly in reshaping the format of a program. Many consultants do have an undeniable talent for boosting ratings. In any event, the use of these consultants shows clearly that news programming on radio and television, like entertainment programming, competes vigorously for an audience. Better ratings mean a bigger share of the market and thus greater profits.

Quality Ratings and Audience Diversity

Generally, whether measuring audiences for radio or television, for entertainment or news, all rating services have problems gaining acceptance in homes. Some people simply refuse to cooperate; others do so halfheartedly or provide flawed data. These forms of resistance distort the results, although the rating services say they try to correct for these problems. No one outside these very secretive and competitive organizations knows for sure how severe these distortions are, because the services do not readily share information about their methods and procedures. (An exception is Arbitron, which publishes a book explaining its methodology.) But regardless of the actual quality of the ratings, they are taken very seriously by the broadcasting industry. Indeed, these ratings sometimes cause major losses in advertising revenues, which can put people out of work and even end their careers.

Although Nielsen and Arbitron dominate the field of broadcast ratings, competitors occasionally emerge to challenge their dominance. As a result of the upsurge of interest in radio in the 1980s, research on the radio audience has prospered. With both stations and advertising agencies eager for more data, several new firms have entered the field of radio research and provided a serious challenge to Arbitron, which once held a near monopoly. One company, TAA, developed a system that could change the way advertisers advertise and networks produce TV programming. Whereas Nielsen and Arbitron ratings show how many viewers watch a particular program, the TAA system attempts to show *how* people watch TV—that is, their degree of intellectual and emotional involvement. This approach begins to get at a qualitative assessment of the broadcast audience.

All of the ratings services try to break down broadcast audiences in terms of the categories we discussed earlier—age, gender, income, ethnic background, and so forth. As we indicated, it is these indicators of diversity that are the matrix within which tastes and preferences are formed and consumer decisions are made. Precise knowledge of such characteristics has become increasingly important as broadcasters try to attract specific kinds of audiences.

In addition to ratings information organized around such categories, various kinds of commercial researchers probe the size and stability of the audience, seasonal variations, hours spent viewing, and consumption patterns. The Axiom Market Research Bureau, for example, uses a large national sample (25,000) to collect information about how people use products and the media and how they make their buying decisions. It offers its subscribers information about some 450 products and services, 120 magazines, 6 newspaper supplements, the nation's major newspapers, network television, and TV and radio usage by type of program. The resulting data can help an advertiser decide which medium to use to sell laxatives, perfume, beer, or some other product.

Readership or viewership and product data are also correlated by W. R. Simmons & Associates Research, which studies the audiences of magazines, newspaper supplements, national newspapers, and network TV programs in terms of selective markets. Other firms, like Opinion Research Corporation, provide selective market information about the reading patterns of groups such as executives and teenagers. Still another firm, Lee Slurzberg Research, focuses on the African-American consumer and black media.

Other market research firms collect and disseminate information about advertising rates and mechanical specifications, advertising volume, and advertising effectiveness. One such firm, Daniel Starch & Staff, Inc., studies readers of consumer magazines, general business and trade periodicals, daily newspapers, and other publications. They also note reading intensities or the reactions of readers to particular typographical devices and approaches.

Individual newspapers or broadcasters sometimes hire firms to probe their audiences in more detail. The circulation losses of U.S. newspapers led to a good many of these studies in the 1970s and 1980s. One study, commissioned by a large metropolitan newspaper, examined what was in the paper and what people read. The confidential report described the study's recommendations in the following terms:

> The prescription outlined here is: It points out what kinds of things might be cut out of the paper to improve readership, and also what kinds of things readers seem to want more of. It points out how differences in readership are related to such things as the subject of a story, its orientation, where it takes place, where it appears in the paper, the writing approach used in the story, the length of the story, the size and quality of its headline, the size of the newshole and the number of items on the page where the story appears, and the size of any photographs used to illustrate the story.[13]

Clearly, specially commissioned studies of this kind offer recommendations that, if followed, would alter the newspaper in the hope of gaining a larger and more dedicated audience. Thus, the various ratings services and market researchers do not provide static indicators of audience preferences but information that can be used to change the content or format of a program or publication.

Most of the information we have been discussing is gathered for internal use by advertisers and media organizations. Sometimes, as in the case of the Nielsen ratings, the information is published widely in the press, but still its main use is internal. The public sometimes sees the consequences of the ratings but rarely knows much about how they were determined or why decisions were made. On rare occasions, a disgruntled ratings service employee might reveal anecdotes about the internal operations of the firm. Beyond this kind of insider's view, however, little is known about these groups that have so much influence on the media.

Chapter Review

- Each of us attends to and acts upon mass communications differently because of our individual tastes, interests, beliefs, attitudes, and values. These are shaped by our social experiences in the different social groups and categories of which we are members.
- The American society is rich in diversity. That diversity is based on historic patterns of immigration from virtually all parts of the globe, through which the population continues to grow and prosper.
- The American population has always been characterized by various internal migrations within the nation's borders. These have included flows of population from east to west, south

to north, farm to city, city to suburb, and from Northern and Eastern states to the Sun Belt. These migrations tended to mix people and eventually produce a general American culture.
- Most U.S. citizens are of European origin. Immigrants from Northern Europe came first, followed by others from Southern and Eastern Europe. In addition, many unwillingly came from Africa as slaves. In more recent times, the greatest numbers of immigrants have come from Latin American and Asian countries.
- Contemporary sources of American diversity are based both on the ethnic and racial mix of the population and on demographic characteristics, such as age, gender, and education. Each

plays a part in determining what people select from the mass media and how they interpret and respond to it.

- The family is the most significant consuming unit, and its trends and current status are important for professional communicators. American families are now smaller and organized differently than they were in earlier times. Relationships have changed between husbands and wives, with the latter gaining in power and economic influence.
- The women's movement of the nineteenth and twentieth centuries has completely altered the role of women in American society. They now exercise considerable economic power as consumers. This was particularly true after the majority of women entered the labor force.
- The media depend mainly on delayed feedback in one form or another to judge how well their messages are being received by their complex audiences and if their goals are being achieved. A variety of groups have developed ways to assess the size and composition of the audiences for each of the media.
- Newspapers and magazines depend on the Audit Bureau of Circulation (ABC) to monitor

their claims about readers and subscribers. These figures are used by advertisers to judge where their print advertising will attract the attention they seek.

- The movie industry depends on box office receipts to judge how well audiences like its products. These data are systematically gathered and reported by *Variety*, an industry periodical.
- Various approaches have been taken to measure audiences for the broadcast media. These methods have changed in various ways through the years and have included passive devices that merely record when the sets are on, diaries completed by samples of people, phone surveys, and more recently the people meter. Any method is likely to be criticized by one group or another. Indeed, all of them have flaws, and none provides completely reliable and valid data.
- Billions of dollars of revenue from advertising and other sources are at stake. Therefore, the assessments of audience size, interest, and behavior are of critical importance to mass communicators.

Notes and References

1. The first Homestead Act was signed by President Lincoln in 1863. In 1909, the amount of free land was increased to 320 acres. Then, in 1916, it was expanded again to 640 acres (reflecting the fact that only less desirable land remained to be awarded). By the end of the nineteenth century, over a quarter of a billion acres of land had been distributed under the Homestead Act.
2. U.S. Bureau of the Census, *Population Projections of the United States by Age, Sex, Race and Hispanic Origin, 1992–2050* (Washington, D.C.: U.S. Government Printing Office, December, 1992).
3. This means that if one were born in 1900, one could expect to live 47.3 years on aver-

age, provided that the death rates prevailing that year remained constant throughout one's lifetime. Of course, that is not the case; the older one becomes, the greater the chance of living on for additional years. This is partly a reflection of the improvements in medicine that constantly take place.

4. U.S. Bureau of the Census, *Vital Statistic Rates in the United States, 1900–1940* (Washington, D.C.: U.S. Government Printing Office, 1943).
5. Sydney Head and Christopher Sterling, *Broadcasting in America*, 5th ed. (Boston: Houghton Mifflin, 1986), p. 227.
6. For a detailed discussion of the history of broadcast audience measurement, see Hugh

Malcolm Beville, Jr., *Audience Ratings: Radio, Television and Cable* (Hillsdale, N.J.: Lawrence Erlbaum Associates, 1988).

7. Albert E. Gollin, review in *Public Opinion Quarterly*, Summer 1987, p. 285.

8. Head and Sterling, op. cit., pp. 373–403.

9. Head and Sterling, op cit., p. 228. See also Head and Sterling's excellent general discussion of audience measurement, pp. 373–403.

10. Elizabeth Kolbert, "Company Promises a No-Effort TV Rating Device," *The New York Times*, December 9, 1992, p. D4.

11. Peter Boyer, "Bewitched, Bothered, and Bewildered, the Networks Adjust to People Meters," *Gannett Center Journal*, Summer 1988, p. 26.

12. Julius K. Hunter and Lynn S. Gross, *Broadcast News: The Inside Out* (St. Louis: Mosby, 1980), p. 280.

13. From a confidential report prepared by a market research firm for a large metropolitan daily newspaper.

Political Controls on the Media

> Politics and media are inseparable. It is only the politicians and the media that are incompatible.
>
> Walter Cronkite, former CBS anchor

Just as the mass media must exist within a particular economic system with all its realities, harsh and happy, so must they cope with government within a particular political system. Once it was easy to distinguish the relationship between media and government in the United States simply by pointing to the former Soviet Union. There, the media were a part of government rather than being independent of it. Under such a system the mission of the media is to promote the goals of government. Information is strictly controlled—the media operate under the direction of propaganda bureaus, supervised wire services, and highly restrictive newspaper, broadcast, and film organizations. Now, with the fall of communism in the former Soviet Union and Eastern Europe, journalism and news media are being reinvented in those parts of the world. New press laws have been drafted that generally give the media a role in society independent of government. Because political conditions have changed radically, the roles of journalists and other communicators are being redefined.

This chapter describes the political conditions that confront the mass media in the United States. We make a distinction between the news and the content of the rest of the mass media, which is mainly directed toward entertainment or advertising. We will discuss both because they are part of an integrated system and are affected by the entire complex of political factors that relate media and government in American society.

American media, whether delivering news or entertainment, are separate from government; they operate independently and are not reliant on government funds. At the same time, it should be said that media systems in Latin America, Asia, and the former Soviet Union, once tightly controlled by government, are moving toward that condition. That is, they are liberalizing, and the once stark contrasts with the United States no longer exist. However, exceptions remain in totalitarian states such as Cuba, North Korea, and China.

By deeply established tradition, the news media in the United States have an obligation to deliver information, debate, and opinion to the public and are often described as a "trustee" or "representative" of the people. They have been labeled the "watchdogs of the public interest" and even the "fourth estate," implying that they are as powerful as a branch of government. Quite often, this role puts the press in conflict with the government, as it did, for example, during the Watergate scandal in the mid-1970s, the Iran-Contra affair in the late 1980s, and the Gulf War in 1991.

Sometimes conflict between press and government centers on particular individuals, for example, by focusing on the alleged sexual or fiscal misconduct of members of Congress or officials in the executive branch. Another area of conflict between government and the press is the coverage of elections, especially presidential elections. As might have been expected, in the 1992 presidential election, all three major candidates and their campaigns at some time were sharply critical of the press, charging bias and unfair portrayals. In other countries, disputes with the press during elections have often led to censorship of a harsh nature. That has not been the case in this country. Politicians who are elected to office sometimes retaliate by withholding information or making the lives of members of the press difficult, but they have only rarely attempted censorship and punitive action. Still, the news media are almost always wary of potential problems of this kind, knowing that the public holds a generally negative view of them. In fact, one recent survey suggested that if the public could reconsider the Bill of Rights in the U.S. Constitution, it would not grant so much latitude and freedom to the press.

Freedom of the press, as guaranteed by the First Amendment to the Constitution, is a basic tenet of American government. The amendment guarantees the rights of assembly and speech, not only to private individuals but also to all who operate the media. This principle has frequently been tested and interpreted by the courts so as to prevent censorship of the movies, to extend rights of free expression to the electronic media, and even to allow advertisers and public relations practitioners to speak their minds—but within certain limits that we will discuss. Thus, in this country, *direct* government control over the media is very limited indeed. But, as we indicated earlier, communication in the United States (and elsewhere in the world) is largely influenced by economic competition, which exerts its own marketplace controls.

The political regime under which the mass media exist in the United States is complex and subtle, and government and the press frequently clash for a variety of reasons. One is the conflict over rights. Another is the desire of private and public interests in the country to communicate directly to the people through the press without any editorial interference. Although much of the content of the media is routine and noncontroversial, some material creates friction. As we saw in Chapter 3, this supports the idea of an adversarial press attempting to check and balance the power of government. Of

THE PRESS AS A REPRESENTATIVE OF MINORITIES:
A Linchpin to Philosophy and Ethnic Studies

It is not uncommon for members of minority groups to criticize bitterly the mainstream American media. Their unhappiness with the press might be reduced to a single word: representativeness. African-Americans, Asian-Americans, Latinos, and Native Americans (as well as other groups that have historically lacked much social or economic power, such as women, the handicapped, the elderly, and gay people) have argued that the mainstream press does not fairly represent them or their interests. Further, they claim, one of the reasons for this state of affairs is that the important decision-makers on the staffs of American newspapers, magazines, and broadcast stations tend not to be representative of any of these groups.

That news content and coverage should fairly and accurately represent what a given group or interest is doing in society does not sound like an unreasonable expectation. Its basis, though, is the cause of some debate both in the media community and in the courts. The question is whether the concept of representation, which enjoys an honorable history in public law and philosophy, squares with freedom of the press. The "command of the press" clause of the First

Amendment states only that "Congress shall make no law . . . abridging the freedom of speech, or of the press." It says nothing about requiring the press to be fair, objective, or representative. Indeed, the framers of the Constitution believed that the rationale for a press unconstrained by censorship was twofold: to give the public a free flow of information and to provide a forum for opinions of all kinds.

Still, the idea of the press as a representative of the people is an assumption on which most journalists operate and that permeates many details of their day-to-day work. This concept was discussed in the 1947 Commission on Freedom of the Press, which declared that the public deserves "a truthful, comprehensive and intelligent account of the day's events." The Commission went further, arguing that the news media should provide "a representative picture of the constituent groups of society."[1] Some scholars have linked this formulation with the concept of representation as it is defined in political science, wherein the press has a role much like that of the more formal aspects of representative government such as the legislature and the executive.[2] In fact, the

course, the government is not without means to fight back. It is this competition that best characterizes the true nature of the way the media navigate in the American political environment.

To survive in our political system, the mass media perform two major functions: First, they provide a forum of communication for the nation, a *commonality of interest*. The daily agenda for public discussion is set by the press and provides a list of topics and issues to talk about. That agenda allows public opinion to form and emerge as people discuss its topics within the information provided by the press. Second, the media serve as both an *advocate* and an *intermediary* for the citizenry as they take positions on issues and serve as a bridge with society's institutions such as business, education, labor, and others.

The first function generally leads to consensus and cooperation, whereas the latter may lead to conflict. The first allows the media to be a central ner-

idea of the press as the fourth branch of government—the fourth estate—is directly linked to the idea of representation.

The great British legal commentator William Blackstone wrote that every person has "an undoubted right to lay whatever sentiments he pleases before the public: to forbid this is to destroy freedom of the press."[3] Blackstone's work provided a legal framework for the integration of ideas from such seventeenth- and eighteenth-century philosophers as John Milton, John Locke, Jeremy Bentham, Thomas Hobbes, and Jean Jacques Rousseau; their views provided a basis for freedom of the press, drawing on such notions as self-expression, tolerance, the free flow of ideas— indeed, freedom itself. Direct links between these thinkers and others as seen in the letters of Cato and in *The Federalist Papers* were said to influence both the framers of the Constitution and subsequent legal commentators. Later such philosophers as James Mill and John Stuart Mill argued that freedom of the press was necessary to representative government.

For a long time the idea of the press as a representative of the people was buried in little-used treatises by philosophers, but in the 1970s the idea emerged again in U.S. Supreme Court decisions. In one case Justice Lewis Powell opined that "the press is the nec-essary representative of the public's interest . . . and the instrumentality which effects the public's right."[4] Recently, the concept of representation is most often invoked as a moral and ethical imperative by critics who argue that the press ought to give the public an accurate picture of what is actually happening in society. This objective, they assert, would be enhanced by a media work force that is culturally more diverse—an idea most major media organizations are committed to at least in theory, if not always in practice.

1. Commission on Freedom of the Press, *A Free and Responsible Press* (Chicago: University of Chicago Press, 1947).

2. Hanna Fenichel Pitkin, *The Concept of Representation* (Berkeley, Calif.: University of California Press, 1972). See also Hanna Pitkin, *Representation* (New York: Atherton Press, 1969); Everette E. Dennis, "Rhetoric and the Reality of Representation," in Bernard Rubin, ed., *Small Voices and Great Trumpets* (New York: Prager, 1980), pp. 67–88; and E. E. Dennis and John Merrill, *Media Debates: Issues in Mass Communication* (New York: Longman, 1991).

3. William Blackstone, *Commentaries on the Laws of England, of Public Wrongs*, Vol. 4 (Boston: Beacon Press, 1962), p. 161.

4. *Saxbe* v. *Washington Post Co.*, 417 U.S. 843, 864 (1974), Justice Powell dissenting.

vous system for the nation; the other is a correcting device that allows the media to represent the people when other institutions need an independent evaluation. For example, a government agency that is performing poorly will not announce its shortcomings to the public, which deserves to know them. It is the responsibility of the press as watchdog of the public interest to report on them.

To understand the press fully, it is vital to realize that for the most part, they see themselves as nonideological entities, or as instruments of fairness and impartiality in a world of self-serving politicians and government officials. Some citizens, especially those who are criticized by the news media, obviously have a different view. But in comparison with news systems that openly declare partisan political allegiances, such as exist in Britain and France, the American press is, to a large extent, politically independent and generally nonpartisan. Occasionally the press may endorse political candidates, but the news media are not part of any political party or funded directly by the government—which cannot be said of many other countries.

Political Protections: The Constitutional Framework

Political as well as economic considerations place limitations on media in all democratic systems. In Great Britain, for example, although newspapers are privately owned, it is a crime to publish anything from public documents unless prior authorization is obtained. Reporters are allowed to report only what is said at a trial, nothing more. Pretrial publicity is not permitted.

In spite of the First Amendment, the government frequently does prohibit the press from printing whatever it wishes. For example, in 1992, the Supreme Court of Minnesota ruled in a lawsuit against a newspaper that printed certain information. The case centered on whether an agreement between a reporter and a source (who had been assured of confidentiality) was a legally binding contract. In *Cohen* v. *The Minneapolis Star Tribune*, a reporter promised a Minnesota publicist that his role in leaking information would be kept confidential. The reporter's editors overruled, revealed the source's name—making him very angry. He sued, and after several appeals, he finally won. The newspaper had claimed a First Amendment privilege to do what it wished with the information he had supplied. On appeal, the court finally ruled that a verbal promise of confidentiality is a contract that must be honored, and ignoring the First Amendment claim, awarded $200,000 in punitive damages to the publicist.[1]

As can be seen in the above legal case, the political environment of the American media has two fundamental elements: First, a guarantee of freedom of the press is *clearly embodied* in the U.S. Constitution. Second, that freedom is *not absolute*. As freedom of the press has come into conflict with other rights and freedoms, legal limitations have been established. We begin an examination of these limitations by looking at the constitutional guarantee of a free press that arose from this nation's colonial experience.

The Historical Legacy

Prior to the American Revolution, governors representing the English Crown were appointed for each colony to ensure that English laws and policies prevailed. With English law came a specific set of legal relationships between the press and the government. One principle embedded in those laws was *prior restraint*, which allowed that the government could not only punish those responsible for illegal publications but also prevent the publication of material it did not like. The government, in short, could engage in censorship.

In England, the Crown had not enforced its prior restraint laws for many decades before the Revolution, although, as noted in Chapters 3 and 4, it had jailed or fined some individuals whose publications it did not like. English pamphleteers and newspaper writers in the eighteenth century often criticized the government without reprisal. But in the colonies, where rebellions were an ever-present possibility, the Crown's governors sometimes required that any comment on the government's activities be reviewed and approved before publication. As was discussed in our history of the newspaper, the governors would occasionally decide to crack down. One case involved Ben Franklin's brother James, who was jailed and later forced to give up his paper for criticizing the government. Another is the celebrated case of John Peter Zenger, publisher of the *New York Weekly Journal*.

Zenger was charged with seditious libel—for defaming the Crown and its governor (Chapter 3, p. 79). At his lawyer's urging, the jury found him not guilty because what he had published, although critical of government, was true. The jury's verdict thus asserted the right of citizens to speak out against the government. The Zenger case did not change the laws regarding libel, but it did put public opinion firmly behind the idea that newspapers should be allowed to print the truth even if it is contrary to the wishes of the government. All during the remaining time of English rule, the principle of prior restraint remained a part of the legal system, but it was seldom enforced.

The First Amendment

Curiously enough, despite the key role played by newspapers, pamphlets, and printed broadsides in mobilizing support for the Revolution, the

Disputes between government and the press have taken many forms and had many levels of significance and complexity. The burning of John Peter Zenger's *Weekly Journal* on Wall Street in 1734 lacked subtlety, but was the beginning of a legal dispute that is of historical importance and symbolic value today. (Brown Brothers)

framers of the U.S. Constitution did not mention freedom of the press in the original document. For one thing, they could neither agree on what the concept meant in practical terms nor see how such a provision could be enforced. In addition, some of the members of the Constitutional Convention argued that there was no need to guarantee such freedoms.

Before the Constitution was finally ratified, however, several states insisted on adding amendments that guaranteed certain freedoms. These were accepted, and we have come to know them as the Bill of Rights. Prominent among these is the First Amendment, which states, "Congress shall make no law . . . abridging the freedom of speech, or of the press." These words are known as the free speech and free press *clause* of the First Amendment. (The amendment also includes guarantees of freedom of religion and freedom of assembly.) At first glance, the clause seems clear and unambiguous. Yet through the years, as additional media have come into being, the press and the government have become enmeshed in a tangle of issues that have confused the public, perplexed the most able jurists, and placed a variety of constraints on those who operate the mass media.

How could such confusion occur? At the outset, you should recognize that even in the first days of the republic, many of the founders had mixed feelings about the merits of a "free press" and the extent to which it should be unfettered. Some had qualms because it seemed obvious that newspapers were instruments of political power. For example, newspaper enthusiasts today are fond of quoting Thomas Jefferson, who wrote, "Were it left to me to decide whether we should have a government without newspapers, or newspapers without government, I should not hesitate a moment to prefer the latter." Less frequently quoted is the qualifying sentence that followed: "But I should mean that *every man should receive those papers and be capable of reading them*" (italics added). And almost never quoted are the bitter remarks of a disillusioned Jefferson after being opposed frequently by the press: "The man who never looks into a newspaper is better informed than he who reads them, inasmuch as he who knows nothing is nearer to the truth than he whose mind is filled with falsehoods and errors."

Almost all Americans will nod vigorously in agreement if asked whether they believe in freedom of the press. It ranks with motherhood and the American flag as a source of national esteem. But when pressed concerning some specific case—involving, for example, pornography, criticism of their favorite public figure, or unfavorable stories about themselves—their enthusiasm for a free press is likely to vanish. Generally, then, support of freedom of the press is often based not on the idea that the government simply has no right to control the press, but on the belief that a free press is the best method for insuring a well-informed public and a stable democracy. When the press appears to be doing a poor job of informing the public, support for its freedom is likely to diminish.

The issue of freedom of the press (media in general) is complicated by issues related to libel, offensive material (such as sacrilegious films or pornography), technical needs to control the airwaves, secrets during wartime, and many other issues. It is further complicated by jurisdictional boundaries between various courts. For example, over the years, most libel cases were fought in the state courts under state statutes. Federal courts rarely intervened to broaden press freedom until well into this century. By then, the debate over freedom of the press had become more complicated, with the appearance of film and the broadcast media.

Are movies, soap operas, and radio programs forms of "speech" and "the press," and therefore protected by the First Amendment? In 1915, the Supreme Court ruled that cinema was a "business, pure and simple, originated and conducted for profit" (*Mutual Film Company* v. *Ohio*). Therefore, the Court continued, it was not protected by constitutional guarantees of free speech and a free press. But in 1952, the Supreme Court reversed this decision, after the state of New York forbade the screening of an Italian film ("The Miracle") in the state because it was "sacrilegious." When the case was appealed to the Supreme Court, it ruled that the state had no power to censor films on religious grounds.[2] The effect was that films gained the protection of the First Amendment.

Radio and television present a more complicated situation. Whereas in principle there are no limits to the number of newspapers that can be published or films that can be produced, the number of frequencies that can be used for broadcasting is severely restricted. This difference between broadcasting and print has provided the basis for a host of government regulations regarding broadcasting. In other words, broadcast regulation has been

No issue has a more colorful history and remains more controversial than freedom of speech, as provided for in the First Amendment. Over many decades, various forms of personal expression and virtually all forms of print, film, and broadcasting have become shielded by this provision. In recent years, a significant controversy arose as to whether burning the U.S. flag as an act of protest should have First Amendment protection. The Supreme Court said yes. Many more controversies about what constitutes personal or mediated free speech can be expected. (© 1992 Ricky Flores, Impact Visuals)

justified by the scarcity of channels. Therefore, government regulates the owners of broadcast stations by granting and renewing licenses, as well as by regulating content to some extent. As we shall see later in this chapter, regulations regarding broadcasting are generally a compromise between the principle that "the public owns the airwaves" and the Constitution's guarantee of freedom of speech.

As the media have developed, the idea of a scarcity of channels is becoming obsolete. New technologies have greatly expanded the means by which messages can be transmitted to audiences. For example, with the advent of cable and direct broadcast satellite, as well as such emerging technologies as fiber optics, we are entering a period not of broadcast scarcity but of *abundance*. Although this has led to a certain amount of deregulation, some of the old regulatory system remains.

The greatest source of conflict over the right to a free press may be that it is only one among many other important rights. The right to a free press sometimes conflicts with society's right to maintain order and security. For example, the press's exercise of its freedom may conflict with the ability of the police and courts to do their jobs or with the government's ability to maintain secrets it deems necessary for national security. Freedom of the press may also conflict with the rights of individuals, such as the right to privacy and the right to a fair trial. As a result of these conflicts, the courts have frequently ruled against the press's right to publish anything it pleases. Some of the more important limitations on the press imposed by the courts concern libel, coverage of trials, obscene material, and government secrets.

Protection from Libel

Injunctions against making false, defamatory statements about others have ancient origins. Among the Ten Commandments is the injunction "Thou shalt not bear false witness against thy neighbor." In ancient Norman law, it was written that "a man who falsely called another a thief or manslayer must pay damages, and holding his nose with his fingers, must publicly confess himself a liar."[3] The idea that a person whose reputation has been damaged by another's untrue public statements is entitled to compensation was passed on to the American colonies and into our contemporary legal system through English law. Today, libel laws protect not only the reputations of individuals but also those of corporations and businesses. With the development of media with huge audiences, it became possible to "bear false witness" and damage reputations on a very large scale, with serious economic consequences.

Libel Laws and the Media

Every year, libel suits are brought against newspapers, magazines, book publishers, and broadcast stations. They constantly test the principle of freedom of the press. The courts must weigh the right of the press to publish freely against the right of people to preserve their privacy, reputation, and peace of mind. The situation is complicated in the absence of any federal statutes concerning libel. It is a matter of state law, and each has its own statutes.

State laws usually give news reporters and the news media some protection against libel suits. They usually allow publication of public records and "fair comment and criticism" of both public figures and public officials. Unfortunately, it is not entirely clear who qualifies as either under the laws of the various states. However, various court cases have defined *public figures* essentially as persons who are well-known. Examples are prominent sports stars, entertainment personalities, widely read novelists, and even well-known scientists.

In recent years, reporters and the media have also received constitutional protection from libel suits. In a 1964 case, *New York Times* v. *Sullivan*, the Supreme Court considered for the first time whether state laws regarding libel might be overturned on the grounds that they violate the First Amendment to the Constitution. During the height of the civil rights conflict in the South, the *Times* had published an advertisement that indirectly attacked the Birmingham, Alabama, commissioner of public safety. An Alabama jury ruled that the *Times* had to pay $500,000 in damages because the advertisement included some misstatements of fact. But the Supreme Court overruled the Alabama jury, holding that its decision violated freedom of the press. Essentially, the Supreme Court held that a full and robust discussion of public issues, including criticism of public officials, was too important to allow the states to restrain the press through their libel law. After 1964, it became very difficult for public officials to claim libel damages. According to the Supreme Court, only when public officials could prove that the press had shown "malice," "reckless disregard of the truth," or "knowing falsehood" could they sue for libel.

By no means was the libel issue decided once and for all in *New York Times* v. *Sullivan*. Since then, courts have repeatedly redefined who *is* and *is not* a public official or a public figure. And in a 1979 case, *Herbert* v. *Lando*, the Supreme Court ruled that courts could inquire into the state of mind of a reporter to determine whether there was malice present as a story was written. Furthermore, there have been many large libel judgments against the media.

Multimillion-Dollar Libel Suits

In the 1980s, certain conditions—mainly economic ones—called attention to the importance of libel as a constraint on freedom of the press. A number of dramatic libel suits captured headlines during the decade. General William Westmoreland, who led U.S. forces during the war in Vietnam, sued CBS for his depiction in a documentary about the conflict but dropped his suit in the last days of the trial; a gubernatorial candidate unsuccessfully sued the *Boston Globe*; and Mobil Oil President William Tavoulareas successfully sued the *Washington Post*. Entertainer Wayne Newton sued NBC and won in a case involving charges that the singer had consorted with members of organized crime. In 1990, the *Philadelphia Inquirer* lost a multimillion-dollar libel suit to a local official. All of these cases had one thing in common: Large amounts of money were involved, either in what have been called "megabuck libel verdicts" or in substantial legal fees. Whatever their outcome, libel suits of this kind are extremely expensive and sometimes take years to litigate.

The rising cost of libel trials is due not only to those judgments of the courts that penalize the media, but also to legal fees and increasing libel insurance premiums. According to Henry Kaufman of New York's Libel Defense Resource Center, damage awards have increased more than 400 percent since *Times* v. *Sullivan* in 1964.

> "Today's average damage award in just a single media libel case where a plaintiff's verdict is entered comes very close to equaling the total of all awards requested in the cases surrounding Times against Sullivan," he claimed. The cost of libel, Kaufman declared, is "onerous and getting worse."[4]

New laws are not being written by the courts, but statutes and court decisions long on the books are being enforced.

Some critics cite an increasingly conservative judiciary as one of the reasons for increasing libel costs, although David Anderson, a law professor at the University of Texas, argues that the media win nearly as many cases as they lose in the courts.[5] Still, win or lose, the legal costs are substantial. Some observers say that increasing costs have been responsible for diminishing investigative reporting (the so-called chilling effect); others say that the costs check the growing power of the media in necessary ways. It should be noted that many large libel judgments are greatly reduced on appeal or by judges. Almost all knowledgeable observers agree, however, that the cost of libel is having a significant effect.[6]

Libel law and libel cases always bear watching because the law in that area is complex, and it is relatively easy to bring a suit. Communication law scholar Donald M. Gillmor of the University of Minnesota points out in a widely cited book that although the media often win libel cases or have them thrown out of court, there is still a great cost in legal fees that can be especially harmful to small publications and broadcasters. Gillmor sees public officials and celebrities as the culprits in many libel suits and proposes to deny protection to those with "high visibility and the resources to communicate with broad sections of the public," saving the tougher provisions of libel law for ordinary citizens who are genuinely damaged by the media with little ability to fight back.[7]

A libel reform movement gained some publicity in 1989 when the Annenberg Washington Program mounted a proposal for libel reform and urged its adoption at the state level. However, there were few takers. Interest in libel reform typically comes from the media after major cases are lost, but to date there has been little public support. More importantly, the legal profession has little enthusiasm for reform, perhaps because lawyers would stand to lose huge fees under any such plan.

Other proposals have been made to circumvent libel cases and other media-public confrontations. One such proposal has been advanced by

Robert Chandler, an Oregon publisher, who has called for community complaint councils that would have less authority than press councils but would still offer a safety valve for public feedback.[8] The Minnesota News Council has also taken up cases on a trial basis in other states and has proposed a modest "nationalization" of their efforts. In the Pacific Northwest, a journalism complaints council has been developed.

Lawyers rightly argue that libel and other legal issues have become increasingly complex in recent years as defendants from other countries have sued American media in foreign courts. For example, in the 1980s, the prime minister of the Bahamas, Lyndon Pindling, sued *Time* magazine in Canada, where the libel laws are more restrictive than those in the United States. There are similar suits against U.S. media in Britain. The media are increasingly global, and they are often susceptible to the laws of the countries where they operate, many of which run counter to press rights under the U.S. Constitution. This is likely to be a growing area of libel litigation.

Libel and the Congress

Members of Congress are virtually immune from libel suits. Statements made on the floor of Congress or in committees are regarded as related to their responsibilities as public officials. Therefore, they can and often do

During the 1950s, Senator Joseph McCarthy (shown here with Roy Cohn) caused an upheaval that had profound consequences in the United States for years. Using public fears that a Communist conspiracy was working to undermine the nation's social institutions, he denounced hundreds of people as "fellow travelers," "sympathizers," and "card-carrying members of the Communist Party" (all of which were perfectly legal). He made effective use of the media for his denunciations and was widely feared. Eventually his tactics were condemned, but many lives and careers had been ruined. (The Bettmann Archive)

make irresponsible public statements about issues and people, protected by the knowledge that they will not wind up in court. The late Senator Joseph McCarthy provides a classic example of such abuse of this protection. In the 1950s, McCarthy gained national and even worldwide attention by claiming that the United States was in the grip of powerful but hidden Communist infiltration. Using the media to whip up public fear of a vast Communist conspiracy, he accused prominent individuals in government, business, education, the military, the film industry and even the clergy of being "subversive," "fellow travelers" or "card-carrying members of the Communist Party." The media gave his outrageous claims worldwide coverage.

McCarthy's accusations helped create a climate of fear that wrecked reputations and ruined careers all over the nation. Finally, however, the media that had helped McCarthy's rise assisted in his downfall. As a result of his accusations, Congress held formal hearings on Communist influence in the Army, which were televised daily to a national audience. McCarthy's tactics were so outrageous that, after seeing him in action, the public concluded that he was an irresponsible demagogue. He lost credibility, and his bid for power came to an end. Since then, McCarthy's name has become synonymous with unfair attacks without evidence. In presidential campaigns, the term "McCarthyism" often re-emerges, as it did in 1992 when then Arkansas Governor Bill Clinton accused then President George Bush of using "guilt by innuendo"—a McCarthy-like tactic.

Trial by Media

The Constitution guarantees freedom of the press, but in the Sixth Amendment it also guarantees a public and speedy trial to defendants. Sometimes publicity about a crime and the suspected criminal seems to make a fair trial impossible. The classic example of how the press can turn a case into a Roman circus and thereby deny the defendant's right to a fair trial occurred in the prosecution of Dr. Sam Sheppard in the 1950s. Dr. Sheppard was a successful osteopathic surgeon in Ohio. One night his wife was brutally beaten and stabbed to death under mysterious circumstances in their suburban home. The police were baffled because there were no witnesses and few clues. Long before the police investigation had been completed, the local newspapers decided that Sheppard was guilty. One headline read "Quit Stalling—Bring Him In"; another asked "Why Isn't Sam Sheppard in Jail?" Numerous editorials and cartoons proclaimed him guilty.

Later, Sheppard was arrested and charged. The trial was overrun with reporters and photographers, and the jury was not adequately shielded from negative publicity about Sheppard. One newspaper even printed a photograph of Mrs. Sheppard's bloodstained pillow, retouched so as to "show more clearly" the alleged imprint of a "surgical instrument." The prosecutor found no witnesses to the murder, and the only evidence he presented was circumstantial (for example, Sheppard was having an affair with another woman). Yet Sheppard was convicted and spent many years in prison before the Supreme Court finally reviewed his case. It declared his trial invalid, largely because of the publicity and improper legal procedures. Ohio tried Sheppard again, and he was acquitted. By this time, of course, his life was shattered. He died in 1970, still a relatively young man.

The American Bar Association (ABA) took action to protect defendants against unnecessary publicity before trial. Because of the Sheppard case and the publicity surrounding accusations against Lee Harvey Oswald (the alleged assassin of President Kennedy), they convened a national commission to establish better rules for the protection of defendants. Led by Justice Paul Reardon of the Supreme Judicial Court of Massachusetts, in the late 1960s, the ABA Commission suggested rules to restrict the release of prejudicial information. For judges, court officers, attorneys, juries, prosecutors, and the police, these rules carried the weight of law once they were adopted by federal and state courts. For the press, the Reardon guidelines were voluntary. Nevertheless, in more than thirty states, beginning in the late 1960s, "fair trial–free press" committees charged with promoting recommended codes of conduct were set up. The guidelines were even issued on little cards for reporters, and for the most part they worked well. Then, in a Washington state case in the late 1970s, a judge used the voluntary guidelines as the basis to restrict press coverage of a murder trial. The fear that this could happen elsewhere quickly unraveled many, though not all, of the codes of the state committees.

Today, few reporters use the Reardon guidelines as such, and there is renewed discussion of the need for some voluntary curbs in a period when television, more often than newspapers, has become more sensational, a phenomenon journalism historian John D. Stevens has called "wretched excess."[9] However, screaming newspaper headlines that might be considered prejudicial are not a thing of the past. In covering many celebrated trials in recent years, supermarket tabloids such as the *National Enquirer* or the *Star*, as well as big-city tabloids such as the *New York Post* or *Boston Herald*, have featured accusatory headlines about such highly visible defendants as William Kennedy-Smith, televangelists Jim and Tammie Bakker, Amy Fisher, and others.

In the case of *Gannett* v. *Depasqualle* (1979), the Supreme Court suggested that the press could be barred from certain portions of trials. An uproar followed, in which many said the decision was a threat to the coverage of supposedly public trials. This was clarified somewhat in a 1980 Supreme Court decision, *Richmond Newspapers Inc*. v. *Virginia*, which gave specific constitutional protection for the media to cover public trials.

The intense publicity surrounding celebrated cases makes it common for defense attorneys to seek a variety of remedies to help their clients get a fair trial. One such remedy used by the courts, in addition to challenging potential jurors and sequestering the jury, is *change of venue,* such as occurred when the trial of the Los Angeles police officers in the Rodney King beating case was moved to nearby Simi Valley. The assumption is that in another location jurors will not have been influenced by prejudicial publicity.

Celebrated trials in recent years—including those of General Manuel Noriega, the deposed leader of Panama; Marion Barry, the Mayor of

Washington, D.C.; and Colonel Oliver North of Iran-Contra fame—doubtless have received considerable prejudicial publicity. Just what can be done about this kind of media attention, which informs the public but also tramples on individual rights, is uncertain. Some commentators have called for new rules for news-gathering and a return to the Reardon guidelines of the 1960s.

Moral Values: Obscenity and Pornography

Do parents have the right to protect their children from seeing advertisements on the street for pornographic movies or pornographic magazines displayed at the local drugstore? Many Americans would answer yes, but the Supreme Court's answers have been ambiguous. The most emotional issue in recent times has been child pornography: magazines and films depicting young children engaged in explicit sexual acts with adults and with each other. Public pressure prompted Congress to hold hearings on the issue in the 1970s, and various laws passed since that time have greatly curtailed the production, distribution, and sale of such material.

Two very different conceptions of the role of government underlie debates about regulation of obscene material. Liberals generally deplore censorship of such material, arguing that government should not attempt in any way to regulate the moral behavior of its citizens as long as the people involved are consenting adults. On the other hand, many conservatives are inclined to see censorship of obscenity as the proper duty of local or even national government. They tend to feel that a safe society can be maintained only through government regulation of personal behavior such as sexual activity or the use of alcohol and drugs.

Over the years, the media have received strange and convoluted signals concerning pornography and obscenity. The Supreme Court seemed to side with conservatives in 1957 when it announced, "Obscenity is not within the area of constitutionally protected speech or press" (*Roth* v. *United States*). That may seem clear enough, but it has not been easy to determine what is or is not obscene. In the 1960s, material could not be declared obscene if it had "any redeeming social value" whatsoever. Then in 1973, the Court made it easier to ban materials by relaxing this standard. Moreover, it stated that material should be judged by local authorities according to standards that "prevail in a given community" (*Miller* v. *California*). Thus, what is considered obscene in one community may not be obscene in another. But since this decision, the Court has overturned some efforts by local governments to ban materials. What can and cannot be censored on obscenity grounds remains far from clear.

In the face of public pressure, the media have censored themselves to some extent. Various industry associations have drawn up codes limiting the treatment of material related to sex. A classic example is the self-regulation of the movie industry in the 1930s, when the Motion Picture Producers and Distributors Association Code became so puritanical that at one point not even butterflies could be shown mating. Later in the 1950s, the comic

One of the most controversial issues that has confronted Americans in the past decades has been the legal status of pornography. Those who approve of it, own or manage porn shops, or show pornographic movies often claim that they are exercising their First Amendment rights. Many critics disagree, claiming that parents have a right to protect their children from exposure to such material and bar its sale or distribution in their neighborhoods. At present, there are almost as many positions on this issue as there are porn shops and movie houses. (Copyright Ken Heyman)

book industry voluntarily (though grudgingly) curtailed production of horror comics in response to a public outcry. (Congressional hearings were held to determine whether such comic books were harmful to children.) Even as late as 1965, the American Newspaper Advertising Code prohibited such words as "girlie," "homosexual," "lesbian," "lust," "naked," and "seduce." It also ruled out horizontal embraces and comments on bust measurements.[10]

Today, the National Association of Broadcasters forbids (rather unsuccessfully) the use of "dirty" words and explicit sexual content. The relative purity of broadcasting, however, is also a result of the Federal Communications Commission's enforcement of the Federal Communication Act's strict rules against obscenity. For example, in 1992, the FCC fined a Los Angeles radio station for airing allegedly obscene and off-color commentary by the controversial radio-TV host Howard Stern.[11] Considerable conflict has flared between feminists and producers of lurid, sexually explicit material. Here the old liberal-conservative split over censorship of pornography has broken down, because many politically liberal feminists believe that pornography is so offensive and damaging to women that censorship is warranted.

Although we have been dealing here with moral values as they are embodied in the law, the role of the media as a moral teacher and "enforcer" of values, too, has come up repeatedly in recent years. Arguing that the media are now taking on the role once filled by the family, church, or school, critics urge more care and accountability among media professionals. However, this is strictly a voluntary effort, not something that can be enforced by the courts or other authorities.[12]

Another area in which there is currently great controversy over freedom of expression is in the relationship between government funding of the arts and what such exhibitors as museums that receive public monies should be allowed to be put on display. Much of this controversy centers on monies provided by a federal agency, the National Endowment for the Arts (NEA), and displays of works by individuals who want to be funded regardless of whether taxpayers and politicians approve of what they say and how they say it. For example, in 1993, a controversy arose over an exhibit on "Abject Art: Repulsion and Desire in American Art" in New York's Whitney Museum (which receives grants from the NEA). Critics objected to the materials on display, saying that the majority of Americans would be offended and should not be called upon to provide financial support. For example, George Will, a syndicated columnist, pointed out:

> "The exhibit, which features such "abject materials" as dead animals, menstrual blood and rotten food, includes a three-foot-high mound of synthetic excrement, a film showing a man pushing his head into another man's rectum, framed samples of an infant's fecal stains and, of course, two hardy perennials—Robert Maplethorpe's "Self-Portrait," a photo of him with a bull whip in his rectum, and Andres Serrano's "Piss Christ," a photo of a crucifix in a jar of Serrano's urine.[13]

This kind of communication, many critics maintain, so grossly transgresses norms of acceptability that it is inappropriate for the artists or museums to demand to be subsidized with public funds, either directly or indirectly. Whatever position one takes on this issue, one thing seems clear. This area of political conflict in public communication—between the legitimacy of demands by artists for financial support and reluctance by taxpayers to subsidize certain forms of expression—will not soon be resolved. Thus, controversies over freedom of speech will continue to develop, as has been the case in the past, as new media and new forms of expression challenge existing boundaries.

The Government's Secrets during National Crises

In times of national crises, such as wars, reporting some kinds of information can give the enemy a clear advantage. The classic example of the "scholarly spy" illustrates this danger. In 1940, before the United States and Germany were actually at war, a German undercover agent was smuggled into the United States on a mission to assess this country's future capacity to produce air armaments. Such knowledge would play a vital part in Germany's preparations for air defense. Ironically, the spy did not need to sneak around airplane factories or army and navy airfields—he simply spent his time reading in public libraries. He carefully scrutinized the *New York Times Index* and the *Reader's Guide to Periodical Literature* for published accounts that mentioned aircraft facilities, plans for factories, and existing air armaments. After making copious notes, he returned to Germany and prepared a report for the high command. The report, later acquired by American espionage agents in Germany, turned out to be an extremely accurate prediction of U.S. production of military aircraft for the years 1941 through 1943. In fact, his assessment was more accurate than that made by the U.S. War Production Board for the same years. Yet, all the spy's data had come from newspapers, magazines, and books readily available to the public.[14]

Recognizing the security risks, Americans have generally accepted some form of censorship during wars. Even many fervent civil libertarians agree that the government deserves and requires protection during wartime. But such censorship obviously contradicts the guarantee of a free press and limits the public's right to know.

In peace and war, government secrecy has led to many controversies. For example, in October 1983, when the United States invaded the small Caribbean nation of Grenada, military commanders barred the press from the island, and thus the war zone. Journalists and broadcasters vigorously protested the government policy as unprecedented and unwarranted censorship; the White House replied that it was trying to protect the lives of the media people. After Grenada, a commission involving military officers, government officials, and representatives of the press was set up. It recommended guidelines for the coverage of military actions and suggested the formation of a press-broadcast pool for future operations.

Only a few years later, in 1989, the press got a chance to test these recommendations while covering the U.S. invasion of Panama, an action resulting in the ouster and arrest of Panamanian leader General Manuel Noriega.

In the United States, the relationship between the press and the armed forces has changed over time. Generally, the military wants the press to report favorably on its efforts. From the Civil War to the Korean conflict, members of the press traveled with the troops and had unlimited access to them. Things went well in general. During the Vietnam War, however, the relationship became strained. Since then, the military has often held the press at arm's length. That was clearly the case during the invasions of Grenada and Panama and the Gulf War. (AP/Wide World Photos)

This time the press had greater access, and the pooling system for electronic media seemed to work. The arrangement in Panama offers a good example of press-government cooperation that balances the interests of both and is generally regarded as serving the public well. In August 1990, when Iraq invaded Kuwait causing the United States to send troops to Saudi Arabia, press access again became an issue in various foreign capitals and on the front lines with the troops.

The 1991 Gulf War against Iraq's forces under Saddam Hussein resurrected the conflict between press and government. From the beginning of what was a very popular war, in contrast to Vietnam, the press complained that the rules concerning access to information from the front were too restrictive and prevented effective coverage. A pool system representing the entire press corps was in effect, and obtrusive military "handlers" accompanied reporters to their interviews. The Pentagon argued that it was simply trying to prevent the release of information that would undermine military operations or endanger the lives of troops. The result was tightly controlled information, released at formal press briefings, and little opportunity for reporters to pursue stories independently, especially if that required access to the battlefield area. At the war's end, there was an almost universal agreement that the media had been kept at bay and, in effect, lost the information war.

Various conferences and meetings followed the war, as well as major reports and studies. A study with which one of the authors of this book was associated, concluded:

> The Persian Gulf War witnessed severe restrictions imposed by the military on the press, including banning access to the war zone. A few media organizations and journalists fought the restrictions in court, but with no success. Though military officials have contended that they will look at each situation differently, they have also said that they plan to use similar controls in any future military conflicts.[15]

Another report, published in Britain, said, "The media and the military have fundamentally opposed information objectives during wartime; the military must protect operational security and the lives of armed forces, while the media seeks to satisfy the public's right to know and in so doing to gain new viewers and readers."[16]

So strong was media dissatisfaction with the restrictions that, after the war, a unified committee representative of U.S. print and broadcast media petitioned the Pentagon and the White House to consider a set of rules and procedures for future wars. Those rules aim at encouraging open and independent reporting, limitation of pools, access to all major military units, and other improvements. And the press agrees to be prudent in not publishing information about military operations that could put troops at risk.[17]

Direct Censorship in Wartime

In past wars, the government has been able to use various indirect methods to protect its secrets. One of the earliest indirect ways used to control information was to deny access to telegraph, cable, and similar facilities. Reporters then either had to let military censors screen their copy or try to transmit it in some other way. For example, when the battleship Maine blew up in the harbor of Havana, Cuba, in 1898, the U.S. government immediately closed the Havana cable to reporters. Similarly, at the outbreak of World War I, Great Britain immediately severed the cables between Germany and the United States. American reporters had to use the British-controlled cables between Europe and the United States and submit their copy to rigid British censorship.

The government has also imposed censorship through codes, regulations, and guidelines. During World War I, the Espionage Act of 1917 stipulated fines and prison terms for anyone interfering with the war effort in any way. For example, criticism of arms manufacturers was said to be unpatriotic. This enraged newspaper publishers, and legal battles over the issue went all the way to the Supreme Court. Such censorship was later declared unconstitutional, but Congress passed new, even stricter laws to control information. The Sedition Act of 1918 made it a crime to publish anything that abused, scorned, or showed contempt for the government of the United States, its flag, or even the uniforms of its armed forces. As a way to enforce the law, such publications could be banned from the mails.

On December 19, 1941, only a few days after Japanese forces attacked Pearl Harbor, President Roosevelt created the U.S. Office of Censorship and charged it with reviewing all communications entering or leaving the United States for the duration of the war. At the peak of its activity, the office employed more than ten thousand people. Its main objective was to review all mail, cables, and radiograms. A Code of Wartime Practices for the American Press was also issued to newspapers, with a request for voluntary cooperation from the nation's editors and publishers. The purpose was to deny the Axis powers any information concerning military matters, production, supplies, armaments, weather, and so on. (The case of the scholarly spy occurred before the guidelines were in effect.) For the most part, those responsible for the content of the print media cooperated very well, often exceeding the guidelines set by government. A related code was issued for broadcasters, and their cooperation was also excellent. The system of codes, regulations, and guidelines in World War II worked because the media cooperated voluntarily. The U.S. government attempted to find a way to deny vital information to the enemy without using official censors, and by and large it succeeded.

Even during peacetime, the press has often censored itself to protect the national interest. In 1960, for example, the Soviet Union shot down an American U2 spy plane. The incident temporarily ended attempts to improve Soviet-American relations. For a year before the plane was shot down, however, James Reston of the *New York Times* had known that American spy planes were flying over the Soviet Union, but "the *New York Times* did not publish this fact until one of the planes was shot down in 1960."[18] Later, as a favor to President John Kennedy, Reston withheld information about the planned U.S. invasion of Cuba at the Bay of Pigs.

Although the First Amendment guarantees freedom of speech, the idea that some speech can be dangerous is advertised by this World War II poster. Defense workers are warned that "loose talk" might inadvertently feed dangerous information to the enemy. (National Archives photo no. 44-PA-1304c)

Challenges to Government Secrecy

Although the press often engages in voluntary censorship, there are many examples when the media and the government have been locked in conflict, disputing the government's right to censor the news. Because a shared belief in the need for freedom of the press became such a tradition very early in the life of the nation, any effort by the government to limit that freedom has always met with hostility.

During the Civil War, for example, the 57th Article of War stipulated a court martial and possible death sentence for anyone, civilian or soldier, who gave military information to the enemy. However, newspapers were an indirect source of military information, and Confederate leaders went to great lengths to obtain copies of major Northern papers because they often revealed the whereabouts of military units and naval vessels. As a result, the

U.S. War Department tried to prevent newspapers from publishing any stories that described the movements of troops or ships. Editors generally ignored these orders. After the war, General Sherman refused to shake hands with Horace Greeley, publisher of the *New York Tribune*, maintaining that Greeley's paper had caused a heavy loss of life by revealing troop movements to the enemy.[19]

Thus, even in wartime, Americans have questioned censorship, asking what kind of controls should be imposed and by whom. Clearly, the government has the need to protect its secrets and a duty to protect the nation. But the press claims a right to inform the public of what government is doing, and maintains that the public has the right to know. Therefore, an inherent conflict exists between the right to a free press and the need to control information that would be damaging to the government.[20]

The conflict between government and the press has grown in recent decades, as the government itself has increased in size. Since World War II, Americans have supported a giant defense establishment, a complex network of foreign relationships, and a powerful nuclear arsenal. Government secrecy grew with all of these developments. The majority of editors and broadcasters cooperate with the government in maintaining secrecy when national security is clearly at stake. But as a host of government bureaucrats classify thousands and thousands of secret documents each year, the press—and the public—often wonder how many of these secrets protect national security and how many protect the government from embarrassment. It is often difficult to determine what is being protected, or at what point a secret becomes so damaging to the national interest that the constitutional guarantee of free speech should be overruled. The historic case of the Pentagon Papers illustrates these questions dramatically.

During the Johnson administration, the Defense Department put together a 47-volume history of American involvement in Vietnam from 1945 to 1967, including secret cables, memos, and other documents. The history, which came to be known as the "Pentagon Papers," was classified as *top secret*. In 1971, Daniel Ellsberg, who had worked on the papers but later opposed the war, leaked them to the *New York Times*, hoping that their release would turn public opinion against the war and help bring about its end. Although the papers were both stolen and classified, the *Times* began publishing a series of articles summarizing the contents and presenting some of the documents themselves.

The Nixon administration went to court to stop the *Times* (and later other newspapers) from printing additional articles based on the papers, arguing that their publication would endanger national security. In response, the courts issued a temporary restraining order stopping the *Times* from continuing its planned series on the papers. In effect, the courts imposed prior restraint.

Eventually, the case went to the Supreme Court, which ruled against the government. The government had failed to convince the Court that publication of the Pentagon Papers constituted a danger severe enough to warrant suspending freedom of the press. Relieved and triumphant, the newspapers resumed their articles. (Ellsberg was later tried for stealing the documents.) However, the Court's decision in the Pentagon Papers case is still regarded as controversial, and it resolved little of the debate between government and the press. Conflict continues over the press's right to publish, the public's right to know, and the government's need to protect the secrecy of some activities.

During the 1980s, the Reagan administration engaged in a contentious tug of war with the press over access to government information. President Reagan proposed sweeping changes in the Freedom of Information Act, which provides public access to the records of various departments and agencies of government. He issued executive orders making access to information from agencies such as the FBI and CIA more difficult. Professional groups such as the Society of Professional Journalists and the American Society of Newspaper Editors campaigned vigorously against these restrictions. In this instance, there was profound disagreement between the government, which claimed it acted in the best interest of the people by limiting access, and the press, which said the public was better served by the free flow of information. This issue re-emerged in 1993 when the same groups urged President Clinton to relax information policies.

The most divisive of the debates between press and government during the Reagan administration centered around what came to be called the Iran-Contra affair. It occurred in 1986 and 1987, when the press revealed covert arms-for-hostages negotiations between Washington and Iran, then classified as a terrorist state. The government at first argued against disclosing the secret negotiations, which involved diverting funds to the opposition Contras in Nicaragua, who were battling the Marxist Sandinistas. Doing so, they claimed, might jeopardize the lives of the Americans held in the Middle East at the time. But critics in the press and government argued that laws may have been violated and that full information about the matter should be reported. One of many such conflicts between the media and the government over the years, the incident illustrates the adversarial role of the press and the controversy over governmental secrecy versus freedom of information.

Protection of Reporters' Sources

While the government claims that some secrets are necessary for its survival, the press makes a similar claim. For example, in 1966, Annette Buchanan, the editor of the student newspaper at the University of Oregon, published a story about marijuana smoking on the campus. A local court asked Buchanan to reveal the names of the people from whom she had obtained much of her information. She refused and was later fined $300. Although this seemingly trivial incident involved neither serious crimes nor harsh punishment, it illustrates the elements of an important controversy regarding freedom of the press. Had Buchanan given the names of her informants to the police, her credibility with her sources would certainly have been destroyed. Similarly, news personnel claim that maintaining the confidentiality of sources is an important part of the machinery of reporting. If reporters are not allowed to keep their sources secret, they will not be able to obtain information that the public should have.

A case with more serious consequences involved Earl Caldwell, a reporter for the *New York Times*. In the 1960s, Caldwell gained the confidence of the Black Panthers, a radical black power organization considered by many people to be militant and dangerous. Caldwell wrote several stories about the Panthers but in a way that did not cost him the group's trust. Later, after David Hilliard, a member of the group, was charged by a grand jury with threatening to kill the President, Caldwell was asked to appear before the grand jury to testify. He refused. In fact, he refused to go anywhere near the grand jury on the grounds that once he entered the closed session, he would then lose the confidence of his informants, who would never be certain of what he had said behind closed doors. Because of his refusal to testify, Caldwell was held in contempt of court—a decision later upheld by the U.S. Supreme Court. The case caused an uproar among journalists. During the Supreme Court's hearing on it, the Authors' League of America argued:

> Compelling a reporter to identify his sources or divulge confidential information to a grand jury imposes obvious restraints on the freedom of the press to gather information. . . . The threat of such interrogation would induce many reporters to steer clear of controversial issues, inducing the "self-censorship" which is repugnant to the First Amendment.[21]

The Caldwell decision appeared to provide a clear basis for legal action against reporters who refused to divulge such information. A few years later, Peter Bridges was the first reporter actually jailed as a result of the decision. In 1972, he remained in jail for twenty-one days because he refused to identify the sources for an article he had written on alleged illegal practices involving the Newark, New Jersey, housing authority.

Since that time, a number of legal measures have been adopted to protect news media and reporters who do not wish to divulge sources. Many states have passed so-called *shield laws*, which specifically exempt journalists from having to reveal their sources.[22] Some journalists and lawyers argue against such laws, saying that they imply acceptance of the Court's interpretation of the First Amendment. Many other lawyers oppose these laws on the grounds that the courts need all the information they can get to protect citizens from wrongdoing and to provide fair trials.

The issue of confidentiality of sources is by no means resolved. In 1978, a New Jersey court jailed Myron Farber, a reporter for the *New York Times*, for refusing to turn over his notes in a murder trial. The defendant's lawyers claimed that they had a right to see the notes. Despite a New Jersey shield law that supposedly protected reporters' confidential sources, the court convicted Farber of civil and criminal offenses, and the *Times* was forced to pay a fine. Both the New Jersey Supreme Court and the U.S. Supreme Court said that in this case the Sixth Amendment, which guarantees a public trial, took precedence over the claims of the press.

Political Constraints: The Agents of Control

We have discussed several specific areas in which freedom of the press as guaranteed by the Constitution is limited, not absolute. But in practice, freedom of the press depends not only on this abstract constitutional framework but also on the daily decisions of courts, bureaucrats, and politicians.[23] The constitutional framework itself continues to evolve as specific problems and conflicts arise. Moreover, in particular cases, the actual freedom of the press may differ from its theoretical freedom. Therefore, we look next at the various agents of political control of the media: the courts, legislatures, the executive branch, and private citizens. These groups may exert both formal controls on the media and informal influence on the flow of information.

The Courts

We have seen that the courts often act as referees in conflicts between the rights of the press, the rights of individuals, and the rights of the government at large. This role is nothing new—as early as 1835, the French writer Alexis de Tocqueville observed, "Scarcely any political question arises in the United States that is not resolved sooner or later into a judicial question." Today, Americans are even more litigious, and conflicts involving the media often lead to lawsuits in local courts. Some of the resulting verdicts are appealed and occasionally wind up in the Supreme Court.

Often, the Supreme Court's interpretations of either prevailing laws or the Constitution itself have broken new ground and established new policies. In recent years, the Court has ruled on a long list of issues affecting the media, including newsroom searches, libel, confidentiality of journalists' sources, regulation of advertising, and laws regarding copyright and cable television. These rulings have often been the center of immense controversy. The prevailing view in the press is that, for many years, the Supreme Court under Chief Justice Warren E. Burger was generally, though not always, hostile to the press and its claims. Dan Rather of CBS News went so far as to claim that the Supreme Court has been "repealing the First Amendment" by its decisions. Many legal scholars, however, disagree.

What we see in the courts when the press is on trial is a legal battle involving private citizens, the media, and the government. It is all a matter of "rights in conflict." As journalist Anthony Lewis said in a 1983 speech:

> We have libel suits because we think a civilized society should take account of an interest besides freedom to criticize. In other words, individuals have rights too; sometimes they conflict with the rights of the press. It is not uncommon to find rights in conflict; that's why we have judges. But sometimes the press sounds as though the Constitution considers only its interests. If a network or a newspaper loses a case, "That's it, the Constitution is gone; Big Brother has taken over." Well, I don't think life is so simple. The interest of the press may not be the only one of constitutional dimension when there are conflicts.[24]

As a social institution, the media pay more than passing attention to personnel changes at the Supreme Court. In 1986, when William Rehnquist became Chief Justice and Antonin Scalia became an Associate Justice, their "press records" were examined carefully by media leaders who predicted rough times for the press with an increasingly conservative and presumably anti-press Supreme Court. From the Nixon administration through the Bush administration (1970–1992), conservative or moderate Republicans were appointed to the high court. In 1993, President Clinton appointed a moderate Democrat, Ruth Bader Ginsburg, to fill the late Thurgood Marshall's seat.

Just what the Rehnquist court will do in the years ahead, however, is anybody's guess. Some media lawyers say they are not eager to take press cases before the U.S. Supreme Court unless there is no other recourse. However, such fears may be unfounded. In a 1987 case involving evangelist Jerry Falwell and *Screw* magazine publisher Larry Flynt, the court found for Flynt, who had written scurrilously about Falwell. Chief Justice Rehnquist himself wrote the majority opinion, proving that it is often difficult to predict what the Supreme Court will do. According to media scholar David Anderson, however, press defendants appearing before the Court, from its beginning two hundred years ago to the present, have generally fared worse than other defendants.[25]

The Legislatures

The Supreme Court is the final staging ground for many media battles, but the first rounds of these battles are fought in state legislatures. These bodies promulgate laws that have considerable impact on the mass media. They may amend or rewrite statutes dealing with libel, misrepresentation, business taxation, newspaper advertising, cable television, and many other subjects. Most major lobbying groups for the media, such as state broadcast and newspaper associations, have representatives at state capitals continuously looking out for their interests.

Congress's influence on the media is greater than that of the state legislatures. Like other businesses, the media can be hurt or helped by congressional decisions regarding postal rates, taxes, antitrust policy, protection of copyrights, affirmative action, and so on. In addition, both houses of Congress have subcommittees that deal specifically with communications issues and policies. In the past, Congress has investigated the financial structure of the communications industry, tried to determine whether television networks pressured producers not to release films to pay-cable systems, written new copyright laws, passed laws on campaign spending in the media, and considered a federal shield law. In the late 1960s, Congress authorized the Department of Health, Education, and Welfare to fund studies of the effects of television, especially the effects of televised violence on children.[26] Congress was also responsible both for passing censorship laws, as during World War I, and for creating the Freedom of Information Act of 1966, which has opened the government to greater scrutiny by the media and the general public than ever before. Finally, Congress established and oversees agencies that regulate advertising and broadcasting.

In its regulation of broadcasting, Congress sometimes is accused of meddling with freedom of the press. On occasion, congressional committees summon network heads, other media executives, and journalists to testify. Some refuse to do so, arguing that having to "report" to the government on their internal operations is an intrusion on freedom of the press. But to date, Congress has taken no draconian measures to force compliance.

The Executive Branch

The web of government influence gets more tangled when we consider the executive branch, which includes the White House and a host of other government departments and agencies. Many bureaucrats in federal departments and agencies exercise formal control over information through the government's classification system. Others exercise informal controls over the flow of information to the press and the public. Both federal and state governments are composed mainly of large bureaucracies that manage their own public relations, anxiously trying to maintain a favorable public image. At the federal level, agencies such as the FBI, the Department of Agriculture, and the Pentagon spend millions each year on domestic public relations. In fact, every division of government has its own information officers and staff, and reporters depend heavily on these official spokespersons for information about the daily workings of government. Reporters often have no way of assessing the validity of this information. Much of the news that is reported about the government is, therefore, what public relations people hand out to the press. Thus, through press releases, news conferences, and interviews, bureaucrats strongly influence news that appears about their agency or group. Obviously, this kind of control limits the ability of the press to gain access to factual information that they need to inform the public. Thus, they must work hard to uncover facts through their own independent investigations.

The White House also exercises informal influence on the flow of information. For example, it is a tradition for the President's press secretary to select a limited number of reporters from the pool of the more than two hundred assigned to the White House beat to cover an important political briefing or social event. The remainder of the pool must then obtain information from those selected. Whether the White House regards a member of the pool favorably or not has a significant influence on that reporter's prospects for first-hand access to information.

There are a number of roundabout ways for the executive branch to influence the press. Former Vice President Spiro T. Agnew demonstrated one of them in 1969. When the media were debating the war in Vietnam, Agnew claimed (in essence) that the news media were dominated by the liberal Eastern elite that did not adequately represent or care about the views of more conservative citizens. He implied that this constituted a "controlled press" and that it was time to "do something about" the situation. Agnew's speech sent shock waves through the media—especially in the television

Since the days of Theodore Roosevelt, who began the tradition of meeting with the press regularly, every U.S. President has developed his own style for these encounters. John F. Kennedy masterfully staged announcements at the State Department. Richard Nixon had a highly adversarial relationship with the press. Ronald Reagan met with its representatives infrequently and mainly in formal settings. George Bush had an informal style and often invited reporters aboard Air Force One, or even to his home in Maine. Bill Clinton faced a highly critical press early in his administration. (Clockwise: AP/Wide World Photos; Doug Mills, AP/Wide World Photos; AP/Wide World Photos; Reuters/Bettmann)

industry, where broadcasters worried that government might revoke their license. In fact, there is some evidence that the networks changed their policies after Agnew's remarks. For example, in 1971, when half a million people flooded into Washington, D.C., to protest the war in Vietnam, the network news media gave the event only minimal coverage. A short time later, they gave thorough coverage to Bob Hope's "Honor America Day," which took a conservative view of the war.[27]

The executive branch also has more formal sources of influence on the media. The President appoints members to the two agencies that have power to regulate parts of the media, the Federal Trade Commission and the Federal Communications Commission. More importantly, the White House can propose new legislation to Congress, as well as lobby for or against any proposals that Congress considers. For example, during the early 1980s, the Reagan administration, in an effort to tighten security, proposed changes in the federal Freedom of Information Act. Also, President Reagan issued a series of *executive orders*—which do not require the approval of Congress—intended to prevent leaks and curtail other activities by government employees. One order alone required more than 100,000 former and current government employees to submit all articles, speeches, and even letters to the editor to their agencies for prepublication review. Although some commentators defended this practice for national security reasons, the American Society of Newspaper Editors called the new policy "peacetime censorship of a scope unparalleled in this country since the adoption of the Bill of Rights in 1791."[28]

Without a doubt, President Reagan's news and information policies were the least popular with the press of any administration's since the Nixon-Agnew years. This was partly due to Reagan's infrequent press conferences and general avoidance of the press. In contrast, President Bush during the early days of his administration seemed eager to court the press. By summer 1990, Bush complained when reporters asked him questions about serious matters while he was vacationing in Maine. And by the time of his unsuccessful 1992 re-election campaign, he was openly at war with the media, claiming that it treated him unfairly. When President Clinton took office, he also established a cordial relationship with the press, but after a brief period, there was such conflict that he reassigned his communications director, the young and telegenic George Stephanopoulos, and replaced him with former Reagan aide David Gergen. Without a doubt, Clinton can expect more ups and downs in the relationship. The likelihood of conflict developing between any president and the press is great.[29]

Regulation and other controls   The Federal Communications Commission (FCC) makes and enforces rules and policies that govern many kinds of communications industries, from telephone companies to TV networks. The FCC's rulings have the status of law and can be overturned only by the federal courts or by congressional action. Its rules govern advertising, ownership of broadcast stations, obscenity, and a number of special circumstances. For example, the FCC and the courts legislated a personal attack law, which gives individuals who are publicly criticized by a broadcast station airtime to respond. The FCC also enforces the equal time rule for political candidates, which states: "If a licensee shall permit any person who is a legally qualified candidate for any public office to use a broadcasting station, he shall afford equal opportunities to all other such candidates for that office in the use of such broadcasting station." Based on the equal time rule, the commission later established the fairness doctrine, which grants equal time to people representing issues and causes. Subsequently, in the 1980s, the FCC dropped the fairness doctrine ruling, stating that it penalized the media and had outlived its usefulness in an era when abundance replaced scarcity of broadcast signals. Some members of Congress maintained that the fairness doctrine inhibited speech on the part of the media and the public, whereas most disagreed and reinstated the doctrine, only to have it vetoed by President Reagan. This convoluted series of changes, and other aspects of broadcast regulation, are still being debated by media people, legal scholars, and legislatures.

Much of the FCC's attention is given to interpreting its own rules as it resolves disputes between various interests. In some instances, these rules are very specific—for example, the equal time rule. But in other instances, they are vague, and the commission frequently wrangles over terms such as "the public interest," trying to determine just what it means in a specific set of circumstances.

The FCC also handles the issuance and renewal of broadcast licenses granted to radio and TV stations. It has the power to revoke licenses, but it rarely does so. In recent years, the government has greatly simplified procedures for license renewal and diminished its demands for detailed information from broadcasters. Still, the FCC is charged with seeing whether and how well a broadcast station is serving the public's interest, convenience, and necessity. Although broadcasters often complain of the heavy hand of government, the FCC has been remarkably lenient in renewing licenses. In fact, one critic compared the relationship between the FCC and the industry to a wrestling match wherein "the grunts and groans resound through the land, but no permanent injury seems to result."[30]

A case in point is the FCC's handling of obscenity. The Federal Communications Act of 1934 gives the commission the power to revoke the licenses of stations broadcasting obscene or indecent material over the airways. Although there have been numerous instances of stations running pornographic films and indecent comedy routines in the past, the maximum penalty usually imposed by the FCC is a small fine.

The deregulation of broadcasting, discussed in earlier chapters, has altered the role of the FCC in recent years. Although the commission has had a major economic impact, its rules on media content, children's programming, advertising, and even obscenity have relaxed considerably. Still, the very existence of a government agency regulating the industry is widely viewed as a constraint on broadcasting. Even with much less rigorous rules today, compared to earlier years, many broadcasters still grumble about the FCC, which they regard as a bureaucratic nuisance. However, the notion that broadcasters are obliged to fulfill the public trust by accepting a government license makes them markedly different from the print media. When he was a federal appeals court judge, former Chief Justice Burger once stated:

> A broadcaster seeks and is granted the free and exclusive use of a limited and valued part of the public domain; when he accepts that franchise it is burdened by enforceable public obligations. A newspaper can be operated by the whim or caprice of its owners; a broadcast station cannot.[31]

Controls by the Federal Trade Commission   In December 1978, the Federal Trade Commission (FTC) began a series of hearings to determine whether the growing concentration of ownership in the media influenced the flow of information. Although the hearings generated no definitive answers, media owners denounced the FTC for its potential interference. Those hearings reflect only a small part of the FTC's interest in mass communication and other industries. Like the FCC, the FTC is an independent regulatory agency of the federal government that exists for the purpose of preventing unfair competition. In relation to the media, this task generally translates into the regulation of advertising.

Since its inception in 1914, the FTC has viewed deceptive advertising as unfair competition. Both the FTC and the FCC have brought suits against manufacturers and the media for false claims or misrepresentations. A classic illustration is the Rapid Shave shaving cream case. Rapid Shave aired a television commercial in which a voice-over claimed that shaving with Rapid Shave was especially easy because it had a "deep wetting" ingredient. A demonstration showed a piece of sandpaper being shaved clean with Rapid Shave. Yet the commercial failed to mention that the sandpaper had been soaked in water for nearly an hour and a half prior to the demonstration. And in another version, a hard plastic surface sprinkled with sand was used in lieu of real sandpaper. The case was in the courts for six years while the commercial continued to be shown. Finally, the Supreme Court banned such trickery.

Another example of deceptive advertising banned by the FTC promoted Profile bread. Its makers claimed that the bread contained special ingredients helpful for dieters and that each slice had one-third fewer calories. Actually, the manufacturer was simply slicing the bread one-third thinner than a standard slice.

The most famous consumer protection case, however, came not from the FCC or the FTC but from Congress, which banned cigarette advertising from television and required manufacturers to label each package with a warning to users that cigarette smoking could endanger their health.

Although the FTC directs its actions mainly against individual advertisers, it has a strong indirect effect on the mass media, which are the channels for advertising. For example, when the FTC ordered Profile bread to stop implying that its product had special ingredients, it clearly influenced the content of all advertising.

In recent times, the FTC has been very active, and has cracked down on a lengthy list of food distributors that have been using such terms as "lite" and "low fat." New regulations have been issued requiring that product labels provide detailed information about such claims and about other ingredients.

The FTC issues warnings before moving to formal orders. Some of these orders have the effect of law, and the commission can and has levied punitive fines on manufacturers, sometimes as high as hundreds of thousands of dollars.

Decisions by the FTC have defined the scope of deception in advertising, discussed the concept of truth in advertising, and denounced puffery, that is, exaggerated claims. The FTC also legislates rules, holds conferences on trade practices, issues guides for advertising and labeling practices, and hands down advisory opinions when advertisers request advance comments about advertisements. In recent years, the FTC has frequently called on communications researchers to help examine issues such as the effects of television commercials aimed at children.

Deregulation of communication Underlying deregulation has been the assumption that competition in the marketplace is the best way to conduct business in the United States and that government rules, even if intended to protect the public, are an intrusion. Recently, both the FCC and the FTC have been more lenient in regulating communications industries. This reflects the general trend toward deregulation of various industries, which we discussed in previous chapters with regard to newspaper and broadcast ownership.

This trend seemed to peak with the election of George Bush, when many supporters of deregulation believed that it had gone as far as it was likely to go, given the transitional enthusiasm in Congress for tighter rules. Compared with the dramatic deregulation experienced by airlines and banks, deregulation in the communications industries, whether broadcasting or advertising, has been somewhat mild. One consequence of this relative deregulation has been less scrutiny of advertising content by the FTC.

By the early 1990s, there was again a call for more government regulation of television. In 1991, former FCC chairman Newton Minow declared, in a speech that revisited his famous "Vast Wasteland" speech of thirty years earlier:

> I reject the view of an FCC chairman in the early 1980s who said that "a television set is merely a toaster with pictures." I reject this ideological view that the marketplace will regulate itself and give us perfection.[32]

Overall, regulation of the media by the FCC and FTC is a complex arena that is constantly evolving. Regulation policies and implementation are shaped by many views, and the uneasy relationship between these government agencies and the media will continue to generate debate.

Other Pressures on the Media

Political influences and pressures on the media do not exist either in isolation or in the narrow confines of a government agency. Private lobbyists and special interest groups attempt to influence the media for their own purposes. Congressional committees sometimes provide them with a forum, allowing testimony in favor of or against a piece of legislation that affects broadcasting and the print media. Over the past few years, lobbies and other special interest groups have tried to influence such matters as the amount of violence on television, hiring policies in the media (especially with regard to women and minorities), election coverage before the polls close, the screening of sexually explicit movies in local theaters, and a variety of other issues. These issues change, but one thing is certain—major public concern about the media will often become a political issue, because public concerns shape government legislation and agendas.

The complexity of communication-related issues causes some scholars and critics to ponder whether the United States needs a more coherent communications policy. At present U.S. policy, if there is one, is diffused among various governmental branches and the private sector. As new issues arise, it is difficult to know whether they should be resolved by the FCC, the FTC, Congress, the state legislatures, or others. Some even argue that many policy issues are simply resolved by the private sector because the government does not take enough of an interest.

In the late 1980s, the issue of high-definition television (HDTV) emerged, as discussed in Chapter 7. Amid global competition from Japan and Europe, U.S. TV manufacturers had difficulty in the race to be competitive, partly because they lacked an overall policy with which to standardize their products. They sought guidance from the FCC, which outlined a policy that Congress is likely to challenge in the future. Without a unified communications policy, it may be difficult for U.S. communications industries to speak with clarity in their dealings with the rest of the world. This problem is likely to persist, and perhaps there will one day be a council of communications advisers, as media lawyer Stuart Brotman has proposed, or at least a presidential commission to make recommendations about how various technical, legal, and economic disputes can be handled and resolved.

The public can pressure the media in ways besides directly petitioning elected officials or testifying before Congress. For example, dozens of groups united in opposition to ABC TV's airing of "Amerika" in February 1987, presenting their disapproval in the media itself. The fourteen-and-a-half-hour miniseries portrayed the United States in 1997 controlled by a United Nations peace-keeping force manipulated by the Russians. Protesters felt the program's intent was to glorify conservative positions and to criticize the Kremlin. ABC did air the program, even though some advertisers pulled out and boycotts were organized amid much negative publicity.

Chapter Review

- Although most Americans approve of a free press and believe the United States has one, the mass media in this country operate in a complex web of limitations arising from politics and government.

- The First Amendment forbids Congress to make laws restricting the freedom of the press, but that freedom often conflicts with other rights, such as the right to privacy and the right to a fair trial.

- Libel laws are intended to protect people from false and damaging statements made about them, and libel suits today can result in awards of millions of dollars.

- The courts have sometimes placed restrictions on the press to try to limit publicity that might prejudice juries, but generally efforts in this area have resulted from voluntary cooperation from the press.

- Obscene material is not clearly under the protection of the First Amendment. Although the courts take action to prevent the publication or broadcast of material deemed obscene, debate continues over what exactly constitutes obscenity and how far attempts to control it should go.

- During wartime, restrictions on the press have ranged from outright government censorship via codes and guidelines to voluntary self-regulation by the media. In peacetime, the federal government may attempt to keep information secret for national security reasons, but the media frequently disagree with this policy.

- Reporters claim a right to keep their sources confidential. Some have been willing to go to jail rather than having to identify their sources when ordered to do so by the courts.

- The courts are frequently referees when freedom of the press and other rights conflict. Legislatures and the executive branch also influence the press, through both formal powers and informal influence over the flow of information. Both bureaucrats and politicians can use informal influence to bias what is reported.

- The FCC has the power to regulate many aspects of broadcasting but is sometimes less than vigorous in doing so. Groups of private citizens as well as public opinion exert other pressures on the media.

- Overall, although the American media are generally free from direct government control or outright censorship, they are greatly influenced by economic and political conditions. As economic conditions, legal interpretations, and political pressures constantly change, so too will the media.

Notes and References

1. This was a complex case that was tried, reversed, and taken to the U.S. Supreme Court, which sent it back to the Minnesota court. The newspaper appealed twice, but the final verdict went to Cohen. See 479 N.W.2d 387, 1992, and 481 N.W.2d 840, 1992, Supreme Court of Minnesota.

2. John L. Hulting and Roy P. Nelson, *The Fourth Estate*, 2nd ed. (New York: Harper & Row, 1983), p. 9.

3. William S. Holdsworth, "Defamation in the Sixteenth and Seventeenth Centuries," *Law Quarterly Review*, 40, 1924, pp. 302–304.

4. "The Cost of Libel: Economic and Policy Implications," conference report, Gannett Center for Media Studies, New York, 1986.

5. David Anderson, "The Legal Model: Finding the Right Mix" in Everette E. Dennis, Donald M. Gillmor, and Theodore Glasser, eds., *Media Freedom and Accountability* (Westport: Greenwood Press, 1989).

6. Everette E. Dennis and Eli M. Noam, eds., *The Cost of Libel: Economic and Policy Considerations* (New York: Columbia University Press, 1989).

7. Donald M. Gillmor, *Power, Publicity, and the Abuse of Libel Law* (New York: Oxford University Press, 1992), pp. 171–172.

8. Robert W. Chandler, "Controlling Conflict: Working Proposal for Settling Disputes Between Newspapers and Those Who Feel Harmed by Them," working paper, Gannett Center for Media Studies, New York, 1989.

9. John D. Stevens, *Sensationalism in the New York Press* (New York: Columbia University Press, 1990).

10. Richard Findlater, *Comic Cuts* (London: Andre Deutsch, 1970), pp. 21–22.

11. "Howard Stern Is the Object of FCC Fine," *New York Times,* October 28, 1992, Section B, p. 3.

12. John C. Merrill, *The Dialectic in Journalism: Toward a Responsible Use of Press Freedom* (Baton Rouge: Louisiana State University Press, 1989). See also Everette E. Dennis and John Merrill, *Media Debates; Enduring Issues in Communication* (White Plains: Longman, 1990).

13. George Will, "Fed Up with Subsidizing Non-Degradable Art" (The Washington Post Writers Group syndicated column), *The Syracuse Post-Standard*, July 22, 1993, p. A-10.

14. Douglas Cater, *The Fourth Branch of Government* (Boston: Houghton Mifflin, 1959), p. 119.

15. *The Media at War: The Press and the Persian Gulf Conflict*, Gannett Foundation Report, New York, 1991. (contents page description of censorship in the Gulf War).

16. Nicholas Hopkinson, *War and the Media*, Wilton Park Paper 55 (London: Her Majesty's Printing Office, 1992), p. 1.

17. Howard Kurtz and Barton Gellman, "Press and Pentagon Set Reporting Rules." *International Herald Tribune*, May 23–24, 1992, p. 3.

18. James Reston, *The Artillery of the Press* (New York: Harper & Row, 1966), p. 20.

19. Frank Luther Mott, *American Journalism*, 3rd ed. (New York: Macmillan, 1962), pp. 326–336.

20. Hulting and Nelson, op. cit., p. 9.

21. "Freedoms to Read and Write and Be Informed," *Publishers Weekly*, December 13, 1971, p. 29.

22. A good example is New York's 1970 law. Essentially, it protects journalists and newscasters from charges of contempt in any proceeding brought under state law for refusing or failing to disclose the sources of information obtained while gathering news for publication. See *Editor & Publisher,* May 6, 1972, p. 32.

23. J. Herbert Altschull, *From Milton to McLuhan: Ideas and American Journalism* (White Plains: Longman, 1989).

24. Anthony Lewis, "Life Isn't So Simple as the Press Would Have It," *ASNE Bulletin,* September 1983, p. 34.

25. David A. Anderson, "Media Success in the Supreme Court," working paper, Gannett Center for Media Studies, New York, 1987.

26. A study that resulted is *Television and Growing Up: The Impact of Televised Violence* (Washington, D.C.: United States Department of Health, Education, and Welfare, December 31, 1971).

27. Fred Powledge, *The Engineering of Restraint* (Washington, D.C.: Public Affairs Press, 1971, p. 46.

28. Tony Mauro, "Reagan Imposes Ironclad Grip on Words by Government Employees," in *1983–1984 Freedom of Information Report* (Chicago: Society of Professional Journalists, 1984).

29. "The Press, the Presidency and the First Hundred Days," conference report, Gannett Center for Media Studies, New York, 1989.

30. R. H. Coase, "Economics of Broadcasting and Government," *American Economic Review, Papers and Proceedings*, May 1966, p. 442.

31. *United Church of Christ* v. *the Federal Communications Commission*, 359 F.2d 994 (D.C. Cir 1966).

32. Newton H. Minow, "How Vast the Wasteland Now?" Freedom Forum Media Studies Center, Columbia University, New York, May 1991.

CHAPTER **10**

Advertising: Using the Media in the Marketplace

Through its ability to
deliver carefully
prepared messages to
targeted audiences,
(advertising) has had an
influential role on all
sectors of society. With
the dawn of a new
century, the increased
demand for sophisticat-
ed information about
goods and services will
put even greater
pressure on the industry
as it strives for greater
creativity and, yes, truth
in its messages.

Stanley E. Cohen, *Advertising
Age*, November 9, 1988

As the English historian and essayist Thomas B. Macaulay wrote, "Advertising is to business what steam is to industry—the sole propelling power. Nothing except the Mint can make money without advertising." Almost without exception, Macaulay's principle holds true for businesses today, and it is especially true for the mass media. Their solvency as businesses depends to a great extent on advertising, and advertising, in turn, depends heavily on the mass media as its vehicle. It is impossible to imagine the American mass media without advertising, for they have grown up together and each depends on the other. Although many people deplore ads on TV or elsewhere, advertising is regarded as the key to persuading consumers to buy particular goods and services. Its persuasive effects result in jobs throughout the entire complex chain of systems that either turn raw materials into finished products or perform service activities for profit.

Advertising is the main source of funds for the American system of mass communication. It is one of two streams of revenue that support American communications industries. Advertisers use communications media to market products and services to consumers, or "end users" as economists call them. Not surprisingly, the other revenue stream for communications are end users themselves—individuals and families who buy magazines, subscribe to newspapers or cable services, and consume records, videotapes, and other media products.

In some societies, advertising plays no such role. Historically, this was the case in the former Soviet Union and the several nations of Central and Eastern Europe that opted for independence in the late 1980s and early 1990s. Along with independence, for better or worse, came advertising, which is now commonplace in these and other former command-socialist economies. Even in authoritarian China, which once forbade advertising as "bourgeois capitalist decadence," commercial messages flourish now. Only in a few places today, such as North Korea, is commercial advertising unknown. Thus, it appears that advertising is essential to the modern market economy. There are no known instances where there is a free market *and* an advertising-free society, though some foreign broadcast systems, such as the BBC, pride themselves on not carrying commercial announcements.

This chapter examines both the content and function of advertising as communication. We look briefly at how it developed and how advertising messages are manufactured. This includes attention to the industry, its messages, its structure, the connection of advertising to public taste, and criticisms of the outcomes it supposedly produces.

Advertising as Communication

Advertising is a social institution in its own right—a deeply established part of American culture. It is not a mere appendage to the mass media. That is, it has a structure and existence of its own, and it is an important factor in the U.S. economy. Moreover, as economic historian David M. Potter wrote:

> Advertising now compares with such long-standing institutions as the school and the church in the magnitude of its social influence. It dominates the media, it has vast power in shaping popular standards, and it is really one of the very limited group of institutions which exercise social control.[1]

Viewed in this broader context, then, advertising is a central feature of our urban-industrial society—one that needs to be understood in relation to society's other institutions and processes. However, advertising takes so many forms that it is not easy to sort out the central principles that need study. For example, consider the following: a television commercial, a catchy slogan, a full-page spread in a magazine, a pencil with the name of a firm embossed on its side, a poster above your seat on a bus or subway. All these are forms of advertising, but what do they have in common? Thus, this examination of advertising begins with a look at its definition, functions, content, and history.

What Is Advertising?

Perhaps the answer many people would give to the question "What is advertising?" would be similar to the common reply to "What is art?" That answer is, "I can't define it, but I know it when I see it!" Nevertheless, it will be helpful to examine attempts to provide a definition and then develop one that incorporates the most essential features.

A dictionary definition suggests that advertising is simply "the action of attracting public attention to a product or business [as well as] the business of preparing and distributing advertisements."[2] Another, provided by the American Marketing Association, states that advertising is "any paid form of nonpersonal presentation and promotion of ideas, goods, and services by an identified sponsor."[3] But neither of these definitions notes the role of the mass media in advertising. To correct this deficiency, a leading advertising textbook defines advertising as "controlled, identifiable information and persuasion by means of mass communications media."[4]

Each of these definitions provides at least a part of the answer. Advertising is *controlled* in that it is prepared in accordance with the desires of the firm or other group it represents. Unlike a person who grants an interview to the press not knowing how his or her words will appear, the advertiser knows exactly what the message will say. Furthermore, advertising is identifiable as *communication*. The message may be subtle or direct, but you know it is advertising and not, for example, news. Advertising can be entertaining, but few would claim that entertainment is its primary goal. If advertising entertains, that is only a means to an end. That end is to increase sales. Thus, advertising tries to inform consumers about a *particular product* and to persuade them to make a *particular decision*—usually, the decision to buy that product. Its avowed goal is to guide and control buying behavior, to move the consumer toward one product instead of another. Thus, it is a form of *social control,* urging the consumer to conform within a range of product choices, "providing norms of behavior appropriate to current economic conditions."[5]

Taking a more theoretical approach, one could define advertising in terms of the meaning construction theory of mass communication's effects presented in Chapter 17. In these terms, it is an attempt to establish, extend, substitute, or stabilize people's meanings for symbols that label the advertiser's products or services. Advertisers seek to influence language conventions, individual interpretations, and the shared meanings associated with such symbols so that people will make choices that are favorable to the advertisers' purposes. In other words, they hope that through communication they can get people to know about, like, and purchase their clients' wares.

Each of these attempts to define advertising has merit. However, each also emphasizes only one or two important features of the process. Thus, in order to set forth clearly what this chapter is about, we can develop the following more comprehensive definition: *Advertising* is a form of controlled communication that attempts to persuade an appropriate audience, through the use of a variety of appeals and strategies, to make a decision to buy or use a particular product or service. Because advertisers make use of many other channels of communication, this definition does not specify that the message must be transmitted via the mass media. However, a huge amount of advertising is presented via mass media, so we focus on that in the present chapter.

The Content of Advertising

To accomplish their ends, advertisers must make a *persuasive appeal*. Sometimes that appeal is simple and descriptive; sometimes it is subtle and sophisticated. Communication scholar James W. Carey says that advertising is persuasive—and thus acts as a form of social control—mainly by providing information.[6] Indeed, some advertising content is direct and makes rational appeals, mentioning characteristics of the product, its relative advantages, and price. A General Tire commercial that features babies, for example, talks about the durability of the tire and its role in keeping the family safe.

Much advertising, however, has little to do with direct information or rational appeals. Instead it attempts to manipulate the consumer by indirect appeals. Research in 1992 on Americans' favorite commercials indicated that those with fantasy scenes, such as the ads for the California Raisins or Kibbles 'n Bits dog food, are more popular than those featuring celebrities. Economic historian David Potter maintains, "Advertising appeals primarily to the desires, the wants—cultivated or natural—of the individual, and it sometimes offers as its goal a power to command the envy of others by outstripping them in the consumption of goods and services."[7] If this is true, advertising may try to get you to buy a product not because of its advantages and not because of your existing needs, but because of a need or desire that the advertisement itself tries to create.

Potter's analysis has much merit. Almost every appeal imaginable has been used in advertising. Some ads have traded on prestige; others have used fear. Some have promised glamour and the good life. Some have embraced fantasy, and others have been firmly fixed in reality. To make these appeals, advertisers associate products, verbally and visually, with other images, symbols, and values that are likely to attract consumers. For example, advertising for the auto rental firm Avis appealed to the love for the underdog when it promised, "We try harder." Historically, another kind of dog—the trustworthy family dog—was used by RCA Victor, an early manufacturer of the record player that advertised its Victrola with the slogan "His Master's Voice" and a picture of a dog listening to recorded music. The starched but debonair look of "the man in the Arrow shirt" provides a model for the well-dressed man. Elegant, tastefully designed advertisements for Cadillacs convey an image of quality and excellence. Coca-Cola's successful "It's the Real Thing" advertisements show happy, fun-loving, youthful people drinking Coke with upbeat music playing in the background—without saying anything about taste, nutritional value, or price.

The advertising industry places a high premium on creativity in finding new images that will appeal to the public. Table 10.1 lists some winners of the 1992 Clio awards, which are given annually to the best, most effective ads. Even the sometimes prosaic area of outdoor or billboard advertising has been on the lookout for striking, appealing ads. In 1992, for example, that industry's Creative Challenge contest sponsored by the Gannett Outdoor Group honored an ad showing a mighty dam holding back a waterfall. Above the dam appeared a single word: "Huggies." Said the *New York Times*, "This unexpectedly imaginative way of advertising one of the most mundane products [disposable diapers] has won a hefty prize in a contest intended to persuade agencies that creativity in outdoor ads is no oxymoronic concept." The winners of the $10,000 prize were three employees of the advertising agency Ogilvy & Mather; the big winner, naturally, was the advertiser itself—Kimberly-Clark, producer of Huggies.[8]

McDonald's "golden arches" have become one of the most durable symbols in American advertising, whose messages typically change rapidly. Anyone who sees these arches easily recognizes the products with which they are associated. Another example of an enduring symbol was the "Marlboro man," who was instantly recognizable to millions. To many, he represented desirable values of individualism and self-reliance. Ironically, the actor who posed for the Marlboro ads died recently of lung cancer. (© Elaine Braithwaite/Peter Arnold, Inc.)

Not all advertising focuses on a specific product, such as diapers. A form called *institutional advertising* is much less direct. For example, a firm that makes paper and other forest products presents a television ad or a colorful full-page magazine ad describing the virtues of a beautiful, well-managed forest. The advertisement shows cute animals but says nothing about its specific product, providing only the corporation's name. The goal is, of course, to get the public to associate the corporation with the "selfless" ad and lovely images.

The visual and verbal content of advertising has changed considerably over time. In the last hundred years, styles have included the ornate and highly decorative soap and cosmetic ads of the 1890s, the clean lines of the art deco designs of the 1920s and 1930s, and the psychedelic posterlike ads of the 1960s and early 1970s. More recently, the clean, orderly, Swiss Gothic look of the 1980s yielded in the 1990s to more traditional and formal design, possibly in response to an economic recession and a serious public mood. It is, says design expert Roy Paul Nelson, all a matter of coordinating art and typography with content.

These changes reflect the efforts of creative professionals and entrepreneurs to fashion effective messages. In order to be effective, an advertisement must appeal to its audience and reflect shared values. Advertising that works is therefore an index of popular culture. That was recognized as far back as 1917, when writer Norman Douglas claimed, "You can tell the ideals of a nation by its advertisements."[9] Thus, changes in advertising over the years have been closely tied to changes in American society as a whole.

Advertising in America: A Brief History

Until recently, social histories all but ignored advertising. Even histories of journalism failed to deal with advertising's role in creating the modern mass media. But the American Museum of Advertising in Portland, Oregon, has examples of advertising going back to the Greeks and Romans and much

Category	Client and Ad (or Series)	Advertising Agency
Local Campaign	WLUP-FM 98; "Smokes/Get Up," "Smokes/Cheer Up," "Smokes/Lively Conversation"	Elsaman Johns & Laws, Chicago, IL
	Seattle Opera; "Don't Know Songs," "It's Boring," "Can't Understand"	Livingston + Company, Seattle, WA
Apparel/Fashion	Reebok; "Kick/Farmer-Patrick"	Coppos Sato Thomas, Los Angeles, CA
Automotive	Chrysler Jeep Eagle; "Snow Covered"	Plum Productions, Santa Monica, CA
Banking/Financial	Visa; "Burro"	Gartner Grasso, Los Angeles, CA
Beverages/Non-Alcoholic	Pepsi Cola Co.; "Summer of Love"	BBDO, New York, NY
	CA Milk Processor Board; "Aaron Burr"	Goodby Berlin & Silverstein, San Francisco, CA
Corporate/Institutional	Goldsmith/Jeffrey Advertising; "Graves"	Moxie Pictures, Hollywood, CA
Personal Items	Swiss Army Watch; "330 Feet"	Margeotes Fertitta Donaher & Weiss, New York, NY
Recreational Items	Lynx Recreational Items; "Ball POV: Miss It"	DDB Needham Worldwide, New York, NY
Public Service	Earth Communications Office; "The Power of One"	Team One Advertising, El Segundo, CA
Retail Food	Little Caesars; "Italian Feast"	Cliff Freeman & Partners, New York, NY
Animation—Cell	Levi's; "Woman Finding Love"	ACME Fireworks, Hollywood, CA
Animation—Computer	Warner-Lambert Co./Listerine; "Arrows"	Pixar, Richmond, VA
Cinematography	Norwegian Cruise Line; "Laws"	Goodby Berlin & Silverstein, San Francisco, CA
Direction	Little Caesars; "Italian Feast"	Cliff Freeman & Partners, New York, NY
Editing	Start Credit Card; "Grandfather"	Tony Kaye Films, Los Angeles, CA
Humor	CA Milk Processor Board; "Aaron Burr"	Goodby Berlin & Silverstein, San Francisco, CA
Music—Adaptations	KLM/Northwest Airlines; "Mr. Sandman"	Macrose Music, New York, NY
Music—Original	Life Savers; "Cool La La"	JSM Music Inc., New York, NY
Performance	John Hancock; "Grandma's Hero"	Daktor Higgins & Associates, Hollywood, CA
Sound Design	Chevy Trucks; "Hulk-Extended Cab"	Machine Head, Venice, CA
Special Effects	Pepsi International; "Algebra"	BBDO, New York, NY

Source: Clio Awards

material from colonial America. Since our country's beginnings, advertising has had an important place in the life of the nation. As historian Daniel J. Boorstin has written:

> Advertising has remained in the mainstream of American civilization—in the settling of the continent, in the expansion of the economy, and in the building of an American standard of living. Advertising has expressed the optimism, the hyperbole and the sense of community, the sense of reaching which has been so important a feature in our civilization.[10]

American society provided one important precondition for advertising: abundance. It seems clear that advertising can thrive only in a society where abundance exists. When resources are scarce, there is little or no need for manufacturers or producers to promote their wares. As economic historian David Potter wrote:

> It is when potential supply outstrips demand—that is, when abundance prevails—that advertising begins to fulfill a really essential function. In this situation the producer knows that the limitation upon his operations and upon his growth no longer lies, as it lay historically, in his productive capacity, for he can always produce as much as the market will absorb; the limitation has shifted to the market, and it is selling capacity which controls his growth.[11]

The United States has usually provided the relative abundance necessary for advertising to be useful. And American businesses, with the help of advertising, have been very successful at increasing sales. The result is what economists have dubbed the "consumer society."

Although historians often date modern advertising to the 1880s, advertising is actually much older than that. The earliest advertising messages were those of criers or simple signs above shops. Modern advertising has its origins in the trademarks used by crafts workers and early merchants to distinguish their wares from those of others. With the advent of printing and expanding world trade, there was even more advertising. The watermarks of printers were distinctive forms of advertising. Coffee, chocolate, and tea, to name a few items, were hawked in messages on broadsides and in newspapers and other periodicals. Proving that advertising could be compelling and useful, the *London Gazette* in 1666 published an advertising supplement to help lost and homeless fire victims get in touch with one another.

In the American colonies, advertisers used many media—newspapers, pamphlets, broadsides, and almanacs. Early communications media thus became factors in the marketplace for goods and services. But advertising was not a very important source of revenue for early newspapers. They depended more on government printing contracts and the price paid by the reader. Advertising in colonial times was somewhat subdued by modern standards and rarely overshadowed the editorial content of the papers. Still, it often received front-page billing, probably because the news often consisted of less-than-fresh reports from distant Europe, whereas the advertising was current and local.

It was the Industrial Revolution, with its huge increase in the production of goods, that made advertising so essential. From the early 1800s on, advertising grew naturally as markets expanded and factories tried to sell their goods. As the nineteenth century progressed, advertising accounted for an increasing proportion of the content of newspapers and magazines—and for more and more of their revenue. Like the press during this time, advertising was fiercely local and was paid for by local merchants.

Around the middle of the nineteenth century, *national advertising* developed. In the United States, the first advertising aimed at a national audience appeared in magazines, which were really the first medium of nationwide communication. Many of the new national magazines appealed to women. Therefore, soaps, cosmetics, and patent medicines were among the products frequently advertised in their pages.

These ads created markets for new products. That is, advertising proved that it could accelerate acceptance of new products and get people to change their buying habits. For example, in 1851, people still bought soap by the pound. Then a soap manufacturer named B. T. Babbitt introduced the bar of soap. When the public was unresponsive to the product, Babbitt introduced a history-making innovation. He offered a *premium*: For every

Advertising strategies are basically the same now as they were in the earliest advertisements. In these examples, advertisers use attention-getting type, images of the products, and appeals to buyers' needs and desires to sell violins and Coca-Cola. (Smithsonian Institution Photo No. 78–19094; "Coca-Cola" is a registered trademark of The Coca-Cola Company)

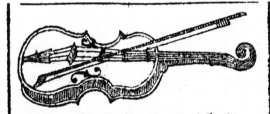

A VIOLINS.

A FEW excellent toned VIOLINS for Sale, at CALLENDER's Ivory Turning & Whipmaker's Shop, juſt below Mr. JONES's Auction-Office, North-ſide of State-Street.

Alſo, a Variety of Phæton & Chaiſe WHIPS, and a few ſilver-mounted cat-gut Whips, all of his own manufacture ; Thongs of all lengths & prices ; a variety of Walking Sticks of all Prices ; India Bambooes ; large and ſmall India Joints, Billiard Balls, Drums and Fifes, with a Variety of other articles in his Line.——CHEAP.

Alſo, a few Elephant's TEETH Black Ebony by the hundred or leſs quantity Letter Wood ; Rattan by the bundle, dozen or yard.

Alſo a very handſome ſett of COUDRILL, made of Pearl.

☞ *Caſh given for Sea-Cow Teeth.*

☞ Turned Work of all Kinds for Houſes, done in the cheapeſt & beſt manner with Thanks for the ſmalleſt Favours.

Wherever you go you will find
AT ALL FOUNTAINS Coca-Cola 5¢
to refreſh the parched throat, to invigorate the fatigued body and quicken the tired brain

twenty-five empty soap wrappers a buyer presented, Babbitt promised a handsome colored picture in return. The lure attracted buyers, and the idea of premiums took hold. We have been living with premiums ever since. They are common today on cigarette wrappers, cereal boxes, and other products.

The nineteenth century saw the use of another advertising strategy: the *testimonial*. Some firms used photos of beautiful or prominent women, such as the First Lady (without her permission), to promote their products. Later, movie stars, athletes, and television stars would lend their names and images to particular products. That has also become part of our culture.

In the late nineteenth century, a combination of new postal rates favorable to regularly issued publications, improved transportation, and the desire of business for nationwide markets stimulated the growth of national magazines and consequently national advertising. Magazine publishers, following the lead of Benjamin Day and the nation's newspapers, adopted the idea that the reader should be able to buy a magazine for a fraction of its actual cost (that is, the cost of production) while advertising revenue should pay for the rest and produce profits. By the 1890s, nickel and dime magazines flourished, even though the cost of production was much higher than five or ten cents.

In the twentieth century, as new mass media were developed, the importance of advertising in promoting products accelerated greatly. Radio and television were ideal as advertising media, and as we have seen in earlier chapters, they soon became dependent on its revenues. Whereas a newspaper or magazine required the receiver to purchase a subscription, broadcast messages were free and difficult to avoid; consequently broadcasting was added to print as a major advertising medium. Thus, as the industrial society developed, a symbiotic relationship provided the financial foundation of the American system of mass communication. It has been said that "Marconi may have invented the wireless and Henry Luce may have invented the news magazine, but it is advertising that has made both wireless and news magazines what they are in America today."[12]

The captains of American business fought vigorous battles for larger sales in an expanding economy. One of their weapons in this war was advertising. At first, essential goods and services were advertised, then luxury items, and then an almost infinite list of products and services. Advertising became the expression of the nation's commercial self. As the advertising industry grew, newspapers and magazines developed advertising departments catering to commercial interests that wanted to buy advertising space. Publications began to compete aggressively for advertisers' business, especially in towns where there were competing media. Large retail organizations placed large amounts of advertising, and eventually they too established advertising departments to plan and place their ads. By the 1930s, intermediaries were facilitating the relationship between the commercial enterprise and the media organization. At first, these intermediaries were merely space brokers who arranged for the placement of ads. Later, they expanded their operations and became the world's first *advertising agencies*—organizations that eventually provided creative and research assistance and advertising strategies to large numbers of clients.

Thus, the main features of the modern advertising industry were established early in this century. Its development both depended on and stimulated the growth of the mass media; it could not have flowered without businesses eager to expand. And, of course, neither of these would have been possible without consumers with money to spend. Thus, advertising has become a great social institution linking the nation's productivity, its mass media, and its consuming public.

The Contemporary Advertising Industry

The advertising industry exists for the purpose of putting businesses who want to market and distribute goods and services in touch with consumers who want to buy and use them. Viewed in this way, the advertising industry today is a kind of facilitator of communication between advertisers and the public. Components of the industry include:

1. Advertising agencies
2. Media services organizations
3. Suppliers of supporting services ranging from public opinion research to commercial art
4. Advertising departments of retail businesses
5. Advertising media, including print and electronic media, outdoor advertising, specialty advertising, direct-mail advertising, and business advertising (also the various departments of these organizations that deal with advertising)

These are only the bare bones of the industry, and everything on the list comes in several sizes. For example, there are massive national advertising agencies with offices in scores of cities in the United States and abroad, and there are small, local agencies with only a few accounts.

Although the advertising industry is made up of independent business interests and is by no means a tightly controlled national entity, it is held together by various voluntary organizations and associations. There are, for example, associations of advertisers and advertising agencies. These include the important American Association of Advertising Agencies (or 4As) and the Association of National Advertisers (the clients of agencies), as well as regional and state groups. There are also media associations concerned with advertising, including the Newspaper Advertising Bureau, the Outdoor Advertising Institute, the Television Bureau of Advertising, and the Cable Advertising Bureau, to name only a few.

These organizations and others produce regular publications that carry news of the advertising industry. Some are general-interest periodicals for advertising (for example, *Advertising Age*); others are very specific (for example, *Art Direction*, which deals with graphics). Each category of advertising (direct mail, outdoor signs, packaging, and so on) has its own publications. Information and research services as well as publishing houses also produce much on the subject of advertising.

All this adds up to a huge industry with a substantial economic impact. As the 1990s began, U.S. businesses were spending $126 billion per year on

TABLE 10.2 The Top One Hundred National Advertisers

Rank	Advertiser	Ad Spending In 1993(millions)	Rank	Advertiser	Ad Spending In 1993(millions)
1	Procter & Gamble Co.	$2,397.5	51	Quaker Oats Co.	246.5
2	Philip Morris Cos.	1,844.3	52	News Corp.	243.5
3	General Motors Corp.	1,539.2	53	Schering-Plough Corp.	233.1
4	Sears, Roebuck & Co.	1,310.7	54	Mazda Motor Corp.	228.0
5	PepsiCo	1,038.9	55	Tandy Corp.	223.1
6	Ford Motor Co.	958.3	56	Federated Department Stores	223.0
7	AT & T Co.	812.1	57	U.S. dairy farmers	215.1
8	Nestle SA	793.7	58	S.C. Johnson & Son	209.9
9	Johnson & Johnson	762.5	59	General Electric Co.	204.8
10	Chrysler Corp.	761.6	60	Mattel	201.1
11	Warner-Lambert Co.	751.0	61	Joh. A. Benckiser GmBH	199.2
12	Unilever NV	738.2	62	Clorox Co.	198.3
13	McDonald's Corp.	736.6	63	Adoph Coors Co.	197.8
14	Time Warner	695.1	64	ITT Corp.	196.2
15	Toyota Motor Corp.	690.4	65	Helene Curtis Industries	192.6
16	Walt Disney Co.	675.7	66	Paramount Communications	185.3
17	Grand Metropolitan	652.9	67	ConAgra	183.2
18	Kellogg Co.	627.1	68	Ciba-Geigy	182.7
19	Eastman Kodak Co.	624.7	69	IBM Corp.	171.8
20	Sony Corp.	589.0	70	Citicorp	169.8
21	J.C. Penney Co.	585.2	71	Broadway Stores	169.5
22	General Mills	569.2	72	Wendy's International	168.3
23	Kmart Corp.	558.2	73	Gillette Co.	167.2
24	Anheuser-Busch Cos.	520.5	74	Goodyear Tire & Rubber Co.	163.1
25	American Home Products Corp.	501.6	75	Roll International	160.1
26	RJR Nabisco	499.4	76	Philips NV	158.3
27	Nissan Motor Co.	413.1	77	Campbell Soup Co.	150.1
28	May Department Stores Co.	403.6	78	Upjohn Co.	146.5
29	Matsushita Electric Industrial Co.	385.1	79	Bayer AG	145.3
30	Ralston Purina Co.	372.8	80	Wm. Wrigley Jr. Co.	144.9
31	Hershey Foods Corp.	366.3	81	American Stores Co.	143.0
32	Honda Motor Co.	354.4	82	American Brands	142.7
33	Coca-Cola Co.	341.3	83	Marriott International	132.6
34	Mars Inc.	337.6	84	AMR Corp.	131.3
35	American Express Co.	324.8	85	CPC International	129.4
36	H.J. Heinz Co.	318.9	86	Apple Computer	129.1
37	Circuit City Stores	308.5	87	Seagram Co.	126.8
38	U.S. Government	304.4	88	Dr Pepper/Seven-Up Cos.	125.5
39	Sara Lee Corp.	299.7	89	Dow Chemical Co.	125.1
40	MCI Communications Corp.	297.4	90	Loews Corp.	124.5
41	Colgate-Palmolive Co.	287.4	91	Visa International	122.5
42	Nike Inc.	281.4	92	Kimberly-Clark Corp.	119.8
43	R.H. Macy & Co.	280.5	93	U.S. Shoe Corp.	118.8
44	Hasbro Inc.	277.3	94	Imasco	117.6
45	SmithKline Beecham	269.7	95	B.A.T Industries	116.9
46	Dayton Hudson Corp.	266.7	96	Daimler-Benz AG	116.6
47	Sprint Corp.	264.8	97	Bally Manufacturing Corp.	115.1
48	Wal-Mart Stores	251.9	98	Pfizer Inc.	114.9
49	Bristol-Myers Squibb Co.	250.2	99	Mitsubishi Motors Corp.	113.4
50	Levi Strauss & Co.	248.9	100	Delta Air Lines	113.1

Source: Advertising Age, *September 28, 1994. Reprinted with permission from the September 28, 1994 issue of* Advertising Age. *Copyright, Crain Communications Inc., 1994*

advertising, including media advertising and such other approaches as direct-mail marketing. (A list of the leading advertisers appears in Table 10.2.) Industry analysts predict that this number will reach $180 billion by 1996.

Of the total amount of advertising spending in 1991, media were getting about 60 percent, with the rest going to sales promotion, direct marketing, package design, and other activities. It was estimated that the top 100 advertising agencies—the principal "middlemen" between advertisers, the media, and the public—were getting about 36 percent of this amount, which represented a slight but noticeable decline. It has also been estimated that more than 226,900 people are employed in advertising, approximately 157,900 of them in advertising agencies in the United States. The 1991 U.S. Bureau of the Census has estimated that there are nearly 14,000 establishments engaged in the advertising business, including 9,800 advertising agencies.

The trend toward concentration into large firms that we have seen elsewhere in the communications industries has also characterized advertising. A list of the top grossing agencies, as shown in Table 10.3, sections A and B, reveals that a small number of giant New York agencies predominate in the industry. To grasp the magnitude of the business that these companies do around the world, remember that the value of billings for each firm is several times that of the income figures displayed in the table.

The various elements of the advertising industry are interrelated parts of a dynamic system in which competition is intense. The image of the harried advertising account executive often presented in movies and on television may be an overstatement, but advertising is a field marked by stress and competitiveness as agencies and other firms do battle for accounts.

Advertising Agencies

Advertising agencies have come a long way since the nineteenth century, when they were essentially space brokers. Today, there are two main types. One is the full-service agency, which performs virtually every aspect of the advertising process for its clients. The other is the boutique agency, which is a much smaller operation.

Full-service agencies The *full-service agency* employs writers, artists, media experts, researchers, television producers, account executives, and others as part of the organization. Advertising professor John S. Wright and his colleagues have identified three main functions for the full-service advertising agency:

1. *Planning.* The agency must know the firm, its product, the competition, and the market well enough to recommend plans for advertising.
2. *Creation and execution.* The agency creates the advertisements and contacts the media that will present them to the intended audience.
3. *Coordination.* The agency works with salespeople, distributors, and retailers to see that the advertising works.[13]

TABLE 10.3   Rankings of Advertising Agencies by Income (in millions)

A. Top Ten U.S. Agencies by Worldwide Gross Income (in millions)	1993	1992	Percentage Change
1 McCann-Erickson Worldwide, New York	$1,003.9	$948.9	5.8
2 Young and Rubicam, New York	936.0	980.1	−4.5
3 J. Walter Thompson Co., New York	876.0	820.2	6.8
4 BBDO Worldwide, New York	856.2	830.5	3.1
5 DDB Needham Worldwide, New York	811.5	783.3	3.6
6 Ogilvy & Mather Worldwide, New York	740.0	755.1	−2.0
7 Lintas Worldwide, New York	722.6	744.2	−2.9
8 Grey Advertising, New York	709.4	673.7	5.3
9 Saatchi & Saatchi Advertising, New York	638.8	644.0	−0.8
10 Foote, Cone and Belding Communications, Chicago	633.7	661.5	−4.2

B. Top Ten U.S. Agencies by U.S. Gross Income (in millions)	1993	1992	Percentage Change
1 Leo Burnett Co., Chicago	$304.8	$313.6	−2.8
2 J. Walter Thompson Co., New York	291.6	268.8	8.5
3 Grey Advertising, New York	282.7	257.7	9.7
4 McCann-Erickson Worldwide, New York	245.2	224.3	9.3
5 DDB Needham Worldwide, New York	231.4	231.2	0.9
6 BBDO Worldwide, New York	229.7	215.7	6.5
7 Saatchi & Saatchi Advertising, New York	227.3	231.2	−1.7
8 Foote, Cone and Belding Communications, Chicago	221.8	219.2	1.2
9 D'Arcy Masius Benton and Bowles, New York	197.0	198.6	−0.8
10 Young and Rubicam, New York	173.3	181.3	−4.4

C. Top Ten U.S. Cities for Advertising by Billings (in millions)	1993	1992	Percentage Change
1 New York	$26,531.9	$25,030.3	6.0
2 Chicago	7,705.8	7,433.6	3.7
3 Los Angeles	5,340.6	4,931.7	8.3
4 Detroit	4,510.0	4,160.2	8.4
5 San Francisco	2,962.5	2,420.0	22.4
6 Dallas	1,748.4	1,448.3	20.7
7 Minneapolis	1,668.3	1,496.4	11.5
8 Boston	1,494.8	1,428.9	4.6
9 Atlanta	1,057.8	952.1	11.1
10 Stamford, Connecticut	1,000.0	871.3	14.8

Source: Advertising Age, April 13, 1994. Reprinted with permission from the April 13, 1994 issue of Advertising Age. Copyright, Crain Communications Inc., 1994.

Within the full-service agency are several major functions and groups:

1. *Account management.* The account executive and his or her staff provide services to a firm or product. An account management director is responsible for relations between the agency and the client.
2. *The creative department.* The creative director supervises writers, directors, artists, and producers, who write and design the ads.
3. *Media selection.* A media director heads a department in which the specific media to be used for particular ads are chosen.
4. *The research department.* Advertising messages are pretested and data are gathered to help the creative staff fashion a specific design and message. The research director supervises in-house research and hires public opinion firms for more extensive national and regional studies.
5. *Internal control.* The administrative operations of the agency, including public relations, are concentrated in one department.

An administrative director runs the agency. Of course, large agencies have a board of directors and the usual trappings of a big business.

Boutiques   A *boutique agency*, unlike its full-service counterpart, has more limited goals and offers fewer services. It is essentially a creative department and may hire other agencies and independent groups to provide other kinds of advertising services for particular clients and products. Often a boutique works closely with an in-house agency—that is, a small ad group or department formed by a business to handle its own products. Most boutiques are small agencies established by people who once worked for full-service agencies.

Once, most advertising agencies and the preponderance of the advertising business were based in New York City, mainly on and around Madison Avenue. Although there were strong regional centers, such as Chicago, Los Angeles, and a few other cities, serious national advertisers usually looked to New York for big-time agencies. In the 1980s and 1990s, with the advance of new technology, many local and regional agencies in smaller cities such as Atlanta, Minneapolis, Seattle, Portland, and Kansas City began to pick up major national accounts outside of their own regions. The industry is still firmly planted in New York, the capital of the communications business, but observers are closely watching the regional developments (see Table 10.3[C]).

Inside the agency   What an advertising agency offers is service, and it is confidence in that service that brings clients to pay 15 percent of their total billings to an ad agency. Just what happens from the initial contact between an agency and a client to the finished advertising campaign varies considerably, depending on the size of the agency and the nature of the account. But, essentially, this is how it works.

The *account management director* either calls on a business—say, a local company that manufactures solar heating devices—or someone from the business contacts the advertising agency. Indeed, the company may contact several agencies and ask all of them for proposals, with the understanding that only one will receive the account. The account management director then selects an *account executive* from within the agency, who arranges a meeting between company executives from the solar heating firm, the account management director, and other appropriate people from the agency. They discuss potential advertising objectives: Who are likely customers for the device? How can they best be reached? Through what medium? With what appeals?

Then the account executive goes to work inside the agency. The *research department* conducts studies or assembles information to answer some of the questions about potential consumers. The agency's *creative department* holds brainstorming sessions, discussing ideas for a potential campaign. *Artists* and *writers* draw up sample ads. These may be rough sketches of newspaper and magazine advertisements as well as broadcast *story boards*, which are a series of drawings on a panel indicating each step of a commercial. Depending on how complex and detailed the campaign will be, a variety of other specialists may be involved, such as sound engineers, graphic artists, lighting experts, and actors.

The result of all this is the sample ad, which is then *pretested* on potential consumers. The agency's research department goes over this pretesting and suggests which of several approaches would be best for the client. In recent years, copy-testing has grown in importance: All elements of a print ad or broadcast commercial are tested for consumer reactions. This process removes some of the risks of advertising and generally pleases the client. The research also guides the agency and client in deciding what media to use. Various options are print, broadcast, outdoor advertising, matchbook covers, buses, and so on.

The account executive then gathers this information and, along with other agency personnel, conducts a *presentation* for the client. But first, potential costs are clearly laid out so that the company can evaluate the proposal. The presentation is often elaborate, with slide and tape presentations and sample ads. Research and creative personnel are called in to discuss the ads, and people from the *media department* discuss the advantages and disadvantages of using particular media for the campaign. Now the ball is in the company's court. The executives either accept or reject the agency's proposal. Their acceptance may, of course, be conditional on various modifications.

Once the go-ahead is given, the account executive coordinates activity within the agency to produce the actual ads and works with the media department to contact the appropriate media and arrange for the advertising campaign to reach the public. The research department prepares to *evaluate* the campaign so that the agency can present evidence about whom the campaign has reached and with what effect—and thus ensure that the account will be renewed in the future. Finally, the advertisement reaches the consumer. The success or failure of the campaign depends on whether an ample number of consumers head toward a local store to buy the product.

Media Service Organizations

Advertisements must be placed in appropriate media, and space or time has to be arranged. Specialized organizations exist that spend their time buying space in the media at reasonable rates and negotiating with advertising agencies for it. Many people in these *media service organizations* once worked for advertising agencies.

One type of media service organization is the national advertising representative, who has special expertise in network television rates and knows the ideal times to display particular kinds of products. Often national advertising representatives buy blocks of television time in advance and then sell the time to various advertising agencies for particular accounts. They get involved with an account late in the game, usually after a lot of planning has been done. Other kinds of media service organizations include independent design firms and television production companies. Usually they work with the advertising agency and not directly with the advertiser.

Advertising Departments

Whole industries, as well as large department stores, sometimes have *advertising departments*. Unlike advertising agencies, which are independent "middlemen" serving several accounts or businesses, the advertising department of a business works with that firm's products and is part of its staff. This department has an intimate knowledge of the business or industry and makes proposals for advertising plans and strategies. Its main concern is the outcome: increasing sales or heightening the awareness of a particular product or service. Advertising departments work closely with advertising agencies, which compete for their business and present alternative proposals for the campaigns. Some retail advertising departments resemble small advertising agencies and place advertising directly with local media. For more complicated transactions that involve research and other specialties, they look to agencies for assistance.

Advertising Media

All of the standard mass media are, of course, advertising vehicles. Newspapers, magazines, TV stations, radio stations, cable companies, and other media outlets have advertising departments. At both the national and the local level, the media compete vigorously for advertising dollars. Each of the major media has some kind of national advertising association that gathers data and tries to show that it is the "best buy" for reaching a particular audience. At the local level, advertising salespeople who work for media organizations sell space to businesses either directly or through an advertising agency or media service organization.

In selecting a medium, the business or advertising agency considers the target audience to be reached, the cost of advertising and the effectiveness of a medium for reaching the desired audience. Various sources report slightly different data, but it is clear that among the traditional mass media, newspapers get the largest share of the advertising dollar (24.1 percent), followed by television (21.7 percent), direct mail (19.3 percent), Yellow Pages (7.2 percent), radio (6.7 percent), magazines (5.2 percent), and all other types (15.8 percent). Table 10.4 indicates how advertising volume in the United States is divided.

The other types of advertising include *retail advertising* (signs and displays in stores), *specialty advertising* (pencils, calendars, and similar items), *outdoor advertising* (billboards and other signs), *transit advertising* (posters on buses and other vehicles), and *business advertising* (special advertising directed to an industry or business, as in trade magazines and trade shows). There is also *electronic advertising* on videotext systems and on-line data services delivered through personal computers. There are even rather exotic forms, such as an electronic headline advertising service in taxicabs, and commercial messages posted over toilets in public restrooms. But this list gives only a hint of the diverse media for advertising. There are firms that specialize in exhibits for trade shows and fairs, firms that do skywriting, and many other outlets.

Not to be overlooked as a major advertising medium is *direct mail*, which is growing very rapidly. It began with post office deliveries of letters, brochures, broadsides, and other materials, but recently has included electronic mail, automatic telephone messages, fax and video appeals. Here new technology is amplifying a long-standing advertising medium.

Since the late nineteenth century, media that carry advertising have dominated the communications industries and have produced the lion's share of media revenues. By 1992 and 1993, however, that certainty seems to be changing. Such segments of the media industry as video rental outlets, pay-

TABLE 10.4 U.S. Advertising Volume*

Medium	1992 Millions of Dollars	1992 Percentage of Total	1993 Millions of Dollars	1993 Percentage of Total	Change (%)
Newspapers					
National	3,602	2.7	3,620	2.6	0.5
Local	27,135	20.7	28,405	20.6	4.7
Total	30,737	23.4	32,025	23.2	4.2
Magazines					
Weeklies	2,739	2.1	2,850	2.1	4.1
Women's	1,853	1.4	2,009	1.5	8.4
Monthlies	2,408	1.8	2,498	1.8	3.7
Total	7,000	5.3	7,357	5.3	5.1
Farm Publications	231	0.2	243	0.2	5.2
Television					
Network	10,249	7.8	10,209	7.4	−0.4
Cable (national)	1,685	1.3	1,970	1.4	16.9
Syndication	1,370	1.0	1,576	1.1	15.0
Spot (national)	7,551	5.8	7,800	5.6	3.3
Spot (local)	8,079	6.2	8,435	6.1	4.4
Cable (non-network)	475	0.4	594	.4	25.1
Total	29,409	22.4	30,584	22.1	4.0
Radio					
Network	424	0.3	458	.3	8.0
Spot (national)	1,505	1.1	1,657	1.2	10.1
Spot (local)	6,725	5.1	7,342	5.3	9.2
Total	8,654	6.6	9,457	6.8	9.3
Yellow Pages					
National	1,188	0.9	1,230	.9	3.5
Local	8,132	6.2	8,297	6.0	2.0
Total	9,320	7.1	9,517	6.9	2.1
Direct Mail	25,391	19.3	27,266	19.7	7.4
Business Papers	3,090	2.4	3,260	2.4	5.5
Outdoor					
National	610	0.5	605	.4	−0.8
Local	421	0.3	485	.4	15.2
Total	1,031	0.8	1,090	.8	5.7
Miscellaneous					
National	12,124	9.2	12,759	9.2	5.2
Local	4,303	3.3	4,522	3.3	5.1
Total	16,427	12.5	17,281	12.5	5.2
National total	76,020	57.9	80,010	57.9	5.2
Local total	55,270	42.1	58,070	42.1	5.1
Grand Total	131,290	100.0	138,080	100.0	5.2

*The McCann-Erickson U.S. advertising volume reports represent all expenditures by U.S. advertisers—national, local, private individuals, etc. The expenditures, by medium, include all commissions as well as the art, mechanical, and production expenses that are part of the advertisers' budgets for each medium.

Source: Prepared for Advertising Age by Robert J. Coen, McCann-Erickson Worldwide.

Controversy over advertising aimed at children—a long-standing issue—took on a new slant in the late 1980s when Chris Whittle's Channel One, a TV service for in-class use, included paid advertising with its programming. Citizens, educators, policymakers, and media researchers debated the implications of commercials in the classroom. (© Eric Sander/Gamma-Liaison)

per-view TV networks, video shopping networks, business information services, and other nonadvertising media have become important factors in the media mix. Nonadvertising media including those described above are already getting notice on Wall Street as vibrant and growing segments of the media industries.

Increasingly, audiences are being asked to pay more of the "freight" for their media fare. For example, newspapers and magazines have recently raised their prices considerably, and pay-per-view productions such as prize-fights and wrestling matches may charge as much as $50 for a single evening's event. Fax newspapers and various specialized newsletters charge hundreds if not thousands of dollars per year. In such a climate, it is probable that advertising will play a slightly less significant role than in the past, and certainly the idea that people pay little or nothing for their media because of advertising will no longer be true.[14]

Research on Advertising

The advertising industry is a great generator of research. Each of the advertising media hires research firms, rating services, and other groups to gather data showing its pulling power. Agencies conduct research on the effectiveness of their ads, awareness of their clients' products, and the public's response to them. And, of course, academics—including sociologists, psychologists, and anthropologists—conduct research on the industry and its effects. They study topics such as marketing, product appeals, the psychology of advertising, and consumer behavior. Marketing researchers probe the effects of different appeals on various audiences, and mass communication researchers examine the role of particular media in communicating advertisements, among other things.

Reports on such research can be found in trade publications and academic periodicals, such as the *Journal of Advertising* and the *Journal of Advertising Research*. Some associations and groups will provide a copy of a research report (for example, on the ability of magazines to sell a particular product) to anyone who asks for it.

Much of the research on the effectiveness of advertising, however, is *proprietary*—owned by those who produce it and hidden from the public. Some of it is gathered by research firms and then sold to the highest bidder; some of it is conducted by a specific company for its own use; some of it is conducted by agencies for particular clients. Moreover, much of this research is self-serving, designed to demonstrate that an advertising agency or business should take a certain action. As a result, there are always questions as to its objectivity. Businesses sometimes hire consultants to help them sort out the various claims of these kinds of researchers.

Studying the Effects of Advertising

Advertising researchers may conduct surveys, panel studies, or experiments. (These and other strategies of communication research are discussed at some length in Chapter 15.) In surveys, researchers systematically gather information about consumer preferences. In panel studies, researchers select a group of subjects and analyze their attitudes or behavior over time. In experiments, they set up "treatment" and "control" groups to determine the effect of advertising messages. But whatever the method, Russell Colley claims, good research on advertising effectiveness must make "a systematic evaluation of the degree to which the advertising succeeded in accomplishing predetermined goals."[15]

What are these goals? If advertising is successful, says Colley, it results in sales, and to do that it must carry consumers through four levels of understanding: (1) *awareness* of a brand or company, (2) *comprehension* of the product and what it will do for them, (3) a *conviction* that they should buy the product, and (4) *action*—that is, buying the product.[16] Colley urges advertisers to use precise research, including the following types, to evaluate whether an advertisement has succeeded:

1. *Audience research* involves gathering basic data on the audience to be reached, including the numbers of people in various groups (based on age, sex, religion, and so on) who see and respond to advertising.
2. *Media research* involves studying the particular characteristics of each medium and what it can do, including comparisons of the pulling power and persuasiveness of various media.
3. *Copy research* consists of making comparisons of audience reactions to particular advertisements. For example, researchers might compare the effectiveness of ads using an underdog appeal with those that arouse fear, instill pride, or reinforce old values.

HOW ADVERTISERS PERSUADED AMERICANS TO SMOKE:
A Linchpin to Public Health and Demography

In 1919, Dr. George Dock, chairman of the department of medicine at Barnes Hospital in St. Louis, called his students together to witness an autopsy. The patient had died of a rare disease. Dr. Dock said that it was unlikely that most of them would ever see such a case again. The disease was lung cancer.

In 1989, an estimated 155,000 new cases of lung cancer were diagnosed in the United States and 142,000 people died from the disease. Cigarette smoking was the cause of an estimated 85 percent of those deaths. Lung cancer has a very low rate of survival. Only one in ten who contract the disease can be cured. The other nine die rather quickly.

If anyone doubts the great power of advertising when it sets out to persuade people to buy a particular product, the case of cigarettes offers dramatic evidence to the contrary. Thus, a considerable lesson can be learned by reviewing the history of cigarette advertising in the United States. We do not do so in order to condemn tobacco companies or to assess the wisdom of those who take up the habit. A purpose more relevant to our analysis is to show that, under certain conditions, advertising campaigns can be extremely effective, with a cumulative influence on individual behavior, demographic trends, and the

public health of the society as a whole, persuading people to behave in dangerous ways.

Before World War I, few people in the United States smoked cigarettes. Men who did so were regarded as effeminate. Real men smoked either cigars or pipes, or they chewed tobacco. In retrospect, both were very unhealthy habits, but they did not lead specifically to lung cancer. Women rarely smoked; those few who did so in public were generally regarded as "loose."

At the turn of the century, automatic cigarette-rolling machines were acquired by major tobacco companies and production rose sharply. Between 1910 and 1919, the number of "tailor-made" cigarettes produced increased by well over 600 percent. More than any other factor, it was the events of World War I that hooked American men on cigarettes. A major tobacco company and a group called the National Cigarette Service Company (a creature of the industry) distributed millions of free cigarettes to the boys in France. They were regarded by the military, from General Pershing on down, as an important factor in keeping up morale. Lighting up was said to provide relaxation under conditions of great tension and anxiety. The use of cigarettes lost their earlier wimpish image. It was replaced by the much stronger

Consumer and Life-Style Research

More accessible than studies of advertising effectiveness is *consumer behavior research*, though some of it is also privately funded and proprietary. From their studies of consumers, researchers help businesses and ad agencies learn who their most likely consumers are and what kinds of advertising are most likely to reach them. They might study how needs, drives, and motives affect consumers' buying, how perception of an advertisement might vary among consumers, and what opinions, attitudes, beliefs, and prejudices should be taken into account in fashioning a message.[17] Some researchers focus on one group, such as children. These specialists might examine children at different stages of their development and then predict what kinds of things children like at certain ages and how they may influ-

one of a soldier under fire coolly lighting up a smoke just before going "over the top." The free cigarette program was repeated during World War II. All field rations provided for the troops in combat contained small packages of cigarettes to be enjoyed with each meal.

During the early 1920s, with the habit firmly established among men, the tobacco companies faced the fact that half of the population did not smoke! The next step was to destroy the concept that women who did so were somehow immoral. Advertisers began their campaigns. Ads began to appear suggesting that it was all right for women to smoke cigarettes. For example, one now famous ad showed a young man and woman, both elegantly dressed, on a grassy river bank enjoying a picnic. The man held a cigarette with a smoke plume rising. The woman was leaning longingly toward the man and the smoke. The ad copy indicated that she was saying "Blow a little my way."

Meanwhile, movies, novels, magazine stories, and virtually every other portrayal of everyday life showed people smoking and offering each other cigarettes. During the 1950s and 1960s, intensive advertising campaigns portrayed smoking as "masculine" for men, but "sophisticated" for women. They touted cigarettes as completely safe, relaxing, and even beneficial to health. Thousands of ads convinced people that smoking would promote digestion, protect the throat, and even help avoid wrinkles. Meanwhile, the death rate from lung cancer rose sharply. In 1930, it was less than 5 per 10,000 of population per year. By 1950, it had quintupled to more than 20. Today, it exceeds 70.

As medical understanding of the smoking-cancer linkage grew, starting about 1960, the federal government and consumer groups began conducting vigorous anti-smoking campaigns. Tobacco companies were prohibited by law from making claims that cigarettes are harmless. They have been barred from advertising on television and forced to label their product as dangerous. As a result, smoking has significantly declined in the United States. By 1985, 41 million Americans had quit smoking.

The implications are that when advertising is unrestrained, and supplemented by public relations efforts, it can be very persuasive indeed. However, when a consistent advertising message is challenged by contrary claims and evidence from authoritative sources, even deeply established habit patterns can be turned around. Advertising, therefore, can have great power, but only over an extended period in which other conditions are supportive and few challenges exist.

Sources: Karen Miller, "Smoking Up a Storm," *Journalism Monographs* 136, December 1992, pp. 1–35; John A. Meyer, "Cigarette Century," *American Heritage*, December 1992, pp. 72–80.

ence their parents' purchases of toys, food, and so on. Advertising agencies may then use this information to prepare commercials for Saturday morning cartoon shows.

Another area of study is *life-style research*, which grew out of surveys studying trends in Americans' living patterns and buying behavior. These studies inform advertisers about the changing attitudes and life-styles that characterize potential consumers at different ages—information that can be immensely helpful in fashioning an advertising campaign. For example, if older people today are moving out of large old houses into small new apartments where they live alone, and if they are interested in simplifying their domestic tasks and having more free time, then they are new potential consumers for several types of goods, such as single-serving frozen food dishes, microwave ovens, and airline tickets.[18] It might be worthwhile, then, for companies producing these items to use ads that have special appeal to older people.

Generally, advertising research is applied research (discussed more fully in Chapter 15). Its purpose is to help stimulate sales. Not surprisingly, this use of research in attempts to find ways to manipulate people has aroused considerable criticism. Although the research tries to demonstrate the effectiveness of particular advertisements and campaigns, no scientific cause-and-effect relationship can be established between a given ad and the product or service it seeks to sell. As social scientists have said, there are just too many uncontrollable variables in any situation to prove that advertising actually works. The important thing, though, is that many people believe it does, and they are the ones making decisions to spend millions of dollars on it. Advertising is part of the corporate strategy of most firms that sell products. Advertising researchers try to gather the best evidence available to show what advertising can do, but their efforts fall far short of absolute proof.

An Age of Market Segmentation

Although advertisers would like to sell their wares to everyone, they know that is not possible, and so they go after a particular *segment* of the market. As we discussed in Chapter 8, that segment may be defined by age, income, gender, education, race, and so on. Once, most advertising was *product-oriented*; that is, the content was mainly concerned with a persuasive message about the attributes of the product. Now most advertising is *user-oriented*, with messages aimed at the specific needs, interests, and desires of particular groups of consumers. As historian Daniel Pope put it:

> Segmentation campaigns are user-focused and concentrate on consumer benefits rather than product attributes. They show people with whom the target audience can identify; people who represent a credible source of authority for them or who express their latent desires and dreams. Marketers hone in on consumers whose lifestyles and personalities have been carefully profiled.[19]

This new emphasis also suggests problems for the ethical presentation of advertising. It is much easier to apply a truth-in-advertising standard to statements about the qualities of a product than to indirect appeals to the desires of a segment of the audience. The trend toward market segmentation has also led to some specialization in advertising agencies and promoted the growth of media that appeal to a specific rather than a general audience.

Recently, a considerable amount of research evidence is emerging from what John Phelan of Fordham University calls "noble hype," or information campaigns focused on good causes, such as the prevention of AIDS, heart disease, and other social problems. A lot of money has been poured into studies of information campaigns that use direct advertising strategies and messages. The dramatic success of the AIDS information campaign—which is credited, in part, for the decrease in sexual activity likely to spread the disease—seems in a preliminary way to bode well for advertising effectiveness. At the same time, other researchers and critics say that AIDS is a special case

In one of the most successful examples of health communication in history, an anti-AIDS campaign raised public consciousness about the disease to the point where most Americans not only knew a considerable amount about it but also rated it the nation's top health threat. (In fact, the death rate from AIDS is relatively low when compared with that from cancer or heart disease.) There has been a longstanding controversy about the effectiveness of health advertising, but the AIDS campaign was definitely evidence of profound media effects. (Courtesy Centers for Disease Control and Prevention)

How much do your children know about AIDS?

Your children need an understanding of what it takes to be healthy. Schools can play an important role. If you'd like to know how you as a parent can be more involved in your school's curriculum, call 1-800-342-AIDS for information. For the hearing impaired, 1-800-AIDS-TTY.

AMERICA RESPONDS TO AIDS

that does not apply generally, since the threat of death is a great motivation in changing behavior.

Criticism and Control of Advertising

Few people doubt that advertising has a significant impact or that it plays an important role in the United States. Most would agree that it reflects the culture and ideals of this country—although many also find that idea disturbing. Noting its importance, however, is very different from granting approval, and advertising has been criticized on many grounds. Some disparage advertising in general for its economic and social effects; others criticize the content of some ads or their effects on some groups. These criticisms, as we shall see, have led to attempts to regulate advertising.

Economic and Social Criticisms

A favorable view of advertising claims that it stimulates competition, which is good for the economy, and encourages the development of new products, which is good for consumers. Proof of the pudding, defenders say, is that people choose to buy the new products. And consumers are happier because they can choose from a great variety of goods—a diversity stimulated by advertising. Advertising helps keep the economy and the number of jobs growing by encouraging people to buy more. And, by giving consumers information, advertising also helps them buy wisely. Advertising, then, is a key cog in the economic machine that can give Americans the good life and the fruits of capitalism—the so-called American dream.

Critics have many answers to these comments. First, a great deal of advertising has nothing at all to do with objective information and does not help consumers make wise choices. Yet, even though they do not benefit, people must pay for advertising because its cost raises the price of the goods they buy. Therefore, they say, advertising is wasteful.

What is more, critics say, rather than stimulating competition, advertising contributes to monopoly. Larger firms can easily afford to invest in expensive national advertising, whereas smaller firms cannot. Larger firms can then perpetuate and even expand their hold on the market. For example, there are few local brands of soft drink that can effectively compete with Coca-Cola or Pepsi-Cola, though there were once many successful local and regional beverages. Even in the absence of an actual monopoly, some economists see advertising as hindering the development of perfect competition and leading to the condition known as imperfect competition. Several consequences may follow, including, according to critic Neil Borden, "improper allocation of capital investment," "underutilization of productive capacity and underemployment," "relatively rigid prices," and increasingly severe cyclical fluctuations in business, from inflation to recession and back again.[20]

According to Borden, even the diversity of goods stimulated by advertising is not beneficial. Consumers, writes Borden, "are confused by the large number of meaningless product differentiations and consequently do not make wise choices."[21] Other critics point to more general effects on individuals and society attributed to advertising. Advertising is often believed to be manipulative and deceptive, indirectly teaching us that other people are objects to be manipulated and deceived. By creating new wants and desires, advertising is also said to distance people from their "true" selves, contributing to their alienation and dissatisfaction, and making life an unending and hopeless quest for trivial goods or the perfect image.

We certainly cannot evaluate point by point either the economic or social analysis advanced by advertising's critics, and we have stated their complaints rather briefly. But, note that advertising depends on mass communication, and the principles we will review in Chapters 16 and 17, regarding the media's influence on individuals and society, apply in general to advertising. That is, you should not assume that advertising messages are "magic bullets" that cause uniform effects among all who receive them. Moreover, you would be ill-advised to consider the people seeing or hearing the messages as passive dolts receiving them helplessly. Nor should you think of advertising as a single, isolated cause of behavior, such as a decision to purchase a product. Reactions to advertising messages are determined by complex causes and influences that we discussed in Chapter 8, related to the nature of the audience. Only a great deal of careful research will reveal the answers.

If you have taken a course in economics, you may recall how little attention textbooks in that field devote to advertising. The distinguished Harvard economist John Kenneth Galbraith said that there is a good reason why such texts downplay its importance. Economists like to believe that consumer wants are held deeply within the human psyche. They subscribe to the idea of consumer sovereignty. But Galbraith writes:

> So long as wants are original with the consumer, their satisfaction serves the highest of human purposes. Specifically, an original, inherent need is being satisfied. And economics as a subject matter or science thus becomes basic to the highest human service. But [this] holds only if wants cannot be created, cultivated, shaped, deepened, or otherwise induced. Heaven forbid that wants should have their source in the producer of the product or service as aided and guided by his advertising agency.[22]

Thus, it would downgrade some of the most basic principles of economics if it were true that consumer wants were actually generated by advertising and not by human nature itself.

Children and Advertising

Few aspects of advertising have generated more concern or research than advertising directed at children, particularly TV commercials. Critics fear that such advertising creates wants that cannot be fulfilled and that it prompts children to ask their parents for innumerable things that they cannot afford. Thus, children's advertising may generate tension and conflict in the family and teach many wrong lessons because children mistake advertisements for realistic portrayals of the world. In defense of such advertising, supporters maintain that it helps children learn to be consumers, a role that is vital to the economy.

Any evaluation of advertising's effect on children requires answers to several questions: To what extent do children pay attention to commercials? What, if any, effects do commercials have on children's thinking processes? Can they, for example, distinguish between fact and fantasy in a commercial? What, if any, influence do children exert on their parents' buying as a result of commercials? Government, foundations, ad agencies, and other businesses have spent a lot of money to answer these and similar questions. Research by advertisers and ad agencies, however, is devoted understandably to one purpose: determining how to make better and more persuasive commercials. Although their results are usually kept secret, we are beginning to get some answers to these questions from outside researchers.

To date, the findings suggest that the younger the child, the fuller the attention he or she pays to commercials. However, trust in commercials declines with age.[23] Very young children do not know the difference between commercials and programs. They pay a good deal of attention even to commercials that would seem to be irrelevant to them, such as ads for beer or household cleaning products. Perhaps they are simply using the commercials to learn about what is unfamiliar to them. As they get older, children pay less and less attention to commercials, and by the time they are adolescents, they usually scorn them. The evidence so far indicates that children do pressure their parents to buy the products they have seen advertised. Overall, however, we do not yet know enough about advertising's effects on children, and many questions have yet to be explored in depth.

Meanwhile, critics, such as Action for Children's Television, are taking their concerns to the government and seeking controls on advertising. In the controversy over advertising appeals to children, particular media (such as television) have debated with consumer groups and government. In 1988, the *Wall Street Journal* noted that while network television had high standards for children's advertising, independent stations usually did not. The networks barred the overglamourizing of a product or the use of exhortative language such as "Ask Mom to buy . . . ," but independent stations were quite lax on these and other points. As criticism mounted, the Better Business Bureau urged local TV stations to be more vigilant, and eventually the board of the Association of Independent Television Stations endorsed guidelines for children's advertising. Later the same year, the U.S. Senate passed legislation to limit the number of commercials aired during children's programs.[24]

An unusual and highly controversial effort at TV advertising began when "Channel One," Whittle Communications' news program for public schools, went on the air in March 1990. The Whittle organization supplied free video

A topic that has generated considerable controversy is the influence of advertising on children. Children often accompany a parent to the supermarket. Products such as breakfast cereals are advertised heavily on TV programs aimed at children. The extent to which preferences created by this advertising influence what parents select from the shelves has been debated for decades. Overall, the relationship of children and advertising is a complex one that varies greatly depending on age. There are no simple answers. (© Jane Scherr/Jeroboam, Inc.)

equipment to thousands of public schools, and they broadcast, into classrooms, news programs complete with paid advertising. Regarded as a boon by some school administrators who readily accepted the equipment and programming, "Channel One" was attacked by others, including the consumer-oriented Action for Children's Television, which found the service odious. What bothered critics was that "Channel One" invaded the public schools with advertising messages. Schools, critics said, should be off limits from commercial exploitation. On the other hand, defenders of Whittle's efforts said that children could learn to be better consumers if they got advertising messages in the classroom where teachers might critique them. School authorities in New York and California barred schools from accepting the equipment or programming. At about the same time, a noncommercial service was started by Cable News Network.

Sources of Control

Whatever the general effects of advertising, the content of many ads has been attacked for poor taste, exaggerated claims, or annoying hucksterism. As a result of these specific sins, some controls on U.S. advertising have developed. Shabby practices led to a gradual erosion of the ancient principle of *caveat emptor* ("let the buyer beware") in favor of *caveat venditor* ("let the seller beware")—that is, toward regulation. Advertisers today live with certain constraints, some imposed by the government and some by the industry itself.

Control by government   As early as 1911, *Printer's Ink*, an industry magazine, called for greater attention to ethics in advertising and proposed a model statute that made fraudulent and misleading advertising a misde-meanor. Before long, with a strong push from the Better Business Bureau, most states enacted it as law. Although there is doubt about its effectiveness, the statute was a statement on advertising ethics as well as a standard-setter. A few years later, in 1914, the Federal Trade Commission (FTC) also set up some ground rules for advertising. In administrative rulings over the years, the FTC has written rules related to puffery, taste, and guarantees and gen-erally has taken considerable interest in the substantiation of advertising claims. At times, the FTC has demanded "effective relief" for those wronged by misleading advertising and levied fines against companies engaging in unfair, misleading, and otherwise deceptive advertising.

As we saw in Chapter 9, the Federal Communications Commission (FCC) also scrutinizes advertising. In addition, several other federal agencies, including the Food and Drug Administration, the Post Office Department, the Securities and Exchange Commission, and the Alcohol and Tobacco Tax Division of the Internal Revenue Service, influence advertising. State and local governments have passed laws on lotteries, obscenity, occupational advertising, and other matters. Government controls over advertising, how-ever, relaxed considerably during the Reagan era of industry deregulation in the 1980s and 1990s.

Industry codes of ethics   In the private sector, various advertising organi-zations and individual industries have developed codes of ethics to govern advertising. The broadcasting industry, for example, has codes that set stan-dards for the total amount of nonprogram material and commercial inter-ruptions per time period. (However, the amount of time commercials could air for each hour of programming for adults was expanded during the dereg-ulation of broadcasting in the 1980s. In fact, say some critics, today some programs are nothing but hour-long paid advertisements. These so-called infomercials, airing late at night or on weekends, promote business-success seminars, real estate deals, "classic" CDs, juicers, personel care items, and phone consultation with psychics.) In many states, local industry organiza-tions such as advertising review committees and fair advertising groups pro-mote truth in advertising. The National Advertising Review Council pro-motes ethical advertising and fights deception, and Better Business Bureaus prepare reports on particular firms and their advertising.

Court rulings   In recent years, both the public and private sectors have fol-lowed closely various court decisions regarding whether or to what degree the First Amendment's guarantee of freedom of speech and the press extends to advertising. To date, the courts have distinguished between advertising that promotes an individual's or group's views, which *is* protect-ed by the First Amendment, and advertising that is designed only for com-mercial gain, which is *not*—although at times it is difficult to separate the two. Typically, courts have stoutly defended what they call "political speech," or expression that promotes public discussion of public affairs. The courts have until recently been less kind to "commercial speech," which is aimed at selling products. Now all that is changing, as commentators recognize that separating public and private speech is difficult at best.

Consumer groups In addition, many consumer groups monitor advertising and protest when they object to particular content. These groups range from the National Consumer Union to religious organizations and environmental groups.

Advertisers have in the past responded to public criticism, and advertising itself has undergone constant change. For example, for many years radio and TV commercials included very few African-Americans, Latinos, or other minorities. When they were featured, portrayals were often trivial or demeaning. But by the late 1960s, advertisements began to include minorities more often and more realistically. Some would argue that such changes are not always for the best. In a recently exposed practice, producers of malt liquors (with a higher-than-normal alcohol content) have allegedly targeted blacks (some say teenaged blacks specifically) with their ads.

Changes have also begun to take place in advertising's images of women, who have traditionally been shown behaving either idiotically in domestic situations or as passive sex objects. Similarly, elderly people, who often appeared as doddering simpletons, are sometimes portrayed more respectfully in today's ads.

Although there have been modest improvements, advertising still often deals with stereotypes. In the 1960s, feminist writer Betty Friedan drew attention in *The Feminine Mystique* to sex-role stereotypes in advertising. Twenty years later, researchers Thomas Whipple and Alice E. Courtney write that there have been only relatively cosmetic changes. In fact, they found that the use of women as sex objects in advertising is on the rise:

> Nudity, seminudity, innuendo, double-entendre and exploitive sex are being used with increasing frequency and intensity in advertising. . . . [It] continues to exploit [women], show violence and aggression against them, and cause widespread offense.[25]

Many advertising professionals would take issue with these critiques, saying that advertising reflects public tastes and that feminism has had a definite impact on advertising content. Other advertisers, as Whipple once stated in an interview, are likely to say, "Gee, I'd really like to avoid these stereotypes, but I've got to use them to survive."[26] Whipple argued that research shows that avoiding stereotypes can be effective and urged a re-education of advertisers.[27]

If a large part of the public becomes unwilling to accept demeaning stereotypes, advertising will probably soon follow that lead. After all, advertisers are not trying to mold society or public opinion—though they may in fact influence both. They are trying to sell goods, and they will change their message if need be to appeal to the public. If critics can arouse the people to complain enough or can convince advertisers that the public is annoyed, they have a good chance of changing specific aspects of advertising messages. Critics argue that they want to raise the standards of ad content, not censor communication.

It is likely that the debate over sexual stereotyping in advertising will continue for a long time. Many advertisers appeal blatantly to sex appeal, and much of what they put before the public is clearly sexist. Occasionally, various groups representing women, religious interests, and other social forces protest and even urge the boycott of particular products. Since advertisers almost always want to avoid controversy—after all, they want to sell products, not enrage consumers—some of these protests have worked.

Formerly, sex appeal in advertising was largely aimed at men and exploited women in the process. However, this has changed in recent years as suggestive poses of men are now commonly featured, displaying males as sex objects in an explicit manner heretofore unknown in advertising. Thus far, few men have objected. Sometimes such advertising has curious origins. For example, in 1992, rap star Marky Mark of the group Funky Bunch was pictured in *Interview* magazine wearing only his underwear, disrobing being one of the trademarks of his performances. Designer Calvin Klein saw the photo and decided to use the irreverent rapper in his ads. Photos done for the ads concurrently appeared in book form in time to compete with a similar photo essay book featuring a teasing nude Madonna.

It is possible, of course, that advertising does not influence people as much as its critics claim. Sociologist Michael Schudson argues that advertising is not nearly as important, effective, or scientifically targeted as either advocates or critics imagine. Advertisers are often quite cautious in deciding on their advertising outlays and take few chances. In the end, says Schudson, advertising rarely has a chance to create consumer wants, and instead reinforces what already exists. In assessing the role of advertising in American society, Schudson makes the following observations:

1. Advertising serves a useful informational function that will not and should not be abandoned.
2. Advertising probably has a socially democratizing influence, but one with an ultimate inegalitarian outcome.
3. The most offensive advertising tends to have the least informational content.
4. Some advertising promotes dangerous products or promotes potentially dangerous products to groups unlikely to be able to use them wisely.
5. Nonprice advertising often promotes bad values, whether it effectively sells products or not.
6. Advertising could survive and sell goods without promoting values as bad as those it favors now.
7. Advertising is but one factor among many in shaping consumer choice and human values.[28]

Critics who object not to specific aspects of some advertisements but to advertising's broader effects on individuals, society, and the economy will not see the changes they desire any time soon. Government is unlikely to impose stringent controls. As long as they think the messages work, advertisers are likely to continue to appeal to people's desires to be attractive, liked, and somehow better than the neighbors—in short, to have more or better of just about anything—whatever may be the psychological, cultural, or economic effects of these appeals. Furthermore, advertisers are likely to continue to engulf us with their messages unless there are monumental changes in the economy and society.

All of the above considerations lead to a reaffirmation of our central thesis: The media, the economy, advertising, and the population as consumers are inextricably linked in a deeply institutionalized way. Thus, advertising is a central social institution in American society.

Chapter Review

- Advertising is a form of controlled communication that attempts to persuade an appropriate audience, through the use of a variety of appeals and strategies, to make a decision to buy or use a particular product or service.

- Advertising is essential to the mass media insofar as it is the principal source of revenue for most of them. Without advertising, Americans would not have the great variety of mass communications from which to choose what they now enjoy.

- The history of advertising is related not only to public taste but also to the growth of the American economy and the mass media. Unless there is relative abundance in a society, businesses are not likely to find advertising worthwhile.

- The nineteenth century saw the growth of national media, national markets, and national advertising in the United States. Advertisers showed that they could create markets for new products, and newspapers, magazines, and broadcast stations eventually became dependent on advertising for most of their revenues.

- As advertising grew, organizations specializing in the production of advertisements developed. Today, advertising agencies are staffed by managers, writers, artists, researchers, and other specialists. Boutique agencies and various media service organizations offer more limited, specialized services, and many businesses and media organizations have departments that deal exclusively with advertising.

- Advertising today is a $126 billion industry that employs nearly a quarter of a million people in the United States. However, concentration into large firms seems to be the trend here as in other industries.

- The advertising industry has many critics. Some economists claim that it is economically wasteful in that it decreases competition, increases consumers' costs, and channels investment away from more productive uses. Other economists claim that advertising promotes competition, diversity, and wise buying decisions.

- Some critics are concerned that advertising somehow debases individuals and cultures. Still other criticism is directed more specifically at advertising that makes exaggerated claims, is in poor taste, is directed at children, or presents negative stereotypes of particular groups.

- Those who recognize the importance of advertising but want it to be carried on with higher standards have set up guidelines to prevent misleading, offensive, and excessive advertising.

- Although advertising can be criticized on many grounds, it will be with us for the foreseeable future. It plays a critical role in promoting the economy's goods and services and is a deeply established social institution.

Notes and References

1. David M. Potter, *People of Plenty*, 2nd ed. (Chicago: University of Chicago Press, 1969), p. 167.
2. *The American Heritage Dictionary of the English Language* (Boston: Houghton Mifflin, 1970), p. 19.
3. John S. Wright et al., *Advertising*, 5th ed. (New York: McGraw-Hill, 1982), p. 6.
4. Ibid., p. 9.
5. James W. Carey, "Advertising: An Institutional Approach" in C. H. Sandage and V. Fryburger, eds., *The Role of Advertising* (Homewood, Ill.: Irwin, 1960), p. 16.
6. Ibid.
7. Potter, op. cit., p. 172.
8. Stuart Elliott, "Awarding Case Prizes to Stamp Out Boredom in Billboards," *New York Times*, September 3, 1992, p. D6.
9. Norman Douglas, *South Wind* (1917), in *Bartlett's Familiar Quotations*, 13th ed., p. 840.
10. Daniel J. Boorstin, "Advertising and American Civilization" in Yale Brozen, ed., *Advertising and Society* (New York: New York University Press, 1972), p. 12.
11. Potter, op. cit., p. 172.
12. Potter, op. cit., p. 168.
13. Wright et al., op. cit., pp. 161-162.
14. *Media Private Market Value Estimates*, Paul Kagan Associates, Inc., 1992.
15. Russell H. Colley, *Defining Advertising Goals for Measured Advertising Results* (New York: Association of National Manufacturers, 1961), p. 35.
16. Ibid., p. 38.
17. Wright et al., op. cit., p. 392.
18. Otto Kleppner, *Advertising Procedure*, 7th ed. (Englewood Cliffs, N.J.: Prentice-Hall, 1985), pp. 301–302.
19. Daniel Pope, *The Making of Advertising* (New York: Basic Books, 1983), pp. 289–290. See also Kim B. Rotzoll and James E. Haefner, *Advertising in Contemporary Society* (Cincinnati: South-Western, 1986).
20. John S. Wright and John E. Mertes, *Advertising's Role in Society* (St. Paul, Minn.: West, 1974), pp. vii–viii.
21. Ibid.
22. John Kenneth Galbraith, "Economics and Advertising: Exercise in Denial," *Advertising Age*, November 9, 1988, p. 81.
23. For an extended discussion of research evidence on television advertising and children, see Robert M. Liebert, Joyce N. Sprafkin, and Emily S. Davidson, *The Early Window: Effects of Television on Children and Youth*, 2nd ed. (New York: Pergamon Press, 1982), pp. 142–159.
24. Joanne Lipman, "Double Standard for Kids' TV Ads," *Wall Street Journal*, June 10, 1988, section 2, p. 1. See also Jeanne Saddler, "Congress Approves Limiting TV Ads Aimed at Children," *Wall Street Journal*, October 20, 1988, section 2, p. 6.
25. Thomas Whipple and Alice E. Courtney, *Sex Stereotyping in Advertising* (Lexington, Mass.: Heath/Lexington, 1983), p. 195.
26. "Advertising Stereotypes," *Washington Post*, December 13, 1983, section B, p. 5.
27. Ibid.
28. Michael Schudson, *Advertising, The Uneasy Persuasion: Its Dubious Impact on American Society* (New York: Basic Books, 1984), pp. 239–241.

CHAPTER **11**

Public Relations: Linking Clients and Constituencies

. . . Information for the
public is first filtered
through publicity
agents. The great cor-
porations have them,
the banks have them,
the railroads have them,
all the organizations of
business and of social
and political activity
have them, and they
are the media through
which the news comes.

Frank Cobb, *The New York
World*, 1919

In early 1990, film star Rob Lowe made the rounds of television talk shows to promote his new movie, "Bad Influence." The guest spots were the actor's first public appearances after weathering a scandal in which he was videotaped in a sexual encounter with two teen-aged girls. In a carefully planned media tour, Lowe sought to redeem his reputation, express remorse for his earlier behavior, and build an audience for his upcoming film. He enlisted the help of public relations specialists and followed an orchestrated strategy to restore his public image as a credible, if sometimes wild, young actor. Much of the credit for Lowe's successful "comeback" is due to the help of public relations professionals, who understand the tools needed to engineer a favorable image for celebrities and other public figures.

Public relations is more than a search for ways to get favorable publicity for individuals and organizations, however. It is a *communications industry* that serves virtually all institutions and individuals in society who seek to convey specific information and ideas to the public. Public relations is based on organized and calculated transmissions of messages on behalf of those wishing to communicate desired sets of meanings to designated target audiences. The goal of such communication is to influence the thoughts and feelings of relevant receivers and sometimes their conduct.

As the quotation from Frank Cobb on the chapter opening page suggests, much of the content in the news is the result of public relations activity. In this sense, those efforts are closely linked to such concepts as publicity, persuasion, and propaganda. As we will explain, some scholars use the term "public relations" in a neutral sense to describe a process, a communications activity, or even a kind of business. However, the term also has strong negative connotations in many people's minds.

Public Relations and the Media

Much of what Americans learn about public affairs—that is, the visible activity of government and the private sector—is the result of the careful planning and dissemination of mass communicated messages of one sort or another by people engaged in public relations. This is seldom obvious. That is, although public relations greatly influences the content of mass communications, we often do not observe public relations activity directly, and leaders in the field are rarely known to the general public.

Although public relations is often regarded with suspicion, or even disdain, our society could scarcely function without it. Public attention to and understanding are often crucial to the success of a government policy or a business practice. In the entertainment world, favorable publicity is essential to the careers of prominent individuals such as rock stars and sports figures. Whether we realize it or not, then, public relations as an industry making extensive use of mass communications is highly integrated into almost every aspect of American society. People from the President of the United States to the manager of a local store depend on it to conduct their affairs successfully. They need effective media strategies to reach and influence the public.

Thus, achieving goals by influencing people through managed communication is what public relations is all about. An author who fails to seek out TV talk shows may never receive the desired publicity for his or her book. A developer who needs local cooperation to complete a project cannot stand by hoping to be invited to speak at the Rotary Club. A newspaper engaged in a libel suit cannot gamble that its own coverage will ensure credibility in the matter. In a highly competitive world, little is left to chance. That explains why people and interests use formal public relations efforts, typically directed by professional public relations specialists, to accomplish their goals. Thus, whether a public relations message is low-key and informal, as in local media outlets, or consists of high-powered national pitches, as in the entertainment media, it is the result of a *deliberately designed communication process*. And this process recognizes that public attention and support are not achieved by accident.

The broad scope of public relations is the inevitable result of the growing complexity of society in general and of the communication system that holds it together. An individual or a unit of society that wants to be known and understood by the larger public must master and use mass communications. This is true for an unknown politician who wants to run for mayor, a federal agency that wants Americans to stop smoking, or a giant chemical company that wants a positive public image. In all these instances, it is difficult to accomplish the desired goal without some access to and receptive treatment from the media.

Individuals or interests that want to achieve a positive public image through the mass media face at least two barriers. First, the media are independent entities with their own goals—which may *conflict* with those of the publicity seekers. For example, a politician's desire for positive coverage on the evening news obviously conflicts with the local TV station's intention to disclose the same politician's alleged wrongdoing. Second, there is great *competition* for limited space and time in the media and other public forums, and many worthy individuals and causes simply cannot receive the media attention and public exposure they desire. Thus, people and institutions seeking public understanding usually cannot achieve it on their own. They need help in seeking it, and it is that set of societal conditions that has given rise to the public relations industry.

Defining Public Relations

As the preceding section suggests, the term "public relations" has a number of meanings, and this makes it difficult to define. However, it is generally agreed that public relations is a *planned and organized communication effort* that links particular elements of society together for particular purposes. To give an example of how complex the problem of defining the field can be, a leading text in the field defines public relations this way:

> The term public relations is used in at least three senses: the relationships with those who constitute an organization's publics or constituents, the ways and means used to achieve favorable relationships, and the quality or status of the relationships. Thus the one term is used to label both means and ends, to name a condition, and to express the conduct or actions related to that condition.[1]

We can add that the term is also used to describe the group of expert communicators who call themselves "professional" public relations practitioners. As we will see, the field does have at least some of the traditional characteristics of a true profession, such as an accrediting process and requirements for formal training. However, later in this chapter, we will examine more closely the word "professional" to see if it realistically can be used to label public relations practitioners. As will be seen, there is some doubt that the field currently meets the full set of criteria required to be a true profession.

The Enduring Problem of Negative Connotations

Complicating the problem of defining public relations is a widespread belief that its practitioners often *mislead* the public. Many people think of public relations as efforts to cover up bad behavior by clients, emphasizing only their positive aspects in efforts to bring the public to view them more favorably. It is this set of beliefs that explains why the term has strong negative connotations in many people's minds. For example, during the "Tailhook" scandal of 1992, when it was reported that drunken naval aviators sexually molested a number of women during a convention, high-ranking officers first tried a public relations "solution"—downplaying reports of the misconduct to try to soften interpretations by the public and the press. In another example, after the huge oil spill from the tanker *Exxon Valdez* in Prince William Sound in Alaska, the Exxon corporation was criticized for devoting more effort to cleaning up their public image than to cleaning up the environment. Thus, for many skeptics, public relations has typically meant putting a "gloss" on a problem by offering a reasonable explanation to justify

The historic oil spill that occurred when the tanker *Exxon Valdez* went aground in Alaska's Prince Edward Sound created a public relations nightmare for Exxon, the vessel's operator. Americans were deeply disturbed that hundreds of miles of beaches were contaminated and thousands of animals were killed. The corporation spent millions of dollars in clean-up efforts as part of its public relations "damage control" campaign. The goal was to clean up its public image as well as the environment. (© Bill Nation/Sygma)

what happened and why. This can be anything from an open disclosure to *damage control*—that is, diverting attention from, or explaining away, a difficult or embarrassing situation after its occurrence.

A classic example of how public relations can "rehabilitate" an image is that of Richard Nixon, who resigned from the presidency in disgrace in 1974. Through skillful public relations, he has rebuilt his image over nearly two decades. After a long absence, and after publishing several books, Nixon re-emerged in the 1980s as an expert on foreign policy and a senior statesman. He bravely spoke before the American Society of Newspaper Editors and what is now the Newspaper Association of America—journalists' organizations with whom he had notably bad relations during his presidency. He appeared in a widely disseminated photo with Katherine Graham, publisher of the *Washington Post*, the newspaper credited with hastening his ouster from office. Thus, as a result of a carefully orchestrated communications strategy, the new Nixon seemed statesmanlike, brilliant, and even responsive to criticism. His eventual place in history doubtless will be positively affected by his creative use of public relations.

Given the less than clear picture of what the field is and what its practitioners actually do, it is not surprising that much debate has centered on the nature of public relations. In particular, its practitioners do not like the negative connotations and often try to define the field in ways that minimize them. For example, Scott Cutlip and Allen Center settle on an upbeat version: "Public relations is the planned effort to influence public opinion through good character and responsible performance, based upon mutually satisfactory two-way communications."[2] To some, this looks like a "public relations definition" of public relations. It describes a desirable goal but is hardly neutral. A somewhat more reflective definition comes from public relations pioneer Edward L. Bernays, who is widely credited with founding the field. He defines public relations as a "profession that deals with the relations of a unit and the public or publics on which its viability depends."[3] Bernays adds that public relations should serve the public interest, but that is equally hard to define.

In 1992, the *Ragan Report*, a respected newsletter for public relations executives, devoted several columns to "defining public relations" and argued that "settling on a single PR definition might well raise the field's status." When the publication asked leading practitioners, publishers, and educators in the field to offer definitions, the result was a "dazzling array of concepts, ranging from profound philosophical reflections to brief, witty aphorisms." Famed expert Frank Lesley wrote that "PR helps organizations and their publics adapt mutually to each other."[4] Professor Mel Sharpe, of Ball State University, called public relations a process that "harmonizes long-term relationships." An irreverent cab driver claimed that "PR is propaganda and common sense properly disseminated." In a more serious vein, James Grunig, of the University of Maryland, writes that true public relations follows the "two-way symmetrical model"—that is, it "uses research and dialogue to manage conflict, improve understanding, and build relationships with publics."[5]

Public Relations versus Advertising

Most of the preceding definitions make public relations and advertising sound remarkably alike. Like advertising, public relations is a communication process; it is planned and organized and depends on the mass media to convey its messages. But unlike advertising, which makes use of purchased slots of media space and time, public relations does not have such easy access to mass communications. Some critics call advertising space "captive media," since an advertiser buys and uses it according to his or her own discretion. Public relations messages are not bought and paid for in the media; instead they are offered persuasively to editors and others, who then determine whether the information is worth using or not.

Although some public relations campaigns involve advertisements, such as those that promote tourism or the general integrity of a corporation, public relations specialists often use more indirect, persuasive means to build a favorable climate of opinion. Moreover, public relations efforts are not always identifiable. We know an advertisement when we see it in a magazine, but we do not always know that the source of a news article or of the staging of a golf tournament, bass fishing contest, or other public event is a public relations campaign. Rarely do public relations people announce exactly what they are doing. Public relations personnel may use advertising as part of their overall activities, but they are much more involved than advertisers in the total process of communication, from initiating the message to getting feedback from the public.

The once reasonably clear distinction between public relations and advertising became clouded in the 1980s when a number of advertising agencies acquired major public relations firms. However, for the most part, the public relations firms have continued to operate somewhat independently under the ownership of the parent advertising agency.

A Formal Definition

Even though the problem of specifying precisely the organization, goals, and activities of public relations may never be solved to everyone's satisfaction, we need a clear statement of what this chapter is about. Therefore, a definition that incorporates most of the central issues we have discussed can be expressed in the following terms:

> *Public relations* is an organized communication process, conducted by hired communicators, in which messages are transmitted via a variety of channels to relevant and targeted audiences in an attempt to influence their beliefs, attitudes, or even actions regarding a client, whether a person or a group.

This rather long definition incorporates the major features of public relations activities. Even so, there are other elements that could be included. For example, as a business, public relations services are provided by specialists who use various ways to get their messages to the targeted public. These include sponsoring various kinds of contests and sporting events (that usually receive media coverage), providing press releases, and holding press conferences to appeal to reporters, editors, and publishers who control media content. Thus, in the final analysis, public relations is a way of *manipulating the meanings* that receivers in the target audience construct for messages about the person or group represented by the communicator. This does not necessarily mean, however, that such manipulation is deceptive.

Historical Background

Some scholars argue that public relations is really an ancient activity, dating back at least to Plato's *Republic*. Whether that is a valid claim is not clear, but it is true that for many centuries much of the purpose behind public discourse and public rhetoric has been for reasons of *publicity*—expanding the number of people who are aware of some policy, program or person. In addition, public relations is often associated with *propaganda*—communications designed to gain people's approval, or, as we might say today, to capture their hearts and minds, concerning some policy or program. (The word "propaganda" originally referred to the Roman Catholic Church's efforts to "propagate the faith" through the communication efforts of missionaries.)

Certainly both publicity and propaganda played major roles in the colonies before the American Revolution, when committees of correspondence sought to win the hearts and minds of the public. Also, many American presidents have had a need to sway public opinion in a favorable direction for their policies. Abraham Lincoln, for example, had a definite public relations problem with his Emancipation Proclamation, which freed all slaves in states and territories at war with the Union. Several states not in the Confederacy were reluctant to give up the idea of slavery, and Lincoln had a "hard sell." During the last century, presidents in that position relied on informants in local areas to gauge public opinion. It was not until well into the present century that formal public opinion polls became an important part of the public relations landscape and a method of taking the public pulse.

The field of public relations partly grew out of reactions to the "public be damned" attitude that characterized big business at the turn of the century. The so-called captains of industry did as they pleased regardless of what people thought. Eventually, however, the public became aroused over their excesses—especially after many of their practices were exposed by the muckraking journalists of the time (Chapter 4). To counter this negative trend, many large corporations began to use public relations in one form or another to head off confrontations. The forerunner of the modern public relations agency was the Publicity Bureau of Boston, founded in 1900 by three former newspapermen. They set an important pattern in that for a fee they would promote a company's causes and business interests. The bureau's early clients included AT&T and Harvard University.

By 1911, the Bureau had died, but other public relations and press agencies quickly formed in its place. For example, publicist and former journalist Ivy Lee, after working for political candidates and the Pennsylvania Railroad, recognized the value for businesses of a positive public image and the possibilities of creating such an image through favorable publicity. He set up an *agency*—a firm providing services that we would now call public relations activities—to help businesses communicate with the public, and his clients eventually included John D. Rockefeller, Jr. and his infamous Standard Oil Company. Another early publicist was Pendleton Dudley, who at Lee's urging opened an office on Wall Street. According to Scott Cutlip, Dudley denied that early public relations efforts were in direct response to the muckraking journalists.

During these early days, public relations specialists were called "publicity men," or sometimes "press agents." In 1919, the newspapers of New York took a census of the number who worked regularly in the city and found that there were about 1,200 actively employed.[6] Furthermore, their functions were well understood by that time. Commentator and author Walter Lippmann noted that it was their task to use the media (mainly newspapers at the time) to provide the public with interpretations of events related to their clients:

> The development of the publicity man is a clear sign that the facts of modern life do not spontaneously take a shape in which they can be known. They must be given a shape by somebody, and since in the daily routine reporters cannot give a shape to facts, and since there is little disinterested organization of intelligence, the need for some formulation is being met by [press agents and publicity men].[7]

Thus, there was a thriving public relations industry by the time of World War I. Its practitioners performed essentially the same services as their

In many ways, Edward L. Bernays is regarded as the father of public relations as a professional field. He ran a famous agency in New York City early in this century, taught the first university public relations course, and wrote the first text for the field. He continued his contributions long after his retirement, writing a regular column in a trade journal and corresponding widely with other professionals. Born in 1891, Bernays died in March 1995 at the age of 103. (UPI/Bettmann Newsphotos)

modern counterparts, although they had only the print media to work with as they attempted to create meanings and images about those whom they represented.

Although public relations has grown into a sophisticated and complex occupational field, with the work carried on by relatively large agencies, some old-fashioned publicity agents (still using that name) continue to operate successfully, especially in New York City. There such high-visibility fields as the entertainment and fashion industries require constant publicity and access to the media. Entertainers and designers thus hire the publicity agents—who often violate all the canons of professionalism that pioneer Edward L. Bernays and other industry leaders have fought for.

Public Relations Today

Public relations practitioners today go by many names, among them public relations counselors, account executives, information officers, publicity directors, and house organ editors. They are found virtually everywhere—in the private sector in business, industry, social welfare organizations, churches, labor unions, and so on, and in the public sector in all levels of government from the White House to the local school or fire station. The number of people employed in public relations is impressive. The U.S. Department of Labor estimates that in 1950 there were 19,000 people engaged in public relations and publicity work. By 1970, this had grown to 76,000, and by 1990, to more than 170,000. These are very low estimates because the figures include only the rather narrow category of "public relations and publicity writers." In contrast, the U.S. Bureau of the Census reported that 465,000 persons were engaged in public relations in 1984; of this number, 44,000 worked for public relations or management firms.

Public relations activities are carried on in a variety of organized ways. Some are activities of individuals, such as consultants. Most, however, are carried on as team efforts by various kinds of groups. Perhaps most common is the *independent public relations counselor* or *agency*. This person or organization operates much like an advertising agency or law firm. It takes on clients and represents them by conducting public relations activities on their behalf. The client may be an individual who wants better understanding from the public or a large company that wants an experienced firm to provide special services such as conducting research and designing publications to help the company's own in-house public relations staff.

Somewhat related is the *public relations department* within a particular businesses or industry. Such a department acts as part of the overall management team and attempts to interpret the firm to the public and internal constituents and to provide channels for feedback from the public to management. The department is expected to contribute to the firm's profits by helping it achieve its overall business goals. The public relations department of General Motors, for example, sets communication goals to support and enhance the corporation's economic goals. Public relations departments of a similar nature also exist within nonprofit and educational institutions. Publicity for organizations such as colleges and labor unions usually involves a range of internal and external activities, from publications to fund drives.

Public relations departments also provide services within governmental agencies, at the federal, state, and even local level. In government, the terms "public information" and "public affairs" refer to any activity that communicates the purposes and work of an agency to the general public or to users of the agency's services. For example, welfare recipients need to know about the policies of the state welfare department, and taxpayers need to know how their money is being spent.

Another form of organized public relations activities is carried on by *specialized consultants*. These range from political advisers who work exclusively on public relations problems during election campaigns to information specialists who are experts in communications in a specific field, such as health, transportation, or insurance.

A related form of organized public relations activity is provided by *policy consultants*. These specialists suggest courses of action to public and private institutions that want to develop a policy for the use of information resources. They may want to influence Congressional legislation or FCC policies or develop an early-warning system to assess and trace the impact of a particular issue or program on corporate clients. This is a relatively new area of public relations that expanded considerably in the 1980s. An indication of its growing importance is *Business Week*'s information management section.

Finally, the field includes communication specialists in technical areas, called *technical specialists*. For example, in Chapter 8, we discussed consultants who try to improve the ratings of a TV station's news programs. Others are specialized firms that work with corporate clients to help them better understand and work with television, training programs for company presi-

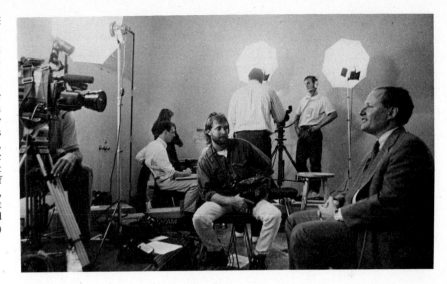

A public relations client can be a small business, a giant corporation, a huge federal bureaucracy, a foreign nation, or a single individual. Specialists in an agency help clients with television presentations, prepare carefully crafted video and print news releases, design brochures, draft speeches for public appearances, and assist with any other form of communication between clients and the relevant publics. (AP/Wide World Photos)

dents who serve as spokespersons, and placement services that get corporate clients on the air in various cities. Technical specialists also include graphics practitioners who provide full-service publication assistance, producing publicity messages that fit into an organization's overall public relations plan.

As in any dynamic industry, new ways of accomplishing public relations goals constantly emerge. For example, a number of advertising agencies have recently acquired established public relations firms or set up new ones within their organizations. Many public relations practitioners and media critics fear that if public relations becomes a branch of advertising, it will become a servant of product promotion, and ethical practices will not be maintained. They assert that the credibility of an independent public relations agency is greater than that of a public relations program under an advertising agency. Only time will tell.

The recent economic upheaval in the communications industries has complicated the world of public relations. Independent public relations agencies are becoming less common as advertising agencies acquire them and subject them to the corporate requirements of the parent company. It is too early to predict whether this trend within the industry will continue and what it will mean for public relations practice. However, the vast majority of public relations activity today occurs in the public relations departments of businesses and the public affairs departments of government.

Public Relations Campaigns

Public relations practitioners or agencies work in systematic ways. Typical of their activities on behalf of clients is the *public relations campaign*, an organized way of communicating carefully designed messages with specific meanings to targeted audiences that are important to the client.

SHAPING A SYMPATHETIC IMAGE OF KUWAIT DURING THE GULF WAR:
A Linchpin to History and Political Science

On August 1, 1990, the forces of Iraq's Saddam Hussein invaded and seized control of the independent nation of Kuwait. Months later, in January 1991, the United States led a coalition of allies and went to war with Iraq to free the tiny, oil-rich nation.

Just how the United States and its allies decided to go to war was influenced by a carefully organized effort by the White House and other interested parties. The image that was successfully propagated was of the government of tiny, overpowered Kuwait helplessly waiting for outside help to wrest its country from Iraq. Not so. The government of Kuwait was closely in touch with U.S. government and military authorities from the beginning and left nothing to chance.

Ten days after the invasion, Dr. Hassan al-Ebraheem, a professor of international politics at Kuwait University, visited the Washington, D.C. offices of the public relations firm Hill and Knowlton Inc. Kuwait thus became a client of Hill and Knowlton and in the next ninety days spent $5.6 million dollars trying to win the hearts and minds of the American people.

It is not unusual for nations, multinational firms, or political movements to use professional public relations firms. In fact, there are few that do not. Because public relations companies, lobbyists, and others doing work for foreign governments in the United States have to file reports with the U.S. Justice Department, detailed information about Kuwait's use of Hill and Knowlton is available. How was the money spent? Apparently $2.9 million was for professional fees and $2.7 was for other expenses, some of which are detailed below:

Research	1,100,000
Video production (probably for news releases)	644,571
Printing (PR kits)	436,825
Advertising	43,217

That so little was spent on direct advertising demonstrates the ability of public relations firms to get free publicity. In the Kuwaiti case, this involved direct lobbying of Congress, governors, and other leaders, rallies on college campuses, and support for an instantly manufactured group called Citizens for a Free Kuwait.

Public relations campaigns become necessary for businesses and other organizations under many kinds of circumstances. Some clients have positive goals in mind; others may not. Several examples provide illustrations: A business has been causing industrial pollution and is gaining a bad reputation. The firm now wants to convince the public that it is dedicated to protection of the environment. A public health organization wants to erase the stigma associated with a physical illness such as cancer or to create greater concern among the public about helping the mentally ill. An educational institution has experienced a bad sports scandal with consequent negative publicity. Enrollments have dropped, and it now wants to attract students and encourage donations. A government agency promoting prenatal child care for the poor wants women to make better use of its services. All these groups achieve their goals with public relations.

According to Cutlip and Center, any public relations program must include four basic steps:

One of the more outrageous aspects of the campaign came in the midst of a Congressional debate when fifteen-year-old Nayirah (only her first name was given) testified before Congress on October 10, 1990. She claimed to have witnessed Saddam's soldiers taking babies out of hospital incubators and leaving them to die on the hospital floor. It was "a PR masterstroke" orchestrated by Hill, Knowlton, according to the *Washington Monthly.* So what was wrong with bringing in the girl to testify about the mass murder of Kuwaiti babies? First of all, the story was manufactured; secondly, the girl was not an ordinary Kuwaiti, as had been reported, but the daughter of the Kuwaiti ambassador to the United States. Only months later was this incident revealed in John R. MacArthur's influential book, *Second Front: Censorship and Propaganda in the Gulf War.* Incidentally, Hill, Knowlton was famous for having considerable influence at the White House, with several of their top people having close ties with President Bush. At the same time, the firm was known for its bipartisan clout: It also employed top Democrats.

Propaganda is, of course, part of virtually every war. Almost as much energy is devoted to this quieter side of warfare as to the actual engagement on the battlefield. In World War I, for example, the British and the Germans both engaged in a vigorous propaganda war that influenced their entry into that conflict. Prior to World War II, the German propaganda machine under Hitler created massive support among the German people. Later, during the Vietnam War, there was a feverish battle to sway public opinion as that war became increasingly unpopular. It was the memory of the loss of the public opinion war at home during the Vietnam conflict that is credited with giving the military in the Persian Gulf a special impetus to supply government-controlled information and cooperate with the Kuwaitis in certain efforts (like those by Hill, Knowlton).

Sources: Susan B. Trento, "Lord of the Lies, How Hill and Knowlton's Robert Gray Pulls Washington's Strings," *Washington Monthly,* September 1992, pp. 12–21; Gary Lee, "Kuwaitis Pay $5.6 Million to Publicity Firm," *Washington Post,* December 19, 1990, p. 21A; John R. MacArthur, *Second Front: Censorship and Propaganda in the Gulf War* (New York: Hill and Wang, 1992), pp. 46–58. For a general treatment of the role of the media in the Persian Gulf War, see Everette E. Dennis et al., *The Media at War: The Press and the Persian Gulf Conflict* (New York: Gannett Foundation Media Center, 1991). An important work in this field is Philip M. Taylor, *Munitions of the Mind, War Propaganda from the Ancient World to the Nuclear Age* (London: Patrick Stephens, 1990).

1. *Fact-finding and feedback.* This stage involves background research on the desired audience, including impressionistic observations by knowledgeable observers and scientific studies of public opinion. The public relations practitioner uses this information to define the problem and to identify the audience to be reached.
2. *Planning and programming.* The publicist also uses the information from the fact-finding stage to plan a broad strategy for the entire public relations program. This strategy includes a timetable, budgets, and possible targets for the message.
3. *Action and communication.* In this stage, the publicist initiates the actual communication process using the media and the appropriate publicity tools. Pamphlets are distributed, speeches are given, news releases are sent to media organizations, etc.
4. *Evaluation.* After the program is carried out, it is assessed in several ways—by measuring changes in attitudes and opinions among particular

publics, counting the number of news clippings or reports on radio and television to evaluate the success of contacts with the news media, and/or by interviewing key opinion leaders. If carried to its logical conclusion, evaluation should affect future public relations activity, depending on what worked and what did not.[8]

In actual practice, a public relations campaign begins with the recognition of a problem or the perceived need for an image change of some sort. Let's say, for example, that the tourism board of the state of New York is unhappy with the state's tourism revenues and thinks the low level of tourism might be due to a poor public image. The group decides to investigate further and hires a public relations firm. The firm conducts research among selected publics, such as regular vacationers, travel agents, and travel writers for newspapers and magazines. Surveys assess what these people know about vacation possibilities in New York State. The results indicate a lack of public awareness, the presence of misconceptions, or concerns that keep tourists from vacationing in the state.

Next, the public relations firm prepares a campaign proposal suggesting a variety of measures likely to increase tourism in New York. Because all audiences cannot be reached through a limited campaign, the firm decides to direct its efforts at travel writers, hoping that they will say something positive about the state as a vacation spot in their articles. To influence the writers, the firm will distribute news releases, hold press briefings, and even organize tours.

As a next step, the firm presents the campaign proposal to the leaders of the tourism board. Assuming that the board accepts the proposal with a few modifications, it then commissions the public relations firm to carry out the campaign. At the end of the campaign, the firm conducts an evaluation that includes another survey of the same groups who provided the initial round of attitudes and opinions to see if these have changed. In addition, the firm looks at subsequent tourism figures and attempts to ascertain whether the campaign had any effect on them.

This hypothetical example reveals one of the real problems with public relations: The people who carry out information campaigns are not disinterested social scientists but *profit-making entrepreneurs* (or perhaps government employees eager to advance in their jobs). Thus, they look for proof that their campaign has worked. If it clearly has not, publicists may try to convince their clients that uncontrollable factors, such as a weak economy, too many crime reports in the media, or pre-existing negative stereotypes about New York, caused the public relations program to fail. Naturally, clients who hire the firm are free to make their own judgments about what worked and what didn't. Scholarly evidence about public relations campaigns—and there is far too little of it—suggests that many such efforts are unsuccessful. However, practitioners dispute this evidence with practical and often compelling examples.

Leaders in public relations are quick to point out that their work involves much more than mass communication. Sometimes they distinguish internal from external communication. *Internal communication* is communication within an organization directed to its members. For example, a labor union communicates to its members through newsletters, meetings, bulletin boards, and other internal media. This kind of communication is aimed at a discrete group of people, not at the general public through mass media. In contrast, *external communication* transmits messages via the mass media to a large, diverse audience or to particular segments of the population outside the organization.

A relatively new kind of organized public relations work is serving as a media consultant to a political candidate's campaign during an election. This kind of organized activity brings together public opinion research, strategic planning, and more traditional public relations. According to Jerry Hagstrom of the *National Journal*, who is an expert on this new form of public relations, there is an elite corps of about forty Washington-based polling and media firms that play a profound role in national presidential campaigns and other races. Similar firms exist across the country and typically serve the Republican or Democratic party.

Robert Squier, who represents Democrats, and Roger Ailes, who represents Republicans, are leading practitioners of political consulting today. Hagstrom states that this new cadre of consultants has virtually replaced state and local political bosses and party chairpersons as behind-the-scenes power brokers. What was once done intuitively by political operatives is now in the purview of consultants. Although consultants usually stay out of the public eye, they occasionally appear on CNN and various network talk shows to speak on behalf of their clients. Typically, such consultants engage in a kind of guerrilla warfare, plotting strategy and modes of attack and designing defensive responses for their clients when they are under fire. They key their efforts to opinion polls. And although national campaigns are the most prestigious races,, Hagstrom observes that the most elite consultants usually center their efforts on statewide campaigns because they are more financially lucrative.

In dealing with the media, campaign media consultants often engage in what has come to be called *spin control* (a term from billiards, where a left or right spin can be put on a ball, making it curve to one side or the other as it moves across the table). They do so by interpreting or reinterpreting situations that arise in connection with their candidate in ways that will reflect a more favorable (or less damaging) image. Thus, they initiate a proper or positive "spin" in their communications on an issue or subject.

One of the masters of spin control is New York public relations executive John Scanlon, who has represented such controversial clients as General William Westmoreland, the editors of the arch-conservative *Dartmouth Review*, Lawrence Tisch (who heads CBS), and the now defunct investment banking firm Drexel Burnham Lambert. All had suffered scandals or received large-scale negative publicity. As one observer noted, "Scanlon works at preserving a client's reputation with the same zeal and sense of purpose a criminal lawyer employs in keeping some miscreant from going to jail."[9] One of the authors of this text arranged through Scanlon a meeting with Tisch. He would not have agreed to the interview without Scanlon's advice that the appearance would be beneficial to him in the midst of a public controversy. People who see Scanlon and others like him at close range understand the clout and importance such consultants have in assuring visibility. Many media people also assign Scanlon a high degree of credibility, because he has access to people they want to reach.

Typical Tasks and Work Assignments

The actual tasks and work assignments of public relations practitioners vary widely from one setting to another. Much depends, of course, on the position of the individual within the power hierarchy of the agency. In some businesses, the vice president for public relations is a high-ranking person who is involved in all major corporate decisions and a part of the policy-making team. In other firms, the public relations officer has less power and is brought in only to provide damage control through publicity. Still other practitioners are the drones of public relations: entry level or low-ranking employees who do the many day-to-day tasks that are necessary in a public relations campaign. Thus, at the top end of the organization are those who engage in tactical and strategic planning and at lower levels are those who perform more routine tasks involved in such plans. Lone practitioners or people in small firms usually do everything, ranging from designing both strategy and tactics to writing copy for press releases.

Top level policy-makers set long-term objectives and usually agree on some realistic expectations for results. This somewhat abstract agreement is then channeled into specific approaches, using publicity tools ranging from sponsored events to TV presentations, press conferences, and information pamphlets. Thus, the complete public relations process involves planning and implementation—both overall thinking and precise technical work that make achievement of the campaign's goals possible.

There are a number of specific tasks that must be accomplished in implementing a *public relations* campaign. In larger firms with a significant division of labor, the work assignments may be highly specialized. For example, one specialist may spend most of his or her time writing news releases for a political candidate. Another may specialize in communicating new, high-tech information to nurses or engineers. In smaller firms, personnel will handle a wider range of duties. However, regardless of the size of a public relations agency or department, certain categories of work assignments are common. Cutlip and Center list the following common tasks and specific forms of work:

1. *Writing*—producing news releases aimed at the general media and drafting copy for specialized publications, brochures, posters, catalogues, and other pieces intended for distribution to the public.
2. *Editing*—revising and checking texts of speeches, company magazines, newsletters, and electronic bulletin boards;
3. *Media relations and placement*—getting clients in the newspaper and on the air and coordinating media coverage of events;

4. *Special events*—organizing media events such as anniversaries of organizations, openings of new programs, sponsored performances, donations of money, dedications of new facilities, and similar ceremonies;
5. *Speaking*—writing and delivering speeches to various groups on behalf of the client;
6. *Production*—working with designers, typesetters, editors, and producers to present material in printed or visual form;
7. *Research*—evaluating programs, developing questionnaires for surveys, and analyzing media coverage of an event or issue;
8. *Programming and counseling*—developing a plan for the client or department and giving advice about how to handle a particular event or limit negative publicity;
9. *Training and management*—providing training services to employees, advising them on how to set a proper climate in a firm, and coordinating employees of varied skills and backgrounds to ensure the success of a program.[10]

In addition to being able to perform the preceding kinds of work, effective public relations practitioners need to have certain personal qualities. They usually have excellent communications and social skills, a thorough knowledge of the media, management, and business, and the ability to function both as problem-solvers and decision-makers. Other common qualities are stability, common sense, intellectual curiosity, and a tolerance for frustration.[11]

Lobbying as Public Relations

A special form of public relations is *lobbying*, although some experts do not see it as part of the field. But lobbying has many similarities to the kinds of activities we have described as constituting public relations. Lobbyists are defined as persons employed "to influence legislators to introduce or vote for measures favorable to the interests they represent."[12]

To achieve their influence, lobbyists rely mainly on interpersonal communication and informal contacts with legislators or regulators. Nevertheless, they are persons or groups paid to engage in efforts to influence the beliefs, attitudes and actions of specifically defined target individuals through the use of deliberately designed messages. In that sense, they fit quite well within the broad definition of public relations. The main differences are that they seldom use the mass media and they focus their influence attempts narrowly on legislators and regulators.

When these influence peddlers were first identified in the nineteenth century as a distinct group, they stood in the lobby of Washington, D.C.'s venerable Willard Hotel—which still stands only a few paces from the White House and a few blocks from the Capitol. When officeholders came through the lobby, these importuners clutched at the legislators' sleeves to try to get their attention (much as had influence seekers at centers of power since organized government began). In time, they came to be called "lobbyists."

The words "lobbyist" and "lobbying" were in use before the Civil War. Many legislators ate lunch at the historic Willard's Hotel, which is very close to the Capitol Building in Washington, D.C. Individuals wanting special consideration waited in a long lobby near the dining room and plucked at the sleeves of politicians as they passed through. Even President Lincoln, who stayed at the hotel for weeks before moving into the White House, received their attentions. The recently restored hotel remains on the same site today. (The Bettmann Archive)

Even today, the Willard Hotel proudly tells its guests that the name was born right there during the time that Lincoln was in the White House.

Lobbyists represent a great variety of groups and interests. These include trade associations, veterans' groups, labor unions, political action committees, consumer advocates, professional associations, churches, foreign governments, and many more. There are literally tens of thousands of organizations and individuals who want to influence the legislative process. A lobbyist might be a lawyer, public relations practitioner, or policy expert who has been hired to influence the work of Congress. Not all work at the federal level. Some represent clients at state and even local centers of government.

Federal law requires that lobbyists register with the Records and Registration Division of the Capitol Hill Lobbying Office. There are over six thousand registered individual and group lobbyists in Washington, D.C. They represent more than eleven thousand active and about twenty-eight thousand inactive clients (those who have not been represented on Capitol Hill for the last three months). Some of the groups identify themselves as lobbying specialists. Others are public relations firms, law firms, and think tanks (various mission-oriented institutes and centers).

Lobbying and lobbyists have always been a subject of controversy. Some critics regard them with deep suspicion. Early in 1993, lobbying got on the public agenda very quickly when Ron Brown, former chairman of the Democratic National Committee, was appointed Secretary of Commerce by President Clinton. Brown had been a member of a well-known and very influential lobbying firm, Patten, Boggs and Blow. The group had represented many special interests in Washington, D.C. over the years. Questions were raised as to whether Brown would favor those whom his firm had represented in the past.

The move by Brown from a lobbying firm to government office—which at some point in the future may be made in reverse—is an example of a situation that is a continuing focus of criticism of lobbying. There is a constant movement of individuals between government service and private influence-seeking roles. A continuing concern is that former government officials or employees will use their inside knowledge and contacts for lobbying purposes, giving the special interests that they represent an unfair advantage. There are now rules that prevent them from doing so for several years after they leave office.

For a number of years, the two largest lobbying and public relations firms in Washington, D.C. have been Hill and Knowlton, Inc., and Burson-Marsteller, Inc., each of which has ties to advertising and public relations groups on a worldwide basis. Clients pay huge fees to be represented by these firms, and their annual billings are in the millions of dollars. Such firms use every conceivable tool and process to promote, change, or impede legislation pending before Congress that can have an influence on their clients. Sometimes even getting a single word changed in a bill (for example, from "shall" to "may" or from "never" to "seldom") as it is passing through a committee can mean millions to a client. Like more traditional public relations groups, these firms organize events, do research, develop communication strategies, and sometimes shape news, on behalf of their clients. Lobbyists at both federal and state levels write articles, make speeches, design campaigns, buy advertising, influence journalists, and guide public officials.

Although lobbying currently has a negative connotation for many critics, some lobbyists provide legitimate and necessary services that go beyond gaining benefits for special-interest groups. Representatives of various causes that are well regarded by the public often bring to officeholders' attention information that can be critical to promoting the well-being of their constituents. Thus, lobbyists can help busy legislators see an issue from a number of perspectives. (Bob Daemmrich, Stock, Boston)

Many critics deplore all lobbying and lobbyists, but others point out that they have a legitimate role in the process of government. They do bring to the attention of officeholders a great deal of information that should be taken into account as laws are formed or modified. They bring together those who have legitimate interests with those who can have powerful influences on those interests. Often, legislators need to know who will be affected by the outcome of bills under consideration. The down side comes when special interests gain an advantage over the public good and scandals arise. Fortunately, consumer groups, the press, and governments constantly monitor lobbyists for ethical and other kinds of violations.

Public Relations as a Professional Field

As the field was being established, no particular credentials were required to become a public relations specialist. Indeed, many of the earliest practitioners were ex-journalists who had an understanding of the workings of the press and how to get stories about their clients into the pages of the newspapers. Moreover, it was all done by the "seat of the pants." That is, there was no body of concepts and principles that had been developed by systematic research. It was a field where intuition, creativity, insights, and lore held sway. Often the guesses and inspirations of practitioners led to success; sometimes they did not.

Today, there is a strong movement among its practitioners and educators to try to transform public relations into a *profession*. Whether this will be successful or not depends on what that label really means. The word "profession" is an ancient one, going back to the Middle Ages, when there were only three basic "learned professions": divinity, law, and medicine. What set them apart from other vocational pursuits were these major criteria: (1) Each had an extensive body of sophisticated knowledge requiring long periods of formal study to learn and master. (2) Their practitioners used that body of knowledge on behalf of the public within a set of ethical norms. (3) Their practitioners monitored each other to insure compliance with the norms, rejecting from their ranks those who engaged in unethical practices.

The label "professional" is now widely applied by the public to designate virtually any specialized occupational group. Thus, we hear of "professional" hair dressers, prizefighters, bartenders and even dog-groomers. However, it is the traditional meaning of the term, and its prestige, to which public relations practitioners and educators aspire, and there is evidence that progress is being made. Today, two major factors are playing a central role in the evolution of public relations as a professional field. One is the increasing establishment and acceptance of courses and degree programs in colleges and universities. The other is systematic research and scholarly inquiry aimed directly at developing concepts, principles, and practical solutions related to the field.

The growth of education and research would appear to satisfy the criterion of developing a body of sophisticated knowledge that requires lengthy training to master. However, whether the field's practitioners use that knowledge for the benefit of the public within an ethical framework is another matter. Furthermore, whether they monitor each other and reject those who transgress the ethical norms is something else altogether. The following section focuses on public relations within the framework of the three criteria for a true profession.

Education and Professionalism

Public relations has been taught in universities since 1923, when Edward Bernays organized the first course at New York University. Early on, it was taught mostly in journalism schools, which were largely newspaper-oriented and not always hospitable to the inclusion of public relations in the curriculum. This prejudice concerning public relations has faded over the years, although a few journalism schools still bar it from the curriculum. Departments of speech/communications have added public relations programs, as have the comprehensive communications schools and colleges. In addition, there are individual courses in public relations at community colleges and industry trade schools.

Today, public relations is a rapidly growing field of study in higher education, and it has also taken other important steps to establish itself as a profession. For example, the organization that periodically examines and approves of journalism curricula in the United States also reviews public relations courses in specific institutions to determine if they qualify as an accredited sequence. (Other regularly reviewed areas of study are news-editorial, magazine, and radio-television news.)

There are several hundred teachers of public relations in journalism and communications schools and in speech/communication programs in the United States, and every year thousands of students major in the field. Student internships are available with public relations firms, businesses, government agencies, and professional associations. Dozens of textbooks and a number of technical journals reporting research results are devoted to the field. Public relations practitioners also have their own national organization, the Public Relations Society of America (PRSA), which has student chapters (PRSSA) as well. The PRSA has an accreditation procedure and formally admits practitioners, although by no means all of them have this certification.

A formal curriculum in public relations at the undergraduate level usually includes substantial work in the liberal arts and sciences. Typically, a public relations major takes an overview course on public relations as a communications field, an advanced course in public relations methods, and other specific courses in various aspects of the field, depending on the size of the program. Public relations curricula at the graduate level usually involve formal research training. In the 1970s and 1980s, public relations became one of the most popular communications majors as students in the information age realized the importance of public relations and other media consulting activities.

The purpose of public relations education is to promote the field as a professional communications activity, to produce a trained work force, and to foster research. However, this does not mean that people who work in public relations must major in public relations at a university or college. Although there is a great and growing demand for people educated in public relations at accredited schools, many still get into the field by working for newspapers or other media. Some people come into public relations as specialists—for example, they may have a background in public health and take up a public relations assignment in that area. Thus, there are many pathways to a public relations career. However, most university-based public relations programs have the advantage of having close links with the industry and are better positioned to help their students get jobs in the field.

Public Relations Research

A second significant area of development in public relations is research. This, too, represents an effort to gain full professional status by fulfilling the criterion of having an extensive body of specialized knowledge. However, as will be clear, that body largely remains to be developed.

Much of the research done in the field stems from practical rather than theoretical considerations. Clients want to see what kind of "bang" they have received for their "buck." Although public relations was once carried out with little formal evaluation, businesses and government departments increasingly require that public relations practitioners document expenditures and provide evidence that some kinds of benefits flow from those costs.

Increasingly, however, much of the impact and influence of public relations can be understood in the general context of high-quality media and communications research. Thus, research on such general topics as persuasion, attitude change, and agenda-setting is pertinent. Moreover, a growing field of applied research more specifically focused on problems and practices in public relations has also emerged. Some public relations agencies and departments conduct in-house assessments simply to take stock of their activities. Other research is done in universities by public relations scholars and is broader in scope and less parochial than the applied research of public relations practitioners. University research typically aims at establishing general patterns, relationships, and theories that help explain processes and effects in the field.

Public relations scholar John V. Pavlik has identified at least three motivations for public relations research: One is understanding public relations *as communication*, which involves building communications theory and studying the effects of public relations activity on the individual, group, and society. A second is *solving practical problems* in the field, including monitoring the public relations environment, measuring social performance, and auditing communication and public relations. A third motivation stems from the need to *monitor the profession*, by taking stock of how public relations practitioners, individually and collectively, are performing technically and ethically.[13]

Much of the in-house public relations research done by agencies gives clients feedback and helps them improve communication with their constituencies. Some critics say that such research is manipulative, but defenders say it is simply the intelligent, systematic gathering of information that can make the client more sensitive to the desired audience. How public relations people use such information is up to them—the hope is that most will use it ethically.

The state of public relations research and its use by people in the field is difficult to ascertain. The largest and most powerful public relations firms and government departments spend a considerable amount of time and money testing their messages and monitoring their campaigns for evidence that they are having some effect. On the other hand, many small public relations firms and individual practitioners make limited use of research in their work. Some publicists do not use research at all, preferring an intuitive approach. Usage on a day-to-day basis of the kinds of public relations research typically reported in academic journals is limited. Yet such research is part of a growing body of literature that can help imaginative and thoughtful practitioners.

New Strategies for Reaching Publics

Another way in which public relations is changing is in the development of new strategies to reach relevant publics. Notice that we do not say "serve" the public—the benefits go to clients who pay the bills. In any case, practitioners seek ways to make use of technological advances in communications within the United States and all over the world. With new media available, public relations specialists have been able to design new formats, such as the video news release, for presenting messages about their clients to relevant receivers.

Using new communications technologies   Today, public relations messages compete with other kinds of information for public attention in an environment that includes both multiple media and a great variety of sources. Fax machines deliver millions of messages daily; through personal computers, people access a vast array of specialized information; electronic mail (e-mail) enables people both within and between groups to transmit and receive information of many kinds; teleconferencing brings small groups together for discussions, even though the participants may be at sites remote from each other.

This continuously evolving world of privatized communication does not rely on mass media at all. It is targeted to specific individuals, within both established groups and new constituencies. Anne Wells Branscomb, a communications attorney and scholar, uses the terms "teletribes" and "telenetworks" to describe those groups of people who are brought together by virtue of modern telecommunications.[14] Through electronic mail and computerized networks on data services, diverse groups such as teen-agers who

Public relations practitioners use many kinds of strategies, events, and media to bring the messages of their clients to the attention of the public. These include sponsoring various kinds of sporting events, such as golf tournaments, fishing contests, tennis matches, and auto races. The implication is that the winner is not only the person who got the trophy but also the product that sponsored the event or the winner. Whether such strategies have any real influence on the public is anyone's guess. (Rob Crandall, Stock, Boston)

gamble, AIDS victims, and collectors of Japanese antiques can communicate very effectively among themselves.

This emerging information society requires new strategies and new tactics for the public relations field. In order to target various sectors of the public successfully, publicists are learning to use the new specialized information services and are finding new avenues of publicity. For example, it is possible to get time on an electronic network to send messages to antique collectors in New Jersey or South Carolina who might like to know about new developments in that field. The electronic services offer a more precise way of reaching a desired audience than, say, the special-interest magazine. In fact, the most specialized publication probably has a more diverse readership than the audiences currently being targeted by new data services. There is also a considerable newsletter industry with annual revenues reaching $7 billion. Special-interest newsletters, often transmitted electronically, reach chocolate lovers, travelers to certain countries, and many other "publics" that desire highly specific information.

The idea of using various kinds of media to achieve public relations goals was well understood by the Chinese students who in 1989 led the pro-democracy protests in Tiananmen Square. They quickly learned to provide information to American and European print and broadcast journalists. But they also used computer networks and fax machines to transmit their news releases and interpretations across national boundaries into the court of world opinion. The Chinese government, which strongly disapproved of their actions, was slow to make use of such channels or even to shut them off. At first, government officials stonewalled requests for information and later tried to persuade reporters and others that the protests were simply

The lessons of American public relations were not lost on the Chinese students in Tiananmen Square in 1989, when they used the "Goddess of Liberty" to capture the attention of television viewers (especially Americans). (© Chip Hires/Gamma-Liaison)

disruptive and illegal. When that strategy failed, the government crushed the protest in a bloody massacre. Many student leaders were subsequently executed, jailed or forced into exile; yet images of the students bravely demanding democracy in the face of violent governmental opposition is likely to be remembered for a long time.

The video news release   A good example of the way in which public relations practitioners constantly search for new ways to present their messages to targeted publics is the *video news release* (VNR)—a self-serving promotion of a person or organization presented on videotape. Originally used by companies to promote their general image or to respond to a crisis, VNRs are now commonly used by political candidates. In 1988, several campaigns at the national and local level used VNRs with limited success, but in 1992, more than 10 percent of television stations used VNR material from the major presidential candidates during the primaries and the general election.

Producers of VNRs control the style, content, and tone of the message, which may be picked up and aired by broadcasters. From the standpoint of

TV stations, VNRs conveniently provide much needed visual material for news programs and reduce filming costs. In some instances, the only way a local station can get direct access to major candidates is through VNRs or satellite news conferences, both of which are paid for by the candidates.

An ethical problem associated with this kind of communication concerns identification of the source. When television stations do not identify the VNR as such, they do their viewers a disservice. Yet stations do not always give the public due warning that self-serving VNR material was produced by the candidate or company represented and was not subject to usual journalistic checks for accuracy.[15]

Video news releases are distributed either on video cassette or via satellite transmission. Like a printed news release that may emphasize favorable elements to convey a positive image, a VNR seeks to communicate a certain point of view or argue a case. For example, VNRs have been used by various industries to dispute environmental claims, and by environmental groups with equal fervor. When a firm is in the midst of a major crisis, a corporate VNR allows the company spokesperson or CEO to put the firm's position forward to employees without press intervention. Supporters of corporate VNRs say that this is an appropriate use of corporate communications in an era when it is difficult for a firm to get its message across without constraints or disruption from the press. Sometimes such VNRs are used to save time and money when a firm wants to get its message across in several markets without extensive travel or personal appearances from its executives. In effect, the VNR is an advisory from an organization making a plea for publicity and understanding. Media organizations are then free to use the material verbatim without comment, edit it heavily, or identify it as a statement from those appearing therein.

Criticisms and Ethical Issues

As public relations continues its struggle to be recognized as a profession, one of its major problems lies in the public image of the field and in developing and enforcing a meaningful code of ethics. As we noted earlier, almost from its beginnings, public relations has had its detractors. Critics charge that public relations activity is manipulative, self-serving, and unethical, that it distorts and blurs issues in its attempts to persuade the public, and that publicists will use just about any means to assure a favorable image for their clients.

There are unscrupulous people in public relations, as there are in any profession. They become especially visible because of the nature of what public relations specialists do. Public-spirited groups and the news media make special efforts to try to ferret out deceptive activities. As a result, public relations practitioners are increasingly in the public eye, often on unfavorable terms. In addition, unethical practices sometimes backfire and harm the image that public relations is meant to polish.

To its credit, the field makes extensive efforts to reduce poor practices. To be accredited by the Public Relations Society of America, those who work professionally in the field must pass tests of communications skills and ascribe to a code of good practice. In addition, many college and university programs include courses on public relations ethics. These conditions are likely to decrease flagrant deceptions of the public.

In spite of these efforts, those who criticize the basic task of public relations focus on a more fundamental problem: whether there is something less than honorable in a business devoted to enhancing the image of a corporation or individual by suppressing truths that would bring criticism and emphasizing only favorable meanings. To the critics this is a serious charge; it is this aspect of the basic mission of many public relations campaigns that is most troublesome. Defenders say that a corporation or individual has every right to put the best face possible before the public. Moreover, public relations provides useful information to people in an increasingly complex and bureaucratic world—although such information should ideally be balanced with information from more objective sources.

Such negative views of the field may change. One reason is that during the past twenty years, an important concept that may help to mute such criticisms has found increasing favor among public relations specialists. A commitment to *public accountability* has received much attention and has been integrated into public relations thinking and practice. The notion of accountability is tied to the idea of corporate social responsibility, which stipulates that a business ought to contribute more to the commonweal than its own economic success. According to this idea, a responsible corporation should make a positive contribution to local communities or the nation as a whole.

As a business, public relations often appears to lack accountability. For example, after Hurricane Hugo hit the Caribbean islands in 1989, promoters of tourism quickly organized information about what islands and resorts were still open for business in the midst of widespread destruction and relief efforts. Although some criticized this seemingly insensitive campaign, others argued that the future employment and prosperity of the islanders depended on sustaining the tourist trade. In such a case, critics of public relations may charge that no one represents the consumer. On the other hand, publicists may counter that their own ethical standards prevent them from deliberately misleading the public, and that the promoters were doing a service by providing accurate information in the midst of rumor and misinformation. There are no easy answers, and there will be none until the canons of ethics for public relations in such complex situations are further developed.

Today, one of the major sore points for critics of the industry lies in the area of public relations during elections. Political campaign consultants often approach and sometimes cross the ethical borderline. For example, Roger Ailes worked for George Bush in his successful 1988 presidential campaign against Michael Dukakis. The campaign Ailes designed ran negative TV ads that many critics said appealed to racial fear in voters. One was the so-called Willy Horton ad, named for a convicted African-American murderer who committed another terrible crime while out on furlough. The ad showed convicts going through a revolving door (representing the furlough policy approved by Dukakis). The meaning conveyed was that Dukakis was an ultra-liberal who was soft on criminals. In addition, Ailes admitted that he planted doubts in reporters' minds about Dukakis, knowing full well that the imputations were false. Ailes and other political consultants who "play hard-ball" in their public relations efforts are often criticized by the press and their colleagues. However, as long as they successfully accomplish their goals in getting people elected, it is doubtful that they will change their tactics.

From an overview of the efforts by the field of public relations to be identified as a profession in the traditional sense, it is clear that public relations has a long way to go. The current status of the field can be assessed against the three criteria discussed earlier: (1) Progress is clearly being made on the first criterion. That is, the field is assembling through research and scholarship a body of complex knowledge. That accumulated knowledge is now being taught in formal courses and degree sequences in colleges and universities. (2) There is less certainty as to how well the second criterion is being met. That is, it could be hotly debated whether public relations practitioners serve the public with their knowledge or only those well-heeled clients who can afford their services. Indeed, many critics believe that public relations campaigns often deliberately fool the public by suppressing damaging information and emphasizing only positive messages about the publicists' clients. (3) Finally, there is, as yet, no codified set of ethical canons to which public relations practitioners universally subscribe, and there certainly is no way in which those who cross the line on ethical standards can be drummed out of the profession. Therefore, it will be interesting to see, in the years ahead, if the field can resolve these problems and gain the public trust that has largely failed to develop over the years.

Chapter Review

- Public relations as communications consists mainly of transmitting organized and calculated messages on behalf of clients wishing to arouse desired sets of meanings in designated target audiences. Public relations campaigns are conducted by hired communicators who transmit messages via a variety of channels to relevant audiences in an attempt to influence their beliefs, attitudes, or even actions regarding a client.

- Most public relations efforts make extensive use of mass communications. Practitioners constantly try to draw attention to their clients by transmitting information through the media in news reports, talk shows, or any form of print or broadcast content that can show their client in a favorable light.

- Some scholars argue that public relations is really an ancient activity, dating back at least to Plato's *Republic*. However, its more modern origins lie in the publicity men, press agents, and agencies that developed in New York City early in this century. Their task was, much as it is today, to improve the image of a client.

- Public relations specialists today go by many names. However, their basic task is to organize communication tactics, strategies, and campaigns that will modify the beliefs, attitudes, and perhaps actions of targeted audiences. Such campaigns include the steps of fact-finding, planning and programming, action and communication, and evaluation.

- The specific work of public relations personnel includes writing, editing, media relations and placement, arranging special events, public speaking, production of brochures, research, training, and management.

■ Lobbying is a special and controversial form of public relations. Lobbyists use a variety of communications techniques to try to influence legislators and bureaucrats as they initiate, modify, and pass laws and regulations that can have an impact on their clients.

■ Today, there is a strong movement among its practitioners and educators to try to transform public relations into a profession. Whether this will be successful or not depends on how well the field meets three major criteria: (1) developing a body of sophisticated knowledge, (2) using that knowledge for the public good within a system of ethical norms, and (3) ensuring compliance to those norms by monitoring practitioners.

■ The accomplishments of the public relations field in education and research would appear to satisfy the first criterion. There is considerable doubt that the field's practitioners always try to use that knowledge for the benefit of the public within an ethical framework. Furthermore, efforts to monitor one another and reject those who transgress the ethical norms have not been impressive, to say the least.

■ Therefore, the field has a number of problems to solve before it can gain professional status in the traditional meaning of that term. It will be interesting to see, in the years ahead, if the field can resolve these problems and gain the public trust that has largely failed to develop over the years.

Notes and References

1. Scott M. Cutlip and Allen H. Center, *Effective Public Relations*, 6th ed. (Englewood Cliffs, N.J.: Prentice-Hall, 1985), p. 4. See also Robert T. Reilly, *Public Relations in Action* (Englewood Cliffs, N.J.: Prentice-Hall, 1987); and David Haberman and H. A. Dolphin, *Public Relations: The Necessary Art* (Ames: Iowa State University Press, 1988).
2. Ibid., p. 16.
3. Edward L. Bernays, "Public Relations," lecture at the School of Journalism and Mass Communication, University of Minnesota, October 19, 1979; also mentioned in his several books on the subject. Other information about Bernays in this chapter comes from several personal interviews and correspondence over a ten-year period.
4. *Ragan Report*, August 1992.
5. Ibid.
6. Frank Cobb, *The New Republic*, December 31, 1919, p. 44.
7. Walter Lippmann, *Public Opinion* (New York: Harcourt, Brace, 1922), p. 345.
8. Cutlip and Center, op. cit., pp. 138–230.
9. Bruce Porter, "The Scanlon Spin." *Columbia Journalism Review*, September/October 1989, p. 50.
10. Ibid., p. 64. See also James E. Grunig and Todd Hunt, *Managing Public Relations* (New York: Holt, 1984), chapter 5.
11. Scott M. Cutlip, Allen H. Center, and Glenn M. Broom, *Effective Public Relations*, 6th ed. (Englewood Cliffs, N.J.: Prentice-Hall, 1985), p. 73.
12. *American Heritage Dictionary of the English Language* (Boston: Houghton Mifflin, 1970).
13. John Pavlik, *What Research Tells Us* (Newbury Park, Calif.: Sage), pp. 15, 23–24.
14. Anne Wells Branscomb, interview with Everette E. Dennis, April 1993.
15. See John Pavlik and Mark Thalhimer, "From Wausau to Wichita: Covering the Campaign via Satellite," in Everette E. Dennis et al., *Covering the Presidential Primaries* (New York: The Freedom Forum Media Studies Center, June 1992).

PART FOUR

THE CONTENT
OF MASS
COMMUNICATIONS

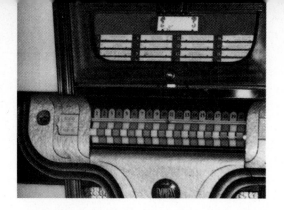

12

> . . . I have never read any memorable news in a newspaper. If we read of one man robbed, or murdered, or killed by accident, or one house burned, or one vessel wrecked, or one steamboat blown up, or one cow run over on the Western Railroad, or one mad dog killed, or one lot of grasshoppers in the winter—we never need read of another. If you are acquainted with the principle, what do you care for the myriad instances and applications?
>
> Henry David Thoreau, 1854

The News Process: The Surveillance Function of the Press

As the quotation from Thoreau on the chapter opening page suggests, some critics have had little interest in the news. However, the overwhelming majority of humankind—from prehistoric times to the present—has found it fascinating. Furthermore, news often brings information that can be of profound importance. The routine events of the mid–nineteenth century, such as those listed in the quotation, were undoubtedly of little consequence, but others reported in the news of Thoreau's time literally reshaped his society. For example, if he had read his newspaper during the 1860s, even casually, he would have gained perspectives on the advancing Industrial Revolution, the expanding frontier, the Civil War, and the end of slavery in the United States. He would also have read about the assassination of President Lincoln, Darwin's controversial new theories, and the laying of wires beneath the Atlantic so as to communicate instantaneously with Europe.

Just as in Thoreau's time, the press today serves as the "eyes and ears" of society. As a result of the gathering, processing, and dissemination of the news, the public comes to comprehend, in greater or lesser degree, an agenda of topics summarizing what has happened in their community, region, nation, and the world. The word "press" today includes all the print, broadcast, and cable media that bring news to the public.

There are many ways to define news, but for our purposes, we can define it in a very simple and common-sense way. *News is current or fresh knowledge about an event or subject that is gathered, processed, and disseminated via a medium to a significant number of interested people.* Of critical importance for understanding the nature of news are the words "gathered," "processed," "disseminated," and "public." It is these four ideas that are at the heart of the *news process*—a series of steps or stages by which accounts of events flow through news organizations and media to the public. Those steps consist of (1) gathering relevant facts or details selectively, (2) preparing them into stories judged to be newsworthy and suitably encoded for particular media, (3) transmitting those accounts via a mass medium to an audience, which then, (4) in varying degrees, attends to, interprets, and evaluates what has been presented.

A broader idea that places the news process in perspective is the *surveillance function* of the press. The main idea here is that the press (news media generally) keeps an eye on what is going on for citizens and, through the news process, gives them reliable reports about what appears to be important. Thus, citizens supposedly have trustworthy information enabling them to make informed decisions about events and issues that are important to them and the society. It is this idealized interpretation of the function of the press in our democracy that is the justification for according the news media special protections and privileges not extended to others.

If the news process works well—that is, if the information presented is reasonably complete and accurate as a representation of reality—the public gets a valid picture of what is going on, creating what should be a close correspondence between what Walter Lippman called the "world outside" and the "pictures in our heads." However, as this chapter will make clear, there are many reasons to believe that the news presented by the press has only a *limited* correspondence with what is actually happening in the real world.

Recognizing the limitations of the news process, as we do in this chapter, is not the same as condemning it. To show that the "pictures in our heads" that we create from the news media's presentations of "the world outside" are distorted is not to say that newspapers, radio, or television deliberately set out to dupe us. An alternative conclusion is that such distortions are an inevitable product of the forces, factors, and conditions within which the press, as it has developed in the United States, must operate to survive. At the same time, as the present chapter will show, in some instances, the press can and should be criticized—strongly in some cases—for policies and decisions that have been made by owners and managers. A major purpose of this chapter, therefore, is to examine the news process objectively so as to provide a better understanding of how well the press actually performs its surveillance function, where it does poorly, and why.

On the whole, the contemporary news industries are impressive. It is quite true that, just as in Thoreau's time, the press reports thousands of events of a trivial nature to the public. However, the press also brings us information about truly significant events, situations, and changes that often have a profound impact on our lives. Furthermore, it does so today with a swiftness and a degree of detail that people in Thoreau's time could not have imagined. Today, the proliferation of media and technologies that permit the gathering, processing, and dissemination of information allows the press to provide far greater coverage of events, gathered from more places, delivered in richer detail, and presented much more quickly than ever before. And as technological development continues, even greater changes in the news process will take place in the future.

The News Process in Earlier Societies

In ancient times, a major means of transmitting the news was by what we might call "news specialists"—that is, messengers of various kinds who developed ways of remembering long accounts with many details. The availability of speech greatly expanded human beings' ability to store information in memory. Studies have shown that people who have only oral language, and who have to remember complex information, develop elaborate techniques that help them recall details. One such technique is the poetic structure. We all keep some details in our heads by memorizing little poems. For example, for recalling the number of days in each month, who can forget "Thirty days hath September, April, June, and November . . ."?

Ancient news specialists, however, had to commit truly important and complex information to memory in such a way that elaborate details could be recalled and retold accurately. To do so, they used several kinds of mem-

Throughout history, people have eagerly sought news about happenings at home and elsewhere. As societies became more complex, political life and commercial activities became increasingly significant concerns. During the sixteenth and seventeenth centuries, demand for both domestic and foreign news grew, but few printed media published timely and detailed information. Thus, social gathering-places, such as taverns and coffee houses, became centers for the diffusion of information by word of mouth. At times, as this engraving shows, discussions of the news could grow heated. (Dept. of Special Collections, Memorial Library, University of Wisconsin–Madison)

DIFFUSION THEORY: THE TWO-STEP FLOW OF COMMUNICATION

Although most people get their news and other kinds of information directly from the mass media, information continues to diffuse through societies by word of mouth. Thus, even in our sophisticated information society, with its satellites, computers, and news media with worldwide reach, word-of-mouth communication is still a part of the mass communication process.

In a now classic study of the role of the mass media in the 1940 presidential campaign between Franklin D. Roosevelt and Wendell Willkie, communication researchers Lazarsfeld, Berelson, and Gaudet rediscovered the importance of the diffusion of information through interpersonal communication. To their surprise, they found that many of the people they were interviewing did not get their information about the issues and candidates from the media at all, but from *other people* who had read about the campaign in the newspapers or had listened to the broadcast speeches of the candidates.

The researchers found that such "opinion leaders" passed on information to many others who had much less contact with the media. As they did so, they had an influence on the way the information was interpreted. Thus, the label "opinion leaders" described not only their activity in transmission but also their role in exerting personal influence. Out of that famous research project came a theory that has come to be called the *two-step flow of communication*. It is important in understanding the word-of-mouth transmission of news to a larger audience than just those who are initially exposed. The two-step flow of communication has been widely studied since it was first formulated in the 1940s.[1]

Most of us can recall learning of some major news

ory devices. For example, in classic times, news was packaged into epic poems (from the Greek word *epos*, meaning "tale"). The standardized verbal rhythms and structures of the poems provided aids to memory, and epics were widely used in preliterate societies. Perhaps the best-known example is *The Iliad*, in which the poet Homer described the Greeks' ten-year siege of Troy, which took place about 1200 B.C. At the time, the Greeks had no written language, and the complex story of Troy had to be remembered with the help of *The Iliad's* sixteen thousand lines of dactylic hexameter.[1]

In the Middle Ages, minstrels and traveling bands of troubadours went from one village and estate to another. They sang, staged little plays, and danced to entertain the local gentry. But more important, they organized songs and recitals around important tidings that they brought from centers of power. It was in this manner that many locals learned of such events as the birth of an heir to their throne, an important marriage among the nobility, or the death of a royal person.

Even today, *interpersonal transmission*—word-of-mouth telling and retelling—is still very much a part of the news process. Today, we call it *diffusion of the news*. Such transmission takes place when individuals who experience events first-hand (or are directly exposed to news stories via newspapers, television, or radio) tell others what they have learned. Their

event this way, but modern research on word-of-mouth transmission of news has shown that it is not a very reliable or accurate method of moving complex information that includes many details. However, it does work well for short messages of a dramatic nature, such as "the space shuttle blew up," "the President has been shot," or "we won the big game." The theory of the two-step flow of communication has been well-verified, and it can be summarized in the following terms:

1. The mass media present a constant flow of information about a great variety of topics of interest and importance to people in contemporary society, but most people attend only *selectively*.

2. Some people, at all levels of society, *attend more fully* to the media than others and become more knowledgeable than their families, friends, or neighbors in certain areas of media content.

3. Among those who attend more fully are people who become identified by others as *opinion leaders*—persons like themselves who are especially knowledgeable and trustworthy as sources of information and interpretation about certain areas of media content.

4. Such opinion leaders often *pass on* information they obtain from the media about specialized topics to others who have turned to them to obtain information and interpretations about those topics.

5. Thus, mass communications often move in *two stages*—from the media to opinion leaders, who attend directly to media presentations about selected topics, and then by word of mouth to other people whom the opinion leaders influence through their information and interpretations.

1. For the original statement of the theory, see Paul F. Lazarsfeld, Bernard Berelson, and Hazel Gaudet, *The People's Choice* (New York: Columbia University Press, 1948).

listeners, in turn, tell still others, and the information moves along through chains of people.

Although word-of-mouth diffusion remains important, the majority of people receive their news via the media, and it is to them that we must turn to understand the news process. It begins with the stage of gathering information from which to construct news stories.

Gathering Facts for News Stories

Reality, of course, is the ultimate source of all news. The problem is reality's mind-boggling complexity. In the words of philosopher William James, the world is a great "blooming and buzzing confusion." Thus, the news is drawn from a reality made of up an enormous variety of issues, events, conflicts, trends, and a host of other happenings. But however perplexing reality is, the first step in the news process is that it must be observed, understood, and interpreted by reporters whose task is to prepare initial comprehensible descriptions for public consumption.

To explain this initial stage of the news process, we need first to look at how reporters reduce the complex world to a limited number of *categories* so as to divide up the task of surveillance. A brief look at each of these categories will help in understanding the nature of news gathering as it is organized by professional journalists.

Monitoring Reality within a Division of Labor

One of the principal advantages of dividing up reality into categories is that it allows for an orderly division of labor in assigning reporters to cover different kinds of events. These divisions have grown out of the practical experience of journalists over the years and have become deeply established by tradition. They are shaped in part by journalists' conceptions of what will interest the public and in part by their beliefs that there are some things that the public should know about in a democratic society.

One important set of categories is the somewhat natural division of geographic *territories*.[2] Thus, facts for news stories come from events that are *local*, *regional*, *national*, or *international*. Each of these rather imprecise territorial definitions refers to different types of facts that hold different levels of interest for particular segments of the public. Some in the audience are "cosmopolitans," who follow the international and national news avidly, but who care little or nothing about what is happening locally. Others are "locals," who keep well informed about what is happening in their immediate community or region but have limited interest in national and international events.[3] These audience preferences have become well understood by professional journalists, who balance their news reports to meet the needs of these different kinds of people.

Within each territory there are additional well-understood classifications based on *specialized topics*. Typical of such topics are politics, the economy, science, education, sports, fashions, weather, labor, business, entertainment, space, crime, and so on through a long list. These play a key role in structuring the nature of the surveillance engaged in by the various media. All journalistic assignment areas, regardless of whether they are territorial or topical, are called beats.

Still another broad category has to do with the *organizations* from which facts for developing news stories are obtained. Thus, at a national level, reporters are specifically assigned to cover the White House, the Pentagon, or the Congress. Assignments at the local level may be the police department, city hall, or a local university.

These categories and subcategories represent different focuses of attention in the ongoing activities of the society, and they represent different subject matters and degrees of interest to various segments of the population. Using them as the basis for a division of labor in a news organization allows reporters to become specialized and thereby expert in one or more categories. Thus, some reporters confine themselves to international affairs, or even to a particular area of the world. Others focus exclusively on a particular kind of activity, such as fashion, science, or education. This kind of specialization helps reporters develop unique skills and perspectives in locating, understanding, and writing about the important facts that are central to given categories.

A different kind of distinction among news stories can be made, within any of the above categories, on the basis of the extension of the story *through time*. Some news happenings are one-time events. For example, at the local level, a house may burn down or an explosion occur. Such one-time events provide *spot news*—a staple of the industry. Spot stories have no history. The event occurs; it provides facts for a news story; the account is prepared; it is disseminated to the public; and that is it. In contrast, other stories can be classified as *developing news*. They occur in stages, like the acts of a play, and a series of news stories is generated as the action or situation unfolds. Eventually, however, it comes to an end and is no longer newsworthy to the same degree. An example at the national level was the highly publicized Palm Beach, Florida rape trial of William Kennedy-Smith. Extensive news coverage began early in 1991, when he was accused by the victim. A new wave of stories was generated when an arrest warrant was issued. A news feeding frenzy took place during the trial in November and early December. He was acquitted on December 12, 1991. That ended the drama, and the media moved on to a new agenda.

Another time-related category is *continuing news*. Here, there is no clear beginning or end, but rather an ongoing series of related happenings. Every time some related event occurs, stories can be generated about the ongoing process. A good example is the issue of abortion. Protests, counterprotests, court cases, and political debates about women's right to have abortions have provided a continuing theme around which stories have been developed for decades. It is a story focus that is unlikely to come to an end. Other examples of continuing news are issues related to the use of drugs, nuclear waste dumps, development versus the environment, the death penalty, and the U.S. trade deficit.

News comes in many forms. A common variety, which is the bread and butter of the industry, is spot news. This refers to stories about real events such as a fire, robbery, or airplane crash, as opposed to "pseudoevents" such as people saying things, planning things, or meeting about things. Spot news stories have no history and are neither developing nor ongoing. The reporter on the spot transmits his or her version of what happened to the newsroom, where it is processed for dissemination via some medium. (AP/Wide World Photos)

Two additional time-related categories can be seen in the distinction between hard and soft news. *Hard news* is what most ordinary people think of as news. Something actually happens on a particular day—a bank is robbed, a murder is committed, a bridge collapses. These are events that occur at a particular point in time. They are news precisely because they are today's fresh happenings, and they must be reported to the public in a timely manner. They cannot be put off until next week. That would destroy their value as fresh information.

Soft news, on the other hand, focuses on situations, people, or events that have human interest. Such stories are seldom sharply focused in time, and they can be used in the news whenever they are needed. An example is the story of a pair of male and female eagles in the Syracuse, New York zoo. Part of a breeding program to reestablish eagles in the wild, the pair finally bred and the mother incubated an egg until a little chick hatched. Then the mother died. Observers predicted disaster. But surprisingly, the male eagle took over the job of raising the newly hatched infant. The father fed the baby regularly, cleaned it, and so on, until it grew large enough to be released in the wild. The local media and the public loved hearing about these events, which provided a series of touching stories—a classic example of soft news.

How News Facts Get Distorted

To what sources do news gatherers turn to obtain facts, and what problems with each can cause a story to depart from reality? In this section, we identify a number of traditional and electronic sources and describe some of the ways facts from such sources can be unwittingly distorted.

Perhaps the source of news facts that most readily comes to mind is *direct observation*. Such "on-the-spot" covering of events or situations presumably gives the news-gatherer the fullest access to the facts. A related source, which is very traditional in news-gathering, is the *reports of witnesses*, who themselves have observed an event and who in interviews can provide eyewitness accounts. Another related source is the *expert*, who may not have observed the particular event in question, but who is knowledgeable about that general class of occurrences.

Many less personal sources are also used. One is the *news release*—a prepared handout provided to reporters by an organization (for instance, the Pentagon) to summarize the issuer's version of some event or situation. Another impersonal source of facts is the many *published documents* news-gatherers use, such as reports of business, educational, or governmental groups; technical journals; census reports; and summaries of economic trends. These can be found in libraries or in many cases via online computerized databases. Finally, *public records*, such as court, tax agency, and property ownership records, are widely used as sources of facts. Some are paper records; others are filed on magnetic tape or another computer medium.

Professional standards prevailing among news-gatherers demand a high degree of accuracy in observing and assembling facts. However, much evidence suggests that unwitting errors, biases, and misrepresentations of reality are inevitable when *any* of the above sources are used. That is not to say that reporters or others in the news industries deliberately falsify the accounts they prepare. On the contrary, the majority try very hard to be factually meticulous. Nevertheless, for reasons that we will show, misrepresentation always occurs to some degree. Furthermore, some sources pose far more problems of this nature than others.

Selectivity in observation by reporters   Contrary to what many people suppose, direct observation of an event by a reporter does not guarantee accuracy in a news story. To see how this can be, you need to understand how a reporter proceeds in trying to observe a situation in order to put together a coherent account of what happened.

Good reporters trying to understand an event that they see do exactly what all human observers do. They focus on what appears to them to be the central details or core of the matter and proceed from there. They cannot possibly notice and comprehend every detail about an occurrence, even if they see it first-hand. Like all human beings, they perceive, interpret, and recall events *selectively*. Exactly what they observe and recall will be a product of their own unique sets of needs, beliefs, attitudes, values, and other cognitive factors, such as memory schemata that inevitably bias their interpretations.

For example, to perceive and make sense out of an occurrence, a reporter must use categories of thought defined by the *language* with which he or she is familiar. To illustrate the point, imagine a reporter who has just arrived on a scene where hundreds of people are watching others milling around, shouting, and looking angry. The term that he or she uses to think about such an event is "mob." Therefore, the reporter "sees" a "mob." Suppose, then, that a handful of the individuals get mad, begin to throw stones or bottles, and even smash a few windows. A word commonly used to describe such behavior is "riot," and the reporter "sees" the behavior through perceptual glasses provided by this term. Suppose further that a few of the people in the crowd decide to run away quickly after seeing stones and bottles being thrown. When this happens, the reporter "sees" people "panic." Putting it all together, the reporter's habitual modes of perceiving and thinking about such events are shaped by the meanings we all share for words in our language. These meanings lead to the preparation of a story about "an unruly mob that participated in a riot and caused people to panic." From the reporter's point of view, those are the *facts*—he or she was there and saw it all first-hand. The additional facts that the majority of the people were merely onlookers, did not throw anything, and did not run away will not be central features in the resulting news story. The members of the media audience on receiving this account will imagine hordes of terrified people fleeing in confusion. They will not imagine that such activity was confined to a few and that the majority were just standing around.

The point is that every first-hand observer perceives and recalls a unique pattern of interpretations and recollections. First-hand reports are always based on selective perception and experience, and they cannot represent the full range of reality as it actually exists. This is not to criticize reporters—who may indeed do better than most of us in describing what happened in a given situation. Nevertheless, news reports prepared by on-the-spot observers always contain biases arising from the selective nature of perception that characterizes all human beings.

Compounded selectivity in reports of witnesses and experts But what about second-hand accounts? That is, for most events in the news, reporters are not eyewitnesses but must rely on the claims of others. Here, we have a situation of *compounded selectivity*. Reporters often try to minimize biased viewpoints by interviewing more than one witness, seeking corroboration from several sources. Yet this is really no guarantee of either accuracy or objectivity. Every actual witness puts together an account based on his or her own unique interpretations and biases. But insofar as witnesses share a similar language and culture, parallels are inevitable. These parallels do not mean that the witness reports accurately reflect reality, even though they appear to corroborate each other. They may be creating the same distortions.

An expert may seem a far better source than an untrained witness. However, if the expert did not personally see the event under discussion, his or her "facts" are but interpretations, conjectures, and assumptions based on past observations that have led to generalizations about what "usually" happens in such cases. No specific event is an exact duplication of a pattern derived from a class of events. The ancient saying *exceptio probat*

The news process begins when a reporter observes an event or interviews eyewitnesses who give accounts of what happened. Whether the reporter's story is recorded on tape or in writing, it contains distortions because all observers see and interpret sequences of events selectively. Reporters are undoubtedly quite objective, but even they perceive events selectively, couch their reports in a particular language, and depend for interpretation on their own attitudes and values. Because these factors introduce bias, the story can never be a full and totally accurate account of what really happened. (Spencer Grant/The Picture Cube)

A troublesome form of "news" comes in the form of releases or conferences carefully crafted for presentation to the press. These accounts may be designed to accomplish whatever goals are on the agenda of the individual or group who presents the information. Often reporters flock to such events and dutifully transmit the message of the sender to their audiences. Here, in a news conference, Gennifer Flowers reveals her alleged relationship to then presidential candidate Bill Clinton. (Reuters/Bettmann)

regula (the exception probes, or tests, the rule) remains true. Thus, whether the opinion of an expert about what usually takes place is a close representation of what actually took place in a particular instance is anyone's guess.

Thus, the reporter interviewing witnesses and experts exercises a second level of selectivity when assembling the results of interviews into a story. He or she may have posed the questions in a biased or leading way or misunderstood or ignored comments by the witnesses. Any witness may be reluctant to disclose some of what he or she saw or heard. The point here is that—even with the best of intentions—the more removed the reporter is from direct observation of the actual events, the less correspondence there will be between the report prepared and the true nature of what happened.

Idealized news releases   Even more troublesome are releases prepared for reporters by an organization. Often, reporters have no opportunity to see the situation or event first-hand or even to interview people who actually were participants. They go to the relevant group's information specialist, who conveniently provides them with a written or verbal account of what the group *claims* took place. Since all groups and agencies have their own agendas, and a need to protect themselves, there is every reason to suspect that such handouts contain idealized or selective accounts of what transpired, perhaps developed for public relations purposes. Again, the distance between the resulting news story and the actual events it presumably represents has increased, and correspondence with reality is an unknown.

Limitations of published reports   Today, few knowledgeable reporters go directly to a library and start rummaging through published reports from government, industry, educators, or other sources. They first undertake searches of online databases for the information they need. The thousands of databases available contain summarized or complete documents pertaining to almost any subject about which someone has published an article or written a book. Many newspapers now maintain subscriptions to such database services as Lexis/Nexis (providing the full text of thousands of news-oriented publications) or BRS (for summaries of hundreds of technical and scientific journals).

Can distortions be present in such documents? Of course they can. Indeed, they can be significant. Just because a document resides in a library or a computer file does not guarantee that it is any more accurate than one obtained from any other source. In particular, summaries and abstracts are by definition abridged versions of originals. As such, they are inherently likely to be selective.

Problems of access to public records   Few can argue, one might say, with an actual document that records a specific public event. Thus, a deed, a military discharge, a marriage certificate, or a loan or mortgage record speaks for itself. The problem with such records is not so much that they can misrepresent reality (which is possible), but that they often provide very incomplete facts. Sometimes a single document can be enough to verify a specific point exposed in a story, and thereby produce a devastating impact. At other times, a single document, or even dozens, may not reveal a great deal.

Another problem with public documents is *access*. That is particularly true with the electronic records produced by public agencies. At all levels of government, records of every kind are increasingly being kept not on paper, which is cumbersome and expensive, but as data on computer tapes. Although the federal government, as well as each of the states, has freedom of information laws, they often do not provide the access to records journalists want. Another problem with computerized records is that it takes expert computer skills and sophisticated computer hardware to get into such tapes and extract complete information. Nevertheless, as we will discuss later, such examinations can uncover the workings of public agencies in ways that were impossible with paper records.

Encoding Strategies for Packaging the News

The second major stage in the news process occurs as stories are *encoded*— transformed within news organizations into versions deemed suitable to present to the public. Modifications and repackaging of news stories occur at this stage for a variety of reasons. These include the need to emphasize certain *news values* in the story, so as to capture and hold the attention of the audience; the need to use certain *formats* for news stories, so as to organize the ways or sequences in which its facts are presented; and the need to fit the *journalistic style* preferred by a particular newspaper, magazine, or broadcast group.

Further modifications of stories arise from the needs of the news organizations themselves, the profit-oriented newspapers, magazines, and broadcasters that make up the news industry. They make the final judgments as to the organization of the daily news presentation *as a whole*. Initial stories received from reporters are placed in a context of advertising and other content, in prominent or more obscure positions in a daily newspaper, a weekly newsmagazine, or a news program for radio or television. Many kinds of judgments must be made by editors, news directors, and others in the chain of command about story size, content, balance with other reports, ethical issues, ideological slant, and general suitability for the particular medium. The end result of this processing by the organization is that the medium's news stories present versions of reality to the public that are still further removed from the actual events that happened. This does not imply a deliberate attempt to mislead the public; the distortions result from solutions to practical problems.

Making the News Interesting and Understandable

In organizing facts into a news story, a crucial requirement is that the account of what happened has to be as interesting and understandable as possible. If the audience finds it either dull or too complex, communication will fail. This requirement influences the ways in which news accounts are prepared.

Journalists have developed convenient criteria for judging the *newsworthiness* (that is, potential interest level) of stories. These criteria are called *news values*, and the account prepared must incorporate as many of them as possible. In addition, the story itself must be packaged in one of the formats that prevail in the relevant news medium, so as to make it understandable while maintaining or increasing its interest. Thus, decisions have to be

News stories must be made as interesting and understandable as possible. They must also be made to fit in the space or time slot available. Therefore, editors refine stories submitted by reporters. Some are too long, others are dull and need to be enlivened, and still others contain passages that need to be altered or deleted for reasons of ethics, potential libel suits, and so forth. When necessary changes have been made, the story is ready for presentation to the public. However, personal and organizational perspectives have introduced departures from actual reality. (Spencer Grant/The Picture Cube)

WIRE SERVICES SPREAD THE NEWS OF LINCOLN'S ASSASSINATION:
A Linchpin to American History

Lawrence Gobright, the Washington bureau chief of the Associated Press, had written his last dispatch for the night and sent it on to New York when a friend burst into his office, shouting wildly. Gobright calmed him down and began asking questions, then hurriedly sent another dispatch: "The president was shot in a theatre tonight and perhaps mortally wounded." Gobright sent five more dispatches through the night, some contradicting the ones that went before, none clear about what was happening. Not until the next morning did War Secretary Stanton send a message to the New York Associated Press that read: "Abraham Lincoln died this morning at twenty-two minutes after seven o'clock." It was April 15, 1865.[1]

Lincoln's assassination at Ford's Theater in Washington, D.C., was one of the great and tragic news stories in American history. Lincoln had successfully defeated a determined effort by the Confederacy to secede from the Union, and he had effected one of the most significant social changes in the nation's history through the Emancipation Proclamation.

Within days, news of the President's death spread across the country. Two decades earlier, word of the tragedy would have taken weeks or even months to reach citizens in the far-flung corners of the nation. In the 1830s and 1840s, news traveled by horse-drawn vehicles, steam or sailing vessels, canoes, or even by foot. In 1865, however, copper wires connected the major communities of the United States in a web of telegraph lines that ran alongside the railroads. It was this network of telegraph wires that gave rise to the Associated Press, the first of the wire services.

The Associated Press (AP) was founded in 1848 by New York newspaper publishers who found themselves spending far more money than they desired to transport foreign news between northern U.S. ports, where it arrived in cannisters carried by boat from Europe and New York City. Since each paper eventually got the same news, there was little competitive advantage to be had in paying top dollar for it, so the publishers met and agreed to share among themselves the cost of transmission. Thus was AP born.

The organization was almost immediately transformed into a shared system linked by the telegraph,

made about the overall story strategy that will be used. Generally, as described in this section, these decisions further shape the way in which stories of events are encoded. As these choices are made, they result in quite different versions of reality.

Journalism's traditional news values   Both print and broadcast journalists use a number of considerations to judge the general newsworthiness of a story. These criteria have been derived over a long period and represent a kind of historically distilled wisdom as to what the public wants to read, hear about, or view in news presentations. Thus, these news values are of considerable importance to reporters when they initially decide what is worth covering and when they prepare their initial accounts of what happened. News values also guide editors and news directors in making final decisions about what to print or put on the air.

At least seven major criteria can be applied in assessing the attractiveness of a particular story as a candidate for presentation to the public. Few stories

and shortly afterward the Associated Press began to transmit domestic news on the wires as well as foreign. As the association grew in number and reach, its members not only shared costs but also pooled and exchanged news. Competing papers that were not members of the Associated Press could not gain access to its news, giving AP newspapers a virtual monopoly in the towns they served.

In 1907 Edward Scripps, who owned a large chain of afternoon newspapers and could not gain membership in AP, started his own news service, the United Press Association. In 1958, it merged with William Randolph Hearst's International News Service to become United Press International (UPI). As a result of its 1991 declaration of bankruptcy, UPI was purchased by owners in Saudi Arabia in 1992, but it continues its operations without significant change. Though there are many news services in the United States today, none compare in their size and reach to UPI and AP.[2]

Most American daily newspapers, even large ones, rely for a substantial portion of their news, and especially their foreign news, on AP or UPI. The news services are often the first to carry a story—AP is powerful enough to insist that all but its largest members publish their stories "on the wire" before running them in their own papers—and they have broken some of the great stories of American and world history. Almost one hundred years after AP sent news of Lincoln's death to a horrified nation, UPI was the first to perform a similarly grim task on November 22, 1963, in telling the world of John F. Kennedy's assassination in Dallas.

Because so many news organizations rely on AP or UPI, when one of the news services gets a story wrong, the consequences of its error can be particularly far-reaching or, at the least, embarrassing. Both AP and UPI have frightening gaffes in their portfolios, but none surpasses the error the United Press Association made in 1918 when it prematurely ended World War I. The United Press general manager in Brest, Germany, mistakenly cabled the United States that the Germans had surrendered, a message that somehow escaped the attention of American military censors. New York City erupted in riotous celebration on November 7, 1918, four days before the war actually ended.

1. Oliver Gramling, *AP: The Story of News* (New York: Farrar and Rinehart, 1940). pp. 52–59.
2. Jonathan Fenby, *The International News Services* (New York: Shocken Books, 1986).

fit all. And, of course, some stories may be of great importance even if they fulfill none. Nevertheless, in a practical sense, the news values listed below provide important guidelines for judging the newsworthiness of any particular story:

1. *Impact.* This criterion refers to the number of people whose lives will be influenced in some way by the subject of the story. For example, if workers in a local bakery decide to strike, it may have only a minor impact on the majority of the community. Some people may be inconvenienced, but most will be little affected. However, if postal workers go on strike, everyone is affected because no one will get mail. Thus, a story about a bakery strike will have less impact than one about a postal strike and will be less newsworthy.

2. *Timeliness.* One of the most important features of news is that it should be presented to the public while it is fresh. News that is "stale" has less appeal. Thus, stories of recent events have higher news value than those

about earlier happenings. Of particular value are stories brought to the public ahead of the competition. An older term for such a story is "scoop." Journalists like to claim, "You read it (or heard it, or viewed it) here first."

3. *Prominence*. Stories about people who are in the public eye have much higher news value than those about obscure people, even if the occurrences are the same. Thus, a story about a well-known sports star who has a major problem would be more newsworthy than one about some unknown individual who had a similar difficulty. An example in recent years was the intense attention paid to Magic Johnson, the professional basketball player who contracted the AIDS virus. If he had been an ordinary citizen, his tragic condition would not have commanded the attention of the national news media.

4. *Proximity*. Stories about events and situations in one's home community are more newsworthy than events that take place far away. A rather grim hypothetical example often used by journalists to illustrate the point is to equate the news value of various numbers of deaths at various distances. If a thousand people drown in a flood in a faraway country, the story has about the same news value as one describing how a hundred drowned in a distant part of the United States. That, in turn, has about the same news value as a story concerning ten flood victims within the state. And finally, a story about those ten has about the same value as one describing a flood that drowns a single person in the local community.

5. *Bizarreness*. An example that illustrates this criterion well is the oft-quoted definition of news attributed to John B. Bogart, who was the city editor of the *Sun* in New York during the 1880s: "When a dog bites a man," Bogart is purported to have said, "that's not news, because it happens so often. But if a man bites a dog, that is news." In any case, odd or peculiar events have always seemed more newsworthy than those of a routine nature. For that reason, the news media can usually be counted on to give space or time to sightings of Bigfoot or UFOs or to disappearances of ships or planes in the Bermuda Triangle.

6. *Conflict*. The rule here is that harmony is dull, but strife is newsworthy. Stories that describe such events as messy divorces or child custody battles, rebellions, personal vendettas, and other kinds of clashes are high in news value. Thus, what transpired at a meeting of an organization devoted to promoting lasting peace might make dull news, unless a fistfight broke out—that would make a good story.

7. *Currency*. More value is attributed to stories pertaining to issues or topics that are in the spotlight of public concern than to those about which people care less. Thus, at the beginning of the 1990s, the Gulf War with Iraq, the savings and loan crisis, and Senate confirmation hearings on Clarence Thomas were high on the public's agenda. Stories related to those topics had high value. They were replaced with an intense preoccupation with the Los Angeles riots, the Miami hurricane, and the presidential election. Those too were replaced with Somalia, Bosnia, and more current concerns in the ever-changing news agenda.

Essentially, then, the news industry greatly prefers stories that journalists' accumulated wisdom identifies as those in which the public will be most interested. The cost of using such criteria to define newsworthiness is that many stories will be ignored that are in fact truly significant from other points of view. For example, discoveries by scientific researchers may be of historical importance, contribute to betterment of the human condition, or advance the frontiers of knowledge. However, they may be judged as dull. If so, they are likely to be found in the back pages or in the last part of the newscast (if they appear at all).

Story organization and format By tradition, the general format for a well-written newspaper story is that it tells *who* did *what*, *where*, *when*, and *why*. These "five w's" set forth the essential features of any good news story, and they are the basic format that every beginning journalism student learns. In large part, they determine the way in which working print journalists package most of their stories. This plan for story organization is also used in broadcast journalism. However, the requirements of radio, and especially television, are quite different from those of print and allow enhancements to the standard print format.

A second traditional way in which news stories are organized is the so-called *inverted pyramid*. It too has long been used by all of the news media, but it is especially relevant to newspaper stories. The basic idea is that the most important ideas should appear first in the story. Journalists learned early that many people read only the headlines. Others read the lead (beginning) sentence, or perhaps the first paragraph or two, and then go on to the next story. Thus, the important ideas need to be set forth at the beginning, and overall the account should both be interesting and make few intellectual demands. Journalists have little confidence in the willingness of the average citizen to linger over complex details or sophisticated analyses. Many maintain that in writing stories they always use the KISS system (keep it simple, stupid).

Broadcast journalists, of course, must also use formats. Radio and television news stories often use the criteria of newsworthiness, the five w's, and the inverted pyramid. However, a radio or TV newscast has much greater flexibility and can use many variations to maintain audience interest. For example, the simplest format for a TV newscast is the *word story*, in which the anchorperson is shown behind a desk telling what happened. A variant is to provide a graphic that appears in the upper corner of the screen, with an identifying phrase keyed to the story. Another TV format is the *VOT* (voice-over tape), in which the viewer first sees the anchorperson but is then switched to a videotape with the anchor's voice over the ongoing picture. Still another format is the *stand-up*, in which the anchor switches to a reporter in the field who makes comments at the scene. The *stand-up with package* is similar, with the reporter interviewing someone at the scene. Several versions of such formats are regularly used in producing TV news in an effort to create audience interest and to provide richer information.

Distinctive Styles of Journalism

A particular set of facts can be combined into a news story in a variety of ways. That is, stories can be written in a number of different general styles and still contain essentially the same basic information. A considerable number of *journalistic styles* have emerged over the years. Some are far more widely used than others, but each has had its period of popularity and has left its mark on the contemporary news industry.

Sensational journalism   This style characterized the press from the 1880s through the 1920s. It stressed shocking details, bizarre events, and sometimes appalling transgressions of the social norms. The newspapers of the time thrived on implications of scandal and sin in high places. For example, if a murder had been committed, the crime was described with special attention to the appearance of the corpse, the look of the blood, suggestions of illicit sex, and the insidious nature of the killer. The sensational style is alive and well in tabloids such as the *National Enquirer* and on TV shows such as "A Current Affair," "Hard Copy," and others.

Objective journalism   Sensationalism gave way to objectivity, which generally prevailed until about mid-century. In 1950, Alan Barth of the *Washington Post* wrote with pride, "The tradition of objectivity is one of the principal glories of American journalism."[4] In reality, that opinion was not universally held; as an examination of the trade journals of the 1940s and 1950s quickly shows, objectivity had been under fire for generations. But for a few years, there was almost complete consensus among American journalists and consumers that objectivity was a vast improvement over the sensational journalism that characterized the earlier press.

Generally speaking, objectivity as a style has traditionally been characterized by three aims:

1. separating fact from opinion,
2. presenting an emotionally detached view of the news, and
3. striving for fairness and balance, giving both sides an opportunity to reply in a way that provides full information to the audience.

By world standards, American reporters had long been and still are very objective. For decades, they have tried hard to separate fact and opinion, keeping factual accounts in the news columns and opinions on the editorial page. But, during the 1960s, an increasing number of critics denied that this could be done, claiming that no human being is capable of complete objectivity. Anchorman Dan Rather even said that objectivity is an impossible goal and urged reporters to adopt fairness as their standard instead.

The challenge to objectivity occurred in part because critics had come to feel that American journalism was lifeless—unemotional and incapable of dealing with great social problems. There is much to be said for this view. For example, during the first half of the century, the press had virtually ignored the predicament of blacks, other minorities, and the poor and the rising tide of frustration over being denied civil rights. In addition, the press in the 1960s trumpeted its virtues energetically enough to help reopen old debates. Many American journalists acted as if objectivity were an established characteristic rather than a yet-to-be-achieved ideal. The typical response to those who said coverage was unfair or inadequate was, "We just report the news." This claim that the press was objective seemed to many to be a rather arrogant refusal to face complaints, and it often enraged critics.

Thus, the press was criticized during the 1960s with a vigor it had not encountered before. In this fate, it had much company; during the same period, most American institutions were challenged by widespread distrust and a search for new approaches. The outcome was that several alternative styles for presenting news stories emerged, and although they did not revolutionize the press, they have influenced contemporary journalism. To understand how, we can examine a few of these alternatives more closely. They include the *new journalism*, the *advocacy style*, and *precision journalism*. Today, the objective approach is still dominant. These newer styles are used to some extent in both the print and broadcast media. However, government regulation makes most of them more difficult to implement in broadcasting.

The new journalism   This style known as the *new journalism* was never of great concern to the public, but it did alter the reigning definitions of news and writing forms within the profession. The first stirrings of this style came from three sources: journalists on newspapers and magazines who felt restricted by the traditional formats such as the inverted pyramid; literary figures, especially novelists, who wanted to say something in a direct way about the nation's discontents; and broadcast journalists eager to explore less conventional sources and language.

Journalists looking for change felt that traditional procedures were not effectively capturing the essence of the great social movements of the day or the changes in life-style. They thought that both the customary reliance on official sources (mainly public officials) and the conventional avoidance of rich description prevented them from capturing the tone of the great changes taking place during the 1960s. As a result, they maintained, it was impossible to give the public the full story of what was happening. For example, the counterculture, which influenced millions of young people during the period, was not presented fully in newspapers and newscasts because it was not tied to authoritative sources. The result was that several young writers began experimenting with new techniques, including:

1. *Scene setting*. The new journalists used many descriptive adjectives to give the reader a sense of being on the scene.
2. *Extended dialogue*. Instead of using a few well-honed quotations, the new journalists used long stretches of dialogue to capture the essence of a person's language.
3. *Point of view*. Rather than trying to be detached and objective, the new journalists sometimes allowed the attitudes or values of their sources to dominate their stories.

4. *Interior monologue*. The thoughts of the people who were the news sources, as they reported them to the journalist, might be included.

5. *Composite characters*. Instead of quoting all sources by name, the new journalists sometimes created a composite character who brought together the characteristics of several people and stood for, say, the average prostitute or police officer.

All of these devices are old tools of fiction writers. The new journalists claimed that these methods allowed them to offer a richer and truer portrait than the traditional news styles permitted. These new journalists were not necessarily political activists; they wanted to observe and report on manners and morals in an exciting way instead of merely quoting official sources. The methods of fiction writers helped them do so.

The new journalism also touched broadcasting. Today, National Public Radio's "All Things Considered" uses creative news-gathering techniques with a literary flair, sometimes re-creating the testimony of news sources with background noises and acting out their roles. Television documentaries, too, sometimes use new journalism techniques. For example, even before the new journalism appeared in magazines, the style was evident in Charles Kuralt's poetic or whimsical interviews with little-known people in out-of-the-way places.

Despite controversy and criticism, the new journalism continues to influence the conventions of the media generally. By the 1980s, the techniques of this style were commonplace in magazines; nonfiction novels were popular; and news writing—for newspapers and broadcasting—was less rigid. For the most part, however, the influence of the new journalism has been not overwhelming or revolutionary but subtle and indirect.

The advocacy style   Another alternative to objectivity is the *advocacy style*. Here, the reporter and the story identify with and advocate—that is, try to promote—a cause or position. Unlike editorial writing, advocacy journalism appears in news columns and is not a simple statement of opinion. In a sense, it is a kind of hybrid news story that promotes a particular point of view. Thus, it departs from both traditional journalism and investigative reporting, which we discuss in a later section.

Advocacy journalism appears mostly in magazines, although a few well-known broadcast journalists, such as Geraldo Rivera, are unabashed advocates, doing stories with no pretense of balance or fairness. Rivera, a controversial figure, is widely known for his exposés of such situations as mental hospital conditions, inner-city corruption, and negligence toward the poor and minorities. Advocacy journalists see themselves as torchbearers for justice and pursue their mission knowing that plenty of people are promoting an opposite point of view. Critics see them as undisciplined mouthpieces for only one side of an issue. Advocacy reporting is not widely practiced, and most studies of journalists show that it is not particularly admired in the field.

Precision journalism   A very different journalistic style that is becoming increasingly important is *precision journalism*. Essentially, it is a way of reporting and writing that makes use of some of the methods of the social sciences to gather and analyze quantitative information for the purposes of preparing news stories. It takes two forms: in *active* precision journalism, reporters conduct their own surveys or other research projects; in *reactive* precision journalism, they use reports already assembled by government agencies, universities, or private firms and develop stories around the data the reports provide.

Although precision journalism is not the same as scientific research, its basic goal is to present to the public understandable and accurate analyses based on quantitative information relevant to significant issues that are in the news. For example, traditional journalists might interview people selected casually or conveniently so as to portray the opinions of "people in the street" concerning a forthcoming bond issue to build a new convention center. In contrast, the precision journalist would interview a sample of citizens, selected according to the rules of scientific sampling, so as to obtain a more representative summary of the views shared in the community.

Precision journalism sometimes makes extensive use of tables and graphs, often supplemented by interviews that serve as examples. It does not replace traditional journalism; it simply makes the news more accurate where quantitative information is important. Reporters using this style must have training in basic methods of the social sciences, including the use of statistical tests and computer data processing. Precision journalism is far more ambitious than computer-assisted reporting (mentioned earlier), which is, in fact, *passive* precision journalism.

Social and Cultural Influences on Decisions in News Organizations

Two sets of social and cultural factors play a significant role in shaping decisions as to what is finally transmitted to the public after specific news stories are passed from reporters to editors and news directors. First, influences arise from the *social organization of newsrooms*. This includes a number of particular editorial and production roles within the teams that decide news policy, selecting the final assortment of stories that will make up the paper or the newscast. The second set of influences is broader, consisting of the *cultural constraints* on news organizations posed by the basic nature of private enterprise itself, as defined within American society.

Influences of the social organization of the newsroom Each news medium—newspapers, magazines, radio, or television—has a pattern of social organization. At the top are those that own the organization as a business enterprise. (We have already reviewed patterns of ownership among the major media involved in news in Chapters 3, 4, 6, and 7.) The owners or their corporate representatives at the top seldom exert direct control over specific news stories, but they set broad guidelines as to which styles of journalism are to be emphasized and where the organization will locate itself along a liberal to conservative continuum.

Managers make up a second stratum. Upper-level managers are generally sensitive to the orientations of the owners. Theirs is the task of running the organization on a day-to-day basis, setting its more specific operating policies and making certain that it achieves its goals. Below them are the middle managers—editors, directors, and producers whose daily task it is to assemble the content of the newspaper, get the magazine ready for the printer, or produce the news program in final form for broadcasting.

News stories flow to the newsroom from reporters, stringers, freelancers, and the "wires." Here they are reviewed and reshaped by this hierarchy of editors and managers. At the core of this reshaping is the fact that so much is happening in the world, the nation, the state, and the local area that there is simply not enough time or space to bring it all to the attention of the public. In producing the daily newspaper, for example, editors must first accommodate the various ads and announcements that provide financial support. If they did not, the paper would soon go broke. Certain other material that is not news must also appear in the daily paper, including weather reports, stock market quotations, editorials, the crossword puzzle, the comics, and so on. As noted in Chapter 3, the space that is left—generally about 20 percent of the paper—is called the *news hole*, and it is into that space that the news of the day must be fit. Since there is always more news than space, only two kinds of decisions can be made to fit the news into the hole: to drop or to shrink stories. The editor, often with a heavy hand, removes details that seem expendable—and again the gap between reality and its description in the news story widens.

To deal with the excessive number of stories that flow into the newsroom via AP, UPI, etc., wire editors read all the stories that accumulate up to a particular time and select ones they view as important and suitable. Once again, through a process of selection, the gap widens between what happened in the "world outside" and what is reported in the newspaper.

In the TV or radio news organization, a similar process takes place. The 30 minutes allowed for the newscast includes time that must be set aside for introductory and closing material, the various commercials that support the program, and mandatory features such as weather and reports on the stock market. The time left can be used for presentation of the news. After the amount of time left over is identified, the editing process begins. News directors review the stories prepared by reporters and those received from network sources. They select the ones to be included and complete the process of fitting the material into the available time. Editors review taped reports, shorten scenes, drop details, and sometimes cut entire stories. The end result is the station's version of what happened today. It may or may not be close to what actually took place. Chances are that it is not.

These processes of selection and elimination of details or even entire stories are called *gatekeeping*. It is a complex process that is a central part of all news editing and production systems. Individuals at different positions—editors, news directors, and others—have to make decisions about including or excluding material from news presentations.[5] Obviously, gatekeeping significantly influences the selective construction of the reality that is reported by the press.

Consequences of the profit motive on news decisions Real people invest real dollars in newspapers, magazines, and broadcast stations or networks. Logically enough, they expect to make real profits. What critics protest is not so much the idea that media owners make a return on investment, but what the owners do to maximize their profits. However, Americans value a profit-driven market economy—enough to avidly support its development in many parts of the world. There is no denying that the profit motive will continue to exert powerful influences on what the public receives as news.

Nowhere is the problem better illustrated than in the case of network TV news. A decade ago, news-gathering and broadcasting were supported by all of the other programming offered by the networks. The news programs themselves were not expected to show a profit. Their ratings were not as high as those of entertainment programming, and advertisers did not flock to news programs as a context for their commercials. Subsidizing of the news was seen as occurring similarly to the way it is done in newspapers. The news part of the paper is not expected to operate profitably on its own. The revenues from the newspaper as a whole provide funding for news gathering, editorial functions, printing, and so on.

However, when cable and the VCR began to eat into audience shares for network television, both corporate leadership and news policies changed significantly. The new bosses declared that the news had to earn its own keep. It had to develop ways of offering the news that would increase ratings so as to make news broadcasts more attractive to advertisers. Under these new policies, the networks pared news teams down sharply to cut costs. Even cameras were automated to save labor costs (Tom Brokaw's three cameras at NBC—privately called "Curly," "Larry," and "Moe" after the "Three Stooges"—are computer-operated; the number of human operators was reduced).

But far more important were corporate decisions to define news program content in different ways. News programs had to be more fun to watch, so as to bring in more viewers. Less funding was to be available for such frills as investigative reporting, on-the-spot coverage, camera teams in foreign lands, and opinion and analysis. Instead, new kinds of programming were designed, sometimes even staging or re-creating news events. For example, when NBC News initiated a series called "Bad Girls," critics called it lurid sensationalism. The same group came up with "Women Behind Bars" and a kind of syndicated tabloid called "A Current Affair," which is openly oriented toward sexual content. CBS News introduced "Saturday Night with Connie Chung," in which actors were hired to play parts. ABC did not go to such lengths, but it did produce "Prime Time Live," in which Diane Sawyer and Sam Donaldson provided entertaining interviews with interesting people. The relationship of such programs to news in a traditional sense is not clear. Indeed, critics use the phrase "trivialization of the news" to describe such programming.

Out of these transformations of news content came a new concept, *info-tainment*—a merging of information and entertainment. Its presence led to new criteria for gatekeeping. From all that is available to news directors and

THE NEWS DISTORTION THEORY OF THE PRESS

In 1922, Walter Lippmann, a journalism scholar, published his now classic work, *Public Opinion*. He developed the thesis that there are often significant differences between the descriptions of events and situations found in newspapers (the only form of the press at the time) and the meanings for those events that were reconstructed by the people who read about them.

Lippmann provided numerous examples of the great gap between the beliefs people entertain about the world and the factual features of that world. He pointed to the outbreak of World War I in Europe (which was a recent situation at the time) and noted that for weeks after that terrible conflict erupted, many people had no idea that it was going on. (The press operated at a much slower pace at that time than it does today with worldwide satellite coverage.) They continued their lives and businesses as

though they were still in peacetime. Later, after the press falsely reported that an armistice had been signed four days before it actually was, people were rejoicing that the war had ended. Meanwhile, the soldiers on both sides continued to fight. Significant numbers of men died on the battlefield while other people at home were celebrating, under the false belief, obtained from the press, that the terrible conflict had stopped. Thus, those who were rejoicing had erroneous beliefs about what constituted reality.

The proper role of the press, said Lippmann, was to create "pictures in our heads of the world outside." But too frequently, he maintained, the process functioned poorly and the pictures presented by the press were false, creating a "pseudo-environment." Inevitably, then, the meanings and understandings people derived from press reports about the events of the world were also false. As a consequence, those false

editors, many selections appear to be made for their entertainment value, rather than because of their newsworthiness or their essential importance to the society.

To a greater or lesser degree, pressures toward trivialization exist in all of the news media, but it is a special problem for the networks. If the emphasis on infotainment becomes the new TV standard—although it has not happened yet—most thoughtful analysts feel that the nation will have been poorly served. Indeed, the reasons for protecting the TV news media with the First Amendment and with a body of shield laws and other legislation unique to this category of business will no longer exist.

Contrasting Conceptions of the Nature and Functions of News
Individual newspapers and broadcasters vary in how they resolve the conflict between the obligation to inform the public fully and the need to be profitable. The choices involved can be very well illustrated by comparing two almost completely opposite prevailing conceptions of the nature and functions of news. These are the *marketing approach,* which avidly pursues the goal of maximizing profits by selling news as a product and sharply limiting public service, and the *adversarial approach*, which sees news as infor-

beliefs often led to behavior by the public that was inappropriate or even tragic in its consequences.[1]

Strictly speaking, Lippmann's *news distortion theory of the press* pertains to the newspapers of his time. However, it is an early version of more contemporary theories that explain the role of all of the mass media in presenting "social constructions of reality" to the public, that is, meanings for the world, which people then use as guides to action. In that sense, the theory is as modern as today's network newscast. Lippmann never put forth his theory as a set of systematic propositions. However, the basic ideas can be modernized somewhat and summarized in the following terms as the news distortion theory of the press:

1. The press continuously monitors events and situations occurring in the physical and social environment to identify potential news stories.

2. To prepare news reports, the press selects from those events and situations those that news personnel believe will be of importance or interest to the populations that they serve.

3. Many factors beyond its control (time, technology, money, or opportunity) limit the ability of the press to investigate, describe, and transmit full details of all events and situations that come to its attention.

4. Because of these factors, news reports are often characterized by selectivity, omissions, and distortions in spite of efforts by the press to be objective, fair, and factual.

5. Thus, when audiences construct their own meanings of news reports ("pictures in their heads") they often have limited correspondence with the facts of reality ("the world outside"), leading people to behave in ways unrelated to the original events and situations.

1. Walter Lippmann, *Public Opinion* (New York: Macmillan, 1922).

mation needed by the public and which emphasizes the watchdog role of the press—often at the expense of profits. These sharply contrasting strategies represent two very different paths the nation's press may follow in carrying out its surveillance function in the future.

The Marketing Approach: News as a Product to Sell

A news organization that uses the *marketing approach* devotes considerable resources to the task of understanding what the audience wants to find in a news medium. Then, it makes certain that it serves those interests. The idea is to market the product—that is, the news—in much the same way as any other commercial commodity, such as beer, soap, or breakfast cereal, is marketed.

This approach begins with extensive market research that assembles statistical data on the interests, media habits, and concerns of the audience. These data are then used as guidelines in determining what material will be offered and, especially, in what manner. Thus, both the content of news stories and the style in which they are offered to the public are selected on the basis of research findings that define what the audience wants most.

In recent years, some news media have relied heavily on the "marketing approach." News is regarded as a product to sell, like any other commodity. Extensive research is conducted to determine what subscribers or audiences want to read or hear about. Here editors choose attention-grabbing photos to accompany stories. Although this strategy may not achieve the goal of a well-informed public, it does ensure that the medium will have audience appeal and improves its chances of making a profit. (© Jeff Albertson/The Picture Cube)

Of course, newspaper editors and publishers for decades have been concerned with what will and will not sell papers. The marketing approach, however, takes this criterion a giant step further. News organizations using this strategy invest a great deal of time and money to find out what the public wants to read about and what formats and styles they like best. The organizations then apply the answers methodically to shape their products. Thus, the marketing approach institutionalizes concern about appealing to the audience so as to enhance revenues, and it gives this concern top priority in the process of selecting and encoding the news.

The marketing approach is not really a new idea. For many years, it was used heavily by broadcasters. Newspapers were actually slow to adopt methods that broadcast stations had used routinely to calibrate their product to their audience. For example, the marketing approach has been applied to TV news almost from its beginning, with changes in format and style often made to attract a larger audience. For years, print journalists often treated this practice with contempt. But in the early 1970s, managers and owners of metropolitan daily newspapers were appalled by their declining circulations per household. There seemed to be many causes: Competition from television, the growth of the suburbs, new life-styles, and a lack of relevance in the papers were all blamed. The newspapers responded with market research designed to diagnose the "ills" causing the decline. Soon print journalists had their own "news doctors."

To end declines in newspaper circulation, the market researchers prescribed *change*, advising the newspapers to add new sections on topics such as life-styles, entertainment, gardening, and housing—sections that help readers "use" their communities and their environment. These new sections are hardly "news." They are edited and written to arouse audience interest and approval—and thus are really a form of infotainment. In some ways, they represent extended and repackaged coverage of topics that have always been in the paper. For example, many newspapers covered real estate for years, but as a result of the marketing approach, some renamed the section "Shelter" or "Home" and began to treat the topic from the consumer's point of view—adding, for example, very personal stories about how to find an apartment or remodel a house. Similarly, in their life-style sections, newspapers print advice from "experts" on how people can solve their everyday problems—from how to get rid of stubborn stains to how to deal with a sulky child or a spouse's infidelity.

The best-known example of a newspaper that relies heavily on the marketing approach is the nationally circulated *USA Today*, which was designed on the basis of market research and which continues to make heavy use of research findings that indicate audience interests. *USA Today* argues that it gives its readers what they want, in both content and packaging, including the use of color, new styles of graphic presentation, and brevity (some say superficiality) in writing.

Does the marketing approach serve readers better, or does it pander to the lowest tastes? Philip Meyer, a leader in the precision journalism movement, suggested that it helps newspapers obtain and respond to feedback from their audiences and thus to communicate with them more effectively.[6] Others maintain that it leads to trivialization of the news, especially in broadcasting. There seems to be more importance attached to the hairstyles of anchorpeople than to the substance of the stories. Perhaps it is too early to predict the marketing approach's lasting effects. If the approach becomes increasingly commonplace, however, the definition of news is likely to shift further away from an emphasis on reports on public affairs and specific events, moving instead toward infotainment-type material that will gratify the audience.

The Adversarial Approach: The Press as Watchdog of the Public Interest

The role of the press as an adversary of government is the one most honored in the traditions of journalism. In this capacity the press has sometimes been called the "Fourth Estate." Thomas Carlyle (1795–1881) attributed the phrase to Edmund Burke (1729–1797), who called the reporters' gallery in the English Parliament "a Fourth Estate more important by far" than the other three estates of Parliament—the lords, bishops, and commons.

It was because the right to speak out freely acted as a check on government, holding it accountable, that the founders of this nation nurtured the principles of freedom of speech and protection of the right to public dissent. Today, the adversarial approach makes a critical contribution to society by increasing accountability and by exposing unsatisfactory conditions in both government and the private sector.

Generally, adversarial journalism has a long tradition and a clear future in the print media. However, it is also found in the world of broadcasting, and one of the brightest spots of television is the weekly CBS News program "60 Minutes." It takes on targets from faith healers to public officials, coming down hard on consumer fraud and corruption, and vividly presenting the conflicting statements of its sources. That for years it has often been number one in the Sunday evening ratings argues against the idea that the public wants merely to be entertained. The continuing popularity of "60 Minutes" shows that people are very interested in having the press serve its traditional role as watchdog of the public interest. That fact seems to have escaped the notice of media managers who are leading the movement toward infotainment.

Traditional investigative reporting   Central to the adversarial approach is *investigative reporting*. This is a kind of news-gathering in which the reporter probes deeply into a situation and assembles the evidence that discloses whether or not there is something unusual, unethical, illegal, or even outrageous going on. The fact-gathering may be done by a single reporter or a team of individuals working together, but the decision to undertake such an investigation is made by editors who must provide the financial support and be ready to disclose and defend what is uncovered.[7]

The professional organization Investigative Reporters and Editors (IRE) defines such reporting in the following terms:

> It is reporting, through one's own work product and initiative, matters of importance which some persons or organizations wish to keep secret. The three basic elements are that the investigation [is] the work of the reporter, not the report of an investigation made by someone else; that the subject of the story involves something of reasonable importance to the reader or viewer; and that others are attempting to hide these matters from the public.[8]

Investigative reporting started in the nineteenth century. Some believe the first such investigation was conducted in the 1840s by James Gordon Bennett, the energetic publisher of the *New York Herald*. Dissatisfied with the usual stories of reporters covering the courts, he sought a way to provide more interesting accounts of serious crimes. He chose the occasion of the spectacular murder of a young prostitute. He personally went to the "fancy house" where she worked, interviewed the "madam," poked through the victim's personal papers, and even examined the unfortunate girl's remains. The resulting story, rich in details about the place and the people involved, made very interesting reading.

Investigative reporting reached dramatic heights late in the nineteenth century. An adventurous young woman writing under the name Nellie Bly (her real name was Elizabeth Cochrane) became famous as a result of her investigative report on an insane asylum on Blackwell's Island, in New York. In an elaborate scheme, she posed as a mentally ill person and was committed to the asylum. There, continuing the deception, she saw first-hand how patients were treated. The doctors and staff had no idea she was a reporter, and she received very bad treatment for about ten days. Fortunately, she had prearranged with her newspaper, Joseph Pulitzer's *New York World*, that it would extricate her. It did so, and her exposé of conditions in the hospital gained worldwide attention.[9]

Early in this century, the journalists of the muckraking era investigated many private and governmental institutions (see Chapter 4). They uncovered and exposed the corruption, abuse, and crime that characterized both private industry and government at the time. The contribution of the muckrakers to American society was far more than just interesting reading matter. Their exposés led to reform and legislation that still affect us today.[10]

An extraordinary example of investigative reporting from the 1970s was disclosures concerning the Watergate scandal involving the Nixon administration. Beginning in mid-1972 and continuing through 1973, the series of stories was developed by investigative reporters Carl Bernstein and Robert Woodward of the *Washington Post*. Their revelations dominated U.S. news media for months, exposing a conspiracy by the White House staff, the CIA, and others to cover up a number of covert illegal activities carried out during the 1972 presidential election by White House aids. The ensuing congressional investigation eventually implicated President Nixon and led to his resignation.

Today, investigative reporting seems to be on the increase in the American press. Although such reporting is expensive, new sources of information and new tools of analysis have become available. Advances in the use of computers for both data storage and information recovery are permitting reporters to develop stories based on a broader body of information than

During the last century, investigative journalism was established as an important function of the American press. One of the pioneers of this tradition was Elizabeth Cochrane, who wrote under the byline of "Nellie Bly." In the 1870s and 1880s, she reported on many deplorable conditions that prevailed among poor working women and other disadvantaged groups. Her greatest investigative work was the exposure of the dreadful conditions that existed in an insane asylum on Blackwell's Island in New York. (The Bettmann Archive)

ever before. Computers are not replacing old-fashioned "shoe-leather" investigations, but they are powerful new tools that are adding a unique dimension to investigative reporting.

Using online information retrieval services We have already mentioned two computer-based technological changes that together are altering the news-gathering process generally and investigative reporting in particular. Online data services, operated by commercial vendors, are especially valuable for obtaining background material for the development of a story or an investigation. And for those who master the essential computer skills, the shift from paper files to computerized electronic public records opens remarkable opportunities for investigating the detailed operations of government agencies. However, for those who lack such skills, this change is increasingly blocking access to what such agencies are doing.

Starting in the 1970s, a few online information services became available. At first, they were used mainly for bibliographic retrieval. That is, a user could find out from a database who had published what in, say, the scientific journals. Today, the thousands of different databases to which access can be obtained for fees contain information ranging from stock market prices and airline schedules to complete files of scientific articles on every conceivable topic. With a desktop computer and a modem permitting telephone access to large mainframe computers at remote sites, a user can retrieve vast amounts of information on virtually any subject.

CAIR: Computer-assisted investigative reporting At the national, state, and even local levels, agencies have been moving away from the preparation and maintenance of vast files of paper toward the use of more efficient electronic storage of records on magnetic tape.[11] This trend actually began during the 1950s, but it was largely ignored by journalists. They had no idea how such records could be examined, or indeed if they legally could be examined even if one knew how. It was not even clear why one might want to undertake such an analysis. During the next decade, Congress passed the Freedom of Information Act (FOIA), which supposedly made almost all government records available for inspection by the public. It was not clear at first whether FOIA also applied to electronic records. As it turned out, it took many court battles before interested citizens could have access to government computer tapes. Agencies preferred to keep their operations from public scrutiny. (Some frustrated would-be users call FOIA the "Official Secrets Act.") However, during the late 1960s and early 1970s, a few pioneering newspapers, such as the *Miami Herald* and the *New York Times*, began to examine local government records using computers to check up on particular agencies and to generate news stories. These and other pioneers made disclosures where irregularities were found. This was the beginnings of *CAIR*, or *computer-assisted investigative reporting*.

The analysis of computerized records is increasingly paying off for those who can access them. Sometimes it is not all that difficult. An oft-quoted example that illustrates the advantages of the procedure is the "School Bus

The tradition of investigative reporting remains one of the most honored in contemporary journalism. It is central to the adversarial approach to news-gathering and to the watchdog function of the press. Investigative reporters often disclose unethical, or even illegal, conduct by individuals, private groups, or public agencies. In recent years, governments have turned to computerized records, which are supposed to be open to public inspection, according to freedom of information laws. A developing journalistic field is computer-assisted investigative reporting (CAIR), in which computers and statistical software are used to analyze the accumulated records of government agencies. (Michael Davis photo/Syracuse New Times)

Driver" story developed in 1985 by reporters Elliot Jaspin and Maria Johnson of the *Providence Journal-Bulletin* (in Rhode Island). Here is what happened: A series of tragic deaths of children in school bus accidents in Rhode Island prompted the newspaper to investigate to find the causes. Jaspin and Johnson began by getting a list of the several hundred school bus drivers in the state. Each had been screened by local authorities who had certified that he or she was a good and moral person with a safe driving record. Wondering if that were true, the reporters obtained the state's tapes of traffic offenses for the previous three years. They matched the bus drivers' names against those on tape and found that a number of school bus drivers actually had dreadful records. Some had driven under the influence of alcohol or drugs; others had invalid licenses, or none at all; some had been in serious accidents more than once. This led the now very suspicious reporters to get the court records of felony trials from the state and again compare names. They found that a number of drivers had felony records, some for very serious crimes. Needless to say, there were a great many red faces among those who had okayed the drivers. The final result was a major shakeup in procedures for certifying school bus drivers in the state.

Massive electronic records are generated at the federal level. Because of their extraordinary size, large and powerful mainframe computers must be used for analyzing them, along with sophisticated software and advanced statistical techniques. This has virtually locked out journalists who want to look into the operation of some of our most important federal agencies. An example of such an analysis is one conducted by Margaret DeFleur working with investigative reporter David Burnham.[12] Their objective was to examine the electronic records of the U.S. federal courts. These consisted of the complete records of all charges brought against individuals and all criminal and civil trials, plus all appeals transactions, for the ninety-two judicial districts in the fifty states for a seventeen-year period. The total was more than five and a half million charges, trials, and appeals. The analysis of such a body of information challenges the capacity of even the largest and fastest supercomputers. The CAIR analysis revealed disquieting trends and comparisons that had never been exposed before. For example, there was evidence that over the eight years, there had been a considerable increase in the use of plea bargaining to dispose of federal cases. In spite of the presumption of equal application of the law, great variations were found among the districts in terms of what types of cases (for example, violent crime, drug offenses, or organized crime) had been pursued by each prosecutor. Using the findings, supplemented by more traditional investigative techniques, reporters developed stories about their communities for a number of major newspapers around the country.

There is a major lesson to be learned from analyses like the school bus story and the large-scale CAIR analysis of federal court records. It is that computer-assisted investigative reporting can reveal situations that could never have come to light using only traditional techniques—that is, leaks from informants, examination of selected paper documents, and personal interviews. These techniques remain valuable, but close examination of an agency's entire computer files opens a Pandora's box and allows many well-hidden trends and situations to come to light. These new technologies give some indication of what investigative reporting will be like in the twenty-first century, when the use of computers will continue to add to the traditional tools of journalism.

Transmitting the News: Unique Features of the Different Media

Once news has been gathered and packaged, a vital next stage in the news process is delivering the information to audiences. In the United States, this is accomplished by newspapers, magazines, radio, and television. We have seen that these include about 1,600 daily newspapers, some 7,500 weeklies, several major newsmagazines, about 5,000 AM and 3,600 FM radio stations, three major TV networks and several smaller new ones, about 1,100 local TV stations, and a large and complex cable system that reaches over half the homes in the country. In short, the news industry operates within a complex media environment. It makes use of all these channels to deliver to the public a daily tidal wave of information about what is happening in the world.

Perhaps the major point to understand in looking at these various channels by which news is transmitted from organizations to the people who make up the audiences is that each does so in a unique way. The daily newspaper, for example, brings a once-a-day cafeteria of news stories and other information to people's homes (or to newsstands or dispensers). It presents its stories in greater detail than do any of the other news media, with the possible exception of magazines. However, it often does so after people have heard about the events from another source. On the other hand, newspapers offer coverage of more events. They contain items of news that would never appear on network or even local television.

The newspaper has certain advantages as a medium. (The newsmagazine has some of the same ones, but newspapers play a much larger role in disseminating daily news.) The newspaper is a channel that can be used at the person's own pace; and the individual can go back and read a story again and again to understand it better. Furthermore, newspaper reading is an activity that shuts other people out. It may be done in a social environment, but full attention is usually given to the printed account. It is a very convenient medium, because it can be carried around and read in almost any context. People read newspapers (or magazines) on the subway, at lunch, at work, in bed, or while eating breakfast.

Because of these features, which help it offer completeness of coverage, the newspaper is thought to be the most effective medium from which people learn about the news. It clearly is slower than radio or television, however, and for that reason people often hear about an event from those media and then get more details from reading a newspaper account later.

Radio, on the other hand, is a medium that presents news in a dissimilar pattern. People seldom sit down for extended periods of time to listen attentively to a lengthy radio news broadcast. They used to before television was available, but today they listen to the radio while driving their cars, perhaps before going to sleep at night, while fixing meals, or while doing something else. Although radio listening is often a secondary activity, it is sometimes more convenient than newspaper reading because it can be done while doing other things with one's hands. Radio newscasters understand this very well, and therefore they present their reports frequently and in brief "bursts." A radio news report offers few details, and opinion and analysis are rare (except on public radio). Thus, radio news presentations touch on the main points and come in the form of news headlines or brief news summaries that seldom last more than five minutes, or ten at the most.

These features all suggest that radio is relatively ineffective compared with newspapers when it comes to audience comprehension of the news. On the other hand, radio does benefit from the factor of immediacy. That is, it can get news bulletins out to the public far faster than any other medium, and when truly significant events take place, such as the outbreak of war, the assassination of a leader, or a serious explosion, the majority of people hear it first on radio or from someone who heard it there.

Television, too, has its own characteristics as a channel for dissemination. Because most sets are not really portable, viewers have to watch at a fixed location, increasingly one linked to a cable. Thus, television is not as convenient as either the newspaper or radio. Like radio, television requires the viewer to receive the information at the medium's pace rather than his or her own. However, since it is a visual as well as an audio medium, it requires the audience members to focus on it more than does radio. It is definitely not something one does while driving, for instance, and one can attend only partially while fixing a meal or doing some other task that requires attention.

Each medium packages the news in a different way and is given different kinds of attention by audiences. Newspapers present a portable cafeteria of news that can be consumed in a variety of settings and at a pace selected by the reader. However, reading requires undivided attention. Radio's news bulletins and brief summaries require only a short attention span and can be heard while people are doing other things. Viewing TV news requires being in place before a set and attending closely to the presentation. There is no chance for review at one's own pace. (© John Blaustein/Woodfin Camp & Associates, Inc.)

Television news viewing, then, has its own pattern. Generally, people sit down to watch the news at the end of the workday or before retiring. However, this often becomes a social ritual as well as a learning experience. People fix drinks, admonish children, munch on snacks, talk to each other during the broadcast, or engage in other kinds of activities that tend to reduce the level of concentration with which they are attending. Thus, even though a TV newscast is usually much longer and more complete than a radio version, it is still a source from which audiences comprehend the news only to a limited extent.

Those who manage each medium understand the complex behavior systems that shape the patterns by which the audience is exposed to the news it delivers. And they package their news in ways that fit in with the reading, listening, and viewing habits of the public as it uses each medium.

The News Audience: Selection, Comprehension, and Recall

The final stages of the news process take place as members of the audience selectively attend to news reports, understand and recall their content to varying degrees, and differentially act on what they see or hear. It is very clear that this is an extraordinarily complex stage. Some people never attend to the news and know very little about what is going on in their community and society. Others pay occasional attention in selective ways, learning about some events but ignoring others. A few are "news junkies," who avidly keep up with the flow of news reports, using a variety of media from which they get multiple exposures.

How Closely Do People Follow the News?

Research on what factors lead people to select and learn about particular news topics does not show consistent results. Also, findings are often at such a general level that they offer little real insight into the news-learning experiences of the audience. Nevertheless, a number of conclusions can be reached regarding what kinds of people attend to the news and what they generally prefer.

One thing that research does show is that people expose themselves to the mass media—both print and broadcast news—to a remarkable degree. However, the situation is perplexing because, whether or not people are exposed to the news, research also shows that the majority of the population actually retains relatively little *knowledge* about individual news stories. Few can explain major social and economic trends (such as changes in foreign policy, interest rates, or the stock market). Most do not appear to have insight into the nature of most events of major political significance (for example, trade treaties, bills passed by Congress, or policies advocated by the President). The majority do not know the names of major public officials (such as the Secretaries of State and Defense, the Chief Justice of the United States, or even the Vice President).

Leo Bogart, who for many years directed research for the Newspaper Advertising Bureau (NAB), is one of those who believe that most Americans attend widely to various media: "In contemporary America, there is almost universal daily contact with the three major media. In the course of an average weekday, 83 percent of the adult public watch some television . . . and 68 percent listen to the radio, while seven of ten read a newspaper."[13] Bogart goes on to note that this high level of attention does not necessarily mean a large audience for the news. Still, he concludes that, on any given weekday, only 8 percent fail to receive news from any medium. Bogart offers evidence to support this claim. He concludes that from 60 to 80 percent of the population (depending on educational level) are "exposed to news." He reaches this conclusion because respondents claim in interviews that they "read a newspaper yesterday." The comparable figures for radio news range from 41 to 61 percent (depending on education); for TV news, the figure is 64 percent for all educational levels.

These figures seem to indicate that people do indeed follow the news closely. However, it is not clear what reading the newspaper (or listening to radio or watching television) "yesterday" really means. Some people read only the comics, watch sports on television, and listen to rock music on the radio, encountering news only incidentally. They may have been exposed "yesterday," but they will likely have trouble remembering any news they saw, heard, or read.

From the above, it is clear that it is difficult to make sweeping statements about the effectiveness of the various news media in keeping the public informed. The overall evidence is inconsistent, to say the least. A better approach to understanding the depth of news exposure in the audience is to look more closely at the personal and social characteristics of different kinds of people and see how such factors can make a difference.

The Influence of Personal and Social Characteristics

A considerable body of evidence indicates that different types of people differ greatly in how much they can remember a news story once exposed. Generally, however, the level of recall is remarkably *low*. Some of this evidence comes from experimental studies of news recall, some from testing people on issues that recently have been well publicized in the news, and some from surveys in which people are interviewed right after seeing a news broadcast on television (these reveal levels of comprehension without regard to day-to-day exposure). There are variations among these findings, but there are a number of consistent patterns. What are the personal and social factors that lead to high and low attention to the news? There are no conclusive answers to that question, but we can put together a kind of general picture.

Essentially, a person's *position in the social structure*, in terms of education and income, and *demographic classification* by age, gender, and ethnicity provide one set of answers as to how likely it is that he or she will attend closely to the news. Still another set of answers comes from the individual's *personal psychological characteristics*—that is, interests, preferences, attitudes, beliefs, and values.

No variable shows a closer relationship with attention to the news than *education*. Simply put, the farther down the educational attainment ladder one goes, the less people know about the news. At the same time, the differences appear to be greater for print news (in both newspapers and newsmagazines) than for televised news. This conclusion has been well-supported by research in a number of countries.[14]

Similar conclusions have been found with respect to *income*. Poor people pay far less attention to the news than do those in the middle class and the affluent. However, this may actually reflect education, which is closely linked to type of occupation and therefore to income. Those at higher socioeconomic levels generally have greater knowledge of news from all media than do those who are less affluent.

The factor of *age* is directly related to high or low exposure to news.[15] Few children younger than fifteen follow the news, except for sporadic attention when adults have the TV set on or when the radio is on in the car. Similarly, although they may read the comics and sports, they seldom read news stories in other parts of the paper. That pattern prevails well into the teens—a segment of the population notorious for its lack of interest in public affairs. Contact with the news increases with age among adults. The older a person is (to a point), the greater his or her attention to the news. The real news addicts are people between sixty and seventy-five.

Although research on the matter is scarce, to a certain degree, *gender* has also been linked to interest in the news, and consequently to patterns of exposure.[16] The limited research available suggests that women have somewhat lower levels of interest in news, especially if it deals with violent themes, and this brings about lower levels of attention.

Still another characteristic that predicts whether a given individual will attend to and retain the news is the person's *race* or *ethnicity*. Generally, members of minority groups are less likely to follow the news avidly than are the more dominant segments of the society. However, this too can be misleading because income and educational levels tend to be lower among minority groups, and the reduced interest in the news may well be due to these factors.

Other factors related to news exposure are *occupation* and *area of residence*. Some people work in situations where they can pay little attention to the news—for instance, on ships, at remote sites, or during odd hours of the day. Generally, urban dwellers have more contact with news than others. However, people may live in an inner-city environment where keeping up with the news is not a cultural tradition. Some people are outside the flow of news simply because the media are not available. Such people may lack a stable home situation. Some are traveling; others are stationed in foreign lands for either business or military purposes; still others are sick or institutionalized.

Another set of considerations arises from the differing psychological make-up of people. The factors discussed above—age, sex, education, and so on—lead to distinctive patterns of *interest* in different news topics. These, in turn, lead to different patterns of exposure. For example, most young males have a heavy interest in sports that is simply not shared by many females. Affluent people may have beliefs, attitudes, and values that lead them actively to seek out business news, which is totally uninteresting to many working-class families. Older people are generally more interested in politics and economic trends than younger. And so it goes. In a complex and heterogeneous society, a host of factors and variables determine the topical interests of various categories of people. The general principle is that interest in different kinds of news is determined by a person's psychological profile as well as by the demographic factors that define his or her position in the society.

Finally, *daily habits* are important in news exposure. For example, the medium one habitually turns to for exposure to the news is a critical factor. Robinson and Levy have examined television versus other media as vehicles for learning the news. It is clear that television is the main source for the majority of people. However, in reviewing fifteen studies conducted over a twenty-year period, it was clear that viewers of TV newscasts were less informed compared to those who depended mainly on print media. This was a result of viewing habits. Many people watch TV news while preparing meals, eating, socializing with the family, and so forth, and their attention is less focused than, say, while reading a newspaper. Television, then, is the main source for news for most people, but it is also the medium from which they learn and retain the least information.[17]

The bottom line is that the *de-facto* audience for the news—people who attend regularly and who learn quite a bit about what is happening on a daily basis—is much smaller than many journalists would like to believe. Only a handful of people are avid news consumers who use all the media and know virtually everything that happens. A large number follow the news very selectively, gaining a grasp of only a few topics. Most people are somewhere in between, regardless of which medium they use.

Chapter Review

- News can be defined in a common-sense way as current information that is made public about an event or subject that is of interest to a significant number of people.

- Information is gathered, refined, and disseminated to an audience through a news process consisting of several steps, including gathering relevant facts, preparing them as stories judged to be newsworthy, and transmitting them to the audience, which, in varying degrees, attends to and comprehends what has been presented.

- People entertain "pictures in their heads" of "the world outside." However, the correspondence between the two depends on many factors and may not be exact, because there are numerous points in the news process where stories are shaped in ways that result in unintentional distortions.

- Reporters who observe events use personal perspectives in writing about what they see. Reporters also use reports of witnesses. Accuracy can suffer substantially because of the selective nature of perception, recall, and interpretation.

- News organizations try to make stories both interesting and understandable. Stories are judged with respect to a set of news values and prepared according to a number of alternative formats. There are various styles of journalism that influence how basic facts are developed into news accounts. These include

sensational journalism, objective reporting, new journalism, the advocacy style, and precision journalism.

- Social and economic influences in news organizations play a central role in decision making about what stories will be disseminated, in what order of prominence, and in what form.

- Two very different kinds of goals are often sought in the development of news, represented by the marketing and the adversarial approaches. The former stresses news as a product packaged to please the audience and maximize profits. The latter is aimed at protecting the public interest by performing the watchdog function.

- Each of the media is used in a different way as a means of disseminating the news. The differences among the media in terms of learning and comprehension of news by those who use them are increased by the different behavior system associated with each.

- Some studies suggest that the majority of Americans are exposed to some degree to news on a daily basis. Other studies reveal very low levels of attention to news. In terms of personal and social characteristics, those who best understand and recall news stories are older, more affluent, and better educated. Television is the main source of news for the majority in the United States, but it is also a source from which comprehension is relatively low.

Notes and References

1. *The Iliad* describes how Paris, the son of King Menelaus of Sparta, brought his father's wife Helen—"the face that launched a thousand ships"—back to Troy with him. To get her back, a coalition of Greek cities sent an expedition (the thousand ships) under Agamemnon (brother of Menelaus) to lay siege to Troy. Finally, the Greeks used a clever strategy, hiding soldiers inside a large wooden horse offered as a gift to the Trojans. As the Greeks sailed away, the Trojans took the horse inside the city. Late at night, the soldiers came out and opened the gates of the city for their forces, who had returned. From this episode, we get the saying "Beware of Greeks bearing gifts."

2. These classifications are based on a similar discussion in Gaye Tuchman, *Making News: A Study in the Construction of Reality* (New York: Free Press, 1978) pp. 23–31.

3. The significance of this distinction between locals and cosmopolitans, and their roles in the formation of media-related opinion in a community, can be found in the classic study by Robert K. Merton, "Types of Influentials: The Local and the Cosmopolitan," in *Social Theory and Social Structure* (Glencoe, Ill.: Free Press, 1949), pp. 387–420.

4. Alan Barth, quoted in Herbert Brucker, "What's Wrong with Objectivity," *Saturday Review*, October 11, 1969, p. 77.

5. The basic concept of gatekeeping originated in social psychology as a means of describing decision processes, but use of the term to identify an important part of the news process stems from an early study by David White of "Mr. Gate," a wire editor who had the task of selecting stories from the Associated Press to include in a local newspaper. See David Manning White, "The Gatekeeper: A Case Study in the Selection of News," *Journalism Quarterly*, Fall 1950, pp. 383–390. See also Phillip Moffat, "The Editorial Process," *Esquire*, April 1980;

Murray Schumach, *The Face on the Cutting Room Floor* (New York: Morrow, 1964) pp. 142–143; Stephan Zito, "Inside Sixty Minutes," *American Film 2* (December-January 1977), pp. 31–36, 55–57.

6. Philip Meyer, "In Defense of the Marketing Approach," *Columbia Journalism Review*, January-February 1978, pp. 60–62. See also Everette E. Dennis, "Can Ethics Survive Business-Editorial Harmony?" in M. Emery and T. Smythe, eds., *Readings in Mass Communication,* 6th ed. (Dubuque: Wm. C. Brown, 1986), pp. 45–50.

7. The authors wish to thank Margaret H. DeFleur for bringing together several of the ideas and citations used in this section. See Margaret H. DeFleur, "The Development of Computer-Assisted Investigative Reporting," Ph.D. dissertation, Syracuse University, 1993.

8. John Ullmann and Steve Honeyman, eds., *The Reporter's Handbook: An Investigator's Guide to Documents and Techniques* (New York: St. Martin's, 1983), p. vii.

9. Iris Noble, *Nellie Bly: First Woman Reporter* (New York: Julian Messner, 1956).

10. See "The History of the Standard Oil Company," in Mary E. Tomkins, *Ida M. Tarbell* (New York: Twayne Publishers, 1974), pp. 59–92.

11. Margaret H. DeFleur, op. cit.

12. See Margaret H. DeFleur, "Supporting the Watchdog: Aiding the Press through Computer-Assisted Investigative Reporting," in Keith R. Billingsley, Hilton Brown III, and Ed Dohanes, eds., *Computer-Assisted Analysis and Modeling on the IBM 3090* (Athens, Ga.: The Baldwin Press, University of Georgia, 1992), pp. 847–863; David Burnham and Margaret DeFleur, *The Prosecutors: Criminal and Civil Cases Brought in Federal Court by the Offices of Eleven U.S. Attorneys from 1980 to 1987* (Syracuse, N.Y.: Transactional Records Access Clearinghouse, October 21, 1989).

13. Leo Bogart, *Press and Public: Who Reads What, Where and Why in American Newspapers* (Hillsdale, N.J.: Erlbaum, 1981), p. 115.

14. Barry Gunter, *Poor Reception: Misunderstanding and Forgetting Broadcast News* (Hillsdale, N.J.: Earlbaum, 1987), pp. 83–109. For a summary of how people in different categories attend to the news in one state, see Pamela J. Shoemaker, "Predicting Media Uses," in Frederick Williams, ed., *Measuring the Information Society* (Newbury Park, Calif.: Sage, 1988) pp. 229–242.

15. Barry Gunter, "News Sources and News Awareness: A British Survey," *Journal of Broadcasting and Electronic Media*, *29*, 4, 1985, pp. 339–406.

16. J. P. Robinson, "World Affairs Information and Mass Media Exposure," *Journalism Quarterly* , *44* (1967), pp. 23–40.

17. John P. Robinson and Mark R. Levy, *The Main Source: Learning from Television News* (Beverly Hills, Calif.: Sage, 1986), pp. 81–83.

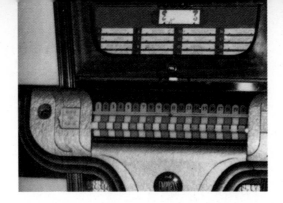

CHAPTER **15**

Popular Culture: Entertainment and Sports

In America, as in all Western societies, the longest and most important cultural struggle has pitted the educated practitioners of high culture against most of the rest of society, rich and poor, which prefers the mass or popular culture provided by the mass media and the consumer goods industries.

Herbert Gans, *Popular Culture and High Culture*, 1974

W hen the Industrial Revolution of the nineteenth century introduced factories with regular workdays, it also defined and expanded people's leisure time. Because larger blocks of free time were available, the demand for amusement and entertainment expanded, and with it came *popular culture*, which we now associate closely with contemporary mass media. Before mass media arrived, the rich and otherwise well-off had their cultural amusements and sports, but people who worked in factories and their families also had their own distinctive brand of entertainment. As historian Richard Maltby writes:

> The city amusements of the late 19th century were prototypes for ephemeral consumption: saloons, dance halls, pool rooms and roller-skating rinks; dime novels and illustrated papers, circuses, amusement parks, burlesque shows and professional sports; melodrama and cheap seats in the theaters and concert halls.[1]

Meanwhile, burgeoning industrial production in the United States and Europe required more consumers to buy products—a development that led to organized promotion and advertising. The means of promoting consumption went hand in hand with the rise of popular entertainment and mass media, which aided in the process of consumption. Eventually, Maltby writes, popular culture became "something you buy" as opposed to traditional folk culture (games, songs, crafts, etc.), which was "something you make."[2]

While considering both the content and supposed impact of popular culture, this chapter also considers the "money connection" because popular culture is big business when it is presented through the mass media.

The Nature and Importance of Popular Culture

The mass media, as they evolved, became players in the creation and promotion of popular culture. Some "media products" such as dime novels provided entertainment; others such as billboards, newspapers, and magazines were vehicles for advertisements that helped sell goods and services. Eventually, much of the entertainment once offered only to small audiences used the media to expand its reach. Thus, cheap novels were also serialized in newspapers and magazines, and live drama eventually made its way into radio, movies, and television. Likewise, sports that began on the playing field quickly became fodder for newspaper stories and electronic media broadcasts.

The Media and Popular Culture

The content of popular culture was, by definition, aimed at large audiences of mainly the middle and lower classes having varied education and income. Thus, there was an attempt to reach the *largest audience possible* with pleasurable, easily understood fare. Critics constantly complained that the popular culture offerings of the media were debasing, drove out so-called high culture, or art, and had an overall negative effect on people.

Early in the debate between the defenders and critics of popular culture, the words "lowbrow" and "highbrow" were coined. They were first used by the journalist and critic Will Irwin in a series of articles in the *New York Sun* in 1902 and 1903. The inevitable "middlebrow" came later. A lowbrow was a person of vulgar or uncultivated tastes. A highbrow was said to aspire (or pretend to) to "a high level of cultivation and learning." A middlebrow simply accepted and sometimes celebrated mediocre fare somewhere between the other two.[3] Scholars, critics, journalists, and others have continued to debate and discuss these terms as they have assessed and examined both the content and effects of popular culture.

Much of the content of the mass media is popular culture that is sold for a profit and is integral to the economics of the media. Audiences are courted to consume popular culture, ranging from popular entertainment to sports and even pornography. People will probably argue forever about whether or not a given image or presentation is popular culture. So, too, will they debate the probable impact of such material: whether or not it is harmful and whether or not it drives out better-quality programs, higher-caliber design, and more elegant writing.

A Definition

But just what is popular culture? Like many other topics of debate, it has been defined in many ways. Critic Ray Browne, who has written several books on the subject, broadly defines popular culture as "all those elements of life which are not narrowly intellectual or creatively elitist, and which are generally though not necessarily disseminated through the mass media."[4] Additional features are provided by scholar David Madden, who writes, "It is

Students of popular culture and its impact on American society take their subject matter seriously. Popular culture, they maintain, is more than simply the most current amusements of the masses. It can shape the ways people think, dress, buy, and relate interpersonally. Moreover, what is regarded as trivial entertainment in one era can become a high art form for later generations. Such figures as Buster Keaton and Charlie Chaplin have come to be regarded as classic representatives of a particular film genre. (The Bettmann Archive)

anything produced or disseminated by the mass media or mass production or transportation, either directly or indirectly, and that reaches a majority of people."[5] Even more inclusive definitions can be found. British historian Lord Asa Briggs wrote a book titled *Victorian Things*, treating such objects as tools, medals, hats, and other artifacts of popular culture.[6] In fact, buttons, such as campaign buttons, and T-shirts are themselves expressions of popular culture. Sociologist Herbert Gans has written musingly about T-shirts and the slogans and legends on them indicating that the messages and advertisements displayed on the ones worn by women tend to be different from those on the ones worn by men.[7]

Some students of popular culture study virtually anything that people use in everyday life—the lettering on cigar boxes, beer cans, and wine labels, advertising in print and electronic media, billboards and so on. The American Museum of Advertising in Portland, Oregon, has exhibits going back to ancient Greece showing how advertising signs and other symbols communicated with everyday people over the years. There is even a set of the once common "Burma Shave" signs from the 1930s, recalling a time when successive phrases on humorous roadside advertisements provided amusement for American motorists. For example, a "Burma Shave" series advertising the now defunct shaving cream proclaims, "Free, free, a trip to Mars [Kentucky] for 500 empty jars!"

Although all of these phenomena of everyday life hold their own fascination, in this chapter we will not discuss in detail elements of popular culture that are not specifically part of the mass media, although some of them, such as fast food and clothing styles, rely on the media for popularization. Somewhat arbitrarily, then, we can formulate a simple definition of popular culture as it will be discussed in the present text:

> *Popular culture* is mass-communicated messages that make limited intellectual and aesthetic demands—content that is designed to amuse and entertain audiences.

Popular culture, in this sense, is presented by all of the print, film, and broadcast mass media. Indeed, the term covers most of what they disseminate. Serious popular culture theorists would probably complain that our definition is too narrowly focused on media popular culture, but it covers what we will address in this chapter—namely, such media presentations as game shows, soap operas, spectator sports, crime drama, movies, and indeed, most of what could be classified as entertaining media content. The next chapter addresses the special category of popular music.

Why Studying Popular Culture Is Important

Debates over the value of the popular arts and the supposed superiority of high culture have gone on for decades, with the idea that much that is popular is unworthy junk. Thus, each generation seems to decry the reading habits, musical tastes, and other popular addictions of the masses. One reason for all educated people to observe and understand popular culture is simply a matter of *keeping up with what is happening in society*. Musician Bob Dylan wrote, in his "Ballad of a Thin Man," a response to attacks on popular culture: "You've been through all of F. Scott Fitzgerald's books/You're very well read, it's well known/But something is happening, and you don't know what it is, do you, Mr. Jones?"

In the 1980s and 1990s, public funding of popular arts led to considerable controversy. Photographer Robert Mapplethorpe received federal funding through the National Endowment for the Arts (NEA) for exhibits of his work. Many people who saw the exhibits were surprised, and some were shocked, to find that some of his photographs showed nude males and homoerotic themes. That federal funds supported the exhibits ignited a national controversy. Conservative senators demanded that funding be withdrawn from the NEA or at least that stricter rules be imposed on the agency. This, of course, raised questions about popular culture and freedom of expression. The debate over the issue has not been fully resolved, and it has implications for the entire issue of what is acceptable in popular art. The Mapplethorpe photographs were widely published in various media, most of them fringe, and were the topic of heavy media coverage.

Some social scientists, such as Japanese sociologist Hidetoshi Kato, maintain that "the mass media can be seen as one of the most decisive factors shaping the populace of a society." Kato continues:

> . . . the belief systems and behavior patterns of the younger generation in many societies today are strongly affected by the messages they prefer to receive (or are forced to receive) either directly or indirectly through mass media.[8]

This kind of influence on audiences is what communications scholar Michael Real calls "mass-mediated culture," and he argues that though it

THE STRANGE, SAD CASE OF AMY FISHER AS POPULAR CULTURE:
A Linchpin to Sociology and Cultural Studies

In 1992, a Long Island teenager named Amy Fisher was arrested for allegedly shooting a woman named Mary Jo Buttafuoco, the wife of a man she claimed was her lover. Thus began a sad and violent story that quickly attracted the attention of racy tabloid newspapers and equally exploitative TV programs. The trial was short, since Fisher admitted guilt and plea-bargained a five-to-fifteen-year prison sentence.

The story had many elements of sensationalism, including sex, crime, and a supposed love triangle. In addition, Fisher was an attractive eighteen-year-old. It also left open many questions: Who was telling the truth and who was lying? What was the role of Joseph Buttafuoco, the alleged lover who denied intimate involvement with Fisher? Was the affair the fantasy of a teenager or a real-life drama?

In December 1992 and January 1993, three made-for-television movies aired on CBS, NBC, and ABC net-

works dramatizing Amy Fisher's story. As a *New York Times* article put it, "Surpassing the expectations of network officials, each of the three made-for-television movies based on the Amy Fisher case . . . was a stunning success, and two of the three are likely to emerge as the most popular television movies of the season."[1] Each movie took sides—one portrayed Amy Fisher sympathetically and blamed Joseph Buttafuoco for her plight, while another took the Buttafuocos' point of view and depicted Fisher as a lying, duplicitous girl with emotional problems.

At the same time, the TV tabloid show "Hard Copy" managed to acquire X-rated videos of Amy and another boyfriend and broadcast them on the air. Before long, popular national talk shows such as "Donahue" and "Geraldo" got involved in the case, inviting the Buttafuocos on the show, where they were heckled and hooted by a studio audience in one

may be distasteful to some, there are good reasons for studying popular (or mass-mediated) culture.[9] These include the following:

1. it offers delight for everyone;
2. it reflects and influences human life;
3. it spreads specific ideas and ideology internationally;
4. it raises far-reaching policy questions, challenging education and research;
5. it is us.

Although these reasons may seem self-evident to today's students, many universities have been reluctant to allow the serious study of popular culture. Author Arthur Asa Berger, for example, had a very difficult time getting his Ph.D. committee at the University of Minnesota to let him write his dissertation on Al Capp's comic strip character "L'il Abner." Few English departments in American universities are interested in having their students study pulp fiction or Gothic romances, though these books command a far greater audience than the most respected literary classics. Art history courses are not much interested in advertising art, although it is produced by an impres-

case and subjected to a mock trial in another. What began as a serious case of domestic violence involving virtually unknown people in a local community was trumpeted in the print and electronic tabloids and became the subject of hundreds of magazine articles, scores of TV shows, and three network TV movies. In addition, deals for paperback books were quickly in the works. The case and its protagonists were suddenly the "stuff" of popular culture. What had been a matter for the police blotter and the courts became everybody's business as people speculated about the parties in the case, their honesty and ethics. Ruth Slawson, senior vice president for movies at NBC, said that the massive public interest "stunned" her. As she put it, "I don't believe there was anything so unique or gripping to this story to make it that special."[2] On reflection, Slawson thought that Fisher's age might have been a factor in luring young viewers.

From the original facts of the case, about which there is disagreement, came fast and loose TV movies that took considerable license in telling the story. What had been a racy but still fairly factual news story became a quasi-fictional treatment as a TV movie and more fodder for what University of Michigan scholar John D. Stevens calls the "wretched excess" that is so common among the tabloid media.

Though none of the people involved in the case were thought to be particularly attractive by newspeople and commentators, their story had taken off as a popular tale and became an artifact of popular culture. Popular culture portrayals like this can have staying power, but many do not and simply recede from public consciousness as new and more gripping stories emerge.

1. Bill Carter, "Amy Fisher Story, A Surprise Smash in Three TV Movies," *New York Times*, Jan. 5, 1993, p. C11.

2. Ibid., p. C18. Also see "Joey, Mary Jo Rip 'Donahue'," *Newsday*, Jan 6, 1993, p. 1. For a useful discussion of sensationalization and its origins, see John D. Stevens, *Sensationalism in the New York Press* (New York: Columbia University Press, 1990).

sively large labor force and is consumed by millions. American history classes do not take note of the meteoric rise of the fast-food industry, although firms like McDonald's have sold so many sandwiches that if you stacked them all up they would stretch from Earth to the outer reaches of the solar system. In other words, the study of popular culture seems "tainted" to most intellectuals even though it influences the public in many powerful ways.

In this chapter, we reject the position that popular culture can just be dismissed with a wave of the hand. Some reasons for taking popular culture seriously in the study of communication are (1) it reaches almost all of the public in one form or another; (2) whether we like it or not, it influences the way we think, act, dress, and relate to others; and (3) it has a tremendous economic impact on the media and strongly influences almost all mass communication content.

Furthermore, today's popular culture might well become tomorrow's high culture. For example, as editor Tad Friend writes in *The New Republic*, "Popular entertainment that outlasts its era gets re-examined by new critics, re-presented to a new audience, elevated and enshrined."[10] Some examples include Mathew Brady's Civil War photographs, the movies of Charlie Chaplin and Buster Keaton, and the music of Patsy Cline and Jim Morrison. And, even though many deplore it, historians often study an era through its popular culture because it tells a great deal about what people liked and enjoyed at that time.

Closely associated with popular culture studies are two kinds of media research. One focuses on *heroes* and the other on *images*. The popular heroes of any period—athletes, rock stars, film sex goddesses, and even some military leaders and major politicians—are "products" of mass media portrayals. Similarly, one learns a great deal about a given culture by its images of women in advertising or images of minority groups such as African-Americans, Latinos, and Native Americans in films and even news photographs. The frequency with which people appear and the way they are depicted says a great deal about the values of a society and the decisions that media people make. In the early 1940s, for example, the *New York Times* and other newspapers mentioned African-Americans mostly under the grisly topic of lynching, rather than covering them for their achievements. Even earlier, many media stereotyped various ethnic groups in denigrating ways, again indicating social values by the content of popular culture.

Popular Culture as Entertainment

It can be argued that some popular culture content, such as advertising, is deadly serious about promoting a product or a point of view. Nevertheless, virtually all popular culture has an entertainment function. It is typically designed to amuse and serve as a pastime. And as we have seen, the media are the important delivery systems for most kinds of popular culture today.

Of the media we discuss in this book, it is the content of television and film that is mostly concerned with entertainment. Newspapers, once a major source of entertainment, now provide utilitarian information, such as TV and movie schedules and listings of local events. However, newspapers do carry a considerable amount of entertainment. When they do, they rely heavily on feature syndicates as sources for material. (The role of feature syndicates in newspaper publishing was discussed briefly in Chapter 3.) Radio, once mostly a news medium, is now mainly devoted to entertainment, with an emphasis on music, talk shows, and sports broadcasts. Cable is both an entertainment and an information medium, but clearly entertainment is the dominant concern. Books, our oldest medium, also deliver both serious information and entertainment.

Media Influences on Consumer Art

One of the most controversial (and most fascinating) social and cultural effects of the media is the invention and spread of a constant deluge of popular songs, cheap paperback novels, formulaic TV drama, low-grade film thrillers, comic strip characters, and other unsophisticated content.

Such material reaches enormous proportions of the population and becomes a part of people's daily lives. People hum the latest popular tunes, suffer the latest problem of a soap-opera heroine, exchange analyses of the latest big game based on news reports, and organize their activities around the weekly TV listings. This media output is at the heart of popular culture. The formulation of well-articulated theories concerning the sources and influences of popular culture is badly needed. Such efforts represent a frontier of theory development that has been widely but not systematically explored. This section looks at this area of mass communications and offers a tentative theory that tries to explain why our media are so preoccupied with this type of content.

People have debated the artistic merits of media-produced culture and its impact on society for generations.[11] Media critics and defenders have disagreed hotly about whether deliberately manufactured mass "art" is blasphemy or blessing. These analyses of mass communication and its products as art forms take place *outside the framework of science*. Media criticism is an arena of debate where conclusions are reached on the basis of personal opinions and values, rather than carefully assembled data. Nevertheless, those who praise or condemn the content of mass communications perform an important service. They offer us contrasting sets of standards for judging the merits of media content. By choosing from among those standards, we can establish our own set of criteria and perhaps reach our own conclusions about the merits of popular music, soap operas, spectator sports, and so on.

In the sections that follow, we review a tentative theory of mass-communicated popular culture derived from discussions of two issues: (1) the merits of various forms of popular culture manufactured and disseminated by the mass media, and (2) the levels of cultural taste that characterize segments of the American population that are served by the mass media. These discussions are based on the *strong opinions*, *clear biases*, and *personal sets of values* of a number of critics. You may find these admittedly biased opinions consistent with your own views, or you may disagree violently. In either case, they illustrate the types of analyses found in debates over popular culture and should help clarify your own thinking about it.

To understand popular culture and why it is so ubiquitous as a form of content in the American media, we need to place it into a more general context of artistic products. Critics tell us that prior to the development of the mass media there were essentially two broad categories of art. These were folk art and elite art.[12] Both, it is said, are genuine and valuable. However, there is an important relationship between the two, according to the popular culture theory we are developing.

Folk art   The category of artistic products called *folk art* consists of those that develop spontaneously among anonymous people. Such art is unsophisticated, localized, and natural. It is produced by many unknown artists who are talented and creative but who receive no recognition for their contributions. It is a grass-roots type of art created by its consumers and tied directly to their values and daily experiences. Thus, villages, regions, and nations develop characteristic furniture styles, music, dances, architectural forms, and decorative motifs for articles of everyday use. Folk art never takes its cue from the elite of society but emerges as part of the traditions of ordinary people. It does not consist of widely known classics.

Elite art   Products of *elite art* represent high culture deliberately produced by talented and creative individuals who often gain great personal recognition for their achievements. Elite art is technically and thematically complex. It is also highly individualistic, as its creators aim at discovering new ways of interpreting or representing their experience. Elite art in the West includes the music, sculpture, dance, opera, and paintings that originated mainly in Europe but appeal to sophisticates worldwide. However, sometimes the boundaries are less than clear. For example, increasingly, original art from Africa, Asia, and Latin America has been sought after by elite museums and collectors. Although elite art has its great classics, it is marked by continuous innovation, as novelists, composers, painters, and other creative artists constantly experiment with new forms and concepts.

Kitsch   In modern times, many critics maintain, both folk and elite art are threatened by a demonstrably inferior category. The rise of privately owned, profit-oriented media brought radical change and created a completely new kind of popular art. With the advent of cheap newspapers, magazines, paperback books, radio, movies, and television, this new form of art made its debut, catering to massive, relatively uneducated audiences with undeveloped aesthetic tastes.

The content of this new art form, say its critics, is unsophisticated, simplistic, and trivial. Its typical literary forms are the "whodunit" detective story and the sex magazine; its typical musical composition is the latest rock hit; its typical dramatic forms are the TV soap opera and game show, the comic strip, and the sexually explicit or violent movie. A term that has been widely used to label such mass-mediated art is the German word *kitsch*. Like the English word "junk," kitsch refers to trashy and garish products that are in bad taste and have no artistic merit. According to the popular culture theory we are developing, it is the unrelenting demands of the media for entertainment content that produce a constant flow of kitsch.

Criticisms of kitsch   Critics charge that in manufacturing kitsch, those who produce it for the media often "mine" both folk and elite art for crass commercial purposes. A mask from rural Zaire, for example, may be reproduced in a limited edition for collectors. Such manufacturers operate "the way improvident frontiersmen mine the soil, extracting its riches and putting back nothing."[13] As Clement Greenburg wrote:

> The precondition of kitsch . . . is the availability close at hand of a fully matured cultural tradition, whose discoveries, acquisitions and perfected self-conscious kitsch can take advantage of for its own ends.[14]

some say that kitsch is a parasite it uses but puts nothing back. it borrows from folk and elite

Why do critics see kitsch as such a problem? They maintain that the older separation between elite and folk art once corresponded to the distinction between aristocrats and common people. Although they do not necessarily approve of the aristocracy, they believe that it was critical to the existence of the most developed forms of art. Prior to the emergence of mass communication, critics claim, folk art and elite art could coexist because they had clearly defined constituencies. Then came the dramatic spread of the media to all classes of society. Their content was aimed at the largest numbers of consumers with purchasing power. The tastes of these consumers were not geared to either folk art or elite art—they were best satisfied with content characterized by low intellectual demand. The result was a deluge of inconsequential kitsch.

Kitsch affects all levels of society and art because it competes for the attention of everyone. Its constant presence and attention-grabbing qualities are the source of its popular appeal. Thus, critics conclude, people who earlier would have read Tolstoy now turn to one of a few dozen formula writers of mysteries and romances. Those who might have found entertainment at the symphony, ballet, or theater now tune in to Madonna or wrestling; those who would have gained political wisdom from modern versions of Lord Bryce and Alexis de Tocqueville now watch the latest "analyses" of Geraldo Rivera.

In other words, popular culture theory states that products in low artistic taste drive out elite art and higher culture, just as bad money drives out good money. In assessing the principal characteristics of popular culture, Dwight MacDonald maintains that:

> It is a debased, trivial culture that voids both the deep realities (sex, death, failure, tragedy) and the simple, spontaneous pleasures. The masses, debauched by several generations of this sort of thing, in turn come to demand trivial and comfortable cultural products.[15]

Furthermore, the theory maintains, kitsch represents a double-barreled form of exploitation. Those who control the media not only rob citizens of a chance to acquire higher tastes by engulfing them with less demanding media products, but also reap high profits from those whom they are depriving.

If true, this theory of popular culture leads to three major predictions: First, kitsch presumably diminishes both folk and elite art because it simplifies their content and, in using them, exhausts the sources of these arts. Second, it deprives its audiences of interest in developing tastes for more genuine art forms. Third, it is mainly a tool for economic exploitation of the masses.

These predictions represent serious charges. To try to see if this theory has merit, we can attempt to determine if the above conclusions are true. To do this, we can look at one aspect of popular culture—the heroes created by the media. Does the presence of media-created kitsch idols tend to diminish the stature of genuine heroes as the theory predicts? Moreover, does a fasci-

THE THEORY OF POPULAR CULTURE

Human beings have always enjoyed light entertainment, simple diversions, and sports, but these activities played only a minor role in the economic affairs of societies until relatively recent times. Before the Industrial Revolution, most ordinary people toiled from daylight to dark on their farms or at other forms of work. They had little leisure time to enjoy entertainment, so there was no great need for popular culture. With the coming of the Industrial Revolution, factory work became scheduled rigidly by the clock, and people began to have at least some leisure time. However, diversions were scarcer than they are now. People could turn to print media if they were literate. Or, if they had an afternoon or day off, they could attend circuses, amusement parks, dance halls, roller skating rinks, and so on.

As leisure time increased, there was a great need for simple forms of diversion that could be enjoyed at home or by traveling a short distance and paying a modest fee. The movies provided just such a form of entertainment, and the movie industry began to produce popular culture after the turn of the century. Then came home radio, with its soap operas, quiz shows, evening drama, comics, sports broadcasts, and other forms of entertainment. With each additional medium came an increasing flood of popular entertainment fare. After television arrived, the airways were flooded with sports, sitcoms, daytime serials, old movies and cartoons, and the age of popular culture became a reality. After cable and the VCR joined the available media, the pace increased even further.

nation with such media-created heroes lessen interest in meritorious accomplishments in real life? Furthermore, is economic exploitation a real factor?

Heroes of the media as kitsch   One way of inferring whether the theory of popular culture has merit is to look at the kinds of heroes that American mass media have created. In early America, critics say, heroes and heroines were extraordinary individuals with rare personal qualities who performed admirable deeds. The list of heroes admired by eighteenth and nineteenth century Americans included such notables as George Washington, Robert E. Lee, Sacajawea, Daniel Boone, Harriet Tubman, Geronimo, and Davy Crockett. These men and women were real people who performed deeds that truly had a significant impact on history. They did not win acclaim because they were pretty or entertaining but because they had powerful determination to succeed in situations requiring courage, dedication, and self-sacrifice.

Even as the media rose in the twentieth century, the tradition of heroes lingered. Alvin York and Eddie Rickenbacker emerged as the great heroes of World War I. But after that (following the rise of the new media) the number of real *heroes of the deed*—such as explorers or pioneers who actually went out and did something—thinned noticeably. Perhaps the last great hero, and one of the most adulated of all time, was Charles A. Lindbergh. His soli-

Thus, popular culture is a product of the public's dependency on mass communication and people's increasing inability to gratify needs for diversion by social contacts with family and neighbors. Today, our society requires a relentless flow of new entertainment content; this plays a critical role in the competitive struggle among the media for audience attention.

Those who produce popular culture draw from any source that can be turned into simple entertainment for the masses. Elite art and high culture are often simplified and used for commercial purposes. Critics maintain that the resulting kitsch debases high culture, exploits the public who must pay, and diminishes interest in real-life heroes who make significant contributions to civilization. These ideas can be summarized as the theory of popular culture, which explains both its sources and its influences on art and the public. Its major propositions are as follows:

1. Privately owned mass media are dedicated to maximizing their *profits*.
2. This locks them into a dependency on attracting the attention of the *largest number of people* who make up the potential audience for a medium.
3. The simple tastes of this audience are not linked to either folk art or elite art, but to media content produced to provide entertainment that makes *limited intellectual demands* on its consumers.
4. To maximize profits from advertising, admissions, or direct sales, the media produce and disseminate an endless flow of such content, that is, popular culture in the form of *kitsch*.
5. Thus, the constant production and consumption of kitsch exploit and drive out artistic products. The result is destruction of both folk and elite art, economic *exploitation* of the public, and a *diminishing* of the significance of real-life heroes.

Source: This theory was developed from the sources cited in this chapter for the purposes of this book.

tary flight across the vast Atlantic in a single-engine aircraft required steel nerves and an iron will. In his single deed were focused all those qualities that Americans admired, and he was the most acclaimed hero of the twentieth century—at least until the full development of film and broadcasting.

When the media became established in this society, American heroes changed. In a classic study, the sociologist Leo Lowenthal examined biographies in popular magazines, believing that ordinary people best understand history and contemporary affairs in terms of famous people. He looked at political, business-professional, and entertainment heroes. Heroes, Lowenthal concluded, are a product of the values and tastes of the time. For example, in the early years of the twentieth century, *idols of production* in fields such as business, politics, and industry dominated magazine biography, but later *idols of consumption*, persons from entertainment, the arts and sports, moved ahead in popular appeal.[16]

Hero study traces its origins to an essay by the historian Thomas Carlyle published in 1885, which demonstrated how forceful personalities have shaped history. Although the great man (or woman) theory of history is now on the wane, scholars and media critics still find the study of heroes useful in examining people's attitudes and values. In effect, heroes become symbols for public hopes and aspirations and, according to cultural critics, serve a social function.

Heroes used to be real individuals who earned a place in the public imagination because of significant deeds. Like Charles A. Lindbergh, perhaps the last American hero of this type, they became universally known and acclaimed. As the mass media developed, other types of heroes replaced them. Today's heroes are individuals who are widely known for their skill in athletics or entertainment or even fictional characters in movies, comics, or TV shows. (The Bettmann Archive; Everett Collection)

Are the days of true or real-life heroes gone? Some people think that they are. As the media assumed a greater presence, many critics maintain, a new *hero of kitsch* began to replace the hero (or heroine) of the *deed*. These new objects of public adulation are not individuals with extraordinary personal qualities. Instead, they are media-created idols known for their sex appeal, their alluring voices, and their athletic or acting ability.

It is greatly to the advantage of the media and those who create and supply popular culture to convince the audience that their products are *truly important*. One way that this is done is through highly publicized "competitions" in which a multitude of awards (Oscars, Grammys, Emmys, Heisman trophies) are presented to media kitsch stars, usually in highly publicized, televised ceremonies. These events powerfully reinforce the illusion that these are the people in our society that really "count." Yet, critics ask, are they simply modern versions of "The Lone Ranger," who was for an earlier generation a heroic figure, but whom many now see in retrospect as a mere creation of the mass media?

Thus, the view posed by popular culture theory is that most contemporary heroes are media kitsch creations whose fame derives not from extraordinary deeds that inspire and benefit society, but from words on paper, images on the screen, and sounds from CDs and tapes. Some are actual people who sing, dance, act, and play sports. Others are pure inventions—imaginary characters who have no real existence outside the movies, soap operas, or prime-time sitcoms. There is ample reason to believe, say the critics, that in treating these illusions as though they are important, our society has merged fantasy with reality in a final commitment to kitsch.

We can identify several categories of such media-created heroes. First, there is the *hero of the ball and stick.* A long list of athletes have been made into celebrities through media attention, from Babe Ruth and Jim Thorpe to today's Michael Jordan and Monica Seles. Clearly such individuals are superb athletes. Yet critics say it would be difficult to account for their immense popularity on any other grounds than the status conferred on them by the media.[17] Striking a ball skillfully with a bat, racket, or club or throwing it into a hoop contributes little to the national destiny. Athletic skill is scarcely the stuff of which advances in civilization are made.

Another significant category is the *hero of the titillating tune.* Famous singers are instantly recognized by millions of fans. Not many members of the older generation in the United States would fail to identify the voices of Bing Crosby and Frank Sinatra. Today, the sounds of Bruce Springsteen and Whitney Houston command instant recognition. The songs that these and other musicians have made famous through the media constitute an important part of today's kitsch. Here, the dependence of popular culture on folk and elite art is especially clear. Many songs that have made the top of the popularity lists are based on either classical music or folk traditions, such as early American ballads and grass-roots jazz.

Of even greater interest are the *heroes of superhuman power.* Characters of the imagination have long intrigued people. For example, one could easily speculate that the various "superheroes" of today's media are the counterparts of ancient mythological deities with fantastic powers who appeared in human form. There is a timeless attraction to fantasies of power and success. Millions have been entertained by the unusual deeds of a long list of fictional characters with superhuman capacities. Generations of readers

One of the first and most prominent heroes of the ball and stick was Babe Ruth, who gained worldwide acclaim in the 1920s for his skill in hitting baseballs. High status was conferred on him by radio, newsreels, the sports pages, and other print media, and as a result, he became an instantly recognizable celebrity. Even today, his name remains a household word, and his feats a benchmark against which those of other such heroes are measured. A recent film portrayed his life story. (UPI/Bettmann)

have admired and coveted the powers of such fantasy creations as Superman, the Shadow, Wonder Woman, and Batman.

Other contemporary media characters have human limitations, but are remarkably capable of combating the forces of evil. Here the critics include the police *heroes of screeching tires,* the cloak-and-dagger *heroes of international spydom,* and the steely-eyed "private eye." The list would not be complete without the *heroes of legal ploy* and the venerable *heroes of suture and scalpel.* What hard-working private eye measures up to Magnum? Who can defeat James Bond or Dirty Harry? The capacities of real people in the real world are pale and flabby by comparison.

How, then, can we evaluate this theory of popular culture? The charge that popular culture draws from elite culture can clearly be substantiated in many cases. However, whether popular culture should be *condemned* for doing so is an open question. The conclusion that the public is forced to pay for popular culture also seems correct, for the public ultimately pays the high salaries of media heroes and heroines because they are added to the costs of advertising and marketing the products of sponsors. On the surface, this does rather look like "economic exploitation of the masses," but the final assessment must be made on the basis of one's personal values.

Finally, the charge that media heroes diminish interest in accomplishments in real life may also have some validity. Most of the significant achievements of "ordinary" people that make the news do so in the back pages of the paper. The accomplishments of scientists, artists, and others who make significant contributions to our culture seldom receive much recognition, while gossip about celebrities often makes front page headlines. Overall, then, the theory of popular culture makes important arguments. However, the degree to which these aspects of popular culture actually represent a *threat* to the public as a whole remains a matter of personal judgment.

Taste Publics as Markets for Media Presentations

The theory of popular culture makes important assumptions about taste levels among the public. Just what are the different levels of taste among those that the media serve, and how are these tastes linked to the production of kitsch? We take a brief look at these issues in this section. However, the analysis of taste publics, like debates about the merits of popular culture, is outside the framework of systematic research and proceeds from individual opinions and standards. Judgments must be made about whether enjoying a particular artistic product represents "high" or "low" taste, or something in between, and judgments about "good" and "bad" taste depend on subjective values, not scientific criteria. Nevertheless, such analyses illuminate significant factors in the basic support system of American media.

Because the task is difficult and the risk that others will disagree strongly is great, not many scholars have analyzed taste publics in the United States. Sociologist Herbert Gans, however, has used the method of qualitative observation to identify five major levels of taste in American society.[18] In this section, we describe these taste publics and the content they tend to prefer.

Our description is based largely, but not exclusively, on Gans's analysis. Education seems most important in defining taste levels, but many other factors are also involved.

The *high culture taste public* likes the products of "serious" writers, artists, and composers. High culture is found in the little magazines, in off-Broadway productions, in a few art-film theaters, and occasionally on public television. It values innovation and experimentation with form, substance, method, overt content, and covert symbolism. Styles tend to change often. Art, for example, has been dominated at one time or another by expressionism, impressionism, abstraction, conceptual art, and so forth. In fiction, high culture emphasizes complex character development over plot. Modern high culture explores psychological and philosophical themes, among them alienation and conflict.

Clearly, this form of culture will have little appeal to the majority of the media's usual audiences. For this reason, it is seldom found in mass communications. Members of the small segment of the public that prefers high culture consider themselves elite and their culture exclusive. They might read elite journals such as *Foreign Affairs* and *Daedalus* and subscribe to on-line databases and specialized newsletters.

The *upper-middle taste public* is concentrated in the upper-middle socioeconomic class—which is composed mainly of professionals, executives, managers, and their families. These people are well educated and relatively affluent, but they are neither creators nor critics. For the most part, they are consumers of literature, music, theater, and other art that is accepted as "good." To characterize the upper-middle-class public, one might generalize that they prefer fiction that stresses plot over characters or issues, and that this group favors stories about people like themselves who have successful careers and play important parts in significant affairs. They tend to like films and programs about likable upper-middle-class people in upper-middle-class settings. They read *Time* or *Newsweek* and enjoy the kind of popularized social science that appears in *Psychology Today*. They might well be familiar with classical music and opera but dislike contemporary or experimental compositions. They purchase hardcover trade books, support their local symphony orchestra, and occasionally attend the ballet. They subscribe to magazines such as the *New Yorker*, *National Geographic*, and *Vogue*.

Although this group is larger than the high culture one, its influence on media content is quite limited. Some TV dramas, public affairs programs, and FM radio broadcasts represent the upper-middle level, but most media content is at the level below it. The reason is that even though these people are relatively affluent as families go, there are simply not enough of them. Taken as a whole, their aggregate purchasing power does not add up to an impressive part of the nation's total.

The *lower-middle taste public* is the dominant influence in mass communication. This is true for two reasons. First, the lower-middle taste public includes the largest number of Americans; second, it has sufficient income to purchase most media-advertised products. People at this level tend to be white-collar workers (for example, public school teachers, lower-level managers, computer programmers, government bureaucrats, druggists, and higher-paid clerical workers). A substantial number are college-educated, many with degrees in technical subjects. This public often consciously rejects the culture preferred by the taste levels above it, but occasionally it uses some of their forms, especially after they have been transformed into popular culture.

The lower-middle taste public continues to support religion and its moral values. It tends to like books, films, and TV dramas in which old-fashioned virtue is rewarded. Thus, it disapproves of positive portrayals of gays, promiscuity, or other alternative life-styles. The lower-middle group likes unambiguous plots and heroes like the late John Wayne, who espoused traditional virtues. Neither complexity of personality nor philosophical conflicts are dominant themes. People of lower-middle tastes commonly read *Reader's Digest* or subscribe to *People*. They also purchase millions of paperbacks with fast-action plots. They enjoy TV programs such as "Knot's Landing," family and situation comedies, cop-and-crook dramas, musical extravaganzas, soap operas, and quiz shows. Earlier, they tuned in to "All in the Family" (many even supported main character Archie Bunker's racial and ethnic biases). In music, Lawrence Welk (recently revived on television) remains the most appealing for older members of this group, and groups such as the Beach Boys for the middle-aged. Such music makes few intellectual demands on its listeners.

The *low culture taste public* consists mainly of skilled and semi-skilled blue-collar workers in manufacturing and hands-on service occupations (factory assembly line work, auto repair, furnace servicing, routine plumbing). Their education level is likely at the vocational school level or less. Younger members of this category attend vocationally oriented community colleges. Although still numerically large, this taste public is shrinking. More blue-col-

Preferences for various kinds of music vary greatly among the distinctive taste publics in the United States. The high culture taste public enjoys experimental music by avant garde composers. The upper-middle group prefers easily recognizable symphony and opera classics. Many in the lower-middle taste public faithfully watched the late Lawrence Welk on television and are now following his reruns. Those in the low culture group enjoy rock in various forms, gospel, country, and ethnic music. (UPI/Bettmann)

lar families are now sending their children to college, and many manufacturing industries are rapidly being replaced.

This taste public dominated media content in the 1950s and 1960s and still plays a part. But because its purchasing power is currently somewhat less than that of the lower-middle level, it is being replaced by that category as the dominant influence on the media. However, the media continue to produce a substantial amount of unsophisticated content for this audience.

The low culture taste public likes action—often violent action—in film and television drama. Thus, to please this public, the media resist efforts to censor the portrayal of violence. This group enjoys simple police dramas, comedy shows, and western adventures. Also popular are programs with a lot of slapstick (older examples are the Lucille Ball and Jackie Gleason shows), as well as "Wheel of Fortune," wrestling, and country-western music. For reading, they like the *National Enquirer,* confession magazines (for women), and *Wrestling* (for men).

The *quasi-folk taste public* is at the bottom of the socioeconomic ladder. It is composed mainly of people who are poor and have little education and few occupational skills. Many are on welfare or hold uncertain or unskilled jobs. A large portion are nonwhite and of rural or foreign origin. Although this group is numerous, it plays only a minor role in shaping media content, primarily because its aggregate purchasing power is low.

The art appreciated at this bottom level of taste resembles that of the low culture level. This taste public tends to like simpler television shows, and in many urban areas, foreign-language media cater to their needs. People in the quasi-folk level also preserve elements of their folk culture. For example, they may hold religious and ethnic festivals and social gatherings and display religious or ethnic artifacts and prints on the walls of their homes. Colorful murals adorn the streets of some urban ethnic neighborhoods.

As suggested earlier, some people may disagree strongly with these categories and may even find them offensive, but they provide a basis for examining one aspect of the theory of popular culture.

Implications of Popular Culture Theory

As the previous sections have made clear, popular culture as media content must be understood in terms of both the aggregate purchasing power and taste preferences of various segments of the public. Regardless of the protests, claims, and counterclaims of the critics, the media *must* continue to produce content that appeals to the largest taste publics because it attracts the attention that is necessary for them to sell time or space to sponsors in order to stay in business. There is little likelihood, given these dependent relationships, that the media will bring about a cultural revolution on their own by emphasizing high or even upper-middle culture. The obvious prediction for the future is that lower-middle and lower tastes will continue to dominate American mass communications. Thus, no matter what the future holds in bigger screens, clearer pictures, more channels, or interactive modes of delivery, the tastes of the lower-middle category will continue to dominate and define the nature of the majority of mass media content. The current popularity of tabloid television and other sensational media is evidence supporting this conclusion.

The Feature Syndicates as Sources for Popular Culture

One of the most durable of the delivery systems that bring entertainment content to the print media are the feature syndicates. We discussed these earlier in terms of newspapers. However, syndication has become widespread in television as well.

As we noted in Chapter 3, the earliest syndicate was organized just after the Civil War. Others quickly followed suit, and by the late nineteenth century, Irving Batchelor and S. S. McClure (who later became famous as magazine publishers) and others organized feature syndicates—formal systems for distributing particular features, such as regular political analyses, comic strips, or gardening columns, to newspapers that subscribed to the service. William Randolph Hearst organized his King Features Syndicate in 1914. By the early 1900s, syndicates were offering opinion pieces, political cartoons, and comic strips as well as columns on fashion, personal problems, politics, and other topics, and there was considerable competition among them. Almost from the beginning, the syndicates played an important role in making the work of particular writers and artists popular among millions of readers.

Unlike the wire services, which distribute their wares to both print and broadcast media, the syndicates aim almost exclusively at the print media. But the major broadcast networks (ABC, CBS, NBC, and Fox) as well as some independent companies distribute material that is to local television and radio stations what syndicated features are to newspapers and magazines. Newspaper syndicates were a model for broadcast syndication, which offers various new and recycled programs for wide distribution to both network affiliates and independent stations.

What the Syndicates Provide

To understand the source of much popular culture that winds up in the media, it is necessary to understand the role of syndicates. In particular, the syndicates provide a great deal of the entertainment and opinion material for newspapers, including serializations of popular books, columns by noted political commentators, comic strips, and editorial cartoons. To the print media, syndicates promise that their material will bring circulation gains, something every newspaper covets, and readership studies indicate that the syndicates are sometimes right.

King Features Syndicate claims to have the greatest array of comic strips for the Sunday papers. This syndicate has feature columnists who cover everything from astronomy to zoos. It offers many old favorites that go back a couple of generations, but it also carries material from the rock magazine

Rolling Stone. In addition, subscribers have access to puzzles and game columns.

Tribune Media Services (formerly the New York Daily News–Chicago Tribune Syndicate) offers "Dear Abby," the nation's most widely read advice column, and a variety of other columnists and comics. Along with crossword puzzles and other amusements, the syndicate carries editorial cartoonists Jeff MacNelly and Wayne Stayskal, as well as "Youthpoll," which keeps track of young people's opinions. Tribune Media Services gets about 60 percent of its revenues from its comics; the rest comes from text features, puzzles, and a graphics service.

Washington Post Writers Group claims to offer "bylines that build readership." Among its services are political commentary by George F. Will and David S. Broder, economic analysis by Hobart Rowen and Jane Bryant Quinn, and media criticism from Sander Vanocur and Charles Seib. This syndicate also provides columns by Ellen Goodman, illustrations by Geoffrey Moss, editorial cartoons by Tony Auth, and the Book World Service.

How the Syndicates Work

A former syndicate editor, W. H. Thomas, wrote, "Of all the outlets available as a market for creative talent, none is so little understood or so ill defined as the newspaper syndicate, that insular and elusive shadow-organization which exercises so much power within the various communications media."[19] Little is written about syndicates, probably because even the largest of them are modest in size and complexity. But in spite of this lack of

Typical of the material provided to newspapers by syndicates is Abigail Van Buren's feature, "Dear Abby." This appears in hundreds of papers throughout the country and is the nation's most widely read advice column. Advice to the lovelorn became a standard feature in American newspapers around the turn of the century. Locked in fierce competition, they increased their circulations by providing syndicated features, many of which remain popular today. (Courtesy Universal Press Syndicate)

publicity and the variations among these organizations, we can make some generalizations about how they work.

Syndicates coordinate many people and tasks, including contracts between the creators of syndicated material and the syndicate itself and contracts between the syndicate and subscribing newspapers. They also handle the flow of money from the newspaper to the syndicate and the payment of royalties to the writers and artists. A production staff prepares material for distribution to various media outlets. Additionally, syndicates promote and market their products through personal contact, advertising, and other means.

Acquiring material   First, the syndicates must acquire the content that they want to distribute. To do so, they maintain regular contacts with writers, artists, designers, and others. Acquisition can be complicated and secretive, as in the negotiations for a President's memoirs. Or it may result from opening the morning mail. Free-lance writers and artists frequently send material to syndicates. The syndicates often serve as representatives for their writers and artists, much as literary agents represent authors. Contracts must be negotiated; the new "property" (strip or column, for example) must be prepared for marketing; then the material is sold to clients.

A syndicate usually offers a newspaper a contract for a variety of materials for a specified time at a specified cost. Like the wire services, the syndicates have a sliding scale of fees; papers with small circulations pay less. Some syndicates make it financially attractive for a newspaper to take several of their offerings, but most often, newspapers buy material from several syndicates. Sometimes there is vigorous competition for a feature.

Managing and marketing   Syndicates must manage and market their wares like any business that produces a product. New items are added constantly; unsuccessful columns and cartoons are dropped. Bob Reed, former president of Tribune Media Services, said in an interview that syndicates are always on the lookout for new talent but are cautious in signing new artists and writers. A property succeeds or fails on the basis of the numbers of papers that agree to run it. Sometimes serendipity plays a role. For example, in the late 1970s, Reed "discovered" editorial cartoonist Jack Ohman, then a sophomore at the University of Minnesota, where he drew cartoons for the *Minnesota Daily*. Ohman, at the age of twenty, moved on to the *Columbus Dispatch*, where his work was syndicated to other papers. In 1981, the syndicate's star cartoonist, Jeff MacNelly, took a year's vacation, and young Ohman was picked to take his place. Instantly Ohman's work began appearing in nearly three hundred newspapers. MacNelly later returned to cartooning, but Ohman continued to draw successfully for the syndicate from his new base, the *Oregonian* (in Portland).

Sometimes syndicate personnel must coordinate many talents. For example, in 1917, John F. Dille was a creative businessperson with experience in advertising when he founded the National Newspaper Syndicate. Although Dille was neither an artist nor a writer, he is credited with originating adventure comic strips. The most notable accomplishment of his syndicate was the science fiction strip "Buck Rogers." Dille got the idea for "Buck Rogers" from a science fiction article in a magazine. He talked the author into writing for a strip based loosely on the article. Then he hired an artist to work with the writer, and "Buck Rogers" was born. Dille's involvement with the strip did not end there. He knew scientists at the University of Chicago and often talked with them and reported their ideas about the future to his artist and writer. Perhaps more important, Dille convinced newspapers to buy the new strip. It prospered, appearing in 287 newspapers at the height of its popularity.

Thus, syndicates are multifaceted organizations that link a wide variety of creative energies to potential outlets. Syndication can be carried out by large organizations or by the self-syndicating efforts of a writer or artist. Syndicates are brokers, but they can also be quite creative, as was John Dille. Some syndicates are responding to the communication revolution and making substantial changes. Tribune Media Services, for example, became an information service with a broader mandate than it previously had, and ceased calling itself a syndicate in 1984.

The Influence of Syndicates

Whether and to what extent feature syndicates have influence is not a purely academic consideration. In the late 1980s, a controversy erupted in Dallas, Texas, when several popular columns and comic strips distributed by Universal Press Syndicate moved from the Dallas *Times-Herald* to the Dallas *Morning News*. The *Times-Herald* lost "Doonesbury" by Gary Trudeau, "The Far Side" by Gary Larson, "For Better or For Worse" by Lynn Johnston, and "Herman" by Jim Unger, as well as "Dear Abby" by Abigail Van Buren, "Erma Bombeck," and "A Conservative View" by James J. Kilpatrick. A lawsuit was filed, and an angry dispute ensued.[20]

This was not the first time that a tug of war between various features would be settled in the courts. The reason? "Syndicates have an enormous influence, especially in competitive markets, and the potential for abuse exists," says Roy E. Bode, editor of the Dallas *Times-Herald*.[21] But this may depend on how many features a given paper gets from a single source. According to Steven S. Duke of the Chicago *Sun-Times*, "I don't think syndicates can dominate newspapers. At least not here. We don't buy that many pieces from a single syndicate. If we lost them all, it wouldn't cause any significant damage."[22] But former editor and publisher of the Oakland *Tribune*, Robert Maynard, comes down somewhere in the middle, writing:

> When I became editor [of the *Tribune*] I found the *San Francisco Chronicle* had exclusive contracts with all their major syndicates. Every feature we wanted, we couldn't have. We sued and finally settled. The settlement enabled us to get all the features we wanted on a phased-in basis. I came to understand that syndicates are middlemen, distributors. Some find and develop powerful features and then control who can buy them. The question is, is it smart business or undue influence? There is no easy answer.[23]

Nevertheless, the debate over the impact and influence of syndicates and their services continues.

Sports as Popular Culture

Sports is a form of popular culture that is deeply rooted in modern society. From neighborhood games to high school, college, and professional sports, it is so pervasive in society that even a presidential debate had to step aside rather than compete for public attention and approval. During the 1992 presidential campaign, the timing of the World Series was a key to scheduling the debates, and no political party would have dared suggest pre-empting a game for a debate to pick the next President of the United States. In the midst of an important tennis playoff a few years ago, the CBS Evening News was delayed for several minutes. In a famous incident, Dan Rather stomped off the set. There was also the so-called Heidi incident of 1968. The New York Jets were leading the Oakland Raiders 32–29 with very little time left in the game when NBC cut away to the movie *Heidi*. The Raiders scored two touchdowns in the last nine seconds to win, and viewers in the Eastern time zone missed it. An extraordinary number of irate callers protested to NBC. As a result, NBC began a policy of broadcasting to the end of all football games. All of these incidents indicate the apparent economic and psychological value sports has for television.

Sports as conveyed in media also has considerable international clout. Several years ago when the United States had no diplomatic relations with China, it was media coverage of ping-pong matches between Chinese and American teams that brought a breakthrough. Sadly, international sporting events can also provide a temptingly large stage for political violence, as occurred at the 1972 Munich Olympics when Israeli athletes were attacked and killed by terrorists. In 1980, President Jimmy Carter blocked U.S. participation in the Moscow Olympics to protest Soviet downing of a Korean aircraft in violation of international law.

The popularity of sports has helped create a whole sports-culture industry, ranging from toys and games to cards, calendars, magazines, sneakers, T-shirts, and other items. The demand for these goods is promoted by media coverage of sports and by advertising that features sports and sports figures. Sports has also been a major source of American heroes. In baseball, figures such as Babe Ruth, Satchel Paige, Willie Mays, Mickey Mantle, and Roberto Clemente cast a long shadow across the sport and American life. In virtually every sport, there have been heroes or heroines, such as Muhammad Ali from boxing and Billie Jean King from tennis. Whether it is hockey, tennis, golf, basketball, football, or baseball, each sport has its heroes, known for their athletic feats and for their personalities. Indeed, as we noted earlier, most Americans know them far better than they do national leaders in politics, science, or the arts or powerful figures from other fields.

If the amount of attention given to an aspect of popular culture is any indication of its importance, then sports heads the list of popular fare. Sports coverage in the media, whether in newspapers or on network, cable, or pay-per-view television, is dominant in terms of the time and space it occupies and the revenues it brings to media. Sports coverage occupies 20 percent of all newspaper space and 25 percent of television's weekend and special-event coverage. Roughly 19 percent of all newspaper reporters cover sports, as do 21 percent of all consumer magazines. No other subject gets as much media attention.

Sports is a vital form of popular culture and has wide appeal. Images of winning and losing, success and failure, pain and pleasure are drawn from sports. Without muscular sports metaphors in the language, American businesses might not communicate at all. The most valuable and expensive advertising time on television occurs during the Super Bowl, World Series, and Olympics. It is estimated that the January 1993 Super Bowl attracted 133.4 million viewers.

The earliest sports journalism in the United States and elsewhere emphasized the pastimes of the wealthy, such as hunting and horse racing. Pastimes of the poor or common people received less attention. Though this has changed greatly over time, sports journalism today has a middle-class bias and covers mainly baseball, basketball, football, and hockey. Upscale sports such as skiing, golf, and tennis also get considerable coverage, but the down-home pastimes of less affluent people—such as bowling, wrestling, and stock car racing—are rarely covered in the sports pages.

In a very real sense, media industries and sports both date from the Industrial Revolution, when people began to have more leisure time. Newspapers at first paid little attention to sports. Some leading editors such as the legendary Horace Greeley seemed ambivalent about sports and its coverage. As historian John D. Stevens points out, Greeley once devoted six columns of coverage to a prizefight and a one-column editorial denouncing the brutality of the sport in the same issue. Still, sports and newspapers grew up together, and as the penny press of the 1830s developed, sports coverage helped draw ordinary people to these inexpensive, highly popular papers.

Henry Chadwick, an Englishman who came to America in 1824 at the age of thirteen, became the first important sports writer in the United States and was especially influential in popularizing baseball. He wrote for the *New York Times*, Greeley's *New York Tribune*, the *Brooklyn Eagle,* and the *New York Clipper*. He covered, promoted, criticized, and helped standardize the rules of the game. Although Chadwick did not invent baseball, he was known in his lifetime as the "Father of the Game." According to John Stevens, until the advent of baseball, there were no specific games that were played uniformly across the country. Baseball at first was an entirely amateur affair, but by the late 1860s, players were being paid, sometimes under the table. The Cincinnati Red Stockings was the first team to admit having professional players, which came after a season of 57 wins, no losses, and one tie.

Chadwick played an important role in covering and commenting on baseball during this period and published the first annual baseball guides. He noted that there was little agreement about the number of players on a team and the specific rules of the game. In his compilations, he summarized rules and helped institutionalize baseball. People in distant places who had never seen the game played learned it from Chadwick's writings. This remarkable

The development of spectator sports was in many ways an outcome of the Industrial Revolution. Individualistic sports, such as hunting and fishing, were carried on in frontier or rural environments. Games such as croquet and tennis began as activities for the family at home. However, as more and more people crowded into urban-industrial areas, sports were needed as diversions for large numbers of spectators who could pay only limited fees. Such games as football and baseball met this need. Henry Chadwick, the first important sportswriter in the United States, popularized baseball and helped standardize its rules. He is widely regarded as one of the "fathers" of the game. (The Bettmann Archive)

man urged the use of gloves and chest protectors for catchers, criticized team owners, and helped organize the first professional sportswriters' organization. Chadwick is credited with helping to make baseball the so-called national pastime, and he was one of the first nonplayers elected to the Baseball Hall of Fame in Cooperstown, New York.

Sports columns like those written by Chadwick became sports pages and eventually sports sections of newspapers. They were also the forerunners of sports magazines. Sports coverage spread over time, and along the way other artifacts of this form of popular culture such as sports books, baseball cards, and other materials appeared. With the advent of radio, actual coverage, including play-by-play announcing, became possible, and the dominant role of sports in the press, while still important, was never the same. Television ushered in a new era of sports as media fare and also a new era of media economics, in which the rights to broadcast games of popular teams, the Olympics, and the Super Bowl generated huge revenues.

Sports broadcasting was largely invented and defined by two important events: David Sarnoff's coverage of the Dempsey-Carpentier championship boxing match in 1921, and the 1958 National Football League (NFL) championship game between the Baltimore Colts and the New York Giants. Author Huntington Williams says the first event launched prizefighter Jack Dempsey, one of the most popular and mythic sports figures of all times, as a hero of popular culture. Later, it helped establish Sarnoff and his fledgling National Broadcasting Company (NBC) as the leader of post–World War I radio—and eventually television. The NFL game coverage established professional football as the first money-sport of the TV era.

The narrators of sports programs on radio and television became legends in their own time as well. In the 1920s, Graham McNamee, who first covered the 1923 World Series, understood the game of baseball and communicated it well to the public with a rich, baritone voice and colorful play-by-play announcing. He was such a popular figure that he once received fifty thousand letters during a World Series. And, of course, he and others who joined him in the broadcasting booths of stadiums all over the country brought their listeners the heroic exploits of great teams and players, which themselves became legends in sport.

In the TV era, ABC Sports, an independent company owned by the ABC network, did not treat sports as mere entertainment or as a subset of news, but as a subject of its own. For live productions of sporting events, the network staged extravaganzas, taking advantage of new technology to dazzle the public with instant replays and other marvels of the electronic age. Under the leadership of Roone Arledge, one of the greatest programmers in modern broadcast history, and with the collaboration of engineer-technologist Julius Barnathan, ABC Sports harnessed satellites, employed minicams, and developed computer graphics long before they were used by other networks for sports, news, or entertainment. Most visible to the public through three decades of television's championing of sports was announcer Howard Cosell, sportscaster for "Monday Night Football." With a distinctive style and personality, Cosell became the most famous figure in TV sports. He dominated the screen with his opinionated interviews, analyses, and play-by-play action. He even appeared in movies playing himself.

Television revenues took professional sports from a mostly local, modest business to a billion-dollar enterprise. By the 1990s, as the television networks fell behind cable as a competitor for the best sports fare, the sports industry was itself again in charge, and television was more of a vehicle for its distribution. The ESPN network, a 24-hour, all-sports service on cable, became a regular feature of most fans' TV diet.

There is no doubt that sports programming will remain as one of the most popular forms of popular culture. Even though there are significant segments of the population who have little interest in, or even detest, spectator sports, the ability of such content to attract attention makes it an advertiser's dream.

Chapter Review

- A great need for popular culture was created by the Industrial Revolution of the nineteenth century. Factories established regular workdays that defined and expanded people's leisure time. With larger blocks of free time available, people demanded entertainment, and it came in the form of mass-communicated diversions and amusements.

- Much of the content of the mass media today is popular culture that is sold for a profit and is integral to the economics of the media. Audiences are courted to consume popular culture, ranging from various forms of entertainment to sports and even pornography. People will probably argue forever about whether a given image or presentation is popular culture or not.

- Somewhat arbitrarily, for purposes of this book, we can formulate a definition of popular culture: It is mass-communicated messages that make limited intellectual and aesthetic demands—content that is designed to amuse and entertain media audiences.

- Some reasons for taking popular culture seriously in the study of communication are (1) it reaches almost all of the public in one form or another; (2) whether we like it or not, it influences the way we think, act, dress or relate to others; and (3) it has a tremendous economic impact on the media and strongly influences almost all mass communication content.

- People have debated the artistic merits of media-produced culture and its impact on society for generations. Media critics and defenders have disagreed hotly about whether deliberately manufactured mass "art" is blasphemy or blessing. These analyses take place *outside the framework of science*. Media criticism is an arena of debate where conclusions are reached on the basis of personal opinions and values, rather than carefully assembled data.

- Folk art, unsophisticated, localized, and natural, is a grass-roots type of art created by its consumers and tied directly to their values and daily experiences. Elite art is technically and thematically complex as well as highly individualistic, as its creators aim at discovering new ways of interpreting or representing their experience.

- With the advent of cheap newspapers, magazines, paperback books, radio, movies, and television, a new form of art called kitsch made its debut, catering to relatively uneducated audiences with undeveloped aesthetic tastes.

- According to the theory of popular culture, media-created heroes—the idols of kitsch—diminish the stature of genuine heroes. Moreover, a fascination with such media-created heroes lessens interest in meritorious accomplishments in real life.

- The theory of popular culture makes important assumptions about taste levels among the public. Several different levels of taste exist among those that the media serve. The largest taste public is the lower-middle group, which has the greatest aggregate purchasing power and therefore its preferences dominate the production of media content.

- One of the most durable of the delivery systems that bring entertainment content to the print media is the feature syndicates. Syndicates coordinate the flow of feature material to subscribing newspapers, and they handle contracts and payments for artists and writers who create the material.

- Sports is a form of popular culture that is deeply rooted in modern society and no other subject so dominates the media. As a result, sports has been a major source of American heroes; it has given rise to a whole sports-culture industry, including cards, magazines, and clothing; and it has attracted audiences to media in numbers that make advertisers happy.

Notes and References

1. Richard Maltby, *Passing Parade: A History of Popular Culture in the Twentieth Century* (New York: Oxford, 1989), p. 8.
2. Ibid., p. 8.
3. William Morris, *Dictionary of Word and Phrase Origins* (New York: Harper and Row, 1977), p. 101.
4. Ray B. Browne, "Popular Culture: Notes toward a Definition," in Ray B. Browne and David Madden, eds., *The Popular Culture Explosion* (Dubuque, Iowa: William C. Brown, 1973), p. 207.
5. David Madden, "Why Study Popular Culture," in Ray B. Browne and David Madden, eds., *The Popular Culture Explosion* (Dubuque, Iowa: William C. Brown Company, 1973), p. 4.
6. Asa Briggs, *Victorian Things* (Chicago: University of Chicago Press, 1988).
7. Herbert J. Gans, "Bodies as Billboards," *New York,* November 11, 1985, p. 29.

8. Hidetoshi Kato, *Essays in Comparative Popular Culture, Coffee, Comics and Communication,* No. 13 (Honolulu, Hawaii: Papers of the East-West Communication Institute, 1976).

9. See Michael R. Real, "The Significance of Mass-Mediated Culture," in Michael R. Real, *Mass-Mediated Culture* (Englewood Cliffs, N.J.: Prentice-Hall, 1977).

10. Tad Friend, "The Case for Middlebrow," *The New Republic*, March 2, 1992, p. 24.

11. The word "culture" is being used here in an aesthetic sense rather than in the way anthropologists and sociologists use the term (and as it is used elsewhere in the present book). The reason is that in the literature on popular culture, the term is used consistently to refer to art, music, drama, and other aesthetic products.

12. Michael Real, *Mass Mediated Culture* (Englewood Cliffs, N.J.: Prentice-Hall, 1977), pp. 6–7.

13. Dwight MacDonald, "The Theory of Mass Culture," *Diogenes*, Summer, 1953, p. 2.

14. Clement Greenberg, "Avant Garde and Kitsch," *Partisan Review* (Fall, 1939), p. 23.

15. Dwight MacDonald, op. cit., p. 14.

16. Leo Lowenthal, "Biographies in Popular Magazines," in Paul F. Lazarsfeld and Frank N. Stanton, *Radio Research, 1942–1943* (New York: Duell, Sloan and Pearce, 1944), pp. 507–548.

17. Paul F. Lazarsfeld and Robert K. Merton, "Mass Communication, Popular Taste and Organized Social Action," in Wilbur Schramm, *The Process and Effects of Mass Communication*, rev. ed. (Urbana, Ill.: University of Illinois Press, 1971) pp. 554–578.

18. Herbert J. Gans, *Popular Culture and High Culture* (New York: Harper Collins/Basic Books, 1974), pp. 69–102.

19. W. H. Thomas, ed., *The Road to Syndication* (New York: Fleet, 1967), p. 12.

20. David Astor, "A Features Controversy Erupts in Dallas," *Editor & Publisher*, August 12, 1989, pp. 42–43; see also "A High-Priced Feature Switch in Dallas," *Editor & Publisher*, September 23, 1989, p. 34.

21. Milt Rockmore, "Do Syndicates Exert Undue Influence?" *Editor & Publisher*, February 3, 1990, p. 18.

22. Ibid.

23. Ibid.

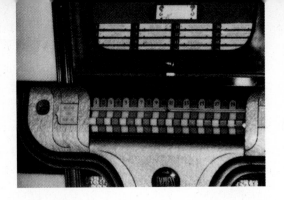

14

The Development of Popular Music and the Recording Industry

> Sweeping across the country with the speed of a transient fashion . . . comes now the mechanical device to sing for us or play the piano . . . in substitute for human skill, intelligence and soul. . . . There will be a marked deterioration in American music and musical taste with the multiplication of various music-producing machines.
>
> John Philip Sousa, *Appleton's Magazine*, 1906

The Beginnings of Popular Music
Work Songs and Folk Music / Ragtime: The First Form of Popular Music / The Blues / Country and Gospel

America Enters the Jazz Age
The "Original Dixieland Jass Band" / The Anti-Jazz Movement

Machines for Recording Sound
Edison's Talking Machine / Significant Technological Developments

Coming Together: Popular Music, the Recording Industry, and Mass Media
The Media and Changing Forms of Popular Music / Popular Music as an Industry

he relationship between popular music, the recording industry, and mass communication is poorly understood by the millions of consumers who listen, sing, hum, and dance to the latest hits every day. The majority give no thought to popular music's origins, to its basic nature as a musical form, or to its deep and mutually dependent relationship with both the record business and the mass media. But an understanding of mass communication must include a grasp of the technologies, development, and current economic situations of these industries. Popular music is a mainstay of contemporary radio. It is also a critical element in motion picture production and in many forms of television content. Furthermore, it supports a related record business that is a significant part of the general economy. In short, it would be difficult to understand the nature of contemporary American culture and the tastes and interests of major segments of American society without insight into the nature of popular music.

This chapter presents an overview of the history and current status of popular music and its relationship to mass communication. It discusses various musical forms that dominated American popular culture at different periods and the ways in which both the recording industry and the mass media captured the fascination of large segments of the American population with those forms. The chapter is less concerned with the latest personalities or current musical hits than it is with the technological, economic, and social developments that at various times have resulted in colorful relationships between popular music, the recording industry, and the mass media.

Today, both popular music and the recording industry are so intertwined with radio, television, and films that it is difficult to separate them. However, that was not always the case. Popular music originated quite independently of both recording technology and the mass media. When ragtime—the earliest form of popular music—got its start, there was no recording industry to promote it and, of course, no radio stations to broadcast the latest releases. Thus, popular music had its own unique beginnings, just as did radio broadcasting and the manufacture and sale of phonograph records. The three did not come together until each was already relatively well established in its own right. Today, of course, they are all part of the overall system of contemporary mass media.

Just what is popular music, and how does it differ from other forms? In many ways, it does not differ. For the most part, it uses the same musical instruments, notes, scales, beats, and so forth, as other kinds of music. The critical difference lies in the way it is produced and the purposes for which it is recorded and performed. There is also a difference in the general nature of its audience. It is not music for an educated and sophisticated elite or for a narrow communal group, but for ordinary people in the mass society.

Popular music, then, can be defined as musical compositions that are written or performed so as to produce commercial services and products that can be sold for profit. Thus, both the performance and preparation of such musical compositions and their production in marketable form (as sheet music, records, compact discs, and so on) are the basis of a large industry. It is this commercial aspect of such music that most sets it apart from musical forms that are more spontaneous in origin, such as folk songs, work chants, ballads, and so on. Although music of one sort or another has been appreciated by the common people since the dawn of time, the production of tunes for profit is a relatively recent phenomenon.

In the sections that follow, we trace the *origins* of popular music, its *transitions* through its major forms, the development of *recording* technology, and the eventual *integration* of popular music, the record industry and the mass media. To do this, we must look at where popular music came from, how its principal forms evolved and changed, and how they were enthusiastically adopted by the majority of Americans. We also investigate the emergence of the mechanical and social inventions that made possible the so-called Jazz Age—in which many say we are still living.

The Beginnings of Popular Music

Music enjoyed by everyday people has always been a part of human life. For example, hymns for religious singing were a powerful influence on the early settlers of New England. The melodies of these songs were preserved mainly by oral tradition in a largely illiterate society.[1] As these religious songs spread from one place to another and were passed on through generations, they often became distorted. This disturbed religious authorities. So to preserve the original hymns, the clergy encouraged "singing masters" to go from town to town providing instruction. These enterprising individuals offered a simple course of a few weeks, during which, for a fee, villagers could learn the rudiments of music and engage in group singing. The sessions were held in local churches, schools, meeting houses, or even taverns.

These singing meetings particularly appealed to the young, because they provided socially approved opportunities to meet and be with members of the opposite sex. This was exciting in the strait-laced farming towns of early America, where there were few distractions from a life of grinding toil. As one young man explained in a letter to a friend in 1782,

> I have no inclination for anything for I am sick of the World and if it were not for the hopes of going to singing meeting tonight and engaging in some of the Carnal Delights of the Flesh, such as kissing and squeezing . . . I should willingly leave it now.[2]

Apparently, the music that provided popular entertainment for people in the eighteenth century had two features that it retains today: a strong appeal to the young, and an association with activities not entirely approved of by the older generation.

Work Songs and Folk Music

As the nation moved into the nineteenth century, the music of ordinary people reflected their daily experiences as they suffered the hardships of a demanding life of bone-wearying labor, little security, and few rewards. With little in the way of machinery, appliances, and amenities to make life easier, most people had to perform hard labor from dawn to dusk. They invented and sang simple, honest songs that needed no musical instruments. The ones that eased the burden of heavy work played an especially important role. Work-gang songs helped focus the energy of men's muscles as they struggled to build canals, railroads, mines, and farms. And from the sea came the chantey, sung by sailors as they pulled heavy rope lines. Even in the following brief segment we can see that the chorus helped them put their backs into the task in unison (every other line is the chorus):

> Cape Cod girls they have no combs
> Heave away! Heave away!
> They comb their hair with codfish bones
> Heave away! Heave away![3]

Similarly, slaves on the plantations developed their own songs—rhythmic "field hollers" and melodic "shouts" that not only helped them do their heavy work but also subtly expressed their emotions. Their lot as slaves and the brutal treatment they suffered left a residue of deep, culturally shared sorrow. In particular, their suffering was intense on the slave ships, as they got their first taste of life under their new white masters:

> At the savage captain's beck
> Now like brutes they make us prance;
> Smack the cat about the deck,
> And in scorn they bid us dance.
>
> > From "The Sorrows of Yamba,"
> > an anonymous eighteenth-century poem

The deep feelings embedded in African-American culture by such experiences would later find expression in the blues, which became a part of popular music early in this century.

Another form of folk music had its origins in the simple songs of those who settled in the isolated Ozark and Appalachian mountains. Based on the English ballads they brought with them, these people's folk songs expressed themes of love, fear, death, and the experiences of their way of life. Today's "bluegrass" had somewhat similar origins in the music of the upper South. In the Southwest and the Great Plains, frequent musical themes were cattle, outlaws, and the personal feelings aroused by the limitless outdoors. Out of that background came the western music and cowboy songs that became popular earlier in this century. In addition, hundreds of ethnic musical forms (jigs, polkas, tangos, etc.) were brought to the New World by millions of immigrants. They sang, danced, and played their instruments long before anyone had ever heard of popular music in the modern sense.

The transition from work and folk songs to written popular music prepared for a market was gradual. Even during the mid–nineteenth century, a few composers were preparing tunes for a small and scattered sheet music market. During the 1850s, Stephen Foster wrote a number of songs that have become a part of this nation's heritage. Although they sound like Southern folk melodies, they were his own creations and he worked in the North. For example, he wrote "Way Down upon the Swanee River" while living in Philadelphia. He never saw the rather muddy Suwannee River, which runs through southern Georgia and northern Florida. In fact, while writing the music he did not even know it existed. His original version used the Pee Dee River, but he decided that he did not like the sound. He consulted his brother, who seriously suggested the Yazoo River ("Way Down upon the Yazoo River"?). Finally, he found the Suwannee in an atlas and shortened the name to Swanee.[4]

Another part of America's musical heritage that helped form contemporary popular music was the minstrel show. This type of show and its music was originated by a group of whites in the 1840s. The players in Lew Johnson's "Plantation Minstrel Company" put burnt cork on their faces to mimic and burlesque the slaves. They played the banjo, beat the drum, shook the tambourine, and rattled the bones to entertain slave owners and their guests with crude humor and gross stereotypes of blacks.[5] After Emancipation, African-Americans themselves continued the tradition—even using burnt cork. (Making a living was not easy in a white-dominated world.)

Even by the end of the Civil War, the social and cultural conditions of the society were such that the development of a popular music industry would not have been possible. None of the economic and technological elements that could provide its foundation were present. In the 1870s, however, the *piano* was slowly being adopted as an instrument of home use—at least among those segments of the population who could afford an instrument. This created a demand for sheet music scored for piano. However, no means of distribution had yet been established to make possible the retail sale of songs and tunes specifically prepared for popular con-

During the nineteenth century, white musicians in "blackface" provided entertainment for white audiences. Their instruments were banjos, bones, tambourines, and a few others. Their routines were simple, and their jokes usually included crude stereotypes of African-Americans. Toward the end of their existence, such shows became more elaborate, and there was often a small orchestra. The influence of the minstrel shows lived on for many years among Tin Pan Alley songwriters and vaudeville entertainers. (The Bettmann Archive)

sumption. What was needed was a form of music that would capture the imagination of the piano-playing public, create a demand for songs to play, and support a system for the production and distribution of sheet music. At the end of the century, that music came from sources that no one could possibly have predicted.

Ragtime: The First Form of Popular Music

During the last part of the nineteenth century, several cities along the Mississippi became important centers of commerce, thanks to their location and to the existence of the great river itself. The farms of the Midwest and the South had begun to produce huge amounts of food and fiber. It was exported down the river. Steamboats brought grains and cotton southward from the nation's heartland and Southern states to the port of New Orleans for shipment to distant markets. In turn, imports from many parts of the world were carried back up the river to be distributed by wholesalers and retailers. This flow of commerce brought great profits to some and high wages to many. With gold jingling in a large number of pockets, it was inevitable that gambling halls, saloons, and bawdy houses would prosper in such cities as St. Louis and New Orleans and even in minor ports along the river.

The "sporting house" piano player   The centers of seamy pleasures in the river towns inevitably attracted clever musicians. There were no juke boxes or record players—only pianos. To provide entertainment, the "sporting houses" employed the most able of the available musicians, the majority of whom were African-Americans. These piano players had extraordinary skill. Even though few could read music, they could make their instruments perform in ways that even piano makers did not know were possible. Playing piano was one of the few jobs that were open to them as musicians, and it was a tough assignment in a tough environment. They had to be *very* good to survive because new candidates eagerly waited in the wings to take their jobs.

The most famous (or infamous) of the sporting houses were in a district of New Orleans called Storyville. The city was the busiest river port of them all, and it was in its red-light district that the most talented and innovative of the entertainers performed in the fanciest establishments.

As a basis for their musical innovations, these entertainers made extensive use of the rhythms and folk music they knew from the society in which they had been raised. They created new piano compositions that incorporated the "rag" dances of the poor blacks who lived and worked along the levee. They also used elements of the "cakewalk" music that had been a part of African-American life on the plantations. (The cakewalk was a competition of fancy, high-stepping dancing. The slave owner usually gave a cake to the winning couple.)

From these sources, with their reliance on polyrhythms that had survived in music brought from Africa, the sporting house musicians created an unusual and very lively form of piano music. It came to be called *ragtime*, and it was widely played in the sporting houses along the great river during the 1880s and the early 1890s. From these colorful beginnings, ragtime would become the first form of popular music in the modern sense of that term.

Scott Joplin and the "Maple Leaf Rag"   One entertainer among the hundreds who played the lively new music was to become the celebrated innovator who brought ragtime out of the sporting house to capture the enthusiasm of the middle class. His name was Scott Joplin, and he was uniquely qualified to bridge the two worlds. Joplin was born in 1868 in a small town in Texas. His father had been a slave and had played the violin for plantation parties. His mother, who was free-born, had a beautiful singing voice and played the banjo.

By the time Joplin was eleven, he could improvise smoothly on the piano, with a keen sense of rhythm and harmonics. Still, he could not read a note. His remarkable ability came to the attention of an old German music teacher living in the town, who gave him free lessons in technique and sight-reading as well as an initial grounding in harmony, musical theory, and classical music.

With few other outlets for his skills, Joplin became a roving pianist, working in the sporting houses and saloons up and down the Mississippi. As a young adult, he took a job as an entertainer in a saloon called the Maple Leaf Club in Sedalia, Missouri. He also studied music at nearby George R. Smith College, which enabled him to produce technically sophisticated compositions.

Joplin began to write down the notes of ragtime pieces that he had composed.[6] He named one of his compositions the "Maple Leaf Rag," after the

Scott Joplin began his musical career as a roving pianist, playing in "sporting houses" up and down the Mississippi River. As a young adult, he studied music formally and learned to score the ragtime tunes he composed. He earned a place in history by bringing ragtime music to the attention of the American middle class. Ragtime spread worldwide, becoming the first form of popular music in the modern sense. (The Bettmann Archive)

saloon. Then he met John S. Stark, a white owner of a music store in Sedalia. Stark bought the rights to the "Maple Leaf Rag" for $50 in 1899 and had it printed as sheet music. Stark was an honest man and included in the purchase agreement a royalty for the composer, just in case the piece made any money after publication. It seemed unlikely, because few outside the saloon world had ever heard of ragtime music.

As it turned out, it was the best investment Stark ever made. First, he distributed the sheet music around the region, and it caught on. Before long, the "Maple Leaf Rag" was selling briskly, even though it was an entirely new musical form, unfamiliar to those who bought it. By 1906, to Stark's and Joplin's mutual astonishment, it had sold over half a million copies.[7] Joplin and other composers quickly produced additional ragtime pieces, and the new music began to attract an enthusiastic national following.

It is difficult to say why ragtime swept the country at the beginning of the new century. Perhaps the public had grown tired of the sentimental ballads, waltzes, and European-type music of the late nineteenth century. Ragtime was very different. Technically speaking, it used rhythmic forms that were not well-known to the established world of music at the time. Ragtime is based on a rhythmic form called *syncopation*. In playing the melody with the right hand, the pianist accents the weak or normally unaccented third beat of a measure while playing a precise and regularly accented bass with the left hand. Complex polyrhythms result—common enough in African drum-dominated music, but a bit startling at the time to middle-class white Americans. Actually, ragtime was far more complex and difficult to play than the ballads and waltzes that were then being published for the home piano. Nevertheless it was exciting and fun.

By the time of Joplin's death at age forty-eight, he had produced a number of famous ragtime compositions and had even written an opera, *Treemonisha,* but it never caught on. In 1974, decades later, the motion picture *The Sting* featured his compositions as its theme music, and Joplin's ragtime composition "The Entertainer" made the top of the charts in the same year.

Tin Pan Alley: Music written to order One contributor to ragtime's wide popularity was its vigorous promotion by a group of New York music publishing houses that came to be called Tin Pan Alley (a name they received later from critics who claimed that their products had the musical qualities of tin pans being banged together). Another contribution came in 1883 when a young man named Charles K. Harris hit on the idea of writing songs specifically for new musical shows. Up to that time such shows had been developed around existing songs that people already knew. Sometimes the music fit the themes of the production, and sometimes it did not. Harris came up with a clever solution to the problem. He opened a small office with a sign outside that said:

Charles K. Harris

Banjoist and Song Writer

Songs Written to Order

Those last four words were the key to what was to become Tin Pan Alley—a completely new approach to the production of music. The songs that Harris produced were sold for profit to specific markets in much the same way as any other commercial enterprise produces and sells a product or service. This concept remains one of the most important features of popular music.

Harris soon had a number of competitors. There was high demand for such music, not only from those producing shows but also from the public. People wanted sheet music for their pianos and the publishing houses that would make up Tin Pan Alley began to produce and sell it even before the ragtime craze got started. Their products were slow sentimental ballads— gushy musical laments about mothers, pathetic little children, unrequited romances, and the like. These ballads were easy to play on the piano and had simple words for the family to learn and sing. Although many found them boring, they did sell. The loosely organized publishing companies had learned how to copyright songs, how to get the scores printed in the form of sheet music, and how to wholesale their wares to national distributors who supplied local retailers. All were necessary elements in the development of a popular music industry.

When ragtime hit they made fortunes. Tin Pan Alley's hustling entrepreneurs eagerly went to work to produce sheet music for anyone and everyone who had the money to buy. Some of their composers were free-lancers who wrote their tunes for a fee plus a share of the royalties. Others worked directly for the companies. Ragtime songs poured into the market; thousands of titles were produced and the snappy new rhythm spread to all parts of the world where pianos were in use. As ragtime reached its peak of popularity, it was not uncommon for a popular tune to sell a million copies. In 1910, more than 2 billion copies of songs were sold in sheet music form.

By this time, the phonograph had been developed and widely adopted, and, as a result, the sale of sheet music began to decline. It was a lot easier to crank up the machine and put on a record than to play a tune on a piano. As the recording companies began to realize the market potential of popular music records, Tin Pan Alley redoubled its efforts to grind out new songs. Soon hundreds of ragtime pieces were being written every month, and millions of records were manufactured every year to meet the demand.

By the time World War I arrived, the country had been virtually saturated with ragtime and people were tiring of it. As the tidal wave continued, it wore out its welcome and simply collapsed. The ragtime craze lasted from just after the turn of the century to the beginning of World War I—only about a decade. However, it left an indelible mark on the country. A taste for popular music had become a permanent part of the American culture.

The Blues

During the same period when the entertainers were playing ragtime piano to amuse the customers of red-light districts, poor black people were singing a different type of song to one another. These songs were not commercially produced but were original folk songs. They were called the *blues* and were a heritage from which a form of popular music with the same name drew its inspiration. The folk blues was music that expressed feelings generated by difficult experiences in everyday life. These were earthy songs about basic human relationships and the hard times that are found at the bottom of the socioeconomic ladder.

Many of the blues songs were poignantly beautiful in their expression of human emotion. Others were intended to be amusing and make people laugh, with words and themes that were sexually explicit, using four-letter words and easily understood metaphors. For example, the title of a blues song first written down in 1896 asked the question "If You Don't Like My Potatoes, How Come You Dig So Deep?" In spite of the humorous and colorful nature of much of this music, the publishing and recording companies of the time avoided it. Four-letter words were absolutely taboo, and even the metaphorical references were not accepted. As a consequence, blues music did not get into record productions until the 1920s or later. Eventually a few pioneering record companies began to overcome their fear of public censure and made records of songs with titles such as: "Please Warm My Wiener," "Your Biscuits Are Big Enough for Me," and "Banana in Your Fruit Basket."

As time went on, the blues were discovered by white society. Like ragtime, they were to reach the general public when a talented African-American musician captured the musical style and its poignant spirit in written form and began using blues themes in his own compositions. Also like ragtime, the blues had disreputable aspects that were to be dropped. What remained were the timeless expressions of people leading a hard life and singing about their sorrows.

The person who did the most to make the blues acceptable to the general public was William C. Handy. Born in Florence, Alabama in 1873, Handy came from a family of preachers, all of whom were dead set against his pursuing a career in music. But young William had a good tenor voice and was fascinated by the soulful folk songs of his people. He was determined to learn all he could about music. When he was about ten, he bought a used rotary valve cornet. He had no money for lessons, but he was able to peek through the open door where other children were receiving musical instruction. He memorized the notes on the blackboard and taught himself to play the music.

By the time he was a young adult, Handy had become a skilled musician. However, finding that jobs for black musicians were scarce, he had to roam around, working wherever and whenever he could. Meanwhile, he continued to study music and to learn about the songs, both sacred and profane, of the South's African-Americans. By 1909, he had written a piece based on black folk music, which was published in 1912 as "The Memphis Blues." Although it never made him any money, it added to his growing reputation as a musician. By then he had established his own small band, and he continued to write and ultimately produce songs that achieved considerable popularity, particularly in the period just before World War I. His "Beale Street Blues," and especially his "St. Louis Blues," became part of the American musical heritage. Thus, today we remember Handy as the "father of the blues." He did not invent the music. But like Scott Joplin before him, he made it accessible.

In the African-American tradition, the blues were sung mostly by women. Often men worked away from home at migratory jobs, and the women stayed behind and missed them greatly. But a number of outstanding male musicians also specialized in the blues. Several African-American performers became famous during the 1920s. "Ma" Rainey, Bessie Smith, Blind "Lemon" Jefferson, and "Leadbelly" Ledbetter were popular figures. Later, Louis Armstrong received world recognition and honor for his role in the development of uniquely American music.

Country and Gospel

What we now call country music is a mixture of several forms that originated in the pioneer folk music of various sections of the nation, although they have evolved to the point that they bear little resemblance to their fore-bears. One early form survived from the isolated life of the early settlers of the Appalachian highlands. These songs were based on English ballads that the pioneers brought with them. They were passed on in the oral tradition—and, predictably, underwent many changes. As time went on, the settlers created their own ballads, and some became widely known. Most of this folk music had a rather simple musical structure so that it could be played easily on the stringed instruments that were available, such as the fiddle, the banjo, and the dulcimer. The lyrics were uncomplicated and usually told a story. These narratives were drawn from the everyday experiences of the people and the times. Like most of their counterparts today, the songs expressed themes that everyone understood. They told of work, play, interesting people or events, and significant human emotions.

Western, or "cowboy," songs were still another form. They too grew out of the everyday life of simple people. The original folk songs were usually sung solo and accompanied by a guitar (adopted from Mexico). Some were ballads that told of dramatic events or famous people; others were used to soothe nervous cattle. In some cases, several instruments were used and the music became more complex, incorporating dance forms such as reels and square dances brought west from the East and South.

In more modern times, the film industry gave the cowboy song an immense boost in popularity. Some cowboy stars of the 1930s not only rode horses, wore white hats, shot the bad guys, and overcame evil, but also played the guitar and sang versions of the old range songs. Roy Rogers and Gene Autry made this type of music a household item in the decade before World War II. In recent times, however the cowboy song has faded as a popular music form.

An outgrowth of the blues, the African-American gospel song grew to maturity during the Great Depression of the 1930s. Times were hard for everyone, even the white middle class, but for black people they were terrible. People of both races often went hungry. Many wandered around seeking even the most temporary kind of work—anything to survive. It was a time of loneliness, heartache, and despair, when religious expression enhanced by gospel songs could stimulate temporary hope. The gospel song is an emotional testimony—a petition to God for help and approval. In other words, the gospel song

> . . . tells the congregation or audience of the singers' problems, needs, or desires—or of their experiences and knowledge of God. It invokes all those within hearing distance, who share or have faced the same problems, to join the singers and to testify to suffering along with them. All are directly singing to each other, yet indirectly speaking to the Almighty, petitioning God or marvelling at His powers.[8]

Sung with great feeling and emotion, gospel songs relieved the frustrations of the members of a congregation and aided them in facing the difficulties and deprivations in their lives.

Gospel songs were not folk music in the true sense. They were deliberately composed, with written scores. But the score was only a rough guide; singers made their own emotional interpretations. Although the basic themes and messages of gospel songs are alike, the singers may use whatever musical style suits their taste. Gospel songs have been written not only in the traditional form but also as blues, jazz, folk, soul, and rock. Gospel music long ago appealed to white as well as black people, and it remains popular among many religious segments of the population.

America Enters the Jazz Age

The word "jazz" was not applied to popular music until 1916. Both the name and the music had their origins in a musical revolution that came out of New Orleans to capture the imagination of Americans and eventually the world. It was the music that displaced ragtime.

The "Original Dixieland Jass Band"

At the turn of the century, New Orleans was full of amateur marching bands. Playing on the streets was popular among both blacks and whites. Almost all social events in the city—prize fights, dances, auctions, barbecues, speeches, funerals, weddings, fish fries—were made more colorful by the presence of live music. The instruments were usually brass, woodwinds, and drums, the basic elements of a marching band. Some groups were large and impressive, with snappy uniforms and whole sections of particular instruments. Others were small enough to fit comfortably on a horse-drawn wagon, as long as the trombonist sat on the tailgate and aimed his slide toward the back.

It was in this environment that the son of an Italian shoemaker grew up to become a leader in changing the nation's tastes in popular music.

Dixieland jazz replaced ragtime just after World War I. It originated among both black and white musicians in New Orleans but was popularized by Dominick LaRocca and his band, pictured here. They coined the word "jazz" and startled people in Chicago and New York with their unusually vigorous playing. Jazz quickly became a worldwide fad. It was later replaced by "swing," a softer, sweeter form of popular music. (Brown Brothers)

Dominick (Nick) LaRocca was born in 1889 and had decided by the age of ten that he wanted to be a musician. His father was outraged, but when he died, Nick promptly quit school, got a job, bought a fancy new silver-plated cornet, and began to play in earnest. Like many amateur musicians in the city, he never learned to read music. Unburdened by preconceptions of the limits of his instrument, he systematically began to gain command of every kind of musical composition, rhythm, and sequence that it could produce.

LaRocca readily found other young men who loved to play and formed a small band. For several years, the group of five eked out a miserable existence playing at sporting events and in saloons and dance halls. Often they had to work at other jobs to make ends meet. Meanwhile, they began to experiment with new styles of music. They were not alone in their attempts at innovation; many groups in New Orleans were experimenting with new musical expressions. But LaRocca's group worked out a very distinctive style of playing, and he began to compose new songs in the innovative technique. These were not written scores; the group practiced them until they could play them perfectly by ear.

In some ways, the new style sounded like musical chaos. Instead of everyone playing together in the traditional manner, following a set melody, each musician improvised in his own way while rigidly maintaining both the beat and the basic harmony. Those who heard the music for the first time often did not know how to react. Some were puzzled; others were angered; still others were frightened. It did not sound like any music they had ever heard before. Each instrument seemed to be playing a different tune in a completely impromptu manner. Yet, somehow, it all fit together into a catchy overall pattern like a musical jigsaw puzzle. Once the initial shock was over, it not only held people's attention but set their feet to tapping as well.

In 1915, a prosperous Chicago nightclub owner heard LaRocca's band at a New Orleans prize fight and offered them train fare and a small weekly salary to come up north.[9] They accepted gladly, and they were an instant sensation. One night while the band was playing enthusiastically and the night club audience was roaring its approval, a tipsy character from Chicago's underworld jumped up and shouted a slang word for sexual intercourse to encourage the band: "Jass it up, boys!" The crowd took up the cry. The next day, the band billed itself as the "Dixie Jass Band" in big red letters posted outside the club. The new music created such interest among Chicagoans that other clubs had to bring in musicians from New Orleans to try to play in the same style. This led LaRocca and his group to call themselves the "Original Dixieland Jass Band."

Al Jolson, a well-known show business personality, helped make arrangements for the band to travel to New York. Within a few days, the verdict was in. New York decided it loved the new Dixieland music. A few newspapers denounced it, but most praised it lavishly. Nearly all misspelled "jass" in every conceivable way. LaRocca finally settled on "jazz," because mischievous boys were defacing the band's posters by crossing out the first letter. Within a few weeks, the Original Dixieland Jazz Band became the talk of New York, and the whole country began to be jazz-conscious. Like it or not, in 1916, America entered the *Jazz Age*. Hundreds of other groups took up the style, and the older ragtime music faded away.

Although the word "jazz" clearly has its origins in LaRocca's music and the name of his band, it quickly became part of the common vocabulary. Indeed, its meaning expanded throughout the world to imply almost all forms of modern popular music. In more recent times, the name "Dixieland jazz" has been used to identify the particular form that originated in New Orleans.

Once the war was over, Americans entered the Roaring Twenties. The older Victorian moral codes that had dominated before the Great War slipped away, and behavior changed. Couples in the 1920s went on dates unchaperoned in cars, drank bootleg liquor, and danced the Charleston. The new phonograph and the budding radio industry helped spread the wild new music. LaRocca's Original Dixieland Jazz Band became the most highly paid and sought-after musical group of the period. With thousands of imitators, they were the Beatles of their time.

The Anti-Jazz Movement

As the twenties roared on, conservatives became increasingly convinced of two things: First, America's moral norms were rapidly being eroded. Second, the bad influence leading to their devastation was jazz. From these two beliefs came a welling up of anger, resentment, and determination to drive out the offending demon. Jazz was the *visible enemy* around which to muster forces for the preservation of good against evil. However, sin was

The 1920s will always be remembered for the Charleston. That decade was a time of new music, dances, styles of dress, and moral codes. The changes were deplored by the older generation, but thoroughly enjoyed by the young. Such a generation gap has existed many times during the twentieth century, as social change has continued and popular music has seen many trends. (Brown Brothers)

clearly winning! The conservatives saw that the phonograph was bringing jazz music right into every home, and the movies were showing seductive visions of immoral life to an impressionable generation. In addition, big city dance halls were becoming increasingly popular as places where the young could come together in an exciting and unsupervised atmosphere of flirtation, illegal drinking, smoking, and dancing. It was clear what *that* led to. The decadence of modern life seemed to know no bounds.

Public leaders of many kinds began to denounce vigorously the growing menace of jazz. Groups such as the National Education Association, the Federation of Women's Clubs, and many religious organizations jumped on the anti-jazz bandwagon and vowed to stamp out the menace. The newspapers spoke out strongly, denouncing this awful threat to the nation's standards of decency. For example, in 1922, the *New York American* published this disturbing item:

JAZZ RUINING GIRLS, DECLARES REFORMER

Chicago, Jan. 21—Moral disaster is coming to hundreds of American girls through the pathological, nerve irritating, sex-exciting music of jazz orchestras, according to the Illinois Vigilance Association.

In Chicago alone the association's representatives have traced the fall of 1,000 girls in the last two years to jazz music.

Girls in small towns, as well as the big cities, in poor homes and rich homes, are victims of the weird, insidious, neurotic music that accompanies modern dancing.

The degrading music is common not only to disorderly places, but often to high school affairs, to expensive hotels and so-called society circles, declares Rev. Richard Yarrow, superintendent of the Vigilance Association.

The report says that the vigilance society has no desire to abolish dancing, but seeks to awaken the public conscience to the present danger and future consequences of jazz music.

By the mid-1920s, jazz was being denounced vigorously on all sides. Church leaders, health authorities, educators, and concerned citizens all joined the assault. In New York City, the commissioner of licenses outlawed all jazz and dancing on Broadway after midnight. Even the phonograph companies joined the crusade. The first jazz record had not been made until 1917 (by the Original Dixieland Jazz Band, a piece called "Livery Stable Blues"). In 1923, the Victor Talking Machine Company, which had been a leader in issuing jazz records, banished the word from its labels and refused to record any more jazz music. Jazz, said the experts, was *dead*.

If it was dead, it was about to undergo a reincarnation. In February 1923, Paul Whiteman, a musician with a background in classical music, had conceived of dressing up jazz in concert form to show that American popular music could be taken seriously. He put together a full symphony orchestra, dressed in tuxedos for the occasion, and gave a historic "Jazz Concert" in the prestigious Aeolian Hall in New York City. It had been advertised as an experiment in modern music, and it certainly was. To begin the concert, the elegantly attired Paul Whiteman raised his baton and the orchestra played its interpretation of Nick LaRocca's "Livery Stable Blues." They went on with symphonic renditions of such familiar pieces at the time as "Yes, We Have No Bananas" and "Alexander's Ragtime Band." The concert finished with George Gershwin playing his new concerto, "Rhapsody in Blue." In the audience were a number of the world's most distinguished musicians and music critics. They loved it.

The event marked the beginning of the end of the older, cruder form of Dixieland jazz played by small groups who could not read music. Within a few years, it went into decline. It would be replaced by a softer and sweeter form played by larger orchestras from carefully arranged music.

In retrospect, the enthusiastic acceptance of jazz music was a *symptom* of cultural change rather than the cause. That is probably true of all new forms of popular music. The twenties were a time when rapid industrialization, urbanization, and modernization brought new values, priorities, and standards to the country. Those changes made it possible for people to accept a radical change in their preferred music.

Perhaps more than any other factor, the rapidly developing technology of the phonograph helped jazz music become popular. During the 1920s, radio began to be a household medium, but it was not much of an influence on the popularity of jazz. But as the radio industry stabilized and home receivers became common, and as the technology of sound recording greatly improved, the combination of the two would play an increasingly important role in the spread of all new forms of popular music. Thus, it was the merging of the medium and the recording industry that ultimately made popular music such a central aspect of contemporary American culture.

Machines for Recording Sound

As we have seen, the early development of popular music in the United States did not depend greatly on the phonograph. The essential medium for ragtime was sheet music. Piano rolls and records played a part, but the home piano was the main factor. Dixieland's basis of popularity was different. To a large degree, the popularity arose from the music's live performance for dancing. However, records eventually promoted the consumption of popular music as the phonograph developed from a novelty to a practical device for home entertainment. After about 1925, home radio and the record industry together provided a combination of content and medium that brought an ever-changing flow of popular music to millions of fans. For that reason, we need to review briefly the evolution of the phonograph and the record industry as they developed over the course of more than a century.

Edison's Talking Machine

Thomas Alva Edison invented so many other remarkable devices that it is easy to forget he was also the originator of the phonograph. While trying to improve the efficiency of the telegraph and telephone, it occurred to him that the human voice might be captured on some sort of recording device. On July 18, 1877, he wrote in his lab notes:

Just tried an experiment with diaphragm having an embossing point and held against paraffin paper moving rapidly. The speaking vibrations are indented nicely, and there is no doubt that I shall be able to store up and reproduce automatically at any future time the human voice perfectly.[10]

By the fall of 1877, Edison had developed a machine that could crudely reproduce the human voice. The speaker turned a crank and shouted into a horn ending in a diaphragm. A needle activated by the diaphragm embossed a hill-and-valley pattern on a tinfoil sheet wrapped around a rotating cylinder. By retracking the needle through the same groove that it made when recording, the thing would talk back.

The first words Edison recorded were "Mary had a little lamb." He wasted no time in demonstrating his talking machine. He took the device to the New York offices of the *Scientific American* and demonstrated it to an enthusiastic group. Later the account was written up in the magazine:

> Mr. Thomas A. Edison recently came to this office, placed a little machine on our desk, turned a crank, and the machine inquired as to our health, asked how we liked the phonograph, informed us that it was very well, and bid us a cordial good night. These remarks were not only perfectly audible to ourselves, but to a dozen or more persons who were gathered around.[11]

The Edison Speaking Phonograph Company was quickly formed to exploit the invention commercially. The phonograph was seen mainly as a curiosity, and it was modestly successful in that form. Showmen could record various sounds on revolving tinfoil-covered cylinders and astonish audiences by playing them back on a machine billed as a Parlor Speaking Phonograph. People could hear voices in Dutch, German, Hebrew, Spanish, and other languages. The barking of dogs was recorded, as was a cock crowing. People sang "Yankee Doodle" or whistled. It was all very entertaining.

Almost at once, Edison and others saw that such a machine might have more serious uses. Edison suggested using it for business dictation, phonographic books for the blind, prerecorded lessons, the reproduction of music, and the recording of family members' voices for posterity. He went on to suggest talking clocks, preservation of the correct pronunciation of languages, and permanent records of important telephone calls. If he had added dancing and the hit parade, he would have anticipated most of its subsequent uses.

None of those applications came about quickly. Soon the novelty wore off and the phonograph fell into disuse. Inevitably, other inventors advanced claims that they, rather than Edison, had produced the first practical machine. Nevertheless, by the end of the 1880s, technology had advanced somewhat. Recording on tinfoil was abandoned in favor of hard wax cylinders. Another innovator brought out a practical disc for recording. It was made of hardened black shellac and was quite durable. A few adventurous musicians from opera and classical music actually recorded their performances.

Efforts to record music proceeded slowly, however. In the 1890s, there was neither a substantial market for the machines nor enough records to play on them. One problem was the poor quality of musical reproduction; another was the brief duration of the recordings (two minutes); still another was that no practical means had been invented for copying a master recording to produce records in quantity. To get multiple copies, the performance had to be repeated over and over, making one record at a time. It was very hard on such groups as the U.S. Marine Band, which played "Semper Fidelis" up to fifty times during one session. Opera stars and other famous musicians had the same difficulty.

Yet in spite of the problems, the technology of recording continued to advance. Developers tried various materials for the records themselves, such as metal and hard rubber. Hardened shellac proved to be the best, and it came into wide use rather early. (In fact, it remained the basic material for the manufacture of records well into the 1940s.) More and more was recorded: Shakespeare's plays, marches by John Philip Sousa, folk music, poems, comedy monologues, and always the venerable opera stars. By the end of the century, American and European firms were marketing thousands of records for various types of machines. Even so, the phonograph was still something of a plaything of the rich.

As the new century began, techniques had been developed for molding multiple records from a master. This was a critical breakthrough because it brought the price of records down sharply. In addition, the disc was rapidly replacing the cylinder, much to Edison's chagrin. Another important advance was that a reliable spring motor had been invented to drive the discs at a constant speed (78 rpm), which remained the standard of the industry until the 1940s.

Within a short time, new sound boxes were coupled to the spring motor, horn, and turntable, and relatively inexpensive phonographs were mass-produced. Twenty-five dollars would buy an improved model. *Victrola* achieved

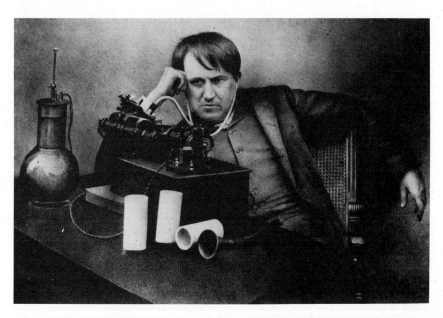

Thomas Edison worked hard to perfect his phonograph machine. He experimented with various devices, such as trumpets and ear tubes to enhance the sound. He even hooked a primitive motor to the machine to replace the hand crank. (The device on the left is a Leyden jar, an early form of the storage battery.) In the 1890s, however, the public showed little interest in Edison's invention. (The Bettmann Archive)

immortality as a generic name for record players when a small machine with that brand name was advertised with an engaging black-and-white fox terrier listening to "his master's voice."

In 1902, the Gramophone Company in England prevailed upon Enrico Caruso, the great opera singer, to cut ten records. By the time Caruso died in 1921, he had earned over $2 million from the venture. His recordings gave the phonograph industry a considerable boost. It was beginning to recognize the potentially large market for recordings and the great profits that could be made by those with imagination. Soon every company in the business was recording Italian opera stars, symphony orchestras, and great pianists. The records sold like the proverbial hotcakes.

Back in the United States, the Victor Talking Machine Company and the Columbia Disc Gramophone Company both began making phonograph machines. They were cheap and reasonably reliable, and there was an increasing repertoire of recordings that people could purchase and play (although little in the way of popular music). Even so, the new machine had its critics. John Philip Sousa, who had been recorded a number of times, decided that the device was a menace and blasted the new craze.[12]

Notwithstanding heavy criticism, by 1910, American and European record companies were producing thousands of titles and selling records in the millions. Victor had introduced its popular "living room" Victrola, which looked like a nice piece of furniture. Other companies brought out similar models. Full symphony orchestras were recording, and opera singers remained a staple. When the dance mania began to sweep the country around 1916, the recording companies all began to market a growing number of titles that fit

ENRICO CARUSO AND THE RECORDING INDUSTRY:
A Linchpin to Music History

Musical entertainment as a part of dramatic theater was highly developed by the time of the classical period. Four hundred years before the birth of Christ, Greek theaters capable of holding thousands of people were used to present tragedies and comedies, with accompanying music. Despite this rich tradition of musical drama, however, the beginnings of opera did not appear in Western Europe until the 1500s. The word "opera" derives from the Latin *opus*, which means "work."

In 1472, a young Italian writer named Angelo Ambrogini produced a verse-drama entitled *La Favola d'Orfeo* that was sung with music on a stage. Many music historians mark this work as a precursor to opera, but it took over a hundred years before Ambrogini's verse-drama was successfully shaped by Claudio Monteverdi into the kind of opera we recognize today: a combination of orchestral music, stage sets, costumes, actors singing their parts, and a larger accompanying chorus. Monteverdi's *Orfeo,* based on the Greek legend of Orpheus, was staged in 1607 (a decade after Shakespeare published and produced *A Midsummer Night's Dream*). Renaissance audiences loved it, and as more musical plays were produced, Italian opera quickly spread as an art form.

During the next three hundred years, increasingly complex and sophisticated operas were written by great musical geniuses from not only Italy but also France, Germany, Russia, and England. A number of different operatic forms developed: *opera buffa, opera comique, opera seria, opera romantique,* and even "operettas" for less complex tastes. By the end of the nineteenth century, opera was prominent among the arts as a widely appreciated form of entertainment. At the time, it had few competitors. It brought together accomplished composers, musi-

the many new kinds of steps—the turkey trot, the one-step, the Boston, and the exotic new tango. By the time of World War I, the 78 rpm record and the spring-driven player had about reached their high point of development. To be sure, the systems could not reproduce music nearly as well as the records we use today. (Both very high and very low frequencies were not reproduced.) Yet they seemed great at the time.

Significant Technological Developments

Because the mechanical phonograph was so simple and reliable, there was no great pressure before the 1920s to bring out an electric machine. But as the basic technology of radio developed, the next obvious step was to adapt its principles to the problem of sound reproduction from records. In 1919, Bell Telephone Laboratories assumed the initiative.

The electric phonograph   The machines that resulted were much more sensitive than the simpler mechanical systems, with a new quality of sound. The early electrical recordings produced a frequency range of from 100 to 5,000 cycles per second. (Even inexpensive stereo equipment today handles

cians, choreographers, and of course world-famous singers for spectacular performances. Both Europe and the United States teemed with opera enthusiasts.

Just when the phonograph was being developed for home use, at the beginning of the twentieth century, an outstanding opera singer was gaining worldwide recognition. In 1901, twenty-seven-year-old Enrico Caruso had already established himself as a star. In later years, he would be known as the greatest singer of his time (and, some believe, of all time). Caruso was fascinated by the new technology of capturing sound. He decided to try recording operatic arias. Singing as loudly as he could, he recorded *E lucevan le stelle* at the primitive studio of the Anglo-Italian Commerce Company. The recording was made on a cylinder that had to be played back at a remarkable 150 rpm (modern LPs play at 33 1/3 rpm). By today's standards of recording precision, it was awful. Caruso and his fans thought it was wonderful.

During the next several years, Caruso and other great performers recorded vocal music on many cylinders and discs. As Caruso became increasingly famous, his recordings were avidly purchased and collected all over the world. Phonographic technology permitted people to hear for the first time in their own homes the voice of the world's greatest tenor.

During the early years of the phonograph, before popular music generated wider interest, it was stars such as Caruso, and elite and classical music more generally, that provided economic incentives for the recording industry. Later, as radio developed into a household medium and popular music increasingly captured the imagination of the masses, opera would be less important. The recording industry turned to jazz, and later to swing, boogie-woogie, and rock and roll as a means of making a profit.

Sources: Donald J. Grout, *A Short History of Opera* (New York: Columbia University Press, 1965); Michael Scott, *The Great Caruso* (New York: Alfred Knopf, 1988); Aida Favia-Artsay, *Caruso on Records* (Valhalla, N.Y.: The Historic Record, 1965).

from about 20 to 25,000 cycles per second, but, in fact, most people cannot hear much beyond the 100 to 5,000 range.) Compared with the old flat-sounding mechanical recording, it was a new listening experience. Deep bass notes could be heard for the first time, as could the higher ranges and overtones of treble instruments.

After much foot dragging, the major record companies and the manufacturers of home machines began making the change to electrical systems in 1925. The whole industry entered a new era. The last half of the 1920s was a period of spectacular growth in the sale of records. Machines that contained both a record player and a radio were being manufactured. The public loved them. The old wind-up victrolas went to the attic. Times were good, and people were eager to spend their money on the new electrical machines and records. Almost every artist who could play an instrument or sing a tune was recorded amid a huge outflow of opera, symphonic works, and popular dance music. In 1927, some 104 million discs were sold in the United States. In addition, Americans purchased some 987,000 record players.[13]

Then came the stock market crash of 1929, and the recording industry crashed along with it. In 1932, only 6 million records were sold in the United States, a drop of nearly 95 percent from the high reached in 1927.[14] The economic factor was clearly a significant cause, as people gave up small luxuries like buying records. However, another significant factor was the soaring popularity of radio as a medium of free home entertainment. In 1925, only about 14 percent of American households had at least one radio set, but by 1935 that figure had shot up to more than 95 percent.[15] By this time, radio stations were filling their broadcast time by playing dance music over the air. In the evenings, people could hear live broadcasts of famous bands from fancy hotels and supper clubs. When popular music could be had for nothing with a mere twist of the dial, why buy expensive records? Indeed, people did not, and by 1933, the recording industry was practically extinct.

Then, with a new administration in Washington, the economy began to turn around. This enabled people to spend just a little on small luxuries, and the phonograph industry started to recover. In 1938, about 33 million records were sold. Also, the introduction of *albums* helped sales, and prices were also greatly reduced. Some classical music records had retailed for as much as $7 before the crash, but comparable discs were on the market in 1940 for $1 apiece. The smaller dance records that had cost 75 cents during the 1920s were selling for 35 cents. As 1941 ended, the record industry was astonished to learn that its sales had reached 127 million records that year. The industry had clearly recovered.[16] However, the Japanese bombing of Pearl Harbor stopped growth, and it did not resume until the war was over.

The juke box   Meanwhile, one application of the phonograph began to play a significant part in promoting enthusiasm for popular music. The original machine was quite simple. A phonograph record (actually a cylinder), a spring-driven player, and a money slot were first combined by Louis Glass of San Francisco.[17] In 1889, he installed such a device in the city's Palaise Royale Saloon. During the 1890s, people could go to a "phonograph parlor," drop a nickel in a slot and hear such favorite performers as John Philip Sousa's energetic Marine Band, an Italian tenor, and John Y. Atlee, the "Artistic Whistler." By 1906, a coin-activated player allowed patrons to *see* the machine change discs.

After record machines became electrified, they spread to all parts of the country. In the South, African-Americans called the machines *juke boxes* for reasons that have never been made clear. By the late 1930s, juke boxes had became a wonder to behold. Typically, they were glowing machines with powerful speakers, brightly lit plastic tubes, sometimes with moving bubbles inside, and a large selection of the latest hits. They could be found in every restaurant, hamburger joint, and drugstore where young people gathered. Soon they also invaded taverns, honky-tonks, and beer halls. The garish, nickel-eating machines pumped new energy into the entire popular music and recording industry and stimulated the spread of new dance forms.

High-fidelity recording   During World War II, the British-owned Decca Record Company was called on by the military to help train naval personnel in tracking German submarines. They were asked to make phonograph records that would capture the very subtle differences in sounds made by U-

The bright, loud, and garish juke box became an important factor in the development of popular music after the early 1930s. For a nickel, one could hear songs that had been identified as the latest hits. The juke box brought lively new dance forms to every hamburger heaven and hangout, increasingly focusing young people's interest on popular music. (UPI/Bettmann)

boats and those made by British submarines. They were able to do so with what they called "full frequency range reproduction." As soon as the war was over, Decca used the techniques to record music. It was a great step forward that brought a new range of sound to the listener.

Yet for all the electronic devices and fancy new sounds, the phonograph record of 1946 was still pretty crude. In fact, in some ways it differed little from what it had been in 1903. Even though it was an electric machine, it retained the 78 rpm of the earlier days, and a record lasted only four minutes at most. Although many improvements had been made, the shellac from which the record was still manufactured was easy to scratch.

Long-playing and stereo records   In 1948, Columbia Records revealed a new kind of phonograph disc, a remarkable product made of new and virtually unbreakable plastic materials. It had "micro grooves" and would play at 33 rpm for an astonishing twenty-three minutes on each side. Not only that, but it incorporated the new full-frequency sound. In a clever strategy, Columbia developed a cheap attachment that enabled existing phonographs to handle the new long-playing (LP) microgroove records, and then hit the market with a stock of recordings already manufactured. The company sold well over a million of the new records in six months. Although Columbia had offered to share the new technology with other recording companies to help standardize the industry, RCA Victor decided to go its own way and brought out an odd little 45 rpm microgroove "single" record, which was cheap to produce and sell.

The main consequence was a great deal of confusion among buyers. Now they had their original collections of 78s, some of the new 33 rpm LPs, and some of the little 45s. In the 1950s, record players had to be built to handle all three record types that were on the market. However, the older 78 rpm shellac discs went into a sharp decline, and production soon ceased. The 45s lasted right up to 1989, when Columbia Records stopped producing them. At present, as we will see, the 33 rpm LPs are also becoming a thing of the past.

Another revolution in recording came with stereophonic sound in the early 1960s. Techniques were developed for recording more than one soundtrack on the disc. Special microphones pick up the sounds of an orchestra or performer from different locations, and stereo equipment can reproduce the separate sounds and send them to different speakers. The result was a distinctive sound experience, almost as though the listener were in the studio with the musicians. Once again consumers had to face the prospect of abandoning their existing records—their monaural LPs—and beginning their collections anew. For a while it looked as if still further changes might come in the form of quadraphonic systems, using four speakers instead of two, and result in yet another problem of obsolescence. However, quadraphonic sound never really caught on.

Magnetic wire and tape   Both wire recordings and magnetic tape came on the market shortly after World War II. Wire recording had been improved by the Germans, who had used it extensively to record radio broadcasts for intelligence analysis. Magnetic impulses were recorded on a small reel of thin wire passed through a recording head. When played back, the sound was of excellent quality, and the wire could play for a long time. However, it could not easily be edited, and it was nearly impossible to repair a wire that broke. Tape filled with metal particles used the same principle, but turned out to have distinct advantages. Both wire and tape, unlike discs, could be played over and over many times without hurting the quality of the sound. However, if a tape broke, it could easily be spliced. Larger and larger reels were introduced, and a big one could play for nearly an hour without interruption. In 1947, experts were predicting the death of the old disc-playing phonograph, just as soon as mass production of tape recordings brought their price down.

The outcome was that wire recording disappeared by the end of the 1940s. Reel-to-reel tapes found a place in the market, especially in music production and among high-fidelity hobbyists. For a short time, the eight-track tape cassette was popular—not really a different technology, but packaged differently and requiring distinctive equipment. Like the wire recorder, it has now become obsolete.

Compact discs and digital technology   Today, LP stereo records are all but obsolete. They are the end of the line for Edison's needle-in-the-track technology. Their replacement, the digital compact disc (CD), uses laser beam technology and has several advantages. It does not wear out no matter how often it is used. It is not fragile like the LP record. Its small size makes storage and handling much easier. It holds about twenty minutes more music than an LP, and it produces no noise other than the music itself.

The use of CDs grew more quickly than anyone anticipated when they first appeared.[18] The discs went on the market in 1983. In 1985, only two years later, over 22 million were sold, and by 1987, annual sales had shot up to just over 102 million. In 1993, the number reached an astronomical 495 million and showed no signs of tapering off at that level. Thus, the acquisition of CDs is following the typical S-shaped curve that describes the adoption of innovations.

As the startlingly rapid adoption of the CD progressed, sales of LP stereo records dropped sharply. In fact, as Figure 14.1 shows, the crossover point, where sales of albums fell below those of compact discs, occurred late in 1986. Many older LP masters are being reissued as CDs, but virtually no record companies continue to produce the records. In addition, record players are not being produced. Turntables can still be included as components in many stereo sets, but the LP vinyl microgroove record will soon be as obsolete as its 78 rpm ancestor.

One technology that has survived—even thrived—is the audio cassette tape. Tapes remain in demand because they are easy to play in cars, in tiny walk-around systems, and in all kinds of portable players. However, the curve of adoption of cassettes (Figure 14.1) already shows ominous signs of impending obsolescence.

Even newer technologies are now coming on line. In 1985, Japanese manufacturers at the Japan Audio Fair in Tokyo began showing prototypes of a new kind of tape, about half the size of conventional cassettes. Based on a technology similar to that used for compact discs, it is called digital audio tape (DAT). The DAT sent shock waves through the audio industry. Its quality of sound is at least that of the compact disc, and its market potential is enormous. Immediately, major recording companies and other vested interests initiated complex legal battles to keep these machines and tapes off the market on the grounds that they will be used for unauthorized copying of recordings. The future of DAT is not easy to predict. However, in 1990, many of these legal obstacles were overcome, and thus opened the way for consumers to buy and use DAT systems. A major shift to DAT technology could produce wrenching changes in the recording industry.

Another innovation that may (or may not) become important in the years ahead is the linking of the audio disc with video recording (CD-V), so that with a suitable player attachment, high-quality music can accompany video on the home TV set. Certainly, the CD-V will be attractive to consumers who want to see as well as hear the music. However, the future of this technology is less than clear.

In the vanguard of the movement to link popular music and television has been the music video. A child of cable television, it has brought a very different experience to the music consumer. It got its start in August 1982,

TABLE 14.1
Sales of Three Types of Recordings, 1981–1993*

Year	Compact Discs	Tape Cassettes	LP Albums
1981	—	137.0	295.2
1982	—	182.3	243.9
1983	0.8	236.8	209.6
1984	5.8	332.0	204.6
1985	22.6	339.1	167.0
1986	53.0	344.5	125.2
1987	102.1	410.0	107.0
1988	149.7	450.0	72.4
1989	207.2	446.2	34.6
1990	286.6	442.2	11.7
1993	495.4	339.5	1.2

*Sales figures are in millions.

Source: Recording Industry Association of America, 1994

FIGURE 14.1
Curves of Adoption for Compact Discs, Tape Cassettes, and Lp Albums, 1981–1993

The increasing use of compact discs by American consumers shows the classical S-shaped pattern associated with adoption theory. After a slow start, the curve is accelerating rapidly and showing no signs of leveling off. In contrast, the LP that it displaced shows a curve of obsolescence that is typical of items being replaced by more effective ones that serve a similar function. The adoption curve for cassettes reflects the miniaturization of players and their relatively inexpensive price. Cassette sales are now declining as CD use increases.

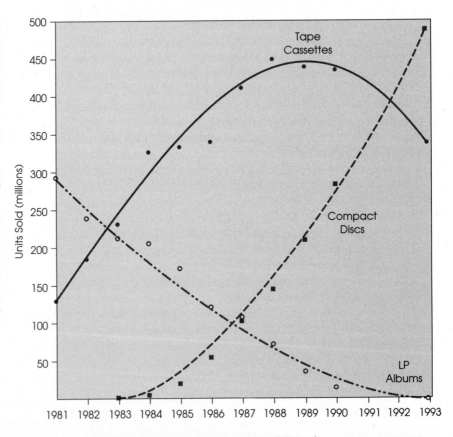

when the Warner Amex Satellite Entertainment Company launched MTV (Music Television). Critics scoffed at the idea of making a profit from a cable channel carrying nothing but rock music, but within two years MTV was serving 15 million households and expanding rapidly through seventeen hundred local cable services. Increasingly, it caught the attention of young audiences, and soon advertisers found it a convenient channel through which to reach a specific market segment.

Coming Together: Popular Music, the Recording Industry, and Mass Media

We have looked at changes in popular music styles and reviewed the evolution of recording technologies. In earlier chapters, we examined the development of the mass media in considerable detail. It was the coming together of all three of these elements that made popular music such a prominent aspect of the general American culture. As the mass media—particularly radio and television—increasingly captured the attention of the public, they became the foundation for sweeping changes in the national taste for popular music. As that took place, the recording industry grew and prospered.

The Media and Changing Forms of Popular Music

As the 1930s began, radio had penetrated the majority of American homes and was playing a growing role in developing the nation's appetite for popular music. Meanwhile, popular music itself had undergone a transformation. Dixieland jazz had faded as bands got larger and larger. Some had as many as thirty musicians, and their music had to be very carefully arranged. Few musicians just played it by ear anymore, and the new *swing music* was softer and sweeter. It was great for romantic dancing or just for easy listening. The radio played more and more records, and the nation became accustomed to having music in the home or car almost constantly.

Broadcasting swing and the big bands   In the late 1930s, the top big bands established their reputations by playing in swanky establishments where people went to eat, drink, and dance. Large hotels in major cities had "supper clubs" that hired the very best dance bands. In New York City there were the Madhattan Room of the Hotel Pennsylvania, the Terrace Room of the New Yorker, and the Palm Room of the Commodore. Also, cities everywhere had well-known "ballrooms" where the big bands appeared from time to time—the Roseland, Savoy, Aragon, Trianon, and Palomar were all famous. If a band was really popular, it played on the stages of major movie theaters, and huge crowds of fans came to hear. The popular music concert had become a reality.

As radio became more technologically sophisticated, the networks broadcast big band music in the late evening hours right from hotels and dance halls where the bands were appearing. People all over the country could tune in and feel that they were in glamorous surroundings, listening to the

During the 1930s and 1940s, the names of big band leaders, such as Tommy Dorsey, became household words. Such groups often had more than twenty musicians playing carefully orchestrated swing music. It was a time when weekly ratings of tunes became a nationwide preoccupation. Live band concerts were widely attended; juke boxes became popular; and a star system brought national recognition to singers. Radio broadcasts brought the big bands into people's homes. (Brown Brothers)

music of Benny Goodman, Jimmy Dorsey, or Glenn Miller. Dozens of band leaders' names became familiar household words. Each band had its own style and special arrangements, often developed around the instrument played by the leader.

Singers were important, too. In fact, some of the vocalists became more famous than the bands in which they got their start. A star system developed as the nation moved through the 1930s and on into the 1940s. Many people still recognize such names as Bing Crosby, Frank Sinatra, and Ella Fitzgerald. Hundreds more were known at the time and had their loyal fans.

In many ways, radio created the popularity of the big bands, along with that of their vocalists and the swing music they performed. During the 1930s, many commercially sponsored programs featured one of the famous bands. Disc jockeys soon established themselves, and playing records over the air helped build the popularity of both the bands and their music. A program called "Make-Believe Ballroom" had particular significance during the 1930s. It attracted a huge and enthusiastic following of young people and remained on radio for many years. From this style of broadcasting came another idea: a weekly poll to see which songs had the greatest appeal to listeners. It was a pretty haphazard survey, but millions tuned in every week to the "Lucky Strike Hit Parade" to hear how the songs were ranked. If this program format sounds familiar, it is because it has been around in one form or another ever since.

Meanwhile, the movies finally discovered popular music. Starting in about 1940, they made a number of low-budget (and low-quality) films featuring the best-known bands and their leaders. Today, popular music plays a central role in movies. Much of the theme music from motion pictures is eagerly exploited by the recording industry and snapped up by consumers.

As a musical style, swing seems innocuous, even innocent, by comparison with what came both earlier and later. Nevertheless, it received its share of criticism. For example, on August 14, 1938, the *New York Times* carried an article suggesting that swing music was responsible for all kinds of human problems, such as emotional unbalance, sexual excess, and even rape. A psychologist was quoted concerning the dangerous hypnotic influence of swing. The grounds for this condemnation were that the music had been cunningly devised around a tempo that was just faster than the human heart. Presumably, by some subtle interaction between music and the body, listeners were being driven toward evil and sin.

Swing was the music of a nation depressed. It was gentle and comforting during a time of economic hardship. During the worst years of the Great Depression, it was just what the nation wanted to hear. Then things started to get better. To be sure, war clouds were gathering in Europe, but the United States was isolated not only by the Atlantic Ocean but by an ideology that focused attention inward rather than on the troubles of foreigners. This all changed on December 7, 1941.

Jitterbugging to boogie-woogie Seemingly out of nowhere came a new kind of music. It had a fast style, and it provided the basis for a vigorous new kind of dancing that would become known as the *jitterbug*. The new musical beat, *boogie-woogie*, actually had its origins in the early 1900s in Chicago, where in obscure saloons in the African-American community, entertainers continued the tradition of improvising new rhythms. They were playing a primitive piano-blues rhythm they called "laying down the beat." The larger world was not ready for boogie-woogie at the time. By 1938, however, the new rhythm became popular in New York's café society, through the startling piano playing of several black musicians who remembered very well how to lay down the beat. Soon the throbbing sound of the fast-paced rhythm, played eight to the bar with a heavy hand on *ostinato* bass figures, had become popular. As the war came, boogie-woogie music and the spirited jitterbug swept an entire generation. It was exciting, pulse-pounding, and just right for an energetic country caught up in a global struggle for survival.

Even then, African-American musicians were developing a new form of music that eventually was called *rhythm and blues*. It retained the basic blues structure but added the pulsating beat of electric guitars. Conducive to energetic dancing, it was played rather loudly, and the vocalist had to shout to be heard. The importance of rhythm and blues was that it provided the basis for the rock-and-roll revolution in popular music that would sweep the younger generation in the postwar years.

Rock-and-roll Popular music is a commodity sold in an intensely competitive mass market. To succeed, the seller must offer the public something it will find new and exciting. Thus, the essence of the popular music industry is *change*. The pressure to produce new sounds, new stars—new product to sell—is intense. After World War II, as technological advances and prosperity increased the market for popular music, musical styles and tastes began to change more rapidly. This was especially evident during the early 1950s, when the division between "black" and "white" music began to blur. Alan Freed, a white disc jockey in New York City, organized concerts featuring well-known African-American musicians in auditoriums and ballparks; teen-

Change is the essence of popular music. Ragtime gave way to jazz and the blues early in this century. Swing transformed the nation's musical tastes in the 1930s and 1940s. By the 1950s, performers such as Elvis Presley had begun the transformation to rock. Rock music has many forms, but as a general category, it has lasted longer than any of the earlier forms of popular music. If the past is an accurate guide, entertainers and performers will bring about further changes in popular music. (Roberts/Photo Researchers, Inc.)

agers of both races attended in large numbers. Freed helped popularize the term *rock-and-roll* to characterize the music the young fans heard. Although it was largely the rhythm and blues that black musicians had been playing for years, the energy of the music took its new audiences by storm.

In 1955, a movie called *The Blackboard Jungle* showcased a song by a white group, Bill Haley and the Comets. The national exposure given "Rock Around the Clock" boosted the popularity of rock-and-roll to a new level. Soon record companies were producing increasing numbers of rock-and-roll records by both black and white artists.

Then came Elvis Presley. He was already something of a star among country music fans when his version of "Hound Dog" achieved a "crossover" success on pop, country-western, and rhythm-and-blues record charts. Presley brought a new personal style to the role of popular music idol. Darkly handsome, with sideburns and slicked-back hair, he sang and danced in a manner that some parents and religious leaders denounced as sexually suggestive. Combining rhythm and blues, country, and other popular music influences, and making confident use of various media—stage shows, recordings, movies, and television—Presley became the first superstar of rock-and-roll. Even today, years after his death, he remains a cult figure with a huge following.

One group stands out in the development of rock. The musical innovation and success of the Beatles formed the touchstone against which all rock acts continue to be measured. Subsequent waves of the so-called British invasion introduced the Rolling Stones, the Kinks, and the Who to American audiences. Detroit's Motown record company created its own distinctive sound with rhythm-and-blues acts such as the Supremes and the Miracles.

Bob Dylan expanded on the protest song tradition; the Beach Boys performed harmonic and carefree surf music. Psychedelic music, largely an off-shoot of the counterculture that grew up on the West Coast, was popularized by Jimi Hendrix and the Jefferson Airplane. Despite its varied forms, much of the music of the 1960s was colored by a political urgency born of the civil rights struggle and the Vietnam War protests.

In the 1970s, much of that variety and urgency drained away. The music industry became more corporate, and musical decisions revolved around what would appeal to the most consumers. The results were sometimes described as "mellow." Critics used a harsher word—"bland." Some performers, such as Linda Ronstadt and Crosby, Stills, Nash & Young, recorded songs with a country music tinge, known as "folk rock." For a while, disco music was wildly popular. Large arenas and stadiums became a standard

In the mid-1960s, a group of young musicians from England became international rock superstars. The Beatles combined American and British musical forms into a unique style that made them media heroes almost overnight. (Zimmerman/FPG International)

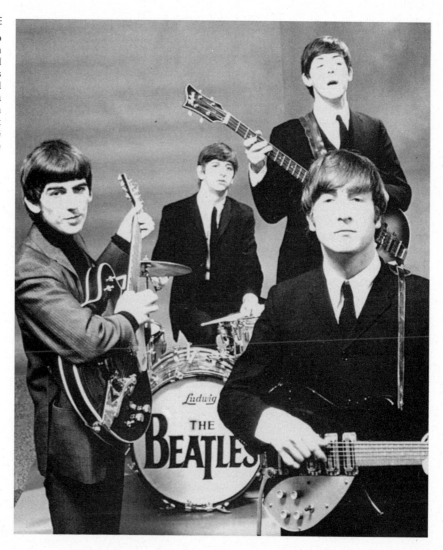

rock-and-roll venue, encouraging the success of performers such as David Bowie and Elton John, whose stage acts were elaborate and showy. But by the end of the decade, punk and new wave bands, led by such groups as the Sex Pistols and the Clash, had begun to puncture some of the emphasis on commercialism and expensive display.

As the 1980s progressed, diversity was once again a hallmark of the music industry. The quick-cut pace of cable's MTV helped create an appetite for musical (and visual) variety, and many different styles flourished. Michael Jackson and Madonna became pop icons through their flamboyant images and polished high-tech sounds. Perennial rock-and-roll favorites, who first achieved success ten to thirty years earlier, drew huge crowds. At the same time, specialized forms of music—heavy metal, reggae, international music (popularly known as world beat), and alternative rock-and-roll—previously not widely heard, became part of the musical mainstream. Country music continued to serve a huge, lucrative market.

Rap   The latest contender for becoming a major category of popular music is *rap*. Like ragtime, the blues, boogie-woogie, and rock, it is a product and expression of African-American life in the United States.[19] It does not, however, express the feelings of the majority of black people. Rap had its beginnings as far back as the mid-1960s in records by James Brown, Melvin Peebles, and Jamaican groups such as U Roy. It developed mainly in New York City, slowly during the 1970s and more rapidly in the 1980s, achieving a distinctive rhythm and unique rhyming vocal patterns. At block parties and other events, local disc jockeys provided a kind of running doggerel and special sound effects over the records they were playing.

By the 1990s, rap messages in musical form were sometimes expressions of anger and despair by young African-Americans. Many of the records that were being made advocated acts of violence. Controversies erupted over the words of such performers as Ice T and his song "Cop Killers," and Sister Souljah, who was said to call for murdering white people. Parents, conservatives, religious authorities, police officials, politicians, and many others—both black and white—began to denounce rap as threatening, antisocial, and unacceptable.

Like other forms of popular music, rap made it out of the black community in which it was developed when recording companies and the media gave it increasing attention. The negative reactions of parents and authorities to rap gave it high appeal to many white middle-class teens, who traditionally are drawn to almost anything the older generation warns them against. Rap records began to be featured on MTV, and a number soared to the top levels of the charts. By the early 1990s, rap was definitely "in," moving well beyond its origins into the white mainstream. About three-fourths of the rap records purchased in 1992 were bought by white youths.

Will rap take over and displace other forms of popular music? It seems doubtful. Its current popularity among white teens seems due more to the negative reactions of parents and others, which provide their own form of gratification, than to the angry expressions contained in the records themselves. The messages of rap about violence as a means to redress the injustices seen by angry African-Americans do not seem to be stirring the majority of white youth to take up their cause. A more likely outcome is that rap, like other forms of music that have become temporarily popular, will wear out its welcome and the tastes of teens will go on to something else.

Popular Music as an Industry

Although the large industry that records, manufactures, and sells popular music as a commercial product is not strictly a part of the mass media, we have shown how it is intricately related. To show how this form of popular culture is generated, we can look at two aspects of the recording industry: how a potential hit record is produced, and how it is distributed and sold.

The anatomy of a hit   What is the process by which a particular recording is produced and brought to the attention of consumers in such a way that it will become a retailing success? Obviously, there is no single set of factors that unfailingly produce a top-of-the-charts recording. There are, however, a number of complex stages through which every successful tune must pass if it is to make it in a big way.[20] These include: (1) beginning with a musical composition that fits contemporary tastes, (2) recording the performance of the musicians with the use of suitable technology, (3) popularizing it by getting it on the air frequently, (4) and distributing it to retail stores where it can be readily purchased.

If everything goes right, in today's market, a highly successful piece of music can sell from 10 to 15 million CDs or cassettes. If that happens, it reaps its performers and producers a fortune. Even if it sells a only a million copies (a "platinum" record), it will be a modest money-maker. But a unit that sells a mere 500,000 units (a "gold" record) may only break even. If sales reach only a paltry 100,000, it will be regarded as a dismal failure. Only a handful of those that are produced every year reach the top of the charts. Many break even, but a very large number lose money for their producers. Thus, music production is a chancy business where profits can be astronomical or where significant losses can easily occur.

Companies that produce and market records are constantly on the lookout for new talent and new compositions. They have little difficulty in finding candidates. There is a huge pool of hopefuls from which to choose. Let us assume, however, that a promising group of performers is under contract, and they will now record one of their new compositions that a major producer will bring to the market. We can follow that new composition through the technological process of recording and through the steps whereby the company tries to maximize its profits from the venture.

Obviously, the first step is to get the song recorded. A decade or so ago, making a record was not all that complex. The band and the singer performed the composition in a specially designed studio, with perhaps several microphones picking up the sound to be recorded directly on a master tape. If the director and engineers felt it necessary, the performance might be repeated several times so that the best version could be picked as the one from which records for retail sale would actually be pressed or otherwise manufactured. Today, the process is far more complex, and very little is left to chance. The object is to use advanced audio technology to produce a composition that is as technically flawless as complex computer-based systems can make it.

First of all, it is highly unlikely that the band will actually play as a group. For one thing, many popular musicians play poorly, and a surprising number of today's stars cannot even read music. Therefore, they need all the technical help they can get to produce a faultless performance. To improve the final product, each instrument may be recorded independently, often several times, on a separate tape "track" so that its sound can be analyzed and carefully adjusted for timing, volume, and pitch before it is added to the others. Parts can be taken from each of that instrument's tapes.

The singer will also perform independently and be recorded on a separate track. This too can be electronically smoothed, tweaked, and peaked to perfection. Then, the producer and the engineers will use the electronic technology to merge all of the separate tracks into a final master version, where all the musicians appear to be playing and singing together. Such technological manipulations limit the risks of faulty performance and make it possible to maximize the sound quality of each of the participants and instruments. The end result is the impressive "natural" and flawless sound that one hears when playing a contemporary cassette tape or compact disc.

It may seem contrary to common sense, but today's popular music is not designed primarily with the retail purchaser in mind. It is designed to appeal to various *gatekeepers* in the radio and music video industries. To be successful at all, a new recording must get by these individuals, or it will forever remain obscure. As Eric Rothenbuhler and Tom McCourt put it:

> . . . radio exposure largely determines which recordings become popular and which remain obscure. Furthermore, because the recording industry measures the value of particular songs in terms of how much airplay they receive—and the sales airplay helps stimulate—popular music is, for the most part, designed to meet the needs of the radio industry rather than individual consumers or the culture at large.[21]

Thus, the actions of program and music directors, or of disc jockeys of radio stations and music video channels, are the first and perhaps the major determiners of which recordings will make it big. These gatekeepers present the song to their listeners, and if the latter hear it often enough and like it, they will buy it at the record store.

As one might suspect, significant marketing efforts are brought to bear on gatekeepers. Music producers supply them with a flow of new recordings in the hope that they will play them. In radio stations, consultants are sometimes involved, but basically the decision to play a particular recording is made by the program director, the music director, or even the on-the-air personality. In small stations, these roles may all be played by one person.

Promoters who are employed by the recording companies push records on these critical people. It was this system that gave rise to the "payola" scandals of the late 1950s and early 1960s, in which promoters bribed radio

Today, the production of a popular recording depends as much on advanced audio technology as it does on the musical skills of the performers. In fact, since many popular artists are relatively poor musicians, technicians often have to refine what is played or sung. Each performer in a group is recorded separately, and his or her part is "tweaked" by technicians to correct for various problems. Later, the separate sound tracks are "mixed" into a master tape from which the recordings sold to the public are produced. (© 1991 Allan Clear, Impact Visuals)

personnel to get their products on the air. Such payoffs are now illegal, but there is every reason to believe that they continue.[22] Today, they may involve drugs, women, specially arranged trips, or well-hidden exchanges of cash.

The relationship between radio or video play and the popularity of a particular song is self-determining. That is, the more a song is "plugged" on the air, the more popular it tends to become among the listening audience. Studies show that music-purchasing decisions are often influenced by exposure to the song or album on radio or television.[23] Thus, the theory of the adoption of innovation fits the situation reasonably well. Media-provided information brings the new song to the attention of potential buyers. That information stimulates significant adoptions of the musical innovation in the form of retail sales. This results in the classic S-shaped curve of adoption shown in Figure 14.2 that starts slowly, rises rapidly, and then reaches a plateau. After reaching a peak, however, continued heavy media exposure produces exactly the opposite effect. The song becomes boring and sales drop sharply. Indeed, that is the fate of most songs that become successful. Their sales rise quickly, for about three weeks. They reach a plateau of brief duration and then drop off rapidly. At that point, the recordings are moved to the "back shelf" at the radio station, and their career as a big money producer is virtually over. Some live on for a time, or even become "golden oldies" that are played now and then. A few find minor continuing sales through special TV offers or mail order record clubs.

Music and records as business   At present, the recording industry is doing very well indeed, with annual sales of over $7.8 billion. Since 1950, when the new LP technology began to take hold, consumers have increased their expenditures for the recording industry's products by over 600 percent. Among the media, only television exceeds its revenues. Adding to the importance of the recording business is its role as a major supplier to the broadcast

**FIGURE 14.2
Schematic
Representation of the
Relationship between
Airplay and Sales**

A modern myth is that radio plays songs that are popular. That is correct only in a limited sense. Closer to the truth is that they become popular because they are frequently played over the air. Thus, airplay, and not the preferences of the audience, is the greatest determiner of the success or failure of a song. As the diagram indicates, those that are played with increasing frequency show a pattern of rising sales. When airplay falls off, sales decline, and the song is sent to the "back shelf," which usually means oblivion.

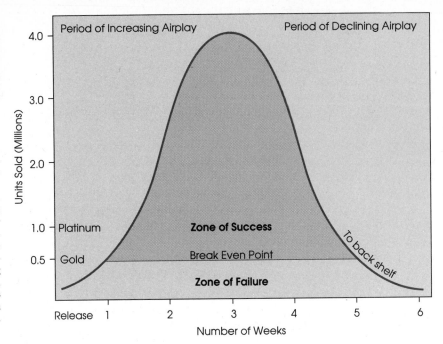

media. As we saw earlier, in face of competition from television, radio stations expanded their music programming in order to continue to attract audiences. Most have vast libraries from which they draw their selections.

The selling of popular music as a product is dominated by a relative handful of so-called *majors* (large producers and marketers of records). In 1993, the six largest were Columbia, Warner Brothers, Capital, MCA, Elektra, and Epic. These companies have vast financial resources that enable them to absorb failures and concentrate on promoting and marketing the limited number of records that rise to the top of the charts. They are so successful that they regularly own and distribute between 75 and 80 percent of the largest-selling CDs and cassettes every year. A key to understanding the role of the majors is that they not only produce the music of artists under contract but also manufacture the discs in the large numbers needed, distribute them to their own wholesale outlets, and in some cases retail them as well. On occasion, the majors also buy up the work of artists who have contracted with smaller companies for production of their recordings. Then the majors manufacture, distribute, and retail the product under their own label.

In contrast to the majors are the independent record companies, or *indies*, as they are called in the trade. Sometimes employing only a dozen or fewer full-time people, these smaller companies have long played a significant role in the development of popular music in this country. The majors concentrate on recording artists who are popular at the moment and whose work will sell in large quantities and have a chance of making a substantial profit. Well-known performers with established reputations are usually under contract with one of the majors, which have the financial means to promote their artists effectively. The indies, on the other hand, are the risk takers. They seldom have the opportunity to produce the works of well-known musicians. Often they have been started by fans of a particular form of music, musicians determined to present their favorite styles, or individuals devoted to the presentation of works by significant but perhaps obscure musicians.[24]

Actually, the word "independent" is somewhat misleading. The indies in fact depend very much on wholesale record distributors, which assume responsibility for distributing, promoting, and selling the music that the indies have produced and manufactured. In other words, the indies find talent, place the performers under contract, arrange to make the recordings, and have the records manufactured. They then sell the records to a network of distributors, which in turn sell them to a network of retailers. The retailers then sell them to the public. It is a very convenient arrangement for the indies, which do not have to maintain a large wholesaling and retailing system. It also allows a large number of indies to stay in business, even though any single one may command only a tiny share of the total sales of records in a given year. And it is a system that provides opportunity for new talent looking for a place in the sun. A performer who can convince one of the indies to make a record has a shot at the big time. It may be a remote chance, but it is a chance nevertheless. Since indies employ only a handful of people, they can keep costs down. But because they account for less than 20 percent of the hit records, the risks are high. If a big hit does come, though, the profits for a small independent producer can be impressive indeed.

Once the records have been produced and manufactured, distribution takes place. Selling the records was much simpler in earlier days, when the system consisted essentially of producers that manufactured the records, wholesalers that distributed them nationally, and retailers that sold them to the public. Today, the separate distribution systems of the majors and indies complicate matters.

One important means of marketing popular music is the *tape/record club*. Currently such clubs account for about 11 percent of total sales of recordings. The clubs (almost all of which are subsidiaries of the majors) offer tapes, CDs, and albums at rather large discounts. They can do so in part because they use large numbers of the roughly 25 percent of recordings offered at retail that are returned to distributors by retailers. Since the majors own the whole system, they can get rid of returns at reduced prices via the clubs, thus recovering some of the expense of excess production. In some instances, the clubs market re-released cassettes and CDs that are specially produced from existing master tapes the majors already own. The low production costs involved make at least modest profits likely.

Direct TV advertising for purchase by mail order is another marketing method. The ad gives a toll free number, and credit cards are the major form of payment. Often advertised as "not sold in stores," such bargains are either leftovers that have been purchased in quantity, a kind of graveyard of old and obsolete recordings that can be combined into "special collections," or special-purchase products bought at discount prices directly from the manufacturer. Here one finds such "classics" as collections of Liberace, over-performed symphonic compositions, long-forgotten tenors, second-rate "oldies," and the "beloved" songs of obscure country singers.

In short, the recording industry, although dominated by a small number of major companies that make the lion's share of the profits, supports an array of competitive enterprises. Dozens of risk-taking independent companies cater to smaller markets and constantly seek new talent to offer the public. The business also extends into such specialized forms as rack-jobbing, record clubs, and TV ads for mail-order purchasing.

Will the system survive? There seems little doubt that it will. In fact, if the past is any indicator of the future, there is every reason to suspect that popular music will continue to capture and hold the attention of people of all ages. In short, the Jazz Age that we entered about the time of World War I may have only begun.

Chapter Review

- Popular music is a commercial product deliberately prepared for sale, as opposed to folk music, which emerges more spontaneously from people's daily lives.

- Black entertainers in the sporting houses along the Mississippi developed ragtime from many musical forms and rhythms brought to this country from Africa. Ragtime made the transition into middle-class living rooms when the works of composers such as Scott Joplin were published in sheet music form.

- As public interest in ragtime waned, Dixieland jazz swept the country. It got its start in New Orleans, where street bands and traditions of musical innovation were strong. An obscure band playing in Chicago and then New York played a key role in gaining public acceptance of the new music and in giving it its name.

- Country music had distinct origins and styles related to pioneering life in various parts of the country. Gospel songs emerged from the trying times of the Great Depression.

- The recording industry grew out of Edison's invention of the phonograph in 1877. As technology and sound quality slowly improved, various companies produced records for a growing market. Recording companies began to produce jazz records, and the market for popular music grew swiftly, interrupted only briefly by hard times and in spite of the efforts of critics.

- By the early 1930s, swing was being played by dance orchestras in major cities. Live broadcasts of the music and the ubiquitous juke box helped make it popular. The era of the big bands flowered just before World War II. As the war started, boogie-woogie and jitterbug dancing became the fashion and added to the excitement of the times.

- High-fidelity recording was developed during World War II. New vinyl materials for records came after the war, and the long-playing microgroove record was the result. Tape won out over wire as a new recording medium. Stereo systems became common, and CDs emerged as the basic recording technology. New digital media lie ahead.

- From its beginnings, popular music has been controversial. Ragtime, Dixieland jazz, swing, and boogie-woogie were loudly denounced as immoral. Rock music has been associated with liberal ideas about drugs and sex. Rap has delighted teenagers but aroused numerous critics.

- As a business, the recording industry is characterized by high risks of capital but the potential for great profit. It is dominated by a small number of major companies, but small independent producers continue to play a part.

Notes and References

1. Steven Urkwitz and Lawrence Bennett, "Early American Vocal Music," *Journal of Popular Culture, 12*, no. 1 (Summer 1978), pp. 5–10.

2. Cited in Irving Lowens, *Music and Musicians in Early America* (New York: Norton, 1964), p. 282.

3. Frank Shay, *American Sea Songs and Chanteys* (New York: Norton, 1948), pp. 5–10, 38.

4. Isaac Goldberg, *Tin Pan Alley* (New York: John Day, 1930), p. 45.

5. Ibid., p. 55.

6. Joplin was not the first to do so; a number of obscure ragtime pieces had been scored a few years earlier.

7. David A. Jason and Trevor J. Tichenor, *Rags and Ragtime: A Musical History* (New York: Seabury, 1978), p. 5.

8. Lena McLin, *Pulse: A History of Music* (San Diego: Niel A. Kjos Music, 1977), p. 116.

9. Harry O. Brunn, *The Story of the Original Dixieland Jazz Band* (Baton Rouge: Louisiana State University Press, 1960), p. 21.

10. Noted in one of Thomas Edison's original (unpublished) laboratory notebooks.

11. *Scientific American*, December 1877, p. 17.

12. *Appleton's Magazine*, December 1906, p. 34.

13. Roland Gelatt, *The Fabulous Phonograph* (Philadelphia: Lippincott, 1954), p. 255.

14. Ibid., p. 255.

15. Melvin L. DeFleur and Sandra Ball-Rokeach, *Theories of Mass Communication*, 5th ed. (White Plains, N.Y.: Longman, 1989), p. 107.

16. Gelatt, op. cit., pp. 267–276.

17. This material is drawn from Ink Mendelsohn, "Magical Music Machines," *South Shore News*, March 27, 1989.

18. The various figures on sales discussed in this paragraph were obtained from both industry sources and such publications as *Billboard*, *Broadcasting*, the *New York Times*, and *Variety*. These publications regularly report trends in the popular music industry.

19. This section incorporates insights provided by the following sources: Tom Bethell, "They Had a Right to Sing the Blues," *National Review*, July 8, 1991, p. 31; David Samuels, "The Rap on Rap: The 'Black Music' That Isn't Either," *The New Republic*, November 11, 1991, p. 24; Alan Light, "Rappers Sounded War," *Rolling Stone*, July 9, 1992, p. 22; "How Hot is Rap?" Newhouse News Service, September 8, 1992.

20. The authors are indebted to Tom Herling, a specialist in audio production and adjunct professor of music recording at Syracuse University, for providing insights into the processes of recording and retailing in the popular music industry.

21. Eric W. Rothenbuhler and Tom McCourt, "Commercial Radio and Popular Music: Processes of Selection and Factors of Influence," in James Lull, ed., *Popular Music and Communication* (Newbury Park, Calif.: Sage, 1992), pp. 101–115.

22. Such payoffs, along with related unethical practices, were made illegal by Congress in amendments to the Federal Communications Act in 1960. See Sydney W. Head and Christopher H. Sterling, *Broadcasting in America: A Survey of Electronic Media*, 5th ed. (Boston: Houghton Mifflin Company, 1987), p. 252.

23. A study by a research arm of the U.S. Congress showed that 79 percent of recorded music purchases in retail stores were not impulse decisions but were made as a result of exposure to particular musical selections encountered on radio or television. See Office of Technology Assessment, *Copyright and Home Copying: Technology Challenges the Law* (Washington, D.C.: U.S. Government Printing Office, 1989).

24. Herman S. Gray, "Independent Cultural Production: Theresa Records, a Case Study of a Jazz Independent," Ph.D. dissertation, University of California, Santa Cruz, 1983, p. 34.

PART FIVE

THE CONSEQUENCES OF MASS COMMUNICATIONS

15

Methods of Mass Communication Research: An Overview

A large and dull literature claims to have overthrown empirical behavioral research. It condemns quantification and controlled observation as arid, naive, banal, and even reactionary and immoral. . . . (However) if knowledge of the world is a good thing to have, there is no other way of acquiring it except by observing carefully with well-designed controls.

Ithiel de Sola Pool, *Journal of Communication*, 1983

Why Is Research Important?
Science as a Source of Trustworthy Knowledge / Reasons for Conducting Research on Mass Communication

The Research Perspective
The Assumptions of Science and the Goals of Media Research / Basic versus Applied Research / Steps in Conducting a Research Project

Major Research Strategies
The Use of Samples / Measuring Variables / Basic Research Designs

This chapter focuses on two major questions concerning research on the process and effects of mass communication. First, why is it important to conduct such research? Second, what are the major perspectives, strategies, and procedures used by researchers who conduct studies of mass communication using the tools of science? The answers to these questions provide an essential foundation for understanding the two chapters that follow. In Chapters 16 and 17, we discuss some of the more important investigations that have been conducted and what they have revealed about the consequences of mass communication for individuals as well as for society and culture.

Why Is Research Important?

We pointed out in Chapter 1 that mass communications and the media that provide them are essential to modern life. They have become an indispensable part of our political, economic, social, and even personal lives. This dependency on media makes it imperative that you understand fully both the process and the effects of mass communication—how it takes place, how it influences individuals, and the impact it has on the entire social system.

Science as a Source of Trustworthy Knowledge

Why turn to research and the procedures of science to understand the process and effects of mass communication? Are there not other valid sources of trustworthy knowledge? The answer, of course, is yes; people over the centuries have used many other sources to answer their questions. But each has its advantages and limitations.

For example, for centuries people have found answers to important questions in *religion*, because it provides revelations from the supernatural. That seems like a reliable source, and for many kinds of questions, it is. However, for something as complex and technical as modern mass media, religion might not provide particularly detailed or helpful information.

Trustworthy knowledge can also be gained from *interpretations by authorities*. In ancient times, those were such individuals as oracles, priests, philosophers, and kings. Today, they might be prominent business leaders, politicians, educators, and other distinguished people. Contemporary society seems to have an abundance of such people instantly ready to provide others with their interpretations and pronouncements about the influences of mass communication. The problem is that these sources are not consistent, and one authority or critic often contradicts another of equal distinction. For that reason, their interpretations have limitations.

Another alternative is *tradition*. People in many societies have long relied on their culturally established beliefs to guide them to truth. Thus, if conventional or traditional wisdom said that the earth was flat, then it was clear to most people that that was the truth. In the case of mass communication, this source is not particularly useful, because the media constantly change and traditions have not had a chance to become firmly established over many generations.

Finally, *common sense* has always seemed a reliable guide to the truth. Common sense tells us that the media are very powerful and that people can be readily manipulated and controlled by advertisers, political campaign strategists, and others who shape media content. A serious shortcoming of this kind of truth is that many such efforts fail because people are not that easy to persuade. They select what they want from the media and interpret it in their own unique ways.

The most reliable source that is left is *research*. This is a relatively new source of knowledge about human behavior. Using the methods of science to conduct research on individual and social behavior in such fields as psychology and sociology extends back no more than a century. And although it has long been recognized that communication is a fundamental form of behavior, media research began a mere sixty years ago.

Research is not confined to the use of labs, white coats, math formulas, test tubes, or delicate instruments. Those may be important parts of the research apparatus in some sciences. But what lies at the heart of research is a set of *logical strategies* for making controlled observations of factors that are assumed to have an influence on whatever is under study. *Controlled observation* is a technique that attempts to limit the influence of errors and to be as precise as possible. Thus, even though the sciences differ in what they study and with what apparatus, there is no difference in the logical foundation of research in such fields as chemistry, biology, physics, and human behavior—including communication. Therefore, *research* in any field can be defined as a set of strategies and procedures (agreed upon by scientists) for gathering reliable information under controlled conditions of observation in such a way that objective conclusions can be reached with a minimum of error.

Research is not infallible, but it has several advantages over less rigorous sources of knowledge. One advantage is that it is conducted with a set of strategies and procedures that, as just indicated, are more or less shared by all sciences. These strategies and procedures are collectively known as the *scientific method*. We discuss their nature more fully in a later section, but the essential features to understand are, first, that the conclusions of researchers using the scientific method must be based on factual observations rather than opinions or other subjective interpretations, and second, that if new observations indicate that previous conclusions are incorrect, those conclusions must be revised on the basis of the new evidence. Alternative sources of knowledge—such as popular opinion, "expert" commentary, or "common sense"—are not committed to these requirements.

Research has many limitations. It is very clear that some people conduct research on trivial and boring subjects. Others do it badly and make mistakes. At least some unscrupulous people (fortunately a very few) deliberately violate the ethical rules of science and fake their findings, perhaps to come up with results that their sponsors want. But, in the main, using scientific procedures and strategies to find answers is the most effective route to reliable knowledge.

Reasons for Conducting Research on Mass Communication

There are three main reasons for doing research on the process and effects of mass communication. One is that the public is deeply concerned about the possible negative effects of the media. People want answers as to whether they and their children are at risk. Another reason is that understanding how mass communication takes place and how it creates effects and influences on people is important in its own right, whether the public is concerned at the moment or not. Finally, research can provide answers to many practical problems of operating the mass media as businesses.

Public concern about media effects This reason for conducting research into the influences of mass media is rather like the reason for which it became important to study the effects of smoking. For a very long time, people liked to smoke and did so with little anxiety. Eventually, however, some people began to worry that smoking might be harmful. They turned to various sources to obtain the truth. Some individuals had *religious revelations* that using tobacco was sinful and that God wanted it to be stamped out. Other people turned for guidance to respected *authorities*—some of whom denounced smoking, while others who were equally respected praised and endorsed it. *Tradition* was also of little help. The use of tobacco was deeply established in society, which seemed to imply that it deserved a legitimate place. *Common sense* seemed to indicate that since it made people cough and be short of breath, it might be harmful—even though it was undeniably enjoyable. In other words, it was difficult to figure out from these sources of knowledge whether tobacco was a problem or a blessing.

Research showed a different picture. When scientific investigation began to uncover the relationship between tobacco and certain diseases, knowledge was significantly advanced. The dangers of tobacco became a matter of *fact* rather than of opinion or speculation. In an analogous way, research can aid greatly in achieving a better understanding of the positive and negative effects of the media on the individuals who "consume" media products and on the culture and society as a whole. Informing the public reliably so that people can make intelligent decisions, then, is one important reason for conducting such research.

Developing theories to explain media influences   Knowledge about the nature and consequences of mass communication in modern society is important in its own right. Such knowledge will aid us in understanding how our society works. Our cultural beliefs and rules for relating to each other are the basis of civilized life. Learning by communicating with others, including attending to the media, is the source from which each individual develops his or her unique human nature. Since the mass media are central to the communication processes of modern society, we need to know as much about them as we can. This means that we need sound explanations for understanding all aspects of mass communication, whether the public is concerned about them or not. Such explanations are called *theories*.

As we will show, theories are not wild guesses, speculations, or "hunches" about how something works. In all scientific investigation, theories are *systematic explanations* of the causes of some condition or situation. They are proposed and developed only after a great deal of objective research. Once formulated, they are tested over and over against observations to see whether they hold up. If they do not, they are abandoned. If they hold up in a partial way, they are revised and tested again. Theories also serve as *guides*, showing researchers how to advance knowledge by conducting certain kinds of research. With carefully gathered evidence, candidate theories can be tested—researchers can show them to be well supported by factual evidence or to be inadequate.

This link between theory and research is the same in all sciences, whether they seek explanations of social, physical, or biological processes—or answers to problems of mass communication. Sometimes it takes decades of research to decide whether a given theory is really adequate. More than once—as we will see—a theory has been abandoned after years of research finally showed it to be deficient.

Solving practical problems   A great deal of communications research is conducted for reasons that are not directly related to either public concern or the development or testing of theory. There are many practical reasons for trying to describe how some form of mass communication has influenced some category of people. These can range from political campaigns that try to convince voters to support a particular candidate to advertising efforts to sell soap, sauce, or soup. Audiences are counted, media are compared, messages and appeals are tested, and various kinds of content are analyzed to see if they will capture and hold attention. At least to some

One of the most important effects of the media, from the standpoint of those who support them through advertising, is the influence they have on consumer decisions. For example, the act of selecting products to purchase is the focus of costly efforts to influence consumers. The same is true for a variety of services. Hundreds of millions of dollars are spent every year to influence the beliefs and actions of consumers. Research that may reveal how their decisions are made or show how they can be influenced is of great potential value to producers and distributors of products. (Bowdan Hrynewych, Stock Boston)

degree, such research is conducted within the general framework of the scientific method.

The knowledge derived from practical research efforts can be critical to the survival of a newspaper, TV network, magazine, or book publisher. As profit-oriented businesses, these media producers need sound guidelines as to how they can do their job more effectively. In the intensely competitive world of profit-making, that usually means reaching larger audiences and exerting greater influence on various aspects of people's beliefs and behavior than their rivals can.

The Research Perspective

Obviously, scientists study many different subject matters. The specific techniques, measuring instruments, and procedures that they use differ greatly from one field to another. At the same time, all scientists have much in common. What they share is a conviction that they can find out what is going on in the physical, biological, or social world by using the scientific method. Thus, even though the specific tools and procedures differ in each field, the scientific method in each is based on the same underlying *logic* for deciding when findings are convincing.

The scientific method is founded on a shared set of very general *assumptions* that set research goals in a broad sense. These underlying assumptions of science, and the various steps for conducting investigations, provide what can be called a *research perspective*. In this section, we look carefully at that research perspective in terms of both the assumptions of science and the several steps involved in conducting scientific investigations. We also look briefly at the distinction between basic and applied research goals.

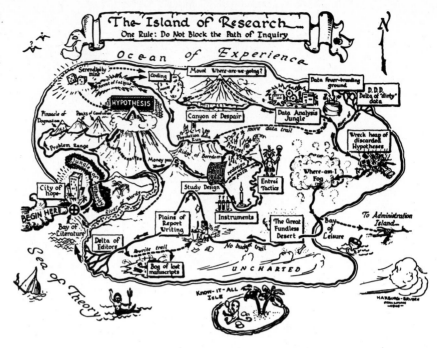

Social research has many pitfalls and obstacles. Here one researcher has illustrated these in the form of a humorous map.

The Assumptions of Science and the Goals of Media Research

In thinking about what they study, scientists of all kinds share a set of basic suppositions about the nature of their subject matter. In a very general way, those assumptions set their ultimate goals. It has been particularly important for media researchers to formulate and understand these basic assumptions clearly, because there have been many critics of the idea that something as ephemeral as people's responses to a TV show or a motion picture can be studied within a scientific framework.

In spite of the critics, media researchers have, for well over a half-century, developed ways to apply the perspectives of science to research on their subject matter. One of the positive consequences of the debates and criticisms has been to make communications researchers acutely aware of the assumptions on which science rests and the goals for which research is conducted. Thus, a logical place to begin in understanding the research perspective as applied to the study of communication is to review three fundamental beliefs that play a key role in all forms of scientific investigation.

The assumption of order   Scientists always assume that the objects, actions, or events that they are trying to study are regular in their behavior and that their activities will form some kind of potentially discoverable *patterns*. The important point here is that assuming such *order* in the physical, biological, or social world provides the beginning point and ultimate reason for the existence of science. If the phenomena of nature, including the communication behavior of human beings, showed only random characteristics, science would have nothing to study.

Thus, one of the initial goals of research is to describe *regularities* in its subject matter. Unless complete and clear descriptions of a process and its consequences have been formulated, little can be done to explain how they got that way. Therefore, in each of the major sciences—from astronomy to zoology—full and comprehensive descriptions of the subject matter under study must be painstakingly assembled before the task of explaining origins and consequences can begin.

For communications researchers, this has meant describing all aspects of the process of communication as well as identifying the media's potential effects on individuals and the social order. For example, some forty years ago, communications scholar Harold Lasswell set forth a brief outline for organizing descriptive research on communication.[1] He stated that communication could be conveniently described by answering the following questions:

Who?
Says what?
In what channel?
To whom?
With what effect?

Most of the studies done by both commercial and academic researchers can be classified rather broadly within this set of questions, and they still represent many of the researchers' primary concerns.

To study the "who" factor, researchers focus on *professional communicators* and describe such matters as ownership trends in the newspaper industry, the management practices of radio, the manner in which decisions are made in the TV newsroom, how magazine publication is changing, and the organization of the film industry.

The "says what" factor is composed of the various categories of *content* of the media—news, entertainment, popular music, advertising, and so forth—that we have described in foregoing chapters. Research of this kind focuses on both quantitative and qualitative assessment of the content of whatever is transmitted through the media. As we will see, procedures for analyzing media content have been well developed by communications researchers. Describing what the media disseminate remains an important research goal. Numerous studies are published every year about such matters as the amount of violence shown on television, the content of children's programming, portrayals of women and minorities in the media, and the content of various kinds of advertising.

To study "in what channel," researchers address such issues as the growth and decline in the use of various *media*. These change constantly as the system of mass communication adjusts to changing conditions in society. New technologies such as cable TV, VCRs, and videotext are described and compared to older channels. Differences and similarities among them are charted in terms of earnings, audience composition, and effects or influences. Also studied are the differences in audience comprehension of particular media content that may be due to the channel used. For instance, is a news story understood and remembered better by members of its audience if they are first exposed to it in a newspaper, on radio, or on television?

The "to whom" factor refers to careful categorizations and counts of the *audiences* of readers, listeners, and viewers of the media. The attributes of such audiences can be described in demographic terms such as age, sex, income, education, and so on. Audiences can also be described in psychographic terms by assessing their psychological characteristics, including their beliefs, opinions, preferences, and attitudes. Such studies can also describe the satisfactions or gratifications different kinds of people obtain when they are exposed to different kinds of media content.

The "with what effects" factor, as we have already indicated in Chapter 1, is the bottom line for much of the research that is done. Certainly, identifying how the media influence the ideas and behavior of people may be the most complex and controversial research goal of all. Communications researchers try to describe a host of *personal*, *social*, and *cultural influences* of the media in terms of such factors as public opinion, shared beliefs, aggression, consumer behavior, political influence, and many more. (We discuss these more fully in Chapters 16 and 17.)

In short, the search for order remains central to studies of mass communication. Whether it fits neatly in Lasswell's scheme or not, much contemporary research is devoted to understanding the underlying patterns—the trends, contrasts, concentrations, and distributions of different kinds of activities, audiences, and consequences that characterize the different media.

The assumption of cause and effect   Scientists assume that it is possible to explain *when*, *how*, and *why* events occur, whether the events are heart attacks, financial recessions, nuclear reactions, or influences on people brought about by watching television. They are skeptical of the idea that things "just happen" in random ways, with no causes at all. Thus, the basic idea underlying the assumption of cause and effect is that any regular event must have some sequence of natural influences that consistently produce it. At any particular time, the causes may be poorly understood, but scientists assume that they are at work and are potentially discoverable.

Many communications research projects are aimed at discovering what features or aspects of media content, interacting with various personal and social characteristics of audiences, result in different kinds of influences on people. Such basic research is theory-oriented—that is, although it rests on adequate descriptive knowledge, it goes beyond mere description. It is designed to uncover or try to verify the merits of potential *explanations* (candidate theories) of what causes certain effects and to use those explanations to make *predictions* about what effects will regularly occur under specified conditions. The reasons why theories are important are discussed in more detail in the next section.

A legacy of fear is the dark side of wide public acceptance of mass communications. While avidly enjoying the media, many people make unwarranted cause-and-effect assumptions that seeing a single film or program can cause individuals to experience major shifts in attitudes and behavior. Protests such as the one shown here indicate that some people believe that the media are to be feared as forces for evil. Only careful research can answer the question of whether mass communications have unwanted social influences. (AP/Wide World Photos)

The assumption that research conclusions are tentative Even if research conclusions have been widely accepted, scientists remain just a bit skeptical. In other words, they do not believe that their conclusions ever provide "final" answers. Instead, they assume that the descriptions and explanations they develop from their research are simply the best that are currently available. Unlike Pygmalion, the sculptor of ancient Cyprus, they do not fall in love with their own creation. They remain somewhat fickle and ready to switch if a better-looking explanation comes along. In other words, they must always be ready to change descriptions or modify their theories if new facts call for revision. Because of this assumption, scientists are constantly seeking new data to test the merits of theories and the validity of conclusions.

Because of this assumption of the tentative nature of scientific conclusions, science is *self-policing*. That is, even if incorrect theories and conclusions developed from them are accepted temporarily, they will be replaced when it is discovered that they really do not explain or predict factual situations validly. No other source of knowledge has this safeguard, which is one of the reasons why scientific explanations resulting from research are superior to other kinds of interpretations and claims.

In a broad sense, then, these three basic assumptions set the goals of science: to provide careful and accurate descriptions of what is under study, to try to uncover what antecedent factors bring about particular consequences, and to test and retest cause-and-effect explanations until they are adequately confirmed.

Basic versus Applied Research

Communications researchers often distinguish between basic and applied research. The distinction is based on the goals or purposes for which investigations are conducted. The two categories sometimes overlap, particularly in the implications of their findings; therefore, it is not always possible to classify a given study neatly as one or the other. Still, the distinction is a useful one, since it shows the reasons for which research projects are undertaken, as well as who pays the bills for the work.

Basic research to develop and test theory   Perhaps the clearest feature of *basic research* is that it is not undertaken to increase anyone's profits. The purpose of such investigations is to *advance knowledge*. Basic research is usually conducted by people in the academic world, vigorously searching for fundamental understandings of the physical, biological, or social world. Universities and colleges recognize a responsibility to the society that supports them to *teach* the knowledge already discovered in fields from astronomy to zoology, but they also understand that they must try to *advance* that knowledge through research. For example, few of us would be content if medical research stopped now and ten years or twenty years from now medical students were taught only what is currently known. Similarly, we cannot be satisfied with existing knowledge in any field. We must go forward in the study of all those features of our environment that have an impact on our way of life. These include the functioning of the media and the influences of mass communication on individuals and society. It is for that reason that academic institutions expect their faculty to conduct research. Without it, their texts and courses would soon become mere repetitions of what was known years ago and out of touch with contemporary society.

Basic research may be simple or complex, and it can make use of any of the procedures available to communications researchers. It may be undertaken to provide a description of some aspect of communication, or it may be aimed at developing a sophisticated theory to explain the causes of some effect of mass communication. Knowledge about the processes and influences of mass communication can be advanced by pursuing any of these goals.

An example of basic research that is purely *descriptive* is the study of the way in which television shows people eating, as portrayed in advertising, movies, situation comedies, and many other kinds of programs. Such research addresses the question "What is the 'television diet' and does it parallel people's actual diets?" That is, what is the selection of foods portrayed daily to millions of viewers, and how is that selection related to the foods that people really eat? This is an important question. Clear description is needed because if these portrayals can be shown to be very similar to what people actually select for their personal diets, that would provide the basis for asking if there is a *causal* connection (a more theoretical issue).

A large number of such descriptive studies have been undertaken. To conduct such investigations, researchers monitor television content in a systematic way over a period of time and classify all food items shown. They then make comparisons with the audience's actual diets through the use of personal interviews and questionnaire procedures.

The foods shown on television would not provide a very balanced and healthful diet for anyone. Heavily represented are fat-laden hamburgers, fried chicken, french fries, pizza, sugary soft drinks, beer, and candies. More healthful foods, low in fat and cholesterol and high in fiber content, are shown very infrequently. Although a steady diet of the fare shown on television would not be a healthful one, to say the least, we cannot simply assume that people who watch television eat that way. Additional research is still needed to determine if such portrayals actually *cause* people to prefer such poor food choices.

Investigators who do basic research do look for causes. They are interested in developing some kind of theory to explain *why* and under *what circumstances* a particular form of behavior will occur as a result of exposure to mass communications. But just what is a theory? In previous chapters, we have introduced a number of theories related to mass communication, so we have already provided examples. However, looking more closely, a *theory* can be defined formally as a set of propositions (statements about how various factors are related) that when taken together provide an explanation of how antecedent conditions or events lead to specific consequences.

To understand the nature of such a set of propositions more fully, we can look at a specific example called the *agenda-setting theory of the press*. The agenda-setting theory is a set of statements (propositions) that shows why audiences for news come to think some stories are more important than others. If this set of statements is true—that is, if the facts fit what the statements say will be the case—the theory has explained that effect. Thus, the theory predicts that if a particular issue is presented prominently in terms of time and space by the press, the public will come to believe that it is important. If research studies verify that people actually behave that way, then the theory is strongly supported by that evidence. In this case, a host of research studies of newspapers, radio, television, and other news sources has confirmed that personal agendas are indeed influenced by reports in the press in this manner.[2]

Communications researchers have developed a number of theories to explain different types of media effects and various aspects of the mass communication process. Selected examples appear in a number of chapters in this book. Some are more restricted and pertain only to, say, television and violence, rather than to all media and all content.[3] Others are very broad and are useful for understanding and explaining several categories of effects brought about by the different media or some aspect of the mass communication process. Some of these will be discussed in later chapters.

Applied research to solve practical problems   There are two major kinds of *applied research*. One, like basic research, is conducted for the purpose of advancing knowledge. This kind of applied research focuses on some practical problem that is relevant to the functioning of a particular

THE AGENDA-SETTING THEORY OF THE PRESS

A theory concerning the influence of the press on people's beliefs and evaluations of the topics reported in the news was first developed by Maxwell McCombs and Donald Shaw. The theory explains how individuals come to regard some events and situations that they encounter through news reports in the press as more important than others. Thus, agenda-setting implies a relationship between the treatment of an issue or event in newspapers or on television or radio news and the beliefs about its importance or significance on the part of individuals who make up the news audience.

The agenda-setting theory grew out of studies of the presidential political campaign of 1968. Its authors studied how people in a community decided which issues, among those that received extended news attention, were important. As it turned out, the public did develop a kind of ranking in their own minds about the importance of the different issues discussed in the news. The authors of the theory found a high level of correspondence between the amount and kind of attention paid to a particular political issue by the press and the level of importance assigned to that issue by people in the community who had received information about it from newspapers and other news sources.

It was the press, therefore, that determined during a political campaign what issues people would discuss among themselves and how much importance they would attach to the different ones. In other words, the press developed its own agenda concerning what issues were news and how much space and prominence to give them. The agenda of the press then became the agenda of those who followed the news of the campaign. This does not imply that the press tells people *what* they should think and decide medium. For example, as we noted in Chapter 12, local TV news stories can be produced in many different formats: word stories, voice-over-tape, reporter-with-stand-up, and so on. An important practical question is whether it is worth the cost to send a reporter to the scene and produce the report in an expensive format. Does it really create greater audience interest in the newscast? Do people actually learn the news better when it is presented this way (as compared with the simpler and cheaper word story)? Controlled experiments with audiences, measuring their interest and comprehension, provide answers to such practical questions.

Another form of applied research is *proprietary research*. This kind of research is usually conducted by or for someone who will benefit financially from its findings. Proprietary research is not classified by scientists as contributing to the body of public knowledge about whatever is studied, because the results of such research are kept *secret*, and other scientists cannot check them out to see if they are true. There is no opportunity, therefore, for the self-policing safeguard of science to work. However, secrecy is important to those who pay for this type of research because the findings may give those sponsors an edge in the competitive business world of

about the issues. However, it does imply that the press tells people what they should think *about* and what issues are important enough to require their decisions.

Hundreds of research projects have been carried out by communications scholars since McCombs and Shaw first published their theory, and its basic ideas have been well-verified.[1] The theory is applicable mainly to the relationship between political issues as these are discussed in the press and the beliefs about their importance by those who follow campaigns in the news. It may not apply to news about other topics. In any case, the basic propositions of the agenda-setting theory of the press are as follows:

1. The press (news media in general) *selects* a number of issues, topics, and events from its continuous surveillance of the environment to process and report daily as the news.

2. Because of limited space and time and because of journalists' convictions as to what is news-worthy, many issues and topics are *ignored* and do not become part of the news.

3. The press gives each of the news stories selected greater or lesser *prominence* in its reports by assigning it a particular position or giving it more or less space or time in print and broadcast news presentations.

4. The selection of stories presented, with their different levels of prominence, space, and time, forms the *news agenda* of the press.

5. Thus, when people attend to these news reports, they will perceive the order of prominence assigned by the press in its agenda of stories and will use it to decide on their *personal rankings of importance* of the issues and topics that make up the news.

1. The original study was Maxwell E. McCombs and Donald Shaw, "The Agenda-Setting Function of the Mass Media," *Public Opinion Quarterly*, 1972, pp. 176-187.

mass communications. Those who pay for proprietary research are such users as corporations, advertising agencies, publishers, consulting firms, broadcasting networks, and public relations firms.

Many different kinds of practical problems are studied in applied research, whether public or proprietary. The problems investigated may be related to print, broadcasting, advertising, public relations, or other areas that make use of mass communications. We will comment only briefly on this type of research, since we want to focus on more basic issues concerning the influences of mass communication.

Applied research for the print media includes investigations of readership, circulation, readability, and typography or make-up. Studies of readership were pioneered by George Gallup, who adapted basic social science research techniques to the study of what people read in the newspaper. The most thorough study of newspaper readership ever conducted was the American Newspaper Publishers Association's "Continuing Studies of Newspapers," in which more than 50,000 readers of 130 daily newspapers were interviewed between 1939 and 1950.[4] The interviews determined what kinds of people (age, sex, income, and so on) read various kinds of content.

Many such studies are conducted today to find out the demographic characteristics of readers, what they select to read, and how much they can recall from their daily newspaper. Researchers make comparisons between readers and nonreaders, between what editors think are good newspapers and what readers think, and between the kinds of gratifications readers get from their papers.[5]

Circulation studies assess the proportion of a *market* (the people who live in a given geographical area or city) that a particular newspaper or magazine reaches. Such information is critical to potential advertisers, who want to use the medium to draw the attention of the largest number of potential consumers. Trends in circulation are also critical. If circulation drops, the medium is in trouble.[6]

Readability refers to how easy or hard a given passage of print is for a reader to comprehend. Exhaustive research has shown that such factors as the number of syllables in words and the length of sentences make some passages more difficult for readers to handle than others. A variety of specific techniques have been developed to assess readability.

Typography and make-up studies focus on different styles of print, headlines, white space, and other physical features of a publication, to see whether these factors make a difference to readers. Such studies can yield important and very practical information about the size and number of illustrations and the amount of text that will elicit the greatest attention from readers and about how headlines, drawings, and other features should be handled to attract attention.

We have already noted how important ratings are in the world of electronic media. A number of firms are engaged in assessing who is watching or listening to what. This is difficult research, because the investigators cannot stay in people's homes and watch how they view television or listen to the radio. Instead, they must depend on a variety of substitutes for direct observation. As discussed in Chapter 8, some use diaries; others conduct after-the-fact phone interviews; still others attach devices to receivers or use the people meter. At best, such procedures provide only partial information.[7] But more accurate alternatives have not been developed.

Advertising researchers study various kinds of message content, themes, and treatments to try to determine their effectiveness in getting people to buy products. What messages, message structures, suggested themes, and stimuli will cause people to buy a product such as cat food, perfume, or razor blades? Probably no field of endeavor is more competitive than advertising, and huge amounts of money are at risk for both parties when national manufacturers seek an advertising agency to design a campaign. In earlier years, research played little part in advertising; decisions were made on the basis of intuition rather than on data and research conclusions. Today, with competition so fierce, proprietary research often gives an edge when decisions have to be made among media, kinds of appeals, and other features of advertising messages.

Public relations research usually focuses on how people think or feel about an organization (or person). It is a difficult and complex process that attempts to assemble information on a number of issues, such as general events in the social environment that may potentially influence the organization, the perceptions some specific group (stockholders, employees, or customers) has about the organization, and the degree to which the organization lives up to its social responsibilities.

Links between basic and applied research   Basic and applied research may seem quite different, but the distinction between them is often blurred and sometimes nonexistent. Many times in the past, a research project has been undertaken to obtain answers to some practical problem, only to wind up making a major contribution to theory. As we will see in the next chapter, a classic along those lines is a study done by the U.S. Army to see how to use motion pictures effectively in training soldiers for wartime service.[8] Its conclusions changed thinking about the whole issue of influencing attitudes and behavior through the use of persuasive films. Thus, even the most practical projects can sometimes reveal fundamental principles or theoretical explanations of the basic nature of mass communication.

Similarly, theoretical research that at first seems to have little to do with such mundane matters as advertising, audience composition, and circulations can sometimes reveal conclusions that become important to people trying to design better media content to attract and interest larger numbers of people. For example, as discussed in Chapter 12, the *two-step flow of communication* was discovered many years ago by basic researchers studying the use of the mass media in a political campaign. They found that some people read newspapers, listened to the radio, or read magazines and then served as sources of information for many others who were not directly exposed to such media. This finding was studied further, and researchers discovered that these *opinion leaders* also influenced their neighbors and friends on many consumer decisions. Naturally, advertisers wanted to devise strategies to make such opinion leaders significant targets for advertising messages, because if the leaders were convinced, they would advise others to purchase the product.[9] In this instance, basic research yielded important practical guidelines for applied interests.

Steps in Conducting a Research Project

An important part of the research perspective is the series of steps or stages that are involved in conducting research according to the scientific method. Designing and completing an investigation of some aspect of mass communication is not a matter of just making observations in some informal way with the hope of uncovering something dramatic. It is a very systematic process. Researchers follow six basic steps as general guides when they plan, conduct, and report research.

Step 1: Specifying the research problem   One of the most difficult steps in the research process is setting forth in writing *exactly* what is to be studied. Essentially, the researcher begins by identifying (1) the *concepts* that will be under study and (2) how he or she expects them to be *related* to each other. For example, in a study of the effects of different ways of producing local TV news stories, a team of researchers identified one concept as "production format." This referred to whether a given news story was produced as an "anchor-only word story," as "anchor's voice-over-tape," as a story including a "reporter-with-a-standup" (an interview on camera), and so on. A second concept was the individual audience member's ability to "recall" the content of the story, and a third was the person's ranking of "story interest." The research sought to understand the relationship between these concepts. That is, do different production formats bring about greater or lesser learning by the audience, and do the formats result in different judgments of story interest? (The answer to both questions is yes.)[10]

A concept has two parts: the name given to the category of objects or events that are being studied, and the definition, which sets forth exactly what qualities or attributes distinguish the objects or events that belong in that category. The idea is less abstract than it seems. Examples of concepts that are used frequently and well understood are "married" (defined by the implied legal relationship) and "employed" (defined by holding a job that provides regular earnings). More complex concepts are ideas such as "level of portrayed violence" (often defined by the number of acts of violence or aggression that can be counted in a given television program) or "audience recall" of a particular news story (usually defined by the number of details of the story that a person can remember).

Some concepts are simply *qualitative* categories, such as "male" or "female," "Protestant" or "Catholic," and "Hispanic" or "Anglo." Others are *quantitative* and *variable*. That is, they can be arranged on a continuum or scale of low to high. "Income" is obviously such a variable concept: a person's income can range from zero to a million (or more) dollars per year. Such concepts are simply called *variables* for short. In fact, the word "variable" is generally used to indicate whatever concepts are under observation in a research project—even those that are actually qualitative.

Once the concepts that are to be studied have been identified, the next step is to try to specify their relationships to each other. Does one set "cause" the other? We saw in our brief discussion of the agenda-setting theory that a variable controlled by the press (the "relative prominence" given to a news item) brings about, or causes, a particular condition in the news audience (the "level of importance" given that item by its members). The variable "relative prominence" is independently controlled by the press; the audience cannot set that level. For that reason, "relative prominence" is the *independent variable* in the agenda-setting theory. By the same logic, the "level of importance" assigned to items by the audience depends on the treatment of those items by the press. For that reason, "level of importance" as seen by the audience is the *dependent variable* in the theory.

In this manner, variables can be identified as independent or dependent on the basis of whether they are assumed to be serving as causes or as effects. In addition, some variables are called *control variables*, because researchers have to keep their influence from distorting the cause-and-effect sequence. To illustrate, suppose we want to study how children respond to advertisements for a particular kind of candy. We can obtain records of their exposure to TV commercials from suitable interviews, and we can record their candy purchases. However, rich kids might have more access to TV sets and certainly have more money to spend on candy than poor kids do. Therefore, we would have to control the factor of family income. We could do this by analyzing the findings separately for the two kinds of children, thereby "controlling" (that is, gaining an understanding of the influence of) income as a variable in the statistical comparisons. The essential idea of identifying the relationships that exist between concepts (variables) is that researchers must carefully identify each factor that is to be observed to determine whether it is an independent, dependent, or control variable. Only in that way is it possible to sort out the implications of the research findings after observations have been made.

If the purpose of the research is simply to describe some pattern, the task of specifying the problem is relatively simple. For example, a researcher might wish to study the amount of violence that is portrayed in children's cartoons on television between 4:00 and 6:00 p.m. weekdays and on Saturday mornings. He or she could specify the problem by indicating exactly which cartoons will be reviewed, what constitutes an act of violence, and how the data will be recorded.

In more complex studies, the researcher may set forth the problem in the form of an *hypothesis*. This is a formal written statement that poses a possible relationship between independent and dependent variables that are to be studied. For example, the researcher might hypothesize that "children of low-income families are more likely to view TV content with high levels of portrayed violence than are children from high-income homes." Here the researcher is predicting that the variables of "family income" and "levels of portrayed violence" will be in a particular relationship. It is important to note that the variables are expected to be *associated*. That is, it is anticipated that when the independent variable of income is high, the dependent variable of viewing of violence will be low, and when the former is low, the latter is expected to be high. This does not really state a causal relationship in a definite sense. It is a relationship of *co-relation* (or, as it is usually stated, *correlation*). In scientific work, researchers make claims of causation only with great caution. When research findings show high correlation, however, it is sometimes possible to infer that the independent variable (or variables) have influenced, or brought about, the state of the dependent variable.

Once one or more hypotheses have been stated, what the researcher needs to study becomes quite clear. That is the great value of proceeding so systematically. For our example, he or she would have to make careful observations of the kinds of children described and their television viewing behavior. After all of the observations had been assembled, the two kinds of children could be compared (in terms of averages and other statistical indices) and a decision made as to whether to accept or reject the hypothesis.

Hypotheses come from many sources. Sometimes they are suggested by earlier research. Others are logical consequences of broader theories. Still others may be little more than informed guesses made by the researcher on the basis of prior studies. However, after the research has been completed, if the observations support the hypothesis it becomes a *generalization*—a conclusion from research that is supported by factual evidence.

Step 2: Reviewing the results of previous research It would be foolish to embark on any research project before finding out whether other people have already studied the question and answered it fully. In the field of mass communication, it is likely that almost any problem related to media influences has been studied to some extent and that at least some knowledge is already available. For that reason, researchers in that or any other field of science turn to a number of different sources to obtain information on previous research.

Literally hundreds of professional and scholarly journals containing the results of communication research appear regularly in the United States (and in other countries). A journal is a kind of technical and specialized magazine—a periodical that is produced by some professional association, university, government bureau, foundation, or other agency. Most are published in the United States and are in English, and the majority appear on some fixed schedule, such as once a month, quarterly, or even annually. Journals contain brief reports of research projects—usually a dozen pages or less for each project—and they often provide a summary (abstract) of each of the articles so that readers can screen them easily.

Research is reported in many other places, including books, professional meetings, and government documents. Researchers must scrutinize all of these sources before making final plans for a new project, to make sure that it does not simply duplicate something that has already been done. This task is made easier by publications such as *Communication Abstracts*, which regularly provides up-to-date summaries of every research report that has appeared in a long list of journals. Best of all, a researcher with the required skills can use a computer to search online information retrieval sources that consist of summaries of articles from hundreds of journals. What once took weeks can now be accomplished by online database searching in a few minutes.

Step 3: Making the necessary observations This is the data-gathering stage, which is in many ways the central feature of the research process. Once a researcher has specified the problem, identified the independent, dependent, and control variables, and selected a general strategy (an experimental approach, a survey, or a field study), observation can begin. Centuries ago, the earliest scientists agreed that *empirical observations* (as opposed to religious experiences, tradition, the exercise of logic alone, or whatever) were the only acceptable basis for reaching scientific conclusions. The word "empirical" means "apprehended by the senses," which is obviously at the heart of the observation process.

Of all the research procedures that have been developed to assess people's beliefs and behavior concerning the mass media, the most effective is the face-to-face interview with individuals who have been selected using a carefully designed sampling technique. This requires tracking people down one by one and coming back, several times if necessary, if they are not home on the first try. Personal interviews of this kind can be expensive to conduct, but they provide highly valid and reliable results. (Delia Flynn/Stock,Boston)

Communications researchers use many kinds of procedures and techniques to assist them in making empirical observations. The assessment of variables in numerical form is often called *measurement*. Once observations have been made, they must be *recorded* so that other scientists can see and understand what the researcher observed, to what degree, and under what conditions. This allows others to repeat the research process if they wish. *Data* literally means "something assumed or known as fact." In scientific work, the term has come to mean "recorded observations." Therefore, empirically obtained and carefully recorded observations are the first product of scientific investigation.

Another problem related to data-gathering is that of *who* is to be observed. One of the important problems involved in studying people is that there are so many of them! Research projects often focus on communication behavior that is common to an entire population, such as that of the United States. But obviously there is no way for investigators to observe all of the people in the country. Therefore, they have to select some smaller and more manageable number. This process of selection is called *sampling*.

Sampling is very important in communications research, and we will discuss it in greater detail in a later section.

Step 4: Data-processing and analysis   Once all of the observations have been made and recorded, they must be *processed* and then *analyzed*. These are two distinct steps, and each can take many forms. If the research is essentially qualitative (based on the personal observations of an investigator who is not using numerically based measuring procedures), the researcher can write the final report on the basis of intuitive conclusions. He or she will need no quantitative analysis or computers to calculate statistical results. Such research can be important in science if it is exploratory—that is, if it investigates complex or difficult problems in a sensitive manner and probes into areas of behavior where quantitative techniques cannot yet be used. However, quantitative research is the norm today, and the procedures followed for data analysis usually involve the use of computers, which enable the investigator to take advantage of complex statistical procedures and probability models for decision making.

After the researcher has completed all observations and transformed them into written records, these records must be made ready for *data-processing*. The first step in such processing is to transform them into a mechanical or electronic form that a computer can accept. Then *data entry* (physically entering them into the computer) can begin. A few years ago, data entry was done by punching IBM cards to record the relevant information in a form that the computer could use to add, subtract, multiply, and divide (which is basically what computers do). The cards were then fed mechanically into the machine. However, the world of computers changes daily, and cards have long been obsolete. Today, there are more efficient means for data entry such as optical scanners and other devices that are used to store observations in memory. Most researchers, however, have to enter their recorded observations into the computer from a keyboard, to be stored in the machine's memory or on magnetic tape for later recovery and use.

Once the data are stored in the computer, *data analysis* can begin. Computer software specially designed to complete various statistical analyses is widely available. It enables the computer to print out different kinds of tables and reports showing the results of various calculations that clarify what the researcher has found. This is an important first step in data analysis. The statistical indices and probability values calculated by the computer allow the researcher to decide whether the hypotheses of the study should be rejected or accepted—or, if the research is descriptive, what the patterns imply.

Step 5: Reaching conclusions and interpreting findings   The payoff in any research project lies in the conclusions that are finally reached. Whatever the nature of the study, whether it is applied, basic, descriptive, theory-oriented, a test of hypotheses, or merely exploratory, the bottom line is *what it all means*. Making such interpretations is the task of the human investigator. The computer cannot help here.

Often the conclusions reached on the basis of research findings result in generalizations, which we described earlier as accurate statements (supported by the research evidence) concerning relationships between the variables. For example, if on the basis of the data, the researcher accepted the hypothesis of our earlier example, which posited a relationship between low income and a tendency for children to watch violent television shows, he or she could form a generalization something like this: "Children of low-income families tend to view more television content portraying violence than do those of high-income families." (Many studies have been done on these variables, and it is a valid generalization.)

Such a generalization does not specify what the researcher found with every child studied. In all likelihood, some poor kids among those investigated watched little violence, and some rich kids may have watched a lot. Nevertheless, on the whole (that is, in general) the statement describes the situation of *most* children who were studied. The statement is therefore truly a generalization, and we can ignore the exceptions, as long as they are not too numerous.

Although such generalizations are normally restricted to the kind of people who have been studied, they do illustrate an important point that we made earlier. Scientists assume that there is order in what they study. A generalization is an expression of that order, so we can infer (tentatively) that the generalization about TV violence may apply to children other than those who were actually investigated. On the other hand, if a researcher claimed that a generalization obtained from a study of children in only one city applied to children all over the world, it would be an example of *overgeneralizing*—extending the rule too far.

The task of reaching conclusions is usually different for various types of research, but it is a process of describing what solutions were found, what generalizations emerged, what hypotheses were accepted or rejected, or what theories were or were not supported. Above all, it is an exercise in *creative insight* within the demanding rules of science. The researcher has to bring the problem that was originally specified together with the findings of other investigators, add the results of the data analysis, and carefully state the implications of this synthesis in the final research report.

Step 6: Reporting the results   Science is a *public* enterprise. A lone genius working in isolation may solve the problems of the universe, but if he or she never publishes those solutions, they do not become part of the accumulated knowledge of science. Other scientists need to scrutinize what was studied and how it was studied, in order to decide what it all means. The community of scholars evaluates each newly published research report within strict criteria to see whether the conclusions are worth taking seriously. This is one of the ways in which science is self-policing.

The factor of publication often sharply separates applied and basic research. We have already indicated that applied proprietary research may be kept secret. Basic research, in contrast, is usually conducted by academic investigators, and the rule is that they *must* publish their results to make certain that their research meets high standards. Professors often complain about the dictum "publish or perish." However, it makes sense if the institutions that employ them are charged by the public with advancing knowledge in the fields they represent. If they did not conduct innovative research and publish their results, soon the field itself—and not just the professors—would stagnate and perish.

It is not easy to get a research report published. Articles reporting findings that are intended to become a part of the accumulating knowledge in a field must undergo rigorous screening. The professional journals that we discussed earlier are *refereed*; that is, a researcher who has prepared a final report sends the manuscript to a journal, and the editors of the journal send the manuscript to several respected experts in that field of research, who read the report, offer critical advice, and decide whether the research is important enough to merit space in the journal. This system of judging reports is operated *blind*, which means that the researcher who sends in the manuscript does not know the names of the referees and the referees do not know the name of the author. This helps to ensure objectivity and standards of high quality. It is a tough competition. Although there are dozens of journals devoted to communications research, some reject up to 95 percent of the manuscripts they receive!

There are other outlets for communications research reports. Hundreds are initially presented as papers to scientific meetings. Often such papers are published later, after the review process has taken place. Projects of large scope, whose reports could not fit into the dozen or so pages of a regular research article, are usually published as research monographs—technical books of varying sizes that are financially supported by governments, foundations, professional associations, university presses, or other publishers who do not expect to make a profit. Their purpose is to add to society's understanding of whatever is being studied. Communications researchers use all of these outlets to present their research reports.

Major Research Strategies

While discussing the general steps involved in conducting research, we mentioned a number of research techniques, strategies, and procedures that merit more detailed discussion. A brief examination of some of the basics of sampling, measurement, and overall research design is helpful for understanding how research on the influences and consequences of mass communication is conducted.

The Use of Samples

Communications researchers often attempt to generalize their results to the entire population of a community, region, or even nation. Quite obviously, it is not possible to study the huge numbers of people that make up such a population, because it would be incredibly expensive and would take an army of investigators. However, in the nineteenth century, researchers studying animal populations, such as marine forms, discovered that if they picked a small number with great care, so that they had the same average characteristics as the whole population, the results found by studying the smaller segment would also be true of the whole. It was soon discovered that the principle applied to people, too. For this reason, researchers adopted sampling. It provides a way to overcome the impracticality of trying to study an entire population, and if it is done well, researchers get about the same results.

Today, the study of populations via samples is not restricted to animals or people. All of the newspapers in the United States make up a "population" of newspapers. The same is true of all TV shows broadcast during a given year or month. Thus, a *population*, in a technical sense, consists of all of the units of whatever the researcher intends to study. The *sample* will be made up of some smaller number of units drawn from that population.

There are many ways to pick a sample to represent a population. The basic rule, however, is to make certain that every unit that exists in the population has an equal probability of being included in the sample. If all goes well and the sample is picked in this manner, its units should have the same basic distribution of characteristics as does the population as a whole. This procedure does not always work, but most of the time it does.

For example, if the population is made up of people, they will have many different social characteristics. A certain percentage will be urban, and a different percentage rural; another group will be well educated, and a different segment will be illiterate; some will be male, some female; and so on. A sample picked under the condition that every person in the population has an equal chance of being selected *should* result in a similar distribution of virtually all such characteristics. If that actually turns out to be the case, the sample is said to be *representative* of the population. A representative sample can be defined as one in which the people in the sample are distributed among major social characteristics in the same manner as people in the population from which they are drawn. The same idea applies to other kinds of populations made up of different types of units. The sample should reflect the overall composition of the population.

How large should a sample be? There is no firm answer to that question, but there are guidelines. Samples of about 1,500 are seldom any less representative than ones three times that big, so national polling agencies often use about that number for studying the entire population of the United States. And they get remarkably accurate results. As sample size decreases from 1,500, representativeness can deteriorate. However, even samples of a hundred or so can offer relatively stable estimates about the characteristics of populations if the basic rules for selection are followed. If not, no one knows what the results mean.

The kind of sample with which all others are compared is the *simple random sample*. It is quite easy to understand. Let us imagine that we could write the name of every person in the United States on a card and then toss all of those two hundred and fifty-three million cards into a big hat—indeed, a very big hat. Then let us imagine that we could stir and toss all of those cards around so that they were fully mixed, and each card's position in the hat was totally governed by chance. Blindfolded, we now approach the hat and draw out, say, 1,250 cards. That would be a simple random sample of 1,250.

In the real world, researchers do not proceed with cards and hats. Researchers drawing a simple random sample must first develop a *sampling frame*, a complete list of the names of every person (or type of unit) in the entire population from which the sample will be drawn. Each person or unit on the list can be given a number. Then, if the researcher needs a sample of 250, a computer can generate 250 random numbers that identify which people (or other elements) are to make up the simple random sample.

The problem here is the sampling frame. How can a researcher get such a list for the entire U.S. population? The answer is that it is not possible. Therefore, simple random samples can be used only in narrower situations where a list of all the units in the population can be obtained. But other ways to get samples are almost as good. Some researchers first select a sample of states, then a sample of counties within those states, and then townships, census districts, or other smaller units within the counties. From there they can select households and then specific people (male head of family, oldest adult female, and so on) within the household. That is called *multistage area sampling*, and it works pretty well.

Some ways to design samples and draw units or people for study from some large population are better than others, and some are terrible. Occasionally, research reports contain terms such as *convenience sample*, which means that the researcher studied whoever was handy—for example, people stopped randomly in the street. Another poor technique is *quota sampling*, in which the researcher hunts up enough people of various kinds so that the final sample has the proportion of males, females, blacks, or whites that he or she deems necessary. There is no pretense that each person has had an equal probability of being selected. Another approach to sampling, useful for initial explorations, is the *focus group*—a dozen or so people selected because they are like those of interest. The researchers will have lengthy discussions with members of such a group about a product, candidate, or issue in the hope that insights will be obtained.

In judging samples, therefore, we need to ask three important questions: (1) Was the sample large enough? (2) Were the units selected according to the rule of equal probability? (3) Did the final sample actually represent the population from which it was drawn? If we cannot answer yes to all three of those questions, then we have to regard the research results as flawed.

Measuring Variables

Measurement is critical in science. It can be defined as the use of numerically based rules to convert subjective sensory experiences—that is, observations—into data symbols that can be counted, added, subtracted, multiplied, or divided. Stated more simply, measurement is observing in a numerically ordered manner. It results in data that are external to the observer, that can be *confirmed* by other scientists, and that can be subjected to *quantitative* analysis.

It is not really possible to conduct empirical research without measurement in some form. Even in qualitative research, the most sensitive observations result in the identification of repetitions of patterns in thought, meaning, and action. At the simplest level, measurement may be little more than deciding whether some attribute or quality is "present" or "absent" in a particular instance of communication behavior. That is essentially a quantitative (1 versus 0) observation. At more complex levels, measurement may involve the use of elaborate scales, tests, or indices based on complex statistical models and designed to assess refined differences among people in terms of their personal or social characteristics. In any case, measurement in some form is at the heart of research.

Two general features of measurement can be used to understand and evaluate the assessment of a particular variable in any given communications research report: the *level* of measurement, and the general *quality* of the resulting data (which means whether they are trustworthy and whether they actually represent what was supposed to be assessed).

Levels of measurement   There are four levels of measurement, each more refined and sophisticated than the one below. It is important to understand the differences among them, because they represent increasingly precise modes of quantitative observation. (See Figure 15.1.)

At the simplest level is *nominal measurement*. As its label implies, this refers to "naming" some category into which objects of study can be classified or categorized. For example, people can be classified as male or female, married or single, Republican, Democrat, or independent, and so on through thousands of such categories. Those words imply important qualities that identify the classifications into which the people will be placed.

Generally, nominal measurement means little more than placing a person (or whatever is being studied) into a named qualitative category. It does not imply "more" or "less" of something. It does mean that the qualities of the named category are *present* or *absent* for a particular individual who is being studied. It is important for the categories to be well defined, nonoverlapping, and exhaustive, so that classification can be accurate and complete. Other than that, nominal measurement is straightforward.

Somewhat more complex are the procedures used for *ordinal measurement*. Most people are familiar with the idea of ranking some set of things or people: The one with the "most" of something is given first place; the one with the "next most" gets second place; and so on down. Positions from first to last are assigned on the basis of some quantitative variable. Again, this is a simple idea that is common in everyday life. A good example is the performance of racehorses, which is reported in terms of ordinal measures: win, place, and show (first, second, and third). Graduates are sometimes ranked as to whether they were first in their class or somewhere down the list, such as one hundred and twenty-third. These are ordinal measures of scholastic performance.

FIGURE 15.1
Levels of Measurement

Nominal measurement
(qualitative categories
for classification)

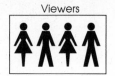

Ordinal measurement
(unequal distances
between points)

Interval measurement
(unknown limits, but equal
distances between points)

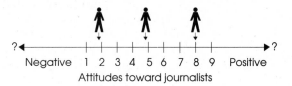

Ratio measurement
(has zero, equal distances)

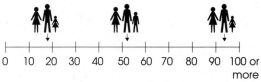

What is not quite so obvious about such ranks or ordinal positions is that the *distance* between positions is probably not consistent. That can be a very important consideration in scientific measurement. For example, a horse may win by a nose, and the third horse, which shows, may lag many yards behind the one that places. Thus, the distance between first and second is not necessarily identical to that between second and third. Why is this important? Because it means that we cannot add or subtract ordinal rank positions. They are positions and not really numbers. That means we cannot add first, second, and third positions and then divide the answer by three to get a real average. The distances between each position are unknown. This flaw is sometimes found in communications research, and it can cause referees to reject a research report that is a candidate for publication. Ordinal measurement has its place—particularly if no other measurements are possible—but it is not equivalent to the more sophisticated levels.

A step above is *interval measurement*, which does provide data that can be added and subtracted (but not divided). Interval measurement is based on the idea of a regular scale, or continuum, somewhat like a common ruler. It has equal divisions along the scale, and individual subjects can be placed at particular points, providing clear numerical values. Communications researchers make wide use of interval scales, especially to assess attitudes, which comprise one of the most frequently studied variables in media-related research.

The basic idea of an interval scale is illustrated by the kind of scoring system that is commonly used in judging sporting events, such as slalom skiing, diving, and figure skating. Typically, a perfect performance in such an event earns the competitor a score of 10 from a judge, which implies "perfectly done in all respects." A truly miserable performance, on the other hand, would presumably earn the athlete a low score, such as 1 or conceivably even 0. Usually, there are several judges, and the competitor's official score is the average of what they individually award.

On this type of scale, there are intervals, or positions on a continuum that have equal distance between any adjacent pair. Thus, the distance between a 2 and a 3 is presumably identical to that between a 5 and a 6, and so on. However, what such a scale lacks is a *true zero point*. Even if a judge thinks the individual is so bad that a 0 is awarded, it does not mean that the competitor has no skills whatsoever. That an athlete appeared at all in the competition testifies that he or she possesses at least some ability. The zero used in the scale, in other words, is rather arbitrary and does not imply an absolute absence of the quality being measured. The significance of this "arbitrary" zero is that the distance between it and a "true" zero is unknown. Nevertheless, it is inevitably a part of any score along the continuum that is awarded by a judge. This means that such score numbers cannot be divided because we do not really know how big they are. In the everyday world, such points along an interval scale are often averaged (as in the case of sporting event judgments) and the difficulty of the unknown zero is ignored. On the other hand, in the world of research, where precision is an important objective, interval measurement has this technical disadvantage.

At the highest level are *ratio measures*. In many ways, they seem to be the simplest, but this is because they are so familiar. Mathematically, however, this is the most sophisticated level of measurement. The idea here is that the underlying ruler, or scale, actually does have a true zero point. It also has the equal intervals as well as the orderly properties of the less complex levels. This eliminates any restrictions on numerical manipulation, such as multiplying and dividing; therefore, ratios can be calculated. Examples of variables that usually provide ratio measures are income, age, years of schooling, and hours of viewing per week. These are measured by simple counts, but they all have a true zero point and equivalent intervals along their separate scales.

Validity and reliability No measurement is perfect. Even in the most exact sciences, where the physical properties of things can be measured with incredibly precise instruments, error still creeps in. In the extremely difficult area of measuring human behavior, especially among communicating human beings, the problem of error is always present.

An important question about any measurement is whether or not the procedure actually measures what it is supposed to measure. This is the issue of *validity*. For example, let us assume that a researcher wants to determine exactly why people select and read certain articles and ignore others in a particular weekly newsmagazine, such as *Time* or *Newsweek*. This is a typical problem for an applied researcher attempting to find out the uses and gratifications of such a magazine for its readers. Let us suppose that the researcher develops a questionnaire that provides a series of reasons why people read newsmagazine articles, and he or she then asks subjects to check the ones that represent their own views. Typically, such a questionnaire would provide about five or six reasons, such as (1) to kill time, (2) to be entertained, (3) to relax or relieve tension, (4) to gain information, and (5) to keep up-to-date. The subject is asked to check one or more of these categories. So far, so good. Now we will assume that in the community under study, unknown to the researcher, a social science teacher in the high school has assigned all his or her students the task of preparing a report on current events and has suggested *Time* as an excellent source of material. Thus, the real reason that many of the young people in town are reading the magazine is to satisfy a course requirement. If these people turn up in the researcher's sample, they will find no box to represent that reason, and they will probably check one of the others. This will result in low validity. The instrument (the questionnaire) has not actually measured what it was supposed to measure for those particular subjects.

Determining the validity of a measure is a difficult problem at best, and not many researchers are able to accomplish it. Yet low validity or lack of knowledge about validity can seriously limit the quality of research findings.

A second common problem in measurement is *reliability*. This refers to the consistency with which the measuring procedure yields similar results if it is used over and over on the same subjects. If a procedure gives one result today and a different result tomorrow on the same variable with the same people, the researcher has a problem! It is doubtful that the results of the research have a clear meaning. In other words, low reliability raises serious questions about the quality of the data obtained in a research project and the conclusions that can be reached.

Validity and reliability are related in a unique way. It is possible to get consistent results with an invalid measuring procedure, as long as it makes the same errors over and over. However, such measures lack validity, so a measurement can have high reliability and low validity. But if validity is high, then reliability must be high.

Generally, then, measuring is a complex way of observing the properties or attributes of something. Researchers have developed many procedures to transform empirical observations into numerically ordered data that can be analyzed in some quantitative way. Qualitative data-gathering has its own uses in science, but even nominal classification has a numerical basis. Each of the four general levels of measurement has its own special characteristics and limitations, and validity and reliability pose additional limits on the quality of a particular measuring procedure.

Money can be saved by using the telephone to contact samples of respondents for surveys. Computers can generate and even dial randomly selected telephone numbers. However, some households do not have phones, and it is sometimes hard to determine if the person at the other end is really the respondent who should be included in the survey. Therefore, telephone surveys often produce results that are less valid and reliable than those from personal interviews. (Kenneth Jarecke/Contact Press Images)

Basic Research Designs

Four general research designs are widely used in communication research: the *experiment*, the *survey*, the (qualitative) *observational study*, and *content analysis*. Each is used for a different purpose and each can take many forms.

Experiments   When people think of research, they often assume that it is mainly a matter of conducting experiments. Although the experiment has long been an important part of science, it is by no means the only strategy, or in many fields, even the most important one. The experiment is mainly a child of the physical sciences. Its logic is rather simple, and it has not really changed for centuries, although it has been adapted for the study of human behavior during the present century. It has become an important tool in certain kinds of communications studies.

The subjects observed in communications experiments are people. This poses a number of important ethical considerations that are of less concern in the physical sciences, where experiments are conducted on inanimate objects, but of critical concern in the biological sciences, where studies are done not only on rats and other animals but also on human beings. Communications researchers often use human beings as experimental subjects, but not in life-threatening situations. Nevertheless, the treatment of human subjects in any experiment must be done with close attention to possible ethical considerations.

The procedures for conducting experiments are quite similar, regardless of what subjects are being used. Typically, in a standard experimental design, some set of subjects is designated as an *experimental group.* (Actually, there can be more than one experimental group.) Another set of matched or similar subjects is designated as a *control group*. The subjects in these groups are assessed or measured in some way before the experiment begins, usually to determine the status of the dependent variable. Then some form of "treatment" is introduced to the experimental group (or groups) only. (Several versions of the treatment may be used if there is more than one experimental group.) Such treatments represent the independent variable. The control group gets either no treatment or some neutral experience that has little to do with the variables under study. Finally, the dependent variable is measured again after the treatment to see if, on average, it changed in the experimental group. If it did, the researcher can infer that the treatment "brought about" some form of change. If it changed in the same way in both experimental and control groups or changed in neither, no causal relationship with the independent variable is implied.

All of these considerations can be illustrated by a classic communications experiment conducted a number of years ago.[11] The researchers wanted to see whether illustrated lectures about dental hygiene and mouth conditions could change the dental practices of high school students. After making suitable arrangements with the school, they carefully assessed with a questionnaire the current dental practices of a large number of students. Then they presented four lectures on dental problems. Three of the lectures provided variations in the independent variable and were designed to provoke different levels of fear arousal (high, medium, and low). The fourth was a neutral lecture on the growth of the teeth and had nothing to do with fear arousal.

Three experimental groups heard the fear-arousal lectures (independent variable) after their initial dental practices had been assessed. One received the high-fear lecture; the second was exposed to the medium-fear presentation; the third got the low-fear treatment. The control group received the neutral lecture on the growth of the teeth. The lectures were accompanied by colored slides that showed various mouth conditions that might result from poor dental hygiene. The low-fear lecture contained a few pictures of bad teeth and cavities. The medium-fear lecture showed some rather scary abscessed gums and bleeding sores. The high-fear treatment included some truly frightening pictures of cancerous jaws, sightless eyes, and gaping holes in people's mouths caused by neglect of the teeth.

The dependent variable (dental hygiene practices) was remeasured for all four groups two weeks afterward. The hypothesis was that the independent variable (fear) would change the dental practices of the subjects according to how much of it they experienced. The control group, of course, was not expected to change.

It did not work that way at all! The low-fear group changed the most, followed by the medium-fear group. The high-fear group changed very little, and the control group did not change. Thus, the higher the fear, the less the change. It was difficult to interpret these findings, and the researchers had to reject their initial hypothesis. They finally decided that the students had mentally shut out the dreadful scenes shown in the high-fear lectures, disassociating them from their personal conditions.

This experiment challenged the wisdom of using strong fear appeals in persuasive communications under the common-sense assumption that this would be effective. It was a fascinating experiment, and it led many experts to believe that a low-fear appeal would always have the greatest persuasive influence on people's behavior. Later on, however, somewhat similar experiments indicated very different findings. High fear *was* associated with high compliance. As additional studies were done, the self-correcting feature of science eventually called into question the idea of a reverse relationship between fear and compliance. The results of the dental experiment are *not* now viewed as particularly generalizable to many communications situations.

Experiments come in many forms in communications research. One form is *laboratory simulations*, where small groups are exposed to various independent variables under highly controlled conditions. The dental research project was a *field experiment*, in which sizable numbers of people are subjected to treatments in more or less normal settings, such as classrooms. In some large-scale field experiments, the subjects are entire communities that are exposed to different conditions, with "before" and "after" measures.

Surveys The survey as a research design is widely used in communications research and is a favorite of those who study the behavior or characteristics of audiences. The best surveys use face-to-face questioning of respondents. In this type of design, a formal questionnaire is often used for two reasons: It standardizes the questions the interviewer poses to the subjects, and it provides for efficient and uniform recording of the observations so that later data-processing and analysis will be simplified.

Interviewing large samples of people face to face is terribly expensive. For that reason, a number of short-cuts have been invented. Unfortunately, they all have limitations that can lead to unreliable results. For example, it is possible to interview people at home on the phone rather than visiting them personally. But one never knows exactly who answers a phone, and the situation is not as flexible as a face-to-face interview. Furthermore, many people have unlisted numbers, and a few do not even have phones. Thus, although this method saves money, it may introduce various kinds of biases and limitations.

Another short-cut is to send questionnaires to people in the mail. Here the problems are even greater. One never knows for sure who filled out the questionnaire. Furthermore, research shows clearly that some kinds of people willingly fill out questionnaires on their own, whereas others do not. The two categories could differ sharply with respect to the independent and dependent variables under study. Finally, mail-back questionnaires have a dismal record of nonreturn. Sometimes it helps to send out letters of reminder, offer a reward, or call people to ask them to cooperate. For the most part, however, researchers can expect their results to be untrustworthy to the degree that questionnaires are not returned. Even worse are the questionnaires that are included in magazines or other publications for people to fill out and return on a voluntary basis. The level of compliance is likely to be so low that no one knows what the results mean in terms of some

THE NOVEL AS QUALITATIVE RESEARCH:
A Linchpin to English and American Literature

A major goal of communications research is to show how the media help shape public opinion and societal values. Such efforts are not always based on the quantitative and statistical strategies of survey research. In fact, some of the most brilliant social commentary and some of the best "qualitative" research on social inequities and social conscience have come through the use of the literary form of the novel. The tradition of using the novel for social commentary is an old and often dangerous one, frequently born of a minority point of view and developed by such great eighteenth-century European writers as Dickens, Tolstoy, Balzac, and Zola, all of whom influenced a later generation of American writers.

Before the middle of the nineteenth century, the United States was still mainly an agricultural nation, and the dominant literary form of the period was the romance—great novels such as James Fenimore Cooper's *The Last of the Mohicans* and Herman Melville's *Moby-Dick*. After the Civil War, however, the country entered an age of industrialization—of booming cities, great entrepreneurs, and miserable poverty. With it came a move to literary naturalism; heroes and heroines were driven no longer by high principle or noble aspirations but by the instinct to survive and the will to prosper. Ever since then the oft-bitter tale of "the American dream," the gap between political reality and democratic principle, has been a recurrent theme in American literature.

In the late nineteenth century, much of that literature drew on the energy of the city for its raw material. Whereas the writers of a generation earlier—Hawthorne, Melville, Thoreau, and Emerson—had all displayed hostility to the growing dominion of the nation's cities, writers of the new age—among them William Dean Howells, Theodore Dreiser, Frank Norris, and later John Dos Passos—immersed themselves in its activity, finding it both rich and terrifying. In their literary rendering of their experience, they re-created the stark contrasts they found there.[1]

In perhaps the most memorable work of this type, Upton Sinclair's 1906 novel *The Jungle*, the Slavic immigrant Jurgis Rudkus and his wife Ona come to Chicago's stockyards looking for a new life. They see the city as "a dream of wonder, with its tale of human energy, of things being done, of employment for thousands upon thousands of men, of opportunity and freedom, of life and love and joy." They find instead, in Sinclair's appallingly brutal account of life in the meat-packing plants, hardship and horror in which the "dream of wonder" becomes a nightmare of death and desperation. At the novel's end, Sinclair's hero at last discovers the promise of American democracy in socialism.

Rarely has a novel caused such a strong public response as *The Jungle*, though to Sinclair's disappointment, it did not win public sympathy for socialism, his principal motive in writing the book. Much of

larger population. The findings and generalizations must be restricted to only those people who do comply, who often comprise only a fraction of those who received the publication. Often, rather unethically, those who sponsor such efforts imply that their "findings" have scientific validity.

Another possible short-cut is to use computerized devices that call people by random-digit dialing. Some are even programmed to "interview" people automatically and record their answers. Researchers who adhere to

the outcry the book caused centered on the unsanitary conditions of the meatpacking industry, leading Congress and President Theodore Roosevelt to create the federal Food and Drug Administration and to enforce new health and inspection regulations.

The theme of social class that inspired Sinclair also inspired other writers. A year after *The Jungle* was published, Jack London's *The Iron Heel* portrayed the laboring classes as a potentially revolutionary proletariat. Theodore Dreiser's novel *An American Tragedy* tells the story of Clyde Griffiths, a poor and somewhat dim young man whose drive to attain social status and sexual fulfillment leads him to murder his pregnant sweetheart and plunge headlong toward conviction and execution. Frank Norris tells a similar tale of broken aspirations in his 1903 novel *The Pit*, which centers on the Chicago Board of Trade. Sinclair Lewis satirized the smug complacency of the middle classes in his novels *Main Street* and *Babbitt*. F. Scott Fitzgerald's novels and stories, most famous among them his 1925 *The Great Gatsby*, focused on "the beautiful and the damned," the virtueless and obscenely wealthy leisure class.[2]

In the 1930s, the Great Depression brought American class inequities into sharp focus once again, and it gave rise to a new political radicalism in American letters. It was a movement that stirred controversy in a way that the naturalists of a generation earlier never did. The most memorable novel of this genre was John Steinbeck's *The Grapes of Wrath*. It is a story of a poor family forced off their farm by the dust storms that devastated Oklahoma during the 1930s. They endured great hardships as they made their way westward to California, the promised land. Their experiences along the way testified to the meanness of an uncaring society. Perhaps no American novel ever struck so deeply at the American conscience. It remains a great classic and has been made into motion pictures twice since it was published.

Generally, then, novels such as *The Jungle*, *Babbitt*, and *The Grapes of Wrath* describe with great sensitivity individual human experience, social conditions, and the problems people face at different levels of society. The portrayals that they provide can be far more sensitive than the numbers and percentages that are the end product of surveys and polls. Their major limitation is that they do not actually describe the lives of real people. They are composites brought together in an author's creative imagination. It can be difficult to tell whether they provide true pictures of the world on which they focus or distorted images designed to alarm or entertain their readers. Nevertheless, carefully researched novels, based on extensive observation by their creators, will remain as important sources from which we can gain insight into the human condition.

1. Grant C. Knight, *The Critical Period in American Literature* (Chapel Hill, N.C.: University of North Carolina Press, 1951), p. vii.
2. Michael Spindler, *American Literature and Social Change* (London: MacMillan, 1983), pp. 135–182.

responsible standards regard computer-obtained samples and interviews as a travesty, but various commercial market-research firms use them and are able to convince clients that the results they provide will offer helpful guidelines as to how consumers feel about the clients' products. Any relationship between the results obtained by such means and reality is totally unknown, and to claim otherwise is unethical. Although these devices are cheap to operate, the old rule prevails: You get what you pay for.

Generally, however, if conducted properly, the survey is a very reliable research design. Sample size must be adequate and sample selection must follow accepted rules. Once the sample has been selected, the best procedure is for the researcher to interview the subjects carefully in person, using a standardized questionnaire.

Observational studies   Observational research was pioneered by cultural anthropologists, who lived with primitive societies "in the field," studying the cultures closely and describing them in detailed ethnographic research reports. For this reason, this type of investigation is sometimes called *field research*. Sociologists who have used this method have joined groups such as prisoners, soldiers, and medical students so as to study them carefully, and they call it *participant observation*. Communications researchers have adapted this strategy to their own needs, sometimes participating in the activities of newsrooms, broadcast stations, motion picture companies, or other media groups to observe them closely.

Although they often yield truly insightful results, observational studies are difficult and time-consuming. The strategy is less formally structured than those that depend on experimental or survey procedures. The investigator may have to spend years with a group to understand everything the group does and why it is done that way.

An observational study now considered a classic was done by David Altheide.[12] For three years, he studied the process by which the daily TV news was selected, edited, and disseminated. He spent months in the newsrooms of three local television stations that were network affiliates and made confirming observations in several others. Then he studied the central managers in the news-making industry, following the way in which they handled several important stories, including a presidential campaign, a war, and a major political scandal. Altheide's research findings revealed a great deal about the day-to-day world of TV news processing of the time. The basic concept he saw in action was what he called the "news perspective," a set of systematic constraints that bring about distortions in the news. These were (1) commercialism, (2) ratings, (3) bureaucracy, (4) lack of real news, (5) the journalist's view of the audience (as essentially stupid), and (6) competition with other media. Altheide's observations showed that commercialism—the need to make a profit—affected the selection and presentation of the news by limiting the amount of time given to stories. Very little time could be allotted to any one story, because time had to be allocated to commercials. News personnel feared a drop in ratings because that would bring a decline in advertising revenue, so the news had to be "interesting," or at least made to appear so, even if it was dull.

A continuing problem with local news (then and now) is that on many days there simply is not anything going on. However, any event that is reported has to be made newsworthy, even if it is a treed cat, a fifteen-cent robbery, or a neighborhood pie-eating contest. Overall, Altheide's work confirmed what many previous researchers had shown in bits and pieces: that a host of factors influence the way the daily news is prepared in the newsroom. Those factors distort the nature of the news that appears on the viewer's screen, so that what happens in the world outside is by no means identical with what the viewer sees there.

Observational research, based mainly on participant observation, is an ideal procedure for obtaining detailed and sensitive information about a complex social process. Researchers can uncover patterns and processes by this means that they could never find by experiments or surveys. Unfortunately, it takes a lot of time, and the observations obtained are usually qualitative rather than quantitative. This limits the degree to which statistical procedures can be used to reveal patterns, as well as the use of probability to accept or reject hypotheses. Nevertheless, observational research has an important place in science, both as a tool of exploratory investigation and as a means of confirming patterns revealed by other means.

Content analysis   This type of research is somewhat unique to communications studies. The basic procedures were devised during World War II, when intelligence units monitored all broadcasts, both civilian and military, that came from Germany. This often produced some surprising insights into the activities of the enemy. For example, it was possible to trace the movements of German troops in occupied countries by studying the popular music played over radio stations in particular areas. If a radio station suddenly changed to music that appealed to German soldiers, it was a good bet that German troops were now being billeted in the area. Similarly, the content of Japan's coded radio transmissions to its navy and land bases was rigorously monitored. The Japanese did not know that the Americans had broken their secret code, so the Americans gained much valuable information that had an important influence on the outcome of various battles and naval engagements.

Starting after the war, procedures for analyzing the content of newspapers, radio and television broadcasts, and indeed any form of communication were more completely developed. Today we can define *content analysis* as a set of systematic and objective procedures for the quantitative study of messages. Presumably content analysis could be used to study any form of message, from telephone gossip to religious scriptures, but it is mainly a tool of research that can reveal underlying patterns in the messages or content that media are presenting to their audiences.

The full range of steps involved in the use of the scientific method are followed in content analysis. Research objectives are defined; previous research is studied; observations are made; data are processed and analyzed; conclusions are reached; and the results are reported. It is in the stage of making observations that content analysis differs from most other research designs, because messages rather than people are observed.

Once researchers have clarified the objectives of their research, they must identify and carefully define *units of analysis*. For example, in a study of the portrayal of sex behavior on prime-time television, researchers must first define exactly what constitutes "sex behavior." Obviously, this could take many forms, ranging from touching to violent rape. The investigators must identify various categories of sexual activity (for example, kissing, embracing, flirting, intercourse), and these categories then become units of analysis. Once such units have been carefully identified and defined, the researchers can count the number of times that each occurs in a given TV show.

If the medium under study is print, the same basic procedures are used. Researchers identify and define units of analysis so that they can be counted, but in this case a unit may be the number of column inches devoted to a particular type of story, such as crime, news about the women's movement, or a political scandal. Or the unit of analysis may be a specific word, theme, or name, which is counted each time it appears on a page.

Although it sounds simple, content analysis can be difficult in practice, particularly for broadcast content. Today, TV shows can be taped and replayed over and over so that the researcher can decide whether a given activity is indeed an instance of, say, flirting. Researchers performing content analyses often try out their procedures many times before deciding how they will define their units of analysis.

Sampling is also a critical aspect of the procedure. It would be too big a task to study *all* prime-time network television, so it is necessary to settle on some representative segment, such as all programs broadcast during a given week or time slot. With print, the sample might consist of randomly selected front pages of a newspaper during a given period. There are an unlimited number of ways to select samples from media content for systematic study.

Once researchers have defined the units of analysis in a workable manner and selected the sample of what is to be studied, they can begin actual observation. They read the stories carefully or review their tapes over and over, to count the number of times each unit occurs. These become their basic data for analysis with statistical procedures.

Content analysis is an excellent way to determine what is being presented to an audience. However, those who use the technique always suggest a number of cautions. First, one cannot tell from what has been *presented* by a medium what has been received or how it might *influence* the audience. For example, if a lot of sexual content appears on television, this does not mean that people will have seen it or that it will increase their sexual activity. Furthermore, inferences about the *intentions* of the communicator may be unwarranted. If a network consistently presents advertisements for candy in children's programming, there are no grounds for assuming that the network is really trying to ruin children's teeth. Unfortunately, many equally silly inferences have been drawn after research has revealed that some form of content is prevalent in a medium.

Generally, then, content analysis is a special way of making observations. It focuses on messages from various media and provides systematic and objective information as to how often particular units of analysis appear in samples of that content. It is widely used in communications research to study what the media are telling their audiences.

The several research designs we have discussed bring together such research strategies as measurement and sampling. They provide orderly plans for designating which variables will be considered independent or dependent and which are to be controlled. Finally, they permit researchers to gather data in such a way that they can make generalizations, test hypotheses, and understand the data's implications (if any) for more general theories. Overall, communications research is a fascinating, creative, and challenging activity that brings us greater understanding of the process and effects of mass communication.

Chapter Review

- Research is a set of procedures for gathering reliable information under controlled conditions of observation in such a way that objective conclusions can be reached with a minimum of error.

- Research provides a way to develop and test theories that explain the process and effects of mass communication. Additionally, it is a means by which media or media-related industries can seek solutions to the many practical problems they face.

- Research on mass communications follows the general pattern of science. It begins with the assumptions that its subject matter is orderly, that cause-and-effect relationships can be found, and that conclusions must always be regarded as tentative and open to revision.

- The scientific method begins with a careful specification of the research problem. Empirical observations are transformed into data, which can then be processed and analyzed by computer so as to take advantage of existing statistical techniques and probability models.

- Getting research reports published can be difficult. Manuscripts are rigorously screened by a blind system of judging, and those that survive appear in journals or as monographs.

- Research strategies include sample selection, measuring variables, and the use of one of several basic research designs.

- A good sample is representative of the composition of its population and large enough to provide for accurate estimates of the way the variables under study are distributed in the population.

- Measurement refers to making numerically ordered observations. The four levels of measurement are nominal, ordinal, interval, and ratio.

- Validity is defined as the degree to which a measurement procedure actually assesses what it is designed to measure, and reliability refers to the consistency with which it does so. Both are important indicators of the quality of a measuring procedure.

- Experiments are the oldest research design, inherited mainly from the physical sciences. Surveys were developed by the social sciences and are heavily used by communications researchers. Qualitative observational studies are difficult, yet they have an important place in communications research. Finally, content analysis is unique to communication research. Its findings can tell with precision what a medium is saying to its audience, but not how the audience will react or what the intentions of the communicator might be.

Notes and References

1. Harold D. Lasswell, "The Structure and Function of Communication in Society," in Lyman Bryson, ed., *The Communication of Ideas* (New York: Harper & Brothers, 1948), pp. 37–51.

2. Donald L. Shaw and Maxwell E. McCombs, *The Emergence of American Political Issues: The Agenda-Setting Function of the Press* (St. Paul, Minn.: West, 1977). See also *Journalism Quarterly, 71* (Winter 1992) (a

special issue in its twenty-fifth anniversary year, with a number of articles devoted to the current status of agenda-setting theory and research).

3. David Pearl, Lorraine Bouthilet, and Joyce Lazar, eds., *Television and Behavior: Ten Years of Scientific Progress and Implications for the Eighties*, vol. 2 (Washington, D.C.: U.S. Government Printing Office, 1982), pp. 287–307.

4. Charles Swanson, "What They Read in 130 Daily Newspapers," *Journalism Quarterly*, *32*, no. 2 (1955), pp. 411–421.

5. Maxwell McCombs, "Using Readership Research," National Newspaper Foundation Community Journalism Textbook Project, 1979. See also Leo Bogart, *Press and Public* (Hillsdale, N.J.: Erlbaum, 1981).

6. William Tillinghast, "Declining Newspaper Reader-ship: Impact of Region and Urbanization," *Journalism Quarterly*, *58*, no. 1 (1981), p. 14.

7. Sydney W. Head and Christopher H. Sterling, *Broadcasting in America*, 5th ed. (Boston: Houghton Mifflin, 1987), pp. 373–403.

8. Carl I. Hovland, Arthur A. Lumsdaine, and Fred D. Sheffield, *Experiments on Mass Communication* (Princeton, N.J.: Princeton University Press, 1949).

9. Elihu Katz and Paul F. Lazarsfeld, *Personal Influence: The Part Played by People in the Flow of Mass Communication* (Glencoe, Ill.: Free Press of Glencoe, 1955).

10. Donna Hayes and Melvin L. DeFleur, "The Influence of Production Formats on Audience Recall and Judgments of Importance of Local Television News Stories," paper presented at annual meeting of the Association for Education in Journalism and Mass Communication (AEJMC), Montreal, 1992.

11. Irving Janis and Seymour Feshback, "The Effects of Fear-Arousing Communications," *Journal of Abnormal and Social Psychology*, *48* (1953), pp. 78–132.

12. David I. Altheide, *Creating Reality: How TV News Distorts Events* (Beverly Hills, Calif.: Sage, 1976).

16

Short-Term Media Influences on Individuals: Limited Effects

(The penny papers) are willing to fan into destroying flames the hellish passions that now slumber in the bosom of society. The guilt of murder may not stain their hands; but the fouler guilt of making murderers surely does.

Horace Greeley, *The Tribune*, 1841

Early Evidence Supporting a Belief in Maximum Effects
Research Begins with the Magic Bullet Theory / The Payne Fund Studies of Movies and Children / Radio Reports the Invasion from Mars

Beyond the Magic Bullet: Selective and Limited Effects
The *Why We Fight* Film Experiments during World War II / Effects of the Media in a Presidential Campaign / The Bases of Limited Influences Theories

Audience Uses and Gratifications in the Selection of Media Content
The Foundation Studies / Assessing a New Medium / Children's Uses of Television

The Issue of Television and Violence
The Report to the Surgeon General / The Second Report to the Surgeon General

The Bottom Line: Most Research Evidence Reveals Only Weak Effects

As soon as the penny papers began to circulate in the nineteenth century, there arose an enormous outpouring of complaints about mass communications. These condemnations focused on the problems that the new papers were supposedly causing, and they were based on the widely held assumption that the media of the time had great power to influence individuals, particularly in unwholesome ways. Similarly, as film and broadcasting arrived during the twentieth century, people became deeply concerned about the problems for society that these new media were presumably creating. These criticisms left in American society a "legacy of fear" that the mass media have immediate, uniform, powerful, and often harmful effects on their audiences.

A critical issue for understanding mass communications today is whether or not these anxieties are *justified*—whether the "legacy of fear" is still a valid perspective for assessing the impact of the media on individuals within our society. More specifically, do mass communications present false pictures of the world to the public? Do the American media promote unacceptable behavior among the nation's children? Can mass media messages be used as instruments of persuasion so as to shape our beliefs, attitudes, and behavior? Are mass communications dominating the political process and limiting intelligent decision-making?

Questions of this kind point to a serious challenge to basic democratic values. If the answer is "yes" to any of them, it follows logically that the broad concept of freedom of the press may not be such a good idea. That is, allowing those who control any medium to print, broadcast, or display any content that they wish, for any purpose that they wish, may not be in the best interests of society as a whole. If some kinds of mass communications unfairly *control* or even *harm* large numbers of people, perhaps the content of the media should be more closely controlled, or even censored so as to eliminate content that creates unacceptable effects. The problem is that such a cure may be worse than the problem. Most Americans would find such controls unacceptable. Obviously, this issue goes to the heart of the issue of freedom of expression and Americans' cherished constitutional guarantees. Therefore, it is little wonder that debates about harmful effects of mass communications are carried on with such vigor.

Another problem is how do we decide whether or not a particular medium or form of mass communication has effects that are personally or socially destructive? Most scholars take the position that among the alternatives, research conducted according to the scientific method provides the most trustworthy answers. It is, as we pointed out, *not perfect*. Research studies can be done poorly, or they can pursue the wrong questions. However, *in the long run*, scientific investigation is the most effective way to gain reliable information to make decisions about complex and perplexing questions, such as those that concern the influences of mass communications.

In this chapter, we review a number of large-scale investigations that have become milestones in the search for trustworthy knowledge about the influences of mass communications on individuals within American society. During the six decades since systematic research began, an interesting mixture of insights emerged from the milestone studies, plus hundreds of others that focused on the process and effects of mass communication. Some yielded conclusions that are still quite correct, but others were inconsistent. Still others (seen in hindsight) were just plain wrong. However, we will see that as the ability to conduct research on the influences of the media improved, additional understandings were provided by each new investigation. Thus, as the "cutting edge" of research moved forward, incorrect conclusions were gradually eliminated, to be replaced with alternatives that more adequately described the realities of mass communications and their influences. It is this *self-correcting* feature of the scientific method that makes it an attractive means of gaining trustworthy knowledge.

This chapter presents a *developmental* view of the increasing understanding of the process and effects of mass communication—a kind of historical tracing of the paths that research took. In particular, it shows how increasingly adequate theories explaining the effects of the media gradually emerged and how inadequate ones were abandoned. This means that we must interpret with caution any one of the investigations to be presented. We cannot simply take the conclusions of a study done long ago, when both the media and the society were much younger, and say that they are perfectly valid for interpreting the influences of the media today. It is the larger picture that counts; the improvement of understanding over time. Thus, in the early studies, the research methods used were crude and often inadequate. The theoretical perspectives developed from them were quite simple, and in some cases, they are now obviously invalid. However—and this is a major point of this entire chapter—during the sixty-year period represented by these studies, *there has been a slow but steady accumulation of knowledge* about how the media function—what they do, and what they do *not* do, to individuals in our society. That kind of development is exactly what research is all about.

Early Evidence Supporting a Belief in Maximum Effects

Empirical research on the effects of mass communication lagged far behind the development of the media themselves. Large-scale studies did not begin until the late 1920s. The reason for the delay was that the necessary research procedures, strategies, and techniques required to conduct such investigations were not available until the century was well under way. By then, research designs and measurement and statistical procedures were sufficiently developed within the social sciences—mainly psychology and sociology—for investigation of the effects of mass communication to become possible.

In the decade following World War I (the 1920s), when the first communications researchers began their work, sweeping changes were taking place in the society as well as among the media. The frontier was gone. Millions of immigrants had arrived. The forty-seventh and forty-eighth states (New Mexico and Arizona) had just been admitted to the Union (in 1916). The U.S. population was not only growing rapidly, but major internal migrations were also taking place—east to west, south to north, and farm to city.

Thus, the nation had become more complex as the so-called master trends of *migration*, *urbanization*, *industrialization*, and *modernization* continued with special vigor. Something like a mass society had emerged—increasingly made up of unlike people with weak ties to each other or even animosities toward people unlike themselves. It did not resemble a traditional society, in which similar people have close personal ties based on long-standing loyalties and family obligations developed over generations. The population of the United States was a jumble of newcomers thrown together, with significant psychological, economic, ethnic, and religious differences that kept them apart psychologically and socially. With communication based on strong interpersonal ties on the decline, it is not surprising

American society was undergoing rapid change in the 1920s. Within a decade, the nation moved from horse-and-buggy technology toward urbanization, industrialization, and modernization. The development of the movies and radio was a significant part of these trends, and their impact on individuals was yet to be understood. (Culver Pictures, Inc.)

that the new mass media played an increasingly important role. People came to *depend* more and more on the mass media, and less and less on each other, for information they needed. The developing mass media were themselves an integral part of the master trends. As the twentieth century began, the movies arrived. Within twenty years, they had become a major form of family entertainment. Radio became a household medium during the 1920s, and in the 1930s and 1940s, new kinds of magazines and television came on line.

It was against this background that large-scale empirical research on the influence of mass communications began. At first it was relatively unsophisticated, and the methods used had many shortcomings. Furthermore, the beliefs that prevailed among social scientists during the 1920s about the basic nature of people and urban-industrial societies guided the investigators. Those beliefs stressed the idea that human beings were guided by their *inherited* instincts and that the social ties between individuals were *weak* because of the heterogeneous nature of the mass society.

As we follow the story of media research across six decades, you need to understand (1) the *basic theories* that researchers developed over the years, (2) how they used increasingly sophisticated *research methods* for studying the effects of mass communication, and (3) how new findings sometimes forced them to *change* or even abandon some of their theories. All of these developments contributed to contemporary understanding of the process of mass communication and its influences on individuals and society.

Research Begins with the Magic Bullet Theory

Around the turn of the century, both social scientists and the public believed that the mass newspapers of the time were powerful instruments that could control and sway the thoughts and behavior of the members of the mass society. As we explained in Chapter 1, in our discussion of dependency theory (pp. 18–19), intellectuals of the period were convinced that people in the modern urban-industrial societies that were developing lived in social isolation from each other in a kind of "lonely crowd." People, they said, lacked the strong ties to neighbors, family, and friends that had characterized the older, preindustrial and traditional societies. It was, as Gustave Le Bon, a French sociologist, put it in 1895, an age of *crowds*, without ties between people, as opposed to an age of *community*, where people were linked by strong social bonds.[1]

A general set of beliefs about media influences that were prevailing at the time has come to be called the *magic bullet theory*. Although it is now formulated in a systematic manner only in retrospect, it represents the prevailing convictions about the features of the new industrial society and indicates why people believed that the mass media had very powerful effects on people. It predicted immediate, direct, and uniform effects on everyone who received a media message. Thus, it was a general theory within which both social scientists and the public interpreted the mass media when empirical research started. As it turned out, these interpretations of the

DARWIN'S INFLUENCE ON EARLY THINKING ABOUT MASS COMMUNICATIONS:
A Linchpin to the History of Biology and Psychology

Are complex human activities, such as work, play, and courtship, driven by internal biological forces beyond our control? Can our behavior be explained by blind motivations we inherit as part of our genetic endowment? These may seem oddly simplistic questions, but they were widely and seriously debated at the turn of the century when psychology was a developing science. The idea that human conduct is dictated exclusively by inherited biological factors no longer has scientific merit, but it still remains in some popular beliefs about the ways people respond to mass communications.

Emphasis on the biological causes of human behavior resulted from the profound impact that Charles Darwin had on the intellectual world when he published his *Origin of Species* in 1854. His theories were seen as a direct challenge to those who believed humankind to be a special life form, created in the image of God, and fundamentally different from other animals. Darwin's explanation was that the human species, like all others, was a product of an evolutionary process. He held that distinctions between species came about as creatures developed specialized qualities and unique ways of coping with the environment in the competitive struggle to survive. Successful species survived because their distinctive characteristics gave them advantages over their competitors. Human beings, with their large brain capacity and opposable thumb, were particularly well adapted.

The ideas Darwin advanced helped shape the earliest theories that behavioral scientists devised to explain the influence of mass communications on human populations. What connected Darwin's theories and the earliest interpretations of the effects of mass communications was the idea of *uniformity* in adaptive human conduct. The reasoning was that animal behavior, including human behavior, was governed by genetics. The key concept was *instinct*. This term identified complex patterns of action controlled

power of the media would not be easy to alter because they seemed so logical and were so widely believed.

The Payne Fund Studies of Movies and Children

Social scientists interested in large-scale research on the effects of mass communication first focused on the movies. There were clear reasons for this choice. During the first decade of the new century, movies were a novelty. During the second decade, they became one of the principal media for family entertainment. By the end of the 1920s, feature-length films with soundtracks had become standard, and the practice of going to the movies for entertainment had been deeply established.

Meanwhile, the public had become uneasy about the influence of the movies on children. In 1929, an estimated 40 million minors, including more than 17 million children under the age of fourteen, went to the movies weekly.[2] Critics raised alarming questions about the potential effects: Were

from within by inherited genetic "clockwork." Instinct was what enabled salmon to return upriver to spawn, birds to navigate unerringly during long migrations, and bees to communicate the location of food far from the hive. Driven by blind biological motivations, all salmon, all birds, and all bees of a given species did these things in exactly the same way. Thus, behavior in the face of stimuli from the environment was thought to be both *automatic* and *uniform*. Human beings could be no exception. Textbooks in psychology just after the turn of the century presented long lists of instincts that explained uniformities in human conduct.

When the mass media began to be a common part of national life, these theories defining animal and human behavior in terms of instinct were ready and waiting. They were used to explain the effects of mass communications: Media messages were assumed to be perceived uniformly by all those who were exposed to them, and the responses audience members made to such messages were assumed to be both uniform and automatic. Media messages, then, were seen as "magic bullets," striking every eye and ear the same way and creating mass behavioral

effects over which people had little control. Thus, it was thought that people could be readily manipulated by the content of the mass media.

Today, these theories are obsolete. The idea that human behavior is a product of instinct was dismissed by scientists during the late 1920s. Some psychologists continue the search for biological influences on human behavior, but in far more sophisticated ways. Contemporary theories of the influence of mass communications stress the influence of both individual learning and culture on people's interpretations of media effects, resulting in *selectivity* rather than uniformity. However, the venerable magic-bullet idea, as influenced by Darwin, is alive and well among some segments of the public. Various groups of citizens criticize the media for airing or publishing content that, they charge, will inevitably corrupt youth, unravel the moral fabric of the nation, or somehow set off uniform and automatic effects of an unacceptable nature.

Sources: Edwin G. Boring, *A History of Experimental Psychology* (New York: The Century Company, 1929); Melvin L. DeFleur and Sandra Ball-Rokeach, *Theories of Mass Communication*, 5th ed. (White Plains, N.Y.: Longman, 1989). pp. 172–179.

During the 1920s, the public became deeply concerned about the influence of the new motion pictures on children. In 1929, more than 17 million children under the age of fourteen attended the movies every week. The films presented stories about crime, love, war, and horror. Especially worrisome were themes that seemed to emphasize immoral behavior. Early research on the influence of films appeared to confirm the public's worst fears. (Brown Brothers)

Early Evidence Supporting a Belief in Maximum Effects ■ **539**

THE MAGIC BULLET THEORY

The earliest general theoretical perspective on the influence of mass communication, widely shared when empirical research began, was what in retrospect is called the *magic bullet theory*. In spite of its colorful name, this theory was based in part on certain basic scientific assumptions about human nature that were heavily influenced by the evolutionary perspectives of Charles Darwin. Earlier, before he published his *Origin of Species* (in 1859), thinking about the nature of humankind emphasized *religious* interpretations. Human beings were said to be unique "rational" creatures formed in the image of God. After Darwin, scientific thinking began to stress the importance of inheritance and biology as causes of human behavior.

Influenced by this genetic perspective, social and behavioral scientists rejected interpretations of "rational" human beings and stressed the *animal* side of human nature. They assumed that there was *continuity* between the behavior of higher animals and that of human beings. For example, animals within a particular species presumably all behaved in more or less the same way because of their *uniform inherited instincts* (derived from their evolutionary history). It was assumed, therefore, that human beings were also uniformly controlled by their biologically based "instincts," and that they would react more or less uniformly to whatever "stimuli" (situations confronting them) came along. Under this conception of human nature, responses made by human beings to stimuli were thought to be shaped either by instincts over which people lacked rational control or by other unconscious processes that were not guided by the human intellect.

the picture shows destroying parents' control over their children? Were they teaching immorality? Films with unwholesome themes—horror, crime, immoral relationships, and the illegal use of alcohol (during Prohibition)—were especially troubling.

No government agency existed to give money to investigators who wanted to assess the impact of films on children, but a private organization (The Motion Picture Research Council) decided to seek research data in order to develop a national policy concerning motion pictures. This organization called together a group of educators, psychologists, and sociologists to plan large-scale studies to probe the effects of motion pictures on youth. A private foundation called the Payne Fund was persuaded to supply the necessary money. The resulting Payne Fund Studies were the first large-scale and multi-disciplinary scientific effort to assess the effects of a major mass medium.

When the thirteen reports were finally published in the early 1930s, the Payne Fund Studies were the best available evaluation of the impact of motion pictures on children. The researchers used approaches that ranged from collecting and interpreting anecdotes to experiments measuring and analyzing responses to questionnaires. But by today's standards of research, many of these studies seem quaint and naive. Later, some became quite

This was a frightening view, and it had a strong influence on thinking about the power of mass communication. It portrayed human populations as being composed of irrational creatures that could be swayed and controlled by cleverly designed mass-communicated "stimuli." This theory led people early in the century to believe that those who controlled the media could control the public. Thus, the magic bullet theory implied that the media have direct, immediate, and powerful effects of a uniform nature on those who pay attention to their content. The theory, representing both popular and scientific thinking, assumed that a media message reached every eye and ear in the same way, like a symbolic "bullet," bringing about the same changes of thought and behavior in the entire audience. Although the magic bullet theory was not set forth formally at the time, in retrospect, its propositions can be summarized in the following way:

1. People in mass society lead *socially isolated lives* with very limited social controls exerted over one another because they are from diverse origins and do not share a unifying set of norms, values, and beliefs.

2. Like all animals, human beings are endowed at birth with a *uniform set of instincts* that guide their ways of responding to the world around them.

3. Because people's actions are not influenced by social ties and are guided by uniform instincts, individuals attend to events (such as media messages) *in similar ways*.

4. People's inherited human nature and their isolated social condition lead them to *receive and interpret* media messages in a uniform way.

5. Thus, media messages are like symbolic "bullets," striking every eye and ear and resulting in effects on thought and behavior that are *direct, immediate, uniform*, and therefore *powerful*.

controversial. Technical details about the way data were collected and the conclusions reached by the researchers were widely criticized by research specialists for a decade. On the other hand, the public did not care about these controversies. They were frightened by the results. The technical criticisms of research procedures seemed to the average layperson like debates over fine points of navigation conducted while the ship was sinking. Above all, the overall results of the Payne Fund Studies seemed to confirm the charges of the critics of the movies and the worst fears of parents. These studies remain important because they established many of the research questions that are still pursued.

To illustrate the approaches, data, limitations, and conclusions of the studies, we can look briefly at two of them. One dealt with the question of how the movies influence the everyday behavior of children. The other tried to find out whether movies change children's attitudes.

Influences of the movies on everyday behavior   One of the most interesting, if least rigorous, of the Payne Fund Studies was done by sociologist Herbert Blumer.[3] Blumer wanted to provide a general picture of how viewing films influences children's play, their everyday behavior (such as dress, mannerisms, and speech), their emotions, their ideas about romance, their ambitions and temptations, and their career plans. His method was simple. He had adolescents and young adults recall in *autobiographical* form influences from films they had seen years before in their childhood. Eventually, Blumer collected accounts from more than 1,200 people. Most were college and university students, but some were office and factory workers. The result was an immense number of recollections about how people *thought* that seeing films had influenced their daily behavior.

Blumer attempted to draw conclusions from these accounts, but he did not subject them to quantitative or statistical analysis. He preferred to "let the facts speak for themselves" by quoting liberally from the autobiographies to illustrate his conclusions. The movies were, he said, a source of *imitation, unintentional learning*, and *emotional influence*.

According to Blumer, the movies had an especially powerful impact on children's play. Youngsters impersonated cowboys and Indians, cops and robbers, pirates, soldiers, race drivers, and every conceivable hero and villain they had seen in films. Re-enacting movie plots, children battled each other with wooden swords, spears made from broom handles, and shields from washboiler tops. They rode horses made of scraps of lumber, shot rifles and pistols made of sticks, and flew airplanes built with apple crates. They dug trenches in their back yards and assaulted forts in vacant lots. They became Dracula, Cleopatra, the dreaded Dr. Fu Manchu, Tarzan, the Red Baron, and Mary, Queen of Scots. Most of it was remembered as fun. For the most part, these activities seemed to have little lasting influence on later life.

More significantly, Blumer concluded that children and teenagers copied many mannerisms, speech patterns, and other behaviors from the people portrayed on the screen. There were hundreds of accounts in the autobiographies of how youngsters had tried to imitate the way a favorite movie star smiled, leered, smirked, laughed, sat, walked, or talked. Their attempts were usually unsuccessful and short-lived, and they often mystified parents.

Although it would seem harmless for children to adopt hair and dress styles from film characters, remember that the 1920s were the age of "flaming youth" and "flappers." The movies showed speakeasies, easy money, powerful cars, and "fast" women. Parents were accustomed to books and magazines that followed the strict standards of the Victorian era. But by the time of World War I, Victorian morality had begun to fade, and the automobile was being used for more than just transportation. When they saw movies mirroring the new styles and the new "looser" morality, many people believed the movies were the *cause* of the changes (a common *non sequitur* in interpreting mass communication). By showing that children copied the behavior they saw in films, Blumer's findings seemed to support this view. This worried parents a great deal.

Blumer's study revealed another facet of the movie experience. Movie viewing was often an intensely emotional experience. His subjects reported that often while watching films they experienced what he called *emotional possession*. As the plot unfolded, they had intense feelings of terror and fear,

Many of the movies produced during the late 1920s alarmed the older generation, whose moral values grew out of the Victorian era. Films that depicted gambling and easy money, fast cars, illegal drinking, and "loose" morals were feared as unwholesome influences on children and young people. (Culver Pictures, Inc.)

sorrow and pathos, thrills and excitement, or romantic passion and love. They often left the film emotionally drained, anxious, or sexually stimulated—depending on the film. This also worried parents and fueled the fires of critics of the movies.

What can we learn from Blumer's research and its conclusions? Can Blumer's study tell us whether the films *caused* certain behaviors? Can it give any objective measure of the influence of films on children today, or even on Blumer's subjects at the time? Can it tell us whether any influence they might have had lasted over the lifetimes of the subjects? The answer to each of these questions is *no*. First, whatever Blumer found out about the first generation of moviegoers has completely unknown applications to today's youth, who have a great deal of experience with other kinds of media and a very different culture. Second, the methods of Blumer's study are not adequate to provide indisputable answers even to his own questions. Notice first that Blumer's *sample*—the subjects who wrote the autobiographies—might have been unrepresentative, or biased, in many ways. Moreover, his ways of measuring influences were merely anecdotal and retrospective.

Stated in more technical terms, Blumer's study falls short in meeting two fundamental criteria for scientific research: *validity* and *reliability*. We saw in Chapter 15 that a procedure is valid if it measures what it claims to measure. We are not certain that Blumer's autobiographies actually show the influences movies had on the children under study. Similarly, a study is reliable if a repetition of the study using the same techniques would yield similar results. Would his findings have been the same if Blumer had repeated his research? Or, if another researcher had duplicated the study, would the conclusions have been parallel? We simply don't know. Yet, in spite of all of its "warts," we don't want to write off Blumer's study as inconsequential. It was very imaginative, and it opened important lines of research that are still followed today. It remains an historic landmark.

Seeing movies changes children's attitudes   Ruth C. Peterson and L. L. Thurstone conducted another of the Payne Fund Studies. The research design and measurement procedure used resemble today's social science research strategies rather closely. They used what we would now call a field experiment and focused on the question of how movies influence children's *attitudes* toward social issues.[4]

First, they reviewed hundreds of films to select a few that dealt clearly with specific issues. To be included in the research, a film had to be recent, acceptable to school authorities, and clearly focused on attitudes toward one of the issues under study. Eventually, the researchers selected thirteen films that depicted attitudes toward (1) the Germans and World War I, (2) gambling, (3) Prohibition, (4) the Chinese, (5) punishment of criminals, and (6) "the Negro" (the term commonly used at the time). In some experiments, they assessed the ability of one film to change attitudes; in others, they measured attitude change resulting from viewing two or even three films.

Each of the eleven experiments had four steps: First, the subjects' attitudes toward an issue under study were *measured*, using specially designed questionnaires. Then the subjects were exposed to an *experimental condition*. (Actually, they were given a free ticket to see one of the selected films at the local theater a day or two later.) The day after they saw the film, their attitudes were *measured again*. In some cases, the attitudes of the subjects were assessed a third time (from two to eighteen months later) to see whether any effects of the films had persisted. The subjects in these experiments were some four thousand junior and senior high school students from small communities near Chicago. For any given experiment, the subjects were just those students who were at school on the day the study began, who went to the movies according to plan, and who were at school the next day, when their attitudes were retested.

The questionnaires used were Thurstone's new attitude scales, which he had only recently developed. The results of the experiments were subjected to careful statistical analyses. But notice that by today's standards there were several obvious weaknesses in the design of the study. To begin with, the researchers took no precautions to see that their sample was not in some way *biased*. Also, they made no attempt to study those students who did *not* complete all stages of the study. Notice, too, that the researchers did not follow one procedure that is now commonplace in such research; they did not use a *control group* in any of the experiments—only experimental groups. Since there were no control groups, it is possible that factors other than the films seen might have altered the subjects' attitudes.

Despite these weaknesses in the study by today's standards, its findings were very influential. Thurstone and Peterson concluded that films could change children's attitudes, sometimes dramatically. In one experiment, for example, the subjects saw a movie called "Son of the Gods," which told the story of Sam Lee, a fine young Chinese-American who was not accepted by his non-Chinese neighbors, and which portrayed Chinese people and their culture in a positive way. After watching the film, the teenagers in the study showed more positive attitudes toward the Chinese. From a statistical point of view, the shift toward more positive attitudes was significant.[5]

Other youngsters in another town watched "The Birth of a Nation" (1915), a classic silent film to which a soundtrack had been added. The movie is clearly anti-black and sympathetic toward the Ku Klux Klan. In this case, questionnaires showed that the subjects' attitudes toward "the Negro" became considerably *more negative* after seeing the film. In tests of the same subjects five months later, the shift toward negative attitudes persisted. Conducting such a study today would be unthinkable! Using a film to provoke negative attitudes toward people would flagrantly violate the ethics of modern research. At the time, however, no one thought it was wrong.

In other experiments, Peterson and Thurstone concluded that attitudes toward war, gambling, and punishment of criminals could be altered with a single film. Furthermore, they found that two or three films dealing with the same general topic could shift attitudes even if any one of the films alone could not. In short, the influence of movies appeared to be consistent with the magic bullet theory.[6]

Implications: Confirmation of fears From the overall findings of the Payne Fund Studies, which were published in the early 1930s, the magic bullet theory seemed to have considerable support, and the conclusions reinforced the legacy of fear. The views of the strongest critics of the media, who argued that the media were both powerful and harmful, seemed justified. But not everyone came to such conclusions. Even when the studies were first published, experts criticized their technical shortcomings, but to the public that seemed like quibbling over unimportant technicalities. The Payne studies *reinforced public fears* that the movies were responsible for bad ideas, bad morals, and bad behavior among the nation's youth.

Radio Reports the Invasion from Mars

On October 30, 1938, horrible creatures from Mars invaded the United States and killed millions of people with death rays. At least, that was the firm belief of many of the 6 million people who were listening to the CBS show "Mercury Theater of the Air" that evening. The broadcast was only a radio play, a clever adaptation of H. G. Wells's science fiction novel *War of the Worlds*. But it was so realistically presented in a newscast format that the many listeners who tuned in late missed the information that it was only a play. They thought that Martian monsters were taking over.

Reactions to the "news" of the invasion If there had been any doubt that a mass medium could have a powerful impact on its audience, that doubt was dispelled by the next day. Among those who believed the show was a real news report, large numbers *panicked*. They saw the invasion as a direct threat to their values, property, and lives—as the end of their world. Terrified people prayed, hid, cried, or fled. A high school girl later reported:

> I was writing a history theme. The girl upstairs came and made me go up to her place. Everybody was so excited I felt as [if] I was going crazy and kept on saying, "what can we do, what difference does it make whether we die sooner or later?" We were holding each other. Everything seemed unimportant in the face of death. I was afraid to die, just kept on listening.[7]

Among those who believed that the Martians were destroying everything and that nothing could be done to stop them, many simply abandoned all hope:

> I became terribly frightened and got in the car and started for the priest so I could make peace with God before dying. Then I began to think that perhaps it might have been a story, but discounted that because of the introduction as a special news broadcast. While en route to my destination, a curve loomed up and traveling at between seventy-five and eighty miles per hour, I knew I couldn't make it though as I recall it didn't greatly concern me either. To die one way or another, it made no difference as death was inevitable. After turning over twice the car landed upright and I got out, looked at the car, thought that it didn't matter that it wasn't my car or that it was wrecked as the owner would have no more use for it.[8]

Such accounts showed that the broadcast was accepted as real by many people who thought they were going to die.

In fact, the Mercury Theater and the actors had no intention of deceiving people. The script was written, and the program was presented, in the tradition of telling ghost stories for Halloween. It was clearly identified as a play

The CBS radio broadcast of the play The War of the Worlds in October 1938 caused millions of people in the United States to believe that the country had been invaded by dreadful creatures from Mars. After hearing the play in its authentic sounding news format, some people panicked and ran or drove away in an attempt to escape. Others barricaded their homes or businesses and stood ready to defend themselves. Here William Dock, of Grover's Mill, New Jersey, stands on guard at his feed store with his shotgun, ready to confront the Martians. (UPI/Bettmann Newsphotos)

before, during, and after the broadcast and in newspaper schedules.[9] But the newscast style, the powerful directing, and the talented performances of the actors conspired to make the presentation seem very real. The result was one of the most remarkable media events of all time. Needless to say, the public, the FCC, and the broadcast industry were deeply disturbed by the broadcast and its aftermath. Although no one was killed in the panic, tens of thousands all over the country felt like fools when they discovered what had happened.

Immediately after the broadcast, social psychologist Hadley Cantril hastily began a research study to uncover the causes of panic in a general sense, as well as explore reactions to the radio broadcast. More specifically, he sought to discover the psychological conditions and the circumstances that led people to believe that the invasion was real. Although the scope of the investigation was limited and its flaws numerous, the Cantril study became one of the milestones of mass media research.[10]

Actually, only 135 people were interviewed in depth. Most were people who had been frightened by the broadcast, and all came from the New Jersey area, where the Martians were said to have landed. Most of the subjects were located as a result of the interviewers' personal initiative. No pretense was made that those interviewed were a representative sample. In addition, just prior to the start of the interviews, two extensive tabulations of listeners' comments, commissioned by CBS, were made available to the researchers. All the mail received by the Mercury Theater, CBS station managers, and the FCC was analyzed, and 12,500 newspaper clippings related to the broadcast were systematically reviewed. The results provided a sensitive study of the feelings and reactions of people who were badly frightened by what they thought was the arrival of Martians.

The researchers concluded that "critical ability" was the most significant variable related to the response people made to the broadcast. Critical ability was defined generally as *the capacity to make intelligent decisions*. Those who were low in critical ability tended to accept the invasion as real and failed to make reliable checks on the broadcast; for example, they did not call authorities or listen to other stations.

Especially low in critical ability were those with strong religious beliefs, who thought the invasion was an act of God and that it was the end of the world. Some thought a mad scientist was responsible. Others were disposed to believe in the broadcast because war scares in Europe (World War II did not begin until 1939) made catastrophe seem more plausible.

Those high in critical ability tended *not* to believe the broadcast was real. They were more likely to be able to sort out the situation even if they tuned in late. These people tended to be more educated than those low in critical ability. In fact, statistical data obtained from CBS revealed that amount of *education* was the single best factor in predicting whether people would check the broadcast against other sources of information.

Implications: Powerful effects, but only on some The conclusions derived from the Cantril study posed something of a dilemma. In some ways the magic bullet theory was supported, but in other ways it was not. For example, it was clear that the radio broadcast brought about some very powerful effects. Yet, *they were not the same for everyone*. This was not consistent with the theory. To be consistent, the broadcast should have had about the same effect on everyone who heard it. But the Cantril study isolated individual characteristics of listeners that strongly influenced their response: critical ability and amount of education. Thus, for the public, the *War of the Worlds* broadcast seemed to reinforce the legacy of fear with respect to the media, but many researchers began to suspect that the magic bullet theory had flaws.

Beyond the Magic Bullet: Selective and Limited Effects

Around the end of the 1920s, both psychology and sociology developed completely new theories of human nature and the social order, which eventually influenced research on mass communication. *Individual differences* became a focus of psychological research and measurement, revealing that variations in people's needs, attitudes, values, intelligence, and other personal factors played key roles in shaping their behavior. Meanwhile, sociologists gave increased attention to the importance of *social categories*. They were concerned with the nature of social structure—that is, the overall organization of society into economic levels, racial and ethnic groups, and social institutions, such as the family, religion, government, etc. They were investigating the characteristics of similar people located at various positions within society as a whole. Researchers quickly discovered that specialized cultures within these categories of people (based on such factors as race, ethnicity, age, and social class) had strong influences on their behavior. This was to become very important for audience theory.

These new understandings of the roles of both individual differences and social categories inevitably were brought to the task of studying the effects of mass communication.[11] New ideas about the media then began to challenge the magic bullet theory. In fact, Cantril's study already shows this change; it looked at individual differences in critical ability and at social categories based on religion and amount of education to account for differences in the effects of a mass medium.

We next review two studies that were milestones in *replacing* the magic bullet theory: one examining soldiers in training during World War II, and the second analyzing the presidential election of 1940. Both studies helped build new ways of understanding how and to what extent the media influence ideas, opinions, and behavior.

The *Why We Fight* Film Experiments during World War II

By the time of World War II, social scientists had developed fairly sophisticated techniques of experimentation, measurement, and statistical analysis. The military therefore felt that these scientists could contribute to the war effort. In particular, the Army formed a special team of social psychologists to study the effectiveness of a special set of films that had been designed to teach recruits about the background of the war and to influence their opinions and motivation.[12]

When the United States entered the war in 1941, many young men were ill-informed about all the reasons for this participation. It was a society that was without television, our main source for news today, and people were generally less educated and less informed. Everyone knew about Japan's attack on Pearl Harbor, but not everyone knew about the rise of fascism, Hitler's and Mussolini's strategies, or the consequences of militarism in Japan. Moreover, the United States was (and still is) a nation with diverse regions, subcultures, and ethnic groups. The newly drafted soldiers included farmers from Nebraska, ethnic men from big cities, small-town youths, and young men from the ranches of the West. All were plunged into basic training, and many understood only dimly what it was all about.

Goals and conduct of the experiments The chief of staff, General George C. Marshall, had decided that the troops needed to be told *why* they had to fight, *what* their enemies had done, *who* their allies were, and why it would be a *tough job* that had to be seen through to unconditional surrender by the Axis powers. Since no one knew about the atom bomb, which eventually ended the war in Japan, everyone thought that the terrible conflict would drag on for several additional years after Hitler was defeated. General Marshall believed that special orientation films could give the diverse and poorly informed recruits the necessary explanations of the causes of the war and provide understanding of why it would not end soon. He hoped that it would also result in more positive attitudes and higher morale.

A top Hollywood director, Frank Capra, was hired to produce seven films—a series called *Why We Fight*. The Army gave the job of studying their effectiveness to social psychologists in the Research Branch of the Information and Education Division. The basic plan was to see if exposure to such a film would result in measurable influences on the understandings and orientations of the soldiers. These included a firm belief in the right of the American cause, a realization that the job would be tough, and confidence in the Allies ability to win. They also hoped that the facts presented in the films would create resentment of Germany and Japan for making the fight necessary. Finally, it was anticipated that seeing the films would foster a belief that through military victory the political achievement of a better world order would be possible.

We can summarize the procedures used rather simply: Four of Capra's *Why We Fight* films were used in a series of well-conducted experiments. Great control over the experimental conditions was possible, because the subjects were under orders to participate in the experiments and were under the watchful eyes of tough sergeants to see that all took it seriously and none "goofed off." (Few experimenters today could match this!) Under such conditions, several hundred men who were undergoing training were given a "before" questionnaire that measured understandings of *fact*, various kinds of *opinions*, and overall *attitudes*. These questionnaires were carefully pretested on at least two hundred soldiers in order to minimize ambiguities in their language. Then the men were divided (by company units of about a hundred men each) into experimental groups and a control group. Each company designated as an experimental group saw one of the four films from the *Why We Fight* series. The control group saw a different film that did not deal with the war. After they had seen a film, all subjects answered an "after" questionnaire. It measured the same variables as the first questionnaire, but the questions were rephrased so that repeated exposure to the test could not account for changes in responses. Thus, by comparing the amount of change in each experimental group with that of the control group, the effect of the films could be assessed.

Actually, no dramatic results were obtained! The films did produce minor changes in their audiences, but they were *very limited*. For example, seeing "The Battle of Britain" (one of the films in the series) increased the recruits' factual knowledge about the air war over Britain in 1940. As a result of knowing those facts, it also changed specific opinions about some of the issues treated in the film. But it produced no broad changes, such as increased resentment of the enemy or greater willingness to serve until the Axis powers surrendered unconditionally. The results were much the same for the other films studied.

Implications: Media have limited effects Generally, the researchers concluded that the *Why We Fight* films were modestly successful in teaching soldiers facts about events leading up to the war. They were also modestly effective in altering rather specific opinions related to the facts covered. But they clearly had no great power to fire soldiers with enthusiasm for the war, create lasting hatred of the enemy, or establish confidence in the Allies. Moreover, the effects were different for soldiers with low, medium, and high levels of education. Generally, soldiers with more education learned more from the films.

These results certainly did not confirm earlier beliefs in all-powerful media. And the finding that variations in education modified the effects flatly contradicted the old notion that communications were magic bullets penetrating every eye and ear in the same way, creating similar effects in every receiver. For all intents and purposes, the older theory of uniform influences and powerful effects *died* at this point. The Army film studies were models of careful research, and they left no room for doubt about either the precision of their methods or the validity of their conclusions.

After World War II, research on mass communication blossomed. Social scientists were armed not only with new theories of the nature of human beings but also with increasingly precise research techniques. Some researchers tried to sort out the factors in communication through simulation experiments. Professor Carl Hovland, for example, launched a large-scale research project involving anthropologists, sociologists, and political scientists.[13] He and some thirty associates explored several broad issues, including the nature of the communicator, the content of the communication, and the response of subjects exposed to messages. But real-life media campaigns and mass communication were not part of this research. It used mostly student subjects. The research produced advances in theory, but the applicability of the program's findings to the real world was not clear.

Effects of the Media in a Presidential Campaign

One major study, conducted in 1940 but published several years later, did focus directly on the real-life media. Professors Paul Lazarsfeld, Bernard Berelson, and Hazel Gaudet probed the web of influences within which voters made up their minds during the Franklin Roosevelt versus Wendell Willkie presidential election campaign. In particular, in a now-classic work called *The People's Choice*, they studied the role of mass communications as influences on voters.[14]

This study is a landmark for two reasons. First, its scale was large and its methodology sophisticated. In fact, even today, few studies have rivaled it in these respects. Second, the findings revealed completely new perspectives on both the process and the effects of mass communication.

Great improvements in research methods Lazarsfeld and his colleagues interviewed some three thousand people from both urban and rural areas of Erie County, Ohio. Interviewing began in May and ended in November 1940, when Roosevelt defeated Willkie. All of the subjects were interviewed in May, and they agreed to give further interviews as the election campaign progressed.

The research strategy used was new at the time and very clever: A random sample of 600 individuals was selected from the 3,000 interviewed and

The presidential election of 1940 was a contest between Wendell Willkie, an able business administrator who had never held public office, and the popular Franklin D. Roosevelt, who was seeking an unprecedented third term. This campaign was the first in which candidates made extensive use of radio and air transportation.
The study by Lazarsfeld, Berelson, and Gaudet of how the media influenced voters in Erie County, Ohio, revealed the important role of social relationships in the mass communication process. (Historical Pictures Service, Chicago)

designated as the *main panel*. The remaining 2,400 were randomly divided into four additional panels (samples) of 600 each. Those in the main panel were interviewed each month from May to November for a total of seven interviews. The other four groups served as *control panels,* and each was to be interviewed only one time. One control panel was interviewed in July, another in August, and another in October. At each point, the results of these interviews were compared with those of the main panel. This procedure allowed researchers to see how *repeated* interviews were affecting the main panel as compared to a fresh panel. After three such comparisons, they found that the repeated interviews were having no measurable cumulative effect, and they decided that a fourth was not necessary. Thus, the researchers could feel confident that their findings were meaningful and not an artificial result of their multiple interviews of the main panel.

Some respondents decided early for whom to vote; some decided late. Some shifted from one candidate to another; some who had firmly decided fell back into indecision. Always the interviewers tried to find out why the voters made these changes. They also focused on the social characteristics of the subjects. Rural and urban dwellers were compared; people at various income levels were contrasted. People of different religious backgrounds, political party affiliations, and habits of using the media were studied. Using complex methods, the researchers found that these category memberships could be used with fair success to *predict* voting intentions and actual voting behavior.

How the media influenced voters   Then, and even more now, much of a political campaign is waged in the media through both news reports and paid advertising. But Lazarsfeld and his colleagues did not find all-powerful media controlling voters' minds. Instead, the media were just one part of a web of influences on voters. People's personal characteristics, social category memberships, families, friends, and associates also helped them make up their minds. Furthermore, the media did not influence all voters in the same way. When the media did have an effect, three kinds of influences were found. The researchers called them activation, reinforcement, and conversion.

Activation is the process of getting people to do what they are predisposed to do by their social category memberships—pushing people along in ways they are headed anyway. For example, for almost fifty years in Erie County, most well-to-do Protestant farmers usually voted Republican; most Catholic, blue-collar, urban workers usually voted Democratic. Indeed, all across the country, many voters tend to have certain socially based predispositions for and against the political parties. Yet, even though as the campaign progressed, many voters in Erie County said they were undecided, the media helped *activate* voters to follow their predispositions. Although activation as a media influence changed no one's mind, it did affect the election's outcome through the following four steps:

1. The political propaganda in newspapers, magazines, and radio broadcasts increased *interest* in the campaign among potential voters.

2. This increased interest led to greater *exposure* to campaign material.
3. But the exposure was *selective*. Personal characteristics (such as age, gender, education) plus social category memberships (such as rich Protestant farmers versus Catholic urban workers) led people to read or listen to the output of just one party.
4. As a result of increasing interest and selective exposure, the voters' intentions eventually *crystallized* in directions that were generally predictable from the voters' personal and social characteristics.

Reinforcement is a different process. Fully half of the people studied already knew in May for whom they would vote in November. They made up their minds early and never wavered. Does this mean that the media had no effect on such voters? Not at all. The media were also important in strengthening the voters' intentions. Political parties can ill afford to concentrate only on attracting new followers; the intentions of the party faithful must be constantly reinforced through communications that show that they have made the right choice. The media are used to provide this reassurance. Clearly, reinforcement is not a dramatic effect. It merely keeps people doing what they are already doing.

Finally, *conversion* was rare. The presidential campaign in the mass media did move a few voters from one party to the other in Erie County, but the number was small indeed. Most people either made up their minds in May, went with the party they were predisposed toward, or paid attention only to the campaign of their own party. Conversion took place among a very small number who had only weak party affiliation to begin with.

Perhaps the major conclusion emerging from this study is that the media had not only selective but *limited* influence on voters. When people talk of the media's power, the ability to convert is what they usually have in mind. But the researchers found that of their subjects, approximately 16 percent showed *no* effect of the media; 9 percent showed *mixed* effects; 14 percent were *activated*; 53 percent were *reinforced* (the largest influence), and a mere 8 percent were *converted*.

Serendipity: The two-step flow of communication One totally unexpected but extremely important finding emerged from *The People's Choice*. It was the two-step flow of communication, which we discussed at some length in connection with the word-of-mouth diffusion of the news in Chapter 12 (see pp. 386–387). Its discovery occurred almost by accident, in a way that scientists call "serendipitous." About halfway through the Erie County study, the researchers began to realize that a major source of information and influence for voters was *other people*. Individuals turned to family, friends, and acquaintances to obtain information about the candidates and the issues. Inevitably, those who provided the information also provided interpretation. Thus the two-step flow of communication between people also included a flow of influence. The researchers called this *personal influence* (in contrast with *media influence*).

Those who served most often as sources of information and influence had two important characteristics: They had given great attention to the media campaign, and their socioeconomic status was similar to that of those whom they influenced. In other words, voters were turning for information and influence to people who were *like themselves* but whom they regarded as *knowledgeable*. Thus, in the two-step flow, content moves from the mass media to opinion leaders, who then pass it on to others whom they inevitably influence. Since *The People's Choice* was published, hundreds of other studies have tried to understand the nature and implications of the two-step flow theory and the personal influence of opinion leaders as part of the effect of mass communication.

Implications of the presidential campaign study Without question, *The People's Choice* opened a new era in thinking about the mass media. Its large scope, sophisticated methods, and impressive findings set it apart as a major milestone in media research. It dismissed flatly the old theory that the media have great power. Instead it supported a new interpretation: that the media have selective and minimal consequences and are only one set of influences on people's behavior, among many. Several earlier studies had pointed in this direction, but this particular study confirmed the need for a completely new theory of the effects of the media.

The Bases of Limited Influences Theories

Meanwhile, as the century progressed, the social and behavioral sciences made great advances in understanding the nature of human beings, both individually and collectively. These discoveries would prove to be important in understanding the process and effects of mass communication.

Psychologists discovered the importance of *learning* in human beings, and developed numerous theories and explanations of how this process played a part in shaping the organization and functioning of the human psyche. It was clear that people varied greatly in their learned beliefs, attitudes, interests, values, and other psychological attributes. The key idea was *individual differences* leading to great interpersonal diversity. No two human beings were organized psychologically in exactly the same way. Each person, as a result of learning in his or her environment, had a different psychological organization through which the individual perceived and interpreted the world.

Sociologists and anthropologists, who had studied the emerging urban-industrial society intensively, also found a picture of great diversity. In this case, it was based on the numerous *social categories* into which people could be classified. Societies had complex social class structures, based on such factors as income, education and occupational prestige. People were grouped into other categories by their race, ethnicity, political preference, and religion. Within such categories, subcultures developed, bringing people within a given category to share many beliefs, attitudes and forms of behavior.

Even more important, social scientists found that people did not live socially isolated lives in a "lonely crowd." They still maintained strong *social relationships*, based on ties to family, friends, and acquaintances. These had truly significant influences on their interpretations and actions toward the world in which they lived.

These sources of diversity—individual psychological differences, social category subcultures, and patterns of social relationships—had powerful influences on the mass communications behavior of individuals. The *People's Choice* research on the presidential election had revealed the foundations for a new general theory of the effects of mass communication based on such considerations. Although the authors of that study did not develop such a general theory, it was formulated within a few years. Known as the *selective and limited influences theory*, it became the basic interpretation of the effects of the mass media as these were revealed by literally hundreds of experiments and surveys completed by social scientists and communications researchers.

As larger and larger numbers of research studies were published, the selective and limited influences theory appeared to be well-supported by the evidence. By 1960, Joseph Klapper stated the case in the following terms when he noted that there was

> . . . a shift *away* from the tendency to regard mass communication as a necessary and sufficient cause of audience effects, toward a view of the media as influences, working amid other influences in a total situation. The old quest for specific effects stemming from the communication has given way to the observation of existing conditions or changes, followed by an inquiry into the factors *including* mass communication which produced those conditions and changes, and the roles which these factors played relative to each other.[15]

In other words, the new theory stated, the media do not have powerful effects, but only minimal influences that are modified by other factors (such as individual differences, social categories, and social relationships) that significantly limit those influences.

In less than twenty years, then, the view of the mass media's influence understood by social scientists changed drastically. No longer were media messages compared with magic bullets. Instead their influence was said to be both selective and clearly limited by a complex set of mediating factors.

Audience Uses and Gratifications in the Selection of Media Content

Between 1940 and 1950, before television was widely available, a number of scholars were trying to understand what *uses* audiences made of the available media and what *gratifications* they derived from exposure to what they selected. Soon, studies began to provide answers, and an explanation was developed. It was called, appropriately enough, the *uses and gratifications theory*. It was not an explanation of the effects of mass communications. Instead, it focused on a part of the process by which specific messages from specific media selectively reached specific segments of the audience. In that

THE SELECTIVE AND LIMITED INFLUENCES THEORY

Research on the effects of mass communication began during the late 1920s with the Payne Fund Studies of the influence of movies on children. At first, the results seemed to support the conclusion that motion pictures had widespread and powerful effects on their audiences. But newer research seemed to offer a different interpretation. The Erie County study during the 1940 presidential election campaign seemed to show that the influence of the media was quite limited. The political campaign as presented by the media did have limited effects. It activated some people to vote who might have stayed home, and it reinforced the views of others. However, very few people were persuaded to change their vote from one party's candidate to the other. In addition, this study led to the conclusion that two kinds of factors were important as influences on what people selected from the media to read and hear. These were their social category memberships and their social relationships with friends and family.

Other research, done by the U.S. Army during World War II, also led to a conclusion of selective and limited effects. Soldiers who were shown the *Why We Fight* films learned a number of facts from their exposure, but they underwent only minor changes in their opinions. They did not change their more general attitudes about the war or their motivation to fight as a result of seeing the films. What changes did occur were linked to their individual differences in such characteristics as intelligence and level of formal schooling.

Following the war, a number of experiments by Carl Hovland and his associates confirmed that exposure to, interpretation of, and response to a persuasive message were influenced by a host of factors. The degree to which a person was influenced was

sense, it extended the factor of selectivity in the selective and limited influences theory.

The new theory saw the audience as *active* in freely choosing and selectively using message content, rather than as *passive* and "acted upon" by the media—as had been the case with the magic bullet theory. That is, it stated that people themselves decided what content they would attend to from what medium, and that their decisions were influenced by their personal interests, desires, values, and habits of seeking gratification of various needs.

The Foundation Studies

In one of the first studies of uses and gratifications, Herta Herzog interviewed those who listened to radio's daytime serials (soap operas). In 1942, she found that they did so for a variety of reasons.[16] Some identified with the heroes and heroines as a means of understanding their own woes better. Others did so to obtain emotional release. Still others engaged in wishful thinking about the adventures of the soap opera characters. Many felt

related both to the characteristics of the message and to the personality of the receiver.

This accumulation of research made it necessary to abandon the earlier magic bullet theory that forecast powerful, uniform, and immediate effects of mass communication.[1] It was necessary to develop explanations that took into account the fact that different kinds of people selected different kinds of content from the media and interpreted it in different ways. Thus, the new theory emphasized both selective and limited influences. Although it was formulated in retrospect, the selective and limited influences theory can be summarized in the following terms:

1. People in contemporary society are characterized by great psychological diversity, due to learned *individual differences* in their psychological make-up.

2. People are also members of a variety of *social categories*, based on such factors as income level, religion, age, gender, and so on. Such categories are characterized by subcultures of shared beliefs, attitudes, and values.

3. People in contemporary society are not isolated but are bound together in webs of *social relationships* based on family, neighborhood ties, and work relationships.

4. People's individual differences, social category subcultures, and patterns of social relationships lead them to be interested in, select, attend to, and interpret the content of mass communications in *very selective ways.*

5. Thus, because exposure to media messages is highly selective and interpretation of content varies greatly from person to person, any specific mass-communicated message will have only *limited effects* on the public.

1. For detailed summaries of the Payne Fund Studies, Erie County study, Army film project, and Hovland experiments, see Shearon Lowery and Melvin L. DeFleur, *Milestones in Mass Communication Research*, 2nd ed. (White Plains, N.Y.: Longman, 1988).

that the serials were a source of valuable advice about how to handle their own family problems.

Another classic study of uses and gratifications was completed in 1945. Sociologist Bernard Berelson conducted an exploratory survey of people's reactions to a two-week strike by those who delivered New York City's newspapers.[17] He found that when people had been deprived of their newspapers for many days, they missed them "intensely." However, when the researcher probed more deeply into exactly what they missed, only a third said it was "serious" news presented by the paper—most kept up with that via radio. Actually, ". . . different people read different parts of the newspaper for different reasons at different times."[18] Some did miss information about public affairs. Others felt deprived because they regularly used the newspaper as a tool for everyday life (seeing what was on the radio log, selecting movies to attend, getting stock market reports, weather, and information from advertising, and even following the obituary notices). All of these categories of newspaper content filled needs and provided gratifications that went unfulfilled during the strike. Other uses were "respite," following the news so as to gain social prestige by seeming knowledgeable,

THE USES AND GRATIFICATIONS THEORY

It seems clear that mass communications have limited and selective influences on individuals who are exposed to a particular message. However, a different kind of question concerns why audiences deliberately seek out some kinds of media content and completely ignore others. That is, why do people buy a particular kind of magazine or book? Why is it that they turn first to a particular section of the newspaper or scan the radio and TV listings to locate certain programs? Why do they peruse the latest advertisements of movies so as to find particular kinds of films?

These are goal-oriented forms of behavior. They indicate clearly that audiences do not simply wait placidly to receive whatever content happens to come their way. Many audiences seek content from the media that they anticipate will provide them with certain kinds of experiences. In other words, they are receivers who want to *use* the information in some way or to obtain *satisfactions* that they anticipate. What is the basis of this kind of deliberate and active selection of media content?

To provide answers, the *uses and gratifications theory* was developed to try to explain why audiences do not passively wait for media messages to arrive. It seeks to explain why, instead, audiences are active, deliberately seeking out forms of content that provide them with information that they need, like, and use.

This theory focuses on psychological factors: Each member of the audience has a structure of interests, needs, attitudes, and values that play a part in shaping selections from the media. Thus, one person, with a particular set of needs and interests, might seek sat-

and gaining gratifications from personal advice columns, human interest stories, and vicarious participation in the lives of the rich and famous.

Other studies during the same period supported the general picture of uses and gratifications provided by the newspaper study. In an extensive study of comic reading, Katherine Wolfe and Margery Fiske concluded that children used comic books for different purposes, depending on their age.[19] In a study of book reading, Douglas Waples and his associates concluded that readers selected their material on the basis of many predispositions that were derived from their individual personalities.[20]

As television swept through the population during the decade of the 1950s, uses and gratifications theory would continue to play a role in guiding research. In fact, as we will see below, one of the largest studies of children and television ever conducted was based on the theoretical perspective of uses and gratifications.

Assessing a New Medium

By the end of the 1950s, television was reaching almost every corner of the country, and just as people grew alarmed over the movies during the 1920s, they now grew concerned about television. What was this new medium doing to them, and, most of all, what was it doing to their children? A trickle

isfactions through exposure to sports, popular music, and detective dramas. Another, with a different psychological make-up, might prefer wildlife programs, symphonic music, and literary classics.

The central propositions of the uses and gratifications theory emerged from a long list of investigations that have been completed over a number of decades.[1] The uses and gratifications theory has not previously been formally stated as a set of propositions, but, in summary, its basic ideas are as follows:

1. Consumers of mass communications do not *passively* wait for messages to be presented to them by the media.

2. Members of audiences are *active* in that they make their own decisions in selecting and attending to specific forms of content from the available media.

3. Those choices are made on the basis of individual differences in *interests, needs, values,* and *motives* that have been shaped by the individual's socialization within a web of relationships and category memberships.

4. Those psychological factors *predispose* the person to select specific forms of media content to obtain diversion, entertainment, and respite or to solve problems of daily life in particular ways.

5. Thus, members of the audience will actively select and *use* specific forms of media content to fulfill their needs and to provide *gratifications* of their interests and motives.

---

1. A detailed discussion of media uses and gratifications can be found in Jay Blumler and Elihu Katz, eds., *The Uses and Gratifications Approach to Communications Research* (Beverly Hills, Calif.: Sage, 1975).

of research in the early 1950s did little to quiet the public's fears. It showed that when a family acquired a TV set, the lives of its children changed in a number of ways. For example, television reduced the time they spent playing, postponed their bedtime, and modified what they did in their free time. Children with television spent less time watching movies, reading, and listening to the radio.[21] But no one knew whether television viewing limited or broadened children's knowledge, raised or lowered their aesthetic tastes, changed their values, created passivity, or stimulated aggression. Research was urgently needed to clarify such issues.

Today, a huge literature has developed on the subject of children and television, but three investigations stand out as landmarks. The first was an early comparison of television viewers and nonviewers. The second was a series of studies on the relationship between portrayals of violence and aggressive conduct by children. The third was not a single investigation, but a synthesis of the findings of hundreds of studies done over a ten-year period and published between 1979 and 1981.

Children's Uses of Television

In 1960, Wilbur Schramm, Jack Lyle, and Edwin Parker published the first large-scale American investigation of children's uses of television.[22] The study was concerned not with what television does *to* children but with what children do *with* television. In that sense, it was in the tradition of the uses and gratifications theory. The researchers looked at the content of TV shows, the personalities of young viewers, and the social setting of TV viewing. In eleven studies, conducted in both the United States and Canada, they interviewed nearly 6,000 children, along with 1,500 parents and a number of teachers and school officials. They used in-depth interviews and standardized questionnaires, with statistical analyses of the results. In the end, they had an impressive mass of quantitative data plus detailed insights on children's viewing patterns and their uses of television.

Patterns of viewing   Very early in the life of the children studied, television emerged as the most-used mass medium (it remains so today). By age three, children were watching about forty-five minutes per weekday, and their viewing increased rapidly with each additional year. By the time children were five years old, they watched television an average of two hours per weekday, and by age eight the average viewing time was three hours. In fact, it startled Americans to learn that from ages three to sixteen, their children spent more time watching television than they spent in school! Only sleep and perhaps play took up as much or more of their time.

Of course, some children watched television much more than the average numbers of hours, and some much less. Compared with light viewers, the heaviest viewers had a characteristic profile: (1) They were in grades six through eight—about eleven to thirteen years old. (2) They were less intelligent. And (3), they were poor.

Children's tastes in television programs varied with their age, sex, and intelligence, but their families were the chief influence on taste. Middle-class children tended to watch realistic, self-betterment programs. Working-class children viewed more programs that provided sheer entertainment or fantasy.

In 1960, little was known about how children used television. Research of the period showed that children increased their viewing sharply with age. By the time they were eight years old, they averaged three hours of viewing per day. From age three through sixteen, children spent more time watching television than in school. Viewing by children has actually increased since that time. (Brown Brothers)

Uses of programs   For several reasons, *fantasy* was one of the most important uses: Used in this way, television gives the passive pleasures of being entertained, of identifying with exciting and attractive people, and of getting away from real-life pressures. It provides pleasurable experience free from the constraining limitations of daily living. Fantasy, in other words, provides both escape and wish-fulfillment.

Children often turned to television for diversion, but in fact they often received *instruction*. This teaching was neither formal nor planned, nor did the youthful viewers intend to learn anything. Such unplanned, unintentional learning is called *incidental learning*. This is a very important concept that continues to be used in evaluating the influence of television on children even today. What is learned is related, of course, to the child's abilities, needs, preferences, and patterns of viewing. The incidental lessons taught by television are not necessarily objective or correct. Television sometimes portrays reality realistically, sometimes falsely. But whatever their validity, such lessons are a significant source of instruction for young viewers.

When the researchers compared children in an American community that received television signals with a similar Canadian community that had no television at that time, they found that children in the community with television had higher vocabulary scores and knew more about current events. This held true even among those with low mental ability. The researchers concluded that television accelerates a child's intellectual development during his or her early years.

Implications: Viewing television poses few dangers   Overall, the findings from this massive study revealed *no truly dramatic problems* arising from television. Although the researchers found that children were preoccupied with viewing, they did not find that they were passive receivers of evil influences from it. Instead the effects of television depended on factors such as the child's family, mental ability, group ties, age, sex, needs, and general personality.

Although the study had some flaws in its methods, its findings remain important. It offered further evidence that television has both limited and selective effects. It showed that the medium's influences vary among children with different individual characteristics and among those of different social categories. In particular, the research evidence supported the central thesis of the uses and gratifications theory. Children actively selected what they viewed and that content fulfilled many needs and provided a variety of gratifications.

The Issue of Television and Violence

The legacy of fear in modern dress was the source of the largest research effort ever aimed at understanding the effects of mass communications in the United States. In American society, as each new medium appeared, vocal critics pronounced it to be the cause of society's mounting ills. The fact that these ills are rooted in the long-term trends of urbanization and industrialization is not readily accepted by most of the public. The media are visible targets to blame. Thus, it is not surprising that many people during the late 1960s saw television as the cause of the nation's rising rates of crime, mounting levels of violence, and changes in values among the young.

The Report to the Surgeon General

As fears of the medium grew, public concern brought pressure on Congress to "do something." In March 1969, Senator John Pastore said he was "exceedingly troubled by the lack of definitive information which would help resolve the question of whether there is a causal connection between televised . . . violence and antisocial behavior by individuals, especially children."[23] With Pastore's urging, Congress appropriated $1 million to conduct research into the effects of television.

The National Institute of Mental Health (NIMH) became the agency responsible for managing the program. NIMH appointed a committee of distinguished communications researchers to design the project and a staff to do the routine administration and to prepare a final report. All the distinguished researchers on the committee, however, first had to be "approved" by the television networks. That is somewhat like asking the fox to designate who will watch the chickens! Some researchers who had published negative opinions about networks were actually blacklisted from participation. Needless to say, many highly qualified investigators thought that such exclusions were unethical and simply refused to play any part in the project.

In any case, the Surgeon General of the United States charged the committee with two goals: (1) to review what was already known about television's effects, and (2) to provide funds to researchers to launch new studies on the subject. Eventually, in 1971, the results of some sixty studies plus reviews of hundreds of prior investigations were published in five volumes and a summary volume.[24] Many issues were addressed, including the impact of advertising, activities displaced by television, and the information learned from television. The focus, however, was on *televised violence* and its *influence on children*. We can review briefly some of the main findings on this topic.

Network television's violent content Just how violent were network television shows at the time of the study? Volume 1 of the research report presented some striking answers. For example, one researcher studied a full week of prime-time television in the fall of 1969. He found that eight of every ten programs contained violence. Even more striking, the hours during which children viewed most were the most violent of all. Violence was carried out on the screen mostly by men who were free of family responsibilities. About three-fourths of all leading characters were male, American, middle or upper class, unmarried, and in the prime of life. Killings occurred between strangers or slight acquaintances, and few women were violent. (In real life most killings involve family members or people who know each other.) Overall, then, television's portrayals of violence were very *frequent* and very *unrealistic*.

Social learning from models for behavior   Television content clearly presents large amounts of violence. But do such portrayals provide models that children imitate and that make them more aggressive? In an attempt to answer this question, one volume of the report to the Surgeon General reviewed all the research that had been published on what psychologists call *observational learning*. This kind of learning is just what the term implies. As a result of seeing the actions of someone else, the observer adopts the modeled behavior, knowledge, attitudes, or values. We will review the idea in detail in Chapter 17, but some findings from research on modeling behavior are important to the issue of whether portrayals of violence on television provide models that stimulate aggression among children.

The most widely known studies of modeling were those done by psychologist Albert Bandura and his associates in the early 1960s.[25] Bandura had children watch a live (or sometimes a filmed) model strike a large inflated "Bobo" doll. In one experimental condition, children saw the model *rewarded* for this aggressive behavior. In a second condition, children saw the model receive *no consequences* for such aggression. In a third experimental condition, the subjects observed the model being *punished*. The children who had received these "treatments" were then left in a room full of toys, including a doll like the one the model had beaten. The children who had seen the model rewarded or receive no consequences showed a great deal of direct imitation: They too beat up the doll. Those who had observed the model being punished for aggression were much less likely to be violent.

Later, to check to see if the subjects had understood the actions of the models, the children in all three groups were asked to show the experimenter what the model had done. They were able to do so without difficulty. In other words, observational learning had taken place regardless of whether the model had been rewarded or punished. The children knew full well that the model had beaten the doll. However, whether the children imitated that behavior depended on what experimental condition they had been in—on what they had observed to be the consequences of being aggressive.

What do such experiments mean? There is no doubt that children often imitate what they see others doing, and most psychologists believe that modeling is an important factor in personality development. But does this mean that children imitate violence portrayed on television? There are no clear answers. Modeling influences in experiments may be very different from the effects of mass communications in "real life."

Television and adolescent aggression   Other studies in the report to the Surgeon General did look at attitudes and behavior in real-life settings. In the section of the overall report entitled *Television and Adolescent Aggression*, eight projects are reported that attempted (1) to measure adolescent use of television, (2) to measure adolescent aggressiveness, and (3) to relate use of television to violent behavior.[26]

Perhaps the most interesting of these studies is one by Monroe Lefkowitz and his associates. This ten-year *longitudinal project* covered one set of subjects over a period of a full decade—unusual in social science. Some 436 children in Columbia County, New York, were tested while in the third-grade and again ten years later. The children were asked to rate themselves and each other on such characteristics as popularity and aggression. The researchers also interviewed the parents. The ratings and interviews revealed that a child who was unpopular in the third grade tended to be unpopular ten years later. It also showed that such children tended both to watch television more and to become more aggressive as they got older. Thus, frequency of viewing violence portrayed on television was related to level of aggression in the group studied, and the effects of viewing TV violence were greatest for those who viewed most often.

Overall, the studies of adolescent aggression found that specific kinds of youths were more likely both to watch televised violence and to be aggressive. These were males, younger adolescents, those of lesser intelligence, and those in lower socioeconomic levels. Thus, among youths in these social categories, viewing violence on television and aggressiveness went together. At the same time, the relationship between these behaviors was not strong enough to imply that television *caused* the aggressiveness. This is an important point in interpreting any research. To show that two things tend to occur together is not the same as showing that one of those things causes the other.

Implications: Television may cause aggression   The final report of the advisory committee, entitled *Television and Growing Up*, contains a summary of the findings of the above and other studies, recommendations concerning further research and public policy, and a statement about the relationship between televised violence and aggressive behavior. After reviewing the entire body of evidence, the Scientific Advisory Committee concluded that televised portrayals of violence *could be harmful to some children*. As they put it, the issue posed a potential public health problem:

> Thus the two sets of findings (laboratory and survey) converge in three respects: a preliminary and tentative indication of a causal relation between viewing violence on television and aggressive behavior; an indication that any such causal relation operates only on some children (who are predisposed to be aggressive); and an indication that it operates only in some environmental contexts. Such tentative and limited conclusions are not very satisfying [yet] they represent substantially more knowledge than we had two years ago.[27]

The committee's conclusions from the research findings created a storm of controversy. Senate hearings were held in 1972 to explore what it all meant. The public, disregarding all the hedges, limitations, and qualifications of the scientists, focused on the idea that *television causes kids to be aggressive*. The TV industry, seizing mainly on the shortcomings of the research and the tentative nature of the conclusions, declared the findings to be *of little importance*. Many media critics were outraged; a number of the researchers charged that their work had been misrepresented. Perhaps the final word went to J. L. Steinfield, the Surgeon General:

These studies—and scores of similar ones—make it clear to me that the relationship between televised violence and anti-social behavior is sufficiently proved to warrant immediate remedial action. Indeed the time has come to be blunt: we can no longer tolerate the present high level of violence that is put before children in American homes.[28]

In effect, then, the Surgeon General of the United States concluded that *televised violence may be dangerous to your health*! However, that conclusion was still hedged with caveats that only certain kinds of children were influenced under certain kinds of conditions.

Perhaps most interesting of all is the clear contradiction between the implications of the findings from the studies of Schramm and his associates, a decade earlier, and those of the report to the Surgeon General. The first suggested that television posed no dangers to children; the second suggested that, for some, the medium could be dangerous. Here, then, is the classic situation that often confronts a scientific community. Which one is the correct interpretation? As we indicated earlier, the answer must lie in further research leading to theories that more closely portray reality.

The Second Report to the Surgeon General

By 1980, the pace of research on the effects of television had increased sharply. In fact, 90 per cent of *all* research ever done on the effects of TV viewing on behavior (up to that time) was done during the decade following the publication of the first Report to the Surgeon General in 1971. So many research findings were available that it was difficult to grasp their overall meaning. Additionally, the report to the Surgeon General on children and violence had created many controversies and left many questions unanswered. Because of these two factors, Julius Richard, then the Surgeon General, asked the National Institute of Mental Health to undertake a *synthesis* and *evaluation* of the mass of research evidence that was then available. Thus, in 1982, a decade after the first report, a second was published.

The increased pace of research The new report to the Surgeon General, entitled *Television and Behavior: Ten Years of Scientific Progress and Implications for the Eighties*, was not based on new research sponsored by the government.[29] Instead, it was a compilation of the main findings of more than 2,500 studies of the influence of television on behavior, most of which had been published between 1979 and 1981.

Overall, this was an enormously valuable synthesis and evaluation of thousands of research studies on television, showing how the medium influenced a number of forms of behavior. Seven broad areas of influence were reviewed: (1) television and health, (2) violence and aggression, (3) prosocial behavior, (4) cognitive and affective aspects of viewing, (5) the family and interpersonal relations, (6) social beliefs and social behavior, and (7) television's effects on American society.

It is not possible to summarize in a few paragraphs the nature of the thousands of studies or the detailed findings of so massive an amount of material. We can, however, focus on that part of the report devoted to studies of violence and aggression. The report noted that television has been and remains devoted to showing violence. By the time of the report's publication, the portrayal of violence on television had continued unabated since the 1950s, with only a few minor fluctuations. In fact, over the decade covered in the report, there was an *increase* in violence in children's weekend programs, which by the end of the period had become more violent than prime-time television.

Implications: Televised violence does cause aggression   A major difference between the first and second reports to the Surgeon General was that there was no longer any question that a relationship exists between exposure to violent TV programs and increased tendencies toward aggressive behavior among individuals viewing such content. However, as is the case in the association between smoking and cancer, one cannot predict on an individual basis. That is, it is not clear whether violent programs will cause a particular person to become more aggressive. However, the totality of evidence for inferring that viewing violent programs raises *rates* of aggression among those children who are heavy viewers was even clearer than it was in the first report to the Surgeon General.

The question for research now, said the report, is not whether exposure to violence raises the probability that a person will engage in aggressive behavior. That conclusion has been well established. The problem remaining is to discover exactly what portrayals of violence, and what psychological factors, lead people with particular social characteristics to become more aggressive after being exposed.

The Bottom Line: Most Research Evidence Reveals Only Weak Effects

In this chapter, we have reviewed a massive body of research that has accumulated over sixty years of investigation into the influences of mass communications. Some of these large-scale studies and projects involved thousands of subjects and numerous specific investigations. There have been literally tens of thousands of additional studies of a smaller scale that have not been included in this review, but their overall conclusions are consistent with what we have discussed. This overall body of research has yielded several rather general conclusions. These can help in understanding the nature of communications research, why it is conducted, and, in a very broad sense, what its "payoffs" have been.

First, it is clear that societal concern with the influence of the media in encouraging unapproved behavior, especially that of children, has been the *driving force* that stimulated several of the largest research efforts. Other very practical concerns of society provided the resources needed to conduct others—persuading soldiers, understanding the role of mass communication in the political process, and probing the relationship between violence shown on television and aggressive behavior. What this focus on public concerns implies is that research is as much a political process as it is a scientific endeavor.

Second, there was a progressive improvement and increasing level of sophistication in the *research methods* used in studying the influences of the mass media. The early studies made many mistakes that now seem naive and glaring. Yet, they were an important part of the development of knowledge about the process and effects of mass communication.

Third, in spite of the back-seat status of basic research, there was between the late 1920s and the beginning of the 1980s a progressive development, modification, and improvement of *basic theories* explaining how people attend to the media, interpret media content, modify their beliefs or attitudes, and shape their behavior because of such exposure. This process of development and modification did not follow a simple or even logical path, but it did take place. It can be reconstructed as follows:

1. *The magic bullet theory was seen as incorrect.* Before empirical studies began, it was believed that the mass media produced direct, immediate, and powerful influences on all individual members of audiences. The earliest research findings did little to challenge that prevailing belief and, in fact, seemed to confirm it.

2. *Selective and limited influence theories replaced the magic bullet perspective.* As research became more sophisticated, the factors causing people to expose themselves selectively to media were found to be *individual differences* (in psychological makeup), membership in various kinds of *social categories* (age, education, gender, occupation, etc.), and finally, patterns of *social relationships* (with family, friends, work associates, etc.).

3. *The audience was found to be active and not passive in selecting media content for personal uses and gratifications.* Influenced by their individual differences, category memberships, and social relationships, people made their own decisions as to what they wanted to read, hear, and view from the media; they were not simply passive members of audiences who were "acted upon."

Thus, the preponderance of evidence about the effects of mass communication that emerged from decades of research led to the general conclusion that *the mass media are quite limited in their influences on people who select and attend to any particular message.* In short, six decades of research revealed an overall picture of weak effects.

Chapter Review

- Large-scale research on the effects of mass communication began with the Payne Fund Studies. These efforts of the late 1920s and early 1930s concluded that motion pictures were having many influences on children. This early research was discredited by experts, but it confirmed the public's belief that the movies were a powerful and potentially dangerous influence on children.

- The Halloween broadcast by the Mercury Theater about a Martian invasion created a panic in the United States as large numbers of listeners were unable to distinguish the play from news. It convinced many thoughtful citizens that radio was a medium with great power to influence people.

- Studies of films during World War II, when they were used to teach soldiers about the war and to try to shape their opinions and attitudes, showed that movies had far fewer influences than was anticipated. They taught facts and modified some opinions, but they did little to create more powerful sentiments and motivations concerning the war.

- A large research project conducted in Erie County, Ohio, of the role of the media in the 1940 presidential election, showed clearly that mass communications were not the powerful influences that people once believed them to be.

- A large, government-sponsored project (the report to the Surgeon General) focused on televised violence and its influence on children and adolescents. In content analyses, experiments, and surveys, all indicators pointed to the conclusion that under specific kinds of circumstances, repeated exposure to violence on television did raise the probability that some kinds of children would be more aggressive. Yet, the findings were not compelling, and debates over the research report triggered more heat than light.

- In a review of some 2,500 research studies of the effects of television (the second report to the Surgeon General) the link between exposure to violence portrayed on television and aggressive behavior (among some types of children) was seen as somewhat stronger.

- Overall, the research of the past sixty years has brought about the demise of the early theory that the media have powerful and uniform effects. Replacing that view are theories of selective influence on an active audience (based on individual differences, social categories, and social relationships) and a general conclusion that mass communications have limited effects.

Notes and References

1. Gustave Le Bon, *The Crowd: A Study of the Popular Mind* (New York: Viking, 1960; first published in Paris in 1895).

2. Edgar Dale, *Children's Attendance at Motion Pictures* (New York: Arno, 1970; originally published in 1935), p. 73.

3. Herbert Blumer, *The Movies and Conduct* (New York: Macmillan, 1933).

4. Ruth C. Peterson and L. L. Thurstone, *Motion Pictures and the Social Attitudes of Children* (New York: Macmillan, 1933).

5. Speaking more technically, this conclusion emerges from comparisons of the distributions, their central tendencies (averages or means), and the probable error of the difference (between means). This was one of the earliest uses of inferential statistics in the study of the effects of mass communications.

6. For a review of this theory, see Melvin L. DeFleur and Sandra Ball-Rokeach, *Theories of Mass Communication*, 4th ed. (New York: Longman, 1982), pp. 144–146.

7. Hadley Cantril, *The Invasion from Mars: A Study in the Psychology of Panic* (Princeton, N.J.: Princeton University Press, 1940), p. 96.

8. Ibid., p. 103.

9. Howard Koch, *The Panic Broadcast Portrait of an Event* (Boston: Little, Brown, 1970).

10. The full account of the study and its findings can be found in Cantril, op. cit.

11. DeFleur and Ball-Rokeach, op. cit., pp. 144–146.

12. C. J. Hovland, A. A. Lumsdaine, and F. D. Sheffield, *Experiments on Mass Communication*, Vol. III of *Studies of Social Psychology in World War II* (New York: John Wiley and Sons, 1965).

13. C. J. Hovland, I. L. Janis, and H. H. Kelley, *Communication and Persuasion* (New Haven: Yale University Press, 1953).

14. Paul Lazarsfeld, Bernard Berelson, and Hazel Gaudet, *The People's Choice* (New York: Columbia University Press, 1948).

15. Joseph Klapper, *The Effects of Mass Communication* (Glencoe, Ill.: Free Press of Glencoe, 1960), p. 5.

16. Herta Herzog, "What Do We Really Know about Daytime Serial Listeners," in Paul F. Lazarsfeld and Frank N. Stanton, eds., *Radio Research, 1942–1943* (New York: Duell, Sloan and Pearce, 1944), pp. 3–33.

17. Bernard Berelson, "What Missing the Newspaper Means," in Paul F. Lazarsfeld and Frank N. Stanton, eds., *Communications Research, 1948–1949* (New York: Harper & Brothers, 1949), pp. 111–129.

18. Ibid., p. 116.

19. Katherine M. Wolfe and Margery Fiske, "Children Talk about the Comics," in Lazarsfeld and Stanton, *Radio Research*, pp. 3–50.

20. Douglas Waples, Bernard Berelson and Franklin R. Bradshaw, *What Reading Does to People* (Chicago: University of Chicago Press, 1940).

21. Eleanor E. Maccoby, "Television: Its Impact on School Children," *Public Opinion Quarterly*, 1951, pp. 421–444; also Paul I. Lyness, "The Place of Mass Media in the Lives of Boys and Girls," *Journalism Quarterly, 29* (1952), pp. 43–54.

22. Wilbur Schramm, Jack Lyle, and Edwin Parker, *Television in the Lives of Our Children* (Palo Alto, Calif.: Stanford University Press, 1961).

23. Surgeon General's Scientific Advisory Committee on Television and Social Behavior, *Television and Growing Up*, Report to the Surgeon General, U.S. Public Health Service (Washington, D.C.: U.S. Government Printing Office, 1971), p. 14.

24. Each volume has the title *Television and Growing Up: The Impact of Televised Violence* with a different subtitle; the subtitles are *Media Content and Control* (vol. 1), *Television and Social Learning* (vol. 2), *Television and Adolescent Aggression* (vol. 3), *Television in Day-to-Day Life: Patterns of Use* (vol. 4), *Television's Effects: Further Explorations* (vol. 5). The various reports were prepared by George A. Comstock, John P. Murray, and Eli A. Rubenstein. They were published by the U.S. Government Printing Office, Washington, D.C., in 1971. The summary volume appeared in 1972.

25. A. Bandura and S. A. Ross, "Transmission of Aggression through Imitation of Aggressive Models," *Journal of Abnormal and Social Psychology, 63* (1961), pp. 575–582.

26. Surgeon General's Scientific Advisory Committee on Television and Social Behavior, op. cit., p. 11.

27. Surgeon General's Scientific Advisory Committee on Television and Social Behavior, op. cit., p. 11.

28. J. L. Steinfield, "TV Violence Is Harmful," *Reader's Digest*, April 1973, pp. 34–40.

29. *Television and Behavior: Ten Years of Scientific Progress and Implications for the Eighties* (Rockville, Md.: National Institute of Mental Health, 1982).

17

I must confess, Lone Ranger, that lately I have been having some uneasy feelings about you and what you did to me. I see now that you were the creation of a commercialized image that made us both believe that reality was something other than what we experienced.

Richard Quinney, *The Insurgent Sociologist*, 1973

Media Influences on Society and Culture: Powerful Effects

hose who study and evaluate the process and effects of mass communications in modern society have long been troubled by a perplexing and recurrent dilemma. When they try to reach conclusions about the influence of mass communications in American society, two *totally contradictory conclusions* can be reached. Both are clearly based on trustworthy sources of information. And—compounding the problem—both of those conclusions seem to be correct!

The dilemma is this: Looking at the research findings that have been produced over a number of decades leads to a clear conclusion that the media have only very *limited influences* on most people's beliefs, attitudes, and behavior. However, anyone who has even an elementary acquaintance with recent American history must reach the quite different conclusion that, frequently, the media have had very *powerful influences* on a number of social and cultural situations, trends, and processes.

This perplexing dilemma has to be resolved. Did the research reveal a false picture of minimal effects? If so, it would contradict the claim that science reveals trustworthy knowledge. Or, is the reading of recent history faulty when it seems to show that mass communications often have powerful effects on people?

To resolve this dilemma, we show in this chapter that *both conclusions are correct!* The media do have weak effects; but they also have powerful effects. That may sound like impossible double-talk. However, the key to understanding this seemingly irreconcilable puzzle lies in recognizing the difference between *short-term* influences on individuals and *long-term* effects on society and culture.

In this chapter, a number of theories are set forth briefly, along with historical examples of long-term influences of the media that they can explain. Included are accumulation theory—a broad formulation. Also included are adoption theory, modeling theory, social expectations theory, meaning construction theory, and stereotype theory. These kinds of explanations of long-term media influences are needed to provide guidelines for continuing research on the process and effects of mass communications.

One problem with such long-range theories is that they go *beyond* what can currently be confirmed by empirical research. That is, they deal with influences and effects of mass communications that cannot be readily uncovered by short-term experiments or one-time surveys. Yet, these theories are more than just opinions and guesses. Powerful media effects can be revealed by careful observation of historical events and trends. To bring these influences under the scrutiny of researchers, not only new theories but also new methods and strategies of investigation will be needed in the decades ahead.

Theories of Long-Term Influences

It is not difficult to show that mass communications can play a vital role in stimulating social and cultural change. In this section, we look at two ways in which the media can be instrumental in bringing about change within a society. The first is by a process of continuous presentation of media-provided interpretations of some particular event or situation in a society, such as generating a political issue, stopping a war, or ameliorating a widespread problem of public health, over an extended period of time. To explain the part played by the media in bringing about such changes, we will look closely at a *theory of the accumulation of minimal effects*.[1] This theory proposes that the impact of any one message on any specific person may be minimal (as the research very clearly reveals). However, it also states that even minor changes among audiences do gradually *add up* over time. They do so as increasing numbers of individuals slowly modify their beliefs, interpretations, and orientations toward an issue that is repeatedly presented by several media that consistently emphasize a particular point of view. When this happens, significant changes take place on a long-term basis.

The second form of change is that which occurs within a society as people gradually adopt (individual by individual) some new form of technology, a new way of solving an old problem, or a particular new way of believing or behaving. That kind of change can be explained in terms of a theory focusing on the *adoption of innovation* over time. According to adoption theory, the media influence social change by bringing innovations to the attention of potential adopters, who, in turn, take up and begin to use new cultural items on the basis of information that is supplied by mass communications.

Accumulation Theory: The Adding Up of Minimal Effects

One way to understand long-term media influences is to identify the factors that must be present before minimal effects can add up. This can show how the media can have a great deal of influence in shaping people's ideas and interpretations of a situation, even though any particular message a medium presents to any one individual probably will have very limited effects in a short-term sense.

There are three factors that must be present in a situation before accumulation theory can explain how significant changes occur over a long period. First, the media must focus *repeatedly* on a particular issue; second, they must be relatively *consistent* in presenting a more-or-less uniform interpretation; and third, the major media (newspapers, radio, television, and magazines) must *corroborate* each other with parallel reports.

But what evidence is there that powerful media effects are brought about under such conditions? Clearly, no such evidence can be derived from either experiments or surveys completed at a particular point in time. However, historical analysis can supply examples that show the theory in action. We can identify very obvious and impressive examples of accumulative effects by looking at changing patterns of public response to certain events that have occurred in recent decades where media played a decisive role.

We begin with the sending of the Marines to Somalia. This episode in recent U.S. history shows very clearly the dramatic consequences to society that can result from *consistent, persistent,* and *corroborative* media attention to a human tragedy. However, to show that it was not something totally unique, we also briefly examine several other examples: Watergate, changing American interpretations of the war in Vietnam, and the transformation of public attitudes and behavior toward smoking. Mass communications played a key role in all of these changes.

Sending the Marines to Somalia Sending the Armed Forces of the United States to invade a foreign country is a drastic step in international

If the conditions necessary for accumulation theory are present, the mass media can have powerful effects on a population. For example, for many weeks before U.S. Marines were sent to Somalia, television and other media repeatedly presented deeply disturbing pictures of starving children and adults. Each of the media conveyed much the same message, and none presented an alternative point of view. When a message is presented repeatedly in this way, with corroboration among the media, it can have a powerful cumulative influence on the beliefs, attitudes, and actions of audiences. (AP/Wide World Photos)

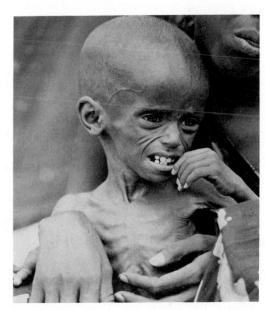

affairs. In the past, when the Marines have been dispatched to another country (such as Nicaragua, Haiti, and China in this century), other nations strongly condemned the action. However, not only did the U.S. Marines "invade" Somalia, but they also received the approval and gratitude of the majority of that country's citizens, and indeed of the rest of the world.

How could this happen? Accumulation theory provides one answer. In 1991 and 1992, night after night on American television, viewers saw pictures of pathetic starving people who looked like walking skeletons. These pictures showed little children in such a wretched state of starvation that it was painful just to watch. The cause of their plight was shown to be the local "war lords" who were preventing humanitarian efforts to bring them food. No one claimed in any of the media that these people deserved their plight, that the war lords were justified, or that the United States should ignore the situation. In other words, the portrayals in all of the media were *consistent*, *persistent*, and *corroborative*. As a result, public sentiment built up to a point that President Bush was able, with a high level of approval, to take the extraordinary step of invading another country—a powerful effect indeed. Much of the world had seen the same pictures. They raised few objections. Indeed, most people in other countries applauded; a number even participated. Without the accumulation of minimal effects, providing a strong base of public opinion, however, it is doubtful that the invasion would have occurred.

Bringing down a president Another clear example is Watergate. The press, that is, the news media in general, were in many ways responsible for the accumulating changes in public opinion and the resulting political pressures that eventually forced a president of the United States out of office. It was the only time that had ever happened in this country's history. Of course, the press did not do it alone. That is, the media did not create the actual events that finally led to the resignation of Richard Nixon from the presidency. The part played by the press was *relentless investigation* and *repeated disclosure* of the unfolding details of the Watergate issue. That disclosure consistently revealed the actions of the people involved, their efforts to cover up what they had done, and the negative interpretations of those who were not sympathetic to Nixon. Eventually, that negative orientation spread to the majority of citizens.

Facts and interpretations about Watergate were reported in the newspapers, on television, in magazines, and even in books, day after day and month after month, as the story unfolded. It preoccupied the entire nation for two years. At first, the public was not aroused, but Nixon slowly lost popularity and support as the reports in the press raised more and more questions about his credibility and honesty. As his public support faded, Nixon's political adversaries were able to move toward an impeachment process in the Congress, and the President resigned rather than face that outcome. Again, a powerful effect!

It all started in June 1972, when a rather clumsy team of five burglars broke into the Democratic National Committee headquarters in the

Watergate building in Washington, D.C. They apparently were looking for material that would be useful in the forthcoming presidential campaign. They were discovered, and two were arrested and convicted. It then became clear that the perpetrators and certain co-conspirators had ties to the CIA and to some of President Nixon's immediate aides in the White House. A persevering investigation by the *Washington Post* eventually revealed a complex plot that included attempts to discredit Nixon's political opponents. There were attempts to cover up the plot and any involvement of the President. At its peak, virtually all the media in the United States gave it extensive coverage. Outrage was expressed by everyone who disliked the President. That included many prominent journalists because Nixon and the press had developed a long-standing antagonistic relationship.

As the story developed, it provided wonderful opportunities for politicians to gain public attention and to posture before the TV cameras. Lengthy congressional investigations were held. The unfolding story made headlines and lead stories on the TV news month after month. Ultimately, Nixon himself was charged with the responsibility for the situation, and impeachment proceedings were initiated. President Nixon resigned and Gerald Ford took over the office. (His first official act was to pardon Nixon.)

It was the slow accumulation of negative interpretations, citizen by citizen, that provided the base for the political actions that were taken. Without that transition, it would not have been possible to force an American president to resign from office. But without the press, it never would have happened. Thus, the news media were necessary but not sufficient conditions in the causal chain.

Redefining a war   Another example of slow but steady accumulation of opinion change in which the media (especially television) were a critical factor was in the gradual disaffection of the American public with the war in Vietnam. Television obviously did not "cause" that change of heart in some unilateral sense. There were many events in the society that played a part. However, night after night, the medium brought bloody war actions and grim "body counts" into American living rooms, along with domestic scenes of protest, draft avoidance, and campus sit-ins against the conflict. All of these portrayals, plus reports and interpretations in newspapers, magazines, radio, and other media, slowly reshaped the shared impressions of Americans concerning the moral nature of the war. As the conflict wore on, the news media portrayed a society in turmoil at home, torn over the meanings and implications of the bloodshed in Vietnam. Support for the war gradually eroded to a point where political leaders had little choice but to terminate it.

Smoking and health   Still a third example of the accumulation of minimal effects is the 25-year campaign against smoking—waged largely in the media. The continuous, consistent, and corroborated portrayal of smoking as harmful to people's health in news and public service campaigns slowly but surely brought about a significant change in the thinking and actions of

THE MEDIA'S ROLE IN DEFINING ENVIRONMENTAL ISSUES:
A Linchpin to Environmental Science

Americans have been assaulting their environment since the first settlers arrived in the New World. Viewing nature as an obstacle to overcome, they cut down forests, drained marshes, diverted rivers, and used agricultural methods that destroyed topsoil while polluting water supplies. By the late nineteenth century, the air of many of the nation's industrial cities was heavily polluted by coal smoke, much of the nation's farmland and forests had been laid to waste, and many species of animals had been wiped out.

These developments received some important attention from philosophers and scientists. Their work, collected in some seminal books of the period, led to strong federal action to protect wild lands and wildlife, particularly during the administrations of presidents Theodore Roosevelt and his cousin, Franklin Delano Roosevelt.[1] But in general there was little sense of public alarm about the environment until the mid-twentieth century. With the publication of a single book in 1962, the environmental movement took root in the public consciousness virtually overnight.

That book was Rachel Carson's *Silent Spring*. In a lyrical prose style, it detailed with scientific rigor the effect of pesticides on animal habitats and life. A marine biologist by training, Carson at first felt ill-equipped to take on such a writing project, but her friend E. B. White encouraged her to go ahead with it. While dying of cancer, she finished the book. First serialized in *The New Yorker* magazine, the book stirred controversy even before its publication. *Silent Spring* became an instant best-seller and aroused the fury of politicians, chemical companies, and scientists alike, all of whom mounted smear campaigns against the book and its author. In time, however, Carson's thesis and her arguments withstood almost every challenge, leading the federal government to ban or restrict use of twelve of the most toxic chemicals the book discussed. But most importantly, perhaps, *Silent Spring* introduced the idea of ecology to the public imagination, taking a seemingly impenetrable topic out of academic circles and giving it a thorough and sophisticated public airing.[2]

Eight years later, in April 1970, thousands of Americans across the country took part in the first Earth Day. TV, radio, magazine cover stories, and newspaper headlines proclaimed the environment a leading public issue. For a time, editors gave the topic great attention and reporters developed expertise in the field. Media coverage of several environmental disasters—such as the 1969 Santa Barbara oil spill, the burning of the Cuyahoga River in Cleveland, the biological "death" of Lake Erie, and the chemical quagmire at Love Canal—all galvanized public opinion. But

large segments of the public. (See Figure 17.1.) Eventually, the public supported a variety of new laws concerning that habit.

Although old movies on television still show everyone smoking, media messages about its dangers became increasingly persistent, consistent, and corroborated across the media. Ultimately, cigarette ads were barred on television, and no messages were deliberately presented to persuade people that credible authorities thought that smoking was healthy and risk-free.

Many additional examples could be cited, showing ways in which effects slowly accumulate when consistent messages about a topic are persistently

the environmental movement of the 1970s had risen to prominence at least partly on the coattails of other issues—civil rights, nuclear weapons disarmament, the Vietnam war—and as they faded, so did environmental coverage.[3]

The environment began to regain salience as a public issue in the 1980s, even as official Washington, under the Reagan administration, virtually ignored it. Nuclear accidents at Three Mile Island, Pennsylvania, in 1978 and then at Chernobyl in the Soviet Ukraine in 1986 illustrated the global effect that a local environmental disaster could have. In 1989, the near ruination of Alaska's Prince William Sound by oil spilled from the Exxon *Valdez* outraged the U.S. public. For weeks TV pictures of the once pristine sound showed oily beaches, wildlife killed on a grand scale, a local fishing economy shattered, and a clean-up effort marred by incompetence and cynicism.

By 1990, the influence of these persistent media images accumulated to the point where concern for the environment had become a leading public issue. In the United States, national opinion polls consistently showed environmental issues to be near the top of the public's concerns. Environmentalism also gained ground in international media. Green Party politics took hold in Western Europe and, with the advent of *glasnost* in the Soviet Union, in Eastern Europe as well. Media coverage of the environment grew in importance for developing nations in South America, Asia, and Africa, where the long-term effects of ill-planned economic development and unbridled population growth became major public policy issues.

Some communications scholars explain this renewed focus on environmental issues as a result of the accumulation of minimal effects theory of media impact. Others argue that, in the United States at least, the many environmental public interest groups are responsible for setting the public agenda and the media are merely second-tier players. Environmental scholars themselves often refer to the attention cycle theory of public interest, noting that worldwide concern for the environment has waxed and waned for nearly 200 years, often with significant effect. In any case, whatever the source of this latest concern, as the United States moves into the 1990s, more media are devoting more resources to environmental coverage than ever before.[4]

1. John McCormick, *Reclaiming Paradise: The Global Environmental Movement* (Bloomington, Ind.: Indiana University Press, 1989), pp. 49–56.

2. Geoffrey Norman, "The Flight of Rachel Carson." *Esquire*, December 1983, pp. 472–478.

3. Allen Schnaiberg, "Politics, Participation and Pollution: The Environmental Movement," in John Walton and Donald E. Carns, eds., *Cities in Change: Studies in the Urban Condition* (Boston: Allyn and Bacon, 1977), p. 466.

4. "Environmental Reporting: Now It's an International Affair," SIPI Scope (New York: Scientists' Institute for Public Information, Spring 1990). Also see Craig L. LaMay and Everette E. Dennis, eds., *Media and the Environment* (Washington, D.C.: Island Press, 1991).

presented and corroborated across media. Such examples include the current emphasis on avoiding fats and cholesterol in one's diet, the increasing preoccupation with exercise, and concerns about the dangers of using drugs and alcohol. At one time, the messages from the media concerning drugs were mixed. Now, the media have placed the negative aspects of these problems high on their agenda and have brought them sharply into focus for the public. Finally, in the same general category, we can note the role of the media in helping to define the dangers of AIDS.

Generally, then, the accumulation theory explains social and cultural changes in society that are influenced by the mass media as a slow adding

THE THEORY OF THE ACCUMULATION OF MINIMAL EFFECTS

After several decades of intensive research, it became widely accepted that mass communications had only selective and limited effects. Hundreds of experiments and other kinds of research studying different kinds of persuasive messages aimed at changing people's beliefs, attitudes, and behavior failed to reveal any really strong influences on those who were exposed to such messages.

At the same time, year after year, changes could be observed taking place in society that many scholars believed were significantly influenced by the media. Thus, there was a dilemma concerning the ability of the media to influence people's ideas and behavior. Scientific research revealed a picture of weak media having only limited influences on people at best. But systematic observation of ongoing events in society suggested a much more powerful role. For example, it appeared to many observers that mass communications played a significant part in bringing about such changes as President Richard Nixon's resignation because of the events of Watergate, the civil rights movement of the 1960s, the redefinition of the Vietnam War that took place in the United States, and many changes related to health behavior.

Clearly, some way of resolving this apparent dilemma was needed. Both the scientific research and the careful observation of historical events seemed to lead to sound conclusions—even if these were completely opposite. Finally, it came to be understood that most of the scientific research was based on short-term studies, making use of brief experiments and one-time surveys. The historical observations of changes in society extended over long periods of time. The resolution of the dilemma came when it was realized that both conclusions could be correct. In a short-term sense, the media may have very selective

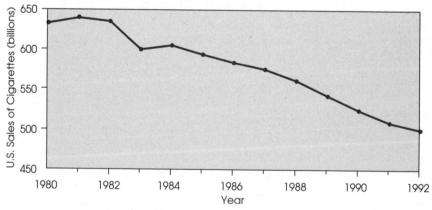

**FIGURE 17.1
Sales of Cigarettes in
the United States,
1980–1992**

As accumulation theory suggests, the behavior of a population can undergo long-term change. For example, Americans' annual consumption of cigarettes fell from almost 650 billion in 1981 to 500 billion in 1992. The media can play a role in such changes by transmitting messages about a topic that are consistent, persistent, and corroborated. For the first time, the number of deaths from cigarette smoking dropped in 1990. (*Sources:* U.S. Dept. of Agriculture; Tobacco Institute)

up of minimal effects. Such effects are brought about when media repeatedly focus on a particular issue, present it in relatively consistent ways, and corroborate each other. The end result can be truly significant changes, with the media playing a relatively inconspicuous but nevertheless powerful role.

and limited influences. But over a long period, small changes in a few people at a time can eventually add up to a significant end result.

As it turned out, it was those issues on which the media focused repeatedly and in relatively consistent ways that changed people over time. If those conditions prevailed, and if the various media—print and broadcast—corroborated each other by presenting the same interpretations, truly significant changes could take place in people's beliefs, attitudes, and behavior.[1] From these considerations, the theory of the accumulation of minimal effects was developed. Its basic propositions are as follows:

1. The mass media begin to focus their attention on and transmit messages about a specific topic (some problem, situation, or issue).

2. Over an extended period, they continue to do so in a relatively *consistent* and *persistent* way and their presentations *corroborate* each other.

3. Individual members of the public increasingly become aware of these messages, and, on a person-by-person basis, a growing comprehension develops of the interpretations of the topic presented by the media.

4. Increasing comprehension of the messages regarding the topic supplied by the media begins to form (or modify) the meanings, beliefs, and attitudes that serve as guides to behavior for members of the audience.

5. Thus, minor individual-by-individual changes *accumulate*, and new beliefs and attitudes slowly emerge to provide significant changes in norms of appropriate behavior related to the topic.

---

1. This theory first appeared in the fourth edition of *Understanding Mass Communication* (Boston: Houghton Mifflin, 1991), pp. 560–565.

Adoption Theory: The Role of the Media

A second perspective that includes a somewhat different type of accumulation process is *adoption theory*. Its basic propositions were set forth in Chapter 3 (pp. 92-93) in connection with the increasing use of the daily newspaper by Americans over a number of decades. In Chapters 4 through 7, we presented the adoption curves of other media. But the adoption process has far-reaching implications that go beyond the specific question as to how Americans took up and began to use radio, television, or the VCR. In contemporary society, we are constantly confronted with *innovations*—that is, new technologies, new ideas, new fads and fashions, and new standards of behavior. Mass communications play a significant part in their fate. Some may be adopted widely (for example, VCRs and air bags in automobiles). Others, such as eight-track audio tapes, may be introduced but never adopted widely.

Invention   The source of many innovations is invention (although they can be borrowed from other societies). *Invention* is a creative process by which an individual or group brings together elements that already exist in the culture, putting them together into some new pattern—an innovation. We discussed the process at length in earlier chapters in terms of individuals combining existing technological elements to develop new devices related to mass communications (for example, the telegraph, the movie projector, the radio telephone). Even popular music is subject to invention. Ragtime, Dixieland, swing, rock, and rap were innovations. When many individuals decide to adopt an innovation and it comes into increasing use in a society, *diffusion* of the innovation has occurred.

Obviously, people do not immediately adopt every innovation as soon as it is available, even if adopting it is logical and beneficial. There is an accumulation process. That is, the innovation comes into use in a slow additive pattern as, individual by individual, people make up their minds to acquire and use it. Decades ago, for example, seat belts for cars were introduced. Many thousands of lives could have been saved by their immediate and universal acceptance. They were not particularly expensive, and they were not much of an inconvenience. Thus, they were good candidates for immediate adoption by all drivers. Yet, the vast majority of Americans simply ignored them. The federal government tried many media campaigns to increase the use of seat belts. Finally, enough people were persuaded that federal legislation requiring that all new cars have them became acceptable. Today, all recently manufactured cars have the devices, and many states have laws making their use mandatory. The majority of Americans apparently now use seat belts, but some drivers still do not use them regularly. Thus, the seat belt is an innovation that has by no means been adopted completely.

But for each such limited success, dozens of other innovations have been rapidly adopted with enthusiasm: the small electronic calculator, the digital display wristwatch, TV dinners, microwave ovens, hot tubs, cable television, home computers, and so on. Other innovations are social rather than material. Around the globe, societies have replaced age-old customs with modern ways. This process of social and cultural change has fascinated scholars and scientists for decades. Media researchers have been particularly interested in the adoption of innovations and have shown that mass communications often plays a significant role in spreading of new ideas, behaviors, and products.

The adoption curve   But how does this adoption process actually take place, and just what is the part played by mass communications? Fortunately, a great deal of information has been developed about the *adoption process*.[2] Studies of the spread of social change go back at least to the nineteenth century, when Gabriel Tarde said that "imitation" explained the spread of new social forms.[3] Later, sociologists made quantitative studies of the spread of such new cultural items as ham radios, hybrid seed corn, new teaching methods, and public health measures.[4] By the 1950s, research on this process was an established tradition in all the social sciences. The adoption of an innovation can be viewed in terms of the *S-shaped pattern* that we described in connection with the growth in use of the major mass media. That pattern is a result of a process among individual adopters. That is, people first become aware of the innovation. Then, a small number of adventurous early adopters try it out. If it seems to work for them, increasingly larger numbers take up the innovation. Finally, the curve levels out, and only a few late adopters have yet to begin using it.

Mass communications play a key role in bringing about the adoption of many innovations, such as the cellular phone, which is coming into widespread use. Not only are such innovations presented by advertisers in many media, but they are also shown in use in many kinds of entertainment formats. This brings them to the attention of large numbers of potential users, who weigh the costs and benefits of an innovation and then decide whether to adopt it. (Bettmann)

Awareness Where do the media fit into this? The answer is that they *create awareness*. The spread of information via the media and the adoption and diffusion of innovations are closely related. In older societies, innovations were adopted in the absence of mass communication; they came to people's attention by word-of-mouth. Today, information about an innovation can spread without resulting in adoption, but the first stage in adoption is *learning about an innovation*. Obviously, then, wide adoption of an innovation requires first that news of its nature and availability be made known. In modern society, the mass media facilitate the fast and widespread presentation of that information and thus stimulate social change.

In the United States today, the mass media present information on a great many possible innovations to large numbers of people. These items range from household products and cosmetics to new models of automobiles. Advertising is an obvious source of information about new consumer products. In addition, various kinds of media, such as magazines and newspapers, regularly report on advances made in medicine, physical science, biology, education, and various kinds of hobbies. Person-to-person communication supplements this media-initiated diffusion of information. As a result, Americans adopt many innovations over varying periods of time. Thus, adoption theory, explaining the communication and behavioral dynamics of the diffusion of innovations, provides an understanding of the contributions of the mass media to this kind of accumulative and long-term social change.

Implications of Long-Term Theories

Both accumulation theory and adoption theory aid greatly in resolving the dilemma that we posed at the beginning of this chapter. It remains entirely true that from a short-term perspective mass communications have very limited and very selective influences on individuals. There is every reason to be confident in that conclusion. However, repeated exposure to a consistent message can change people. The change may be less than dramatic for any particular person, but it does happen, and such changes add up. Among large populations repeatedly exposed to relatively consistent messages that are corroborated across media, an accumulation of individual influences eventually results in significant change.

Socialization Theories: Incidental Lessons on Social Behavior

We noted in Chapter 16 the preoccupation of researchers with the issue of televised portrayals of violence and their influence on children. This focus came about because parents and others have been concerned about the socializing influence of television—the *lessons* the media present to youthful audiences and the degree to which youngsters *learn* from them the rules of behavior that prevail in the society. The fear is that television legitimizes the use of violence as a means of settling disputes between people. There are some grounds for that fear. As we saw, with repeated exposure over a long period of time, certain kinds of children do appear to become somewhat more aggressive as a result of their attending to violence portrayed on television.

Although this set of relationships—between portrayed violence, selected youthful audiences, and their actual behavior—illustrates the idea of socialization, it is only one form of media content and one kind of behavior that comes within the broad concept. Socialization is a long-term process that every human being undergoes as he or she becomes a functioning member of society. It certainly includes much more than just learning from television. Socialization refers to the internalizing of *all* of the lessons from many sources concerning ways of behaving that are approved and expected by society, as individuals mature through every stage in the life cycle. Thus, as people pass from infancy to old age, they must constantly acquire new habits, new ways of thinking about themselves, and new understandings of the groups in which they must participate. Briefly defined, then, *socialization* is that extended learning process by which the rules of behavior of a society, and all of the demands of its culture, are incorporated into the psychological organization of the individual participating in its social order.

To illustrate the long-term influences of mass communications, we review two different theories about how socialization is influenced by portrayals in media content. The first focuses narrowly on individual members who are exposed to depictions of certain forms of behavior that are seen as attractive and worth copying. This modeling theory explains that many activities observed in media portrayals serve as guides to behavior for persons undergoing socialization and will be adopted as part of their personal repertoire of habitual actions. The second theory about socialization is much broader, and it focuses on the rules and expectations for patterned social behavior that are shown as the media portray or describe people acting within groups. Social expectations theory focuses on media-provided lessons about what constitutes acceptable behavior in various group settings. Both of these perspectives illustrate very well the idea of a long-term accumulation of influences.

Modeling Theory: Adopting Behavior Portrayed by the Media

Because the dramas and other kinds of portrayals commonly found in the movies or on television show many aspects of human life, they provide a rich source of depictions of behavior that can be imitated by members of their audience. To a lesser degree, this may also be the case when behavior is described verbally in radio or in print. But in either case, media portrayals *model* many kinds of actions and situations by displaying them on the screen or in other ways. Adopting such modeled behavior is one form of socialization.

The word "model" can apply either to the person who portrays an action or to the depicted action itself. Thus, under certain circumstances, members of an audience may imitate or reproduce behavior they find modeled in media sources. One of the most impressive findings of the Payne Fund Studies of the movies, undertaken in the late 1920s, was the extent to which children of the time readily imitated forms of behavior that they saw modeled on the screen. The same is true in more modern times of what people are shown doing on television. There is a great deal of imitation.

A theory has been developed by psychologist Albert Bandura to account for the acquisition of virtually any kind of behavior that people see being performed by others. In its more general form, it is called *social learning theory*. This is not specifically focused on mass communication, but attempts to explain how people take on new forms of behavior when they see them performed by others, whether through direct observation or in media portrayals.

The term *modeling theory* has come into use to indicate the application of the more general social learning theory to the case where people acquire behavior forms that they find modeled in the media.[5] An important feature of modeling theory is that it can help explain long-term influences of mass communications. That is, it can help in explaining why minor changes take place among individuals, eventually to accumulate in major changes in society.

To illustrate modeling theory, we can cite an incident that actually happened: A middle-aged woman was invited by friends to accompany them on a shopping trip to a nearby mall. After making a number of purchases, one of the group suggested that they stop at a cocktail lounge for a drink. The others seemed enthusiastic and the woman agreed, even though she had only limited experience with alcoholic beverages. Once seated in the lounge, the question arose as to what each person wanted to drink. As the others were ordering, the woman realized that she did not know the name of a single drink, and she was embarrassed to display her ignorance. However, she suddenly remembered the soap opera that she had watched

MODELING THEORY

The mass media, and especially television and movies, present many depictions of people acting out patterns of behavior in various ways. These can be ways of speaking, relating to members of the opposite sex, dressing, walking, or virtually any form of meaningful action. These depictions can serve as models of behavior that can be imitated, and people who see an action depicted may adopt it as part of their own behavioral repertoire.

One explanation of how and why this can take place is *modeling theory*. It was derived from a more general perspective called social learning theory, originally formulated by psychologist Albert Bandura. Social learning theory provides explanations of the acquisition of behavior as a result of seeing it performed by someone else, whether the media are involved or not. When applied to learning or adopting forms of action portrayed in the media, it has come to be called modeling theory.

The reason that modeling theory is particularly relevant to television and motion pictures is that they actually *show* actions performed by persons (models) who, in the course of various kinds of dramas or other content, can be seen behaving in various kinds of social settings. Thus, the modeled behavior is depicted more realistically than if it were only described in verbal terms, as would be the case with radio or print.

Modeling theory does not imply any *intentions* on the part of the model, or even on the part of the viewer. The adoption of a form of action after seeing it portrayed in the media may be wholly unplanned and unwitting. Certainly, there is no implication that

the previous day, in which a young couple met in a bar to discuss their marital difficulties. She recalled that the woman was quite attractive, and she wished she were like her. In any case, the young woman in the drama ordered a "Brandy Alexander." This was a colorful name, and it stuck in the woman's mind. Therefore, when it was her turn to order, she asked for a Brandy Alexander. As she discovered, it was a rather pleasant drink and she enjoyed it. Thereafter, on similar shopping trips when the group stopped for drinks, she always ordered a Brandy Alexander.

The essential conditions   This anecdote illustrates several essential features of modeling theory. It shows that the behavior was modeled in the media, where the woman encountered it. She saw the actress as attractive and identified with her. She recalled the name of the drink and used it to solve an immediate problem. That was a rewarding experience—both in the sense that it provided a solution and that the drink was pleasant. She adopted the behavior as a more or less permanent solution to the problem when it rose again. Those are the essential stages and conditions of modeling theory, but the concepts of identification and adoption are particularly critical.

those who designed or performed the media depictions intended them as models for others to adopt. Thus, viewers may imitate a behavior pattern whether or not the people who created the portrayal intended it to serve as a guide, and the effects of viewing a model can be completely unrecognized on the part of the receiving party.

The modeling process proceeds in stages. The receiver first encounters the model depicting the behavior. If the person identifies with the model, he or she may reproduce the form of action portrayed by it. But, before permanently adopting it, the observer must perceive some positive benefit. If that is the case, the behavior may be tried out, and if adopting it solves some problem for the person, it may be used again and again in similar circumstances.[1]

Stated more formally, modeling theory can be summarized briefly as the following propositions:

1. An individual *encounters a form of action* portrayed by a person (model) in a media presentation.

2. The individual *identifies with the model*, that is, believes that he or she is like (or wants to be like) the model.

3. The individual *remembers and reproduces* (imitates) the actions of the model in some later situation.

4. Performing the reproduced activity *results in some reward* (positive reinforcement) for the individual.

5. Thus, positive reinforcement increases the probability that the person will *use the reproduced activity* again as a means of responding to a similar situation.

1. For a discussion of social learning theory and the modeling process, see Alfred Bandura, *Aggression: A Social Learning Analysis* (Englewood Cliffs, N.J.: Prentice-Hall, 1973).

Identification with the model   The second stage, *identification*, is central to modeling theory, but the term is not easily defined. In general, it refers to circumstances in which the observer approves of the portrayal and either wants to be like the model or believes that he or she already is like the model. In some cases we can add another possibility: that the viewer finds the model different but attractive and therefore sees the modeled behavior as a suitable guide to his or her own actions.

Imitating and adopting the portrayed behavior   A great deal of controversy has centered around the last two stages of the modeling process. That is, under what circumstances will a viewer imitate a form of activity observed on television or in a movie? And, even if the person imitates the action once, what will lead him or her to adopt it on a more permanent basis? One answer is that on at least some occasions a person is confronted with a situation to which some sort of response *must* be made, but he or she lacks an appropriate, previously learned way of acting to handle the problem. As in the anecdote, a mode of response remembered from a mass media presentation may seem worth trying. When that happens, and if it works as a way of responding to the situation, that alone provides positive reinforcement of

Modeling theory suggests that portrayals of violence on television can foster aggressive behavior among children. Thousands of research studies have addressed this question. The weight of evidence suggests that, at least among some children (who lack counteracting adult supervision and teaching), long-term repeated exposure to such depictions of violence may increase the probability of such behavior. However, the issue remains controversial; for most children, viewing violence on television does not uniformly result in aggressive behavior. (© Frank Siteman 1992/The Picture Cube)

the imitation. If the response generates even more valued rewards, such as approval from others or a strong feeling of self-satisfaction or achievement, then the reinforcement is even stronger.

Social Expectations Theory: Learning Group Requirements

Another way of looking at an accumulation of influences on media audiences is to note how, over time, people learn the rules and requirements for acting out parts within various kinds of groups by seeing them portrayed in media content. This, too, is an important part of the socialization of the individual. But here the focus is not on isolated specific acts that are acquired from mediated models, but on developing an understanding over time of the *pattern* of customs and routines of behavior expected within specific groups by seeing their portrayals in the media.

More specifically, what is it that must be learned by a particular individual for effective participation in a group or for acceptance in any kind of social setting? In every human group there is a complex *set of understandings* that must be acquired before the individual can act effectively in such circumstances. To describe this process, we can begin by noting that groups are made up of people who come together to accomplish a *goal* that they deem important—and that cannot effectively be accomplished by the same number of individuals acting alone. Thus, it is the *coordination* of their actions into an organized teamlike pattern that gives the advantage to the group over solitary action. It is the rules of that teamlike coordinated behavior—often called the group's *social organization*—that set it apart from actions taken by individuals alone. Without such a pattern of social organization, learned and followed by each member of the group, their collective actions would be chaos. Thus, groups—from the smallest family to the largest government agency or corporation—have rules and expectations that define and govern the activities of each of their members so that goals can be accomplished.

What are the major components of such a collective and shared pattern of social organization, and how do human beings acquire their personal knowledge of such requirements? Briefly stated, social organization can be defined as that pattern of general *group norms, specialized roles, ranking positions* (indicating differences in prestige and power), and the set of *social controls* used by the group to ensure reasonable conformity to its requirements. Each of these components of organized social activity is important in stabilizing a group and getting it to work effectively for whatever goals brought its members together in the first place.[6]

Group norms   Every group has a set of general rules that all members of a particular group are expected to follow. These may have to do with the way people dress, use certain specialized language, greet each other, and so on, through literally hundreds of activities that make up the behavior performed in the group. They differ greatly according to the type of group. The norms of Army life are very different from those of a high school, and both are very different from the norms followed by members of a local labor union. Nevertheless, all groups have some set of general norms that all members must learn, understand, and follow to a reasonable degree.

Specialized roles   There are specialized rules that apply only to persons playing particular parts or defined positions in the group. Such role definitions must be understood not only by the person performing a particular role but also by those who must relate their own roles to it. For example, imagine a baseball team in which the batter, pitcher, and each other player understands only what he or she is to do, but not what each of the other players are supposed to do under various circumstances. There would be chaos, and the goal of winning could never be accomplished. Thus, the key ideas regarding roles are *specialization* and *interdependence*. That is, in most groups, the role requirements for each position in the group are not only different (specialized), they are also interlinked with the specialized activities of other members. It is this feature—a coordinated division of labor—that makes groups far more efficient than the same number of uncoordinated individuals.

Ranking   There are few groups, if any, in which every member has precisely the same level of authority, status, and reward. Even in informal groups of friends, some members are leaders and are looked up to, and others are followers and command less prestige. In large and complex groups, many lay-

Portrayals of various kinds of groups and social situations on television or in the movies or other media provide lessons on social organization to audiences. That is, the norms, roles, ranks, and controls that govern many kinds of human social behavior are acted out or depicted in the mass media. Social expectations theory predicts that most people learn from the media how one is expected to behave in various settings, whether they have participated in such situations or not. (Dennis Hallinan/FPG International)

ers of rank exist. People at different levels have varying amounts of power and authority, and they receive different amounts of respect and rewards. Such differences in ranking arise from many sources. Who is at the top? Those who take the greatest responsibility, who possess scarce but critical skills, who have had extensive experience, and who are not easily replaced. Those with opposite characteristics tend to remain at the bottom.

Social controls   Maintaining the stability of a group takes place through the use of *sanctions*. These are the rewards and punishments used by a group to prevent excessive deviation from and reward conformity to its social expectations. They can range from mild sanctions, such as words or gestures of approval and disapproval, to really significant actions of control, ranging from awarding medals to those who perform in a significantly positive way to executing those whose deviations are too great to tolerate. Many groups allow limited deviation from norms, some personal variability in the manner in which people fulfill role requirements, or even disregard for rank, but there are always limits beyond which sanctions will be invoked.

People in societies without media learn these social requirements by a slow process. Older members in the society teach the young, or they acquire the needed knowledge by a process of trial and error, which can sometimes be painful. In a media society, however, an enormous variety of groups and social activities are portrayed in mass communications. These can serve as a rich source of learning for their audiences. Social expectations theory explains that knowledge of norms, roles, ranks, and controls can be acquired through a process of incidental learning by exposure to media portrayals of many aspects of social life and kinds of human groups.

An important caution is that such media portrayals of group life may be misleading, inconsistent, or just plain wrong. Nevertheless, they often provide audiences with *beliefs* about the requirements of many kinds of groups that they may have to deal with at some point in their lives.

Implications of Socialization Theories

Socializing the young is an important kind of long-range influence of mass communications in American society. Media portrayals show people performing particular actions that can serve the needs of those who see the models. Through a process of observational learning, those actions can be made a part of the behavioral repertoire of those who adopt the modeled behavior. In a broader sense, the media portray hundreds of different kinds of groups. Those patterns of social expectations can be observed and learned by members of the audience who may later actually enter such groups. Through such learning experiences, they will have acquired from the media beliefs about what is acceptable or unacceptable social behavior. That knowledge, right or wrong, can provide them with personal definitions of a group's norms, how they should play their roles, how to show deference to authority or accept the decisions of those in positions of power, and what they can expect in the way of rewards or punishments for either exemplary or deviant behavior. In this way, depictions of social activity and group expectations in mass communications can have long-range, subtle, accumulative, but significant influences on the behavior of individuals.

Meaning Construction Theories

Do the media faithfully portray reality as it "really is"? The answer is obvious—as our discussions of meaning distortions in the news (Chapter 12, pp. 406–407) showed clearly, they do not in many cases. In other words, *misrepresentations* occur in many forms of content, such as the daily soap operas, movies, the evening news, advertisements and commercials, and even in children's books about Dick and Jane. But so what? If the media misrepresent reality, what difference does it make? What kind of impact do portrayals of reality of any kind have on people's beliefs and behavior?

In this section, we look at two major ways in which mass communications provide people with both labels and meanings for reality that help shape their personal and shared interpretations of the physical and social world around them. We also discuss what difference it makes in terms of the influence of language on behavior. The first way in which mass communications influence personal conceptions of reality is in *shaping the relationships between labels and meanings* for many words people use to describe and think about things, events, and situations. The second way is by stabilizing the "clusters of meanings" existing in the language for categories of people—that is, *stereotypes*—that have long existed as part of the culture. People learn such stereotypes during the process of socialization, and they are passed on from one generation to the next. As we will indicate, the media are one major channel by which this "passing on" takes place.

SOCIAL EXPECTATIONS THEORY

One of the most important features of the socialization of the individual is the process by which he or she learns how to take part in, or at least to understand, various kinds of groups. These range from the family and peer groups early in life to increasingly complex groups as the person goes on to school, begins work, and generally must understand and deal with a wide number of groups in the community.

Every human group has its own set of rules that must be followed—its customs and expectations for many kinds of social behavior. If the individual does not conform to these social expectations, he or she risks social criticism and even rejection.

But what are the sources from which people acquire knowledge about such social skills and learn the social expectations of others? The answer is that there are many. Obviously, individuals learn from their families, from peers, from schools, and from the general community. But in the modern world, there is another source from which to acquire a great deal of information about the social expectations of people who are members of various kinds of groups. That source is the mass media.

By watching television or going to a movie, or even by reading, people can learn the norms, roles, and other components of social organization that make up the requirements of many kinds of groups. People can learn what is expected of a prisoner in a penitentiary, a father or mother, a nurse in a hospital, or a corporation president conducting a board meeting. Or, they can find out how to behave when at the horse races, in combat, gambling in a casino, or hav-

Constructing Personal and Shared Meanings

An important explanation of certain long-range influences of mass communications on habits of perception, belief, and behavior among their audiences is called the *meaning construction theory of media portrayals*.[7] This interpretation of the influences of mass media sees the meanings people hold for various words as strongly influenced by their exposure to the content of mass communications. Those meanings, in turn, shape their understandings of, and actions in, situations with which they must cope in the real world.

Personal meanings for features of our physical and social environment are shaped in a variety of communication processes in which our understandings for labels—that is, words in our language—are shaped, reshaped, and stabilized so that we can interact with others in predictable ways. These communication processes take place in families, among peers, in the community, and in society at large. But each is different from one society to another. In traditional societies, word-of-mouth is the main source of information. In modern society, the mass media are a very important part of these communication processes. In a media-saturated society, not only do people attend to content directly from mass communications, but as we noted in discussing the two-step flow of communication (Chapter 16, pp.

ing dinner at an elegant restaurant (even if they have never been in such places).

There is, in short, an almost endless parade of groups and social activities—with behavioral rules, specialized roles, levels of power and prestige, and ways of controlling their members—portrayed in the media. There is simply no way that the ordinary individual can actually participate in most of these groups, so as to learn by trial and error the appropriate forms of conduct. The media, then, provide broad if unwitting training in social expectations.

This analysis of the influence of the mass-communicated lessons on social activities that are transmitted through the media can be termed the social expectations theory of media effects.[1] Its essential propositions can be summarized in the following terms:

1. Various kinds of content provided by the mass media often portray *social activities* and *group life*.

2. These portrayals are *representations of reality* that reflect, accurately or poorly, the nature of many kinds of groups in American society.

3. Individuals who are exposed to these representations receive *lessons* on the norms, roles, ranking, and social controls that prevail within many kinds of common groups.

4. The experience of exposure to portrayals of a particular kind of group results in *incidental learning* of behavior patterns that are expected by others when acting within such a group.

5. Thus, these learned expectations concerning appropriate behavior for self and others serve as *guides to action* when individuals actually encounter or try to understand such groups in real life.

1. This theory was first developed as the "cultural norms theory" in Melvin L. DeFleur, *Theories of Mass Communication*, 2nd ed. (New York: David McKay, 1970), pp. 129–139.

553–554), they also discuss such information in conversations and pass on news and interpretations in a process of diffusion.[8] It is in these exposures and exchanges that people's meanings for words are constantly shaped, reshaped, and reinforced. Thus, exposure to mass communications plays a singularly important part in forming habitual ways of perceiving, interpreting, and acting toward the outside world. Therefore, we need to look briefly at the meaning construction theory of media portrayals. Its basic ideas flow from the nature of words and how the media play a part in shaping their meanings, which in turn influence people's actions.[9]

Words as constructions of meanings for reality   Words are the basic units of communication with which we perceive, understand, and communicate about what we believe to be true. The meaning for every word and grammatical pattern can be understood as consisting of personal experiences previously recorded (imprinted) in neural cell structures in the brain. Thus, meanings are subjective experiences that each person has in his or her head, so to speak. We really do not know if they are actually the true features of what exists in the world outside.

For every word in our language, we have constructed a pattern of subjective meanings that are undoubtedly different in some ways from the detailed and objective characteristics of the thing or situation for which the word stands. This is because no word or other kind of symbol can capture *all* aspects of the objective reality to which it refers. Therefore, we do not communicate about actual realities; we communicate by referring to our own subjective meanings aroused by words. Others who receive our messages construct their interpretations of our words from their own subjective experiences.

We also think and understand in terms of such word-linked meanings. That is, after learning a word, we soon become accustomed to following the shared rules of the culture concerning the subjective experiences that it is supposed to arouse in each person. Then, we use the word not only to communicate with each other but also to *perceive* and *think about* the reality for which it is a substitute. Thus, words separate us from actual reality, focusing our attention on our own personal constructed meanings. This may be a complex idea, but it is critically important to understanding truly important influences of mass communications.

From the above, we can conclude that *the word itself becomes far more important to people in many ways than the objective reality for which it originally was a substitute*. In fact, most of us have never had any first-hand contact with the realities to which the majority of the words we freely use refer! For example, only a few of us have ever put on scuba gear and dived to a tropical coral reef. Yet, because of the learned meanings we have acquired, we feel that we have a reasonably good understanding of what the scuba diving experience is like and what we would encounter upon reaching the reef. Another example is going to the dentist. Many children have never been there, but they "know" what it is like. They can confidently confirm that it is a painful experience to be dreaded. In reality, modern dentistry is not actually painful. It may be uncomfortable and certainly expensive, but cleanings or even fillings are not painful. Nevertheless, children share the meaning that dental treatment is a terrible experience.

What is happening here? We have never actually experienced many kinds of activities for which we have meanings. However, these meanings permit us to talk and think about reefs and diving, the agonies of dentistry and a thousand other situations, actions, and things. What is happening is that in thinking and talking about such matters, we respond to our *subjective representations* of reality—meanings that we have acquired in processes of communication—rather than to the objective realities of actual experience. Participating in society's communication processes enables us to acquire and share *conventions* of meaning about almost anything that can be described in language or shown in media portrayals—life in the Arctic, ancient Greece, marriage, physicians, cowboys, and even beings on other planets. We "know" what these are because we participate in communication, even though we may never have been in the far North, visited Greece, been married, gone to medical school, or been a cowboy—and we certainly have not encountered people from another planet!

The important principle underlying the meaning construction theory of media portrayals is that the personal and subjective interpretations we experience for words constitute the world to which we adjust. We cannot relate accurately to the objective world of reality itself because our access to that world is both selective and limited. In the absence of direct experience with many aspects of that world, we create both our cultural and private worlds of meaning through communication. It is through these shared representations—the "pictures in our heads"—that we perceive, think, and shape our responses to the "world outside."[10] In short, the heart of the whole idea is that subjective and personal *meanings shape behavior*.

Media portrayals as influences on meanings   How are these principles specifically related to the mass media? The obvious answer is that by presenting endless portrayals of reality, mass communications provide experiences from which people collectively shape their meanings for words. Meaning theory explains that people learn or modify at least some of the meanings they associate with words through exposure to portrayals encountered in mass communications. Then, in their interpersonal communications, the meanings they derive from the media are further shaped, and reshaped, into conventions about what words are supposed to mean, which they share with others so that they become part of the general language and culture. The media also play a key role in stabilizing these meanings. Thus, the mass media are a source both of *changes* in language, as they modify meanings for individuals, and of *stabilization*, as they reinforce conventional usages. These may be subtle influences of media content, but they are of profound importance.

As an example of how meanings can be linked to a label by a medium in a forceful way, consider a deodorant commercial that was shown on network television. The commercial opened with a desert scene showing a gang of Mexican bandits on horseback galloping up to the foreground. When they stopped, the camera focused on their leader, who was a big, burly, hairy, and very dirty bandit. While glaring meanly into the camera, he reached into his saddle bag and pulled out a can of (a particular brand of) deodorant. Just as he was about to spray it under his arm, a voice in the background proclaimed, "If it can help him, think of what it can do for you!" The portrayal implied, of course, that Mexicans (the label) are the meanest, dirtiest, and, presumably, smelliest people imaginable (the meaning). Needless to say, the commercial offended many people, and it was hastily withdrawn by the advertiser.

Through such portrayals, the media can modify the relationship between a symbol and the subjective experiences aroused by that symbol within an individual. In other words, the media can shape meanings for people exposed to their content and establish similar meanings among large audiences. The media may not *intend* to do this, any more than members of the audiences intend to be influenced by them when enjoying their content.

Types of meaning modification   The influence that the media have on meanings may be simple or complex. For example, by exposure to print, film, and broadcasting, audiences can learn new words with new meanings or can acquire new meanings for old words. For example, in recent years,

THE MEANING CONSTRUCTION THEORY OF MEDIA PORTRAYALS

One of the oldest explanations of human behavior is that people act on the basis of what they believe to be real. That is, knowledge shapes action. Furthermore, people obtain knowledge—their beliefs, understandings, and meanings for the realities to which they must respond—from social sources in a process of communication. Both of these principles go back at least as far as the fourth century B.C., when Plato set them forth dramatically in his *Republic*, in the famous "Allegory of the Cave."

Today, we still deal with the world on the basis of knowledge derived from social sources. But unlike people in Plato's time, we have the mass media as a central part of the process. The meanings that each of us associates with various words are significantly influenced by the ways in which the mass media present images, depictions, and interpretations of those aspects of reality to which our words refer.

As we are exposed to the content of mass communications, the experience of reading, hearing, or viewing can *establish* meanings for new words that we learn (for example, "modem" and "carjacking"). That experience can *extend* the meaning of words we already know, by providing additional meanings (for example, "desert storm" and "star wars"). It can *substitute* different meanings for more traditional ones. For example, media reports on computers make use of terms such as "bits" and "chips," which have very different traditional meanings. The same is true in news about sports, in which terms such as "bowl" and "blowout" have little to do with their original meanings. Finally, the experience of exposure to the media can *stabilize* the relationship between familiar words and their customary meanings through repetition of standardized word-meaning linkages. Thus, the media present to us a complex flow of language and mean-

the media brought us "nerd," "dweeb," and "yuppie," with complex denotative meanings. We have learned that substances called "carcinogens" cause cancer and that some things are "biodegradable." We acquired foreign words, such as "perestroika" and "ayahtollah," as part of our everyday vocabularies. Today, such words arouse more or less parallel meanings in the memories of millions of Americans. Media audiences also learned new meanings for old words. Today, we know that "neat" may not mean orderly, as it once did, but likeable; that "heavy" may not simply mean weighty in a physical sense, but important or significant; and that describing someone as "gay" does not necessarily mean that that person is jovial and light-hearted. The American mass media have had a significant influence in transforming these symbols by adding denotative meanings that are now widely shared.

According to meaning construction theory, there are at least four ways in which media portrayals can play a part in shaping the process whereby we achieve new or modified social constructions of meanings for reality. These can be called establishment, extension, substitution, and stabilization. Each term refers to a relationship between a symbol and the learned subjective experiences of meaning to which that symbol refers. These can be explained briefly.

ings that enriches, alters, and sometimes even confuses our interpretations of words.[1]

In more specific terms, how does this process take place? That is, how do the meanings of an individual become modified or stabilized by media exposure? The process of learning meanings from the media, which then serve to guide actions, is not difficult to understand. We can summarize the basic stages of the meaning construction theory of media portrayals in the following terms:

1. By presenting depictions of reality in print, audio, or visual form, the media describe objects, events, or situations in ways that link *labels* (language symbols, such as words) to *meanings.*

2. A member of the audience perceives such a portrayal and either *undergoes some change* in his or her personal interpretation of the meaning of a particular label or has a meaning *stabilized* around existing conventions.

3. The individual communicates with others using the label and its media-influenced meaning. In this interpersonal communication, such media-derived meanings are *further shaped* and/or *stabilized.*

4. This participation in mass and interpersonal communication is an important part of the development and maintenance of *cultural conventions* of meaning in the language community.

5. Thus, individual behavior toward objects, situations, or events is *guided by the meanings* people hold for them. In this way, the media have played an indirect but significant long-term role in shaping people's thoughts and actions.

---

1. This theory of the influence of mass communications on meanings and actions was first developed in Melvin L. DeFleur and Timothy G. Plax, "Human Communication as a Bio-Social Process," a paper presented to the International Communication Association, Acapulco, Mexico, 1980.

Establishment is a process by which new words and new meanings become part of the language system through audience exposure to media portrayals. For example, the acronym AIDS meant nothing to most Americans a decade ago. Because of extensive media presentations of the term as a dread disease, it is now a part of American vocabulary. Another word of clear media origin is "Rambo." Originally a name of a movie character, it has been established as a term to describe any person who takes bold and audacious, but reckless, action. In this way, individuals acquire meanings for symbols that they were not familiar with before.

Extension, that is, an expansion of meanings, can also take place as an outcome of media portrayals. In this way, people learn additional meanings that can be attached to symbols with which they are already familiar. For example, a few years ago, the word "crack" meant a physical defect that one found in a surface. Introduced in a story in the *New York Times* in 1985, it now has extended meanings referring to a dangerous drug. Similarly, before the 1991 military action in Kuwait, "desert storm" referred to a weather disturbance in a dry region. Its new meaning refers to complex military activities.

Substitution consists of a displacement of older meanings for a word in favor of newer ones as a result of media portrayals. For example, prior to

Meaning construction theory predicts that the mass media play an active role in the constant modification of the linkages between words and the ways people collectively use them to understand and interpret their physical and social worlds. The media establish meanings for new words and extend, substitute, or stabilize meanings for others. For example, the word "rambo" had a clear origin in the film character portrayed by Sylvester Stallone but is now routinely used and recognized as indicating actions that are bold and reckless. (Sygma)

about 1980, the term "Vietnam veteran" implied a person who had served his or her country in the armed forces during a particular period in a particular place. Then for years the news media, entertainment television, and the film industry presented content that modified at least some of the implications of that term. They did so by giving a great deal of attention to the psychological problems of some of those who served in Vietnam. The result was to provide the public with alternative meanings for the term "Vietnam veteran." Instead of simply meaning courageous people who served their country in a difficult time, the term came to represent individuals with deep psychological problems. The connotative meanings imply mental instability, raising questions about their suitability as employees, husbands, and so on.

Stabilization, or standardization, of meanings is still another outcome of certain kinds of media portrayals. In this case, members of the audience already share a more or less similar set of meanings for symbols in the portrayal. By repeatedly showing the accepted meanings for these symbols, the media reinforce (that is, more firmly establish) the conventions regarding their interpretation. For example, the public now holds certain beliefs about young black males living in the inner city. Many white Americans think they are dangerous and aggressive. Certainly some are, but the majority clearly are not. This may be a result of endless TV shows and movies in which this category of persons has been portrayed as repeatedly engaged in drug-dealing, shootings, theft, and other deviant acts. Even the local TV news plays its part when it shows the evening round-up of crime stories. Many who are shown in the hands of police are young male African-Americans.[11]

Generally, then, the ways in which the mass media link words and people's personal and shared meanings through their depictions and portrayals of reality play an important part in changing and stabilizing the language. Because people's actions are shaped by the labels and meanings they use in responding to the world around them, the media have subtle, complex, long-range, and significant influences on behavior.

Stereotype Theory: Negative Meanings for Minorities

A special case of the more general meaning construction theory of media portrayals can be used to analyze specific ways in which the mass media reinforce existing patterns of attitudes and behavior toward minorities in American society. The special case is what we will call *stereotype theory*, which brings together meaning construction theory and the older idea of rigid beliefs that are a part of Americans' shared culture.[12]

Stereotypes are clusters of negative meanings that are shared by many people concerning minority groups or other categories of people in society. Generally, such negative meanings make it easier for the dominant segments of society to keep minorities in subordinate positions. For example, prior to the civil rights movement of the 1960s, it was to the advantage of whites to keep alive the idea that African-American citizens had low morals, were stupid, lazy, happy-go-lucky, musically inclined, and without ambition. Such beliefs seemed to make it reasonable to keep blacks from voting, going to school with whites, living in white areas, and taking many kinds of jobs. Thus, to maintain their power and prestige advantage, dominant people perpetuated stereotypes in the media about African-Americans and many other religious, ethnic, and racial groups.

But what kind of evidence can be assembled to see if this theory has any validity? One answer is extended and systematic observation of the content of mass communications as various categories of people are being portrayed. For example, before World War II, virtually all American media were heavily involved in the portrayal of gross stereotypes about various kinds of minorities. In the movies, African-Americans were shown as either servants or buffoons. They were never main characters playing significant roles. On radio, such characterizations as "Amos 'n' Andy" (two white actors in blackface) brought the stereotypes of the earlier minstrel show tradition into the twentieth century. Newspapers seldom printed photos of African-Americans, unless they were criminals (who were identified as "Negroes"). Even in sports, the players and teams covered were white. The "Negro League" scores were seldom reported, and photos of its players were almost never found in the sports page. The list could go on and on: Italians were portrayed as gangsters; Asians were sly and cruel; Native Americans were treacherous and always lost to the cowboys; Mexicans were lazy, and so forth.

After various reform groups and activists spoke out strongly against such portrayals and omissions, the American media sharply reduced their fre-

THE STEREOTYPE THEORY

The word "stereotype" comes from the world of printing—full pages of metal type were cast into a cylindrical form and attached to the roller of a printing press. As the paper passed through the press, the stereotype produced thousands of pages that were exactly alike. Walter Lippmann adopted the term in the 1920s to describe rigidly formed ideas, usually of a negative nature, that people hold about a minority group and use as a justification for treating all members of the group exactly alike.

Beginning in the 1930s, the concept was intensively studied by generations of social scientists. Commonly, they defined a stereotype as a structure of negative meanings thought to be characteristic of every member of a particular category of people. On the basis of such a structure of beliefs, each member could be treated in the same manner (usually rejected or discriminated against). Thus, a stereotype is a *schema* stored in memory—a set of beliefs held by individuals, but shared with others as a part of a culture. It was an important concept for explaining both prejudice and discrimination, and it came into common usage within that context.

Stereotypes function to keep members of minority groups in positions of low power and prestige. For example, following slavery and well into this century, many whites were able to keep alive shared beliefs that African-Americans were intellectually backward, lazy, oversexed, criminally inclined, and generally characterized by a long list of negative attributes. Therefore, they claimed, it was justifiable to deny them opportunity and to treat them as inferiors. The same was true of a number of other minorities. To maintain their advantaged position in the social order, dominant people perpetuated such stereotypes about many religious, ethnic, and racial groups.

During early decades of this century, the movies were often criticized for their stereotyping of minority quency. However, many kinds of stereotypes have survived. For example, older people are often portrayed unsympathetically as cranky and forgetful, if not downright senile. All during the Cold War, Soviet characters were portrayed as grim dullards that we all loved to hate.

As the twentieth century draws to a close, the incidental lessons offered by media-portrayed stereotypes are undoubtedly less blatant than the mass-communicated curriculum of earlier decades. But the process is still there, allowing exposure to mass communication content to serve as the foundation from which meanings leading to prejudices and biases toward various categories of people can be learned. An instructive example that seems to have a life of its own is the stereotyped portrayal of the mentally ill on televison.

The Mentally Ill: A Case Study in Stereotype Theory

To illustrate the implications of stereotype theory, we can consider how the mentally ill have been portrayed on television in recent decades. The discus-

groups. Up until about mid-century, African-Americans were routinely shown in subservient or comic roles. Italian-Americans were shown as gangsters, and Asians were depicted as sly and sinister. Native Americans were most often shown as savages attacking wagon trains, who were regularly defeated by the cavalry.

A theory of the influence of media depictions on stereotypes can be derived as a special case of the more general meaning construction theory of media portrayals.[1] It can be used to analyze specific ways in which mass media reinforce existing patterns of attitudes and behavior toward minorities in American society by perpetuation of stereotypes in their content. The essential ideas of the stereotype theory can be expressed in the following propositions:

1. In entertainment content, and in other messages, the media repeatedly present *portrayals* of various categories of people, such as the aged, women, and major racial and ethnic groups.

2. Those portrayals tend to be *consistently negative*, showing such people as having more undesirable attributes and fewer positive characteristics than members of the dominant groups.

3. Such portrayals are similar among the various media—providing *corroboration*.

4. These portrayals provide *constructions of meaning* for members of the audience, particularly for those who have only limited contact with actual people of the relevant categories.

5. Thus, members of the audience incorporate those meanings into their memories as relatively inflexible *schemata*—stereotypic interpretations—that they use when thinking about or responding to any individual of a portrayed category, regardless of his or her actual personal characteristics.

1. This theory as applied to long-term influences of mass communications was formulated by the authors of this book. However, its basic ideas were first presented by Walter Lippmann, in his book *Public Opinion* (New York: Macmillan, 1992.)

sion is intended to show some of the ways that portrayals in mass communication link meaning to particular symbols and to show how meaning construction theory in general explains how mass communication may influence a particular set of interpretations and shared cultural beliefs. Our example will focus on the mentally ill because they make up one category of people whom the media continue to portray in grossly stereotyped ways. As we will see, the media have by no means invented the idea that mentally ill people are to be regarded negatively. What the media continue to do is to perpetuate, stabilize, and reinforce an ancient and deeply established aversion to the mentally ill and to keep alive traditional meanings of insanity.

Traditional meanings of insanity   The mentally ill have long been treated as social outcasts. To explain this pattern of social rejection, we need to look very briefly at the history of meanings for mental illness. In this way, we can show the power of culture over individual interpretations and behavior and then illustrate the role of the media in perpetuating this particular set of stereotypes.

In medieval times, attitudes toward those we would now call mentally ill were far more benign than they are today. Later, during the Renaissance, the situation changed, and "madness" came to be feared and despised. The "mad" were often confined on ships that moved from place to place, exhibiting the "crazies" to people for a small fee:

> "Ships of Fools" crisscrossed the seas and canals of Europe with their comic and pathetic cargo of souls. Some of them found pleasure and even a cure in the changing surroundings, in the isolation of being cast off, while others withdrew further, became worse, or died alone and away from their families. The cities and villages which had thus rid themselves of their crazed and crazy, could now take pleasure in watching the exciting sideshow when a ship full of foreign lunatics would dock at their harbors.[13]

Practices such as confining people to ships of fools reinforced and stabilized the meaning of madness among Europeans. It became a repulsive state—an inherited curse to be concealed, a condition to be punished and dreaded. Children or other relatives who suffered such conditions were hidden in attics, confined to dungeons, or even killed, to keep people from knowing about "bad blood" in the family.

Establishing the medical model As the eighteenth century ended, changes had taken place. A few humanitarians successfully agitated for better treatment of the insane. The concept of providing them with sanctuaries, or asylums, was slow to come. However, during the last part of the nineteenth century, the belief spread that they should be placed in hospitals rather than be chained in dungeons. In the early 1900s, psychoanalysts and other medical authorities provided a new view of insanity, arguing that it was not a curse indicating possession by demons or inherited bad blood but a sickness. This *medical model* of mental impairment was widely accepted by professionals by the early twentieth century. It redefined the insane as *sick*, as people with "syndromes" capable of being cured by *treatment*. This meant, of course, that after successful therapy, they would be able to return to normal social roles.

Unfortunately, public attitudes lagged far behind these developments in the medical profession. Even today, they have been slow to change. Mental illness is still a dreadful stigma, and those that have been successfully treated have enormous difficulty in getting accepted as "normal," even though they behave in ways no different from other people. In fact, former convicts have better economic and social prospects for acceptance in American society than former mental patients. An important question is *why?*

Although the meanings associated with mental illness today differ greatly from those of earlier times, many elements of the older beliefs persist. In recent years, the problems of the mentally ill have been compounded by the closing of many of the state-supported mental hospitals and asylums. This trend began when hospital costs began to rise dramatically and new drug therapies were discovered and used to control some of the symptoms of mental illness. Under such therapy, many patients who were in such institutions were able to function adequately in home settings—as long as they received medication.

Unfortunately, not all continued such therapies when they were turned out, and some now roam American cities with little or no support network. Many of today's homeless are people who either received institutional care at an earlier time or would be in such settings if the older system of hospitals and asylums still prevailed. Even though the old system had many negative aspects, the nation has not as yet developed a satisfactory alternative for providing even basic care for such people. There is widespread apathy toward these unfortunate people, and they appear to have little hope of leading a normal life-style.

In any case, both those who were once mentally ill (and have recovered) and those still afflicted suffer a considerable stigma. The term "mentally ill" remains a powerful label that is applied by the untrained public more or less uniformly across all categories of former and current patients. That label triggers strongly negative meanings that are widely shared. Above all, the stereotype implies that such a person is likely to be *dangerous*. A person so labeled is instantly stigmatized as one who is likely to exhibit bizarre, unpredictable, and dangerous behavior and is avoided if at all possible.

Objective reality does not fit this picture. The facts assembled by responsible medical and psychiatric research show clearly that mentally ill people as a whole are far *less* dangerous than the normal population as a whole! For every one of the handful whose crimes make headlines, thousands live obscure lives that pose no dangers to others whatever. It is the "normal" people who are a problem! The truly dangerous segment of the population consists of clinically normal, young, urban males who are between sixteen and twenty-five. These "normal" people account for the lion's share of murders, rapes, and other crimes of violence committed in the United States. The mentally ill account for about the same proportion of crimes as adults over sixty-five—which is a tiny share indeed. But in spite of the factual situation, the stereotype of the "mental patient" (including the "ex-patient") is one that continues to arouse fear.

How the meanings of the stereotype are reinforced today   Why does the idea that mentally ill people are dangerous persist? What are the modern counterparts of the "ship of fools" that continue to demonstrate that the mentally ill are mindless lunatics, only a hair's breadth away from deviant and dangerous behavior? One important factor is very clearly the way the *news media* report on mentally ill killers. Even though they are very rare—a few every year out of the 253 million citizens in this country—the press gives them enormous coverage. That tradition was established as early as the 1880s, when the relatively new mass newspapers gave great attention to Jack the Ripper. The public was both fascinated and horrified, but the bottom line was that the stories sold newspapers. In fact, the public is still fascinated with the Ripper case more than a century later! Since World War II, there have been several notorious cases. The Boston Strangler, Charles Manson, the Son of Sam, John Gacy, Wayne Williams, Ted Bundy, Jeffrey

Dahmer and similar individuals have received *intense* attention from the modern media. This handful of men seems to represent, for many people, about all one needs to know about the mentally ill. The fact that millions of other people who suffer mental illness are totally different and entirely harmless is ignored.

All the mass media play a significant part in maintaining the stereotype attached to mental illness. Books, movies, the comics, and especially television frequently portray the mentally ill in very negative ways. Their depictions are meant to amuse us, but unwittingly they are influencing the "pictures in our head"—our conventionalized constructions of meaning for reality.

An example: Television's portrayal of the mentally ill   To illustrate how stereotype theory aids in understanding the kinds of media portrayals that stabilize these meanings, we can review very briefly the results of a small study of television dramas completed several years ago.[14] The goal was to examine the portrayal of the mentally ill in all crime-adventure dramas

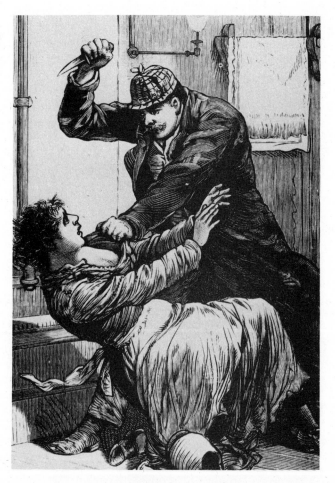

The media started focusing attention on the mentally ill during the last century. By emphasizing bizarre cases, such as that of Jack the Ripper, they created high interest. However, they also strongly reinforced the stereotype that mentally ill people, even those who have recovered, are unpredictable and dangerous. According to meaning theory, this is the reinforcement function of media portrayals. (The Bettmann Archive)

broadcast by the major networks during a four-month period. First, a small pilot study was conducted. It showed that few other types of TV programs at the time had content related to mental illness. The mentally ill were mentioned (negatively) in a few news stories, and there had been a recent documentary and a movie dealing sympathetically with mental illness, but the overwhelming concentration of depictions of mental illness were found in the evening police and detective shows. For this reason, the study focused on thirteen action series in which various kinds of private detectives or police officials sought weekly to outwit the bad guys.

Overall, the researchers carefully analyzed seventy-five episodes of one-hour, prime-time dramas in which official or unofficial representatives of law and order acted against wrongdoers or forces for evil. Thirty-one of these programs (41 percent) had content in which people portrayed as mentally disturbed openly committed serious, deviant acts. A total of thirty-four such portrayals of mentally ill wrongdoers were identified and analyzed. (Several programs had more than one portrayal.) Thus, portrayals of the mentally ill as villains were very frequent. Each program was analyzed in terms of (1) the details of the plot, and the attributes of the characters, (2) descriptions of how the mentally ill were shown, and (3) a complete list of labels, words, and phrases used to describe or communicate about the mentally ill. For the control programs (explained below), a similar procedure was followed. In addition, the programs were studied as "whole plots" so that the meanings of actions, labels, and incidents could be interpreted within their context.

In addition to those showing deranged criminals, twenty-one of the programs depicted serious deviance but *no* mental illness. These programs served as a control. The number and quality of negative labels used to describe these "normal" villains were carefully analyzed in order to see what *level of dangerousness* was implied for deviants who were not mentally ill. This was an attempt to determine if mentally ill villains were portrayed in a more negative way than just plain crooks.

Assessing the level of dangerousness implied by each portrayal of wrongdoing allowed numerical comparisons of the actions of the mentally ill villains with the behavior of the non–mentally ill ones. In addition, the programs were classified into three "nominal" categories: (1) those in which people were *verbally* identified as "crazy," "nuts," and so on, as they were shown carrying out deviant acts; (2) programs in which only *nonverbal* cues—such as close-ups of strange-looking eyes, fixed grins, odd twitches—indicated that a character engaged in deviant acts was "nuts"; and (3) programs that made extensive use of the *vocabulary* of madness but did not show mentally ill people acting in deviant ways.

Overwhelmingly, these nightly portrayals of mentally ill people were *unsympathetic* (to say the least). The scriptwriters were clearly using the mentally ill as the bad guys. They were murderers, rapists, slashers, snipers, and bombers. In other words, the cues, either verbal or nonverbal, that identified the characters as mentally ill were linked to activities that were extremely harmful to others. Moreover, by comparison with the (presumably sane) regular villains, the mentally ill were shown as *far more dangerous*.

These portrayals were vivid. They provided powerful lessons that the meaning of mental illness includes elements of severe danger to others. The mentally ill offenders were not only shown to be dangerous, but were also portrayed in ways calculated to arouse *fear* in the audience. While the mentally ill on the screen were conducting deviant acts extremely harmful to others, they grimaced strangely, had glassy eyes, or giggled incongruously. Some laughed weirdly and then sobbed or cried. Others mumbled incoherently or screamed irrationally. One bared his teeth and snarled as he jumped on his victims to suck blood from their jugular veins. Still another squeezed raw meat through his fingers and rubbed it on his gun as he prepared to kill his next victim. Unusual music often accompanied these scenes to enhance the effect. In some shows, dark scenes and carefully timed actions were used to startle and frighten the audience.

In addition to showing the overt behavior of the mentally ill in very negative terms, the stories made abundant use of the popular *vocabulary of madness*. Any kind of behavior that was unusual, eccentric, or merely difficult to explain with the facts at hand was likely to be categorized by the non–mentally ill characters as that of "kooks," "chuckleheads," "fruitcakes," "cuckoo-birds," and so forth. More technical terms for neurotic or psychotic conditions, such as schizophrenic and paranoid, were used far less frequently.

The essential conclusion from the analysis of these TV programs was that scriptwriters for these crime-adventure shows openly used the mentally ill to represent *evil*, against which the forces for right and justice could fight to protect society. Since the heroes and heroines of such shows were virtually invincible, the mentally ill never got away with their foul deeds. They were hauled off night after night to "hospitals for the criminally insane," where they presumably would remain forever.

Partly because of the reinforcement of the stigma attached to the mentally ill by the mass media, our daily language continues to also play a part in perpetuating the stereotype. Colloquial expressions that we all use continue to describe irrational behavior as "nuts," "kooky," "kinky," "freaky," "wacky," "loony," and so on. Furthermore, many of us quickly judge as "sick" or "weird" any behavior of which we do not approve. The list could go on and on. The point is that anything that departs from what someone thinks is normal—anything that seems alien, irregular, or merely inexplicable—is described in the terms that we use for the mentally ill. Thus, by repeatedly emphasizing the connection between the symbols for mental illness and what we define as bizarre, we stabilize our meanings for madness. And the mass media continue to play a central role in the stereotyping process.

Implications of Meaning Construction Theories

The basis of all complex communication is the link between words or other symbols and the subjective meanings that they arouse within each of us. Insofar as those meanings ("pictures in our heads") are governed by shared conventions, we are able to communicate with each other more or less adequately. Given those conditions, it is clear that the part played by mass communications in establishing, extending, substituting, and stabilizing the links between words and meanings is of critical importance to the society.

One of the continuing problems in any society is that of developing meanings for words that adequately reflect and incorporate the true characteristics of reality. There is considerable concern that the mass media are often doing just the opposite. Their portrayals emphasize ties between meanings and words that *misrepresent* the real physical and social world. The media clearly perpetuate incorrect and even harmful stereotypes that have come down from the past. This was very clear in the research on portrayals of the mentally ill. The perpetuation of such stereotypes may be one of the ways in which mass communications can have powerful effects that are quite harmful to people. Although the portrayals of deranged and dangerous criminals in the crime-detective shows were meant to be entertaining, millions of people who are, or once were, mentally ill may continue to suffer if the medium continues to reinforce ancient stereotypes.

Chapter Review

- Two seemingly contradictory conclusions about the influences of mass communications on their audience can be derived. From massive research evidence, it seems clear that they have only selective and minimal influences on people. From observing events in society, such as Somalia, Watergate, and the smoking controversy, it appears that their effects are actually very powerful.

- This dilemma can be resolved by looking at media influences from two different perspectives. In a short-term and immediate sense, exposure to mass communications has limited effects on any particular individual. Over a long term, however, accumulation theory predicts that where information and interpretations supplied by the media are relatively persistent, consistent, and corroborative, minimal changes in individuals can add up over time to significant changes in populations.

- Adoption theory explains a long-term process in which significant social and cultural change takes place as large numbers of individuals gradually take up new technology and new ways of behaving. The media are a significant source for bringing a flow of innovations of

many kinds to the attention of the public, and therefore they are a necessary but not sufficient condition of the adoption of innovations.

- In contemporary society, mass media play a central part in the overall socialization process by which individuals obtain their personal understandings of the culture and their knowledge of the social order. That socialization shapes everyone's patterns of perception, thought, and action.

- Modeling theory explains that one way in which people acquire new modes of acting is by observing behavior portrayed in mass communications. Such behavior is adopted if the individual identifies with the model and receives positive reinforcement for trying out the behavior.

- Another significant form of socialization is the acquisition of understandings about the requirements for behavior in groups. Social expectations theory explains that through exposures to media portrayals of social life and human groups, individuals learn about norms, roles, ranking, and controls.

- In their portrayals of the social and physical world, the mass media present meanings to their audiences for specific words, for social situations, and for categories of people. Meaning construction theory concludes that, once learned, those meanings and general interpretations of the physical and social world provide a basis for people's behavioral decisions. This theory points out that every word in a person's vocabulary provides him or her with an associated set of understandings concerning some aspect of reality. Through their portrayals, the mass media help create and modify those understandings. Thus, mass communications influence people's structures of meaning by establishing, extending, substituting, and stabilizing the meanings for words.

- An important application of meaning construction theory to stereotypes aids in understanding how the media help perpetuate certain clusters of belief about particular categories of people. This is illustrated by examining the way in which television portrays the mentally ill, reinforcing the incorrect idea that all who are or have been mentally ill are extremely dangerous.

Notes and References

1. This particular theory has been developed for the purposes of this text and it does not appear by this name in the theory literature.
2. Everett M. Rogers and F. Floyd Shoemaker, *Communication of Innovations: A Cross-Cultural Approach* (New York: Free Press, 1971), p. 100.
3. Gabriel Tarde, *The Laws of Imitation*, trans. E. C. Parsons (New York: Holt, 1903).
4. Rogers and Shoemaker, op. cit., pp. 52–70.
5. For a discussion of the general social learning theory from which modeling theory has been drawn, see Albert Bandura, *Social Learning Theory* (Englewood Cliffs, N. J.: Prentice-Hall, 1977).
6. For an extended treatment of these features of social organization and how they shape behavior for the members of human groups see "Social Organization," in Melvin L. DeFleur et al., *Sociology: Human Society* (New York: Random House, 1984), pp. 72–104.
7. For a detailed discussion of several meaning theories, see Melvin L. DeFleur and Sandra Ball-Rokeach *Theories of Mass Communication*, 5th ed. (White Plains, N.Y.: Longman, 1989), pp. 228–269.
8. For a summary of the literature on the diffusion of the news, see Melvin L. DeFleur, "The Growth and Decline of Research on the Diffusion of the News," *Communication Research, 14*, no. 1 (Feb. 1987), pp. 109–130.
9. This theory of the function of media portrayals was first developed in Melvin L. DeFleur and Timothy G. Plax, "Human Communication as a Bio-Social Process," paper presented to the International Communication Association, Acapulco, Mexico, 1980.
10. Walter Lippmann, *Public Opinion* (New York: Macmillan, 1922). See Chapter 1, "The World Outside and the Pictures in Our Heads," pp. 1–19.
11. Robert M. Entman, "Blacks in the News: Television, Modern Racism and Cultural Change," paper presented at the annual conference of the International Communication Association, Chicago, 1991.
12. Although the study of stereotypes began many decades ago in social psychology, and a large literature has accumulated concerning their nature and functions, the term "stereotype theory," in the context of a meaning theory of media effects, was developed for the purposes of this book.
13. Michel Foucault, *Madness and Civilization* (New York: Random House, 1965), p. 11.
14. See Briggitte Goldstein, "Television's Portrayals of the Mentally Ill," MA thesis (in sociology), University of New Mexico, 1980.

CHAPTER **18**

Ethical Issues in Mass Communication

The June 28 issue of *People* contained a story on a new diet product called starch blockers. On rechecking his tapes, reporter David Scheff found that he misquoted Dr. J. John Marshall. Dr. Marshall did not say that the writer Cameron Stauth was a "dirty rotten scum who got very greedy." What he said was, "He's an unscrupulous little (pause) gentleman."

People, 1982

As the correction notice quoted on the chapter opening page suggests, accuracy, and therefore credibility, is very important to journalists. Indeed, these qualities are important to most of the communications industries. As previous chapters have shown, those who present the news, direct public relations and advertising campaigns, and produce other media content want the public to believe that they are telling the truth and that they are transmitting their messages within ethical bounds. After all, professional communicators know only too well that if the information, opinion, and even entertainment they present to the public lacked believability, it would quickly erode public confidence and they would lose their audience. Communications in a civilized society must be not only competent but also credible to be valuable to people. Thus, ethics is more than an arcane topic that is debated by religious authorities, do-gooders, and philosophers. It is a deeply practical concern across all of the communications industries. When ethical norms are violated, it upsets most professional communicators because it threatens their livelihood.

The issue of ethics affects not only professional communicators but everyone who is in public life. Members of Congress have been involved in a number of ethical controversies in recent years. Ethics was clearly on the public agenda at the beginning of 1993 as a new administration arrived in Washington, D.C. President Bill Clinton announced especially high ethical requirements for people in his administration, and even went so far as to publish a set of standards to avoid conflicts of interest. Ethics was often cited in the 1992 presidential campaigns of Clinton and George Bush, and Clinton lost no time in making clear his position that public officials should adhere to a high standard of conduct without even the *appearance* of conflicts of interest. Ironically, only a year earlier, as governor of Arkansas, Clinton fought his own ethical scandal when the supermarket tabloid *Star* detailed an alleged extramarital affair with a woman named Gennifer Flowers. Ethical problems continued to arise after he became President, as they have in other administrations. There seems little doubt the media during the Clinton administration will keep ethics on the front burner and scrutinize the government very closely.

Concern over ethics is a lively one in American society. It is not uncommon for a charge of breach of ethics to be front-page news, whether the charge involves government, business, other institutions, or individuals. In the 1980s, critics worried about Wall Street greed, government corruption, and hypocrisy in the lives of politicians, televangelists, and other people in the public eye. In 1992, three United States senators were accused of sexual harassment. One was driven from office by newspaper and TV accounts of his transgressions. Another made front-page news when several women accused him of numerous instances of sexual misconduct over the years. In the third case, the charge was quietly withdrawn by the accuser after she was satisfied that media publicity had adequately "punished" the senator.

It has been suggested that for some reason interest in the moral behavior of people is exceptionally high in the 1990s, especially in the face of such great social problems as AIDS and homelessness. It seems, in fact, that there is no field that is exempt from ethical concerns, as various conferences and seminars have pointed out. Ethical conduct is on the docket in businesses, churches, schools, and other institutions. By extension, this national preoccupation with ethics—the subject of a 1992 *Time* cover story—also affects the media.

Although public preoccupation with ethical issues across so many fields is rare, media ethics has long been a subject of public discussion. Some critics ridicule the idea that competitive and profit-driven media can operate within an ethical framework. But most people disagree, saying that no media system can exist very long without public confidence, and that requires accurate, honest, and believable communications. As we have made clear in previous chapters, this does not mean that the media industries are always reliable or that all of them share the same values or ethical standards.

Growing Concern over Media Ethics

As a general field, ethics is a branch of philosophy that tries to promote good values and good will as opposed to mean-spirited or venal behavior. Some critics believe that the issue of media ethics is too broad and illusive to have much meaning. For example, no unified field of media ethics offers rules or standards that apply to all media organizations. What is taboo for a newspaper reporter may be business as usual for an advertising salesperson from the same organization. Ethics, say critics, is simply a matter of personal integrity. This ties the question of ethics for the media and media organizations to personal standards of forthright, honest, and competent behavior.

Others say that ethics is a collective concept and that corporations, networks, and newspaper publishing chains have a responsibility to see that they are honest and competent. The value of this may seem obvious, but in a society where the business environment is often described as "dog eat dog," the idea that the media industries should be socially responsible and good corporate citizens might be dismissed as wishful thinking. Indeed, some argue that the phrase "media ethics" is an oxymoron—a contradiction in terms. The reason it should not be is that media organizations and their people clearly have a self-interest in being ethical, especially in the sense of being moral and credible. Their stock in trade is the quality of the content they deliver, wheter it is information, advocacy, entertainment, or advertising.

Ethical behavior in a general sense is not hard to define. It simply means that people should not lie, steal, cheat, or commit other antisocial acts. Ethics is doing what is right, but the problem is that "right" is defined differently by different people. Thus, the need exists for serious attention to media ethics in a society increasingly concerned about the ethics of all occupational groups and professionals, including lawyers, doctors, architects, and journalists. A commitment to basic ethical standards is what binds us together as a society, distinguishing us as socially responsible as opposed to self-serving individuals.

All of the media and their supporting systems—including the news, book publishing, movies, cable television, advertising, public relations, and other enterprises—are governed by general business ethics. Moreover, most of them also have codes of ethics, or standards of conduct and acceptable practices for their employees. Most people who work in the media, ranging from financial writers to videographers, agree to abide by certain standards or rules that embody ethical values. Most of these standards, however, include few explicit ethical values beyond those taught generally in the family, church, or school.[1]

At one time, some areas of communication were virtually exempt from ethics. For example, people did not apply the same standards of fact-checking and verification of sources to advertising and public relations that they did to newspapers and magazines, arguing that advocates should have license to make the case for their clients to the point of exaggeration. Whether justified or not, people therefore tended to discount a "public relations approach" or self-serving political or ideological appeals. Similarly, religious observers proclaiming their faith were not necessarily expected to be fair and impartial.

Now that is changing, partly because of the blurring and merging of the various functions of the media. For example, as we noted in an earlier chapter, it is no longer possible to distinguish easily between informational news and entertainment. News programs increasingly use entertainment devices and dramatic language to present information, even if the story does not warrant it. Thus, ethics are sometimes a casualty in the competitive struggle for a good story.

A recent example of competitiveness pushing aside ethics occurred in 1991. It was widely reported that when President George Bush visited a supermarket he was "utterly amazed" by an electronic scanner he supposedly saw for the first time. The truth of the story was less dramatic. Actually, the President was visiting a mock supermarket counter at a grocers' convention in Florida. Reporters present said that Bush saw the technology demon-

A continuing ethical concern about the news media is that their presentations often focus on entertaining audiences rather than providing full and accurate reporting of news that is truly important in the long run. If a scientist discovers a cure for a troublesome disease, that may be reported in a small article in the back pages of a newspaper or in a brief note in a magazine. On the other hand, if a sensational event occurs in the world of entertainment or sports (such as the case of figure skaters Tonya Harding, shown here, and Nancy Kerrigan), stories about that situation will often crowd out news that is more lasting significance. (© Craig Strong/ Gamma Liaison)

strated but didn't appear to be impressed. Later, a news story claimed that Bush had "a look of wonder" on his face. This exaggerated interpretation fit into a then-prevalent stereotype of a rich president out of touch with the recession and unfamiliar with the supermarket lines regular people know only too well. Then, in a paraphrase of what Admiral Dewey said at Manila Bay, it was "Damn the ethics, full speed ahead (to create a good story)." Given the fact that few presidents have ever done their own shopping, the story stuck that President Bush was amazed at the device, and it is widely believed to this day.[2] This minor ethical transgression may be dismissed, but it illustrates the same principle that was at work when Parson Weems created the story about George Washington and the cherry tree—another fiction that was "clearer than truth."

Sometimes, careless attention to ethics brings confusion as to just what constitutes news. In recent years, electronic media executives and critics worried about the injection of entertainment values into the news, especially as tabloid TV shows such as "Hard Copy," "A Current Affair," and "America's Most Wanted" won viewer allegiance. At the same time, a Times Mirror survey indicated that many Americans had trouble distinguishing news and entertainment fare on television. And no wonder, for in the 1992 presidential campaign when Vice President Dan Quayle attacked the fictional TV character Murphy Brown for undermining family values by having a baby out of wedlock, Quayle's criticism quickly became news. When the producers of the series responded to Quayle in a pointed and critical episode, the press covered both the show and the Vice President's response as news. (Quayle spent the evening watching with a group of unwed mothers.) One critic called the incident an example of "the entertainmentization of information."

Similarly, it is difficult to sort out whether a particular article or program is news, entertainment, opinion, or even advertising. The blurring of lines between the traditional functions of the media is creating an ethical dilemma. Under conventional "rules," there are clear ethical definitions of what news is supposed to be. It is clearly to be separated from opinion. Opinion has great latitude to do and say what it will, though there is typically a standard of "intellectual honesty" applied. Entertainment fare also has wide latitude and may engage in almost any kind of fiction. As these forms merge, the role and function of ethics appear to get lost in the confusion.

Comic artists and editorial cartoonists have often faced the problem of crossing the line between information and entertainment. Comic strips, such as "Doonesbury," have so enraged some people that they have been the subject of libel lawsuits.

As new media industries evolve, ranging from business information services to pay-per-view TV programming and home shopping services, the question of what is ethical often arises. In 1992, CNN financial commentator Lou Dobbs was criticized for appearing in a promotional tape for a brokerage house. Some critics believed that Dobbs violated the public trust he had as a financial commentator and newscaster on the cable network.

Ethical expectations and demands are crossing national boundaries as a result of worldwide concern about honesty, ethics, and accurate information. For example, although China's political news remains highly suspect, its financial information is now more accurate, for the international market expects and demands it and no market economy can function on unreliable information. Thus, the issue of ethics is here to stay, and it will probably play a greater role in all kinds of media—and not only in conventional news media, but in new media that under earlier standards might not have been held accountable.

To many commentators, media ethics really refers to journalistic ethics, or the moral conduct and behavior of journalists doing their work as newsgatherers, editors, and disseminators of information to the larger society. Journalists are expected to produce reliable and believable information gathered under scrupulously honest conditions and checked along the way for accuracy. On occasion, an ethical breach in journalism receives publicity. For example, in 1989 *TV Guide* deliberately printed a misleading photograph of Oprah Winfrey's head on actress Ann Margaret's body. Realizing that misrepresentation and deception are almost universally regarded as unethical behavior and that the photo might jeopardize *TV Guide's* credibility as a serious and respected publication, the magazine later recanted. In 1993, the NBC program "Dateline" used faked footage of a GM pickup truck catching on fire, suggesting that this proved that the vehicles were unsafe. GM fought back, and there was a public furor that led to the resignation of NBC News president Michael Gartner.

As the foregoing examples illustrate and as we have shown elsewhere in this book, certain controls influence what the media do and how they do it.

In the spring of 1993, many U.S. newspapers ran a wire service story about a $200 haircut given to President Clinton by Beverly Hills stylist Cristophe aboard Air Force One while it sat on the runway at Los Angeles International Airport. An unnamed FAA spokesman was quoted as saying that other planes were forced to circle the airport while waiting and departures were delayed for up to twenty-five minutes. This was not true. Investigative analysts at *Newsday* obtained FAA records under the Freedom of Information Act and found that there were no circling planes and no backed-up runways. One plane was delayed—by two minutes. (Reuters/Bettmann)

These controls include economic, political, and legal factors, but they also include cultural and philosophical forces. Media ethics is one such force.[3] The manner and method used by the various media of communication to conduct their business and carry on discourse with the rest of society are often under scrutiny.

Here the media do not stand alone, but function in the context of social responsibility in general. Concern with ethics and ethical behavior has focused on business, government, religion, news media, and other institutions. Generally, then, some of the growing concern over media ethics has come from outside critics. However, some has also come from internal sources who want to elevate and advance the work of newspapers, magazines, radio, television and cable, databases, advertising agencies, public relations firms, and other media organizations or support services.

As our discussion has shown, media ethics is not an obscure or irrelevant topic, but something that arises daily as citizens observe the way media organizations relate to their communities as participants, observers, and critics. Ethical dilemmas also arise over the content of the media—whether it is entertainment, news, opinion, or advertising—as well as over the behavior of media people. In a simple sense, ethical choices are between right and wrong, good and bad, actions that are genuinely in the public interest and those harmful to the common good.

Complicating the problem of examining and understanding media ethics is the fact that as simple as choices may seem at first, they typically are not. Ethical decisions involve complex human relationships and often pit values cherished by the media against those preferred by other people. The media are concerned with communicating to the rest of society, whether in news stories that emphasize conflict, in opinion journals that feature debates, or on entertainment programs that often promote consensus and reinforce values. Different media obviously have different purposes, yet most want to be considered ethical. Sometimes though, the media context involves information about a person or organization that was previously protected from outside scrutiny. In such instances, a person's right to privacy conflicts with the media's interest in public disclosure. There is often no legal issue here, but an ethical one—a matter of personal choice between doing what is good for society and doing what is good for an individual.

Special Privileges; Special Responsibilities

Are we being unreasonable when we demand that our press be fair and act ethically? The answer to that question is less clear than many might suppose. By consulting legal authorities, one may learn a good deal about the range and scope of the *rights* of news organizations and the people who work for them. First, there is the general franchise for freedom of the press laid out in the Bill of Rights, specifically the First Amendment. Then, there are rights set out in state constitutions, statutes, and various court decisions that have been described and celebrated in various books. Far less sharply defined are the *duties* and *responsibilities* of the protected press and mass media. In fact, in 1947, when the famed Hutchins Commission on Freedom of the Press suggested that the press has such obligations, the press protested strongly and denounced the commission's report.

The Hutchins Commission was a privately financed effort to look carefully at freedom of the press in the United States in the years immediately following World War II. The commission, made up of philosophers, legal scholars, and other intellectual and cultural leaders, wanted publicly to encourage a system of expression that was responsible to society at large yet free to practice without constraints. It made recommendations for the government, the press, and the public, none of them binding but all intriguing as statements of social criticism and as a plea for ethically sensitive media. Among other things, the commission proposed *press councils* made up of responsible citizens that would monitor the press and provide for feedback to the media and other mass communication agencies. Over the years, the Hutchins Commission's report has gained respect and is now regarded as one of the most important documents in the history of American media. However, it has no official standing.

Under the First Amendment to the Constitution of the United States, there is no requirement that the media be fair, responsible, or accurate. The courts have stated this quite explicitly, yet increasingly a higher standard of media performance is evident in libel cases and other legal actions against the mass and specialized media. It is not uncommon these days for those suing the press to bring expert witnesses into court to testify that a particular story or program did or did not meet "normal ethical standards." Although there is no accepted norm for such standards, courts have looked to witnesses for guidance. In fact, some critics feel that such cases may establish an ethical code for media institutions, perhaps without constitutional authority.

Beyond the First Amendment

If the mass media derive their legal authority from the First Amendment, they derive their moral authority from holding the public trust. From the beginning, the media have claimed to play two roles: that of the *social conscience* of society, or a representative of the people in a nonlegalistic sense, and that of a *profit-making business* that needs to survive to fulfill its first obligation. Newspapers have long cultivated this kind of self-image. In contrast, because of government regulation, broadcast and other electronic media have been regarded as less free than the print media and therefore required to serve the public "interest, convenience and necessity" as stated in the Federal Communications Act. However, just where legal requirements end and ethical ones begin is not clear.

Other media industries, such as advertising and public relations, have also laid claim to moral authority and assert that they pursue ethical ends in their work, although this claim may rest on shaky ground and is often disputed. Media support services, such as wire services and syndicates, have generally been guided by the standards of the news media. Their value is in the quality of the work they produce, whether it is accurate news reports or entertainment matter such as comics, columns, and puzzles. Some media organizations, such as newspapers and newsmagazines, regard themselves as having more elevated ethical standards and concerns than do advertising agencies or political public relations consultants.

The Long Struggle for Professionalism

Institutional media ethics have evolved considerably since the press of the nation's early years—an era sometimes called the dark ages of American journalism. In Chapter 3, we saw that the early press was often scurrilous, making unwarranted partisan attacks on political figures with little regard for truth or accuracy. Later, a sensational press played on the public's morbid curiosity to stir it up and attract readers. The press was known to engage in deliberate deception. For example, even Benjamin Franklin, sometimes with tongue in cheek, made up interesting characters to illuminate the columns of his newspaper. Later, there was the famous "moon hoax" of 1835, in which the *New York Sun* claimed that a Scottish astronomer had observed lifelike creatures on the moon through his telescope.

As the press became more responsible in the late nineteenth century, editors urged a dedication to the public interest and proclaimed statements of noble purpose. Although some of these statements were platitudes that would have been hard to enforce, they did establish the tradition of a public-spirited rather than a self-serving press. Eventually, it was generally believed that newspapers and magazines had obligations of fairness and impartiality that went far beyond those of typical businesses. Although there was no enforcement clause for such assumptions, they were later

WHO IS NOAM CHOMSKY AND WHY IS HE SAYING SUCH AWFUL THINGS ABOUT THE MEDIA?
A Linchpin to Linguistics, Philosophy, and Literary Criticism

Noam Chomsky is considered one of the foremost intellectuals in America today, but few in the general public would recognize either his name or his ideas. Like other intellectuals who have become celebrities of sorts, Chomsky occasionally surfaces in *The New York Review of Books* or in other well-regarded journals to advance his ideas, many of which focus on the media and on media issues.

A linguist of great distinction, Chomsky published in 1957 a revolutionary book called *Syntactic Structures*, which had a profound impact on the field of linguistics. In it, Chomsky introduced a new linguistic theory that took issue with the dominant structural view, which most often tied language to human behavior and the conditions of particular societies. Instead, Chomsky's new linguistics posited that language was more innate and was connected with logical structures in the mind. In proposing "transformational" rules of language, Chomsky said that any number of sentences could be turned into actual language by a simple substitution of basic sounds for symbols. In time,

Chomsky's theories, called Cartesian linguistics, had far-reaching effects.

Chomsky continued to teach linguistics at MIT. where he holds a major chair and became a leader of radical New Left politics in the 1960s, when he strongly opposed the Vietnam War.[1] Later, Chomsky and his colleague Edward S. Herman, a professor at the Wharton School at the University of Pennsylvania, produced a controversial book called *Manufacturing Consent: The Political Economy of the Mass Media*. In much the same way as Chomsky approached the innate nature of language, this work suggests that press treatment of issues and ideas is inevitably determined by the political and economic structure of the media. (The book was the basis for a 1992 documentary film titled "Manufacturing Consent: Noam Chomsky and the Media.") This was not the authors' first encounter with the topic: their 1979 book *The Political Economy of Human Rights* and various articles also have lambasted media for a complacent lack of self-criticism.[2]

supported by codes of ethics and books extolling the idea of a virtuous press crusading to rectify wrongs in a world where corruption and foul play were rampant. Journalism organizations ranging from publishers' and editors' societies to education groups also proclaimed concern for ethics and public accountability.

Media Criticism and Media Ethics

If there has been a consistent voice promoting media ethics over the years, it has been published *media criticism*, which dates back to the nineteenth century. Critics typically charged the press with violating common decency and obscuring the truth. Many American presidents have criticized the press for what they regarded as irresponsible reporting. For example, during the period of muckraking (Chapter 4) just after the turn of the century, journal-

What Chomsky would like to see is a science of pressology—that is, the study of journalism as a full-blown institution. He asserts that the press is largely responsible for public attitudes toward foreign policy, politics, and social issues, attitudes he believes are often wrong-headed or unexamined. This problem could be addressed, he thinks, if members of the public better understand the "manufacturing" process of American journalism—its structure, methods, philosophy, ethics, and general approach. As critic Carlin Romano says, Chomsky and Herman argue that U.S. media conform to a propaganda model whose purpose is to inculcate and defend the economic, social, and political agendas of "privileged groups that dominate the domestic society and the state." We are governed, they say, by a system of presuppositions that make radical criticism of the press difficult.[3]

The trouble is that Chomsky, never a man with ambivalent thoughts, has a rather blunt view of just how the press works. Many of his critics charge that his ideas are not based on the most rigorous research or understanding of media. Chomsky's view of media certainly is much criticized, and some argue that its selectivity and dogmatism have led to his diminished influence as a critic and writer. As an article in *Mother Jones* noted, Chomsky's work is no longer reviewed in the mainstream press. In this he is not unlike an earlier press critic, George Seldes, who also infuriated mainstream media to the point where he was virtually banished, he claims, from most newspapers and magazines for decades.

Although Chomsky's rather savage and uncompromising critique of the press is not widely accepted by people who manage and work in American media, it is a useful perspective that contributes to the literature of the ethics of mass communication. Ethics is a branch of philosophy engaging in critical thought and analysis; for the media, this includes close attention to the "text," or content, of communication as well as to the behavior and motivation of those who produce media.

1. See Chomsky, Noam (1928–), in *Webster's American Biographies* (Springfield, Mass.: Merriam-Webster, 1984), pp. 198–99.

2. Noam Chomsky and Edward S. Herman, *Manufacturing Consent: The Political Economy of the Mass Media* (New York: Pantheon, 1988).

3. Carlin Romano, "Slouching toward Pressology," *Tikkun*, 4, no. 3 (May–June 1989), pp. 41–123.

ists crusaded to clean up sweatshops and reform corrupt businesses and governments. Soon afterward, the press confronted considerable criticism led by President Theodore Roosevelt, who thought muckraking journalism was far too negative and bad for the nation. Critics such as Upton Sinclair began to attack the press for its internal inconsistencies and conflicts of interest, and even went so far as to claim that the press itself was corrupt and deliberately poisoning information. Much of this reproach concerned ethics, for rarely was it suggested that the transgressions of the press were illegal.

Journalism schools established in the years before World War I often had professional practice courses that promoted ideal or ethical behavior. The public outcry over ethics also led to a variety of codes and voluntary guidelines for the media. (The *Printer's Ink* statute aimed at deceptive advertising mentioned in Chapter 10 was one set.) The American Society of Newspaper Editors issued the "Canons of Journalism" in 1923. This was followed by similar codes promulgated by the American Newspaper Publishers Association, the Associated Press Managing Editors, various broadcast organizations and stations (including the CBS network), and public relations organizations. Over a fifty-year period from the 1920s to the 1970s, then, the bulk of American media developed ethical codes. Most were strictly voluntary but some were part of the work rules of media organizations. Employees who violate the codes of their organization today may be disciplined or even fired.

A Double Standard

Media criticism that centers on institutional, individual, or content-related ethics generally distinguishes between the editorial and business functions of the media. Editorial employees were once expected to avoid conflicts of interest, check their work for accuracy, and act as professionals at all times. Typically, this meant keeping their distance from such newsmakers as politicians and not mixing their personal views with the news. On the other hand, publishers and other business-side personnel faced no such prohibitions. They could seek public office and otherwise participate in community affairs without being considered guilty of a conflict of interest or unprofessional behavior.

This situation would later be challenged, largely unsuccessfully, by such scholar-critics as Philip Meyer, who wrote a book titled *Ethical Journalism* that urged an institutional model for media ethics in which all employees would have the same high standards. To Meyer, it was unthinkable that reporters and editors should be held to one standard with respect to conflict of interest, while advertising managers, publishers, and others were not.[4]

The Link to Individuals and Content

Media ethics is rarely concerned with abstract institutional behavior, but is instead tied to the "blood and guts" of daily decision-making and various disputes that later come to the attention of the public. Although journalistic inventions and fakery are not unknown in American history, the public was shocked in 1980 when it learned that *Washington Post* reporter Janet Cooke had faked a gripping story about "little Jimmy," an eight-year-old heroin addict in Washington's African-American community. No such person existed. Cooke claimed that the portrayal was a "composite." To its considerable embarrassment, the *Post* (which won a Pulitzer Prize for the story) had to admit the deception. The prize was returned, and the newspaper, to its credit, launched a major internal investigation of the ruse and released its findings to the public.

Later, the now-defunct National News Council, with a grant from the Twentieth Century Fund, produced a book about the "little Jimmy" controversy and its impact on American journalism and journalistic ethics in general. The deception shook American journalism to its roots, as people worried about the accuracy of stories in the press and the ethical standards of reporters. Commentators scrutinized the press's institutional responsibility to prevent this kind of behavior in the future, calling for routine personnel procedures and checking of résumés (which had sometimes been inflated or faked).

The same issue of public deception arose in 1989 when ABC News aired film footage allegedly showing a U.S. diplomat passing secrets to the Soviets. The grainy and authentic-looking footage was actually staged and featured actors as reporters! The story was based on allegations in news reports, but anchor Peter Jennings later apologized to the American people for the newscast, which was a deliberate deception. By the 1990s, simulations on network news were largely a thing of the past, though they are still common on other TV shows, especially tabloid fare such as "America's Most Wanted."

Of course, the fakery of Benjamin Franklin differs greatly from that of ABC News because news standards and social values have changed since colonial times. The press was a primitive instrument in Franklin's day; now, it is a large and powerful enterprise that has considerable influence through its information, opinion, and entertainment functions.

Dimensions of Ethics for the Media

Typically, media ethics have centered on three major issues: (1) *accuracy* and *fairness* in reporting and other activities, (2) the *behavior of reporters*, especially in relation to their sources, and (3) avoiding *conflict of interest*.

Accuracy and Fairness

It is often said that the first rule of journalism is "accuracy, accuracy, accuracy." Burton Benjamin, a longtime producer at CBS News, got caught up in an accuracy and fair-play conflict in the 1980s when CBS was accused of deliberately distorting information about the Vietnam War and General William Westmoreland in a news documentary. Criticism from outside the media as well as from media people themselves was so fierce that CBS executives commissioned Benjamin to investigate the charges and deliver a report. He found his network colleagues guilty of violating their own stated (and written) news standards and later wrote a book about the incident titled *Fair Play.*[5] In contrast, in the 1993 GM case mentioned earlier, NBC News commissioned outside lawyers to evaluate what happened.

Reports like Benjamin's (which are rare) and other critiques of media performance—favorable and unfavorable—constitute a kind of common law of ethics. For almost every ethical dilemma in the press, there is a history and context, but unfortunately the press has little institutional memory and often ignores the past or reinvents the proverbial wheel.

The Behavior of Reporters

The second area of ethical concern, the behavior of reporters, has to do with an important aspect of professionalism—whether reporters and other media personnel conduct themselves honestly and with integrity. This usu-

Another general concern about media ethics is that accuracy is sometimes sacrificed in the effort to get the story. That is, the media sometimes deliberately engage in fakery. For example, in 1993, NBC News produced a segment that showed a GM pickup truck bursting into flames when struck by another vehicle. It came out later that devices had been placed in the truck in order to start a fire upon impact. This faking of footage for a news report created a considerable controversy. (AP/Wide World Photos)

ally means being honest and aboveboard to *sources* about the purposes of gathering information. For many years, it was thought to be unethical to misrepresent oneself deliberately to obtain information—for example by claiming to be someone else such as a lawyer or police officer. Yet, the precise relationship that should exist between journalists and sources has never been fully understood or established. In a 1989 article in *The New Yorker*, Janet Malcolm scored her fellow journalist Joe McGinniss for misleading a famous news source, Dr. Jeffrey MacDonald, who was convicted of murdering his wife and children. As Malcolm wrote:

> Every journalist who is not too stupid or too full of himself to notice what is going on knows that what he does is morally indefensible. He is a kind of confidence man, preying on people's vanity, ignorance, or loneliness, gaining their trust and betraying them without remorse. Like the credulous widow who wakes up one day to find the charming young man and all her savings gone, so the consenting subject of a piece of nonfiction writing learns—when the article or book appears—his hard lesson. Journalists justify their treachery in various ways according to their temperaments. The more pompous talk about freedom of speech and "the public's right to know"; the least talented talk about Art; the seamiest murmur about earning a living.[6]

The cause for Malcolm's agitation was that she believed McGinniss had convinced MacDonald that he was his friend and would do a book that was beneficial to his case. The issue of whether a journalist seeking full cooperation from a news source is prone to deceiving the source was widely discussed at the time. People joined both sides, some condemning McGinniss and others accusing Malcolm of having committed similar breaches in the past. Malcolm's observations led to a lively nationwide debate in the journalistic community, in which the obligations, if any, of reporters to sources were thoroughly discussed. However, there was no clear resolution. Ironically, Malcolm lost a suit in 1993 in which she was accused of manufacturing quotes used in an article in *The New Yorker*.

Conflict of Interest

Conflict of interest is a third area of ethical concern. The term typically refers to engaging in activity that compromises one's integrity in the performance of one's professional or public duties. It is, for example, difficult to be engaged in partisan politics while writing impartially about politics. By the same token, media people have been urged to avoid cronyism, nepotism, and other conflicts that can compromise their integrity or give the appearance of such compromise. A closely related area is *checkbook journalism*, in which news organizations pay sources to give interviews. This is a violation of journalistic norms, although there are times when media people do it and defend the practice. In the case of newspaper people, conflict of interest usually involves a reporter or editor covering a story in which he or she has a personal stake—a family member may be involved, the reporter may do work on the side for a company being scrutinized, and so forth. Such conflict of interest is strongly discouraged, even to the point where some reporters are fired for it.

Alternative Approaches to Ethics

Standardized codes of media ethics are difficult to establish because there are few ethical imperatives that work in all situations. Also, most codes of ethics and guidelines are so general that they are not always applicable to specific circumstances. For these reasons and others, a system of situational ethics has long been advocated for the media.

Situational Ethics

A decision based on *situational ethics* is made not with respect to a universal or "one-size-fits-all" code, but within the context of the specific situation. The media person's actions are examined in light of all relevant circumstances. Within this perspective, media ethics, like all other ethical considerations, is linked to human choices that involve doing the right thing at the right time. For example, in following up a report on a political candidate's secret sex life, a reporter may invoke "the people's right to know" (about the character of their public servants) as an ethical reason for violating privacy and digging deeply into the individual's private affairs. In the case of a private citizen with similar secrets, however, that standard may not make sense. Publicizing details about such a person's private life may simply be unethical snooping.

The Continuing Search

The search for alternative answers to the question of what is ethical has been a topic of lively debate among journalists for a long time. One thing is certain: The issue of media ethics remains on the agenda and is often discussed both within and outside the communications industries. Many industry seminars probe ethical issues and dilemmas. Fred W. Friendly has produced a public television (PBS) series on ethics with several programs devoted to the media. And network correspondent Bernard Kalb started a media criticism show called "Informed Sources" on CNN in 1992.

Journalism schools have taught journalistic ethics intermittently since the 1920s and have established scores of new courses. There are at least ten relatively new texts on the topic. Various study centers and think tanks are working on media ethics issues, and some are singlemindedly devoted to this topic. There is even a quarterly, *Journal of Media Ethics*, which takes up important issues and offers case studies.

Most of the efforts to encourage media ethics have been less intellectual and more action-oriented. Earlier, we mentioned press councils—small groups of responsible citizens organized at the local, state, or national level as feedback mechanisms. Although only partially successful, these efforts nonetheless represent models for accountability and ethical review.

In one form or another, various codes of ethics have spread to virtually every part of the communications industries. Once mainly in the purview of journalism, there are now formalized ethical standards in advertising, public relations, opinion polling, market research, sports writing, and other areas. That they exist, however, does not mean that they will be followed. These generalized documents are not usually enforced or enforceable, but they still represent symbolic concern about ethics.

Credibility Studies and Market Research

Perhaps the most important efforts to promote media ethics have been *credibility studies*, which probe public attitudes about the news media and dredge up concerns and problems ranging from sensationalism to reporters' rudeness. A media credibility movement emerged in the 1980s because it was perceived that news organizations in particular were losing ground as believable and trustworthy agencies. This probably stemmed from worry that a loss of credibility would both impair the medium's moral authority and undermine its economic might. At a time of feverish competition among print and broadcast media for audiences and advertising, there was real reason to deal with matters of credibility and ethics.

Market research is also a force that perhaps unwittingly promotes media ethics. Market and audience research provides media organizations and others in the communications industries with certain kinds of feedback about public tastes, preferences, and concerns. Often this feedback centers on matters that have an ethical connection.

The issue of television's preoccupation with violence has been debated since the medium first entered American households. Thousands of research studies have suggested that viewing violence can lead some children to behave more aggressively. Whether this is true or not, the majority of Americans believe that violence on television is excessive. In 1993, network proposals to provide warning labels for programs with obscene language, violence, or explicit sex were welcomed by some, but seemed like a half-hearted compromise to many critics. (By Dana Summers; © 1993, Washington Post Writers Group. Reprinted with permission.)

As we suggested, a concern with ethics now stretches across all media fields. Opinion makers—whether talk show hosts, media consultants, advertising executives, or entertainment producers—have standards and codes of conduct. Authors have ethical concerns and so do those who produce and manufacture their work. It is still most common to tie ethics to professional rather than to technical functions, but even that distinction has broken down. Television camera operators had better have ethical standards, or the work they direct might be tainted. The same is true with printers, operators of desk-top publishing systems, cartoonists, and others. It is true that the ethics of each of these categories of people will differ, reflecting varied concerns and values.

Ethics, Technology, and the Future

New technologies of communication, especially in the last ten years, have raised a variety of ethical questions and controversies. In 1989, following the U.S. invasion of Panama, a split-screen device allowed TV viewers to see President Bush's news conference on one part of the screen while the unloading of soldiers' bodies in caskets was featured on the other. The result was an ethical fiasco. The news conference was jocular and amusing, and the smiling President did not know that viewers were at the same time seeing a somber and tragic scene. It was little wonder that the broadcast was much criticized as a thoughtless use of technology. It embarrassed both the President and the media and brought unnecessary grief to those mourning for the fallen soldiers.

Other ethical breaches using technology are linked to privacy, including hidden cameras and microphones and the use of databases to mine personal information about individuals. For example, with distant sensing cameras, it is easy to "spy" on news sources. Various audio and video recorders make this even easier.

Satellite communication allows for easy movement over national boundaries and into the midst of world crises and conflicts. This can result in ethical chaos. In December 1992, a circuslike atmosphere occurred when U.S. Marines waded ashore in an amphibious landing at Mogadishu, Somalia, to begin their mission of protecting food shipments to the starving. While the Marines were following their carefully rehearsed procedures for large-scale assault landings, they were met on the beach by one hundred or more journalists with bright TV lights and a forest of microphones that were shoved into the faces of the landing party. The whole event was ridiculed by elements of the press, even though both the journalists and the Marines were carrying on their normal activities.

Because it is now relatively simple to capture news events on video cameras, many people have footage for sale. They range from amateur local "news hounds," who tape potential news events and try to hawk their footage to TV stations, to free-lancers who are more professional but nonetheless not under the control of an established news organization. Determining the veracity of this material and the qualifications and proficiency of the person who presents it is not easy.

This has led to various deliberate or inadvertent problems for television. Just after the nuclear accident at Chernobyl, for example, American networks bought taped reports purportedly showing the crippled Ukrainian plant. Actually, it was a nuclear power plant in Italy. It was alleged in 1989 that CBS anchor Dan Rather broadcast free-lance footage from Afghanistan that was faked and done in Pakistan. Such examples abound in both print and electronic media, and technology enhances the ability to deceive. For example, a device called the "electronic darkroom" makes it possible to create authentic-looking pictures of couples embracing, although the people have never met each other.

These are only a few examples of ethical problems raised by new communications technologies. The speed and reach of these new tools makes them both liberating and dangerous devices. Again, they affect virtually all aspects of the media industries and much of society.

As the twentieth century draws to a close, much of the discussion of media ethics is still locked firmly in the matrix of the past. However, it is also clear that much of the debate charts new ground and moves beyond established rules. Considerable thought, therefore, must go into determining (1) what should be codified as a lasting part of institutional and individual rules carried over from the past, (2) what should be left to situational decision-making in order to maximize freedom of expression, and (3) how ethical considerations need to be re-evaluated to take into account new technologies. Whatever those decisions, any system of accountability—no matter how modest—always impinges on freedom of choice. Of course, sometimes that infringement is warranted and even desirable.[7]

An important principle for the future is that voluntary methods of resolving ethical dilemmas are typically preferable to legalistic means by which problems eventually end up in the courts. Although many ethical matters are not immediately legal concerns, in this litigious society, one might guess that if they are not they soon might be. To date most of the impetus for media ethics has come internally from the media industries themselves and from communications education. This might not always be the case. It is easy to imagine courts or legislative bodies mandating a system of ethics that would be onerous, especially if it were developed during a period of unpopularity for the media. In fact, the idea of licensing journalists and giving them a required code of ethics has actually been proposed. It was quickly dismissed, however, because of the seeming violation of the First Amendment.

Today, media ethics is something of a cottage industry, the subject of scores of professional seminars held for journalists, broadcasters, public relations people, and others. Many universities now offer courses in media ethics and have a rich literature on which to draw—consisting of not only many books, monographs, and articles, but also case studies that point to the dilemmas and decisions that people face in a modern society, many of them relating directly to ethics.

That cottage industry may be leading to significant changes in media ethics. Communications law scholar Donald Gillmor maintains that such changes come in cycles. In the 1920s, there was an ethics movement in the media, which waned and later resurfaced about every twenty years. Perhaps with a continually improving system of information storage and retrieval, that will not happen again. Ethical dilemmas abound, and they seem to compel enough human attention from both media professionals and the consumers of mass communications that there will likely be a period of maturation and development for this new and still uncharted field.

Chapter Review

- Some critics ridicule the idea that competitive and profit-driven media can operate within an ethical framework. But most people disagree, saying that no media system can exist very long without public confidence, which requires accurate, honest, and believable communications.

- Ethical behavior in a general sense simply means that people should not lie, steal, cheat, or commit other antisocial acts. Ethics is doing what is right, but the problem is that "right" is defined differently by different people. Thus, the need exists for serious attention to media ethics in a society increasingly concerned about the ethics of all occupational groups and professions.

- Media ethics is not an obscure or irrelevant topic, but something that arises daily as citizens observe the way media organizations relate to their communities as participants, observers, and critics. Ethical dilemmas also arise over the content of the media—whether it is entertainment, news, opinion, or advertising—as well as over the behavior of media people.

- Under the First Amendment to the Constitution of the United States, there is no requirement that the media be fair, responsible, or accurate. The courts have stated this quite explicitly, yet increasingly a higher standard for media performance is evident in libel cases and other legal actions against the mass and specialized media.

- Institutional media ethics have evolved considerably since the early years of American journalism. The early press was often scurrilous, making unwarranted partisan attacks on political figures with little regard for truth or accuracy. Later, a sensational press played on the public's morbid curiosity to attract readers.

- A consistent voice promoting media ethics over the years has been media criticism. Critics typically charged the press with violating common decency and obscuring the truth. This has kept public attention focused on the need for ethical standards.

- Typically, media ethics has centered on three major issues: (1) accuracy and fairness in reporting and other activities, (2) the behavior of reporters, especially in relation to their sources, and (3) avoidance of conflict of interest.

- Standardized codes of media ethics are difficult to establish because there are few ethical imperatives that work in all situations. Also, most codes of ethics and guidelines are so general that they are not always applicable to specific circumstances. For these reasons and others, a system of situational ethics has long been advocated for the media.

- In one form or another, various codes of ethics have been developed in virtually every part of the communications industries. Once mainly the purview of journalism, there are now formalized ethical standards in advertising, public relations, opinion polling, market research, sports writing, and other areas. That they exist, however, does not mean that they will be followed.

- New technologies of communication, especially in the last ten years, have raised a variety of ethical questions and controversies. The speed and reach of these new tools make them both liberating and dangerous devices. They affect virtually all aspects of the media industries and much of society.

- An important principle for the future is that voluntary methods of resolving ethical dilemmas are typically preferable to legalistic ones. To date, most of the impetus for media ethics has come internally from the media industries themselves and from communications education. This might not always be the case.

Notes and References

1. Everette E. Dennis, Donald M. Gillmor, and Theodore Glasser, eds., *Media Freedom and Accountability* (Westport, Conn.: Greenwood, 1990).
2. "Dear Reader—Facts Must Not Give Way Even When Fiction Is 'Clearer Than Truth,'" *The Post Standard*, Syracuse, New York, March 4, 1992, p. A6.
3. Edmund B. Lambeth, *Committed Journalism: An Ethic for the Profession* (Bloomington: Indiana University Press, 1986).
4. Philip Meyer, *Ethical Journalism* (White Plains: Longman, 1987).
5. Burton Benjamin, *Fair Play* (New York: Harper & Row, 1988).
6. Janet Malcolm's work first appeared in *The New Yorker*, March 13 and March 20, 1989, and was later published as *The Journalist and the Murderer* (New York: Knopf, 1990).
7. John C. Merrill, *The Dialectic in Journalism: Toward a Responsible Use of Press Freedom* (Baton Rouge: Louisiana State University Press, 1989).

Glossary

Account executive Advertising agency executive who arranges meetings between a client's executives and the account management director and other agency personnel to discuss potential advertising objectives.

Account management director Advertising agency executive who is responsible for relations between the agency and a client.

Accumulation of minimal effects theory The view that the impact of any one message on any specific person may be minimal, but consistent, persistent, and corroborated (between media) messages result in minor changes among audiences that gradually add up over time to produce significant changes in a society or culture.

Accuracy principle The principle that the lower the level of fidelity between the intended meanings of the sender and the interpreted meanings of the receiver is, the less effective the act of communication will be.

Activation The process of getting people to do what they are predisposed to do by their social category memberships. For example, one effect of a mass media voting campaign is to persuade (activate) voters who are predisposed to support a political candidate to go to the polls and vote.

Adoption of innovation theory The view that the media influence social change by bringing innovations, whether borrowed or invented, to the attention of potential adopters, who often, in turn, take up and begin to use new cultural items on the basis of information that is supplied.

Adversarial approach (to journalism) A style of reporting that sees news as information needed by the public and that emphasizes the watchdog role of the press—even at the expense of profits. Contrast with *marketing approach*.

Advertising A form of controlled communication that attempts to persuade consumers, through the use of a variety of appeals and strategies, to buy or use a particular product or service. Advertising messages are often presented via mass media.

Advertising agency An organization that provides, for a fee, creative and research assistance and advertising strategies to clients.

Advertising department In a newspaper organization, the part of the staff that handles both display advertising from merchants and businesses and the classified section containing such announcements as apartments for rent, used autos, and help wanted. In a store or business, the part of the staff that produces advertising for the firm's products.

Advocacy style An alternative journalistic approach in which the journalist openly advocates or promotes a cause or position.

Advocate Media's role of taking a stand on issues and representing the people when other institutions need an independent evaluation.

Agenda-setting theory of the press A set of statements showing why audiences for news come to think some stories are more important than others. This theory predicts that if a particular issue is presented prominently in terms of time and space by the press, the public will come to believe it is important.

Applied research Research that focuses on some practical problem, either for public knowledge or for private use.

Audience-assessment information Data about readers, listeners, or viewers in terms of size, composition, interests, tastes, and purchasing power. The data are gathered by various agencies and services using such means as circulation audits, ratings, and polls.

Audience research A study of the audience to be reached, including the numbers of people in various demographic groups who see and respond to a medium or to advertising.

Audiometer Device attached to a television that records how long a television set is on and what channel the set is tuned to. Data from the device are delivered to a central computer for analysis.

Audion A type of vacuum tube, said to have been invented by Lee De Forest in 1906, based on a three-element circuit, allowing more sophisticated circuits and applications and the amplification of radio signals.

Auteurs Movie directors who have created films with a distinctive style.

Authorized newspaper A newspaper whose content is controlled and screened prior to publication by a governmental authority.

Barter syndication The process by which television program syndicators sell their wares to independent, non-network stations.

Basic research Scientific investigation undertaken to advance knowledge, rather than to increase anyone's profits. It is usually conducted by people in the academic world and may be descriptive or have the goal of investigating a theory.

Beat reporters Journalists assigned to particular areas of societal activity, such as courts, police, schools, or centers of government.

Blacklisting The practice of listing people for being involved in some activity, such as being Communists, and threatening to boycott advertisers that sponsor shows or any other media from hiring those on the list.

Block booking Outlawed studio practice that required theater owners to take and show a set of studio films (both bad and good)—or receive none at all.

Blues A form of folk music, originating among poor blacks, that expressed feelings about the difficult experiences of everyday life. During the early twentieth century, blues became a form of popular music.

Boogie-woogie A style of jazz music with a fast-paced rhythm, played with eight beats to a bar and with heavy *ostinato* bass notes.

Boutique agency A small advertising agency that has more limited goals and fewer services than a full-service agency. This type of agency has a creative department and may hire other agencies or groups to provide other kinds of advertising services to clients.

Business advertising Special advertising directed to an industry or business, as in trade magazines and trade shows.

Business department (newspaper) The portion of newspaper organization that handles such things as accounting, personnel, and building maintenance.

Business magazines Magazines that cover particular industries, trades, or professions and go mainly to people in those fields.

CAIR Acronym for Computer-Assisted Investigative Reporting. The use of systematic strategies for computer analysis of the electronic records of government agencies at all levels to develop news stories about their activities.

Change of venue The movement of a court trial to another location under the assumption that jurors in the chosen location will not have been influenced by prejudicial pretrial publicity.

Checkbook journalism The practice, in violation of journalistic ethics, of paying individuals who are sources of news for interviews.

Cinema vérité A style of film making, most often associated with documentaries, which uses spontaneous, direct filming of events.

Circulation The number of copies of a magazine or newspaper sold through paid subscriptions plus other sales by mail or single copies.

Circulation department The portion of newspaper organization that is responsible for arranging for home or mail delivery or sale by street vendors.

City editor (metropolitan editor) The newspaper employee responsible for news coverage in a community or city, including making assignments for local reporters.

Codes of law Formal (written) guidelines for behavior that specify punishments for deviance. One of the earliest examples is the Babylonian king Hammurabi's code of 282 laws, developed almost 4,000 years ago.

Commercial newspapers An early form of American newspaper that recorded commercial transactions and business matters, such as shipping and foreign economic news, which mainly interested merchants.

Commercialism The determination of a company's offerings based on a focus on profitability.

Community (grassroots) press Weekly newspapers that originated as rural or suburban papers featuring life-style stories, local events, or subscribers' correspondence. Urban weeklies concentrate on neighborhoods or review topics such as politics and the arts.

Composition (of population) The number of people in the population of a certain age, gender, education, income, race, ethnicity, or other demographic category.

Compositor A company that sets manuscript into type.

Compounded selectivity Selective interpretation of an event that occurs when a reporter interviews a witness of an event who has put together an account based on his or her own unique interpretations and biases. The reporter then reinterprets that event from the witnesses' accounts, using his or her own interpretations and biases, compounding the selectivity. See also *selectivity*.

Concept A named category of objects, events, or situations, as defined by their distinguishing qualities or attributes.

Consultant (in radio or television news) Individual or firm who, for a fee, analyzes a station's news operation and suggests ways to improve the station's ratings and share.

Consumer behavior research Studies of consumers that help firms learn who are potential customers and what kinds of advertising are likely to reach them. Research may include how consumers' needs, drives, and motives affect their buying and how their perceptions of advertisements vary.

Consumer magazine Type of magazine that is readily available to the public by subscription or through direct purchase at newsstands.

Content analysis Set of systematic and objective procedures for the quantitative study of the characteristics of messages, used mainly to reveal underlying patterns in the information that media present to their audiences.

Continuing news News events that have no clear beginning or end, but are an ongoing series of related events. For example, the disposal of nuclear waste issue provides continuing news of protests, counter-protests, court cases, and political debates.

Control group A set of subjects used in a research study that receive either no treatment or a neutral experience that has little to do with the variables under study. This group is compared with the *experimental group* before and after the study to see if the experimental group's treatment had a measurable effect.

Control variable Factor, condition, or situation that must be identified and measured or controlled in such a way that it does not affect the cause-and-effect sequence being studied in a research project.

Controlled observation An observational procedure that limits the influence of errors and is as precise as possible.

Convenience sample A means of selecting subjects for study in which the researcher simply uses those who are handy, for example, students in a college class.

Convention A well-established rule agreed upon by those involved.

Conversion The process of changing a person's beliefs from one position to another. For example, a study of an election campaign found that the mass media had limited ability to convert a person's support from one candidate or political party to another.

Copy editor The print media employee responsible for editing a manuscript. Some work in the newspaper industry; others edit copy for magazines and books.

Correlation (from co-relation) A relationship between two factors in which changes in one variable are paralleled by similar changes in the other. That is, when one rises, so does the other; when one falls, so does the other. This relationship does not necessarily imply cause-and-effect.

Correlation function (of mass communication) A medium's role of interpreting society and its parts, projecting trends, and explaining news by bringing together fragmented facts.

Creative department The part of an advertising agency that develops ideas for an advertising campaign and designs the advertisements.

Credibility studies Research that probes public attitudes and concerns about the news media, such as concerns about completeness, accuracy, sensationalism, or reporters' rudeness.

Critics People who judge a film by artistic and theoretical criteria and try to ascertain its social importance.

Crystal sets Early, very basic, radio receivers that could be put together at home from simple parts.

Cuneiform writing A system of writing developed by the ancient Sumerians. The characters were made by jabbing a wedge-shaped stick into a pad of soft clay to form little drawings (or later) stylized symbols.

Curve of adoption Patterns of adoption and use of inventions introduced into society or borrowed from other societies. Typically, the accumulation of adoptions over time forms an s-shaped curve. See also *adoption of innovation theory*.

Daguerreotype The first practical form of photographs that came into wide use. Produced first by Louis Daguerre in 1839, the process imprinted an image on a polished copper plate coated in silver iodide. The pictures were clear and sharp but no copies could be made as there was no negative.

Damage control Diverting public attention from (or explaining away) a difficult or embarrassing situation after its occurrence.

Data Sensory observations obtained in research projects and recorded as symbols, often numerical in nature.

Data analysis The manipulation of data (usually by computers today) to obtain various calculations, reports, and tables.

Data entry The physical process of putting data into a form readable by a computer. Data entry may be done by typing in information on a keyboard or by using an optical scanner or other device.

Data-processing The analysis of data, usually in terms of statistical procedures, so as to identify central tendencies, variability, contrasts, and relationships between variables.

Delayed feedback Reverse communication that has a time lag, such as letters to the editor or phone calls to a studio following a broadcast.

Demographic characteristics and trends Characteristics of the population such as age, gender, income, education, race and ethnicity, family composition and place of residence, and the changes in relative percentages of individuals identifiable by certain characteristics.

Dependent variable A factor, condition, or situation that is influenced or caused by one or more prior conditions, situations, or factors. See *independent variable*.

Detailed coverage and analytic function Newspaper's function to provide detailed information about news events, such as relevant background details, explanations of related events, and analyses of their importance and implications.

Developing news News events that occur in stages, like the acts of a play, and that are covered by a series of news stories. Developing news will eventually come to an end and no longer be newsworthy. An example is a series on a crime. The stages might be the arrest of a suspect, that person's arraignment, the trial, and sentencing.

Diffusion The increasing use of an innovation in a society as larger and larger numbers of members adopt the item.

Diffusion of the news The transmission of news through word-of-mouth networks.

Direct broadcast satellite A technology that uses a small disk, about the size of a large dinner plate, to receive transmissions directly from networks via a satellite transmission, rather than from local stations.

Direct mail Advertising medium using letters, brochures, electronic mail, automatic telephone messages, and fax and video appeals.

Dixieland jazz A form of popular music in which each musician improvises while rigidly maintaining both the beat and the basic harmony. It became very popular about 1915 and remained so through the 1920s.

Dual identity of newspapers The two, sometimes conflicting, functions of a newspaper: (1) to serve as a quasi-public institution charged with being the watchdog of the public interest and often an antagonist of government or other powerful forces, and (2) to make a profit while functioning as a member of the business community.

Editor-in-chief (editor, executive editor) The head of the editorial department of a newspaper, who is responsible for all the paper's content, except advertising.

Editorial operations The portion of the newspaper business that includes those who acquire and process the information going into the paper's news stories and other editorial (nonadvertising) content.

Editorial page editor (associate editor) The newspaper employee responsible for the editorial page and the "op ed" page; reports directly to the editor-in-chief.

Electronic advertising Advertising displayed in online services used by personal computer owners.

Elite art Artistic products that are technically and thematically complex, highly individualistic, and inventive. These products represent high culture.

Empirical observations Literally, observations that are "apprehended by the senses," rather than being based on tradition, logic, or other sources. Such observations are essential to scientists when conducting research.

Encode (encoding) To formulate and produce intended meanings in media messages by the use of words, visual images, sounds, and other means.

Entertainment function Providing diversion to an audience as opposed to explanation or interpretation. For example, newspapers amuse and gratify readers with human interest stories and such content as crossword puzzles, recipes, gardening hints, sports scores, and advice.

Establishment The process by which new words and new meanings become part of the language system through audience exposure to media portrayals of the meanings of words.

Ethnic press Both foreign-language papers and papers written in English but aimed at a particular national, racial, cultural, or ethnic group. Such newspapers have a long history among immigrants to the United States.

Executive order An order issued by the President that does not have to be approved by Congress. For example, President Reagan issued a series of such orders intended to prevent leaks of information by government employees.

Experimental condition The form of treatment given in a research project (the independent variable). The experimental group is studied before and after exposure to the experimental condition and compared to a control group that does not receive the treatment.

Experimental group The set of subjects in an experiment who receive some form of treatment (the independent variable). They are compared with the control group both before and after the experiment to see if the treatment produced some effect.

Extension The expansion of meanings that are attached to familiar symbols, which can occur as an outcome of media portrayals. For example, the word "crack" used to mean "a physical defect in a surface," but now it also refers to a dangerous drug.

External communication Communication via the mass media to an audience or to particular segments of the population outside an organization.

Feature syndicates Commercial groups that contract with publishers to provide a great many of the features used in today's newspapers, such as national and international news, editorial cartoons, comic strips, columns, and crossword puzzles. Syndication is common in broadcasting as well.

Feedback A reverse communication by the receiver back to the sender that indicates to the sender whether the message is getting through or needs to be modified for clarification.

Feedback principle The principle that if adequate feedback (reverse communication) is provided by the receiver, fidelity will be increased.

Field experiment Experimental research in which sizable numbers of people in day-to-day circumstances are subjected to treatments in more or less normal settings. Large-scale field experiments may have entire communities as subjects.

Field research Qualitative research design, also called observational study, in which an investigator lives or works with subjects or is a participant observer.

Focus group Group usually composed of up to twenty or so people selected because they have certain desired characteristics thought to be significant as they examine or discuss a product. For example, a focus group may be used to review and discuss a movie before the final edit and recommend changes to it.

Folk art Artistic products and styles developed spontaneously as part of the traditions of ordinary people; these products are unsophisticated, localized, and natural.

Format Organization or sequence in which facts are presented in a news story or other type of media message.

Full-service agency An advertising agency that performs virtually every aspect of the advertising process for its clients—including planning and researching advertising, creating advertising and contacting the appropriate media to present the advertising, and coordinating the work of salespeople, distributors, and retailers.

Gatekeepers Those who select which news items, music, or other content for a medium will be presented to the public.

Gatekeeping Process of selection of items for release in a medium (such as newspapers and television news broadcasts).

General American culture The overall pattern of living in the United States that has resulted from the mixing of diverse ethnic groups in ways that reduce their differences.

General assignment reporters Journalists who cover a wide range of news as it happens, regardless of the topic.

Generalization A conclusion from research indicating a trend or tendency that is supported by factual evidence.

Genre A category of films with the same basic story type, including typical characters, settings, and plots. Examples include the gangster film, war film, musical, and Western genres.

Group norms Generalized rules that all members of a particular group are expected to follow.

Hard news News about events that occur at a particular point in time and must be reported in a timely manner, so as not to diminish their value. Examples include murders, robberies, and disasters. Contrast with *soft news*.

HDTV High-definition television. A broadcasting and receiving system that provides for a much sharper image and wider picture than that of standard contemporary television sets.

High culture taste public Those who like the products of serious writers, artists, and composers and value innovation and experimentation with form, substance, method, overt content, and covert symbolism.

HUT Households using television. The number of households in an area with the television on, divided by the total number of televisions, multiplied by 100.

Hypothesis A formal statement that poses a possible relationship between independent and dependent variables to be studied in a research project.

Identification (in modeling theory) Circumstance in which an observer approves of the portrayal of behavior and either wants to be like the model or believes that he or she is already like the model.

Ideographic writing (pictographic writing) A form of writing that uses simple graphic representations or symbols with standardized meanings. For example, a wavy line could indicate "water," a foot could indicate "walking."

Incidental learning Unplanned, unintentional acquisition of ideas and behavior from media presentations designed as entertainment.

Independent public relations counselor (agency) A person or organization that operates much like an advertising agency or law firm, representing clients by conducting public relations activities, including research and publications design.

Independent variable A factor, condition, or situation that is independently controlled and that influences or causes some consequent or dependent condition. See *dependent variable*.

Indies Small, independent record companies, which have long played a significant role in the development of popular music. Although called "independent," these companies do depend on wholesalers for distributing, promoting, and selling the music they produce.

Individual differences Differences among people in their personal psychological organization of beliefs, attitudes, values, tastes, and interests.

Information (as in physical information) Events in the real world that conquer time or distance and can be apprehended by the receiver. For example, written communication consists of patterns of light that form visual stimuli.

Information function Newspaper's activities in informing readers with news, weather forecasts, and stock market reports.

Infotainment A merging of information and entertainment in news presentation.

Innovation New technologies, ideas, fads, fashions, or forms of behavior that are borrowed or developed by a society and possibly adopted. See *adoption of innovation theory*.

Instantaneous rating reports Reports indicating the audience size at a particular moment.

Institutional advertising Advertising with the goal of associating a corporation with a selfless, responsible image.

Intermediary Media's role of serving as a bridge between society's institutions, such as business, education, and labor.

Internal communication Communication within an organization directed to its members.

Interpersonal transmission Word-of-mouth telling and retelling of messages.

Interval measurement Classification of objects or variables using a scale that has units of equal size; the scale does not include a true zero point.

Invention Process by which an individual or group brings together elements that already exist in the culture, putting them together into some new pattern (innovation).

Inverted pyramid style Format for news stories, originally developed for wire transmittal. The reporter explains who, what, where, why, and how and gives the most important elements first, then the next important, and so on.

Investigative reporters Journalists whose probes help the press fulfill its vital watchdog role.

Investigative reporting News-gathering style, begun in the nineteenth century, in which reporters probe deeply into a situation and assemble evidence to expose unusual, unethical, or illegal activities.

Jitterbug Fast, vigorous kind of dancing that became popular in the 1940s.

Journalistic style The way in which a particular set of facts is combined into a news story. For example, stories can be written in a sensational, objective, or advocacy style.

Juke box A coin-operated electronic record player that offered a variety of the latest songs and allowed patrons to see the discs being changed. By the late 1930s, the juke box was found in restaurants, drugstores, taverns, and beer halls, where it helped pump new energy into the popular music industry.

Kinetoscope One-viewer-only peep-show device developed by Thomas Edison to exhibit his moving pictures.

Kitsch Art forms that are low-quality, unsophisticated, simplistic, trivial, and in bad taste. Many media critics charge that the demands for entertainment have resulted in a constant flow of kitsch in the form of popular culture.

Laboratory simulation Experimental research in which small groups are exposed to various independent variables under highly controlled conditions in a laboratory-like setting. The research aims to reproduce (simulate) some real-life social process or condition.

Law of large numbers The view that the greater the size of an audience for a medium, the greater is the profit that the medium can make for advertisers and thus for the owners of the medium.

Libel The act of deliberately and maliciously publicizing untruths that tend to damage someone's reputation.

Life-style research Studies of trends in living patterns and buying behavior. These studies inform advertisers about changing attitudes and life-styles of potential consumers at different ages.

Linear communication model A model of the process of communicating that divides the process into six stages: deciding what to communicate, encoding intended meanings, transmitting the message, perceiving the incoming message, decoding and interpreting the message, and influencing the receiver.

Lobbying Attempting to influence legislators to introduce or vote for measures favorable to the lobbyist's organization.

Longitudinal project A research study that follows the behavior of a group of subjects over an extended period of time, such as several years. The study systematically notes changes in the behavior that can be attributed to known influences.

Low culture taste public Those who prefer unsophisticated art and media content with action (often violent) and slapstick-type humor.

Lower-middle taste public Those who prefer artistic products in which old-fashioned virtue is rewarded and that do not have complex personalities nor philosophical conflicts. The majority of the public falls into this category.

Magazine Originally, a storehouse of different items, usually military supplies, explosives, etc. In reference to the printed medium, a collection of writings about various topics. Magazines are published periodically, but less frequently than newspapers, and are usually manufactured in a different format with better paper and binding.

Magic bullet theory Theory that predicted immediate, direct, and uniform effects on everyone who received a media message. Thus, communications were seen as "magic bullets" penetrating every eye and ear in the same way. This theory is no longer considered valid by scholars, but many segments of the public still believe it to be true.

Majuscule letters Capital letters which we continue to use today. They were developed by the Romans and were kept in the upper case of type by early printers.

Managing editor The newspaper employee responsible for the day-to-day operation of the newsroom, including hiring, firing, and supervising specialized editors. The managing editor reports directly to the editor-in-chief.

Market The people who live in a given geographical area or city and who can be reached by a medium, such as television or radio.

Marketing approach (to journalism) Approach to journalism that pursues the goal of maximizing profits by selling news as a product, devoting considerable resources to audience research, and sharply limiting public service. Contrast with *adversarial approach*.

Mass communication An essentially linear, multistage process in which professional communicators design and use media to disseminate messages widely, rapidly, and continuously in attempts to influence large and diverse audiences in a variety of ways.

Mass media Devices used to accomplish mass communication. The major mass media in modern society are print (including books, magazines, and newspapers), film (motion pictures), and broadcasting (radio, television, cable, and videocassettes).

Meaning A sender's intended understanding of an outgoing message and a receiver's interpretation of that message. A communicator assigns meanings to symbols by searching his or her memory for a specific trace configuration of experience appropriate to the perceived symbol.

Meaning construction theory of media portrayals The view that the meanings people hold for various words are strongly influenced by their exposure to the content of mass communications. These meanings, in turn, shape people's understandings of, and actions in, situations with which they must cope in the real world.

Measurement The use of numerically based rules to convert subjective sensory experiences (observation of variables) into data symbols, usually of numerical form that can be manipulated mathematically.

Media department The part of an advertising agency that selects specific media to be used for particular ads.

Media dependency theory An explanation of the relationship between the content of the mass media, the nature of society, and the communication behavior of audiences. It states that people in urban-industrial societies are dependent on mass communication for the information they need to make many kinds of decisions.

Media influence Changes in people's beliefs, attitudes, or behavior brought about by messages received from the media. These changes can range from trivial to profound.

Media research Advertising study of the particular characteristics of each medium and what it can do, including comparisons of the pulling power and persuasiveness of various media.

Media service organizations Specialized organizations that buy space in the media at reasonable rates and then sell the use of the space to advertising agencies. These organizations may have expertise in choosing the best times to display advertising for particular kinds of products.

Medical model The assumption that a problem behavior (such as alcoholism, drug addiction, or crime) is a manifestation of a "sickness" that was acquired by the individual (and can be cured by treatment), rather than a deliberate moral choice or a manifestation of other causes, such as a curse indicating possession by demons or inherited bad blood.

Medium (plural, *media*) Any object or device used for communicating a message by moving physical information over distance or preserving it through time. The medium links the sender to the receiver. A medium may be as simple as a carved stone or as complex as a satellite-linked television system.

Medium of public record Special function of newspapers to publish a legislative body's acts, resolves, advertisements, and notices.

Memory A function based in the central nervous system that allows humans to recover prior experience, meanings, and rules and that is essential to communication.

Migration Population movement from one area to another.

Minuscule letters Non-capital, or lower-case, letters developed by the Romans and refined under the influence of Charlemagne in the eighth century.

Modeling theory The view that one way in which people acquire new modes of acting is by observing behavior portrayed by other people or in the mass media. Such behavior is adopted if the individual identifies with those portraying the behavior and receives positive reinforcement for trying out the behavior. Modeling theory is an application of more general social learning theory.

Muckraking A term applied by President Theodore Roosevelt to characterize journalists whose reporting aimed at exposing the dark and seamy side of political, social, and economic conditions in the United States.

Multistage area sampling A process in which samples (subsets) of a large population are selected, and then samples within those samples, and then samples within the smaller samples. For example, researchers might select a sample of states, then a sample of counties within the states, and then a sample of townships or other smaller units such as households within the townships.

National advertising Advertising in a medium used across the country and aimed at a national audience.

New journalism Alternative reporting format, begun in the 1960s, that used fiction-writing techniques, such as scene setting, extended dialogue, personal point of view, interior monologues (the thoughts of news sources), and composite characters, rather than actual ones.

News Current or fresh knowledge about an event or subject that is gathered, processed, and disseminated via a medium to a significant number of interested people.

News distortion theory of the press The view that the meanings constructed by news audiences often have limited correspondence to the facts of reality because news reports are often characterized by selectivity, omissions, and distortions due to limits on the press. As a result, people may behave in ways unrelated to the original events and situations.

News editor The newspaper employee responsible for supervising copy editors, preparing copy for insertion into the newspaper, designing pages, and deciding placement of stories.

News hole The portion of the newspaper that is actually devoted to the news of the day; generally about 20 percent of the paper.

News process A series of steps or stages by which accounts of events flow from reporters through news organizations and media to the public.

News release A prepared handout provided to reporters by an organization to summarize the issuer's version of some event or situation.

News values The criteria used by news personnel to judge the newsworthiness of a story. Criteria include potential impact of the event on the audience, timeliness, prominence of those involved, proximity of the event to the audience, bizarreness, amount of conflict, and currency (of public concern).

Newsboys Youngsters who bought newspapers in lots of a hundred and sold them for a profit.

Newsmagazine A term coined by Henry Luce and Briton Haddon when they founded *Time*; refers to a national magazine that provides weekly summaries of news and interpretation.

Newspaper A publication produced regularly on a mechanical printing press that provides news of general or specialized interest, is available to people of all walks of life and is readable by them, and is stable over time.

Newsworthiness The potential interest level of a news story.

Nipkow disk An early technology in the transmission of images. Developed by Paul Nipkow in 1884, the rotating disk had small holes arranged in a spiral pattern. Aiming a strong light at the disk, so that light passed through the holes, produced a very rapid scanning effect. The disk could produce electrical impulses that could be sent along a wire so as to transmit pictures.

Nominal measurement Classification of objects into non-numerical (named) categories; for example, people can be classified as male or female, married or single.

Objective journalism Reporting format that generally separates fact from opinion, presents an emotionally detached view of the news, and strives for fairness and balance.

Observational learning The acquisition of ideas, behavior, knowledge, attitudes, or values by watching the actions of someone else. See *modeling theory*.

Observational study Qualitative research design, also called field research, in which an investigator lives or works with subjects or is a participant observer.

One-reelers Early motion pictures that lasted ten to twelve minutes and told a story; they were produced on a variety of topics ranging from prize fights to religious plays.

Opinion leaders People who pay particular attention to the media, thus becoming more knowledgeable about news events, and who influence others through their interpretation of the news as they pass it on.

Option An agreement giving a producer the right to purchase a story at a later date.

Ordinal measurement The classification of objects by some quantitative attribute into order from first to last. The distance between the objects ordered does not have to be consistent. For example, the finalists in a race would be ordered, first, second, third, and so on.

Overgeneralizing Extending a conclusion too broadly, such as assuming that a generalization that applies to teenagers also applies to the entire society.

Paperback A less expensive and smaller paperbound version of a book.

Papyrus A large reed that was pounded, pressed, and dried into a paper-like surface by the ancient Egyptians. The surface could be written on with brush or reed pen, and the sheets could be joined together and rolled up on a stick to produce a scroll.

Parchment An early writing surface made of the tanned skin of a sheep or goat.

Participant observation A method of conducting research in which the investigator joins a group and makes detailed observations of the group while acting as a member.

Partisan paper A newspaper that consistently argues one point of view or is controlled by a political party.

Penetration (saturation) The number of television or radio receivers in working order in relation to the total number of households in a particular area.

Penny press The first mass newspapers. Originating in the early 1830s in New York, they sold for a penny in the streets, made a profit from advertising, and were oriented toward less-educated citizens. Early penny papers were often vulgar and sensational, but later ones carried basic economic and political views, financial information, and editorial comment.

People meter A device used to monitor people's television watching. The users press buttons to record times and stations of the shows they say they are viewing. The device consists of a small box on top of the television and a hand-held gadget; the information recorded is immediately sent to a central computer.

Perception The mental activity by which sensory input (from eyes, ears, touch, etc.) is classified into recognizable categories and meanings. In other words, interpreting sensory stimuli in meaningful ways. For example, when perceiving a spoken sound, humans must identify the incoming pattern of physical events as a known language symbol. Its meaning can then be established via a rapid memory search.

Personal influence Changes in people's beliefs, attitudes, or behavior brought about by messages received by personal, face-to-face communications.

Persuasion function A medium's function of altering or reinforcing the beliefs and opinions of its audience by supporting political candidates, promoting public policies, endorsing programs, and taking positions in their editorial content. As part of the persuasion function, a medium may provide favorable or unfavorable coverage of institutions, candidates, and issues.

Persuasive appeal A theme or meaning incorporated into a message intended to convince people to buy or use a particular product or to behave or believe in some other way desired by the sender.

Phonogram A graphic symbol linked to a specified sound by a convention or rule that prevails among those who speak a particular language. A good example is the letters in the alphabet.

Pirating The illegal copying of any mediated message, such as movies for film and videocassette distribution abroad.

Pocket people meter Small device, worn by an individual in an audience sample, which is used to monitor automatically what the person is listening to on radio or viewing on television, at home or elsewhere.

Policy consultants Public relations consultants who suggest courses of action to public and private institutions that want to develop a policy for the use of information resources.

Popular culture A broad term implying anything produced for wide use by the public. This includes mass-communicated messages that make limited intellectual and aesthetic demands—their content is designed to amuse and entertain media audiences, rather than to educate or uplift them. Examples include soap operas, movies, or popular music.

Popular music Musical compositions that are written or performed so as to produce commercial services and products that can be sold for profit.

Population (in research) All the units of whatever a researcher intends to study.

Precision journalism Reporting and writing form that makes use of some social science methods to gather and analyze quantitative information for news stories. Precision journalism may be *active*, in which reporters conduct their own surveys or research, or *reactive*, in which reporters use information (such as census data) already assembled by government agencies, universities, or private firms.

Premium Advertising method in which a company attempts to lure customers by offering something in exchange for a specified number of a product's labels or product codes.

Press council A group of responsible citizens brought together formally to monitor the press and provide feedback to the media and other mass communication agencies. The Hutchins Commission recommended that such councils be formed to ensure the media met ethical standards.

Pretesting Trying out on a small scale some procedure or product so as to eliminate problems before using it more widely. For example, presenting a sample ad to potential consumers to see its effectiveness.

Prior restraint Legal restriction that allowed government to engage in censorship by examining proposed news stories before publication.

Product-oriented advertising Advertising whose content is a persuasive message about the attributes of a product.

Production department The part of a newspaper organization responsible for typesetting and printing.

Profession Currently, almost any specialized occupational group. Traditionally, a vocational pursuit based on commanding an extensive body of sophisticated knowledge which requires long periods of formal study to master. Its practitioners use the body of knowledge on behalf of the public within a set of ethical norms and monitor each other to insure compliance with their norms.

Program rating The number of households receiving a program divided by total TV households in the market area, multiplied by 100.

Pronunciation Socially accepted ways to make the sounds of words.

Propaganda Communications designed to gain people's approval concerning some policy or program.

Proprietary research Studies that are owned by those who produced them and are not available to the public. Such research may be gathered by a firm and then sold to the highest bidder or conducted by a company for its own use. Much of this research may be self-serving and lack objectivity.

Public accountability Idea that a responsible corporation should make a positive contribution to local communities or the nation as a whole.

Public figure A legal term designating a person who is well known, such as a media personality, politician, or scientist.

Public relations A planned and organized communication process, conducted by communicators hired by a client, in which messages are transmitted via a variety of channels to relevant and targeted audiences in an attempt to influence the audiences' beliefs, attitudes, or even actions regarding that client, whether a person or a group.

Public relations agency A firm that helps clients communicate with the public and develop a positive public image.

Public relations campaign Organized series of carefully designed messages with specific meanings to targeted audiences. The campaign is intended to resolve a problem or provide an image change.

Public relations department A department within an agency, organization, or firm that acts as part of the overall management team and attempts to interpret the group to public and internal constituents and to provide channels for feedback from the public to management. The department helps the group achieve its overall goals.

Publicity Messages intended to expand the number of people who are aware of some policy, program, or person.

Quasi-folk taste public Those who like simple, unsophisticated media content and other items of popular culture. Such items often preserve elements of their ethnic culture.

Quota sampling Sample selection process in which the researcher picks certain subjects to make the sample meet the predetermined proportions of various kinds of subjects. It is not a probability sample because people in the relevant population do not have an equal probability of being selected.

Ragtime Music originating in sporting houses along the Mississippi in late 1800s, incorporating syncopated polyrhythms from Africa, elements of folk music, "rag" dances, and "cakewalk" music. This music swept the country at the beginning of the 1900s and remained popular until about the beginning of World War I.

Ranking (of group members) The relative level of authority, status, and reward of a member of a group.

Rap A form of popular music that is a product and expression of urban African-American life in the United States. Rap combines a distinctive rhythm, unique rhyming vocal patterns, and special sound effects. It often has messages of anger and violence.

Ratings Surveys and polling techniques used to determine the size of audiences and/or their preferences for particular types of media content.

Ratio measure A scale that has equal units and a true zero point, allowing multiplication and division of its measures to form ratios.

Readability How easy or hard a given passage of print is to read and comprehend.

Refereeing A system of judging research articles submitted for publication in technical journals in which each report is critiqued by experts in that field. To maintain objectivity, the researcher and reviewers do not know each other's identities.

Reinforcement Process of strengthening tendencies, preferences, or intentions already held. For example, one effect of a mass media election campaign is to increase the commitment of voters who attended to the political messages of their favored party or candidate.

Relative audience size The share of total audience that is tuned to a station at a given time.

Reliability An assessment of the consistency with which a measuring procedure yields similar results if it is used over and over on the same subjects. For example, a tape measure used to measure a given board will give very consistent (reliable) results. An IQ test given to a person on different occasions may give less consistent results.

Representative sample A sample in which the elements selected for study are distributed in the same proportion as those of the population from which they were drawn. Thus, the sample reflects the overall characteristics of the population.

Research A set of strategies and procedures (agreed upon by scientists) for gathering reliable information under controlled conditions of observation in such a way that objective conclusions can be reached with a minimum of error.

Research department The part of an organization, such as an advertising agency, that conducts studies or assembles information to answer questions of potential clients or customers.

Research perspective The assumptions underlying science and the various steps used in conducting research and interpreting results from scientific investigations.

Rhythm and blues A style of blues music that added a particular pulsating beat. It was the basis for rock-and-roll.

Rock-and-roll Popular music that evolved from rhythm and blues, country, and other popular music influences.

Role-taking A sender's assessment of which symbols and nonverbal cues will work best to arouse the intended meanings in a receiver; that is, the sender evaluates how the message looks from the receiver's point of view.

Role-taking principle Principle that the fidelity (accuracy) will increase in communication situations in which the sender can engage in sensitive role-taking.

Royalties An agreed-upon small percentage of a publisher's earnings from selling books that is given to the author of the book.

Sample A subset selected from the population. Ideally, its characteristics are representative of the whole population. For example, a sample of a community should have the same proportion of ethnic groups, gender, income levels, and age groups as the community as a whole.

Sampling The selection by a systematic or random procedure of research subjects out of a larger population relevant to a research project.

Sampling frame A complete list of the elements in a population from which a sample is to be drawn.

Sanctions Rewards and punishments used by a group to prevent excessive deviation from, or to reward conformity to, its social expectations. Sanctions range in nature from mild, such as words or gestures of approval or disapproval, to significant, such as awarding of medals for outstanding performance or execution for intolerable deviation.

Scientific method A set of strategies and procedures, shared by the sciences, which are used for research.

Scriptoria Commercial establishments that manufactured and sold hand-copied books following the Dark Ages.

Scroll A sheet of paper rolled up on a stick; an early, but cumbersome book.

Sedition Publishing or speaking so as to promote disaffection with government; inciting people to revolt against constituted authority.

Selective and limited influences theory The view that the effects of any particular mass-communicated message on individuals are minimal and that the messages to which people attend are influenced strongly by their individual differences, social relationships, and social categories.

Selectivity (in perception) The principle that what a person observes, understands, and recalls is a product of that individual's unique sets of needs, beliefs, attitudes, values, and other cognitive factors.

Sensational journalism Style of newswriting, characteristic of a number of major newspapers from the late 1800s to about 1920, that emphasized shocking details, bizarre events, and (sometimes) appalling transgressions of social norms.

Sex ratio The number of males divided by the number of females in the population times 100.

Share The percentage of audience presumed to be viewing the programming offered by a particular station at a particular time. It is calculated as the number of households tuned to a particular station divided by the number of households in the area with the television on, multiplied by 100.

Shield law A law that exempts journalists from having to reveal their sources, even to courts or the police. These laws are opposed by some on the grounds that the courts may need such information to protect citizens from wrongdoing and to provide fair trials. Yet without such laws, many reporters fear that being compelled to reveal their sources will inhibit their ability to get confidential information.

Shoppers Free-distribution newspapers that contain advertisements and may have news and entertainment material, calendars of local events, and various features.

Simple random sample A sample in which every element in it had the exact same probability of being included.

Simultaneous feedback Immediate reverse communication, which takes place in face-to-face or interpersonal communication.

Situational ethics A code of behavior that is based on the context of a specific situation. For example, reporting on a political candidate's secret sex life may be considered within "the people's right to know" and thus ethical, but reporting on a private citizen's sex life would not be ethical.

Social categories The organization of society into groupings of similar people defined by such factors as economic level, age, gender, education, and racial and ethnic identities.

Social controls See *sanctions*

Social expectations theory The view that knowledge of norms, roles, ranks, and controls can be acquired through a process of incidental learning. This learning takes place through exposure to media portrayals of many aspects of social life and kinds of human groups.

Social organization The rules and expectations (norms, roles, ranks, and controls or sanctions) that coordinate behavior in a group and govern the activities of each of its members so that the group's goals can be accomplished.

Social relationships People's ties to family, friends, and acquaintances which have truly significant influences on their interpretations and actions toward the world in which they live.

Socialization The extended learning process in families, among friends, in school, and in the community at large by which the rules of behavior of a society, and all of the demands of its culture, are incorporated into the psychological organization of the individual participating in its social order.

Soft news News stories that focus on human interest situations, people or events and do not need to be reported in a timely manner. Contrast with *hard news*.

Specialist reporters Journalists who cover well-defined fields such as fashion, business, or science.

Specialized consultants Public relation specialists who work in a specific area, such as political consultants during campaigns or experts in communications in a specific field, such as health, transportation, or insurance.

Specialized roles Particular rules for behavior that apply to persons playing well-defined parts or positions in a group.

Specialty advertising Advertising using items such as pencils or calendars.

Spin control Interpreting or re-interpreting situations that arise in connection with a candidate or issue to reflect a more favorable image. The term "spin control" is taken from billiards, where a left or right spin can be put on a ball to make it curve one way or the other as it moves across the table.

Spot news News stories that are one-time events, such as a house burning down. The event has no history behind it — it does not occur in stages.

Stabilization The standardization of meanings. By repeatedly showing accepted meanings for symbols, the media reinforce the conventions regarding their denotative and connotative interpretations.

Stand-up Television newscast format in which the anchor switches to a tape of a reporter in the field who makes comments at the scene of an event.

Stand-up with package Television newscast format in which the anchor switches to a tape of a reporter interviewing someone at the scene of an event.

Stars A term originating in early motion pictures, in which movie actors and actresses were publicized by producers as important artists and personalities.

Stereotype A term that described the type used in early roller printing presses. Today, a set of rigidly formed ideas or generalizations, often negative, about a minority group or other category of people that is used as justification for treating all members of the group in the same way.

Stereotype theory The view that the mass media reinforce the dominant segment of society's existing patterns of attitudes and behavior toward minorities by perpetuating rigid and usually negative portrayals, which can have the result of keeping minorities in subordinate positions.

Story board A series of drawings on a panel indicating each step of a commercial or story.

Substitution The displacement of older meanings for a word in favor of newer ones as a result of media portrayals. For example, "gay" once meant light-hearted and jovial rather than a sexual orientation.

Surveillance function The news media's function of keeping track of events in society and, through the news process, giving the public reliable reports about what appears to be important.

Survey Widely used research design in which a sample of people are contacted (directly, by phone, or by mail) to respond to an interview or a questionnaire designed to measure variables under study.

Swing music A softer form of popular music that replaced dixieland jazz in popularity in the 1930s. Swing brought in the era of the Big Bands who popularized the form via radio and records. Audiences enjoyed it for romantic dancing or easy listening. Swing as popular music was eventually displaced by rock-and-roll.

Symbol A word, action, or object that stands for and arouses a standardized internal meaning in people who are members of a given language community.

Syncopation Musical technique in which pianist plays melody with right hand and shifts the musical accents from the strong to the weak third beat of a measure, while playing a precise and regularly accented bass with the other hand. Syncopation played a key role in ragtime music.

Syndicates See *feature syndicates*.

Syntax Rules for ordering symbols in combination so as to make their meanings clear.

Tabloid A newspaper printed on paper of a special size (usually twelve by sixteen inches or five columns wide). Originally, tabloids were of low quality and had sensational or bizarre content, but today tabloids include papers that mix sensationalism with professionalism.

Talkies Motion picture with a full sound track, developed in late 1920s.

Testimonial An advertising strategy in which a famous or beautiful person endorses or promotes a product.

Theory A set of propositions that, taken together, provide an explanation of how antecedent conditions or events lead to specific consequences. Theories vary in the degree to which they have been supported by factual evidence from research.

Total fidelity A perfect match between the meanings of communicating parties.

Trace Some aspect or element of experience that is stored in the brain in such a way that it can be recalled.

Transit advertising Advertising that is displayed on buses, subway cars, and other vehicles.

Tuning inertia The degree of viewer loyalty to a particular program.

Two-step flow of communication (diffusion) theory The view that mass communication is attended to directly by opinion leaders, who then tell others and interpret the news topics they have selected.

Upper-middle taste public Those who are consumers of literature, music, theater, and other art that is accepted as "good"; these people are usually well-educated and relatively affluent.

Used-book trade System in which college bookstores buy back textbooks from students to be resold at high profit levels to other students the following semester.

User-oriented advertising Advertising with content aimed at the specific needs, interests, and desires of particular groups of consumers.

Uses and gratifications theory The view that each individual in the media audience is active, freely choosing and selectively using message content, rather than passive and acted upon by the media. Each audience member chooses and uses media messages based on his or her own structure of interests, needs, attitudes, and values.

Validity The degree to which a given form of measurement actually provides an assessment of what it is designed to measure. For example, a tape measure can provide a rather valid measure of a person's height, but an SAT test may be a less valid measure of a person's actual intellectual ability.

Variable Any concept under observation in a research project that can take more than one value.

Vellum An early writing surface that resembled parchment but was made from the skin of a young calf, rather than a sheep or goat.

Victrola A commercial brand of early wind-up phonograph; the term became a generic name for record players.

Video news release (VNR) A self-serving promotion of a person or organization, presented on videotape and distributed either on videocassette or by satellite transmission. A VNR seeks to communicate a certain point of view or argue a case. Media organizations that receive VNRs from candidates or organizations may use them verbatim without comment, edit them heavily, or identify them as a statement from those appearing therein.

Visual persistence (visual lag) A process, discovered by Dr. Peter Mark Roget, that results in a series of still pictures that capture a moving object in progressively different motions being perceived as smooth motion. The viewer "sees" an image for a fraction of a second after the thing itself has changed or disappeared. When two images are presented in a row, the first image fills in the time lag between the two, so they seem to be continuous.

Vitascope Early motion picture projection system developed by Thomas Edison and Thomas Armat.

VOT Voice-over tape. Television newscast format that first shows the anchorperson but then switches to a videotape with the anchor's voice heard as the viewer sees the ongoing picture.

Wire service Associations formed to transmit stories to newspapers throughout the country via the telegraph line.

Wire service editor (news service editor) The newspaper employee responsible for selecting, editing, and coordinating the national and international news from the wire services.

Word story The simplest format for a television newscast story in which the anchorperson tells what happened while sitting behind a desk (rather than being on the scene).

Yellow journalism A late nineteenth-century type of newspaper publishing that placed profit above truthfulness, emphasizing sensationalism, human interest and reader appeal at the expense of public responsibility.

Index

Coca-Cola, 321
Cochrane, Elizabeth, 410–411
Code of Wartime Practices, 301
Cohen v. The Minneapolis Star Tribune, 286
Colley, Russell, 337
Collier's, 130, 131
Columbia Broadcasting System (CBS), 198, 224, 225, 231, 274
Columbia Disc Gramophone Company, 471
Columbia Records, 475
Commercial newspapers, 80
Commercialism, 59
Communication. *See also* Mass communication
  accuracy of, 13–14
  of complex messages, 12–13
  contribution of memory to, 11–12
  effects of instantaneous, 85–86
  external, 365
  face-to-face versus mass, 29–33
  internal, 365
  linear model of, 5–11, 244
  origins of language and, 3–5
  revolutions in, 4, 6–7, 15–20, 39–40
  use of symbols in, 5
Communicators, professional, 21, 22, 31
Community (grassroots) press, 101
Compact discs (CDs), 476–479
Compositor, 65
Compounded selectivity, 392–393
Computer(s), 105, 373–374, 411–412
Computer-Assisted Investigative Reporting (CAIR), 105, 412–413
Concept, for research, 510
Conrad, Frank, 193
Consultant, 275–276
Consumer art, 430–438
Consumer behavior research, 338–339
Consumer groups, and advertising, 347
Consumer magazine, 134
Consumer's Guide to New Magazines, 135
Consumption, unit of, 263
Content analysis, 529–530
Continuing news, 389
Control group, 524
Control variable, 510–511
Controlled observation, 496
Convenience sample, 518
Convention, 5
Conversion, 553
Cooke, Janet, 618
Cooke, Wilhelm, 187
Copy editor, 108
Copyright law, 69

Cornish, Samuel, 102
Corporation for Public Broadcasting (CPB), 205
Correlation, 511
Correlation function, 133
Cosell, Howard, 449
Country Gentleman, 124
Country music, 462–463
Courtney, Alice E., 347
Cowboy songs, 463
Creative department, 332
Credibility studies, 622–623
Critics, of movies, 178–179
Cro-Magnon, 4, 6–7
Crystal sets, 191
Culture, 26–27. *See also* Popular culture
Cuneiform writing, 45
Curve of adoption, 89, 90, 197, 198. *See also* Adoption of innovation theory
Cutlip, Scott, 355, 358, 362, 366

Daguerre, Louis, 149
Daguerreotype, 149
Dailies, 100–101
Daily Courant, 77
Dale, Edgar, 159–160
Damage control, 355
Darwin, Charles, 538–539
Data, 513
Data analysis, 514
Data entry, 514
Data-processing, 514
"Dateline," 612
Davis, Peter, 165
Day, Benjamin, 82, 326
de Antonio, Emile, 165
De Forest, Lee, 190
Decca Record Company, 474
Decoding, of media messages, 25
DeFleur, Margaret H., 413
Defoe, Daniel, 115
Delayed feedback, 265–268
della Porta, Giovanni, 184
Demographics, 243, 418
Dempsey, Jack, 448
Dependency theory, 18–19
Dependent variable, 510
Deregulation, 313
Detailed coverage and analytic function, 104–105
Developing news, 389
Diario, El, 102
Diffusion, 385–387, 580
Diffusion theory, 386–387, 509, 553–554
Digital audio tape (DAT), 477
Dille, John F., 444–445
Direct broadcast satellite, 237, 290
Direct mail, 334
Divorce rate, 262
Dixieland jazz, 464–468
Dobbs, Lou, 612
Documentaries, 164–165
Donaldson, Sam, 405
Dorsey, Jimmy, 480
Dougherty, Philip, 134

Douglas, Norman, 322
Douglass, Frederick, 102
Dudley, Pendleton, 358
Dukakis, Michael, 377–378
Duke, Steven S., 445
Dylan, Bob, 427

Eastman, George, 149
Ebony, 130
Edison, Thomas Alva, 151, 468–469
Editor-in-chief, 108
Editorial operations (newspaper), 108–109
Editorial page editor, 108
Education
  and critical ability, 547
  development of universal, compulsory, 55, 121–123
  in Hellenistic Greece, 46–47
  and media effects, 550
  of news audience, 418
  and printing, 54–55
  of U.S. population, 254, 256–257
Electromagnet, 187–188
Electronic advertising, 334
Elite art, 432
Ellsberg, Daniel, 303
Emery, Edwin, 75, 78
Empirical observations, 512
Encoding, 5, 21, 22
Entertainment function, 103–104
Environmental issues, 576–577
Epic poems, 386
Espionage Act of 1917, 301
Establishment, of meaning, 595
Ethics. *See* Media ethics
Ethnic press, 101–102
Ethnicity, and news audience, 419
Ethnocentrism, 46
Executive order, 310
Experiment, 523–525. *See also* Research
Experimental condition, 544
Experimental group, 523
Expert, use of, 390, 392–393
Extension, of meaning, 595
External communication, 365
Exxon Valdez, 354, 577

Fairness doctrine, 311
Falwell, Jerry, 307
Families, changing characteristics of, 258–263
Farber, Myron, 305
Farnsworth, Philo T., 215, 216
Feature syndicate. *See* Syndicates
Federal Communications Act, 195, 297, 311, 615
Federal Communications Commission (FCC), 195, 214, 226, 236, 297, 310–312, 346
Federal Radio Commission (FRC), 194
Federal Trade Commission (FTC), 310, 312–313, 346

Federalist Papers, 285
Feedback, 14
  delayed, 265–268
  loss of, with mass media, 30
  simultaneous, 265
Feedback principle, 14–15
Feinberg, Cobbett, 173
Fell, John L., 167, 168
Fessenden, Reginald A., 190
Fidelity, total, 13
Field experiment, 525
Field research, 528
Film, 29. *See also* Motion pictures
Film makers, 159, 166–169
First Amendment, 287–290, 614–615. *See also* Freedom of the press
Fisher, Amy, 428–429
Fiske, Margery, 558
Fitzgerald, Ella, 480
Flaherty, Robert, 165
Flynt, Larry, 307
Focus group, use of, 270
Folk art, 431–432
Folk music, 456–457
Folk rock, 483
Ford, Gerald, 575
Foreign Affairs, 140
Format, 399
Forum, 128
Foster, Stephen, 456
Fourth Estate, 409
Fox network, 231
Franklin, Benjamin, 78–79, 116, 287, 615
Franklin, James, 78, 287
Freed, Alan, 481–482
Freedom of Information Act, 303, 307, 310, 412
Freedom of the press, 79, 283, 286–290
  and advertising, 346
  courts' control of, 306–307
  and executive branch, 308–313
  and government secrecy, 298–304
  legislative control of, 307–308
  and libel, 290–294
  and obscenity and pornography, 296–298, 312
  and press responsibilities, 284–285, 614–616
  and protection of sources, 304–305
  and trials, 294–296
Frequency, 190
Frequency modulation (FM) broadcasting, 201–202, 204, 209
Friedan, Betty, 347
Friend, Tad, 429
Friendly, Fred W., 622
Full-service agency, 329, 331

Galbraith, John Kenneth, 343
Gallup, George, 507
Gannett Corporation, 96, 235